Health and Medicine

1995

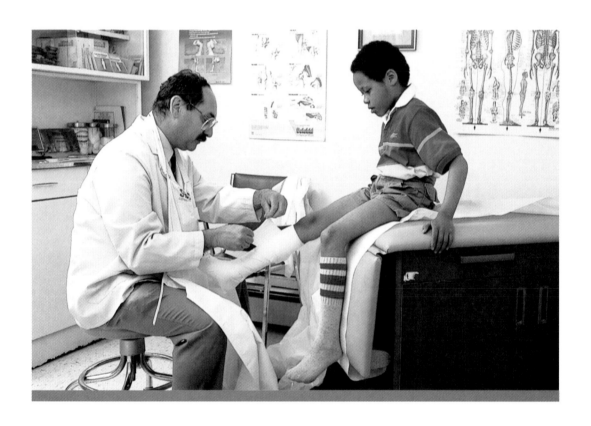

Health and Medicine

1995

Copyright © 1995 by Grolier Incorporated

ISSN: 1061-6446   **ISBN: 0-7172-8451-4**

Printed and manufactured in the United States of America

Contributors

SUE BERKMAN, Freelance writer specializing in medicine
HEALING THROUGH HYPNOSIS

JAMES A. BLACKMAN, M.D., M.P.H., Professor of Pediatrics, University of Virginia; Director of Research, Kluge Children's Rehabilitation Center, Charlottesville, VA
EMERGENCY MEDICINE
PEDIATRICS
SEXUALLY TRANSMITTED DISEASES

EDWARD E. BONDI, M.D., Professor of Dermatology, University of Pennsylvania Medical Center, Philadelphia, PA
SKIN

BRUCE BOWER, Behavioral Sciences Editor, *Science News*
MENTAL HEALTH

LINDA J. BROWN, Freelance writer specializing in environmental and health topics
ENVIRONMENT AND HEALTH
GETTING INTO THE SWIM

ROBERT BUTTERWORTH, Ph.D., Clinical psychiatrist, Los Angeles; Member of the American Psychiatric Association Media Psychology Division
HOUSECALLS: PSYCHOLOGY

KAREN S. CASTAGNO, Ph.D., Education consultant; instructor, University of Connecticut, Storrs, CT
SPECIAL OLYMPICS: SPORT, SPIRIT, SPLENDOR

AL CICCONE, M.D., Spokesperson, American Academy of Family Practitioners; Associate Professor, Department of Family Medicine, Eastern Virginia Medical School, Norfolk, VA
HOUSECALLS: MEDICINE AND THE HUMAN BODY

DAVID M. CLIVE, M.D., Associate Professor of Medicine, University of Massachusetts School of Medicine, Worcester, MA
KIDNEYS

DONALD W. CUNNINGHAM, Science writer in the Washington, DC, area, specializing in kidney and urologic diseases for the National Institutes of Health
UROLOGY

GODE DAVIS, Freelance writer based in Warwick, RI
AGING

JOSEPH C. DeVITO, Freelance writer
TODAY'S HEALTH CLUBS:
LOOKING FOR THE TOTAL WORKOUT

HERBERT S. DIAMOND, M.D., Chairman, Department of Medicine, The Western Pennsylvania Hospital, Pittsburgh, PA
ARTHRITIS AND RHEUMATISM

MICHELLE M. EMERY, R.Ph., Drug Information Specialist, University of Rhode Island Drug Information Center, Providence, RI
coauthor, MEDICATIONS AND DRUGS

DIXIE FARLEY, Staff writer, *FDA Consumer* magazine
IN-HOME TESTS

R. E. GAENSSLEN, Ph.D., Professor and Director, Forensic Sciences, University of New Haven, West Haven, CT
FORENSIC MEDICINE

SUE GEBO, M.P.H., R.D., Consulting nutritionist; author, *What's Left to Eat?* (McGraw-Hill, 1992)
ALL ABOUT OILS

MARIA GUGLIELMINO, M.S., R.D., Consulting nutritionist and exercise physiologist in private practice in Woodbury, CT
HOT AND HEALTHY
NUTRITION AND DIET

MARY HAGER, Correspondent, *Newsweek* magazine
HEALTH-CARE COSTS

KEVIN W. HARRIS, M.D., Ph.D., Assistant Professor, Department of Medicine, University of Texas Health Science Center at San Antonio, TX
BLOOD AND LYMPHATIC SYSTEM

MARIE HOFER, Associate Editor, *Special Report*, Whittle Communications, Knoxville, TN
HOUSEPLANTS: POTIONS IN A POT?

LINDA HUGHEY HOLT, M.D., Assistant Professor, Northwestern University, Evanston, IL
OBSTETRICS AND GYNECOLOGY

ERIN HYNES, Freelance writer based in Austin, TX
JUST PART OF THE GANG

IRA M. JACOBSON, M.D., Associate Clinical Professor of Medicine, Cornell University Medical College, New York, NY
LIVER

JAMES F. JEKEL, M.D., M.P.H., Professor of Public Health, Yale University School of Medicine, New Haven, CT
AIDS
PUBLIC HEALTH

KENNETH L. KALKWARF, D.D.S., M.S., Dean, The University of Texas Health Science Center at San Antonio Dental School, San Antonio, TX
TEETH AND GUMS

JENNIFER KENNEDY, M.S., Certified Health Education Specialist, Johns Hopkins Hospital "Live for Life" health-promotion program, Baltimore, MD
HOUSECALLS: FITNESS AND HEALTH

CHRISTOPHER KING, Managing Editor, *Science Watch*, Institute for Scientific Information, Philadelphia, PA
IMMUNOLOGY
THE MEDICAL NAME GAME
NOBEL PRIZE: PHYSIOLOGY OR MEDICINE

ROBERT L. KNOBLER, M.D., Ph.D., Professor of Neurology, Department of Neurology, Jefferson Medical College, Thomas Jefferson University, Philadelphia, PA
BRAIN AND NERVOUS SYSTEM

PREETHI KRISHNAMURTHY, Freelance writer based in New Haven, CT
EMTs: MEDICAL CARE ON THE MOVE

ARNON LAMBROZA, M.D., Assistant Professor of Medicine, Division of Digestive Diseases, Cornell University Medical College, New York, NY
DIGESTIVE SYSTEM

DYLAN LANDIS, Contributing editor, *Metropolitan Home* and *American Homestyle* magazines; author, *Checklist for Your New Baby* (Perigee, 1991)
THE NEW RULES OF THE GAME

SUZANNE M. LEVINE, D.P.M., Attending physician, The New York Hospital-Cornell University Medical College, New York, NY
PODIATRY

JAY D. MABREY, M.D., Assistant Professor of Orthopedic Surgery, University of Texas Health Science Center at San Antonio, TX
> BONES, MUSCLES, AND JOINTS

THOMAS H. MAUGH II, Medical writer, *The Los Angeles Times*
> GENETICS AND GENETIC ENGINEERING

ELIZABETH McGOWAN, Freelance writer based in New York
> FOR GOODNESS' SAKE!
> JURY PSYCHOLOGY

ALISON A. MOY, M.D., Procter & Gamble Pharmaceuticals, Sharon Woods Technical Center, Cincinnati, OH
> ENDOCRINOLOGY

RICHARD L. MUELLER, M.D., Clinical instructor in medicine, The New York Hospital-Cornell University Medical College, New York, NY
> HEART AND CIRCULATORY SYSTEM

WILLIBALD NAGLER, M.D., Professor and Chairman, Department of Rehabilitation Medicine, The New York Hospital-Cornell University Medical College, New York, NY
> REHABILITATION MEDICINE

ALICE NAUDE, Freelance writer
> RETIREMENT ON THE HORIZON

SUSAN NIELSEN, Freelance writer specializing in consumer advocacy and health issues
> IN-LINE SKATING

MARIA L. PADILLA, M.D., Associate Professor of Medicine, Pulmonary Division, Mount Sinai School of Medicine, New York, NY
> RESPIRATORY SYSTEM

RUTH PAPAZIAN, New York City-based writer specializing in health and medical topics
> TRACE YOUR FAMILY TREE

DAVID A. PENDLEBURY, Analyst, Research Services Group, Institute for Scientific Information, Philadelphia, PA
> OSTEOPATHIC PHYSICIANS:
> DOCTORS WITH A DIFFERENCE

DEVERA PINE, Freelance science writer and editor
> DRUG INTERACTIONS
> THE VALUE OF VITAMINS

ABIGAIL POLEK, Freelance writer and editor
> MEDICAL TECHNOLOGY
> SMOKING IN THE '90s

EDMUND A. PRIBITKIN, M.D., Assistant Professor, Department of Otolaryngology, Thomas Jefferson University, Philadelphia, PA
> EAR, NOSE, AND THROAT

MICHAEL X. REPKA, M.D., Associate Professor of Ophthalmology and Pediatrics, Johns Hopkins University School of Medicine, Baltimore, MD
> EYES AND VISION

CYNTHIA P. RICKERT, Ph.D., Assistant Professor of Pediatrics, Department of Pediatrics, University of Arkansas for Medical Sciences, Little Rock, AR
> CHILD DEVELOPMENT AND PSYCHOLOGY

RAYMOND L. RIGOGLIOSO, Contributor, *Harvard Health Letter*
> WHEN HIV HITS HOME

MACE L. ROTHENBERG, M.D., F.A.C.P., Assistant Professor of Medicine, Division of Medical Oncology, University of Texas Health Science Center at San Antonio, TX
> CANCER

JAMES A. ROTHERHAM, Ph.D., Senior Associate, Chambers Associates, Inc., Washington, DC
> GOVERNMENT POLICIES AND PROGRAMS

JESSICA SNYDER SACHS, Science and health writer based in Atlanta, GA
> AMBULATORY SURGERY:
> OPERATION WITHOUT ADMISSION

C. ANDREW SALZBERG, M.D., Assistant Professor of Plastic Surgery, New York Medical College, Valhalla, NY
> PLASTIC SURGERY

KAREN M. SANDRICK, Freelance medical writer
> HEALTH PERSONNEL AND FACILITIES

DODI SCHULTZ, Freelance writer based in New York City
> CANDY: HOW SWEET IT IS!

NEIL SPRINGER, Freelance writer covering health and science issues
> OCCUPATIONAL HEALTH

ROBERT K. STOELTING, M.D., Professor and Chair, Department of Anesthesia, Indiana University School of Medicine, Indianapolis, IN
> ANESTHESIOLOGY

CHERYL A. STOUKIDES, Pharm.D., Director, University of Rhode Island Drug Information Center, Providence, RI
> coauthor, MEDICATIONS AND DRUGS

MONA SUTNICK, Ed.D., R.D., Spokesperson, American Dietetic Association; consultant in nutrition communication and education
> HOUSECALLS: NUTRITION

ROBERT M. SWIFT, M.D., Ph.D., Associate Professor of Psychiatry, Brown University Medical School, Providence, RI
> SUBSTANCE ABUSE

FRANK M. SZIVOS, Freelance writer based in Fairfield, CT
> THE YOUNG MAN'S CANCER

JANET C. TATE, Freelance writer based in Knoxville, TN
> DOING SOMETHING ABOUT DIABETES

JENNY TESAR, Freelance science and medical writer; author, *Global Warming* (Facts on File, 1991), *Scientific Crime Investigation* (Watts, 1991)
> DON'T TOUCH!

ELLEN TREVOR, Freelance writer based in New York City
> FEET FIRST

LINDA TROIANO, Freelance health writer based in New York City
> TOOTH BLEACHING: IS IT SAFE?

MILAN TRPIS, Ph.D., Professor, School of Hygiene and Public Health, Department of Molecular Microbiology and Immunology, Johns Hopkins University, Baltimore, MD
> TROPICAL MEDICINE

GEORGE VALKO, M.D., Instructor, Department of Family Medicine, Jefferson Medical College, Thomas Jefferson University, Philadelphia, PA
> HOUSECALLS: PRACTICAL NEWS TO USE

JO ANN WHITE, Freelance writer and editor based in Tuckerton, NJ
> BOOK REVIEWS

CONNIE ZUCKERMAN, J.D., Assistant Professor of Humanities in Medicine and of Family Medicine, State University of New York Health Science Center, Brooklyn, NY
> MEDICAL ETHICS

Contents

Review '95

The face of medicine and health care is changing dramatically as a result of scientific advances, consumer behavior, and financial constraints. Many of the changes are positive, leading to longer, healthier lives. Death rates from cardiovascular diseases and certain cancers continue to decline. Polio appears to have been eradicated—not only in the United States, but throughout the Western Hemisphere. An experimental new drug seems to slow the fatal progression of Lou Gehrig's disease. New vaccines raise hope that malaria, one of the world's deadliest scourges, and chicken pox, one of the most common childhood diseases, may soon become preventable.

Thanks to improved techniques and better medications, surgery often can be avoided. And when surgery is needed, recovery is quicker and less painful than ever before. Endoscopic surgery—performing operations through needle-sized holes—has become commonplace in adults, and is even being used on fetuses. More and more surgery is being performed on an outpatient basis: the patient is admitted, has an operation, and goes home the same day. In 1980 outpatient surgery accounted for 16.4 percent of all surgeries in the United States; by early 1995 the figure was around 60 percent, and included such procedures as gallbladder removal, hernia repair, tonsillectomy, and eye surgery.

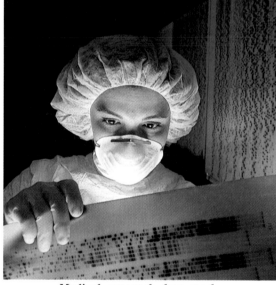

Medical research has made tremendous advances in recent years, thanks in part to discoveries in the field of genetics.

Perhaps more than ever before, people recognize the critical roles they themselves play in protecting their own good health. In general, people are smoking less . . . and eating more broccoli. Many participate in sports and regular fitness programs. And people are paying attention to new medical findings, such as the discovery that what a pregnant or nursing woman eats has more influence on her child's behavior and mental development than how much the mother eats.

Nonetheless, too many people continue to cling to bad habits. Recent reports indicate that the number of overweight Americans has increased significantly. People are ignoring high blood pressure and failing to take in sufficient amounts of essential vitamins and minerals. Almost 60 percent of American babies are not given all the immunization shots they need during the first seven months of life. Also worrisome is the still-high pregnancy rate among teenage girls; the aversion to exercise expressed by many teenagers; the increased use of marijuana among high-school students; and the prevalence of binge drinking among college students.

Fatal and nonfatal injuries from violence continued to increase. "We have an epidemic of firearms death among young men," says Mark Rosenberg, M.D., director of the National Center for Injury Prevention and Control. The drug trade is a major factor in the enormous increase in homicide deaths among adolescent males, but drug dealers are not the only ones who are armed; many other young people have started carrying guns around their neighborhoods and to their schools.

Familiarity with Alzheimer's disease increased following the announcement by former President Ronald Reagan that he was afflicted with this devastating ailment. Some 4 million Americans have Alzheimer's, for which there is no known cure. New studies provided some hope. Research hinted that nonsteroidal anti-inflammatory drugs (NSAIDs, including ibuprofen and other medications commonly used to treat arthritis) and estrogen-replacement therapy (ERT) may protect against Alzheimer's.

Sometimes, what is extolled by one study is found to be worthless or even harmful by another study. During 1994 heavy use of NSAIDs was linked to kidney failure, as was usage of acetaminophen, which accounts for almost 50 percent of the nation's over-the-counter pain-reliever sales. ERT has been linked to increased risk of uterine cancer, while many other studies indicate that it reduces the risks of heart disease and bone fractures.

No medical field is as confusing to consumers as nutrition, which is rife with claims and counterclaims about the value of various nutrients. In recent years, much attention has focused on antioxidants (beta-carotene and vitamins C and E) and evidence that they protect against cancer and heart disease. Because of these studies, people increased their intake of vitamin supplements. But two carefully controlled studies reported in 1994 failed to find any evidence that antioxidant supplements guard against cancer and heart disease. Researchers emphasize, that while the case for supplements is unproven, people should eat lots of fruits and vegetables, the major food sources of antioxidants. The researchers point out that there are many differences in the structure and properties of various antioxidants; also, the protective benefits noted in some studies may be due, not to known antioxidants, but to as yet-unrecognized chemicals in fruits and vegetables.

As research fills gaps in our medical knowledge, future advances in the prevention and treatment of health problems are likely. Large-scale trials of two experimental vaccines against HIV (human immunodeficiency virus), which causes AIDS, were scheduled to begin in 1996. People already infected with HIV may benefit from new discoveries about the interaction between the virus and the body's immune system.

Particularly exciting have been developments in the field of genetics. During the past year, researchers reported the discovery of genes that may be responsible for polycystic kidney disease, skeletal disorders, many cancers, and some cases of obesity. It is hoped that such discoveries eventually will have practical applications, as have similar, earlier discoveries. In 1994, for example, doctors attempted the first gene therapy for vascular disease, inserting genes that stimulate the growth of new blood vessels into a patient who suffered from severe blockage of his leg arteries.

Researchers also are producing a growing body of evidence that everyday events impact health. For instance, they reported that stressful and irritating experiences can increase people's vulnerability to colds and other infectious diseases, while pleasurable experiences protect against disease by boosting the immune system. So, to all our readers, we say: May you have a nice day!

The Editors

Health and Medicine: Features '95

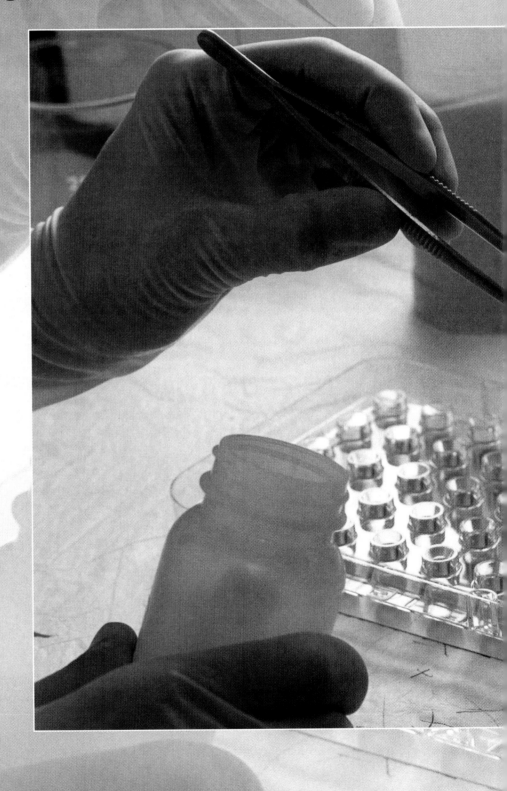

MEDICINE AND THE HUMAN BODY

CONTENTS

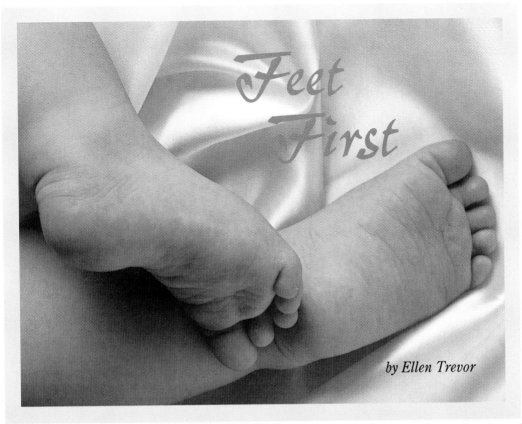

Feet First

by Ellen Trevor

Well-fitting shoes, regular exercise, and diligent attention to foot hygiene can do wonders toward returning your feet to "baby perfect" condition.

Talk about your feet and, heaven forbid, your toes, and most people will get a little uneasy. Take off your shoes and socks, and they'll beat a path out the door. This is not so in other cultures, where bare feet are as normal as bare hands. The results of this are painfully clear: our feet hurt. But podopain is not inevitable. With the right shoes, a few preventive measures, and some simple treatments, your feet will feel like dancing on easy street.

Let's face it: most of us take our feet for granted. Studies show that 62 percent of Americans think it's normal for their feet to

hurt, and 80 percent have foot pain regularly. Yet fewer than 3 percent of Americans visit a podiatrist.

Your feet deserve better. As complex as hands, feet are biomechanical masterpieces. With every step, they synchronize nearly one-quarter of all the bones in the body. They also endure your body weight. Walking puts some stress on your feet (though not nearly as much as running). But since feet are

A runner continually transfers his or her entire body weight from one foot to the other. At least once per day, every person—athlete or not—should carefully inspect his or her feet for anything amiss.

surely designed to withstand that stress, what's causing all these aches and pains?

It's Only Fitting

In shoeless tropical cultures, only about 3 percent of the population have foot ailments. In countries where feet are "protected" with shoes, the number goes up to 80 percent.

"Most foot problems only show up when you're not wearing the proper shoes," says New York City podiatrist Mayde Lebensfeld, D.P.M., a foot consultant for The Rockport Company. Two-thirds of foot problems can be attributed to ill-fitting shoes, she says. "The wrong shoes can cause a host of problems, like irritations, abrasions, and blisters," explains Daniel M. McGann,

D.P.M., a podiatrist in El Monte, California, and the author of *The Doctor's Sore Foot Book* (Morrow, 1991).

The answer isn't to move to Bora Bora and forget about shoes altogether—it's to wear the right shoes.

When picking a pair, remember that the heel, toe box, arch support, and flexibility should feel good in the store. Also, beware of high heels. Every inch of heel height increases the force on the ball of your foot by 25 percent and raises your chances for foot problems.

Know Your Feet

Once you have the correct shoes, you are all set, right? Not so fast. Healthy feet require regular exercise and careful attention.

Meet Your Feet

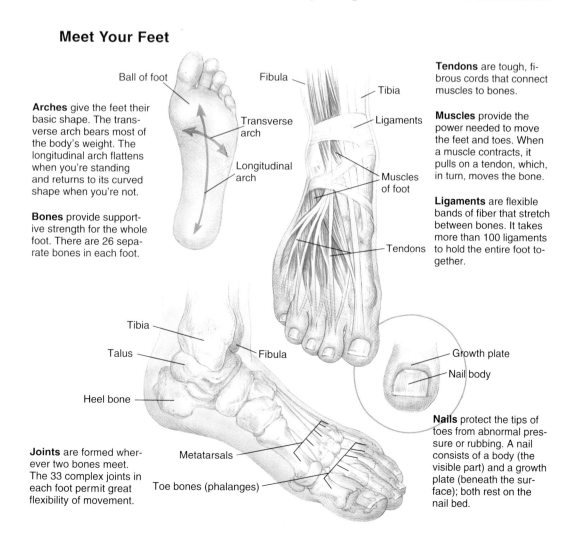

Arches give the feet their basic shape. The transverse arch bears most of the body's weight. The longitudinal arch flattens when you're standing and returns to its curved shape when you're not.

Bones provide supportive strength for the whole foot. There are 26 separate bones in each foot.

Ball of foot

Transverse arch

Longitudinal arch

Fibula

Tibia

Ligaments

Muscles of foot

Tendons

Tendons are tough, fibrous cords that connect muscles to bones.

Muscles provide the power needed to move the feet and toes. When a muscle contracts, it pulls on a tendon, which, in turn, moves the bone.

Ligaments are flexible bands of fiber that stretch between bones. It takes more than 100 ligaments to hold the entire foot together.

Tibia

Talus

Heel bone

Fibula

Metatarsals

Toe bones (phalanges)

Growth plate

Nail body

Joints are formed wherever two bones meet. The 33 complex joints in each foot permit great flexibility of movement.

Nails protect the tips of toes from abnormal pressure or rubbing. A nail consists of a body (the visible part) and a growth plate (beneath the surface); both rest on the nail bed.

Keep your feet active—walking boosts circulation and builds muscles. Also, take the time to get up close and personal with them. "Inspect your feet every day as soon as you finish your walk," says Lebensfeld. Check the length of your toenails. They should be no longer or shorter than your toes. Check your foot for red spots, cuts, blisters, excessive wear, or anything else unusual. (Of course, nothing looks unusual if you don't know your feet.) This routine should also help you determine if your walking shoes are causing any problems. Try a bit of petroleum jelly on an irritated spot to reduce friction before you head out for your next walk.

Next, enjoy a foot soak for 10 to 15 minutes in warm water with Epsom salts or an effervescent bath soak as often as possible. Ahhhh, it feels great and helps reduce swelling, improve circulation, and fight infection. Dry your feet well and apply a moisturizer.

Since the skin on your feet is the thickest on the body (three times thicker than the skin on your palms, and 15 times thicker than facial skin), it is a good idea to use a lotion made specifically for feet. (To prevent fungus growth, avoid rubbing lotion between your toes.) You may even want to smooth down rough spots with a pumice stone. Don't trim the skin with scissors or blades—if you go too deep, you could end up with an infection. Finally, treat yourself to a foot massage (see the box below).

Now the bad news: even if you take care of your feet, they may still get irritated from time to

Five-Minute Foot Massage

This minimassage takes only a few minutes per foot, but will make you feel relaxed and rejuvenated all over.

- Sitting comfortably in a chair or on the floor, bring one foot toward you. Rest the outside of your ankle on the opposite knee, or set your heel on the edge of your seat.
- Starting at the heel, use your fingers to press and knead the bottom of the foot, working your way toward the ball. Continue pressing and kneading, moving from the ball toward the big toe and then to the little toe.
- Wrap your hands around the sides of your foot at the arch so your thumbs are on top and your fingertips are on the bottom. Press your fingers into your instep while working your palms outward. Let your thumbs travel from the center out to each side. Repeat this procedue until you have covered the entire surface of your foot.
- Place your palm under the tips of your toes and gently pull back, flexing your foot. Hold for a few seconds, then let go and point your foot, feeling the stretch.
- Return to the top of the foot and work your thumbs in a circular motion along the outer edge of your foot, traveling from the toes to the ankle. Continue massaging around the back of your heel, then on the inside of your foot.
- Gently pinch the Achilles tendon (the "cord" running up the back of your heel) between your thumb and forefinger. Pinching the tendon with light pressure, run your fingers up the back of your heel, ending just above the ankle.
- Switch feet and repeat.

time. When that happens, it is generally safe to self-treat the problem at first. For example, if you are getting a blister, protect the area with a press-on ring, or "doughnut," made of moleskin. Most pharmacies carry preparations that can help relieve minor ailments.

"If you're older, it may not be a good idea to self-treat foot problems, since the skin on your foot is thinner than it is on younger people," says McGann.

If a foot problem persists, see a podiatrist. A consistent soreness could indicate a biomechanical problem with your gait or a flaw in your bone or muscle structure. If your feet are even slightly out of alignment, you could damage them seriously and eventually hurt other parts of your body, including your knees, hips, or back. These problems are common, but they can be helped: an insert called an orthotic may be the answer. If you and your doctor have exhausted every conservative measure available, foot surgery can be an effective last resort.

My Foot Hurts

For those who have a problem telling a corn from a callus, here is a glossary of the 12 most common foot aches and pains—plus treatments.

Corn. A painful growth of toughened skin on top of, or between, toes; often kernel-shaped.

Cause: Friction. A corn is natural padding that develops in response to friction over a bony prominence.

Treatment: Do not cut it. A warm soak and a pad will make it feel better. If a corn causes great discomfort, a podiatrist can remove it surgically.

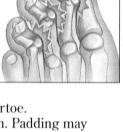

Hammertoe. A toe in a claw shape—raised at the middle—usually accompanied by a corn where it rubs the shoe; this condition is typically extremely painful.

Causes: Arthritis, genetics, an injury, or tight shoes. A long second toe will often become a hammertoe.

Treatment: Treat the corn. Padding may help, but surgery may be necessary. A podiatrist can operate on the tendon to elongate the toe or trim the bone.

Callus. Thickened skin on the bottom of the foot.

Cause: Excessive pressure and friction on a weight-bearing bone, often from ill-fitting shoes.

Treatment: Try a warm soak and then a pumice rub or an over-the-counter preparation containing salicylic acid to reduce the thickness of the hardened skin; also try padding. If you treat the callus, but your shoes still rub, the callus will come back. You may need an orthotic to correct your gait if your shoes fit and you still get calluses. In extreme cases the bone may be surgically trimmed.

Neuroma. Indicated by stabbing pain in the ball of the foot with no obvious bumps, cuts, or bruises. Also called Morton's neuroma.

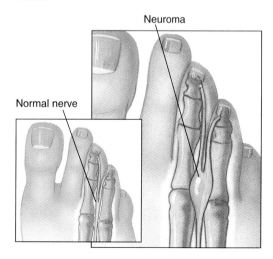

Neuroma

Normal nerve

Cause: A nerve between the toe bones (metatarsals) is rubbed until scar tissue forms. The thick tissue causes the bones to press on the nerves. Older walkers should check for deterioration of the fat pad at the ball of the foot—the problem may be poor padding, not a neuroma.

Treatment: Try a pain reliever, and wear shoes that fit loosely across the ball of your foot (if your foot is pressed from the sides, the bones rub more) to relieve pain; definitely seek help. A podiatrist will try steroid injections, a finger-shaped pad to push the bones apart (neuroma plug), or surgery to remove the scar tissue.

Heel Spur. A calcification or bony growth that extends forward from under

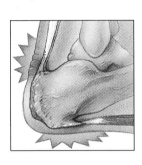

your heel and pulls on the heel-cushioning plantar fascia tissue, causing the painful inflammation known as plantar fasciitis. Indicated by tremendous pain on the bottom of the foot at the base of the heel, especially when you wake up in the morning.

Causes: Occurs in people who have sagging arches or are 10 to 20 pounds overweight. The problem tends to be worse if you have extremely tight calves or Achilles tendons.

Treatment: Try an anti-inflammatory pain reliever, and ice your heel for 20 minutes to reduce swelling. If tightness is the cause, heel-cord stretches (standing up on your toes as high as possible) will help alleviate pain. A podiatrist can diagnose heel spurs with an X ray. Spurs can improve with steroid

shots, hydrotherapy, ultrasound, massage, or analgesic medications. An orthotic may be appropriate.

Bunion. A painful bony bump protruding from the outside joint of the big toe; more common among women.

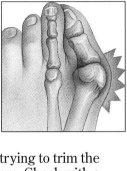

Cause: Usually a genetic condition exacerbated by tight shoes rubbing against the bone.

Treatment: Try a bunion pad. Don't bother trying to trim the skin—that's not the problem. Check with a podiatrist about biomechanical problems that may require an orthotic. Treating your gait may keep bunions from getting worse. In advanced cases the bone can be trimmed surgically.

Ingrown Toenails. Inflammation of the soft tissue at the corner of the toenail.

Cause: Improper cutting; nail digs into the skin as it grows, resulting in irritation.

Treatment: It helps to soak your feet frequently and moisturize around the nail with lotion or cuticle cream. See a podiatrist if the toe is infected.

Prevention: Cut toenails straight across.

Plantar Warts. A group of warts that are bunched together or in a string formation on the bottom of the foot, differentiated from calluses by a tiny black spot.

Cause: Probably a virus.

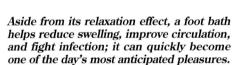
Aside from its relaxation effect, a foot bath helps reduce swelling, improve circulation, and fight infection; it can quickly become one of the day's most anticipated pleasures.

Treatment: May disappear on their own. If not, try a preparation containing salicylic acid. A podiatrist can also remove them.

Athlete's Foot. Peeling, itchy skin.
Cause: A fungus that thrives on moist, warm feet; commonly picked up off the locker-room floor.
Treatment: Wash your feet frequently, wear dry socks, expose feet to dry air and sun (it kills the fungus) as often as possible, and try an over-the-counter medication. If the problem persists, consult your doctor.
Prevention: Keep your feet dry, use powder on sweaty feet, and wear sandals in the gym shower.

Blisters. Pockets of liquid under the skin, usually on heels.
Cause: Friction on skin from loose shoes or damp socks.
Treatment: Use a sterile needle to pierce the blister near the base and drain the fluid out. An Epsom-salts soak may help dry out a large blister. Apply an antibiotic cream and bandage. Never cut away the skin—the underlying area is too sensitive.
Prevention: Wear shoes and socks that fit, and keep them dry. If you're prone to blisters on one spot, use petroleum jelly to reduce friction.

Black-and-Blue Toenails. Toenails become bruised.
Cause: Pressure on the toes from a shoe or

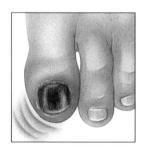

a blow to the foot; bleeding occurs under the nail, a blood clot forms, and the area turns black.
Treatment: A podiatrist can drain the fluid under the nail if the pressure is unbearable. Your toenail may eventually fall off. If this should happen, it is important to protect the exposed area with a clean bandage.
Prevention: Put petroleum jelly on your toenails to reduce friction. Make sure there's room to wiggle your toes in shoes before you buy them.

Do I Need An Orthotic?

One of the easiest ways to alleviate foot pain is to wear an orthotic device, according to David B. Alper, D.P.M., a podiatrist in Belmont, Massachusetts. Unfortunately, when most people hear

the term "orthotic," they think of those expensive shoe inserts, custom-made by podiatrists. Well, think again. Over-the-counter orthotic devices (arch supports, innersoles, and inserts) sold at your local drugstore for $10 to $25 may be all your feet need to feel better. Prescription orthotics are not necessary for most people.

Alper suggests that almost anyone with achy feet start with a store-bought orthotic. "An orthotic attempts to let the foot move in a neutral position, one in which the leg, ankle, and foot are lined up in a 90-degree angle," he explains.

If foot pain continues after wearing store-bought orthotics for a week or two, it is time to consult a podiatrist.

Pump Bump. An often-uncomfortable bump at the back of the heel.
Cause: Constant rubbing of heel and shoe; may indicate a biomechanical problem.
Treatment: Put an insert under your heel to lift the bump above the edge of your shoe. An orthotic can correct a gait problem, but surgery may be needed to remove a well-developed bump.   ◇

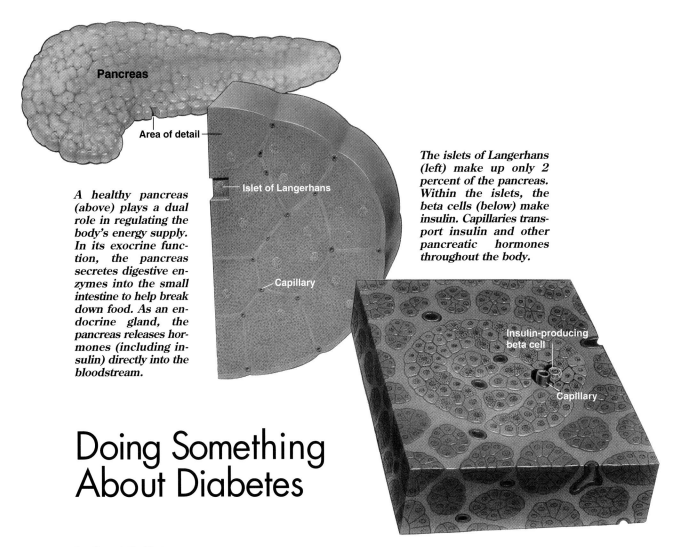

A healthy pancreas (above) plays a dual role in regulating the body's energy supply. In its exocrine function, the pancreas secretes digestive enzymes into the small intestine to help break down food. As an endocrine gland, the pancreas releases hormones (including insulin) directly into the bloodstream.

The islets of Langerhans (left) make up only 2 percent of the pancreas. Within the islets, the beta cells (below) make insulin. Capillaries transport insulin and other pancreatic hormones throughout the body.

Doing Something About Diabetes

by Janet C. Tate

The first decade of the 21st century may well mark a victory over diabetes. Researchers are experimenting with different approaches to prevent the onset of this chronic disease and, at the very least, to prevent the development of its deadly long-term complications. Avenues of research range from new drug therapies and drug-delivery systems to surgery as futuristic-sounding as a bioengineered islet-cell transplant. No matter what course is eventually taken toward preventing diabetes or finding a cure, there is no question that the future looks brighter than it ever has before for the estimated 14 million diabetics in the United States, and the millions more throughout the world.

What Is Diabetes?

Diabetes mellitus, a disorder of the pancreas, is the fourth-leading cause of death by disease in the United States; 160,000 Americans die from it annually, and thousands more face diabetes-induced blindness, kidney dysfunction, or amputation. A much rarer type of diabetes, "diabetes insipidus," can result from damage to or diseases of the pituitary gland.

Diabetes mellitus is itself a broad term for two different diseases. About 1 in 10 diabetics have the more severe form, known alternately as insulin-dependent, Type I, or juvenile-onset diabetes. Though this type of diabetes can develop at any time, it typically does so in childhood or young adulthood.

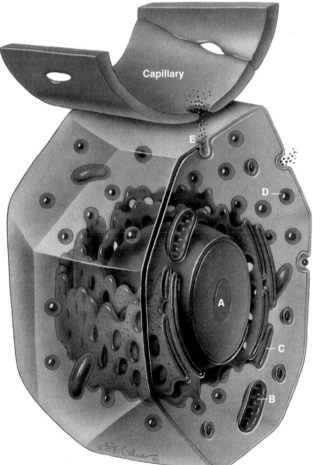

Inside the nucleus (A) of a beta cell (above), DNA directs the manufacture of an insulin precursor chemical, using energy from the mitochondria (B), the cell's power source. In the Golgi apparatus (C), the insulin precursors are broken down into insulin and encapsulated. The insulin capsule (D) then travels outward to the cell membrane (E). At that point, the capsule fuses with the cell membrane and releases its insulin into the blood.

It results from the body's own immune system reacting to the pancreas's insulin-producing cells, called beta cells, as though they were foreign tissue, and destroying them. This leaves the patient without in-

sulin, a hormone needed to maintain normal levels of sugar, or glucose, in the blood.

Most Type I diabetics require a lifelong program of insulin injections to overcome the deficiency and thereby prevent life-threatening complications such as dangerously high blood-sugar levels, cardiovascular disease, and the degeneration of small blood vessels.

The more common and generally less severe type of diabetes is known as non-insulin-dependent, Type II, or adult-onset diabetes. It generally develops much more slowly than Type I diabetes, typically in overweight persons over age 40. The Type II diabetic has a functional pancreas that usually produces normal or even elevated amounts of insulin. However, the tissues in his or her body have grown insulin-resistant—that is, they no longer respond to the hormone. As a result, ever greater amounts of insulin are needed to maintain normal blood-sugar levels, and eventually the pancreas cannot meet the demand.

In most cases, Type II diabetics do not require insulin injections. The disease can usually be controlled with a combination of healthy diet, weight reduction, and oral medication.

A small number of women develop yet another form of diabetes—called gestational, or Type III, diabetes—during pregnancy. If it goes undetected, this can be a life-threatening condition for both mother and baby. Fortunately, most cases of gestational diabetes can be controlled, and most disappear after the baby is born. In some cases, pregnancy appears to "unmask" an already existing form of diabetes (Type I or II), which then becomes a lifelong condition.

What Causes Diabetes?

Recent medical research indicates that diabetes can be the result of a combination of

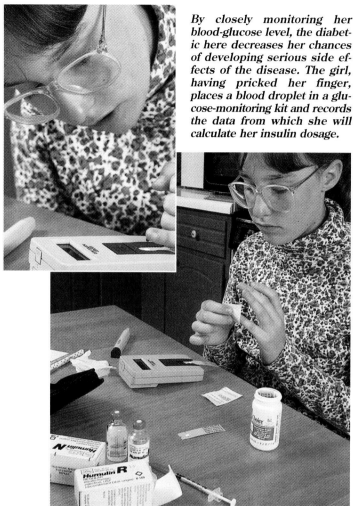

By closely monitoring her blood-glucose level, the diabetic here decreases her chances of developing serious side effects of the disease. The girl, having pricked her finger, places a blood droplet in a glucose-monitoring kit and records the data from which she will calculate her insulin dosage.

nent of the body's insulin-producing beta cells; the immune system revs up to attack the virus, but at the same time attacks the beta cells, mistaking them for foreign viruses.

Type II diabetes may have a stronger genetic component. Most people who have a hereditary predisposition to the disease go on to develop it in later years, primarily if they become overweight. Losing excess weight and maintaining a healthy weight are very important for both preventing the onset and reducing the severity of Type II diabetes.

Symptoms and Management

The initial symptoms of either type of diabetes include fatigue, frequent urination, weight loss, and excessive thirst. But while Type I diabetes usually surfaces abruptly and dramatically, people with Type II diabetes can remain symptom-free for years. Type II diabetes is frequently diagnosed only when a routine physical exam reveals high blood sugar, or when a middle-aged person seeks medical help for a circulation or vision problem that turns out to have been caused by a long-standing, undiagnosed case of diabetes.

genetic, environmental, and immune-system factors. Michael Brownlee, M.D., the Anita and Jack Saltz Professor of Diabetes Research and codirector of the Diabetes Research Center at the Albert Einstein College of Medicine in New York City, explains: "If you have identical twins who are susceptible to Type I diabetes, and one of them develops the disease, the other twin will get diabetes only 50 percent of the time. Now, as identical twins, they both have the susceptibility, but one of them got triggered into diabetes by something in the environment."

A viral infection may be one type of environmental trigger. Researchers theorize that a virus could resemble some compo-

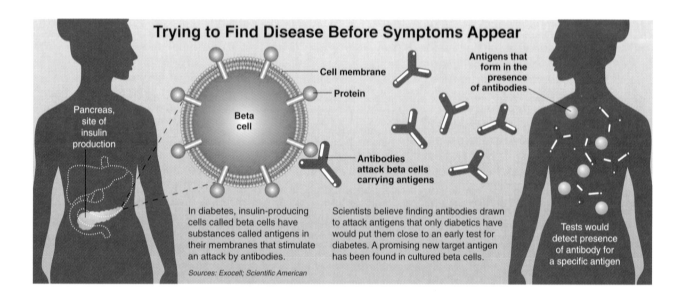

Trying to Find Disease Before Symptoms Appear

Pancreas, site of insulin production

Cell membrane

Protein

Beta cell

Antibodies attack beta cells carrying antigens

Antigens that form in the presence of antibodies

Tests would detect presence of antibody for a specific antigen

In diabetes, insulin-producing cells called beta cells have substances called antigens in their membranes that stimulate an attack by antibodies.

Scientists believe finding antibodies drawn to attack antigens that only diabetics have would put them close to an early test for diabetes. A promising new target antigen has been found in cultured beta cells.

Sources: Exocell; Scientific American

Type I diabetics receiving regular insulin injections and most Type II diabetics do not suffer immediate physical limitations and can enjoy most activities, despite their condition. As mentioned, Type II diabetics can usually manage their disease by watching what they eat and by keeping a tight control on their weight. They may also need to take oral hypoglycemic agents.

The Type I diabetic faces the unfortunate day-to-day reality of blood checks and insulin injections. Every day—sometimes three or four times a day—Type I diabetics must prick a finger and place a drop of blood on a small piece of paper, which is then analyzed by a blood-glucose monitoring device. Depending on the reading, the patient must adjust his or her diet and insulin level (usually through daily self-injections) accordingly.

Failure to take insulin injections can quickly lead to ketoacidosis, in which rising blood levels of sugar and ketones (an acidic substance) can precipitate a gradual loss of consciousness, and eventual coma. Early-warning

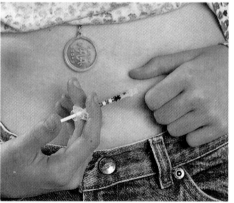

Some diabetics "burn out" on the seemingly never-ending regimen of blood checks, diet adjustments, and self-injections.

symptoms of ketoacidosis include increased thirst and urination, nausea, abdominal pain, and sweet-smelling breath.

On rare occasions, Type I and Type II diabetics fall into comas due to low blood sugar that is caused by an overdose of insulin or hypoglycemic drugs.

Long-Term Consequences

A variety of long-term complications are associated with diabetes. Circulation problems, for example, can reduce sensation in the extremities, especially the feet. In some cases a small injury may progress unchecked, sometimes to the point of requiring amputation. Kidney disease, which affects about 35 to 45 percent of Type I diabetics, often leads to the need for dialysis or kidney transplant.

The most common diabetic complication, particularly for Type II diabetics, is retinopathy, a condition in which changes in the small blood vessels of the eye result in retinal detachment and other visual impairments, including blindness. Ninety percent of diabetics who have had the disease for 20 years or more suffer from some form of retinopathy. Diabetics are also more likely than non-diabetics to experience heart attack, stroke, and diseases of the smaller, peripheral arteries and veins.

Diabetics must constantly plan what, when, and how much they eat. They must also be conscious of how exercise and other activities affect their changing need for

People who maintain a healthy weight decrease their chances of developing Type II diabetes.

insulin and food. Diabetics are encouraged to improve their condition by exercising and by avoiding obesity.

The taxing day-to-day monitoring of food intake and exercise levels, coupled with repeated blood-sugar monitoring, frequently lead to what practitioners call "diabetes burnout." Mary Brown, R.D., M.P.H., an Oak Ridge, Tennessee, registered dietitian who specializes as a nu-

The Exercise Prescription

The American Diabetes Association (ADA) urges people with non-insulin-dependent diabetes mellitus (NIDDM) to do three things: eat healthy food, exercise regularly, and take insulin or oral diabetes medications as prescribed. According to the ADA, exercise can help these patients to maintain a more constant level of blood glucose, lose weight, use fewer medicines, and reduce their risk for heart disease.

Because strenuous exercise can aggravate preexisting conditions (for example, by precipitating episodes of arrhythmia or ischemia in someone with heart disease, or by damaging the arthritic knees of an overweight person), the ADA recommends having a thorough medical examination before embarking on an activity program. And proper equipment is essential: diabetes often reduces circulation and sensation in the feet, for example, and the ADA emphasizes that people with NIDDM must wear properly fitting shoes and inspect their feet for injury after exercising. It is also important to start slowly, work out at regular intervals, and increase the length and intensity of the sessions gradually.

The best time to exercise is when blood glucose is within normal limits, because when the level is either too high or too low vigorous activity can cause problems. If blood sugar is higher than 300 mg/dl,

exercise can make it rise even higher. When the level has been very low (as from excessive insulin or oral medication), exertion can cause it to plummet—which can ultimately lead to unconsciousness and coma. Fortunately, there are a few simple precautions that a person can take to head off episodes of low blood sugar—and promote speedy resolution, should this problem occur:

• Testing blood glucose before and after working out to determine exercise's effect.

• During and after exercise, noting any signs of low blood glucose—dizziness, rapid heart beat, increased sweating, confusion, or hunger.

• While exercising, carrying hard candies, glucose tablets, or some other readily absorbed form of carbohydrate that can be used if signs of low blood glucose appear.

• Taking extra fluids or skipping exercise on particularly warm days to avoid the risk of dehydration.

• Carrying a medical alert card or a bracelet to identify one as having diabetes.

• Taking these steps can make regular physical activity a safe component of NIDDM care, and a way of helping to manage the disease and prevent some of its most serious complications. And one can lose a few pounds along the way.

trition consultant for dialysis and diabetic patients, explains that diabetics sometimes feel so overwhelmed or fatigued by everything they have to do that "they go on a rampage where they're just not going to do anything; they just don't care." This, of course, sets the stage for diabetes' most devastating long-term complications.

The Control and Complications Trial

Fortunately, incentive does exist to abort a "diabetic rampage" before it occurs. Recent findings have verified that stringent control of the Type I diabetic's blood-sugar level, diet, and exercise patterns is extraordinarily successful in lessening diabetic complications. Sponsored by the National Institute of Diabetes and Digestive and Kidney Diseases, the nine-year-long Diabetes Control and Complications Trial (DCCT) studied 1,441 diabetics throughout the United States and Canada—the largest study of its kind ever conducted.

cent lessening of diabetic complications for these patients.

Unfortunately, the success of the study carried with it a rather unrealistic price tag. In addition to the added health-care costs and availability of resources needed to implement this type of program on an individual basis, many physicians wonder: Is such a tightly controlled regimen a practical solution for the general diabetic population? "The short answer is no," says Dr. Brownlee. "The medical facilities and the expertise to help patients do this are still just not as widely promulgated as they could be." Still, what remains clear is that this disease can be successfully controlled by keeping a patient's blood-sugar level as close to normal as possible.

Other Studies, Other Treatments

Clearly, prevention is preferable to any treatment for diabetes. Clinical trials are underway to determine ways

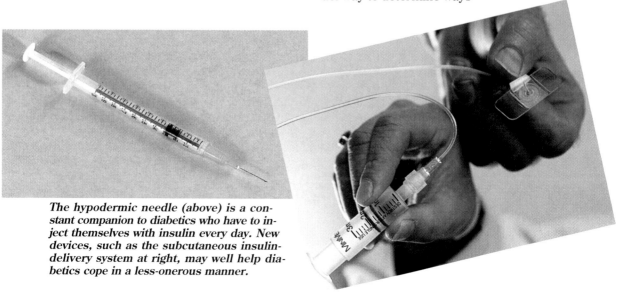

The hypodermic needle (above) is a constant companion to diabetics who have to inject themselves with insulin every day. New devices, such as the subcutaneous insulin-delivery system at right, may well help diabetics cope in a less-onerous manner.

The subjects involved were continuously monitored and managed by specialized treatment teams, had daily consultation with dietitians and other health-care professionals, tested their blood-glucose levels four to eight times per day, and, as necessary, received numerous daily insulin injections. Researchers were astounded at the force of their findings: a 50 to 75 per-

by which practitioners might measure antibodies in the blood in order to predict, three or four years in advance, when a person is going to develop Type I diabetes. "The antibodies don't cause the diabetes, but they signify that damage is going on," explains Dr. Brownlee. Alerted to this early damage, physicians of the future may learn ways to halt the immune destruction. Other studies are also underway to better understand Type II diabetes and to find the best ways to prevent it.

In terms of health management, improved blood-sugar tests may enable the Type I diabetic to better maintain normal levels of insulin in his or her blood. On the drawing board is a device that uses a laser beam to measure blood sugar. Also, researchers are experimenting with a tiny computer that employs infrared radiation to read a patient's blood-sugar level. The computer would automatically trigger a pump to inject the appropriate amount of insulin into the diabetic.

The insulin pump worn by the diabetic equestrian above keeps her insulin and blood-sugar levels stable, even during vigorous exercise.

Meanwhile, researchers seek ways to deal more effectively with some of diabetes' more devastating long-term complications, such as kidney failure. A group of drugs known as angiotensin converting enzyme (ACE) inhibitors have long been used to treat congestive heart disease and high blood pressure. One ACE inhibitor in particular, captopril, has recently proved effective in slowing down the relentless kidney damage that can result from diabetes. ACE inhibitors work by suppressing the production of a certain blood vessel-constricting enzyme. The resulting normalization of blood pressure apparently helps slow kidney deterioration. It is possible that even if a patient does not have detectable high blood pressure, blood pressure may nonetheless be elevated in the kidney's blood vessels. And ACE inhibitors are unique in having a special action on the blood pressure inside the kidney.

In one large clinical study, some patients whose kidneys were starting to show signs of damage took captopril while others took nothing. Those who received captopril showed a 50 percent reduction in the rate of kidney decline. Captopril may be able to double the time that a person can function before they require dialysis or a kidney transplant.

Some of the more intriguing work being done on diabetes management involves the transplantation and genetic engineering of islet cells, groups of cells in the pancreas that contain the insulin-producing beta cells—the ones targeted for destruction by the diabetic's immune system.

One of the problems with transplantation, however, is that it requires the use of potent toxic drugs to suppress the patient's immune system, which would ordinarily destroy any foreign tissue. The risk of using such drugs is considered justifiable in a life-or-death situation, such as with a heart, kidney, or liver transplant, but not with a diabetic who is otherwise healthy.

Another major obstacle: there just are not enough of these precious islet cells to go around, rendering transplantation at this time essentially unfeasible. "We're trying to figure out a way to make these cells grow in a laboratory," says Dr. Brownlee. His research center is one of perhaps two worldwide currently working on the bioengineering of cells for diabetes treatment.

"It's not going to happen tomorrow," Dr. Brownlee says, "but a lot of progress is being made. This is an ongoing approach to actually treating or curing both types of diabetes." ◇

AMBULATORY SURGERY:
Operation without Admission

by Jessica Snyder Sachs

"Fifteen years ago, all my surgery patients spent a few days to a few weeks in the hospital," says orthopedic surgeon Peter Amadio, M.D., of the Mayo Medical Center in Rochester, Minnesota. "Now I rarely hospitalize anyone. Most are home by sunset."

Orthopedic surgeons are not alone in the trend toward ambulatory, or outpatient, surgery. Today tonsillectomy, hernia repair, tumor biopsies, face surgery, vasectomy, tubal ligation, even gallbladder removal, can be done on a same-day basis. A patient checks into a surgical center several hours before his or her operation, and leaves for home later the same day.

"In all, about 60 percent of surgery in this country is now performed on an outpatient basis," says Stephen Sharnick, M.D., medical director of One-Day Surgery Services at Danbury Hospital in Connecticut.

Ambulatory surgery has become the norm largely because new surgical instruments allow surgeons to operate through tiny incisions, says Dr. Amadio. Through these small openings, surgeons slip viewing tubes called endoscopes, special microscopes, or microsurgical tools.

With less cutting involved, such "keyhole" surgery results in far less bleeding, trauma, and risk of infection. Many patients can literally walk away from surgery.

New anesthesia procedures and drugs have also minimized postsurgery recovery time. Even when general anesthesia is used recovery no longer takes as long, notes Dr. Sharnick. "Some of the new, short-acting drugs allow us to have a patient fully awake within minutes of completing an operation," he says. The new anesthetics are also less likely to cause serious complications such as heart attack and kidney damage. So there is less need to hospitalize patients overnight for observation.

Even surgery done with traditional instruments and drugs is more likely to be done on an outpatient basis now. "Studies show that most people recover better at home, both physically and psychologically," says Dr. Sharnick. Sending a patient home after surgery also costs far less than overnight hospitalization.

What to Expect

Same-day surgery is usually performed either in an outpatient suite within a hospital or at a separate "surgicenter." A relatively new concept, private surgicenters are designed to be less intimidating than hospitals, and, in some cases, they offer lower cost. In-hospital surgery suites have the advantage of quick access to emergency care should complications arise.

The Week before Surgery. Since ambulatory surgery usually involves elective—not emergency—procedures, preparation usually begins a week or more before the big day. First the patient schedules an office visit with the surgeon, who explains the procedure and asks about any medical conditions that could complicate surgery. The patient also needs to tell the surgeon about any drugs that he or she is taking. The doctor's staff then schedules the surgery as well as any necessary presurgical testing.

Anesthesia. Except for the simplest form of anesthesia—local without sedation—all anesthetics and sedatives are administered by an anesthesiologist or nurse-anesthetist. These specialists remain in the operating room throughout surgery to monitor the patient's comfort and vital signs.

With local anesthesia the site of the operation is numbed with an injection. A surgeon may use local anesthetic to remove a mole or a small breast lump, or to perform plastic surgery on a small area.

Regional anesthesia is used when a larger area, such as an entire arm or leg, must be numbed. The injection is placed near a major nerve, and so blocks feeling to the body part served by that nerve.

With both local and regional anesthesia, the patient remains awake during the operation. These anesthetics are often combined with sedating drugs to keep the patient relaxed.

General anesthesia, administered either by inhalation or intravenous injection, puts the patient "to sleep." A tube is then inserted in the throat to assist breathing. General anesthesia is reserved for long operations, for operations involving an area that is not easily numbed, and for patients who may become agitated during surgery if awake.

The Day of Surgery

Patients receiving sedation or general anesthesia are usually asked not to eat anything within 10 hours of surgery, to help prevent vomiting. Water or other clear liquids are sometimes permitted up until three hours before surgery.

Several hours before surgery, the patient checks into the hospital or surgery clinic. Check-in usually entails some paperwork and a brief checkup by a nurse or physician's assistant. The patient then disrobes, removes any contact lenses or false teeth, and puts on a surgical gown and slippers.

If an anesthesiologist is involved in the operation, he or she meets the patient before surgery and performs several brief pre-operative checks. The patient may ask any questions or voice any lingering fears, which the anesthesiologist can address.

When the surgeon is ready, the patient is brought into the operating room, helped onto the operating table, and covered with sheets. Arms may be gently strapped into place so that blood-pressure cuffs and intravenous lines can be attached.

Before the operation begins, the area of the incision will be shaved (if necessary) and then swabbed with disinfectant. The staff don clean gowns and masks and bring out sterilized instruments and supplies.

Once anesthetic and sedation have been given, the surgeons begin their work. A patient who remains awake may feel pressure and tugging at the site of surgery. Any sensation of pain should be reported so that more anesthetic can be given.

Postoperative Recovery

Patients who receive general anesthesia are moved to a recovery room. On waking, they may feel extremely chilled, as body temperature can drop during general anesthesia. Other side effects include sore throat, nausea, and, occasionally, vomiting. The site of the operation may be immediately painful. Fortunately, the recovery-room nurses have prewarmed blankets, heat lamps, and pain medications at hand.

Once the general-anesthesia patient has recovered sufficiently, he or she is moved to the discharge area. Patients who have received regional anesthesia move through the recovery room briefly before entering the discharge area. Those receiving local anesthetic go directly to the discharge room.

Typically the discharge room is furnished with recliners where patients can rest comfortably and rejoin their companions. The area is staffed by nurses who can administer pain medication. They also instruct the patients and their family members on how to perform post-surgery care such as bathing, changing dressings, and emptying drainage tubes if needed.

All patients remain in the discharge room until their surgeons and anesthesiologists decide they have recovered well enough to go home. This may vary from a few minutes to an hour or more, depending on the extent of the operation and the form of anesthesia used.

Importantly, a patient who has received general anesthesia or sedation should not drive the same day. Most centers will not release such patients without a companion. It is best for all patients to have someone to assist them, at least through the evening.

In parting, the surgeon will give the patient a prescription for pain medication, and a phone number to call should problems such as bleeding or fever arise. The doctor will also advise as to how quickly the patient can resume normal activities, and when to return for a follow-up examination. ◇

The Young Man's Cancer

by Frank M. Szivos

U.S. Testicular Cancer Trends (per 100,000 men)

Young men are most susceptible to testicular cancer, a disease whose incidence has been steadily increasing (graph). The disease has a very high cure rate, although at the cost of the cancerous testicle (its tumor shown in cross-section above). Many survivors nonetheless go on to father children.

Three days after his 25th birthday, Tom Best awoke doubled over with pain. His left testicle had swollen to three times its normal size. A few days earlier, he had felt a mild soreness in his testicle, a discomfort he wrote off as a slight muscle pull from skiing the previous weekend. Now the pain was intense.

Tom had never experienced anything like this before. After he struggled to pull on his clothes, his wife drove him to the emergency room of the local hospital. A urologist called in to examine him ordered a battery of tests.

Within hours, Tom's worst nightmare had come true—he was diagnosed with testicular cancer and required immediate surgery. How could this be? Tom had never been seriously sick and he was in the prime of his life—married for only three years and planning to start a family. But now he had cancer, and the pain was excruciating.

"In the emergency room, I couldn't think once they told me I had cancer," Best said. "I was scared and in a lot of pain. It was a shock for me and my wife. I never doubted that the doctor wanted to get me back to normal. But it was a long, rough road."

Tom's testicular cancer was somewhat atypical of the usual scenario, given the intensity of his pain and the urgency with which he required surgery. Still, Tom, like the majority of testicular-cancer victims, survived. Indeed, if there is any good news about testicular cancer—the so-called "young man's cancer"—it is the fact that when detected early, the cure rate for this type of cancer is about 95 percent.

A Widespread Problem

Oddly enough, while the mortality rate from testicular cancer is dropping, the incidence of the disease is rising at an alarming rate. Testicular cancer now strikes about two men in every 100,000 annually, and the ratio keeps on rising. Richard Kaplan, M.D., a senior investigator for the National Cancer Institute (NCI), calls the rise in the disease "a real phenomenon." Some physicians argue that the rate is not rising, but rather that the diagnosis of the condition is being made more frequently.

Whatever the case, there's no question about one fact: testicular cancer is the most common malignancy in males between the ages of 18 and 35 in the United States, and is responsible for 3 percent of all deaths related to cancer in this age group. In 1994 there will be an estimated 7,000 new cases of testicular cancer diagnosed in this coun-

try; approximately 400 young men will die of the disease.

"It's an emotionally laden subject," Kaplan says. "It compares to breast cancer in women. It's not talked about enough because it affects a 'private' part of the body. It also seems odd that cancer would strike young men, who would seem less vulnerable to it. Fortunately, we're starting to get the message out."

Baseball fans got the message in 1991, when Philadelphia Phillies first baseman John Kruk was diagnosed with the condition early in the season. Nicholas Viner, M.D., the chief of urology at Bridgeport Hospital in Connecticut, knows firsthand that the publicity from Kruk's testicular cancer helped get the word out about the disease: Dr. Viner received a rash of calls from concerned males shortly after Kruk's problem became public.

Perhaps the best result of this publicity was the public's increased awareness of the symptoms of testicular cancer. Unfortunately, in the early stages, testicular cancer is virtually always symptomless. But when symptoms do occur, they include: a lump on a testicle; slight enlargement of one tes-

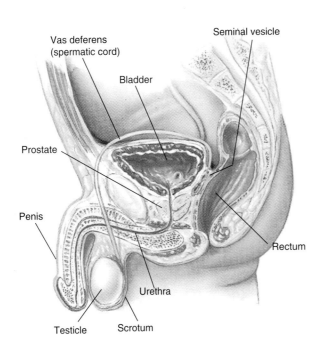

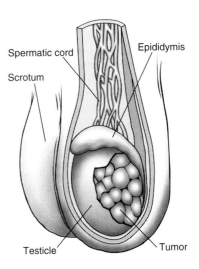

The testicles produce sperm and secrete various hormones—two essential functions of the male reproductive system (left). A testicular tumor (above) usually begins its development in the sperm-producing cells.

ticle; a sensation of heaviness in the testicles or groin; and/or a dull ache in the lower abdomen or groin.

If you have any one of these symptoms, see a doctor at once. It is also essential to do regular self-examinations (see the box at right) and to receive yearly checkups by a physician.

Causes

The causes of testicular cancer still baffle physicians. It is clear, though, that a correlation exists between a child born with one or both testicles undescended or partially undescended and his likelihood of developing the disease. In fact, the reason an undescended testicle does not "drop" into its normal position is probably because it is not perfectly healthy. Children born with this condition run a five-times-greater risk of developing a testicular tumor later in adulthood than do boys whose testicles are properly in place at birth. Fortunately, if the problem is corrected surgically in infancy, the risk of developing testicular cancer drops to near-normal levels.

Evidence also suggests that prenatal factors may contribute to the development of testicular cancer. For example, sons born to women who experienced an unusual amount of bleeding and extreme nausea during pregnancy run a higher risk of developing the disease. Children of women who took diethylstilbestrol (DES), a drug designed to prevent miscarriages, also have a high incidence of testicular cancer as adults. Some research has shown that electric blankets may raise a youngster's testicular temperature, and perhaps contribute to problems later on. And interestingly, while testicular cancer is most common among young white males, it is virtually unknown among blacks.

A recent Danish study has raised evidence that environmental factors could predispose men to the disease. Danish researchers note that during World War II, German occupation troops isolated Denmark from outside commerce. This event somehow significantly lowered the rate of testicular cancer in Danish men born during the war years. The study suggests that

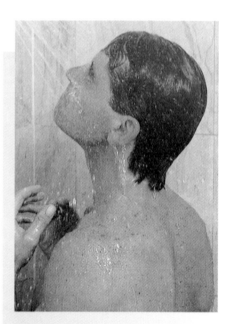

Examine Yourself

Nicholas Viner, M.D., chief of urology at Bridgeport Hospital in Connecticut, recommends that all men conduct a monthly testicular self-examination in the shower. "Young men need to know that they should do a testicular self-exam regularly," Viner says. "Testicular tumors are often painless."

To start the self-examination, glide the fingers over soapy skin, which is more elastic, making it easier to feel the texture underneath. Examine the testicles first, slowly rolling them between the thumb and fingers and applying slight pressure to detect any hard, painless lumps. Next, check the epididymis, the comma-shaped cord behind each testicle. It is common for the epididymis to feel slightly tender to the touch; it is often the spot where most noncancerous problems occur. Continue the examination by searching for any lumps along the vas deferens, the sperm-carrying tube that runs upward from the epididymis. The vas normally feels like a firm, movable, smooth tube.

Dr. Viner notes: "If you feel something, it ought to be checked. Even if it turns out to be the worst possible scenario of cancer, the cure rate is in the high 90 percent range."

Other Testicular Problems

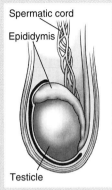

Spermatic cord

Epididymis

Testicle

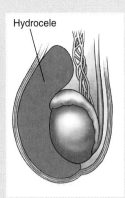

Hydrocele

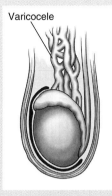

Varicocele

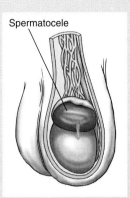

Spermatocele

Physicians warn that men may develop various testicular problems besides cancer. Here is a list of the more common testicular disorders.

• *Hydroceles*, or fluid accumulations around the testicles, are common in boys and men, especially after a trauma to that region of the body. In newborns the condition often disappears spontaneously within a year. Children with hydroceles often require surgery; adults may need surgery if the hydrocele is very large or uncomfortable.

• *Varicoceles* occur when the veins leading from the testicles increase in size. They account for about 15 percent of benign testicular problems and are a prominent cause of male infertility. Treatment commonly involves surgery.

• *Spermatocele* refers to a cyst that forms on the epididymis, the structure next to the testicle that carries sperm. Physicians commonly monitor the condition, and recommend surgery only if the condition is uncomfortable to the patient.

• *Epididymitis* is an infection of the epididymis, which can be treated with medication.

• *Orchitis* is an infection of the testicles, often treated with drugs. This condition can result from mumps, which causes the testicles to swell and become tender. It is not uncommon for the testicles to shrink after the infection subsides.

• *Hematocele* describes a swelling of the testicles caused by a buildup of blood in the scrotum. This is a rare condition often resulting from trauma.

---

maternal changes, probably in diet, altered the rate of fetal precancerous cells (carcinoma in situ).

Still, no one really knows what causes testicular cancer. "A lot of evidence is circumstantial," Dr. Kaplan says. "We still aren't sure about the causes. More research is needed."

Types of Cancer

There are two basic kinds of testicular cancer: seminoma and nonseminoma. The former, a slow-growing cancer, accounts for about one-third of all testicular tumors. If it

is detected early, surgery and radiation can yield a near 100 percent cure rate. Nonseminomas are aggressive tumors. In 60 to 70 percent of these cases, the cancer has metastasized (spread) to the lymph glands.

Surgery is the first line of treatment for both types of testicular cancer. But before that, physicians request blood tests to determine the levels of alpha-fetoprotein and beta-chain HCG (human chorionic gonadotropin)—substances that may be produced when there are nonseminomatous testicular cancerous cells in the body. The tests are helpful in determining the extent of the disease. X rays and CAT scans are commonly used to determine if the cancer has metastasized to other parts of the body. In the actual operation, the surgeon makes an incision in the lower abdomen and removes the testicle out of the scrotum.

With seminoma tumors, physicians commonly use radiation to ensure eradication of any residual cancer. Nonseminoma tumors, of which there are four kinds—embryonal-cell carcinoma, teratoma, teratocarcinoma, and choriocarcinoma—also require surgical removal of not only the testicle, but also of nearby structures, including the epididymis and the spermatic cord. In addition, a rigorous chemotherapy treatment is prescribed to clear any metastatic cells that may have spread to other parts of the body.

A common result of the surgery and follow-up treatments is the reduction of fertility in men. Nonetheless, males can remain sexually active with one testicle, and may still be able to father children. Moreover, there is only a slight chance (about 5 percent) of developing a tumor in the other testicle. Since chemotherapy can cause infertility, men are offered the option to deposit their sperm into a sperm bank before they embark on treatment.

Surviving Testicular Cancer

In 1985, when Fred Reiss of Santa Cruz, California, was 29 years old, he was diagnosed with a seminoma tumor and underwent testicular surgery and radiation therapy. He knows the fear of having this cancer, and the unpleasant side effects of radiation treatment. A professional comedian, Reiss had little to laugh about as he battled the disease and his anxiety.

"Even though the cure rate is over 90 percent, the statistics mean very little when your life is on the line," Reiss says, echoing the lament of many cancer patients. "It's weird when you have something inside of you that could kill you. I was angry at this disease coming at me. I talked to it. I visualized flying saucers (radiation waves) going through my body and bombing the hell out of the cancer cells. Radiation was the hero that came to help me."

Reiss endured four weeks of radiation, five times a week. The treatment often left him weak and nauseous, and he had difficulty concentrating. During the course of treatment, he often slept 18 hours after a round of radiation, and he lost about 20 pounds. But within six months of his surgery, he felt stronger and more energetic.

Because Tom Best had the more serious nonseminoma tumor, he underwent four weeks of fatiguing daily chemotherapy treatments. When the chemotherapy finally ended, his immune system was depleted so severely that he needed to spend the following week in the hospital, battling pneumonia. He lost 40 pounds, his hair fell out, and he experienced only partial sensation in his fingers and hands.

Dr. Viner says the psychological effects of chemotherapy treatment for testicular cancer can be devastating. Most patients endure it and recover. But he once had a rare case involving a 32-year-old patient who underwent testicular surgery followed by chemotherapy treatment. Despite the fact that the drugs were working, he refused to take any more drugs once he developed cancer in his remaining testicle, a truly rare occurrence.

"Chemo pushes you to the brink," Dr. Viner says. "We're talking about young men for the most part, who are strong, and they struggle to endure the treatment."

A brush with testicular cancer changed the lives of both Fred Reiss and Tom Best. Reiss stopped writing for newspapers and became a full-time comedian. He plays tennis often and has learned to surf. Best, an avid Notre Dame sports fan since childhood, visited the college with his wife as soon as he felt strong enough. After he recovered from his illness, he made a career change and became an insurance agent. He and his wife are in the process of adopting a child. "I do a lot more things on the spur of the moment," Best says. "I don't hold back. I went to South Bend, Indiana, to watch Notre Dame play basketball. It's something I'll always remember. I've been cancer-free for seven years. On my fifth anniversary, we had a party. That was great." ◇

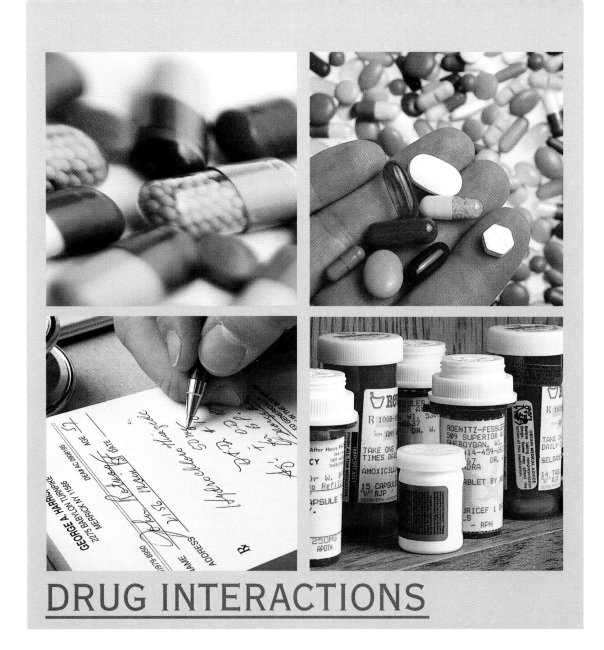

DRUG INTERACTIONS

by Devera Pine

Marsha recalls the terror of waking in the middle of the night, roused by the pounding of her own heart. It was racing so fast and beating so hard that she felt it might burst right out of her chest. The pounding continued for hours, leaving Marsha exhausted and fearing for her life. "What happened to me?" she asked her doctor in the morning.

After backtracking through the events of the previous day, Marsha and her physician solved the mystery. She had been taking the antibiotic erythromycin, which her doctor had prescribed for a bacterial infection.

Then her allergies flared in the afternoon, and she took her prescription antihistamine terfenadine (Seldane), which she had received from her allergy specialist. The combination of the two drugs produced a side effect: an abnormal and potentially fatal heart rhythm, or arrhythmia.

Unfortunately, Marsha's experience is not unusual. Given the thousands of medicines now available—both by prescription and over-the-counter—there are thousands of possible interactions when a person takes more than one drug at a time. Sometimes the consequences are deadly serious.

Drugs can likewise interact with alcohol, tobacco, food, and even sunlight to cause unwanted side effects.

Rarely, dangerous drug interactions occur when a physician inadvertently prescribes two incompatible drugs. More often it is a case of miscommunication. A patient seeing more than one physician may neglect to tell each doctor the sum total of the medications that other doctors have prescribed. A patient on medication should also check with his or her physician or pharmacist before taking any over-the-counter drugs, and patients certainly should never self-prescribe medications borrowed from a friend or saved from a previous illness.

Chemical Combos

Whenever two or more drugs are circulating through the same body, a number of things can happen. Simple drug interactions occur when the effects—and side effects—of various drugs collide.

Drugs with opposite results may effectively cancel each other out. For example, diabetics often suffer from hypertension (high blood pressure). Some diuretic-type hypertensive drugs may increase the level of glucose in the blood, and so counter the action of antidiabetic medicines.

The consequences of such "antagonistic" drugs are not always negative, however. Antihistamines may have the side effect of making you drowsy, while decongestants may have a stimulating effect, notes Kathryn Grant, Pharm.D., assistant clinical professor at the University of Arizona College of Pharmacy in Tucson. Some clinicians believe the combination makes for a decongestant-antihistamine that may be less sleep-inducing.

Conversely, the effects of two drugs can be additive—but the total may not always be what you expect. "One plus one could be three," quips Jack M. Rosenberg, Pharm.D., Ph.D., professor of pharmacology at the Arnold and Marie Schwartz College of Pharmacy and Health Sciences at Long Island University in Brooklyn, New York. A dangerous example is the combination of the tranquilizer diazepam (Valium) and sleeping pills. The resulting sedation can be deadly.

Physicians and pharmacists must also take into consideration the possibility of more-complicated drug interactions. One drug may change the rate at which a second drug passes from the digestive system into the bloodstream. For instance, the painkiller codeine slows digestion, and as a result reduces the speed at which other medications are absorbed. Conversely, the prescription heartburn medicine metoclopramide (Reglan) can speed digestion and the rate at which drugs are absorbed.

Drug interactions can also alter how fast medications pass from the bloodstream into the tissues or organs that they affect. For instance, certain proteins in the blood have a tendency to bind to various drugs. Drug manufacturers realize this, and so adjust the dosages that they recommend for their medicines. But problems can arise if a second drug alters the above equation. In other words, if drug "B" binds with the blood proteins, then drug "A" may be left entirely unbound and active. In effect, this may increase the dosage of drug "A" a dangerous level.

This is just the type of problem that can occur with the over-the-counter pain reliever ibuprofen and other nonsteroidal anti-inflammatories (NSAIDs). In effect, NSAIDs increase the effect of certain drugs such as the anticoagulant warfarin. The result can be unwanted side effects such as internal bleeding.

Drowsiness is just one of the potential side effects that may occur when a drug interacts with alcohol, tobacco, food, sunlight, or even another drug.

Problems can likewise arise when one drug changes the way the body metabolizes, or breaks down, another medication. For instance, doctors and pharmacists know that the antiulcer drug cimetidine (Tagamet) inhibits certain enzymes in the liver. This can slow the rate at which the liver breaks down a wide variety of other drugs. As a result, these drugs remain active in the body longer than is desired. In some cases the results can be deadly. For instance, the unfortunate combination of

Your pharmacist is a valuable source of knowledge about prescription and nonprescription medications. Many drugstores supply special data sheets that give information concerning dose, storage, and possible side effects.

cimetidine and the antiasthma drug theophylline can result in seizures and death.

Similarly, a few medicines can change the rate at which the kidneys excrete other drugs. The combination of some diuretics and lithium, for instance, can act on the kidneys to slow the elimination of lithium. Conversely, various medications speed up the rate at which the body breaks down or excretes other drugs, leaving less of the second drug active in the body.

Food-Drug Interactions

Food, alcohol, and tobacco use are likewise known to alter the action of many drugs. A meal may simply slow a drug's absorption in the digestive tract. For this reason, common medications such as penicillin, tetracycline, digoxin, acetaminophen, and levodopa are best taken on an empty stomach, two hours before or after eating.

In other cases, food-drug interactions affect more than just the absorption. One of the most serious of these effects occurs when monoamine oxidase inhibitors (MAOIs) mix with foods containing tyramine. The result can be a fatal change in blood pressure. MAOIs include the antidepressants Marplan, Nardil, and Parnate; the antibiotic Furoxone; and the anticancer drug Matulane. Tyramine is found in wine, aged cheeses, chocolate, and many other foods (see chart).

MAOIs can also cause a deadly reaction when combined with the ingredients of many over-the-counter cold, allergy, and diet drugs. These over-the-counter ingredients include pseudoephedrine, phenylephrine, and phenylpropanolamine. As a group, they are known as sympathomimetic amines.

If you've ever been prescribed the antibiotic tetracycline, you've probably been told not to take it with milk or other dairy foods. This is because tetracycline and calcium (which is present in abundance in dairy products) form compounds that are not well absorbed in the digestive tract. This greatly reduces the amount of tetracycline available to fight an infection.

Even the vitamins in your food can trip up some medicines. For example, leafy green vegetables, tomatoes, and other foods rich in vitamin K can interfere with the anticoagulant warfarin. People on warfarin should either monitor their intake of these foods or ask their doctor to adjust their dosage accordingly.

Interactions with Tobacco and Alcohol

Smoking or chewing tobacco speeds up the metabolism of many drugs, and thereby reduces their effectiveness. For example, smokers sometimes need twice the usual dose of the antiasthma drug theophylline. Tobacco also interacts with oral contraceptives to increase the risk of stroke, heart attack, and blood clots.

Various other medications perform poorly in the presence of tobacco smoke. These include the antianxiety drugs Librium and Valium, most antidiabetic drugs, anticoagulants such as heparin and warfarin, the antihypertensive drug propranolol (Inderal), and tricyclic antidepressants.

Alcohol and drugs are another bad mix, producing effects ranging from increased

Foods That Contain Tyramine

The naturally occurring chemical tyramine can interact with monoamine oxidase inhibitors (MAOIs), such as certain antidepressants, blood-pressure drugs, antibiotics, and anticancer drugs. The result is potentially fatal changes in blood pressure. The following is a partial list of foods that contain tyramine:

Avocados
Bananas
Beer
Caffeine (any food with caffeine such as coffee, tea, cola, chocolate)
Caviar
Cheese (aged)
Chicken liver
Fava beans
Figs (canned)
Herring (pickled or dry)
Liver
Meat, cured (salami, bologna, pepperoni, etc.)
Meat tenderizers and extracts
Raisins
Raspberries
Sour cream
Soy sauce
Wine
Yeast extract
Yogurt

Food-Drug Interactions

Many foods react with drugs to alter their effectiveness or cause unwanted side effects. For instance:

• **Acidic foods** such as citrus fruits, colas, pickles, tomatoes, vinegar, and wine can slow the absorption of ampicillin, erythromycin, penicillin, and other antibiotics.

• **Dairy products** and **calcium supplements** can impair the absorption of tetracycline.

• **Natural licorice** contains the chemical glycyrrhiza, which can interact with blood-pressure drugs to actually increase blood pressure.

• **Caffeine** in chocolate, cola, coffee, and tea can interact with the antiasthma drug theophylline to increase theophylline's stimulant effects.

• **Diet**, especially high-protein, low-carbohydrate ones, and charcoal-broiled beef can likewise interact with theophylline to decrease the drug's effectiveness.

Vitamin-Drug Interactions

• **Phenytoin (Dilantin)**, an anticonvulsive drug, can cause deficiencies in folic acid and vitamin K.

• **Vitamin B$_6$** can block the action of the anti-Parkinson's drug levodopa.

• **Vitamin D** can interact with barbiturates (such as phenobarbital).

• **Vitamin K** can block the effects of the anticoagulant warfarin (Coumadin).

• **Cholestyramine (Questran)** and other drugs prescribed to reduce high triglycerides can lead to deficiencies in fat-soluble vitamins such as A, D, E, and K.

Drug-Drug Interactions

This is only a partial list of drug interactions. Consult your doctor and pharmacist to be certain the medicines you take are compatible.

Analgesics and Antiinflammatory Drugs

• *Aspirin and alcohol:* Can cause bleeding in the intestinal tract.

• *Aspirin and anticoagulants:* Can increase the effect of anticoagulants.

NSAIDs (nonsteroidal antiinflammatories) (including ibuprofen, naproxen)

• *NSAIDs and aspirin:* May reduce blood levels of NSAIDs.

• *NSAIDs and anticoagulants:* Can increase bleeding in gastrointestinal tract.

• *NSAIDs and beta-blockers:* Can decrease the effectiveness of beta-blockers.

• *NSAIDs and diuretics:* Can decrease the effectiveness of diuretics.

Antacids

• *Antacids and tetracycline:* Can hamper the absorption of tetracycline into the blood.

• *Antacids with aspirin:* May cause "time-release" aspirin to be "released" too soon.

Antibiotics

• *Erythromycin and theophylline:* May decrease effectiveness of erythromycin and increase blood levels of theophylline.

• *Erythromycin and digoxin:* May increase toxic effects of digoxin.

(Also see other categories.)

Antihypertensive Drugs

• *Antihypertensives with diuretics:* Can increase effect of the blood-pressure medicine.

• *Antihypertensives with tricyclic antidepressants:* Can increase the effect on blood pressure.

• *Beta-blockers with cimetidine* (Tagamet): Can slow the metabolism of the beta-blocker, increasing its effects.

• *Beta-blockers with theophylline:* May block the action of theophylline.

Antihistamines

• *Astemizole* (Hismanal) *with erythromycin:* Can cause arrhythmias.

• *Astemizole* (Hismanal) *with antifungal drug Nizoral:* Can cause arrhythmias.

• *Terfenadine* (Seldane) *with erythromycin:* Can cause arrhythmias.

Antidepressants

• *Tricyclic antidepressants* (Elavil, Asendin, Norpramin, and others) *with cimetidine* (Tagamet): May slow the metabolism of the antidepressant, increasing its effect.

• *MAOIs with sympathomimetic amines* (including over-the-counter cold, allergy, and diet medicines that contain pseudoephedrine, phenylephrine, or phenylpropanolamine): Can cause serious—possibly fatal—reaction involving severe headaches, dangerously high blood pressure, and abnormal heart rhythms.

Antiulcer Drugs—Histamine H_2 blockers (including cimetidine—Tagamet—and ranitidine—Zantac)

• *H_2 blockers with anticoagulants:* May inhibit the metabolism of the anticoagulant.

Antianxiety Drugs

• *Antianxiety drugs* (such as benzodiazepines and barbiturates) *with MAOI antidepressants:* May increase the effect of the antianxiety drug.

• *Barbiturates* (phenobarbital, Nembutal, and Seconal, for example) *with beta-blockers:* Can decrease the effect of the beta-blocker.

• *Barbiturates with calcium channel blockers:* May decrease the blood levels of the calcium channel blocker.

• *Barbiturates and anticoagulants:* May decrease the anticoagulant's effectiveness.

---

intoxication to death. Before prescribing H_2-blockers, doctors warn ulcer patients that the medication reduces the amount of the stomach enzyme that metabolizes alcohol. Therefore, any alcohol consumed will be more intoxicating than normal.

Even more dangerous is the combination of alcohol with sedatives or tranquilizers. It was Valium and alcohol that put Karen Ann Quinlan into her coma. Any medicine that depresses the central nervous system—including antihistamines, barbiturates, tran-

Sun-Drug Interactions

The following classes of drugs include brands that can cause photoallergic reactions (hives) in some people:
- Antibacterial and antifungal soaps and creams
- Antihistamines
- Diuretics
- Sunscreens
- Tranquilizers

The following classes of drugs include many brands that can cause phototoxic (sunburn) reactions in some people:
- Acne medicines (etretinate, isoretinoid, tretinoin)
- Antiarrhythmia drugs
- Analgesics and antiinflammatory drugs
- Antibacterials
- Antibiotics such as tetracycline
- Antifungals (some)
- Diuretics, including thiazides (some)
- Oral contraceptives (some)

Tobacco-Drug Interactions

Tobacco can affect the action of many medicines, including the following:

Antidiabetics (some, not all)
Tranquilizers (some, not all)
Oral contraceptives
Estrogens
Heparin
Lidocaine
Propoxyphene (Darvon, Dolene)
Propranolol (Inderal)
Theophylline
Tricyclic antidepressants

Taking the correct dose at the proper time is important, especially when using more than one drug. A weekly pill dispenser (above) helps many people keep themselves on schedule.

quilizers, and psychotropic drugs—can interact dangerously with alcohol. Alcohol can also counter the effects of medications such as antidiabetic drugs.

Drugs can even increase a person's sensitivity to sunlight. Some antibacterial and antifungal soaps and creams can produce hives and other allergic reactions if the person taking them spends time in the sun.

Drugs that increase your likelihood of a sunburn are known as phototoxic. Common phototoxic drugs include the antibiotic tetracycline, many oral contraceptives, and some diuretics and antifungals.

Staying Safe

The average patient can't be expected to keep track of all the possible interactions that medicines can cause. However, to learn about the medications that they are taking, many people find it useful to consult one of the many reference books available in stores and libraries.

More important, be sure to ask your doctor and your pharmacist about any possible interactions a drug may have with food, drink, sunlight, or other drugs—including nonprescription products. Whenever possible, fill all your prescriptions at the same drugstore, so that the pharmacist can track all the medications you take. Today many pharmacies use computer programs to alert them to possible problems.

Finally, if you think that you're experiencing a drug interaction, call your physician or pharmacist immediately!   ◇

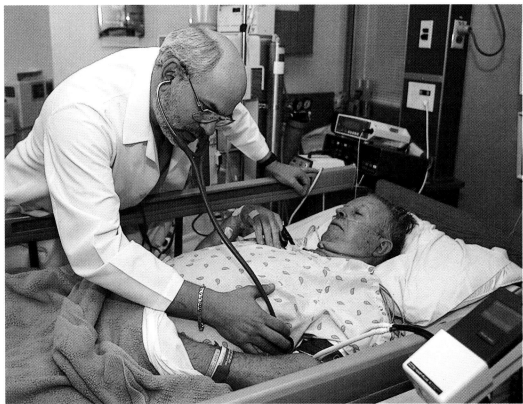

A doctor of osteopathy (D.O.), like a doctor of medicine (M.D.), must complete four years of post-college classroom and clinical training, as well as an internship and residency program. Also like an M.D., a D.O. (above) can practice everything from family care to surgery.

Osteopathic Physicians:
Doctors with a Difference

by David A. Pendlebury

"When is a physician not an M.D.?"

It sounds a bit like a question on a quiz show or some kind of riddle, but there is a simple answer: "When the physician is a D.O."

D.O. stands for Doctor of Osteopathy. It is the degree earned by students who have successfully completed their medical education at one of the 16 accredited osteopathic medical schools in the United States. Graduates of osteopathic medical schools, like their counterparts who earn medical degrees from institutions granting the title M.D., must successfully complete four years of classroom and clinical training, a year of hospital-based internship, and a residency program of varying duration (generally two to six years).

Both D.O. and M.D. students must also pass rigorous examinations throughout their studies to finally receive a license to practice medicine. Like M.D. physicians, D.O. physicians can practice all types of medicine from family care to surgery, and they do so in every state of the nation and in all branches of the U.S. military. And like M.D. physicians, D.O. physicians use all types of modern medical, surgical, immunologic, pharmacological, psychological, hygienic, and technological procedures to treat disease and injury.

Important Distinctions

Such are the similarities between M.D.s and D.O.s, but there are important differences, too. As a group, osteopathic physicians tend to choose primary-care or general medicine over specialties such as cardiology, dermatology, or urology. This tendency arises in part from osteopathic medicine's philosophy of "treating the whole person," which itself reflects a recognition of the importance of the interrelationships among different organ systems. D.O. physicians are trained to think of their patients as more than the sum of their individual body parts or specific symptoms. And, more than anything else, what sets osteopathic, or D.O., physicians distinctly apart from their so-called allopathic, or M.D., colleagues is their special emphasis on the role of the musculoskeletal system in health and in disease.

Osteopathic medicine views body structure and body function as intimately related and indivisibly linked. Osteopathic medicine holds that defects in the musculoskeletal system can have adverse effects on the proper functioning of the circulatory system, the nervous system, the lymphatic system, and other organ systems. In keeping with this perspective, students of osteopathic medicine receive special training in physical diagnosis and in using their hands, not only to detect abnormalities in the musculoskeletal system, but also to correct these defects through osteopathic manipulative therapy (OMT) of the spine, neck, and other parts of the body. M.D. physicians, on the other hand, give the musculoskeletal system no more or no less emphasis than other organ systems, and they are not trained in manipulative therapy.

Since its principles were first propounded by Andrew Taylor Still, M.D., in the late 19th century, osteopathic medicine has moved gradually from the periphery of medicine into the mainstream, and it has done so despite determined opposition from representatives of the older allopathic medical establishment and its professional organization, the American Medical Association (AMA). Last year in the United States, more than 100 million patient visits were made to the offices of D.O. physicians, according to the American Osteopathic Association (AOA) in Chicago, Illinois. Thus, osteopathic medicine, now just over a century old, can be viewed only as a success professionally, especially since other alternative medical systems have failed to be accepted, let alone legally sanctioned. Yet, in many parts of the nation, osteopathic physicians are largely unknown, significantly misunderstood, or consistently confused with chiropractors, who perform manipulative therapy of the spine, but who are not trained as physicians. Within

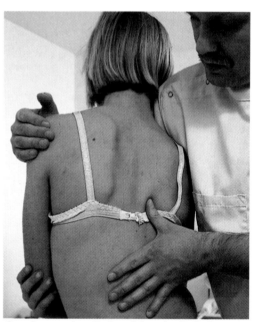

One feature that distinguishes the D.O. from the M.D. is the former's emphasis on using the hands to detect abnormalities in the musculoskeletal system.

American medicine today, D.O. physicians, although legally equal to their M.D. colleagues, stand apart and represent both a numerical and a social minority.

The Osteopathic Philosophy

The philosophy that supports osteopathic medicine starts with the view that the body is an integrated unit, that each organ system is dependent on the others, and that the natural processes of the body are self-regulating. For the body to function correctly, its structure must be correct, say osteopathic physicians. So, for example, for the circulatory system to supply the body's organs with blood, its flow must be unimpeded, and for the nervous system to act effectively, its communication network should not be restricted. Therefore, the physical structure of the body—the musculoskeletal system, comprising bones, muscles, tendons, and ligaments—must be properly aligned for optimal body function; misalignment can both cause and contribute to disease processes. A specific symptom may be ameliorated or corrected altogether by first correcting structural problems. This can be accomplished by osteopathic diagnosis and OMT, a set of hands-on techniques for detecting defects in the structure of the body and adjusting them to their proper position.

Bob E. Jones, executive director of the Oklahoma Osteopathic Association, has provided a detailed description of this procedure, from diagnosis to treatment, in his book *The Difference a D.O. Makes.*

An experienced D.O. can detect minute changes in the tissue at each segment of the vertebrae.

"When employing osteopathic manipulative therapy in diagnosis, the D.O. will use his hands. During the examination, the physician will probe the back and extremities of the individual with his fingers. In affected areas, the reflex mechanism of the nervous system will have produced a change in the tissues surrounding the related vertebral segment. Years of training will allow the physician to sense relatively minute changes in the tissue at each segment of the vertebrae—for example, the tissues may feel doughy or tight, or there may be abnormal warmth. Joints will also be checked for restriction of motion to determine if there is pain upon motion or malalignment. The doctor will additionally feel to detect soreness and spasm in the muscles. Tenderness or abnormal tension in the muscles, tendons, and ligaments will indicate abnormalities. It is possible that X rays will be used to confirm the findings. The diagnosis completed, the physician will make an appraisal and decide upon the appropriate steps for correction."

"Finally," Jones notes, "[there is] the treatment. This will include massaging and stretching to relax the muscles and to calm the excitement existing in the affected part of the nervous system. In addition, the physicians may need to use corrective thrust forces to relieve malalignments and restriction of motion in joints."

It is important to note that not all D.O. physicians routinely use OMT in their practices. Some do not use OMT at all. In fact, very few D.O. students choose to specialize in osteopathic manipulative therapy in their residency years (in 1993 only 11 of some 4,419 students specialized in OMT). Yet OMT remains the most distinctive feature of osteopathic medical practice. For those who employ OMT, they do so in combination with drugs, surgery, and other therapies to treat disease.

Research into the physiological effects of OMT has been pursued since the earliest days of the profession. Most of these studies have been based on clinical observations of OMT's effects, such as improved range of motion and cessation or pain, but there have been experimental investigations of the basic physiological effects of OMT as well. One challenge in such studies is controlling for the so-called placebo effect: the benefit that patients can derive from a particular therapy, because they believe in its efficacy. This is especially true in the case of manipulative therapy where the physical contact is likely to evoke a positive emotional response from the patient. But that, too, osteopathic physicians maintain, is part of the benefit of OMT.

Beyond the use of OMT, D.O. physicians generally bring to their practices a holistic approach to medicine, which in no small part represents their inheritance from the father of osteopathic medicine, A. T. Still.

The Early Days of Osteopathy

The founder of osteopathic medicine, Andrew Taylor Still, was born in Virginia in 1828. He was the son of a Methodist minister who was also, at various times, a physician and a farmer. By 1851, Still had decided to make medicine his career. He did not attend a medical school—which were relatively few in number at the time, and not the well-organized institutions they are today—but rather, served an apprenticeship under his father to acquire his medical knowledge. At the beginning of the Civil War, Still served as a hospital steward, and later, after the war, became a licensed medical doctor.

The practice of medicine in 19th-century America was, in retrospect, a frequently brutal enterprise, with undereducated and undertrained physicians often delivering as much harm to a patient as healing. There were few anesthetics, no antibiotics, and a

Key Dates in the Development of Osteopathic Medicine

1828 Andrew Taylor Still born in Virginia.
1854 Still begins medical career.

Andrew Taylor Still (1828–1917) developed the principles of what is now called osteopathic medicine.

1862–64 Still serves as physician and surgeon in Union Army during Civil War.
1874 Still begins to develop principles of osteopathic medicine.
1892 Still opens the American School of Osteopathy, Kirksville, Missouri, later named Kirksville College of Osteopathic Medicine.
1896 Vermont is first state to formally recognize practice of osteopathic medicine.
1897 American Association

for the Advancement of Osteopathy founded; renamed the American Osteopathic Association in 1902.
1901 *Journal of the American Osteopathic Association* introduced.
1910 Flexner report on medical education in U.S. critical of osteopathic schools.
1920 Osteopathic medical education lengthens to equal that of M.D. institutions.
1923 AMA Judicial Council declares consultation of M.D.s with D.O.s unethical.
1936 Establishment of accreditation system for osteopathic hospitals.
1938 AMA House of Delegates forbids M.D.-D.O. professional relationships.
1957 Osteopathic physicians allowed to serve in armed forces and civil service.
1961 AMA permits D.O.s in California to "convert" to M.D. status.
1969 First state-supported school of osteopathic medicine established at Michigan State University (others established subsequently by other states).

1979 Number of osteopathic schools in U.S. reaches 14, up from 5 in 1969.

1994 Total number of osteopathic schools: 16; total number of D.O. students: 7,600; total number of D.O.s in practice: 35,000.

Dr. Ronald R. Blanck, the head of military medicine in the United States, is an osteopathic physician.

Sources: American Osteopathic Association, Chicago; N. Gevitz, *The D.O.'s: Osteopathic Medicine in America*, Johns Hopkins Univ. Press: Baltimore, 1982; B. E. Jones, *The Difference a D.O. Makes: Osteopathic Medicine in the Twentieth Century*, Times-Journal Publishing Co.: Oklahoma City, 1978.

range of drugs and potions administered that were often toxic to the patient, such as arsenic, antimony, and strychnine. Civil War surgeons were mostly occupied with amputations in field hospitals. Later their patients often died from infections they acquired in the field or during surgery, or from other medications they were administered. Dr. Still became increasing dissatisfied with the medical practice in his day. After meningitis claimed three of his own children—despite all remedies of physicians whom he summoned—Still's mind was set against medical orthodoxy.

Still's achievement in developing the principles of osteopathic medicine from 1874 onward can be seen as an outgrowth of his own distaste for surgery and the materia medica (as the battery of drugs used by physicians was then known), as well as his own belief in the self-regulating powers of the body. He must have also been influenced by ancillary and alternative medical therapies of his time, such as bonesetting

and healing by laying hands on a patient. In particular, the enthusiasm in the last quarter of the 19th century for "magnetic healing," as propounded by the 18th-century physician Franz Mesmer (1734–1815) and Still's contemporary Andrew Jackson Davis (1826–1910), probably influenced Still. Mesmer and Davis asserted that displaced magnetic fluids in the body were in whole or in part responsible for disease. "Though Still never embraced all of the ideas of these contemporaries," notes Norman Gevitz of the University of Illinois, Chicago, author of the authoritative history of osteopathic medicine, "a number of central tenets of magnetic healing made a strong impression on him: the metaphor of man as a divinely ordained machine; health as the harmonious interaction of all the body's parts and the unobstructed flow of fluid; and, of course, the use of spinal manipulation." Dr. Still, instead of attributing disease to obstructed or displaced magnetic fluid, believed that the restriction of blood flow was

Comparison of D.O. and M.D. Physicians

	D.O.	M.D.
Number of practicing physicians in U.S.	35,000	600,000
Percent of total physician population in U.S.	5.5	94.5
Number of students enrolled in medical school	7,600	66,500
Percent of total medical students in U.S.	10.3	89.7
Number of accredited medical schools	16	126
Percent of total physician population in military	10	90
Percent of total physician population in rural areas (population less than 10,000)	15	85
Total years spent in medical school	4	4
Years spent in hospital-based internship (sometimes combined with first-year residency)	1	1
States recognizing degree and licensing	50	50
Name of professional association	American Osteopathic Association, Chicago	American Medical Association, Chicago
Association membership	25,000	290,000
Association publications	Journal of the American Osteopathic Association	Journal of the American Medical Association

Sources: American Osteopathic Association, Chicago; American Medical Association, Chicago.

the cause of disease. Few would deny that Still's conception of osteopathic medicine was original, and to point out its synthetic elements in no way erodes that originality.

Dr. Still became a nontraditional physician, an itinerant practitioner of osteopathic treatment. He eventually found welcome in Kirksville, Missouri, and over time his therapy attracted more and more patients. In 1889 Still established a permanent clinic in Kirksville and pondered a name for his new philosophy of medicine: "I began to think over names such as allopathy, hydropathy [and] homeopathy." Finally he decided upon osteopathy, drawing on the Greek word for "bone" and the English word "pathology."

Fight for Full Status

The institutional origins of osteopathic medicine began in 1892 with the establishment of the American School of Osteopathy in Kirksville (the school was later renamed the Kirksville College of Osteopathic Medicine). Still took on 18 students that first year. Gradually, and despite opposition from M.D. physicians and the powerful and influential AMA, osteopathic medicine grew briskly in the 1890s. Soon other osteopathic medical schools were established: in Kansas City in 1895, in Los Angeles and in Minneapolis in 1896, in Philadelphia in 1899. Schools in other cities soon followed. In 1896 Vermont became the first state to recognize and regulate osteopathic medicine. North Dakota was next in 1896, followed by 13 more states by 1901. In quick order, osteopathic medicine established a professional organization (1897), started a professional journal (1901), adopted a code of ethics (1904), worked to improve instruction, and attempted to guard its reputation against impostors and charlatans who claimed miraculous cures from their osteopathic treatments or who offered osteopathic degrees by mail. By 1904 approximately 4,000 students had earned

D.O. degrees from sanctioned osteopathic medical schools and were practicing throughout the nation.

But with growth and success came increasing opposition from traditional allopathic medicine. Many leading M.D. physicians branded osteopathic, or D.O., physicians as "quacks" and "not qualified to practice medicine." These were merely the first attempts to either break osteopathic medicine or to incorporate it within the allopathic framework, and such efforts continued intermittently for decades.

A famous report on the condition of medical education in the United States appeared in 1910, written by Abraham Flexner of the

In the treatment of disease, those osteopathic physicians who use OMT (above) do so in combination with drugs, surgery, and other therapies.

Carnegie Foundation for the Advancement of Teaching. Flexner surveyed the conditions, curriculum, facilities, and faculty of osteopathic medical schools, and found them to be woefully inadequate, but his findings regarding most allopathic schools were not much better. The osteopathic schools did much in the following years to improve conditions, as well as to set uniform standards to bring their schools more in line with allopathic medical schools.

Significant obstacles were placed before osteopathic physicians during the 1920s,

1930s, and 1940s. D.O. physicians were denied the opportunity to serve as physicians and surgeons in World War I and World War II. The most daunting challenge to the profession's survival, however, was the AMA's declarations in 1923 and in 1938 that it was "unethical" for M.D. physicians to consult with D.O. physicians. In 1938, when this became official AMA policy, many D.O.s lost their hospital privileges. The result, during the late 1930s and 1940s, was the establishment of many small community osteopathic hospitals. Little by little, osteopathic physicians regained their privileges at allopathic hospitals. Finally, in 1973, the last few states to deny D.O.s licenses as full physicians and surgeons changed their laws, providing D.O.s with the same privileges as M.D.s throughout the U.S.

> *Since 1973, every state has accorded osteopathic physicians the same privileges as medical doctors.*

The increasing similarity between D.O.s and M.D.s led some within both professions to consider merger. In the early 1960s, a merger occurred in California, where 85 percent of D.O.s "traded in" their degrees for M.D.s. Though merger did not occur elsewhere, the AMA did eventually concede it was ethical for M.D.s and D.O.s to cooperate professionally. In 1957 D.O. physicians were permitted to serve in all branches of the military and in the civil service (D.O.s now make up 10 percent of all physicians serving in the military, which is about twice their representation within the general population). In the 1960s and 1970s, the number of osteopathic medical schools increased from 5 to 14, with the establishment of many new state-funded institutions. In other words, after about 100 years, osteopathic medicine had achieved a legal status equal to, but still separate from, allopathic medicine.

The Future of Osteopathic Medicine

Today, amid calls for health-care reform and a marked increase in the delivery of health services through health-mainte-nance organizations (HMOs), the osteopathic medical profession finds itself well placed to participate fully in the reshaping of American medicine. Osteopathic medicine's emphasis on primary care, health maintenance, and prevention of disease matches closely the organizational structure and goals set forth by most HMOs. HMOs and other managed-care systems are increasing and, in an effort to contain health-care costs, are using more general-practice or primary-care physicians to serve as gatekeepers for other medical services. Many of these gatekeepers are osteopathic physicians.

The U.S. government has called for more physicians to choose general practice or primary care rather than specialty medicine, and it has adjusted in the favor of primary-care physicians the amount paid for their services under Medicare and Medicaid programs. Some in the osteopathic profession have called for the AOA to explicitly identify itself with primary-care medicine and to discourage D.O. students from choosing a specialty. Others warn against making specialization versus general practice the point of differentiation between D.O.s and medical doctors (in fact, there is evidence that an increasing number of M.D. students are now electing general practice for their residencies). For these people, it is the osteopathic philosophy that is the hallmark of the profession: the body's essential unity, a holistic approach, and the use of manipulative therapy of the musculoskeletal system.

In any case, such a debate within osteopathic medicine is itself a sign of the profession's success. The question of equal status, which occupied the profession for so many years, seems to have finally been displaced. New questions have arisen over what makes osteopathic medicine distinctive, of why and whether it should be seen as different from allopathic medicine. The answer to this question is not without its practical implications, but survival of osteopathic medicine as a profession is no longer a crucial issue. If anything, osteopathic medicine shows more signs of robust growth and good health than it ever has before. ◇

For generations, as reckless boys and girls have climbed trees, walked on high walls, and leaned out of windows, the cry from nervous parents and frazzled baby-sitters has been the same: "Watch out—you could fall and break your seventh cervical vertebra." And what child, engaging a friend in a mock sword fight with perilously sharp sticks, has not heard the warning, "Hey, you're going to put out someone's sclera, iris, and retina with those sticks!"? Even more familiar is the timeless rhyme spoken by children as they skip down the sidewalk: "Don't step on a crack, or you'll damage your mother's intervertebral fibrocartilage."

O.K.—maybe those aren't the exact phrases we remember. Most of us are not in the habit of using such precise medical terms. In the respective examples above, of course, we would be far more inclined to say "neck," "eye," and "back." But these general names do not begin to hint at the richness and complexity of the terms used in describing human anatomy.

The human body has been the subject of relentless study. Since ancient times, learned anatomists have probed deeply into the body's structures and functions—examining, describing, cataloging, and, above all, *naming*. Every imaginable part of our bodies, inside and out—from the largest, strongest bone to the tiniest cell—has been given a name. In some instances the names derive from classical languages such as Latin and Greek. Sometimes the term for

Vesalius (above), a Renaissance anatomist, laid much of the groundwork upon which other scientists developed today's lexicon of medical terminology.

The Medical Name Game

by Christopher King

the body part commemorates the name of the first scientist to describe it (or at least the first to get credit for describing it). In other cases, names have been taken from a more fanciful source, such as literature or mythology. Names have also been conferred on the countless diseases and maladies that afflict the human body. In fact, so numerous and varied are the terms employed in anatomy and medicine that attempting to learn them all could easily cause pressure and pain within the cranial cavity (or, in other words, a mighty big headache).

Classical Origins

The recorded history of medicine goes back thousands of years. The Egyptians in particular were famous for their medical skills, as Erwin H. Ackerknecht notes in *A Short History of Medicine* (Johns Hopkins, 1982). Although medical practice was deeply rooted in the supernatural, Egyptian physicians and dentists did manage to maintain a level of health far superior to that seen in eras and civilizations that would follow. Similarly, ancient China gave rise to forms of medicine that are still practiced today. And in ancient India, physicians busily classified human ailments—naming, for example, 66 diseases of the mouth and five of the earlobe.

However, the real story of modern medicine begins in ancient Greece with the physician Hippocrates (460–379 B.C.), who is known as the "father of medicine." With his observations and writings on diseases

Hippocrates, the distinguished physician of ancient Greece, lent his name to the Hippocratic Oath, a pledge still taken by doctors today to symbolize the ideals for which the physician should strive.

and their treatments, Hippocrates moved medicine away from magic and superstition toward the realm of science. His name survives in the "Hippocratic Oath," the pledge administered to physicians in ancient times that, even today, symbolizes the physician's devotion to duty and ethical conduct.

In the 2nd century before Christ, Greece was conquered by the powerful Roman legions, for whom Latin was the dominant language. But the tradition of Greek medicine continued, most notably in the person of Claudius Galen (A.D. 131–201), a Greek-born physician whose early medical career included administering to gladiators, a job that "would have given him a good opportunity to see gaping wounds and flowing blood," as Jonathon Miller observes in his book *The Body in Question* (Random House, 1978). Later Galen went to Rome and served as the physician to the emper-

or Marcus Aurelius. Galen also set about building a knowledge of human anatomy and physiology that would enshrine him as the world's greatest medical authority for the next 1,400 years. Through the dissection of pigs and monkeys (and, on one occasion, an elephant), Galen greatly advanced the knowledge of muscles, bones, and nerves. And he recorded his observations in voluminous writings, coining many medical terms that are still in use today.

Galen's original writings were in Greek, but were widely translated into Latin and Arabic. Throughout the centuries, even as the civilizations of Greece and Rome declined, Latin flourished throughout the world. At that time, Latin was the language of Christianity, and it spread with the religion. Latin was also the international language of scholars and scientists—the tongue by which they could communicate across national boundaries. Although Latin predominated for centuries as the language of academics, Greek would eventually mount a comeback in the 17th century.

Latin and Greek give us much of the terminology of medicine and anatomy. A few examples of terms from Greek include: *skeleton* (from a Greek word meaning "dried up," used by the Greeks in connection with mummified bodies; the sense of skeleton as the bony framework of the human body was an English invention in the 16th century); *pneumonia* (from Greek words meaning "a gas" or "a breath" and "breathing"); *bulimia* (meaning "the appetite of a bull"); *tetanus* (meaning "stretched," referring to the

The works of Galen, a Greek-born physician who flourished during Roman times, formed an important base for the evolution of modern medicine. Nearly all of his findings were derived from the dissection of animals.

involuntary muscular contraction first observed by Hippocrates in connection with the infectious disease that now bears the name); *sclera* ("to harden," the name given to the outermost covering of the eye); *iris* ("rainbow," adopted in the 18th century as the name for the thin, circular membrane encircling the pupil of the eye, because of the membrane's many colors); and *artery* (from the words "air" and "I carry," a reflection of the ancient belief that arteries carried air, not blood).

Early anatomists also put Latin to use in inventively descriptive ways. *Vertebra,* the term for each of the segments making up the backbone, for example, derives from the Latin *vertere,* meaning "to turn." *Cervical* comes from the Latin *cervix,* for "neck" (cervix also serves as the name for the constricted, necklike portion of the female uterus). *Cartilage,* of which one variety is known as *fibro-cartilage,* derives from the Latin car-tilago, meaning "gristle." *Muscle* comes, in part, from the Latin *musculus,* meaning "little mouse." Apparently the rippling movement of muscles suggested the movements of a tiny mouse under the skin. Other Latin names based on animals include *vermis* ("worm"), describing a wormlike structure in the brain, and *cochlea* ("snail"), a snail-shaped formation in the inner ear.

So pervasive was the influence of Latin that scholars were expected to take a Latin name upon earning their advanced degrees. In one such instance, a Belgian anatomist named Andreas van Wesele (1514–64) become known as Vesalius. Acknowledged as the "father of modern anatomy," Vesalius dissected human cadavers in his quest to advance knowledge of the body. Working on humans allowed him to correct many of the errors made by Galen, who had been forced to make assumptions about human anatomy based on his animal dissections. Ironically, despite his great achievements and stature in medical history, Vesalius has not become associated with any particular body part. The same is not true of his students. One, an Italian named Gabriele Fallopio (1523–63), adopted the Latinized name Fallopius.

Who's in a Name?

Although Fallopius made many key observations regarding the ear (introducing, for example, the term *cochlea*), he is primarily noted for his description of the female reproductive system. In particular, he described the uterine tubes, or oviducts, through which the egg travels on its way from the ovaries to the uterus dur-

In a 1543 treatise, Vesalius published the engraving above, the first accurate depiction of the human system of veins. Despite his numerous contributions to medical knowledge, no body parts are named for Vesalius.

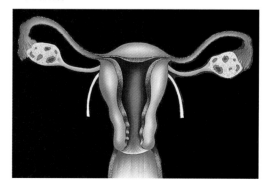

Fallopius (right), a student of Vesalius, described the female reproductive system (below) in such detail that one of its main structures—the Fallopian tubes—bears his name.

GABRIEL FALLOPPIVS MVTINENSIS AN.

AB ANNO 1551   AD ANN. 1565

ing the monthly female cycle. As Henry Alan Skinner notes in *The Origin of Medical Terms* (Hafner, 1970), other anatomists, including Galen, had described the oviducts prior to Fallopius. The description provided by Fallopius, however, proved to be the standard. So close was his association with this pair of anatomical features—the Fallopian tubes—that, for all intents and purposes, they still bear his name today.

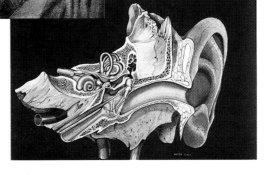

In the 1500s, Eustachius (left) published the most complete description of the inner ear (below) up to that time. A century later, another anatomist coined the term Eustachian tube to describe the connection between the pharynx and the middle ear.

One of Fallopius' contemporaries, Bartolommeo Eustachio (1524–74), took the Latinized name Eustachius. This Italian is credited with several anatomical discoveries and key descriptions, including those of the adrenal glands, the larynx, and the optic nerve, among others. But it was his descriptions of the inner ear that immortalized him in medical terminology. As was the case with Fallopius and the oviducts, other anatomists had dissected and described the *auditory tube*—the connection between the pharynx and the middle-ear cavity. Eustachius' description, however, achieved the status of a classic. A little over 100 years after the death of Eustachius, another anatomist published a work devoted entirely to the ear. He referred to the auditory tube as the "Eustachian tube."

Fallopius and Eustachius and the anatomical structures by which they are remembered—along with Hippocrates and his oath—all provide examples of "eponyms"—a term or phrase derived from a person's name (the word *eponym* comes from two Greek words: *epi*, meaning "upon," and *onyma*, meaning "name"). Throughout the history of science and medicine, one of the most significant forms of recognition and reward has been the practice of attaching the name of a scientist to his or her discovery—a practice known as "eponymy." There is perhaps no greater reward for a scientist, who seeks above all to make a completely original and lastingly significant contribution to knowledge. "In this way," writes the sociologist and historian of science Robert K. Merton, "scientists leave their signatures indelibly in history; their names enter into all the scientific languages of the world."

For hundreds of years, physicians and scientists managed to leave their signatures all over the human body. On the underside of the brain, for example, beneath the frontal lobe, one can locate the *fissure of Sylvius*, a structure named for French anato-

Staining methods developed by Italian anatomist Camillo Golgi (above) allowed him to describe the cell (below) in such detail that a cellular structure came to be known as the Golgi apparatus.

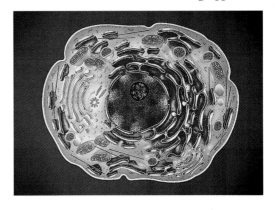

mist Jacobus Sylvius (1478–1555). In the pancreas, which is the organ that lies below the liver and stomach, there are the *islets of Langerhans*, named for German physician and anatomist Paul Langerhans (1847–88). These so-called "ductless cells" secrete the hormone insulin into the blood. At an even smaller level, the Italian anatomist Camillo Golgi (1844–1926) is remembered for his contributions to knowledge of structures within individual cells. By introducing the technique of using silver nitrate to stain nerve cells, he was able to discover several key cellular features that now bear his name. One such cellular structure is the *Golgi apparatus*, a network of threads in the cytoplasm, the region outside the nucleus of a cell. Golgi's name was also attached to specific types of cells found in the brain and nervous system. If those eponyms weren't reward enough, Golgi also received the Nobel Prize in Physiology or Medicine in 1906.

Dueling Eponyms

The few examples above discuss scientists honored for discoveries involving the healthy human body. A whole other branch of eponymy deals with observations of disease. "I have Bright's disease," wrote the humorist S. J. Perelman in one of his magazine sketches, "and he has mine!" It is uncertain whether Perelman was actually familiar with the work of English physician Richard Bright (1789–1858) and the kid-

Thomas Hodgkin (left) first described the lymphatic condition now known as Hodgkin's disease; his name is also incorporated into the term for another disease, non-Hodgkin's lymphoma. Irish physician Robert James Graves (below) first described goiter, an autoimmune thyroid-gland condition now called Graves' disease.

ney disorder named after him. Another Englishman, Thomas Hodgkin (1798–1866), observed a condition involving enlargement of the lymphatic glands associated with enlargement of the spleen. After his death the condition became officially known as *Hodgkin's disease*. Not only has this eponym endured until today, but it has given rise to what might be termed a non-eponym: the name for the malady known as *non-Hodgkin's lymphoma*.

Eponyms have sometimes caused controversy. In one case an Irish physician, Robert James Graves (1796–1853), described a condition known as *goiter*, the enlargement of the thyroid gland on the front and sides of the neck. In Britain the ailment became known as *Graves' disease*. However, a German anatomist named Carl Adolph Basedow (1799–1854) published his own account of the condition. In Germany, therefore, the affliction was known as *Basedow's disease*.

Richard Bright (right) gave a classic description of a type of kidney failure now known as Bright's disease.

This was far from the first instance of dueling eponyms, or of arguments about who was first to make an anatomical discovery. The English anatomist William Cowper (1666–1709), for example, published a description of glands near the upper end of the male urethra, the tube through which urine passes from the bladder. These were subsequently named *Cowper's glands*. Controversy erupted when it was revealed that Cowper had borrowed a little too heavily from the work of another anatomist. Nevertheless, the glands—also known as bulbo-urethral glands—are still described as Cowper's glands.

Many anatomical terms could not possibly cause confusion or conflict between scientists, since they do not derive from the name of any human discoverer. Mythology, for example, has provided many anatomical and medical terms. The *Achilles tendon*, for example, refers to the Greek hero Achilles, who was dipped by his mother into the magical River Styx and rendered invincible—except, of course, for the tiny spot on the back of his foot where she'd held him. Eventually his rival Paris inflicted a lethal wound in that very spot. Thus, Achilles gave us not only the name for a tendon, but an expression, "Achilles' heel," that can stand for any crucial flaw or weakness. Venus, the Roman goddess of love, has her name commemorated in the decidedly unromantic term *venereal disease*, which refers to any number of sexually transmitted afflictions. The opiate drug *morphine* takes its name

Many medical terms owe their derivation to mythological characters. The Achilles tendon in the back of the heel recalls the legend of Achilles (left), a Greek hero who died from an arrow wound to the only vulnerable part of his body: the back of his heel. Venus (below left), the Roman goddess of love, gave her name to venereal diseases—infections transmitted during the act of love. The drug morphine is named for Morpheus (below), the Greek god of sleep.

from Morpheus, the Greek god of sleep.

Works of literature have also given names to some rather strange maladies. Patients who invent and fake illness in order to receive care and attention in a hospital are said to be suffering from *Munchausen's syndrome*. The name refers to a German cavalry officer whose improbable adventures formed the basis of a book that became a best-seller in England in the late 1700s. Conceivably, a patient suffering from Munchausen's syndrome might be treated in the hospital by a person suffering from *Walter Mitty syndrome*—someone masquerading as a doctor. The name refers to the title character in a famous short story by James Thurber about a timid man whose constant daydreams of heroism and adventure contrast with his drab and henpecked life.

Geographic locations have also provided the source of medical terms. For example, *Lyme disease*, a form of arthritis caused by tick-borne bacteria, was named for the town of Lyme, Connecticut, where the first cases were observed. Another tick-borne ailment with a geographical name is *Rocky Mountain spotted fever*. The recent hantavirus outbreak was dubbed "Four Corners disease," for the region in the southwestern United States where incidence of the illness was initially concentrated. Other maladies have often been attached—accurately or not—to countries or regions. Typhus, an infectious disease marked by fever and by mental and physical depression, was once known

Physicians John Cheyne (left) and William Stokes (below) are both honored in the term Cheyne-Stokes breathing, a breathing abnormality caused by serious disorders of the heart, lungs, or central nervous system.

as the *Hungarian disease*. Other examples, generally out of use today, include *German measles* and *Polish influenza*.

Keep My Name Out of It

Some historians of medical terminology have noted the imprecision and confusion caused by medical eponyms based on the names of scientists. In his book *The Language of Medicine* (Harper & Row, 1983), John H. Dirckx records a few common errors. One is the tendency to mistake an eponym for an ordinary word—saying "charcoal joint," for example, instead of *Charcot joint*, a term for osteoarthritis named after French physician Jean Martin Charcot (1825–93); or using the term "change-strokes breathing" in place of *Cheyne-Stokes breathing*, a condition of irregular respiration whose discovery is credited to two clinical observers, John Cheyne (1777–1836) and William Stokes (1804–78).

Sometimes the opposite error occurs, when a writer will mistakenly create an eponym where none exists. "Caisson's disease," for example, implies the name of a discoverer, when in fact the proper name is

Charcot's joint, a painful joint lesion, and Charcot's triad, a group of three multiple-sclerosis symptoms, take their names from French clinician Jean Martin Charcot (left).

caisson disease. A caisson is a boxlike compartment used for underwater work in building tunnels and bridge supports. Workers removed too rapidly from the pressurized interior suffered bubbles of air in their blood, causing headache, dizziness, and joint pain (the condition is familiar to underwater divers as "the bends").

Beyond these kinds of careless mistakes, some observers find more-troubling flaws in the practice of eponymy. Stephen M. Stigler, a statistician at the University of Chicago in Illinois, made a study of eponyms, and came to the following conclusion, which he formulated in terms of a scientific "law": *No scientific discovery is ever named after its original discoverer.* Having a little fun with eponymic tradition, Stigler even named the law after himself: "Stigler's Law of Eponymy." The Chicago statistician noted that names for discoveries tend to be conferred, not by historians of science, but by scientists themselves—in other words, by people who possess no particular expertise in history and who might tend to make errors in assigning credit. Another critic of eponyms, Mark M. Ravitz of the University of Pittsburgh and Montefiore Hospital, Pittsburgh, Pennsylvania, determined that, in many cases involving eponymy, the eponymous person wasn't the first describer of the discovery, or didn't really understand the discovery. In some cases, Ravitz observed, there was no historical basis whatsoever for attributing discovery to the eponymous person.

An investigation into one famous eponym seemed to bear out some of these concerns. A medical historian reportedly made a study of Hodgkin's work, and surmised that fewer than half of the patients whom Hodgkin observed in describing the condition named after him actually had Hodgkin's disease.

Because of such ambiguity, historical fuzziness, and the fact that eponyms usually offer no descriptive quality, there has been some movement in recent times to discontinue their use. In 1955, for example, the International Congress of Anatomy at Paris adopted an official list of anatomical terms from which all eponyms had been eliminated. Despite continuing in popular usage, the term "Fallopian tubes" has fallen from official use. Yet many eponyms persist. *Down syndrome*, for example, named for British physician J. L. H. Down (1828–96), is the eponym for *chromosome 21 trisomy syndrome*. In this disorder an extra chromosome causes birth defects that include mental retardation. The term Down syndrome has actually gained in popularity, as the old term, "mongolism," has faded.

Science or Senselessness?

As knowledge in science and medicine has accumulated and grown, medical terminology has expanded as well. Unfortunately, as Dirckx notes in *The Language of Medicine*, accuracy and clarity have not kept pace. Physicians, Dirckx laments, often employ important-sounding jargon that actually conveys no useful information—using the term *pharyngitis*, for example, to refer to a sore throat; or slinging around such broad, vague terms as colitis, kidney infection, or low blood pressure when they may have no real bearing on the problem at hand. "The unbridled proliferation of ambiguous, unorthodox, and unpronounceable scientific words," he writes, "is not progress but decadence, not science but senselessness."

Doctors and scientists continue to invent terms using Latin and Greek, but with little sensitivity to the subtleties of the original languages. The suffix "-pathy," for example, has been particularly overworked. Based on the Greek word *pathos*, meaning "suffering" or "a distressed state," "-pathy" figures in such terms as *psychopath* (incorporating the Greek word *psyche*, meaning "the mind" or "spirit"; thus, a "distressed mind"—a mentally ill or unstable person) and *neuropathy* (with the Greek word for "nerve," indicating, of course, something wrong with a nerve).

But what are we to make of such modern coinages as coagulopathy, endocrinopathy, and consumptive opsoninopathy? We could, of course, get into the spirit of anatomical names and observe that such terms cause excessive torsion of the *dorsum linguae*.

Or we could just call them tongue twisters. ◇

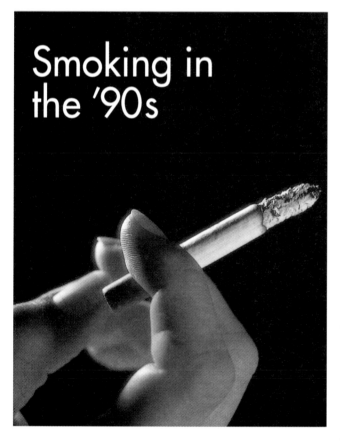

Smoking in the '90s

by Abigail Polek

Stan sipped his coffee, opened his newspaper, and lit his first cigarette of the day. Almost immediately his eyes stopped at a small headline near the bottom of the front page: "Smokers Arrested for 'Lighting Up' in Restaurant." The article described an incident in which people publicly smoked cigarettes in defiance of the federal law banning it. Stan sighed, stubbed out his cigarette, and turned the page.

If you think this scenario could happen only in the future, you are out of touch with current events in the United States. In 1994 the Clinton administration backed legislation to ban smoking in all public buildings regularly entered by 10 or more people at least one day a week (not including residences). The Smoke-Free Environment Act, as the legislation is known, would also prohibit smoking near building entrances. Its introduction follows two similar bills presented in Congress earlier in 1993 and

1994: one bans smoking in federal buildings; the other bans smoking in any buildings that house children's programs financed by the federal government. Each of these two latter bills has been passed by either the House or Senate and is awaiting approval by the other governing body.

The United States stands to save $6.5 billion to $19 billion a year in medical costs and lost wages if the Smoke-Free Environment Act becomes law. More important, however, its resolution could annually save the lives of 33,000 to 99,000 smokers—a significant percentage of the nearly 450,000 people who die each year from smoking-related diseases such as cancer and cardiovascular diseases, and various respiratory disorders, including emphysema and bronchitis.

The new legislation could also save the lives of 5,000 to 9,000 *non-smokers* annually. This statistic represents one of the major motivating factors behind the recent no-smoking legislation. Since 1964, when the U.S. surgeon general first advised Americans that smoking is dangerous to their health, most U.S. smokers have been aware that they are putting themselves at risk for some health problem. Only recently, however, have nonsmokers learned that they, too, are at risk from exposure to cigarette smoke. Some 50,000 people are thought to die each year as the result of diseases caused by secondhand or passive smoke—smoke from someone else's cigarettes.

Several million Americans— many of them adult males— have quit smoking since the 1960s.

Smokers at Risk

For years, doctors have warned the public that smoking causes diseases of the heart and lungs—in particular, heart attacks and lung cancer. More recently, researchers have established a link between smoking and other types of cardiovascular disease and cancer:

• A 1994 study published in the *American Journal of Epidemiology* states that current female smokers are more likely to die of fatal breast cancer, either because smoking adversely affects their survival rate or because they are not diagnosed early enough for successful treatment. The association of current smoking with fatal breast cancer increases with the number of cigarettes smoked per day and the total number of years smoked.

• Leukemia also has been added to the list of cancers caused by smoking. The United States Office on Smoking and Health, a division of the Centers for Disease Control and Prevention (CDC), announced in mid-1993 that a form of myeloid leukemia, an uncontrolled proliferation of a particular type of white blood cell, appears to be linked to smoking. The report, which was based on the results of 21 related studies, found that people who smoke are 1.5 times more likely to develop myeloid leukemia, and, "since the causes of leukemia are largely unknown, this [makes] smoking the leading known cause of leukemia." The study also suggested that lymphocytic leukemia might be caused by smoking, but the evidence currently available is inconclusive.

• Nearly one-fifth of all U.S. deaths caused by cardiovascular disease are now smoking-related. When a person inhales smoke, platelets in the blood become stickier and levels of fibrinogen, a natural clotting substance, become higher. This increases the chances that a blood clot will develop and block the blood supply to part of the brain, resulting in an ischemic stroke. A 10-year study (financed by 15 states) of healthy male physicians found that the smokers in the group were nearly twice as likely to suffer a stroke than those who did not smoke. The chances of a stroke were also related to the number of cigarettes smoked per day. For example, the doctors who smoked fewer than 20 cigarettes a day had a stroke risk 1.8 times that of nonsmokers, while those physicians who smoked more than 20 cigarettes a day had 2.4 times the nonsmokers' risk of suffering a stroke. Smoking also raises blood pressure, and high blood pressure, or hypertension, is the most common cardiovascular disease in the U.S. Hypertension creates a predisposition to stroke.

Nonsmokers at Risk

Scientists have suspected for some time that secondhand smoke is a significant health hazard for nonsmokers, in particular for pregnant women and their unborn

From abominable...

Cigarette smoking did not become widespread until the turn of the century. Back then, it was socially unacceptable for women to indulge (left). By the 1930s, smoking had become the habit of choice in fashionable circles (above).

babies. Numerous studies suggest that children born to women exposed to passive smoke experience slight problems with speech, language, intelligence, and attention span. Babies born to women who actively smoke during pregnancy exhibit more-serious side effects, including low birth weight, prematurity, and impaired mental development.

Until recently, however, researchers did not have the clinical evidence they needed to prove that smoking adversely affects nonsmokers. Most data on secondhand smoke are difficult to validate, because the test subjects have been exposed throughout their lives to a variety of potentially toxic substances, usually without knowing it. That makes it difficult to pinpoint whether a particular illness or condition has been caused specifically by exposure to passive smoke. In February 1994, however, the *Journal of the American Medical Association (JAMA)* published a study containing the first biochemical evidence that secondhand smoke reaches unborn babies. In the *JAMA* study, researchers examined hair samples from newborns for nicotine and cotinine, a substance the body produces from nicotine. These infants could have been exposed to nicotine only while in their mothers' wombs. The scientists discovered that the babies of women exposed to secondhand smoke during pregnancy had twice the levels of cotinine found in the infants of women not exposed. (These levels were one-quarter of those of babies born to women who actively smoked during pregnancy.) Gideon Koren, M.D., professor of pediatrics, pharmacology, and medicine at the University of Toronto in Canada, and director of the division of pharmacology and toxicology at the Hospital for Sick Children in Toronto, the lead author of the study, noted that "hair accumulation of cigarette smoke constituents reflects long-term exposure to these toxins and therefore may be well correlated with perinatal risks." He went on to say that secondhand smoke might harm a developing fetus only if combined with other risk factors such as lack of oxygen. Smoke produces carbon monoxide in the blood, which can reduce the supply of oxygen a fetus receives.

A 1992 Environmental Protection Agency (EPA) report prepared by agency and contract researchers using data extrapolated from various statistical studies found that environmental tobacco smoke causes 2,500 to 3,300 lung-cancer deaths a year in former smokers and people who never smoked. Secondhand smoke is also believed responsible for 150,000 to 300,000 lower-respiratory-tract infections a year in children less than 18 months old.

... to fashionable;

During World War II (left), the per-capita consumption of cigarettes by Americans exceeded 3,000 per year for the first time. Cigarette consumption came to an all-time peak in the early 1960s, thanks in part to the tobacco industry's effective use of print and broadcast advertising (right).

The 1994 edition of the American Heart Association's (AHA's) *Heart and Stroke Facts: Statistical Supplement* estimates that 37,000 to 40,000 people die annually from cardiovascular disease caused by second-hand smoke. The supplement also indicates that mothers who smoke 10 or more cigarettes a day can cause up to 26,000 new cases of asthma in their children each year. One of the most alarming statistics reported by the study is that babies are three times as likely to die from sudden infant death syndrome (SIDS) if their mothers smoke during and after pregnancy.

Nicotine Addiction

The recent U.S. legislation to ban smoking in public places is a sweeping attempt to resolve the health crisis that smoking has created. But this crisis cannot be solved merely by enacting new laws to prohibit public smoking. Such legislation raises issues that must be addressed now, before the proposed bills are signed into law. Banning smoking not only endangers the civil rights of the 54 million adults who currently smoke, but it also ignores the bigger problem of nicotine addiction. In fact, nearly half of heavy users of cocaine, heroin, and alcohol say that the urge to smoke cigarettes is equal to or greater than the urge to use the drug of their addiction.

Lynn T. Kozlowski, Ph.D., an addiction expert at Pennsylvania State University in State College, defines addiction as "the repeated use of a psychoactive drug which is difficult to stop." The American Psychiatric Association (APA), and the World Health Organization (WHO) determine the addictive nature of a substance based on nine criteria, which include unsuccessful attempts to quit, persistent desire, and craving; continued use, despite knowledge of harm to oneself and others; and marked tolerance in which the amount needed to satisfy increases at first before leveling off. Based on these criteria, nicotine is at least a mildly addictive drug.

Early research on addiction suggested that, to be addictive, a drug must produce a high level of pleasure, or intoxication, in the user—as heroin and cocaine do. But Dr. Kozlowski notes that today a more important measure of addiction is how hard it is for a user to give up the substance. Since surveys of cigarette smokers show that two-thirds to four-fifths of them want to quit but cannot, this indicator would suggest that nicotine is highly addictive.

Another measure of addiction is the ability of users to control when and how often they use a substance; in other words, how many people are casual users versus how many are regular users. Of people who use

from hazardous...

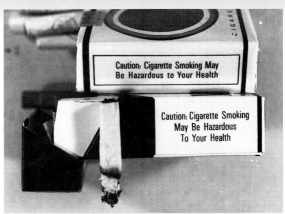

In 1964 (left), the publication of the surgeon general's report that linked smoking to lung cancer began to turn public opinion against smoking. Not long after, cigarette packages started to carry mild warnings of possible danger (above).

heroin and alcohol, many are occasional users, while only a small percentage use the substance regularly. Ninety percent of cigarette smokers, however, are persistent daily users, while only 10 percent smoke occasionally.

The Food and Drug Administration (FDA), which is responsible for regulating controlled substances (drugs) such as heroin and cocaine, is now reviewing the scientific data about the effect of nicotine on humans. This action comes after a federal advisory panel concluded that nicotine is addictive and that it is the major reason people smoke cigarettes. If nicotine is declared to be addictive, it could be classified and regulated as a drug.

Tobacco-Industry Viewpoint

Representatives of the tobacco industry dispute the addictive qualities of nicotine. In spring 1994, seven key executives from tobacco companies testified before a congressional subcommittee that nicotine is not addictive. They based their statements on the "ambiguous" definition of addiction.

Domenic Ciraulo, M.D., a psychiatrist at Tufts University, Boston, Massachusetts, spoke for the Tobacco Institute—the trade industry of the tobacco industry—at the federal advisory panel hearing. While emphasizing that he did not wish to promote smoking, Dr. Ciraulo believes that there are important differences between cigarettes and addictive drugs. The two most important distinctions are the ability of addictive drugs, but not cigarettes, to produce intoxication (which impairs a person's judgment) and euphoria (an intense, pleasurable feeling that occurs after taking a drug). Intoxication from drugs like alcohol leads to a dramatic change in the user's behavior, and has been linked to violence. Euphoria, as produced by cocaine, may make the drug the primary focus of the user's life, often at the expense of family and occupation. Because of these differences, according to Ciraulo, the approaches to treatment for drug dependence is different than those for smoking cessation.

Yet these statements seem to contradict the actions of some tobacco companies. In mid-1994, the Brown & Williamson Tobacco Corporation was forced to admit to the FDA that it had secretly developed a genetically engineered tobacco with the highest nicotine yield known—6.2 percent, compared to 2.5 to 3.0 percent in regular tobacco. Brown & Williamson initially refused to acknowledge that they had developed the tobacco—until the FDA discovered that more than half a million pounds of it had been shipped to the company in 1992. The company then claimed

... to unacceptable.

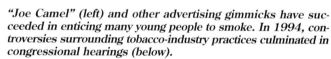

"Joe Camel" (left) and other advertising gimmicks have succeeded in enticing many young people to smoke. In 1994, controversies surrounding tobacco-industry practices culminated in congressional hearings (below).

that the tobacco was to be used only as part of a blend of tobaccos that would yield the amount of nicotine typically found in regular cigarettes. Five brands of cigarettes using the new tobacco were marketed in the United States in 1993, but they were discontinued in 1994 due to the FDA inquiry.

Another controversial report concerning nicotine in cigarettes also appeared in 1994. Tobacco companies released a long-secret list of 599 ingredients added to tobacco to enhance cigarettes. Included on the list were several ammonia compounds, which, according to tobacco-industry documents, change the acidity of tobacco, and free nicotine so that nearly twice the usual amount inhaled enters a smoker's bloodstream.

Testing Flaws

Methods to measure the tar and nicotine in cigarettes are behind the times, according to the Federal Trade Commission (FTC). Typically the tests use machines that hold cigarettes by the filter. The machine draws air through the cigarette in two-second puffs, repeating the puffs once every minute until the cigarette burns to the filter.

Since the FTC first started using these machines to measure cigarette tar and nicotine levels, however, cigarettes have been redesigned to dilute the amount of smoke that can be drawn through the filter. Tiny holes are now punched either close to or in the cigarette filter paper. When the testing machine puffs on the cigarette, it receives less tar and nicotine because air is drawn in through the holes, thus diluting the smoke.

In reality, many smokers cover the tiny holes in cigarettes with their fingers or lips because they find that the diluted smoke is too mild. Some also inhale more often and more deeply; the end result in each case is that smokers ingest higher levels of tar and nicotine than are listed on cigarette labels.

Tobacco companies do not deny that nicotine is what makes their products attractive to smokers. They say that when the amount of nicotine in cigarettes is too low, cigarettes do not satisfy smokers. This fact was discovered when tobacco companies began reducing the amounts of other harmful substances, such as tar, that are contained in cigarette smoke. Nicotine levels, they claim, were reduced by the process as well, a claim now being disputed (see sidebar). To adjust the levels of nicotine without raising the levels of tar, tobacco companies say they must use tobacco blends—as Brown & Williamson claimed to be doing.

The official stand of the Tobacco Institute continues to be that tobacco companies control the tar and nicotine in cigarettes to conform to federal regulations and to produce "a consistent product that their customers have come to respect, just as [companies] do with coffee and alcohol."

Smoking Declining in the Population
Despite its best efforts to counter the negative evidence against smoking, the tobacco industry has watched its customer base shrink, as millions of Americans, many of them adult males, have quit the habit since the 1960s. Researchers estimate that with this decline in adult smoking, "almost 1 million new smokers, 3,000 per day, of whom most will be children and adolescents, must be recruited to fill the void." A study pub-

lished in *JAMA* in 1994 indicates that efforts to recruit new, younger smokers began in the late 1960s and early 1970s, when young women and teenagers were targeted.

Between 1967 and 1973, when cigarettes aimed at women (such as Virginia Slims and Eve) were heavily promoted, the rate of girls younger than 17 who started smoking grew sharply—from a 110 percent increase for 12-year-old girls to a 55 percent increase for 16-year-old girls. During the same period, the rate of boys younger than 17 who started smoking declined. This rate has since evened out. The Office on Smoking and Health, a division of the Public Health Service, estimates that today more than 1 million children under 18 smoke cigarettes regularly, and 19 percent of high-school seniors are smokers.

More-recent efforts to attract younger smokers have included the use of a controversial cartoon character known as Joe Camel. Although R.J.R. Nabisco, the producer of Camel cigarettes, denies that Joe Camel was created to appeal to children, several recent studies have proven otherwise. The authors of one of these reports concluded that "Joe Camel cartoon advertisements are far more successful at marketing Camel cigarettes to children than to adults."

Where Do We Go from Here?

While the government ponders legislation, and the tobacco industry continues to promote its products, other groups are moving forward on their own to curtail smoking in the United States. In 1993 the National Cancer Institute (NCI) and the American Cancer Society began a five-year, 17-state project on smoking education. Abbreviated as ASSIST, the American Stop Smoking Intervention Study for Cancer Prevention program hopes to "reduce adult smoking to 15 percent or less by the year 2000," according to John Seffrin, Ph.D., executive vice president of the American Cancer Society.

Using community groups and cancer-society volunteers, the hazards of smoking will be brought home to the public in programs held in schools, health-care settings, and work sites, and in the mass media. The program will emphasize the importance of not selling cigarettes to children under 18. In addition, health-care professionals will be supplied with information to help smokers quit, including the names of effective cessation programs. Proponents of ASSIST believe that the proposed legislation to prohibit smoking in public places will help prevent reformed smokers from relapsing.

In the meantime, researchers continue to look for medical ways to help smokers quit the habit. The nicotine skin patch slowly releases a predetermined amount of nicotine into the blood to stop the craving for a cigarette. A 1994 *JAMA* study from the Center for Tobacco Research and Intervention at the University of Wisconsin in Madison found that 25 percent of smokers who used the nicotine patch to quit were still smoke-free six months later.

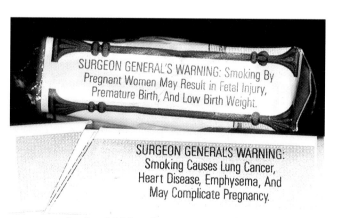

In the 1980s, the government mandated that cigarette packages carry a series of rotating warnings. The warnings reflect research that links smoking to a number of medical disorders.

An antismoking spray not yet approved by the FDA may someday also help those who want to quit smoking. The nasal spray, which contains nicotine, is considered a more successful (although potentially addictive) aid than the nicotine patch because it delivers nicotine to the bloodstream more quickly—within 10 minutes. The spray is available in five European countries. ◇

Housecalls

by Al Ciccone, M.D.

Q *Why do doctors sometimes give you injections in the upper arm, while other times they inject you in the buttocks? Wouldn't it make more sense just to always give the injections in a vein, so the medicine would get immediately into your bloodstream?*

A Injections into a blood vessel have immediate, but often short-lived, effects. Injections into a large muscle, such as the upper arm or buttocks, allow medicines to diffuse more slowly into the bloodstream. Clinicians will inject drugs intravascularly (IV) when they want the medications to take effect as quickly as possible, as is the case with a clot-dissolving drug for a heart attack. Clinicians inject drugs intramuscularly (IM) that need to maintain an effective level for a longer period of time, as is the case with antibiotics. Injecting a bolus of liquid medicine into a small area of muscle tissue can cause pain and swelling, so clinicians use the buttocks rather than the arm for larger intramuscular injections.

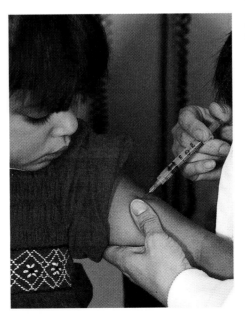

Q *My wife recently underwent a procedure called a "D&C." She mentioned that the procedure was very uncomfortable. What is a D&C? Why is it done?*

A D&C stands for dilation and curettage, a procedure in which a physician uses an instrument called a speculum to open the vaginal canal and cervix, and then takes a scraping of the lining of the uterus. The patient usually receives painkilling medication for the short-lived discomfort of the procedure.

A D&C can help determine the cause of bleeding from the uterus. Also, the procedure is important in searching for abnormal tissues, such as tumors.

Q *Does the risk of suffering a burst blood vessel run in families? Do these vessels only burst in the brain? Can the tendency be discovered before disaster strikes?*

A Burst blood vessels are most commonly caused by aneurysms, or weaknesses in the wall of the vessels that bulge out and then burst. The most likely site for aneurysms is in the brain, where the event can occur in a variety of different vessels, or in the abdomen and chest cavity, where the aorta is usually the site. Aneurysms can be deadly, but they can be repaired surgically before or just after they burst.

Pain, due to the pressure of the bulging aneurysm, is often a warning sign. Using various imaging techniques, doctors can spot aneurysms before they rupture. But doctors need a high incidence of suspicion, based on the patient's pain and other risk factors, before they recommend these sometimes-expensive tests, which include magnetic resonance imaging (MRI), computerized tomography (CT) scans, contrast-die studies, and X rays.

Apparently some people inherit a predisposition to aneurysms. For example, in 1990 researchers at Thomas Jefferson University in Philadelphia, Pennsylvania, studied families with histories of aortic aneurysms. They found a causative mutation in a gene for production of collagen (the primary constituent of connective tissues in such blood vessels). Brain aneurysms are also apt to run in families.

Q *Are the growth disorders that cause dwarfism and giantism curable nowadays? Are such disorders detectable during pregnancy or infancy?*

A A hormone deficiency causes dwarfism, properly referred to as short-stature disorder. Usually the deficiency is based in the pituitary gland, but it can also originate in the thyroid or adrenal gland. The problem is not usually detected until well into a child's first decade of life. Fortunately, the problem is usually curable, through pituitary growth hormones and other supplements.

Conversely, giantism (or, more properly, gigantism) is due to an overabundance of such hormones. Unfortunately, this condition is not usually apparent until the individual is in young adulthood. Treatment may include medication, surgery, or radiation to the overactive gland.

Q *My youngest son seems to have a strong tendency to get strep throat. Should I worry that he might contract one of those deadly strains of strep that I've heard about? Would it help to have his tonsils removed?*

A The necrotic, or flesh-killing, forms of streptococcus bacteria that have received so much attention lately are rare. These bacteria enter the body through skin infections. They are not a cause for concern with regard to strep throat.

Strep, while serious, painful, and contagious, is universally responsive to antibiotics. Although many families of bacteria, including tuberculosis and staphylococcus bacteria, have developed drug-resistant strains, strep has not. For this reason, physicians still consider an occasional course of antibiotics safer than a tonsillectomy, a surgical procedure that requires general anesthesia and has other risks associated with it. In addition, a tonsillectomy is no guarantee against strep throat, which can infect the back of the throat, roof of the mouth, and other areas aside from the tonsils. In general, doctors today will agree to a tonsillectomy only if, over the course of a year, a patient has had several infections in the tonsils despite adequate treatment each time.

Q *What is the function of the spleen? What are the symptoms of a ruptured spleen? Is it possible to live after having your spleen removed?*

A The spleen has several functions, including the following: storing blood cells and helping to process red blood cells that have died; breaking down foreign matter in the blood; and helping to form certain types of white blood cells.

A ruptured spleen is usually the result of trauma, although an infection such as mononucleosis can make the spleen so large that it may rupture. As blood leaks into the abdomen, symptoms can include pain, weakness, and anemia.

A person can live a normal life without a spleen, but he or she will have a decreased ability to fight infections. Individuals who have had their spleen removed must take appropriate precautions, including making certain to have all the immunizations they need.

Q *What causes chronic low blood pressure, and is it as dangerous as high blood pressure? Is it treatable?*

A Low blood pressure, or "hypotension," may become chronic for a variety of reasons. Some people appear to have a tendency toward long-term low blood pressure, possibly due to genetic factors. The characteristic may become more apparent as the person ages, because, in some people, aging also causes a drop in blood pressure.

Blood pressure that is on the very low side of normal may not be so bad. Some authorities think that it may even lead to a longer life span. Individuals with this condition should keep their fluid intake high, and they should be aware that they may pass out easily. If their blood pressure becomes too low, they may need medication to raise it to acceptable levels.

Low blood pressure can also be caused by an adrenal-gland hormone deficiency; dehydration, blood infection, or chronic blood loss; and as a side effect of diuretic or antihypertensive medications.

Do you have a medical question?
Send it to Editor, Health and Medicine Annual, P.O. Box 90, Hawleyville, CT 06440-9990.

NUTRITION

CONTENTS

HOT AND HEALTHY

Peppers come in a wide range of shapes, sizes, colors, and flavor intensities. A healthy food choice, peppers are fat-free, cholesterol-free, low in calories, high in fiber, and rich in vitamin C and beta-carotene. A chemical found in hot peppers even has potent analgesic properties.

by Maria Guglielmino, M.S., R.D.

An amazing gastronomic event occurred in 1991: sales of salsa exceeded sales of ketchup by a stunning $40 million, making salsa the most popular condiment in the United States. The ascent of salsa parallels another trend in American eating habits: the appearance of "chiliheads"—an affectionate term for people who simply cannot get enough of chili (also spelled "chile") peppers. According to David DeWitt, editor of the bimonthly magazine *Chile Pepper*, Americans now buy $3 billion worth of chili peppers and chili-pepper products each year. It's no wonder that words like *jalapeño, serrano, habanero,* and *pablano* roll off the tongue these days just as easily as meat and potatoes did not so long ago.

The chili "mania" in the United States evolved in step with the upsurge of immigrants from Mexico, Asia, and the Caribbean that began about 50 years ago. Along with their other contributions to American culture, these immigrants brought with them their hot-and-spicy cuisines. Before long, Mexican, Indian, and other ethnic restaurants sprang up around the country. Soon mainstream grocery stores and roadside farmers' markets started carrying an array of hot peppers and pungent spices. Today home chefs everywhere prepare spicy dishes using some form of chili pepper as a prime ingredient.

Perhaps the best news about chili peppers is that they are good for you. Chili peppers are fat-free, cholesterol-free, low in calories, high in fiber, and rich in vitamin C and beta-carotene. And even beyond their nutritional benefits, chili peppers are revealing themselves to have a whole host of important medicinal properties.

Hot Stuff

Chili peppers hold the distinction of being the only food that can cause pain when eaten. A single bite can elicit burning in the mouth, profuse sweating, and tearing of the eyes, symptoms that occur with varying intensity depending on the hotness of the pepper and the tolerance of the individual. Despite these reactions, millions of people around the world take great pleasure in eating chilies on a daily basis—despite the fact that they bite back.

Contrary to what might be expected of such a fiery food, chili peppers are fruits, not vegetables. They belong to the nightshade family, siblings of eggplants, potatoes, and tomatoes. Botanists classify hot and sweet peppers in the genus *Capsicum*. Capsaicin is the odorless and tasteless chemical that makes chilies hot. In the pepper plant itself, capsaicin is found in the placenta, just below the stem. The seeds of a chili pepper are attached to the placenta, and are therefore hot as well.

Paul Rozin, Ph.D., a psychologist at the University of Pennsylvania in Philadelphia, has studied the effects of capsaicin on the human body, looking for answers to the chemical's apparently addictive quality. He theorizes that when a person eats a hot pepper, capsaicin irritates nerve endings in the tongue and mouth, causing them to release "substance P," a neurotransmitter that alerts the brain to the pain. Substance P triggers the brain to release endorphins, natural opiates (also linked to "runner's high") that block the pain. Every bite of a chili pepper results in a dose of endorphin, producing a pleasurable high that keeps the chili eater coming back for more.

A daring diner feasts on the hottest of hot peppers, the habaneros (Capsicum chinense). Spicy dishes using various forms of chili peppers have become increasingly popular in the United States.

Origins of the Chili

Wild chili peppers probably originated in South America. Various artifacts found in Peru, Central America, and Mexico, and dated from A.D. 400 to 1400, reveal that peppers were an important part of ancient American cultures. The Aztec, Maya, and Inca civilizations worshiped chili peppers for their healing powers; chilies were also eaten to cure colds, arthritis, and other mal-

Laborers (left) in southern New Mexico harvest hot peppers, several hundred varieties of which are cultivated in warm climates. Gloved workers (above) sort cayennne peppers (Capsicum annuum longum).

adies. A warm beverage made from hot chilies and chocolate is said to have been the drink of choice for Mexican priests.

Thinking that chilies were variants of the black pepper *(Piper nigrum)*, Christopher Columbus erroneously named chilies "peppers." He brought back pepper seeds to Europe; via the trade routes, the seeds reached the Far East. Chili peppers quickly became an important part of the cuisines of China, Thailand, Korea, and India. Today India has the highest per-capita chili consumption in the world. Thus, in a noteworthy twist, the "traditional" hot dishes of these Asian cultures owe their pungent qualities to the New World.

Nutrition and Pungency

Hot peppers grow in a variety of colors, shapes, and sizes. Colors vary from warm tones of orange, bright yellow, and scarlet to deep purple, lavender, forest green, and even black. By weight, fresh red chilies have the same amount of beta-carotene as carrots do. All chilies rival citrus fruits in their vitamin C content. In fact, by weight, chilies have about three times more vitamin C than do oranges. One 45-gram chili contains 109 milligrams of vitamin C.

Chilies vary a great deal in hotness. The bell pepper is the mildest (not hot at all); the fiery habanero from the Yucatán is the hottest. Fortunately, there are some loose rules of thumb for estimating, before you bite into it, how hot a chili will be. For the most part, the smaller the pepper, the hotter it will be. Exceptions do exist however, as in the case of the habanero, which is large in comparison to the less pungent Tabasco chili. Cooking also changes the hotness of peppers. Fresh chilies lose some "heat" when cooked, while dried peppers get hotter. Some peppers, notably Thai peppers and Tabascos, sting the mouth and lips longer than others.

"Chiliheads" in the U.S. buy $3 billion worth of chili peppers and chili-pepper products each year.

How Hot Is Hot?

When extracted from a chili-pepper plant, pure capsaicin is so potent that humans can detect it in a solution of 1 part capsaicin to 1 million parts water. In 1912 Wilbur Scoville, a pharmacologist, even developed a standard, which is called the Scoville Organoleptic Test, for measuring the pungency of capsaicin in chilies. According to this scale, bell peppers rate zero Scoville units, while habanero peppers rate 300,000 units. Pure capsaicin flies off the charts, measuring 15 million Scoville units.

It's no wonder that capsaicin spray is used in lieu of tear-gas sprays by over 1,200 police departments and the Federal Bureau of Investigation (FBI). A person sprayed with this preparation will not soon forget the experience—capsaicin makes the eyes shut and causes the respiratory system to go into spasms lasting up to 45 minutes.

Scoville's test was the standard for chili growers, manufacturers, and pharmacologists until the 1980s, when it was superseded by high-performance liquid chromatography. Although more expensive, this method, which does not rely on human tasters, is considerably more accurate. Human tasters (who made the Scoville pungency determinations) become tolerant of capsaicin, and so are unable to judge the potency of chilies after tasting a series of samples.

Tolerance for hot peppers varies from person to person. Some individuals cannot tolerate hot peppers at all. In an "emergency," milk, yogurt, or frozen yogurt may neutralize the capsaicin reaction, thanks to these foods' casein and lipoproteins, substances that prevent capsaicin from binding to pain receptors in the mouth. Breads, tortillas, rice, beans, and other starchy foods can also provide relief. Oddly enough, water does nothing to put out a capsaicin fire, although ice can be comforting.

Healing Fire

The study of phytochemicals (plant chemicals) and their medicinal qualities is an expanding area of research today. A multimillion-dollar project, "The Designer Foods Program," funded by the National Cancer Institute (NCI), is currently studying the disease-fighting properties of phytochemicals. Capsaicin, a phytochemical, has found a place for itself in modern-day pharmacopoeia because it may effectively treat a number of medical conditions, including diabetic neuropathy, osteoarthritis, post-herpetic neuralgia, and pruritus.

Topical Ointment. Capsaicin, available as a cream called Zostrix (manufactured by GenDerm Corporation, Lincolnshire, Illinois), has been shown in clinical trials to be a powerful pain reliever. Researchers believe that it may work by a simple mechanism of interference. Application of topical capsaicin to the skin first stimulates the nerves to release substance P. Initially a burning sensation occurs. Continued applications, however, inhibit the

Chili and Cancer

In early 1994 a study conducted in Mexico City inadvertently focused negative media attention on chili peppers. Researchers reported that "heavy" chili-pepper eaters were 17 times more likely to develop stomach cancer than were those that rarely ate chilies. According to Robert Dubrow, M.D., Ph.D., epidemiologist from Yale University, New Haven, Connecticut, who conducted the survey, further research is needed to confirm the findings of his survey, which was, in fact, the first study to examine the possibility of a link between chili peppers and stomach cancer from an epidemiological standpoint.

Peter Gannett, Ph.D., associate professor of medicinal chemistry at West Virginia University in Morgantown, theorizes that the capsaicin in chilies may actually lower the risk for cancer. Capsaicin appears to act as an antioxidant, neutralizing cancer promoters, such as nitrosamines. In Gannett's work, when capsaicin was mixed in a test tube with cancer-promoting substances, the carcinogenic process was extinguished.

Capsicum peppers, which include both sweet and hot peppers, are grown throughout the warm regions of the world. Some popular varieties are the long and conical chili peppers (left); the familiar, sweet, bell-shaped peppers (below, at left); and the fiery-red habanero pepper (facing page, top), whose color seems to warn of its distinction as the hottest of the hot.

nerves from secreting substance P, thereby suppressing pain, and possibly reducing inflammation.

Diabetic neuropathy, also called burning-foot syndrome, affects nearly 50 percent of people with diabetes. This condition causes excruciating burning pain of the bottom of the feet, sensitivity to touch, tightness, and coldness. Some people suffer such discomfort that they find walking and sleeping problematic.

A study published in *Diabetes Care* in January 1992 reported the effects of topical capsaicin on 277 men and women suffering from diabetic neuropathy. Either a placebo or a 0.075 percent capsaicin cream was applied to the subjects' painful areas four times a day. Pain evaluations were made at the start of the study and at two-week intervals for eight weeks. Nearly 70 percent of the patients treated with the capsaicin cream reported they experienced less pain.

Handle with Care—Cooking with Chilies

Handling chili peppers may produce a burn that can hurt for days. The burn will not blister like a heat burn (except in highly sensitive people), but it's uncomfortable nonetheless. The best precaution is to always wear gloves when picking chili peppers in the garden or when cooking them.

Although the outside skin of a chili pepper does not contain capsaicin, a small bruise in the pepper's skin can allow the chemical to leak out and make contact with your skin. Cooking experts recommend wearing thin surgical gloves when working with small amounts of peppers, and heavier disposable gloves for added protection when picking or cooking a large batch. Be very careful to avoid touching your skin, eyes, lips, or nose until you have removed and disposed of the gloves and have washed your hands thoroughly with soap and water.

If you accidentally get burned from a chili pepper, the gel from the aloe vera plant or a bit of calendula ointment will soothe the affected area.

About 26 percent of those subjects had improvement in walking, and almost 30 percent had less difficulty sleeping.

"There are no known internal or systemic side effects with topical capsaicin, as there are from most of the oral medications used to treat diabetic neuropathy," says George Dailey, M.D., chief investigator of the study and head of the division of diabetes and endocrinology at Scripps Clinic and Research Foundation in La Jolla, California.

The only side effect from capsaicin is temporary (at times, severe) burning of the skin where it is applied, but this lessens with continued use. "There are several types of diabetic neuropathy that are fairly deep and may not benefit from capsaicin," adds Dr. Dailey. "Capsaicin is most beneficial for superficial burning pain. It should be given a two-week trial, applying it three to four times per day for results."

Capsaicin appears to do the trick for sufferers of rheumatoid arthritis, osteoarthritis, and athletes with "runner's knee," an overuse injury. In a 1991 study, 48 people with arthritis rubbed capsaicin onto their knees four times a day for four weeks. Another 45 subjects with arthritis applied a placebo cream four times a day for the duration of the study. Of the capsaicin users, individuals with osteoarthritis had a 33 percent decrease in pain at the end of the study, and those suffering from rheumatoid arthritis reported a 57 percent reduction. Subjects who received the placebo cream experienced only minimal benefit.

At the 55th annual meeting of the American College of Rheumatology in November 1991, researchers from the Medical College of Wisconsin in Milwaukee reported on the effectiveness of capsaicin for relief of pain and tenderness in arthritic fingers. In a study of 21 patients who used capsaicin cream for their osteoarthritis, 30 percent reported a decrease in tenderness, and 40 percent had a reduction in pain in their finger joints compared to those treated with a placebo.

Post-herpetic neuralgia (PHN) is an extremely painful condition that can follow shingles, an illness caused by the virus herpes zoster. PHN, which appears in nearly 50 percent of people over 60 years old who develop shingles, may persist for months or even years. Capsaicin cream has been shown to provide consistent relief for the intense pain which otherwise is difficult to treat.

Capsaicin is currently being studied to treat other forms of herpes. Preliminary findings suggest that it has antiviral properties—possibly inhibiting the virus from moving from the nerves to the skin, where it causes lesions.

Capsaicin has been a boon to individuals with pruritus, a chronic-itching syndrome.

In some patients, topical capsaicin ointment, which is prepared using chili peppers, effectively relieves pain caused by osteoarthritis, diabetic neuropathy, and a variety of other conditions.

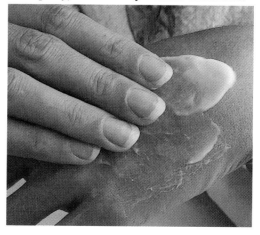

Jalapeño, habanero, and salsa have become household words in the United States, thanks in part to the chili "mania" that has swept the country. For a true fanatic, shops even exist that sell only chili-pepper food products and gift items (left). Below, chefs prepare their favorite hot and spicy recipes as they participate in a chili cook-off sponsored by the International Chili Society.

For unknown reasons, people on hemodialysis for kidney failure are especially prone to this ailment. In a study published in January 1992 in the *Journal of the American Academy of Dermatology*, eight out of nine subjects experienced significant improvement or complete relief following the use of topical capsaicin four times daily for six weeks.

Nasal Spray. Imagine using a hot-pepper nasal spray for a stuffed-up nose. Though not yet commercially available, at least one company, GenDerm, the maker of Zostrix, is working on developing such a product. Capsaicin spray has shown promising results in preliminary research for the treatment of rhinitis, an ailment that causes nasal blockage, frequent sneezing, itching, and, not surprising, a red nose. Capsaicin spray has also shown some promise as a treatment for cluster headaches.

Does eating foods containing hot peppers have any health benefits? Chilies and other pungent foods—such as mustard, horseradish, and garlic—were used by ancient healers to treat a number of respiratory problems. According to Irwin Ziment, M.D., professor of medicine and an expert on traditional remedies at the University of California at Los Angeles (UCLA), capsaicin's chemical structure is similar to that of guaifenesin, a drug used as an expecto-

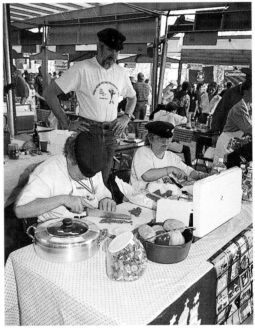

rant in many cough syrups and cold medications. Capsaicin, like guaifenesin, causes glands lining the airways to secrete watery fluids. This action helps loosen congestion, drains the sinuses, and moves mucus along so that it can be expelled. Dr. Ziment prescribes hot foods for a number of respiratory problems, including chronic bronchitis, sinusitis, and colds with nasal congestion. ◇

ALL ABOUT OILS

Consumers are understandably bewildered when it comes to choosing a "nutritionally correct" oil. Olive oil, available in a variety of flavor intensities (above), is the oil of choice for most nutritionists.

by Sue Gebo, M.P.H. R.D.

We've come a long way from the day when lard was the kitchen fat of choice. Today most consumers understand that, in general, it is healthier to use vegetable fats, or "oils," than animal fats in our food. But many people are understandably confused by the nutritional messages conveyed by the media. First we're told that margarine is "healthier" than butter. Then we hear that margarine is "bad." Once even olive oil was considered unhealthy. Now it's the top choice of many nutritionists.

Some people throw their hands up in despair, claiming that tomorrow's health news may undo everything we learned today. But wait. Though our scientific understanding of human nutrition will continue to evolve in coming years, we already know enough to make wise choices today.

The Different Types of Oils

Generally the word "oil" refers to fat that becomes liquid at room temperature. Fish oil is an example of a healthful oil from the animal world. But, by far, most oils come from vegetable products.

When bought by the bottle, the most popular oils in the United States are olive, canola, soybean, corn, peanut, safflower, sunflower, and various blends of these and other oils. Hydrogenated oils such as margarine are another major source of fat in the American diet.

Much of the oil that modern Americans consume arrives hidden in processed foods such as cookies, crackers, chips, popcorn, and prepared dinners. Some of these products contain tropical oils, which are now considered less desirable from a health standpoint. More-unusual oils, such as walnut, sesame, and almond, are typically used in tiny quantities for flavor.

It is important to remember that all oils are 100 percent fat. They all contain approximately 9 calories per gram, or about 120 calories per tablespoon. So, from a weight-management standpoint, all oils are equally "fattening." But some oils offer advantages over others, primarily in terms of cardiovascular health.

Oils are made up of fatty acids, which in turn come in three forms: saturated, polyunsaturated, and monounsaturated. In urated" is especially high in polyunsaturated fatty acids, and so on. The more saturated fatty acids a fat contains, the harder, or more solid, it will be at room temperature.

What Makes Oil "Healthy"

Researchers have found that our bodies react differently to the saturated, polyunsaturated, and monounsaturated fats in our food. When we eat saturated fat, our liver is stimulated into producing cholesterol, which then circulates through the bloodstream. As a result, a diet high in saturated fats can elevate a susceptible person's cholesterol levels. (For little-understood reasons, this is not true for everyone.)

Unfortunately, elevated levels of blood cholesterol—particularly the artery-clog-

The traditional way of extracting oil from palm kernels is still practiced in parts of Nigeria (at left). Tropical oils contain high levels of artery-clogging saturated fat, however, and have thus fallen out of favor with Americans.

chemical terms, fatty acids are long chains of carbon atoms, with various numbers of hydrogen atoms attached to each chain. A saturated fatty acid contains as many hydrogen atoms as its carbon chain can physically hold. A polyunsaturated fatty acid has a carbon chain with two or more spaces free and available for hydrogen bonding. The carbon chain on a monounsaturated fatty acid has only one pair of unbound carbon atoms.

Most oils are a mixture of the three types of fatty acid. An oil considered "polyunsat- ging LDL, or low-density lipoprotein, cholesterol—can lead to a condition in which the arteries become clogged with plaque (atherosclerosis, more commonly called "hardening of the arteries"). This in turn increases a person's risk of heart attack and stroke.

The good news is that by substituting polyunsaturated fat for saturated fat in the diet, a person can usually lower his or her levels of total cholesterol. However, diets high in polyunsaturated fat can have the additional effect of reducing the level of "good" HDL, or high-density lipoprotein, cholesterol in a person's blood. HDL actually helps carry cholesterol out of the bloodstream, and high HDL levels are associated with a lower risk of heart disease.

Studies suggest that diets high in monounsaturated oils can result in lower total cholesterol levels without lowering levels of healthful HDL.

Of late, a great deal of emphasis has been placed on cutting fat and oil from the diet. However, a completely fat-free diet would be very unhealthy. In particular, we need oils that contain two essential fatty acids that the human body does not manufacture for itself. These two essentials are linoleic acid and linolenic acid. All polyunsaturated vegetable oils (as well as various nuts and green leafy vegetables) contain substantial amounts of linoleic acid. But few oils contain significant amounts of linolenic acid.

Butter, with its higher content of saturated fat, is less nutritionally desirable than margarine. Soft margarine is better than the stick form.

Good sources of linolenic acid are soybean oil and canola oil.

Both essential fatty acids are now thought to be important for cardiovascular health. Linolenic is used by the body to produce substances that help "thin" the blood, and thereby reduce the risk of blood clots and heart attack.

The Scoop on Margarine

As mentioned earlier, margarine—which is made of vegetable oils—was once considered a healthful alternative to butter—which is made of milk fat. Margarine's reputation took a major tumble in the early 1990s, thanks to the results of several studies. In one particularly well-publicized 1993 study, researchers at Harvard Medical School in Cambridge, Massachusetts, reported that women who eat four or more teaspoons of margarine a day had a 50 percent greater risk of developing heart dis-

Fats and Oils Comparison Chart

This table compares the fat content of selected fats and oils, ranging from those with a low saturated fat content to those with a high saturated fat content. All fats and oils are high in calories, 115 to 120 calories per tablespoon.

Product (1 Tablespoon)	Saturated Fatty Acids (Grams)	Cholesterol (Milligrams)	Polyunsaturated Fatty Acids (Grams)	Monounsaturated Fatty Acids (Grams)
Rapeseed oil (canola oil)	0.9	0	4.5	7.6
Safflower oil	1.2	0	10.1	1.6
Sunflower oil	1.4	0	5.5	6.2
Corn oil	1.7	0	8.0	3.3
Olive oil	1.8	0	1.1	9.9
Hydrogenated sunflower oil	1.8	0	4.9	6.3
Margarine, liquid, bottled	1.8	0	5.1	3.9
Margarine, soft, tub	1.8	0	3.9	4.8
Sesame oil	1.9	0	5.7	5.4
Soybean oil	2.0	0	7.9	3.2
Margarine, stick	2.1	0	3.6	5.1
Peanut oil	2.3	0	4.3	6.2
Cottonseed oil	3.5	0	7.1	2.4
Lard	5.0	12	1.4	5.8
Palm oil	6.7	0	1.3	5.0
Butter	7.1	31	0.4	3.3
Palm kernel oil	11.1	0	0.2	1.5
Coconut oil	11.8	0	0.2	0.8

ease than women who eat margarine less than once a month. The suspected culprit: trans-fatty acids, a type of fat that is formed when liquid oils are hydrogenated, or hardened, to form margarine and shortening.

During hydrogenation, hydrogen atoms are attached to fat molecules in an unusual, unnatural pattern. When eaten, trans-fatty acids signal the liver to raise total cholesterol levels, just as saturated fat does. To make matters worse, hydrogenated fats also appear to lower blood levels of "good," or HDL, cholesterol. And this further increases a person's risk of heart disease.

Despite the real concerns raised by the Harvard study, more studies are needed to confirm its findings. The American Heart Association (AHA) still stands behind its position that butter, with its higher content of saturated fat, is a worse artery clogger than is margarine. The AHA encourages consumers to reduce their intake of all fats, including butter and margarine. When choosing margarine, the association says, consumers should opt for the softer types, which are less hydrogenated. These include margarines sold in tubs and bottles, rather than sticks. Also look out for "hydrogenated vegetable oils" in the ingredient lists of prepackaged snacks, desserts, and other processed foods.

Spotlight on Popular Oils

Olive Oil. Olive oil's recent popularity in this country may have started with reports that people in Mediterranean countries (where copious amounts of this oil are used) have lower heart-disease rates than do those in North America. True to its reputation, olive oil is high in "heart-healthy" monounsaturated fatty acids.

Olive oil comes in a variety of flavor intensities. Traditional olive oil has a deep-yellow hue, a mild yet distinctive flavor, and a pleasantly pungent aroma that permeates the air when the oil is heated.

Olive-oil makers also produce a "light" olive oil for recipes that call for a milder flavor. On the other end of the spectrum is "extra-virgin" olive oil, recognized by its greenish tint. This intensely flavored oil is traditionally used as a condiment, for dipping bread, and for drizzling over salads, cooked vegetables, potatoes, or pasta. Because of its flavor intensity, small amounts of extra-virgin olive oil are enough to impart flavor—a boon for people seeking lots of taste for the minimum of calories.

Canola Oil. Processed from a plant called rapeseed, canola oil is a relatively inexpensive and mild-tasting oil. It has become popular among health-conscious consumers because it is exceptionally low in saturated fat, while being very high in monounsaturated fat and the essential fatty acid linolenic acid.

Canola is a special type of rapeseed, specially bred and processed to contain a minimum of a very undesirable fatty acid, erucic acid (a suspected carcinogen),

Consumers have a wide variety of oils from which to choose; all are 100 percent fat and contain approximately the same number of calories. Nonetheless, certain oils are more healthful than others.

Popcorn

"Hold the butter!" you say while ordering your popcorn at the concession stand. Little did you know that even "butterless" movie theater popcorn is permeated with artery-clogging saturated fat, according to the Center for Science in the Public Interest (CSPI), a nutrition watchdog group.

Of the theaters that CSPI studied, 70 percent were popping their corn in coconut oil, the most highly saturated fat available. Popcorn samples obtained from 12 chain theaters in San Francisco, Chicago, and Washington, D.C., were analyzed by an independent laboratory. The figures revealed that a medium tub, which holds 16 cups of popcorn, contained an average of 900 calories, a large proportion of which came from saturated fat—and that was without any butter topping.

Even a kiddie-size bag, with 5 cups of the fluffy stuff, contained an average of 14 grams of saturated fat. The recommended intake for an adult is less than 20 grams per day.

CSPI found that some theaters were openly promoting their "healthy" use of canola oil for popping. "Foul play," cried the watchdogs, for the canola "oil" being used was actually hydrogenated canola shortening.

What's a moviegoer to do? Since the headline-grabbing study broke, the United Artists theater chain, with 450 locations nationwide, has begun offering air-popped popcorn in addition to its regular fat-laden fare. Loews/Sony theaters now offer "Healthier Choice" popcorn popped in liquid canola oil. And other theaters are expected to follow suit.

As for home fare, air-popped is the best choice nutritionally, with 25 fat-free calories per cup. Try enhancing the taste with spices, garlic powder, butter-flavored sprinkles, or raisins and cinnamon.

Microwave popcorns vary widely in fat content, and most contain hydrogenated oil. So look carefully at the "Nutrition Facts" label on the box. Aim for 2 grams or less of total fat per cup. A nice surprise: butter-flavored microwave popcorn is usually no higher in fat than the non-butter-flavored option.

which occurs naturally in the rapeseed plant. Occasionally you'll see canola listed on ingredient labels as LEAR, for "low erucic acid rapeseed."

Corn Oil. Popular and moderately priced, corn oil has a mild flavor that produces a pleasant odor when heated. Corn oil is low in saturated fat, and high in polyunsaturated fat. It also contains moderate amounts of monounsaturated fat and a tiny amount of linolenic acid.

Soybean Oil. Another popular cooking oil, soybean oil shares many of corn oil's characteristics. It is a paler color than corn oil,

Stir-fry meals, which contain plenty of fresh vegetables, small portions of meat, and only a minute amount of cooking fat, represent a great "heart-healthy" alternative.

and some cooks prefer its slightly milder flavor. It is nearly identical to corn oil in its content of polyunsaturated, monounsaturated, and saturated fat. But soybean oil is higher—nearly as high as canola oil—in linolenic acid.

Safflower Oil. Safflower oil's mild flavor and pale color make it a versatile choice in the kitchen. It has been widely praised by nutritionists as low in saturated fat. But it is lower in desirable monounsaturated fat and linolenic acid.

Peanut Oil. Used in many Chinese stir-fry dishes, peanut oil gives off a pleasantly nutty aroma and flavor when heated. It contains slightly more saturated fat than the previously mentioned oils, and virtually no essential linolenic acid. Nonetheless, peanut oil is still considered a healthful choice, with its moderately high content of monounsaturated fat.

Cottonseed Oil. A product of pressed cottonseed, this bland oil is most often found in processed foods and vegetable-oil blends, and is often hardened, or "hydrogenated." Even before hydrogenation, cottonseed oil is somewhat higher than the previously mentioned oils in saturated fat. It is moderately high in polyunsaturated fat, and low in monounsaturates.

Tropical Oils. Tropical oils include coconut oil, palm oil, palm-kernel oil, and cocoa butter. As a group, they have largely fallen from favor, due to their high levels of artery-clogging saturated fat. The most saturated is coconut oil, with about 90 percent saturated fat. The saturated-fat content of palm-kernel oil is about 85 percent; cocoa butter, about 60 percent; and palm oil, about 50 percent.

Here in the United States, tropical oils have been widely used as inexpensive ingredients in processed foods. They are useful taste and texture enhancers, and have a longer shelf life than less-saturated vegetable oils. However, in response to consumers' demand for healthier food products, many manufacturers are replacing the tropical oils in their recipes with polyunsaturated and monounsaturated products.

The Bottom Line on Oils

Moderation is the key when it comes to oils. Here are a few specific guidelines:

Limit your intake of fats to 40 to 60 grams per day, so that they account for no more than 30 percent of your daily calories. Remember to count the fat that comes in processed foods, meat, and whole-milk dairy products, nuts, olives, avocados, and processed snack foods.

But don't go too low! At least some of your daily calories should come from some form of fat, ideally unsaturated oils.

Select a variety of monounsaturated and polyunsaturated oils for home use to ensure adequate intake of the essential fatty acids.

Use nonstick cookware and cooking sprays to limit the need for oil in frying and baking.

Choose soft and liquid margarines rather than stick margarines and butter for your table. Try substituting oils for butter and margarine in recipes, and try cutting back on the total amount of oil called for in most recipes. ◇

Candy: How Sweet It Is!

by Dodi Schultz

The Arabs' word for it was *qandi*, from *qand*, a lump of cane sugar. It came down to us, virtually intact, through successive European languages: Old Italian (*zucchero candi*), Old French (*sucre candi*), Middle English (*sugre candy*). In the 1800s Americans called it "sugar candy." Now it's just plain candy.

Sometimes it is indeed virtually entirely sugar, with a few minor glamorizers tossed in for color and zip. That's true of sour balls, for example. A representative label listing of ingredients, which the Food and Drug Administration (FDA) requires on all packaged foods, reads: sugar, corn syrup, citric acid, artificial flavor, Red No. 40, Yellow No. 5, Yellow No. 6, and Blue No. 1. (The last four are simply specific FDA-sanctioned food colorings—synthetic additives to which a few people are allergic, but which otherwise pose no threat to health.)

The word "candy" doesn't cover only pure-sugar concoctions, but also includes an array of tasty confections combining sugar or similar substances with other compatible ingredients such as fruits, nuts, or chocolate. And the most popular of these, as most Americans will confirm, is chocolate. When we think of a "candy bar," what generally comes to mind includes chocolate—usually milk chocolate, although it often contains nuts, along with a variety of sugars, fats, and flavorings.

Candy as a Food

Candy has not had very good press. In his *Reflections on Ice-Breaking,* poet Ogden Nash remarked dismissively that "Candy is dandy, but liquor is quicker." (He didn't reflect on the health risks of either.) In the realm of serious discourse, the sweet stuff has been used as a symbol of weakness. For example, speaking to the Canadian Parliament during World War II, Winston Churchill described the stalwart British by saying, "We have not journeyed all this way across the centuries, across the oceans, across the mountains, across the prairies, because we are made of sugar candy."

Lollipops, a perennial favorite of children, are virtually all sugar, with a few minor ingredients added for color and zip.

Although some may be loath to concede the fact, candy is a food. Its basic elements are included in the U.S. Department of Agriculture's (USDA's) "Food Pyramid" (in the small triangle at the top labeled "Fats, Oils, & Sweets—Use Sparingly"). Short on vitamins, minerals, protein, fiber, and other desirable nutrients, candy is instead a prime source of fat and sugar. And calories.

Candy is either entirely sugar or a tasty combination of sugar and fruits, nuts, or chocolate.

As Michelle Smith, Ph.D., of the FDA's Center for Food Safety and Applied Nutrition (CFSAN) observes: "Calorie content is a recognized nutritional value, and, in some parts of the world, that may be a significant advantage. Many people in this country are—well, not at a deficit for calories."

Some candies—those containing milk or nuts, for example—do offer some beneficial food values in addition to the calories. All foods contain calories, of course. A calorie is neither "good" nor "bad" in and of itself, but simply a heat unit. "Calories, of course, are needed by the body as a source of energy," points out Virginia Wilkening, R.D., a colleague of Smith. "They are needed by some people more than others—teenage boys, for instance. Others should limit their calorie and sugar intake in order to consume foods that are sources of a wide variety of nutrients."

You have a sort of nutritional "budget," Wilkening explains: "In order to maintain the right weight, and take in the energy you need for your daily activities, you need a certain quantity of calories; that quantity varies from one individual to another. Within that 'budget,' you need a variety of other nutrients—vitamins, minerals, protein, and so on. If you're going to use up some of your allotment on a candy bar, watch what else you're eating the rest of the day: skip desserts; consume plenty of fruits and vegetables. We don't recommend shunning any food. The message is: Eat a variety of foods, in moderation."

Sweet Substitutes

How about low-calorie or noncaloric substitutes for the sugar and fat in candy? Of course, sweetness is the essence of candy, and the traditional source is sugar. And the fats in chocolate are what lend it the texture prized by candy lovers.

The idea of introducing substitutes for these ingredients is relatively recent, says George Pauli, director of the CFSAN's division of product policy's office of premarket approval: "The Food, Drug, and Cosmetic Act's provision prohibiting nonnutritive substances in candy was, for a long time, interpreted to bar such additives as nonnutritive sweeteners; actually, the intent was to screen out inedible components of the products. Congress later clarified this point: substances added for 'technical effect' are permitted. FDA policy takes this term to include colorings, as well as artificial sweet-

Although perfectly safe for adults and older children, small, hard candies pose a choking risk for children under five years old.

Chewing Gum & Gum Chewing

The United States is a major producer of chewing gum, and Americans are major consumers—chewing an average of 183 sticks of gum per person annually. However, the love affair with this chewing confection is not restricted to the geographic borders of the United States. After a slump in the mid-1980s, chewing-gum sales rebounded. Gum has now emerged as a multibillion-dollar commodity with worldwide popularity.

Currently, gum chewing is marketed as part of a healthy lifestyle. Both manufacturers and researchers proclaim its benefits: gum chewing helps reduce plaque buildup when brushing is not an option; it temporarily hides bad breath; and it even improves concentration and relieves the boredom associated with long-distance driving. In addition, gum chewing is promoted as an alternative to such bad habits as overeating and smoking.

Gum was long believed to contribute to tooth problems because of its high sugar content. Now it is enjoying a redemption of sorts. Recent studies show that gum chewing stimulates saliva flow, which helps rid the mouth of food particles that ultimately contribute to decay. In fact, the studies show that chewing a stick of gum for 15 minutes after eating can prevent dental cavities. Another study suggests that you need not chew sugarless gum to derive benefits. Researchers say that the sugar in gum is quickly rinsed out of the mouth by saliva, and therefore is not a factor in tooth decay.

Chewing gum is made with three main ingredients: gum base, sugar, and corn syrup. (The gum base is especially strong and elastic in bubble gum.) The desired appearance and taste are achieved with the addition of natural and artificial colors and flavorings (most often fruit, cinnamon, or mint). In general, 90 percent of the sugar and 50 percent of the flavor is released during the first few minutes of chewing.

eners, and a number of the latter have been approved for use in candy. In a chocolate bar, however, simply using a sugar substitute would not cut the calories significantly, since the caloric content of chocolate is very much dependent on its fat content."

What about that fat? Devising acceptable substitutes isn't easy, Pauli observes:

"The problem with chocolate is both fat and total calories. There are two kinds of substances that might be considered fat substitutes. One would be a fat mimetic, a nonfat—it might be based on fiber, or starch, or protein—with the properties of the fat in question. With chocolate, you would want the desired texture, as well as another crucial feature: melting point—chocolate melts at mouth temperature, but not at room temperature. It has been hard to devise substances with these properties.

"A second kind of substitute for the fat occurring naturally in chocolate would be fat that's less readily absorbed by the body—perhaps only 5 calories per gram, as opposed to 9, for instance. Manufacturers have been addressing this issue very intensively, trying to reduce absorbable fat content without losing taste and texture. So far, such products haven't penetrated the market significantly."

The problem, then, is essentially a marketing challenge. The FDA looks at candy's health-and-safety aspects and its labeling as a food; the agency also establishes certain definitions and standards for chocolate (see the sidebar beginning on page 84).

Can Candy Hurt You?

By and large, candy isn't considered a threat to health, with the exception of the hazard of dental caries, or tooth decay. By definition, candy contains sugar, which is the prime source of sustenance for the ever-present bacteria responsible for cavities.

Some people are also convinced that in children, sweets are a major culprit in causing hyperactivity and other behavior and cognitive (learning) problems. Recent evidence suggests that sweets are not to blame. Results of a study examining this issue, funded by the National Institutes of Health (NIH), were published in the *New England Journal of Medicine* in February 1994. Two groups of youngsters—one suspected of being sugar-sensitive, the other presumed not to be—were fed a variety of carefully calibrated diets, including one high in sucrose (table sugar). The researchers concluded that the higher-than-normal sugar regimen had no significant effect on either group of youngsters. Despite this conclusion, some physicians feel there may be isolated cases of unusual sensitivity in some children, whether to sugar or to some other dietary element. The child's doctor is the best source of advice, and he or she should be consulted before any dietary manipulation is attempted.

Sometimes, as with any food, health-and-safety hazards may crop up in candy, notes

All About Chocolate

Chocolate, like most fruits and nuts, comes from trees. The seed of the "chocolate tree," as it's sometimes called, can be spun off in a number of guises. Those derivatives can be further altered in flavor, consistency, and nutritional value through combination with such items as sugars and dairy products. Thus, standards have been devised so that consumers who prefer the creamy lightness of milk chocolate, for instance, to the zestier bite of bittersweet can satisfy their cravings.

To "promote honesty and fair dealing in the interest of consumers" (to quote the Federal Food, Drug, and Cosmetic Act), the FDA's Center for Food Safety and Applied Nutrition (CFSAN) has the authority to set standards of identity for just about every processed food, including chocolate. This means that both producers and consumers can know with certainty that milk chocolate, for example, consistently refers to chocolate containing set minimum quantities of both chocolate and milk solids.

What makes milk chocolate different from dark chocolate? All chocolate (as well as cocoa) is derived from the seeds (beans) of the cacao tree, *Theobroma cacao*, native to the American tropics. The heart of the beans, called "nibs," are contained in foot-long pods and are additionally protected by individual outer shells. When finely ground, nibs become "chocolate liquor," consisting of both cocoa solids and cocoa butter, which are separable. Proportions of these constituents used in chocolate products can be important to the consumer (one chocolate form or variety may, for example, contain more fat than another), as well as to the manufacturer (one may be more or less costly than another). These proportions also affect flavor.

The FDA standards for cacao products were updated in 1993, and the final amended regulations were published in the May 21, 1993, *Federal Register*. Those rules are highly technical, down to prescribing analytic techniques and specifying approved processing methods. Specifications for cacao nibs themselves are offered (they may

Cacao-bean pods mature on the trunk and lower branches of the cacao tree (above). The pods, which contain cacao beans, are harvested year-round.

contain "not more than 1.75 percent by weight" of residual shell), as are the definitions of intermediate and end products, including chocolate liquor ("contains not less than 50 percent nor more than 60 percent by weight of cacao fat," among other requirements). There are also standards for breakfast cocoa, sweet chocolate, semisweet or bittersweet chocolate, milk chocolate, skim-milk chocolate, and so on.

Most popular, as examination of any candy counter will attest, is milk chocolate, with the semisweet, darker variety a distant second. Milk chocolate's main ingredients,

States, unless you've recently sampled certain candies now being test-marketed. The test-marketing is taking place under temporary permits that took effect for a 15-month period starting in February 1994.

Under those permits, issued by the FDA in November 1993, two manufacturers were granted permission to market chocolate that deviates from the present standards for chocolate products. The manufacturers are test-marketing their products on a limited regional basis, to assess consumer acceptance. (The candies otherwise conform to existing chocolate-

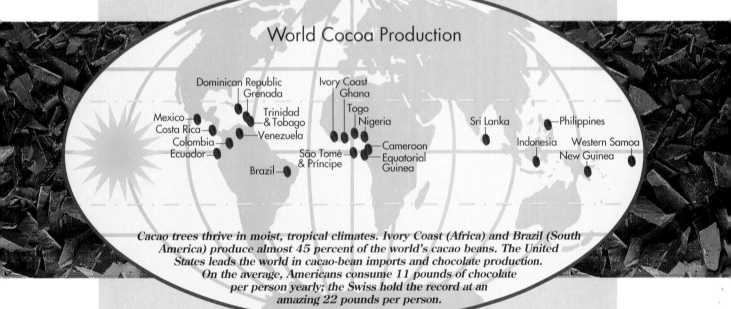

World Cocoa Production

Cacao trees thrive in moist, tropical climates. Ivory Coast (Africa) and Brazil (South America) produce almost 45 percent of the world's cacao beans. The United States leads the world in cacao-bean imports and chocolate production. On the average, Americans consume 11 pounds of chocolate per person yearly; the Swiss hold the record at an amazing 22 pounds per person.

besides the chocolate, are sugar, cocoa butter, and milk; all three may be present in greater quantity than chocolate itself. Semisweet chocolate has a relatively higher proportion of chocolate (a minimum 35 percent chocolate liquor is specified). Both may also contain such optional ingredients as emulsifiers (stabilizers) and flavorings.

And then there's "white chocolate." Or is there? You may think you've eaten something called "white chocolate," but you haven't—at least not in the United

product standards, and all added ingredients—such as sugar, dairy products, flavorings, and preservatives—meet FDA standards; all current labeling regulations apply.) White chocolate, as defined by the permits, contains only the fat (cocoa butter), not the nonfat components (which also contain the color), from the ground cacao nibs; sugar, milk fats, and milk solids are also present in prescribed proportions.

The test products being offered for consumer reaction are Polar Bears, distributed

Chocolate is stirred and blended in a special procedure called conching (left) until it attains the desired texture required for candy.

If there isn't any current standard, what is the product you ate awhile back that looked like white chocolate? It was very much like what's being test-marketed, explains Nan Rainey, chief of the CFSAN's food-standards branch, except that it couldn't properly be called "white chocolate." It might actually have been called "white confectionery," says Rainey, or perhaps it might have been labeled with such a legend as "This is what Europeans call white chocolate."

Finally, what about candy that contains alcohol, such as liqueur-filled chocolates? That depends mainly on state regulations. The Federal Food, Drug, and Cosmetic Act (which applies only to products in interstate commerce, not to those produced and sold only within a state) says that alcohol not in excess of one-half of 1 percent by volume derived solely from the use of flavoring extracts is allowed in confectionery. Beyond that, alcohol is deemed an impermissible adulterant—except that the rule doesn't apply "if the sale of such confectionery is permitted under the laws of the state in which such confectionery is intended to be offered for sale."

by Ganong Brothers of St. Stephen, New Brunswick, in Canada; and Hershey's Hugs, distributed by Hershey Chocolate of Hershey, Pennsylvania.

Will this "chocolate"—a pale stepchild to some chocolate lovers, despite its legitimate cacao heritage—attain a place in the FDA's official list of chocolate varieties? That will depend on agency review of petitions filed by Hershey and by the Chocolate Manufacturers Association, and on the reports filed by Ganong and Hershey, which will supplement the petitions with the test-marketing data.

Gene Newberry, acting director of CFSAN's office of field programs, the center's enforcement arm, which is on the lookout for such introduced hazards. Carelessness in quality control and sanitation—violation of the good manufacturing practices on which the safety of all packaged foods depends— might, for example, result in contamination with microorganisms that could cause illness. But this has happened, according to Newberry, only on rare occasions; in most cases the contamination has been discovered before the product has reached the public, so people have not been harmed.

"Responsible manufacturers," says Newberry, "keep up constant vigilance, especially at key points in production at which the product is particularly susceptible to accidental contamination. If safety deviations are discovered, production is halted, and the situation is corrected immediately." The FDA backs up this basic manufacturers' responsibility with its own unannounced plant inspections, taking random samples for analysis.

The FDA also looks closely at all imported foods, including candy, to be sure that they contain no substances, such as flavors and coloring agents, not approved by the FDA as safe for human consumption.

Another important candy safety hazard is the risk of choking, especially in small children. In some cases the risk is inherent in the product: a hard candy such as a sour ball or lollipop, or a cluster of nuts, while perfectly safe for an older child or adult, could easily block an infant's or toddler's far narrower windpipe. Such products should be off-limits for youngsters under the age of about 5 years.

Otherwise-safe candy can be made unsafe when potentially harmful nonfood components are introduced; the FDA can ban such components as unsafe adulterants. Here the FDA's authority is limited to elements not of "practical functional value" to the product, according to the Federal Food, Drug, and Cosmetic Act. Thus, for example, the FDA cannot ban lollipop sticks, which serve an essential functional purpose, but can prohibit items that are not truly functional. If a manufacturer attempts to incorporate prizes or trinkets inside a food product, for instance, the FDA can take action.

Candy plays into many holiday celebrations. The Halloween haul (above) illustrates the vast variety of candies available to today's consumer.

Food labels, which include an ingredients list, calorie content, and nutrition facts, are required for all packaged foods—including candy.

"Importers from time to time attempt to bring in such products as chocolate Easter eggs with small toys inside," Newberry reports. "We don't want them on the market, because they're a real choking hazard. We can, and do, prohibit them as nonnutritive substances that are definitely not essential to the product itself."

Label Requirements

By law, all packaged foods must bear a label listing ingredients in order of predominance, and candy is no exception. Every package of hard candies and every chocolate bar you buy must offer such a listing.

As part of the new food-labeling rules under the 1990 Nutrition Labeling and Education Act, manufacturers must include substantially more nutrition information on labels than in the past. As of May 8, 1994, every candy product (along with other packaged foods) must have on its label an ingredients list plus a new-format data summary, headed "Nutrition Facts," designed to help consumers best relate content to nutrition concerns. The new labels include such information as calorie content; such elements as carbohydrates, fats, and protein; key vitamins and minerals; and, for each, its daily value percentage on the basis of a 2,000-calorie diet. For example, the label on one popular brand of chocolate-with-peanuts bar, using the new format, includes the information that it provides 280 calories, 8 percent of the daily value for carbohydrate, and a significant 34 percent of the daily value for saturated fat.

So now, if you decide to indulge your "sweet tooth," you know exactly what you're biting into! ◇

In the United States, chocolate is the favorite flavor for candies, ice cream, and other sweets.

THE VALUE OF VITAMINS

by Devera Pine

You thought you wanted a simple multiple vitamin, but now you're not so sure. Shelves of vitamin supplements stretch before you at the store. There are formulas that promise to battle stress or age. Next to them are others that trumpet special ingredients: "beta-carotene" or "antioxidants." One type of multiple-vitamin supplement is labeled "complete," another "advanced," and a third "high-potency." Some are "natural," others sugar-free. And next to the multivitamins are rows and rows of individual vitamin supplements—A, B complex, C, D, and so on—an alphabet soup of choices, all in different doses and forms. What's right for you?

If you're confused, you're not alone. In fact, when it comes to choosing vitamins, confusion pretty much reigns. There are all sorts of vitamins in all sorts of formulations, some making all sorts of health claims. For most of us, sorting out exactly which vitamins we need to stay healthy is a tricky business indeed.

"There's a lot of misinformation out there," says Tammy Baker, a registered dietitian and spokesperson for the American Dietetic Association (ADA). To separate hype from fact and determine which vitamin supplements—if any—you should take, you need to know what vitamins are and what they can and can't do.

Vitamin ABCs

An old proverb describes how, for lack of one horseshoe nail, a horse and its rider came to an untimely end. In a way, vitamins are like that nail—they may seem insignificant because they are present in the body in such minute amounts, and yet they are essential to life. "You only need very small quantities, but without them, you wouldn't be healthy," says Felicia Busch, a registered dietitian and spokesperson for the ADA who has a private practice in St. Paul, Minnesota.

Neither an energy source nor a component of any body tissue, vitamins help form essential enzymes that act as catalysts in the body, enabling vital processes to occur. For example, vitamin A plays a key role in the formation of skin and mucous membranes. Vitamin B_{12} helps the body develop red blood cells and maintain nerve tissues.

Because vitamins are essential to so many body processes, lack of them can spell trouble. The classic example is vitamin C, which helps the body form connective tissue such as collagen. Too little vitamin C results in the deficiency disease known as scurvy, a condition in which the gums bleed, the body bruises easily, and joints swell. Scurvy was once the bane of sailors who, on long voyages, went months without the fruits and vegetables rich in this vitamin. British sailors learned to prevent scurvy by eating limes and lemons—and thereby earned the nickname "limeys."

Sailors knew of the connection between citrus fruits and health more than a century before the first vitamin was identified, however. That happened in 1912, when researchers discovered vitamin A. Today we know of 13 vitamins. These vitamins are classified in two groups: fat-soluble and water-soluble.

The distinction is more than academic; it affects the ways in which we need to obtain different vitamins. Fat-soluble vitamins—A, D, E, and K—must team up with fat to be absorbed into the body, and may be stored in the body's fatty tissues. Water-soluble vitamins—C and the B vitamins—don't require fat for absorption. And because these vitamins dissolve in water, the body can't store them for very long. Amounts that aren't needed immediately by the body are simply excreted.

The body manufactures a few of the vitamins it needs. In response to sunlight, for instance, the skin makes vitamin D. Likewise, bacteria in the intestine make vitamin K, biotin, and B_5 (pantothenic acid). However, we need to get most vitamins from food—and just how much of various vitamins we need is the focus of growing debate. The U.S. government sets Recommended Dietary Allowances (RDAs) for most vitamins—daily amounts that average people need to prevent deficiencies. The RDAs are broken down into separate categories by age and sex, with different values for each group. In recent years, however, researchers have begun to discover that vitamins can do much more than simply prevent deficiency diseases, and that has changed some people's thinking about RDAs.

Vitamins play an essential role in the maintenance of good health.

Vitamins and Disease

Some studies indicate, for instance, that certain vitamins may actually help head off heart attacks and cancer. Most of these studies involve the so-called "antioxidant" vitamins —C, E, and beta-carotene (a precursor, or preliminary form, of vitamin A). A study of 30,000 Chinese by the National Cancer Institute (NCI) found that supplements containing vitamin E, beta-carotene, and the mineral selenium helped reduce the risk of

Freshly squeezed orange juice is a delicious way to supply the body's need for vitamin C. Strawberries, broccoli, and red peppers are other excellent sources.

cancer by 13 percent. Preliminary results from another study at Harvard University, Cambridge, Massachusetts, indicate that beta-carotene may reduce the risk of heart disease.

The reason seems to be that antioxidants prevent substances called free radicals from "oxidizing," or damaging, cells and tissues, says Tammy Baker. Free radicals are reactive molecules produced during normal body functions and in response to ultraviolet light and environmental pollutants such as cigarette smoke, car exhaust, and ozone. Left unchecked, they can attack DNA, which carries the genetic blueprint of the body. As free radicals proliferate, genetic repairs that the body normally makes cannot keep pace with the damage.

Research on antioxidants has yielded generally positive results. "The evidence continues to be remarkably consistent and compelling in demonstrating that antioxidants quench free-radical reactions, which are indeed harmful," says Jeffrey Blumberg, Ph.D., professor of nutrition at Tufts University in Boston, Massachusetts. Epidemiological studies have demonstrated that people who consume generous amounts of antioxidants have a significantly lower risk of developing chronic diseases. Less clear is how effective the antioxidants might be in people who are already sick.

Past claims about vitamins' protective effects have often been controversial and difficult to prove. For example, although thousands of people ingest large quantities of vitamin C in the hope of warding off colds, no one has ever substantiated Linus Pauling's original conclusion (set out in his 1970 book *Vitamin C and the Common Cold*) that the vitamin has this preventative effect. "At megadoses [more than 10 times the RDA], vitamin C tends to act like an antihistamine, so it might stop a runny nose and watery eyes. But it doesn't make a cold go away," says Busch.

Nonetheless, researchers are finding new links between vitamins and good health. Studies have tied a low intake of vitamins B_6, B_{12}, and folic acid to an increased risk of heart disease. Although the precise relationship isn't known, the three vitamins help regulate levels of homocystine, an amino acid in the body. Elevated levels of homocystine are a risk factor for heart disease and stroke, notes Blumberg.

Pregnant women who get enough folic acid can head off neural-tube defects (such as spina bifida) in their unborn children. Folic acid is so effective at preventing this birth defect that public-health officials are now considering fortifying foods such as flour with folic acid. Research on other vitamins is equally promising. Along with the mineral calcium, vitamin D plays an important role in heading off osteoporosis, a weakening of the bones that plagues older people, especially women. Vitamin B_6 may help slow the decline in the immune system that many scientists believe occurs as people age.

Many people obtain their daily vitamin requirements from specially fortified foods.

The RDA Riddle

For years, nutrition experts advised people to get their vitamins from food, not from supplements. As long as you ate a balanced diet of at least 1,600 calories a day, the belief was, you would meet all the RDAs. These days, however, most experts have modified that advice to reflect the reality of our busy, fast-food lives.

"It is misleading to say you get everything from a healthy diet," says Blumberg. "Ninety percent of Americans don't eat a healthy diet."

In fact, if vitamins have the disease-fighting powers that recent research suggests, it may be difficult to get the levels you need from food alone. To ward off neural-tube birth defects, for instance, a pregnant woman has to eat 400 micrograms of folic acid a day. "Few people get 400 micrograms in their diet," says Blumberg. "You would have to be eating lots of spinach." Likewise, the levels of antioxidants that have been shown to protect against disease are anywhere from double to 10 times the RDA. It may not be practical or even healthy to get these amounts from food. For instance, vitamin E is found in fats, which pose health risks. It makes sense to get extra vitamin E from a supplement instead.

With mounting evidence of vitamins' potent effects on health, some people are questioning whether the RDAs are in fact too low. They argue that the RDAs should not just prevent deficiencies, but should also promote health and head off degenerative diseases. This suggestion is controversial; many nutrition experts believe that the RDAs are high enough to promote good health in most people.

Baker, for one, contends that the RDAs are already higher than the amount needed to prevent deficiencies: "The RDAs are recommendations that include a substantial margin of safety that provides for variation in requirements among individuals. The RDAs should well meet the needs for normal body function in a healthy adult." This does not mean that supplements are not useful, says Baker. "The average American does not always eat right and may not meet the RDA for some nutrients. In these cases, a multivitamin supplement may be beneficial."

Megadosing vitamins creates risks because, at such high levels, vitamins no longer function like vitamins. Megadoses of one vitamin can throw off the absorption of other vitamins and nutrients and interfere with the absorption and action of certain drugs, notes William Goldman, Pharm.D., associate director of pharmacy at Maimonides Medical Center in Brooklyn, New York.

Because the fat-soluble vitamins like A and D are stored in body tissues, they can build up to toxic levels. That's not the case with water-soluble vitamins—but megadoses still can have harmful effects. Too much vitamin C can contribute to kidney stones. Too much chewable C can erode tooth enamel. And if you consistently megadose on C and then suddenly stop, you may wind up with rebound scurvy, says Busch. Because your body adjusted to the megadose, it will have a temporarily increased need for C. When you suddenly stop the vitamin, you may develop cracked and bleeding gums, a slowed ability to heal wounds, a tendency to bruise easily, and other symptoms of scurvy.

Such concerns make the decision to increase the RDAs a tricky issue. The Food and Nutrition Board of the National Academy of Sciences (NAS) will soon look at the issue when it undertakes its periodic review of the RDAs. But whatever the board con-

Fresh vegetables, especially when eaten raw, steamed, or stir-fried, are good sources of vitamins A and C, beta-carotene, and several B vitamins.

Vitamins: Charting Your Course

VITAMIN	MAJOR FOOD SOURCES	U.S. RDA*
A	Milk, eggs, liver, cheese, fish oil. (Fruits and vegetables that contain beta-carotene provide vitamin A. You need not consume preformed vitamin A if you eat foods rich in beta-carotene).	5,000 international units (IU), women; 10,000 IU, men 1 cup milk = 1,400 IU
Beta-carotene (not a vitamin but converted to vitamin A in the body)	Carrots, sweet potatoes, cantaloupe, leafy greens, tomatoes, apricots, winter squash, red bell peppers, pink grapefruit, broccoli, mangoes, peaches.	No RDA; experts recommend 3 mg (milligrams) 1 medium carrot = 12 mg 1 sweet potato = 15 mg
C (ascorbic acid)	Citrus fruits and juices, strawberries, tomatoes, peppers (especially red), broccoli, potatoes, kale, cauliflower, cantaloupe, brussels sprouts.	60 mg 1 orange = 70 mg 1 cup fresh orange juice = 120 mg 1 cup broccoli = 115 mg
D	Milk, fish oil, egg yolks, fortified margarine; also produced by the body in response to sunlight.	5 mcg (micrograms) or 200 IU; 10 mcg or 400 IU, before age 25 1 cup milk = 100 IU
E	Vegetable oil, nuts, margarine, wheat germ, leafy greens, seeds, almonds, olives, asparagus.	8 mg, women; 10 mg, men (12–15 IU) 1 tbsp canola oil = 9 mg 1 tbsp margarine = 2 mg 1 ounce peanuts = 2 mg 1 cup kale = 6 mg
K	Intestinal bacteria produce some of the K needed by the body. The rest is supplied by leafy greens, cauliflower, broccoli, cabbage, milk, soybeans, eggs.	60–65 mcg, women; 70–80 mcg, men 1 cup broccoli = 175 mcg 1 cup milk = 10 mcg
B_1 (thiamine)	Whole grains, enriched grain products, beans, meats, liver, wheat germ, nuts, fish, brewer's yeast.	1–1.1 mg, women; 1.2–1.5 mg, men 1 packet oatmeal = 0.5 mg
B_2 (riboflavin)	Dairy products, liver, meats, chicken, fish, enriched grain products, leafy greens, beans, nuts, eggs, almonds.	1.2–1.3 mg, women; 1.4–1.7 mg, men 1 cup milk = 0.4 mg 3 ounces chicken = 0.2 mg
B_3 (niacin)	Nuts, meats, fish, chicken, liver, enriched grain products, dairy products, peanut butter, brewer's yeast.	13–19 mg 3 ounces chicken = 12 mg 1 slice enriched bread = 1 mg
B_5 (pantothenic acid)	Whole grains, beans, milk, eggs, liver.	No RDA; experts recommend 4–7 mg
B_6 (pyridoxine)	Whole grains, bananas, meats, beans, nuts, wheat germ, brewer's yeast, chicken, fish, liver.	1.6 mg, women; 2 mg, men 1 banana = 0.7 mg 1 cup lima beans = 0.3 mg
B_{12}	Liver, beef, pork, poultry, eggs, milk, cheese, yogurt, shellfish, fortified cereals, fortified soy products.	2 mcg 1 cup milk = 0.9 mcg 3 ounces beef = 2 mcg
Folacin (a B vitamin; also called folate or folic acid)	Leafy greens, wheat germ, liver, beans, whole grains, broccoli, asparagus, citrus fruits and juices.	180 mcg, women; 200 mcg, men 1 cup raw spinach = 100 mcg 1 packet oatmeal = 150 mcg 1 cup asparagus = 180 mcg
Biotin (a B vitamin)	Eggs, milk, liver, brewer's yeast, mushrooms, bananas, tomatoes, whole grains.	No RDA; experts recommend 30–100 mcg

*These figures are not applicable to pregnant or nursing women, who need additional vitamins and should seek professional advice.

WHAT IT DOES	POTENTIAL BENEFITS	SUPPLEMENTATION
Promotes good vision; helps form and maintain skin, teeth, bones, and mucous membranes. Deficiency can increase susceptibility to infectious disease.	May inhibit the development of certain tumors; may increase resistance to infection in children.	Not recommended, since toxic in high doses.
Converted into vitamin A in the intestinal wall. As an antioxidant, combats adverse effects of free radicals in the body. Best known of a family of substances called carotenoids.	May reduce the risk of certain cancers as well as coronary-artery disease.	6–15 mg (equal to 10,000–25,000 IU of vitamin A) a day for anyone not consuming several carotene-rich fruits or vegetables daily. Nontoxic.
Promotes healthy gums and teeth; aids in iron absorption; maintains normal connective tissue; helps in healing of wounds. As an antioxidant, combats adverse effects of free radicals.	May reduce the risk of certain cancers, as well as coronary-artery disease; may prevent or delay cataracts.	250–500 mg a day for smokers and for anyone not consuming several fruits or vegetables rich in C daily. Larger doses may cause diarrhea.
Promotes strong bones and teeth by aiding the absorption of calcium. Helps maintain blood levels of calcium and phosphorus.	May reduce the risk of osteoporosis.	400 IU for people who do not drink milk or get sun exposure, especially strict vegetarians and the elderly. Toxic in high doses.
Helps in the formation of red blood cells and the utilization of vitamin K. As an antioxidant, it combats the adverse effects of free radicals.	May reduce the risk of certain cancers, as well as coronary-artery disease; may prevent or delay cataracts; may improve immune function in the elderly.	200–800 IU. No serious side effects at that level.
Essential for normal blood clotting.	May help maintain strong bones in the elderly.	Not necessary.
Helps cells convert carbohydrates into energy. Necessary for healthy brain, nerve cells, and heart function.	Unknown.	Not necessary.
Helps cells convert carbohydrates into energy. Essential for growth, production of red blood cells, and health of skin and eyes.	Unknown.	Not necessary.
Aids in release of energy from foods. Helps maintain healthy skin, nerves, and digestive system.	Large doses lower elevated blood cholesterol.	Megadoses may lower blood cholesterol. May cause flushing, liver damage, and irregular heartbeat.
Vital for metabolism of food and production of essential body chemicals.	Unknown.	Not necessary. May cause diarrhea.
Vital in chemical reactions of proteins and amino acids. Helps maintain brain function and form red blood cells.	May boost immunity in the elderly.	Megadoses can cause numbness and other neurological disorders.
Necessary for development of red blood cells. Maintains normal functioning of nervous system.	May reduce the risk of cervical cancer.	Strict vegetarians may need supplements. Despite claims, no known benefits from megadoses.
Important in the synthesis of DNA and RNA, in normal growth, and in protein metabolism. Adequate intake reduces the risk of certain birth defects, notably spina bifida.	Unknown.	400 mcg, from food or pills, for all women who may become pregnant, in order to help prevent birth defects.
Important in metabolism of protein, carbohydrates, and fats.	Unknown.	Not necessary.

Fish (above) is renowned as a rich source of B vitamins. Whole grains, eggs, meats, nuts, and leafy greens also contain ample amounts of these vitamins.

Besides being rich in vitamin C, berries, grapes, cherries, and citrus fruits are good sources of folic acid, a B vitamin known to reduce the risk of certain birth defects.

cludes, don't expect any dramatic changes in the near future.

One change that is likely to come sooner rather than later is the creation of RDAs for a few special groups. Smokers, people over 50, vegetarians, and those under medical stress may all need more vitamins than the RDAs currently suggest.

Smokers, for instance, need twice as much vitamin C as nonsmokers because smoking interferes with the absorption of the vitamin. Pregnant and lactating women require extra amounts of several vitamins, including folic acid, B_6, C, and D. Strict vegetarians who eat no animal products may need to supplement vitamins D and B_{12} (in addition to minerals such as calcium, iron, and zinc). People over 50 have different vitamin requirements than younger people because the body's ability to absorb nutrients may decrease with age.

Making a Choice

With what we know today about the health benefits of vitamins—and about the average American diet—it is probably safe to say that most people could benefit from a daily multivitamin and mineral supplement. Back at the store, with the vitamin selection before you, what will you choose? Your first concern should be safety, says Baker. "Stick to something that's under a megadose or 10 times the RDA," she says. "That way, you may get the extra benefits without really endangering your body." Stay away from megadoses, and don't try to design your own combination of individual vitamins. Check with your doctor first if you have any medical conditions or if you are taking prescription drugs.

For the most benefits, be sure that the vitamins you choose are of a high quality. This does not mean that you have to spend a lot of money. "A good generic brand is as good as an expensive brand-name vitamin," says Busch. "If you're spending more than $10 a month on vitamins, you're spending too much."

To check for quality, first look at the expiration date on the

Most Americans could benefit from a daily multivitamin supplement.

package to be sure it will not have passed before you use up the contents. Vitamins lose potency when they sit on the shelf, says Baker, especially when they sit there for extended periods.

Do not worry about whether your vitamin is "natural" or whether it claims to contain no sugar or starch. "These terms really do not influence the nutrient's effectiveness," says Baker. "And elaborate terminology may be used to hike up the price." Neither sugar nor starch, for instance, affects a supplement's health benefits. And sometimes the synthetic version of a vitamin is actually absorbed more readily than the natural form.

Also be wary of vitamins that make special claims, such as antistress. Studies have shown that the B-complex vitamins are helpful during major-trauma stress (for instance, when an individual has major burns), but that doesn't mean that the same vitamins are helpful against everyday mental stress.

In fact, sometime in 1995, the U.S. Food and Drug Administration (FDA) is expected to issue new regulations governing what labels on vitamin supplements say. Much like the new labels for food, supplement labels will display information in a standardized form. "The main purpose is to give consumers an easier way of comparing products," says Brad Stone, a spokesperson for the FDA.

The FDA will also regulate the health claims made for supplements. If there is "significant scientific agreement" that a claim is true—for instance, that a calcium supplement may help prevent osteoporosis—the agency will allow the statement to appear on labels. In hazier areas—such as claims that a supplement helps bolster the immune system—the FDA will either disallow the claim or require a disclaimer on the package. In that case, the label might read: "This statement has not been evaluated by the FDA. This product is not intended to diagnose, treat, prevent, or cure disease." The FDA is in the process of determining which health claims it will allow manufacturers to put on labels. "It may come down to looking at things on a case-by-case basis," says Stone. "It's a question of how far a claim can go."

Pills or Food?

No matter what claims the FDA allows— and no matter what evidence researchers uncover in the coming years—experts stress that vitamin supplements cannot make up for a consistently poor diet. "Everyone wants an easy solution to good health. But you can't eat a poor diet, take a supplement, and assume it will make up for your deficiencies," says Baker. "Take supplements as added protection, not instead of eating right."

One important reason for a well-rounded diet is that foods provide other substances that researchers are now connecting to good health. Bioflavonoids and similar "phytochemicals" in fruits and vegetables may help prevent diseases, for instance. "You cannot get all the anti-disease benefits of food simply by taking vitamins," says Blumberg. "We now have science to demonstrate that vitamins are more important than we ever thought. But they're not the only compounds in food that contribute to the health-promoting effects." ◇

Vitamin D is produced by the body in response to sunlight. Just 15 minutes of sunshine a few times a week meets the body's vitamin D requirement.

Nothing to Lose

by Peter A. Flax

Flipping through the pages of any glossy magazine, it seems hard to escape a world where thin is in. Waif-like fashion models lounge about the pages of advertisements in exotic designer clothing. Photographs of slender, successful athletes—whether runners, dancers, or gymnasts—are as ubiquitous as ads for diet books, exercise videos, and weight-loss pills. Countless articles chronicle the growing incidence of obesity among Americans. These images and messages have not fallen upon deaf ears or blind eyes. Asked to assess the perils of being too thin, many people might likely reply, "I wish that was my biggest problem."

For some people, however, excessive thinness *is* a big problem. While obesity is certainly the more prevalent condition in this country, it is still a surprise to realize how many people are lighter than they should be. Researchers estimate that approximately 10 percent of the American populace—more than 25 million people—need to gain weight. Some of these people have whittled themselves away in the zealous pursuit of a slimmer self. Many more are too thin for a host of other reasons: metabolic dysfunction, illness, poor nutrition, or strenuous exercise. The difficulty of surmounting these conditions presents a weighty challenge.

How Thin Is Too Thin?

A person is considered medically underweight when weight drops more than 10 percent below normal levels for that person's height, as set out in government tables such as the chart on page 99.

But it is debatable as to whether marked thinness is in and of itself a problem in a healthy person—particularly if that person's skinniness is lifelong. "We no longer believe that people need a 'reserve fund' of fat," says Eric Tangalos, M.D., head of geriatrics at the Mayo Medical Center in Rochester, Minnesota. Indeed, some studies suggest that people who remain thin their entire lives actually live longer than heavier people.

However, it is not common for a healthy person to fall far below what is considered a normal weight range, says Charles Halsted, M.D., professor of nutrition and metabolism at the University of California, Davis. "While some people are below normal weight and healthy, in most cases, extreme thinness is a red flag for a serious medical problem, such as an eating disorder or underlying illness," he says. Fortunately, most people return to normal weight when the underlying medical problem is diagnosed and resolved.

Something to Gain

Illness is perhaps the most common—and most dangerous—means through which a person loses a precipitous amount of weight. Most of us can recall the lack of appetite that accompanies a bad cold or a bout of flu. During a protracted fever, an individual's appetite decreases while calorie "burning" increases. Weight loss can be rapid and dramatic. Nonetheless, most people's weight rebounds quickly once a short-term illness has passed.

Much more alarming is the weight loss that accompanies life-threatening illnesses such as cancer, AIDS, and tuberculosis. Aptly named "wasting diseases," such disorders take a heavy toll on the body, and, in doing so, sap weight and energy reserves.

Weight loss is also a common sign of thyroid and gastrointestinal diseases. In hyperthyroidism, a person's thyroid gland (located at the base of the throat) overproduces the hormone thyroxine, which speeds body function, or metabolism. Like a car with a racing engine, the patient with hyperthyroidism rapidly burns fuel. The result is weight loss despite a hearty appetite. Hyperthyroidism can usually be treated with medication to slow or counteract thyroxine production. Occasionally some or all of the thyroid must be surgically removed. While treatment helps restore weight, a diet with supplemental calories and protein is prescribed when weight loss has been severe.

Weight loss can also be a sign of a gastrointestinal disorder such as Crohn's dis-

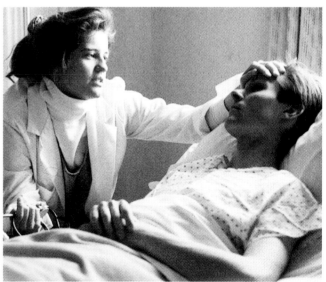

Acute weight loss may suggest a serious illness. Luckily, such weight loss can often be reversed if the underlying medical problem is identified and treated promptly.

ease or colitis. Both involve a chronic inflammation of the bowel. The result is poor absorption of food nutrients and accompanying diarrhea. Gastrointestinal disorders are treated with a variety of medications and occasionally surgery to remove part of the bowel. Liquid food supplements and, in very severe cases, intravenous feeding are sometimes needed to restore weight and health.

Medications can produce excessive weight loss in various ways. Amphetamine-type drugs can accelerate the body's metabolic rate so that calories are burned faster than they are consumed. Such drugs often have the additional side effect of depressing appetite. Examples include not only prescription amphetamines, but also the over-the-counter "pep" pills used commonly by long-distance drivers, college students, and others wanting to stay awake longer than their bodies would normally allow.

Appetite can likewise be severely dampened by medications that produce nausea. A notorious example is chemotherapy drugs, which cause extreme nausea and loss of appetite in many (if not most) patients.

Excessive dieting is to blame for a large proportion of unhealthy thinness, says Dr. Halsted. In an era of acute body-image consciousness, people often forget that the oft-counted calorie, like the much-maligned fat gram, is an important source of energy.

Many Americans embrace unsound dieting practices in an effort to become slim and thus comply with the array of unhealthy images that bombard the public eye. Many fad diets are designed to help people lose weight fast at any cost, often by eschewing sound nutritional guidelines. Followers can wind up suffering from undernutrition.

Eating disorders such as anorexia nervosa and bulimia are characterized by dieting in

The public is besieged with images of athletes, fashion models, and other people whose extreme thinness is equated with beauty, sophistication, and success.

its most extreme form. Although these conditions can affect people of all ages, they occur most commonly in women between the ages of 13 and 25 who tend to be plagued by an obsessive concern with weight loss, a distorted self-image, and mental depression. Anorexia nervosa is characterized by severe self-starvation. Bulimia, a disorder that often appears as an extension of anorexia nervosa, is typified by eating large amounts of food (binging), and then purging this food, usually by self-induced vomiting or through the use of laxatives.

Older adults are particularly vulnerable to weight loss. One study indicates that a quarter of all seniors are at high risk of malnutrition.

The medical implications of eating disorders are grave, warns Dr. Halsted. Adolescents can permanently retard their growth, women often lose the ability to menstruate, body temperature can sink dangerously low, metabolic and hormonal imbalances often develop, and the risk of heart disease and critical nutritional deficiencies rise sharply. Today, eating disorders are treated as potentially life-threatening illnesses. In general, the course of action involves a combination of medical therapy, psychiatric counseling, and nutritional guidance.

Malnutrition is sometimes the unwitting result of an insufficient or unbalanced diet. The U.S. government spends millions of dollars each year to help disseminate information about the size and components of a healthy diet. Despite such ambitious promotion, millions of Americans do not get the message. People with small appetites who are not careful to select nutritious foods may not realize that their diets may be deficient in important vitamins, minerals, and protein.

Some people suffer from nutritional problems because they cannot afford to purchase enough foods to satisfy their body's needs, and either cannot or do not receive

How Slim Is Thin?

In 1994 the U.S. Department of Agriculture (USDA) released revised guidelines for body weight. The new guidelines present a recommended range of body weight for various heights and two age groups. Anyone weighing less than the bottom end of the scale is, by USDA standards, underweight. Following these standards, a 5-foot, 8-inch 40-year-old would be considered underweight if he or she weighed less than 138 pounds. The revised recommendations acknowledge the growing belief among doctors and researchers that it is healthy for a person to gain weight as he or she ages—perhaps as much as 1 pound a year—particularly after the age of 40. "It's the body's way of protecting itself against disease as you age," says Edith Hogan, R.D., a nutritionist based in Washington, D.C.

HEIGHT without shoes	WEIGHT without clothes	
	Age 19 to 34*	35 and up*
5'0"	97 -128	108 -138
5'1"	101 -132	111 -143
5'2"	104 -137	115 -148
5'3"	107 -141	119 -152
5'4"	111 -146	122 -157
5'5"	114 -150	126 -162
5'6"	118 -155	130 -167
5'7"	121 -160	134 -172
5'8"	125 -164	138 -178
5'9"	129 -169	142 -183
5'10"	132 -174	146 -188
5'11"	136 -179	151 -194
6'0"	140 -184	155 -199
6'1"	144 -189	159 -205
6'2"	148 -195	164 -210
6'3"	152-200	168 -216

*Women or Men

Principles for Weight Gain

Whether you follow a nutritionist's comprehensive program or pursue a self-help diet routine, the fundamental key to gaining weight remains the same: follow a more nutritious and *plentiful* diet. In general, nutritionists recommend an increase of some 500 to 1,000 calories per day for people seeking to gain weight. Sometimes, attaining such a goal can be easier said than done. Many underweight people have a limited appetite and feel as though a large increase in food consumption would be an uncomfortable experience. Others are simply apprehensive about gaining excessive body fat.

Nutritional experts therefore recommend that individuals identify and build a diet around nutrient-dense foods such as dried fruits, nuts, breads, pasta, cereals, and potatoes. Underweight people are also encouraged to liberally use sauces, gravies, and embellishments such as jelly, butter or margarine, and salad dressing. Those uncomfortable with eating large meals may prefer a daily regimen of frequent snacks.

Although water is one of very few beverages that actually has no calories, adequate consumption of this fluid is critical to proper nutrition. Washington, D.C.– based nutritionist Edith Hogan, R.D., notes that "hydration is an often forgotten component of undernutrition. People who don't drink enough fluids have a more difficult time processing the nutrients that they do eat." Medical experts recommend that people drink a minimum of 3 quarts of fluids daily. Those who are seeking to gain weight, however, should try to minimize drinking beverages during a meal, because fluids will take up stomach space that could accommodate energy-dense foods. Instead, individuals should try to drink plenty of water between meals.

Below are six tips for gaining weight:

1. Drink plenty of fluids throughout the day, but minimize fluid intake immediately before and during meals.

2. Try to eat a snack before bedtime (along with a large meal for supper).

3. Eat nutrient-dense foods first during a meal, and then foods containing fewer calories.

4. Eat quickly, but chew food thoroughly.

5. Exercise to stimulate appetite and build body muscle.

6. Snack frequently on foods high in energy, such as dried fruits and nuts. However, snacking should not interfere with regular meals.

government assistance to bridge this gap. The threat of chronic malnutrition is particularly grave for older adults. One survey conducted by researchers at the Boston University School of Public Health in Massachusetts found that roughly 25 percent of 8,000 older adults questioned stood at high risk of malnutrition.

"Something as seemingly trivial as broken dentures can lead to weight loss in an elderly person without adequate care," says Mayo's Dr. Tangalos. Many others are physically unable to go to the grocery store, or are afraid to venture out of their homes. Alzheimer's, Parkinson's, and similar cognitive disorders can also lead to malnutrition in an elderly person, who may literally forget to eat.

While the outward sign of malnutrition is extreme thinness, far more serious is the unseen effect on the immune system. "Studies in Third World countries show that malnutrition depresses the immune system, which results in an increased incidence of infections," says Tim Kramer, Ph.D., a nutrition and immunity researcher with the U.S. Department of Agriculture (USDA).

Exercise. While most doctors and nutritionists would hesitate to categorize physical activity as potentially unhealthy, intense exercise can in some instances lead to extreme weight loss. For starters, the human body needs to burn fuel—food, that is—to sustain exercise. Some endurance athletes such as marathoners must eat hundreds, even thousands, of extra calories a day to compensate for their heavy exertion. In fact, some athletes eat twice the U.S. government's recommended daily allowance (RDA) of calories—and still fail to maintain normal weight.

The key to gaining weight is to follow a more nutritious and plentiful diet.

"When energy needs surpass energy intake, the immune system suffers," reiterates Dr. Kramer, citing his own research with underfed soldiers undergoing demanding physical training. The result is like that of malnutrition: increased susceptibility to illness.

These dynamics may also affect casual athletes. A half-hour jog, for example, burns roughly 400 calories. Exercisers who are already at risk of being underweight may fail to add an equivalent amount of calories to their diets. As a result, some weekend warriors do not supply themselves with the extra energy they need. Often these people develop an exaggerated association between exercising and fatigue. While the exertion of two sets of tennis or a 1-mile swim may be tiring, the strain on a body that lacks the proper energy reserves may be even more exhausting.

Some exercisers combine overzealous activity with unsound eating habits, a combination that can yield perilous results—severe weight loss, fatigue, undernutrition, and illness.

Gaining Weight Intelligently

First and foremost, the medically underweight person needs to be evaluated for underlying medical conditions, says dietitian Brenda Knutson, R.D., of the Mayo Medical Center. Physicians and nutritionists also need to look for psychological and social problems that can interfere with adequate food intake.

Underweight people who are not in need of medical intervention may find sufficient advice in nutrition books that address the issues of underweight people; such publications are becoming increasingly numerous in local libraries and bookstores.

However, an individual who is 15 pounds or more underweight should seek the guidance of a physician, who may recommend the services of a dietitian or nutritionist. Such professionals can help design a personalized diet plan that matches the nutritional needs and lifestyle of an underweight individual, and they can offer helpful structure and support during the difficult process of following such a diet. Individuals should seek out a registered dietitian (R.D.)—a certification created by the American Dietetic Association (ADA)—or a professional with a graduate degree in clinical nutrition. To find a nutritionist in your area, ask your doctor for a recommendation or call the ADA at 1-800-366-1655.　◇

Housecalls

by Mona Sutnick, Ed.D., R.D.

Q *I have always washed fresh vegetables and fruits before eating them. Does such washing get rid of pesticides and other contaminants that might be present?*

A Washing fruits and vegetables with a little diluted detergent will eliminate some of these substances. For peel-waxed produce, such as apples and cucumbers, scrub the food with a brush and then rinse the food well. The wax, though harmless, will prevent you from washing off any sprays that might be underneath it. Either way, the fruit or vegetable may have absorbed a certain amount of pesticides and other chemicals that cannot be washed away.

In 1993 the Environmental Protection Agency (EPA), the U.S. Department of Agriculture (USDA), and the Food and Drug Administration (FDA) announced an unusual joint effort to comprehensively revamp policies on pesticide use. The effort is moving toward stricter safety standards for pesticides, reducing the use of such chemicals by farmers, and a ban on the practice by certain American companies of selling pesticides overseas that have been deemed unsafe for use in the United States (and that sometimes end up back on American dinner tables in the form of imported produce).

Keep in mind that the benefits of generous amounts of fruits and vegetables in your diet far outweigh the risks from any trace contaminants that might be on them. To minimize your risk:

• Eat a variety of fruits and vegetables, rather than just one or a few exclusively.

• Buy locally grown produce. Although not necessarily pesticide-free, it will at least be less likely to have certain post-harvest treatments, such as antifungal sprays. Also look for organic produce or grow your own.

• Limit imported fruits and vegetables to no more than a small portion of the produce you eat.

Q *I am a 12-year-old girl. I am 5 feet tall and weigh about 120 pounds. I would like to lose weight, and I think diet pills might be the fastest way of doing so. What do you think?*

A You are about average height for your age, but are in about the 90th percentile for weight. Although these differences can come partly as a result of body build, it is likely that you do need to either lose some weight or grow into your weight.

Diet pills are a fast way, but not a good way, to lose weight. They work for only a limited time and do not address long-term needs. Over-the-counter diet pills usually contain stimulants, and are controversial from a safety perspective.

At your age, it is most important to learn lifelong healthy habits and learn them well. That means following a balanced diet and getting plenty of physical activity. Pills or other means of crash dieting bring on cycles that send your weight up and down like a yo-yo; they are not healthy.

Many people need help and encouragement in setting up a healthy diet-exercise regimen for themselves. Consult your doctor or school nurse, or a registered dietitian for advice. Enlist the support of your family, too.

Washing fruits and vegetables with soapy water reduces the potential for ingesting pesticides and other contaminants.

Q Are U.S. troops still issued chocolate bars as part of their rations? Is the food served to troops in mess halls and the like nutritionally balanced?

A Troops still get chocolate occasionally in their "Meals Ready to Eat" (MREs), the term now used for the individual, prepackaged, U.S. military field rations. Some MREs include candy.

The military strives to deliver nutritionally balanced mess-hall meals, according to the U.S. Quartermaster School in Fort Lee, New Jersey. There, under the supervision of registered dietitians, the staff develops a monthly master menu. The menu gives a daily recommendation of food to be served at all military installations. The various bases, however, have flexibility in this, and can use some discretion in what they serve.

The military has developed its own nutritional recommended daily allowances (RDAs). The military RDA is generally consistent with the civilian RDA, adjusted for certain military needs. The military uses the U.S. dietary guidelines for nutrition education and to work toward having a maximum of 30 percent of calories from fat, a goal it has not yet reached.

Q I recall hearing that red wine can help prevent heart disease. Is this still considered true?

A A fairly solid body of evidence correlates moderate alcohol use with a lowered risk of heart disease. It is not known whether this correlation represents a cause-and-effect relationship.

To date, nothing special about red wine has actually been confirmed. However, a research team had reported the discovery in purple grapes of a substance called resveratol that lowers blood cholesterol, but this finding needs further investigation before scientists can draw any firm conclusions.

Recommending that people consume alcohol makes many experts nervous, because there appears to be a narrow line between the amount of alcohol consumption that may be beneficial and that which is detrimental.

A dietary strategy based on the healthy cardiovascular status of a number of southern European populations, called the Mediterranean pyramid, specifically advocates red wine (one or two glasses per day), but most authorities want to see more research before making such a recommendation.

Q My daughter drinks truly enormous amounts of diet soda. Is she doing herself any harm? Is there any connection between soda consumption and thinning of the bones?

A Sodas contain two problem ingredients: caffeine and phosphorus. For caffeine to affect a person's bones, though, the individual must consume very large amounts of it. Therefore, for the vast majority of people, the bigger problem in sodas is more likely to be the phosphorus content.

High amounts of phosphorus in the diet can influence bone metabolism through an effect on the parathyroid gland. Here's the key, though: the danger of this harmful effect is decreased if the person has adequate dietary calcium. Unfortunately, many Americans don't have enough calcium in their diets. For this reason, soda drinkers—especially women—need to keep their calcium intake up.

Also bear in mind that sodas (diet and otherwise) have no nutrients. It would be wise for your daughter to drink juices, water, skim milk, or flavored seltzers in place of some of the soda.

Do you have a nutrition question?
Send it to Editor, Health and Medicine Annual, P.O. Box 90, Hawleyville, CT 06440-9990.

FITNESS AND HEALTH

CONTENTS

Special Olympics:
SPORT · SPIRIT · SPLENDOR

by Karen S. Castagno, Ph.D.

would never talk or be able to take care of himself, they took Charlie home and cared for him the same way they did their other five children.

As Charlie grew older, he did learn to talk and walk and run. His parents began to see that their son had the same needs and interests as most children his age, including a strong interest in sports. They also heard of a brand-new program that seemed to be a perfect match for Charlie's need to run and jump, and for their need to let Charlie interact with children of his own age and with other members of his community. Special Olympics, with its training and competition in track and field and swimming, had come to the Larsens' community.

Personal Milestones

Almost before the family knew what happened, Special Olympics had become part of their lives. Charlie practiced and participated in local competitions, and before long he was determined to compete against athletes of his same ability at state competitions. Next stop: the 1983 International Special Olympics Summer Games held at Louisiana State University in Baton Rouge, Louisiana, where Charlie joined 4,000 other athletes from every state and 50 foreign countries for the Opening Ceremonies. When these athletes and their coaches marched into Tiger Stadium, they were cheered by an enthusiastic crowd of more than 60,000 people!

Four years later, Charlie returned for another international competition, this time at the University of Notre Dame in South Bend, Indiana, broadcast nationally on ABC's "Wide World of Sports." Charlie returned from those games with a new passion for athletics.

At the 1995 World Games in New Haven, Connecticut, Charlie will have completed

In 1960 Charlie Larsen was born with Down syndrome, a condition usually accompanied by varying degrees of mental retardation. Parents in similar situations at that time were often urged by family and friends to give up their newborn child to the care of an institution. Though the Larsens had to deal with the possibility that Charlie another personal milestone: he will be a track official, certified by The Athletics Congress (TAC), officiating at the same type of international track competition he participated in only 13 years earlier.

It is not easy to become a TAC official. Rules and regulations governing track-and-field competition from the local to the international levels must be memorized and understood. "The test was hard," recalls Charlie. "I had to learn the whole book, but I passed it."

At the 1995 World Games, Charlie hopes to be assigned the job of marshal, the official who guides the athletes from the staging area to their events. "This way I still get to meet the athletes and talk to them," he says. And with Charlie's experience as a former athlete and as a dedication official, the 1995 World Games could not make a better choice.

The History of Special Olympics

The first Special Olympics Games were held in 1968, but the movement to introduce individuals with mental retardation to

Eunice Kennedy Shriver, shown above teaching swimming to children with mental retardation, was instrumental in launching Special Olympics.

the benefits of physical fitness and sports began more than two decades earlier.

The origins of Special Olympics lie with the Joseph P. Kennedy, Jr., Foundation, founded in 1946 to help improve the lives of people with mental retardation and to provide assistance to the medical community in its quest to prevent mental retardation. The foundation, named in memory of the late President John F. Kennedy's elder brother, awards grants to programs that improve the care and lives of people with mental retardation.

Soon after completing a fact-finding trip throughout the United States on behalf of the foundation, Eunice Kennedy Shriver began to formulate the concept of Special Olympics. By the early 1960s, Eunice Kennedy Shriver had started to put this concept to work by inviting more than 100 local children with mental retardation to her home in Rockville, Maryland. She began a summer camp in her own backyard, using her personal sports and recreation experience and the energy and interests of her children and other volunteers to pilot this program of recreational games, obstacle courses, and swimming.

Tim Shriver, son of Eunice and Sargent and now the president of the 1995 Special Olympics World Games, remembers fondly those early years. "I can remember playing a kickball game with people who were never allowed to play before. . . . No one would have dreamed back then that this would be the start of an incredible movement."

The program was so successful in improving these children's lives that similar programs were developed throughout the country. From 1963 through 1968, the Joseph P. Kennedy, Jr., Foundation awarded more than 80 small grants to public and private community groups for the express purpose of developing sports-oriented day camps for individuals with mental retardation.

The next step was to give these individuals an opportunity to compete, and to thus show their family, friends, and the world how hard they had trained. Mrs. Shriver's concept now needed only a name. She

Equestrians train for the upcoming Special Olympics World Games, to be held in New Haven, Connecticut, during July 1995.

chose *Special Olympics*, the only program authorized by the International Olympic Committee to use the word "Olympics" in its title worldwide.

On July 20, 1968, more than 1,000 Special Olympics athletes from 26 states and Canada marched into Soldier Field in Chicago, Illinois, to participate in track-and-field, floor hockey, and swimming events at the First International Special Olympics Games. The idea born over 20 years ago had become a reality.

Today Special Olympics serves more than 940,000 athletes in programs conducted in more than 130 nations. These programs offer year-round training and competition in over 23 winter and summer sports, including aquatics, gymnastics, soccer, volleyball, figure skating, and alpine skiing. All children and adults with mental retardation are qualified to participate.

Enriching Experiences: Unified Sports
In the late 1970s, a recent college graduate, Robert ("Beau") Doherty, was employed by a state institution for people with mental retardation in Massachusetts. His job was to provide recreational activities for the men who resided at the institution. He encouraged the men to be as active as possible, and, calling on his own enjoyment and knowledge of the games, he started to

The Special Olympics Philosophy

The mission and philosophy of Special Olympics is clearly articulated in the *International General Rules of Special Olympics*, a publication that spells out the rules and regulations for conducting Special Olympics programs. The mission of Special Olympics is:

"To provide year-round sports training and athletic competition in a variety of Olympic-type sports for all children and adults with mental retardation, giving them continuing opportunities to develop physical fitness, demonstrate courage, experience joy, and participate in the sharing of gifts, skills, and friendships with their families, Special Olympics athletes, and the community."

Special Olympics is founded on the belief that individuals with mental retardation can participate in individual and team sports, and can enjoy the thrill of participation and competition. With proper training and encouragement, and adapting activities to meet the specific needs of individuals with mental and physical limitations, Special Olympics athletes can enjoy the benefits of sports participation.

Special Olympics believes that proper and consistent training is of the utmost importance to develop skills necessary for participation in sports. Competition should be conducted among individuals or teams of equal ability as the best indicator of testing skills, measuring progress, and providing incentives for personal growth.

Special Olympics believes that participation in an organized Special Olympics program promotes growth physically, mentally, socially, and spiritually; the family is strengthened; and the community benefits from observing the significant accomplishments of individuals with mental retardation.

coach his players in the skills necessary to play floor hockey and soccer. Soon Beau brought in students from a nearby college campus to help play on "integrated" teams. "We would have competitions between teams at the institution, half the team made up of men who lived there, half made up of the college kids. The college students really began to see these individuals with mental retardation in a more positive light. It was sports that brought them together." Little did these individuals know that they were to become the model for an exciting new component to Special Olympics: Unified Sports (a registered trademark of Special Olympics).

This model—teams comprised of equal numbers of Special Olympics athletes and peer athletes of similar age and ability without mental retardation—was brought to the attention of Eunice Kennedy Shriver in 1987. Mrs. Shriver, who had always embraced the idea of community involvement in Special Olympics, was cautious at first, but soon agreed to have the Unified Sports model tested in the field.

In 1989 the Unified Sports Program was introduced throughout the country. It includes sports like basketball, bowling, running, soccer, softball, and volleyball. While Unified Sports gives Special Olympics athletes who have developed the necessary sports skills an additional challenge and opportunity to play sports, it also allows the athlete to make friends and to be further integrated into the community.

Fifteen years later, Beau Doherty, now executive di-

Special Olympics athletes competing in track-and-field events (left) undergo arduous training in preparation for big races. Coaches (below left) offer moral support in addition to athletic instruction. Softball and other sports can be customized to accommodate specific disabilities (below).

rector of Connecticut Special Olympics, is still involved, coaching and playing on a Unified Sports softball team. "I'm not surprised at how much Unified Sports has grown since 1989. I am sure that it is the future of the Special Olympics organization."

Enriching Experiences: Motor Activities Training Program

Although Unified Sports, traditional Special Olympics training, and organized competition offer many children and adults with mental retardation the opportunity to learn new skills and make new friends, there are individuals with severe mental retardation or multiple physical disabilities who need a program that is customized to their abilities. In 1989, after five years of field testing and with the input of countless physical educators, therapeutic recreationists, and physical therapists, the Motor Activities Training Program was introduced.

This program emphasizes training rather than competition. Its purpose is to provide motor-based recreational activities for athletes with severe disabilities, so that, through practice, they strive to achieve their personal best. While this program does not always prepare athletes to participate in traditional sports, it does give the athletes the opportunity to learn the motor skills necessary for aquatics, and provides individually prescribed activities for the development of mobility, dexterity, striking, and kicking.

Training

Athlete Selection. Special Olympics requires that an individual must be at least five years old to participate in training, and at least eight years old to participate in competitions. With no upper age limit, many community programs involve individuals in their 70s and 80s in sports like boccie and bowling. Individuals also must be identified by an established agency or professional as having mental retardation or a cognitive delay (deficiency) as determined by a standardized test; or significant learning or vocational problems due to cognitive delays that require or have required specially designed instruction. While athletes with multiple disabilities are eligible to participate in the program, the athlete must have mental retardation or a cognitive delay.

Nearly half a million athletes participate in the United States; a nearly equal number participate in programs in Canada, Africa, Asia, Europe, Latin America, the Middle East, and the Caribbean.

Coach Selection. In the United States alone, over 125,000 individuals volunteer to

A Special Olympics gymnast (left) develops a high degree of grace and agility through her training. Skiing (below) is a highlight of the Special Olympics Winter Games. The next international winter competition is scheduled for 1997.

coach Special Olympics programs. Coaches come from all walks of life: high-school and college coaches, parents, teachers, people involved in business. All of these people share a genuine desire to help other people, and a love of sports.

While coaches are not required to have experience in the principles of coaching individuals with mental retardation, they are encouraged to attend specifically designed coach-certification courses that discuss such topics as the fundamental principles of coaching, fitness and conditioning, safety, first aid, and the specific rules that govern Special Olympics competition.

With an estimated 250,000 coaches worldwide and a 15-year emphasis on training and certifying coaches, athletes are demonstrating higher skill levels in more sports than ever before in the history of Special Olympics.

Psychological and Physiological Benefits

Research into the effects of a Unified Sports program on the self-concept of both Special Olympics athletes and their teammates without mental retardation has consistently shown positive results.

In one case, 35 members of a middle-school Unified Sports basketball program were given the Martinek-Ziachkowsky Self-Concept Scale to measure their self-image before the first practice. The test was readministered after the 10-week practice session and the Unified Sports basketball tournament had concluded. Similar children not involved in Unified Sports also were given the test as a control group. Significant improvement in the self-concept of both Special Olympics athletes and their peer teammates was found as a result of their involvement in the basketball program.

In addition to improved self-image, involvement in Special Olympics has been shown to promote greater self-confidence on the playing field, in the classroom, and in work situations. It increases and strengthens friendships and provides additional recreational opportunities .

Physiological benefits also have been observed. Improvements in physical fitness have been documented for athletes in-

volved in organized practice sessions that take place at least three times a week for a minimum of eight weeks.

Carefully designed comprehensive coaching programs have also been found effective in improving sports skills for Special Olympics athletes. These athletes may have the physical ability to perform a specific skill, but they require coaching that "task-analyzes" the skill—having it broken down into small steps that permit the athlete to better process the information.

World Games

The First International Special Olympics Games were held in 1968 at Soldier Field in Chicago, Illinois, with 1,000 athletes from the United States and Canada participating in track-and-field, floor hockey, and swimming events. Eunice Kennedy Shriver wanted these games to emulate the Olympics in their grand pageantry, Opening Ceremonies, spirit of sportsmanship, and dignified presentation of awards and Closing Ceremonies. Though medals are presented to the top three finishers in each competitive division, ribbons are ceremonially awarded

The opening ceremonies of the Special Olympics World Games always feature a dramatic parade in which athletes march beneath the flag of their home country.

SPORTS OFFERED AT THE 1995 SPECIAL OLYMPICS WORLD GAMES	
Aquatics	Power lifting
Athletics	Roller-skating
Badminton	Sailing
Basketball	Soccer
Boccie	Softball
Bowling	Table Tennis
Cycling	Team Handball
Equestrian	Tennis
Gymnastics	Volleyball

to athletes who place fourth through eighth. Thus, the love of participation for its own sake is fostered and encouraged.

It did not take long for the idea of Olympic-type competition for athletes with mental retardation to catch on worldwide. In 1970, 550 athletes participated in the French Special Olympics Games, the first instance of international participation outside North America. Since 1975, International Summer Special Olympics Games have taken place every four years.

The winter sports of alpine and cross-country skiing, figure and speed skating, and floor hockey were introduced to international competition in 1977 at the First International Winter Special Olympics Games in Steamboat Springs, Colorado, where more than 500 athletes participated. Like the Summer Games, the winter competitions are held every four years.

In 1993 the international winter competition was held outside the United States for the first time when more than 1,600 athletes competed in the Fifth Special Olympics World Winter Games in Schaldming/Salzburg, Austria.

The 1995 World Games

The Special Olympics oath will be recited by nearly 7,000 athletes from more than 130 countries at the Opening Ceremonies of the Ninth Special Olympics World Games at Yale University in New Haven, Connecticut, during the summer of 1995. The lighting of the Flame of Hope, which will burn throughout the Games, will symbolize the theme of what will be the largest sports event in the world: "Sport, Spirit, Splendor." Athletes, coaches, family, and friends from as far away as China will stay with Connecticut residents for three days before the Games begin, to give them the opportunity to experience true Americana.

Then it's on to the city and suburbs of New Haven for 10 days of excitement and athletic competition. Peter Wheeler, executive director for the 1995 Special Olympics World Games, is excited about the response of officials from the international sports federations whose sports will be featured at the World Games. "We will have world-class officials from over 50 nations assisting us with the sports offered at these games."

Officials will come from Russia, the United Kingdom, Uganda, and Puerto Rico to help with table tennis. Soccer officials—including some who refereed during the 1992 Summer Olympic Games in Barcelona, Spain, and the most recent World Cup Soccer competition—will come from the United States, El Salvador, Poland, Peru, and Bolivia.

Looking forward to all this excitement coming to Connecticut in the summer of 1995, Tim Shriver says, "Since 1989 I have seen an incredible change in the public perception of what individuals with mental retardation can do. Special Olympics is something exciting and wonderful; it's something you want to share with others; it is celebrating people who are different."

For Special Olympics veteran Charlie Larsen, the 1995 World Games can't begin soon enough. "I can hardly wait." ◇

Getting into the Swim

by Linda J. Brown

As her 50th birthday rolled around, Carol Adams grew decidedly melancholy. Age had never bothered her before, but this birthday seemed to hit her like a sledgehammer. Carol decided she had to do something to shake her blues away. So, a full 35 years after her girlhood swim-team days, Carol jumped into the YMCA pool in her Massachusetts hometown.

Like a duck to water, Carol quickly regained her old swimming form. She joined a Masters swim team and began competing in meets. Looking for more competition in her age group, she swam in one regional meet, then in a national meet, and finally in a worldwide event, earning a collection of medals along the way.

The medals are incidental, she says, compared to the wonderful physical and mental benefits she has reaped in the nine months since taking to the pool. She shed the extra dozen or so pounds that had stubbornly held on for years, her blood pressure (for which she took medication) has returned to normal, and she now has a whole circle of new swimming friends. Perhaps most important, Carol's outlook has been buoyed by a strong sense of accomplishment and fulfillment. She now says unequivocally that "50 has been one of the most positive years of my life, in no small measure due to swimming."

Carol is just one of millions of people who have taken the plunge and discovered the

many fringe benefits derived from swimming. During a recent study done by Perrier, the bottled-water company, researchers found that 27 million Americans swim on a regular basis. Why do so many folks get wet? "Swimming is the closest thing on this Earth to a perfect sport," writes Jane Katz, Ed.D., in her book *Swimming for Total Fitness*. "It exercises all the major muscles of the body; it's the inexpensive, fun, social, graceful, sensual, safe, gentle way to achieve fitness—and it's an activity that you can enjoy for a lifetime."

Heart Health

Swimming is a great way to stay fit. As an aerobic exercise—one that causes a marked temporary increase in respiration and heart rate—swimming can condition your heart and lungs. More specifically, the American Heart Association (AHA) maintains that regular exercise, such as swimming, improves the blood circulation throughout the body. Through regular swimming, the lungs, heart, and other organs and muscles work together more efficiently. Swimming also improves the body's ability to use oxygen, thereby providing the energy needed for physical activity. "When you exercise aerobically, your lungs actually increase in size, capacity, and efficiency.

Twenty-seven million Americans enjoy the benefits of a regular swimming program.

Your heart becomes more powerful, more fit with exercise, just like any other muscle," writes Katz.

To reap this improvement, the AHA recommends that you swim for at least 30 minutes, three or four times a week, at more than 50 percent of your exercise capacity. (To calculate your exercise capacity, begin by subtracting your age from 220; the resulting number is your maximum heart rate. Your exercise capacity is 65 to 85 percent of that number. Calculate your heart rate by taking your pulse for 10 seconds right after you stop swimming, and multiply that number by 6.)

By increasing your cardiovascular fitness, you may help protect yourself against

Masters Swimming

Once you feel comfortable with your stroke and stamina, you may want to join a Masters swim team. Masters swimming began in the early 1970s, and has grown in popularity ever since. Its membership currently numbers more than 29,000. Some members choose to swim alone; many others join one of the 435 clubs nationwide for the camaraderie and structure. For those who like to test their skills, there are approximately 550 Masters swim meets each year. About 30 percent of Masters swimmers compete regularly.

For a free brochure about Masters swimming, send a self-addressed stamped envelope to U.S. Masters Swimming, 2 Peter Avenue, Rutland, MA 01543, or call 508-886-6631 for the lcoation of a Masters group nearest you.

heart disease (the leading cause of death and disability in the United States for both men and women), even if you have other risk factors. Regular physical activity may also help prevent high blood pressure, and may even reduce existing high blood pressure. Moreover, swimming may raise the level of "good" cholesterol (high-density lipoprotein, or HDL) in the blood, levels linked to a lower risk of coronary-artery disease.

According to Phillip Whitten, Ph.D., author of *The Complete Book of Swimming*, "The connection between swimming or similar forms of exercise and protection against heart disease is very well-documented." At age 28, his blood pressure was 140/96, his total cholesterol was 229, and his heart rate was 64. Now, 23 years—and countless miles of swimming—later, those same numbers have dropped to 116/74, 209, and 42, respectively.

The Strength Connection

Just one look at the powerful, fluid, muscular bodies of elite swimmers attests to the fact that swimming improves a person's strength. "Swimming is the single best exercise for toning your arms, shoulders, waistline, hips, and legs all at once," writes Katz. She also points out that swimming works the body's muscles in a balanced way, unlike tennis, golf, and other sports that focus more on one side of the body than on the other.

The effort of pushing against water helps build strength. In fact, the AHA claims that overcoming water resistance is roughly equivalent to working out with weights. The faster you swim, the more resistance you will encounter. Of course, it stands to reason that swimmers who move through the water at a snail's pace do not face much resistance. "But if you're swimming [at an energy level] equivalent to running a seven- or eight-minute mile, which is a decent pace, you have to generate strength, and it comes not just from your legs but from your entire body."

Though top swimmers look toned and tight, their bodies are not muscle-bound, bulky, or inflexible. In swimming, flexibility is essential, given that the goal is to stretch out and streamline your body so that each stroke is executed with maximum efficiency. Furthermore, the mere mechanics of swimming works to increase range of motion and flexibility. "Swimming's long, sinuous motions, along with the increased range of movement that your body has in the water, actually elongates your muscles while strengthening them," says Katz. "Swimming will help loosen you up—both in the water and after you're out."

Through the Ages

Swimming knows no age barrier. What other sport can be enjoyed whether you are 5 or 75 years old? Not only do people swim into their golden years, but they race as well. In this country, Masters swim meets are geared for people age 19 and up, in five-year age groups. In 1993, for the first time, a 100-plus age group was created for several competitors.

For years, gerentologists have believed that once past age 25, people experience a 1-percent decline each year in strength, speed, and maximum oxygen uptake. Regular swimming seems to change all that. Evidence of swimming's effect on the aging process comes from Dr. Whitten, who has been analyzing the timed swim-meet performances of several groups of Masters swimmers since 1975. His findings show that the decline each year among these swimmers is only a small fraction of 1 percent. It does not reach a full 1 percent until

Swimming knows no age restrictions. Programs designed for specific age groups have lured young and old alike into pools everywhere.

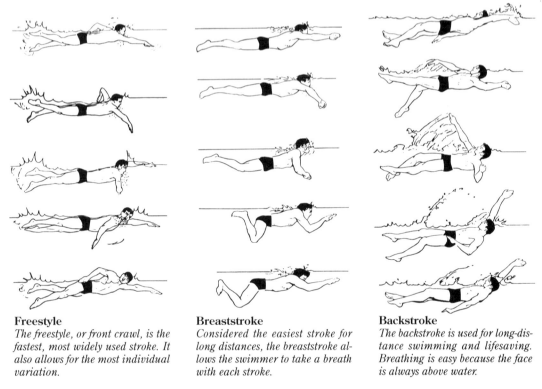

Freestyle
The freestyle, or front crawl, is the fastest, most widely used stroke. It also allows for the most individual variation.

Breaststroke
Considered the easiest stroke for long distances, the breaststroke allows the swimmer to take a breath with each stroke.

Backstroke
The backstroke is used for long-distance swimming and lifesaving. Breathing is easy because the face is always above water.

James E. Councilman."The Science of Swimming" © 1968. Adapted by permission of Prentice-Hall, Inc.

the swimmers are in their early 70s. Also, a swimmer's physical decline does not begin at the age of 25, but rather in the mid-30s. According to Dr. Whitten, "The evidence is overwhelming that most of the decline associated with aging is caused by inactivity rather than the aging process itself. Folks who swim regularly can perform physically at levels typical of much younger individuals in the general population."

On the Mend

Swimming is the ultimate no-impact sport. "Because water provides so much natural buoyancy, exercise in water is easy on the joints and tendons," writes Dr. Whitten. "You can work out as aggressively as you like without concern that you will be disabled by aching feet, blisters, shinsplints, tennis elbow, or runner's knee." Indeed, swimming injuries are quite infrequent. Those few injuries that do occur usually afflict the shoulders or knees as a result of overuse (which Dr. Whitten says rarely happens to adults) or incorrect technique.

A Beginner's Workout

Below is a sample workout from Phillip Whitten, Ph.D., that is sure to boost a beginner's fitness level. If the entire workout is too difficult, just do part of it, working your way up to 900 yards.

1. Swim 100 yards at an easy warm-up pace (1 lap equals 25 yards).
2. Kick 100 yards (use a kickboard).
3. Rest 2 minutes.
4. Kick 100 yards.
5. Rest 2 minutes.
6. Swim 300 yards.
7. Rest 3 minutes.
8. Kick 50 yards.
9. Rest 90 seconds.
10. Kick 50 yards.
11. Rest 90 seconds.
12. Pull 150 yards (use a buoy or just avoid kicking as you swim).
13. Swim 50 yards at an easy warm-down pace.

Water therapy is often prescribed for people recovering from injury or surgery, or for those with muscle or joint diseases. Water's buoyancy facilitates exercises that help to preserve joint function and range of motion while increasing muscle strength and overall flexibility. Webbed gloves, water dumbbells, and other equipment can be used to toughen a workout.

Given its no-impact nature, water therapy is almost invariably the sport of choice for people recovering from injury or surgery. "You can't pick up a medically based journal or physical-therapy magazine without finding something about the water in it," says Lynda Huey, author of *The Complete Waterpower Workout Book*, and director of Total Aquatic Rehab in Santa Monica, California. "It's considered the progressive leading-edge therapy right now." Huey has worked in this area for 12 years with laypeople and celebrity athletes alike.

Water therapy can benefit shoulder, wrist, hip, ankle, elbow, neck, back, and knee injuries, broken bones, and even those recovering from heart surgery. "It's also good for neurological problems such as muscular dystrophy and cerebral palsy," says Huey. She puts people through their paces in both deep and shallow water, prescribing aerobic workouts that strengthen various parts of the body. As people get stronger, they graduate to webbed gloves, water dumbbells, and other resistance equipment that provides the equivalent of weight training in the pool. The process often begins in neck-deep water, where the patient "weighs" only 10 percent of his or her on-land weight, and thus experiences only a fraction of the stress on the body that physical therapy on land might produce.

The Weight Debate

While there's no question that swimming is great exercise, there has been speculation as to whether it is a good way to lose weight. Some studies have shown that running and other forms of exercise burn more calories than swimming. Phillip Whitten, Ph.D., believes that these studies just compare different levels of exertion. Typically, he says, a study lists calories burned while running a seven-minute mile and a 10-minute mile. Then the study gives two figures for swimming: the faster one usually corresponds to the 10-minute-mile running pace and the slower one correlates to a 24-minute-mile run (which hardly qualifies as a "run" at all). A more accurate comparison would be to consider that the calories burned swimming one mile approximately equal the calories burned running four miles. "What happens when you compare the amount of calories burned at the proper levels is that there's very little difference," contends Dr. Whitten. He does admit that there may be some truth to the theory that water cools the body and thus triggers a hunger response, making the swimmer more likely to eat after a workout than, say, a jogger would after a sweaty run.

Water's buoyancy and cooling properties combine to make swimming an ideal activity for pregnant women (right). For a person with a disability (below), water therapy can be a central part of the rehabilitation program.

Gradually the swimmer moves to chest-deep water, where his or her apparent weight increases somewhat.

For people suffering from arthritis, gentle exercise in warm water helps them preserve joint function and range of motion. Out of water, their lives may become easier and less painful with the added flexibility and muscle strength.

Women recovering from breast-cancer surgery may find water exercise a good way to regain strength and increase range of motion, especially in those areas in which scar tissue will likely form after the operation. The YWCA conducts a national support-group program called ENCOREplus for women under treatment or in the process of recovering from breast surgery. The program features a variety of water exercises as well as peer-group support and other activities.

The physical condition of pregnant women also lends itself to swimming and water exercise. Moms-to-be must avoid getting overheated when exercising, and "water provides a natural air conditioner for you and your baby," says Katz, who also wrote *Water Fitness During Your Pregnancy*. Swimming is a safe and comfortable activity that lets women take the weight off their feet, back, and internal organs. And even with the balance changes brought on as the pregnancy progresses, women need not worry about falling when swimming.

The New World of Water Exercise

Water exercise for fitness was initially geared to older women, but has since di-

Take a Dip

The American Red Cross holds swimming classes nationwide. You can call the Red Cross at 202-737-8300 for more information.

If you're interested in trying a water-exercise class, check into local pools or contact the Aquatic Exercise Association (AEA) at 813-486-8600; the AEA will also refer certified instructors. The AEA has a free instructional newsletter called *Water-well* for those who want to go it solo. For a copy, send $1 to AEA, P.O. Box 1690, Nokomis, FL 34274.

The Arthritis Foundation offers aquatic exercise programs at community pools nationwide. To find out the programs in your area, call 1-800-283-7800. The Arthritis Foundation also offers a Pool Exercise Program (PEP) video for $29.95 plus $4 shipping. Call 1-800-497-6137 to order.

versified tremendously; it now counts athletes, men, and young people among its adherents. Jane Katz, for instance, teaches water-exercise techniques (based on her book *Water Exercise Techniques*) to New York City police and firefighters at John Jay College of Criminal Justice in New York.

Water exercise may involve aerobic activity, toning or strengthening moves, stretching to increase flexibility, and can be done alone or with a group. For some a great part of the appeal of water classes is the chance to socialize. "People can talk, laugh, and see each other, unlike lap swimming," says Katz.

Aquatic exercise initially featured simple, low-intensity choreographed routines to music. Today water workouts assume many different forms. There are shallow-water workouts and nonimpact deeper-water workouts where participants typically wear flotation belts. Aqua-step classes use special steps, similar to step-training classes on land. Circuit training combines strength training and aerobic activity at different stations around the pool. Interval training mixes high-intensity bursts with extended light training periods. Some classes focus solely on water walking or water jogging; others stress muscle conditioning.

Getting Started

The evolution of equipment designed for water exercise use has also taken off. "Ten years ago, there wasn't a lot available, and people were using homemade-type things like milk jugs [as flotation devices or for resistance training]," says Julie See, president of the Aquatic Exercise Association. "Now there's something for just about any type of class." Equipment consists of two basic types: flotation equipment (foam dumbbells, ankle cuffs, or flotation belts), and equipment geared to increase resistance to the water for strength training (webbed gloves, ankle cuffs, or water dumbbells).

If you opt for traditional horizontal swimming, you will probably need a pair of goggles and a bathing cap. The basic strokes are freestyle (also called the crawl), backstroke, breaststroke, and butterfly. You may opt to swim sidestroke or elementary backstroke.

If you don't know how to swim, and want to learn, you have several options. Joining a class at a local pool is an excellent choice. Many helpful books and videos exist to guide you. Most important, if you're over 35 and not a regular exerciser, check with your doctor before embarking on a swimming program. ◇

Today's HEALTH CLUBS

LOOKING FOR THE *total* WORKOUT

by Joseph C. DeVito

You need not join a health club to get in shape. Jogging and power-walking require only a good pair of running shoes, and old standards like push-ups, sit-ups, and leg lifts yield results through motivation, not fancy equipment. Home-workout devotees can use everything from exercise videos to dumbbells, treadmills, and ski simulators to achieve their fitness goals. Television "infomercials" tout an amazing array of devices for living-room use.

While working out at home can be enjoyable and effective, it doesn't work for everyone. For some, the problem is self-discipline. For others, it can be the constant distractions or the lack of privacy. Whatev-er the reason, some people need to create a specific slot in their daily routine in which to pursue physical fitness. For such people, health clubs can offer the ideal alternative.

To begin with, clubs provide an escape from the distractions of the day, a luxury few find at home, where the magnetic pull of the couch often scuttles plans for a quick jog, and the road paved with good intentions often leads to the refrigerator. In the focused health-club environment, many find it easier to concentrate and derive motivation from those around them.

Home training also tends to fixate on one exercise. Clubs offer the benefits of "cross-training"—working all the body's muscles

For some members, regular workouts would be impossible without the availability of child care; some clubs even offer "strollerobics" (left). In recent years, martial arts have punched and kicked their way onto the health-club scene.

without overtraining any one group. Clubs can also develop personalized training programs, offer nutritional recommendations, and enlist expert personnel—things virtually no individual could afford to do alone.

And the word "club" need not imply elitism. Many communities have subsidized workout centers that offer weight lifting, aerobics classes, and a range of other activities. Local YMCAs and YWCAs often incorporate family-oriented fitness clubs that include swimming pools; basketball, tennis, squash, and racquetball courts; sports leagues; martial arts; and other activities—all available for a modest membership fee.

Exclusive . . . and All-Inclusive

Still, more than a few people join a health club to enjoy the level of luxury and service that is all but impossible to achieve in a nonprofit setting. At New York City's prestigious Printing House Fitness and Racquet Club, appealing to a discriminating clientele has made the difference. "We've never been a 'weight-lifting' gym," says membership representative and weekend manager Sarah Hamilton. "What sets us apart from other clubs in the city are our amenities and the way we use premium space."

In New York, older buildings were not built for the noise or pounding of gym use, so many of the city's clubs are banished to dungeonlike basements. Not so at Printing House: the club offers five squash courts, three racquetball courts, and two aerobic studios on its lower levels; upstairs the spacious 15,000-square-foot, glassed-in fitness center overlooks the Manhattan skyline. Like many other clubs, Printing House offers state-of-the-art Cybex, Nautilus, free weights, and cardiovascular equipment. But unlike its competitors, this top-of-the-line facility has a sundeck and a seasonal pool.

You could also call the locker rooms at Printing House panoramic, what with the shampoos, soaps, hair sprays, deodorants, lotions, and towels provided to remedy the effects of the most harrowing of workouts. "The amenities are key in New York," Hamilton adds, "because you can find good equipment anywhere." In addition to the in-house physiologist and podiatrist, staff members must all have a degree in fitness and an American College of Sports Medicine (ACSM) certificate.

"Many of our members are from higher-rent areas, so the costs aren't a major concern," Hamilton confesses. While rates may seem high when compared to suburban clubs, she offers a simple formula: an annual membership is still comparable to one month's rent.

While Printing House remembers the finer things, Chicago's East Bank Club offers almost every service imaginable—and more. The massive 400,000-square-foot facility occupies two entire city blocks and includes four levels and a garage, car wash, two indoor and outdoor pools, a 250-seat restaurant with gourmet take-out service, a beauty salon, and a clothing shop, as well as the usual exercise equipment. East Bank acknowledges that time and money are high priorities for today's families, and members need to accomplish many tasks at once to fit exercise into their schedules.

According to director of club services Betty Sacks, the East Bank Club asks its 9,000 members for guidance through regular surveys and questionnaire mailings. Member responses have led to such additions as an outdoor adults-only pool, a second basketball court, and an additional cardiovascular-training center. "At East Bank, three generations can enjoy their own type of workout, then meet to watch a sporting event over dinner," Sacks says.

Given the club's size and large membership, Sacks hesitates to refer to East Bank Club as "exclusive." Still, the 14-year-old establishment does have a certain country-club appeal. "The surroundings are very gracious and designed to make the whole family comfortable," she explains. "You'll find a lot of plants here, but no neon."

Hard Work for Heart Work

Be it the Y, the basement of the local town hall, or an exclusive members-only establishment, there's one thing that virtually every health club has: a room full of sweat-soaked people happily bouncing to the beat. For Kim Stevens, a professional instructor specializing in low-impact and step-circuit aerobics, it takes boundless enthusiasm, smooth technique, and much imagination to keep those people smiling.

Low-impact aerobics is the most popular club class today, in forms that range from funk dance to sliding on special plastic mats. "The earlier, high-impact aerobics classes were overdoing a good thing, and

For an extra fee, many clubs offer personal trainers. At right, a trainer assesses a member's condition before developing a personalized program.

resulted in knee and joint injuries from the bouncing and jarring," says Stevens. Her classes require that at least one foot remain on the floor at all times, and that movements are fluid and controlled. The step-circuit class uses an adjustable stepping board with lightweight dumbbells and elastic resistance bands in lieu of dance moves.

By combining a 35-minute cardiovascular workout with upper-body and abdominal exercises, Stevens isolates major muscle groups while stimulating the most important muscle, the heart. Students can set their own intensity levels.

"Maintaining your target heart rate for at least half an hour is the key to maximum cardiovascular benefit," Stevens says. With that in mind, she stops the class at intervals to measure pulse rates to make sure everyone is within his or her proper range.

Like many instructors, Stevens bases her routines on the T-steps, straddles, turn steps, and lunges that are the building blocks of aerobics classes. Drawing from classes she audits, TV, music videos, and her imagination, she has developed a signature "funky" style. "The hardest part is keeping the class interesting so students don't lose their enthusiasm," she adds, "so

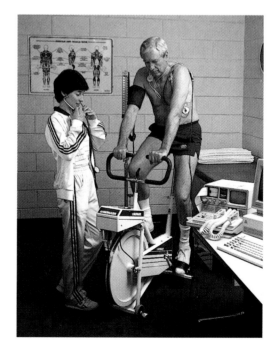

Choosing a Club

Your choice of a health club should not be based entirely upon price. Although metropolitan-area clubs command fees of more than $1,000, annual memberships at most fitness centers range from $300 to $500. Here are a

few questions that can help you find a gym that's right for you:

What is the culture of the gym? Any fitness center may be perfect for one person and inappropriate for another. Some folks look for Spandex and a chance for romance; others prefer grubby sweatshirts and baseball caps. Keep in mind that some gyms cater to those who are already in shape, while others appeal to beginners. If the members are huge hulks guzzling milkshakes between 400-pound bench presses, you may be disappointed with the aerobic offerings. On the other hand, a serious athlete may lose motivation in a sea of pink leotards.

What is the service attitude? Once you purchase a membership, are you on your own, or is the staff friendly, able to answer questions, and available to demonstrate equipment? Some gym employees are eager to interact; others prefer to admire themselves in the mirrors and chat at the front desk. Look for membership in IDEA (International Dance and Exercise Association) or other trade associations to make sure you will get the quality support you need.

What kind of facilities does it offer? Do you prefer stimulation (TV monitors, booming disco, mirrors that let you spy on the aerobics classes), or will your headset and some conversation keep you happy? Are the equipment options enough to hold your interest? Do you demand the latest technology?

Keep in mind that even the best equipment is useless if it's not working properly. If you see any "out-of-order" signs, ask how long the repairs will take, and look

for upholstery or carpeting that is worn-out or ripped. Run your hand across the top of a machine to check for dust, as this sign of poor housekeeping can also collect in machine gears over time. A good gym will clean the equipment with disinfectant at least once a day.

What are the financial conditions? Beware of clubs that ask for a large initiation payment up front, or suggest graduated payments that decrease after the first year. These gyms are usually focused on selling memberships instead of maintaining their facilities, and derive their profits from members who pay for services they will never use. Keep in mind that memberships can't last longer than the club itself, so look out for signs of instability or outrageous promises.

You may have the option of paying in advance or of having monthly billing drawn directly from your checking account, but be careful when giving out your credit-card number. Annual memberships will always be discounted over month-to-month costs, but both depend upon your commitment (read: showing up) to provide the best value.

What is the cancellation policy? As with other binding contracts, you'll probably have a few days to change your mind for a full refund. Veto policies that make no allowances if you are injured or if you move far from the club. Some clubs will let you freeze your membership for a nominal fee, or let you sell it to a third party at a below-market rate. If the club has recently changed hands, ask how it honored outstanding memberships.

What happens before and after the workout? Visit at rush hour (usually from 5:00 P.M. to 7:00 P.M. weekdays) to make sure the number of parking spaces and lockers is adequate. You'll also want clean showers and bathrooms with a good supply of soap and shampoo dispensers, paper towels, and paper cups.

it's important to change the combinations every few weeks." Stevens also selects her own music, which she has a disc jockey calibrate to match the pace of the class.

"It sounds obvious, but a well-trained staff of approachable, friendly instructors and floor people is crucial," Stevens says. She is certified in cardiopulmonary resuscitation (CPR) and accredited through the National Dance and Exercise Instructors Training Association (NDEITA), credentials reputable clubs require. "People's money and their bodies are two very personal things," she adds. "Clubs can't just hire people who look good." She believes an instructor should be "approachable, open to questions, and able to motivate people regardless of their experience or fitness level." An instructor should also have good form and be able to cue the next steps, so the students won't risk injury from unnatural moves or combinations.

Like many other instructors, Stevens is devoted to her class. "Teaching and interacting with the students provides a great release from the stress of the day," she says. Her muscular physique offers no evidence that she's in the fourth month of pregnancy and has had to ease up on her workouts. Although pregnant women who exercise regularly usually have healthier babies, Stevens must now carefully monitor her temperature and heart rate. "I hope to stick with the class as long as I can," she says.

One-Stop Fitness Shopping
As clubs face greater competition, the challenge is to offer the greatest value. "The goal of larger clubs is to provide one-stop health services," says Lyle Schuler, part-owner of five Gold's Gyms in Connecticut and New York. (The Gold's Gym organization has more than 400 clubs in the United States and abroad.) Three of Schuler's clubs feature on-site physical-therapy and sports-medicine centers that offer injury rehabilitation, body-fat analysis, athletic training, fitness evaluations, and massage. "Ten years ago, no one had a professional dietitian on staff," Schuler says. "Now that's a part of the greater role we play in helping members initiate a lifestyle change."

Health-club personnel should be familiar enough with their establishment's equipment to readily answer any questions a member may have.

Bright and busy with the newest high-tech equipment, the club even offers mounted television sets near the cardiovascular equipment. "People want a lot of stimulation for their money," Schuler says. "Today they are more demanding of new gear, more-attractive facilities, and greater variety." In addition to the usual free-weight and circuit-machinery fare, Gold's Gym offers several styles of aerobic classes, sessions devoted to toning and abdominal training, martial arts, and cardiovascular equipment. "Treadmills are hot right now, but it could be stair climbers tomorrow," Schuler adds. "Clubs must be chameleons and stay on the lookout for the most-innovative features."

The conversion of the former in-house restaurant and several racquetball courts to aerobics and nursery space illustrates the commitment to constantly changing customer needs. Even though nearly 10 million people still enjoy racquetball for the workout and for competition, the numbers have nonetheless dropped steadily since 1985. "The decrease in racquetball's popularity is part of a national trend," Schuler says. "Many clubs are converting to smaller squash courts or classroom space."

In addition to continuous investment in equipment, larger clubs also underwrite community events, sports tournaments, and guest speakers from the world of fitness and bodybuilding. Gold's Gym actively sponsors local road races and triathlons in addition to organizing member holiday parties and open houses.

The Personal Touch

Schuler believes today's enthusiasts have too many demands on their time to become fitness experts themselves. "In the '90s, it's acceptable to buy in-depth personal instruction that goes beyond the membership," he adds. "The attitude is, 'Here's the money—now you train me.' " Gold's Gym works with an outside firm that offers individual training for an additional fee. The trainer not only develops a customized program, but also provides hands-on assistance and close progress monitoring.

With the increase in public awareness, personal training has become very popular. At the Houstonian Club in Houston, Texas, the personal-training staff has increased from 6 to 20 over the past four years. According to personal trainer manager Shaun Fiedler, as many as 15 percent of the members schedule $50-an-hour sessions, selecting their trainer by area of expertise (strength, flexibility, conditioning). "Many of the members say they wouldn't come if it weren't for the trainer," Fiedler says. "By

Some health clubs whose facilities include an indoor swimming pool offer such innovative activities as "waterpower workouts" (below).

improving the safety and level of encouragement during their workouts, members can optimize their workout time."

Although the Houstonian Club's trainers must meet revenue quotas and frequently work 12-hour days, there is no shortage of qualified personnel. "Now that the public is well informed, they want certifications in addition to a good personal relationship," Fiedler adds. "With all the competition, it's a lot easier to choose well-trained people."

Ron Fuller, president of Future Fitness, Inc., and a certified U.S. Army Master Fitness Trainer, stresses that an expert recommendation can make the difference when choosing a club. "Price wars and promotion of the latest equipment drive the advertising battles, but neither may have anything to do with the trainee's needs," he maintains. By harmonizing specific training goals, budget, and preferences with the local facilities, Fuller can provide a perfect match. "We also conduct computerized analysis for strength, flexibility, diet, and metabolism, among others," he adds.

Fitness on the Cutting Edge

Step aerobics, circuit training—who dreams up the latest fitness craze? Much of the credit is due to Manhattan's Crunch Fitness, recognized as the leader in innovative club programming. In its six years, Crunch Fitness has worked with internationally regarded dance troupes, gospel choirs, and hip-hop classes with live rappers in a quest for new and different programs that meld the fitness craze and the arts.

"Our diversity drives the publicity and keeps people excited," says Crunch president Doug Levine. Each year the club is approached with more than 100 new programs, of which two or three are selected.

Levine is also active in marketing Crunch Fitness itself, drawing 40 percent of its 1994 profits from clothing sales, and is actively pursuing videotapes, jeans, and shoes bearing the Crunch label. In fact, 40 percent of clothing sales are to nonmembers who simply come to shop, undoubtedly providing free advertising in the other clubs they attend. A television program on the cable channel ESPN is also in the works. ◇

STRETCHING
...THE TRUTH

Flexibility, the ability to move your joints through their full range of motion, is one of the key elements of fitness, along with cardiovascular endurance and muscle strength. Flexibility varies from person to person as well as from joint to joint. The way to maintain or improve flexibility is to stretch.

Numerous studies have shown that the muscle elasticity afforded by stretching increases the range of motion of joints and may enhance physical performance. But stretching is not just for joggers, ballet dancers, and athletes. More than anyone else, sedentary people need the relief from muscle tension and stiffness that regular stretching provides. Stretching, when done the right way and regularly, feels good. Improper or excessive stretching, however, may actually increase the likelihood of injury. So the trick is to stretch correctly and to stretch in moderation.

Basic Types

Experts recognize three basic types of stretching:

Ballistic stretching, which is done by many beginners, is generally the type to avoid. It involves stretching to your limit and performing repetitive, bouncing movements, usually quickly. This may do more harm than good, actually shortening muscles (because of a protective reflex contraction) and increasing the risk of tiny muscle tears, soreness, and injury.

In contrast to the ballistic variety, two types of stretching are highly recommended because they are slow and gentle:

Static stretching calls for gradually stretching through a muscle's full range of movement until you feel resistance or the beginning of discomfort. You hold the maximum position for 10 to 30 seconds, relax, then repeat this several times. In static toe touches, for instance, you slowly roll down (with knees bent) toward your toes and hang in the down position without bouncing. Then you slowly roll up.

Proprioceptive neuromuscular facilitation stretching, like its name, is more complicated. One type is called contract-relax stretching. In this routine, you first contract a muscle against a resistance, usually provided by another person, then relax into a static extension of the muscle (see butterfly stretch described in the box). Because it brings the opposing muscle into play, contract-relax stretching is a good way to increase muscle flexibility.

Prelude to a Stretch

Stretching should always be *preceded* by a brief (5- to 10-minute) warm-up, such as jogging in place, riding a stationary bicycle, or a less vigorous rehearsal of the sport or exercise you are about to undertake. Warming up prepares you for your chosen

THE BASIC STRETCHING SESSION

1 *Neck Stretch. Tilt head to right, keeping shoulders down. Place right hand on left side of head. Gently pull head toward right shoulder for 10 to 30 seconds. Switch sides and repeat.*

2 *Calf Stretch (for gastrocnemius and soleus muscles). Stand about 3 feet from a wall, with feet perpendicular to wall, and lean against it for 10 to 30 seconds. Move left foot forward and lean into wall. Make sure rear heel stays on floor. Switch legs and repeat. Variation: keep rear knee slightly bent during stretch.*

3 *Hip Stretch (for hip flexor). From a kneeling position, bring right foot forward until knee is directly over ankle; keep right foot straight. Rest left knee on floor behind you. Leaning into front knee, lower pelvis and front of left hip toward floor to create an easy stretch. Hold for 10 to 30 seconds, then switch legs and repeat.*

4 *Thigh Stretch (for quadriceps). Placing left hand against a wall for balance, grab right ankle with right hand and pull heel gently toward buttocks for 10 to 30 seconds. Do not arch back. Switch sides and repeat.*

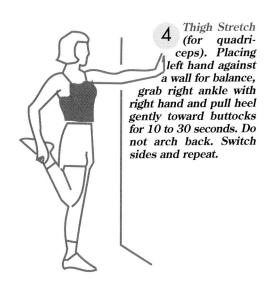

5 *Outer Thigh Stretch (for iliotibial band). Placing left hand against a wall for balance, place left foot behind and beyond right foot. Bend right knee and lean into wall. Hold for 10 to 30 seconds, then switch and repeat.*

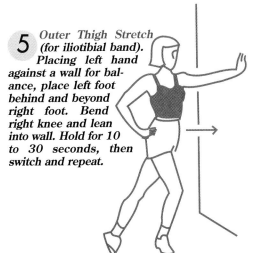

exercise by gradually increasing your heart rate and blood flow and by raising the temperature of muscles (and ligaments and tendons), all vital for elasticity and optimal functioning of muscles and connective tissue. Stretching while muscles are cold may sprain or tear them.

Home Stretching Programs

Before beginning a regular regimen of stretching, consider the following 11 tips:

1. Try to stretch at least three times a week to maintain flexibility. If you are recovering from an injury, your doctor or physical therapist may tell you to stretch more often—perhaps several times a day.

2. An optimal session should last 10 to 20 minutes, with each stretch held at least 10 seconds, working up to 20 to 30 seconds. This routine will maintain flexibility; to increase flexibility significantly, stretches should be held for one to two minutes.

6 *Butterfly Stretch (for adductor muscles in groin). Sit on floor, bringing heels together near groin and holding feet together. Have a partner gently push your legs down at the knees; hold for 5 seconds. Try to bring your knees upward as partner provides resistance. Relax, then have partner gently push down again for a greater stretch. Repeat. You can do the first part without a partner, simply by lowering your knees as far as possible.*

7 *Crossover Stretch (for lower back). Lying on back, bend left knee at 90 degrees and stretch arms out to the side. Place right hand on left thigh and pull that bent knee over right leg. Keeping head on floor, turn to look toward outstretched left arm. Pull bent left knee toward floor; keep shoulders flat on floor. Hold for 10 to 30 seconds, then switch sides and repeat.*

8 *Thigh Stretch (for hamstrings). Lie on back with both knees bent. Grasp behind the right thigh with both hands and pull toward chest. Slowly straighten leg to a vertical position, keeping foot relaxed. Hold for 10 to 30 seconds, then lower leg, switch legs, and repeat.*

9 *Spinal Twist (for back and sides). Sit with right leg straight out, and left knee bent, with left foot placed on the outside of right knee. Bend right elbow and place it on outside of upper left thigh, just above knee, to keep that leg stationary. Place left hand behind you, slowly turn head to look over left shoulder, and twist upper body toward left arm. Hold for 10 to 30 seconds. Switch sides and repeat.*

10 *Lumbar Stretch (for lower back). Lie on back with both knees bent. Clasp one hand under each knee. Gently pull both knees toward chest, keeping lower back on floor. Hold for 10 to 30 seconds, relax, then repeat.*

3. Stretch before exercising or playing a sport to limber up and help prevent muscle strain, and perhaps injury.

4. Besides a general stretch of major muscle groups, stretch the specific muscles required for your sport or activity.

5. If you experience any pain, stop. At worst, any discomfort should be mild and brief.

6. Try not to bounce. Stretching should be gradual and relaxed.

7. Focus on the muscles that you want to stretch, and try to minimize the movement of other parts of your body.

8. Do not hold your breath as you perform each stretching sequence.

9. Remember, always warm up first.

10. Stretch after exercise to prevent muscles from tightening up quickly.

11. Consider taking up yoga, since one of its benefits is to enhance flexibility.

What Stretching Cannot Do

Stretching before a workout, it used to be assumed, decreases the risk of injury, because tightness makes muscles (along with ligaments and tendons) susceptible to pulls and tears if they are forced beyond their normal range. But a few years ago, a study from McMaster University in Hamilton, Ontario, Canada, found that runners who said they never stretched before running were no likelier to be injured than those who said they always stretched. Even more surprising, those who *only sometimes* stretched had the highest risk for injury. These results raise some questions about the conventional wisdom of stretching before exercise.

Since the McMaster study depended solely on a questionnaire, with only very general questions about stretching, it is hardly definitive. Moreover, the runners, especially those who stretched only occasionally, may not have been stretching correctly—and some types of stretching are ineffectual or perhaps even counterproductive. Also, paradoxically, injury-prone athletes are more likely to stretch, which may skew the results. Although there is a very credible theory to explain why stretching should be protective—and countless anecdotal reports claim that it is—studies on the link between stretching and injury prevention have yielded contradictory results. One thing is clear, though: cold muscles are more likely to tear than warmer ones, so warming up is an important way to prevent injuries.

Stretching *after* a workout cannot head off delayed-onset muscle soreness—the kind that generally occurs the day after unaccustomed strenuous exercise. This does not mean you should forgo stretching after a workout. Stretching does, in any case, promote flexibility, and can keep your muscles from tightening up quickly.

Stretching: Mind/Body Workouts

Stretching may affect your mind as well as your body. When done in a slow and focused manner, an extended stretching routine can be an excellent relaxation method and stress reducer. For many Western practitioners, this is one of the main attractions of yoga.

Among the numerous studies on this subject was a recent one in the *Journal of the Royal Society of Medicine*, in which researchers found that a stretching-and-breathing routine was as effective as other means of relaxation, but at the same time increased the subjects' perception of mental and physical energy and alertness. Two studies in the *Journal of Behavioral Therapy and Experimental Psychiatry* suggest that stretching could help tense people reduce anxiety and muscle tension, as well as lower blood pressure and breathing rate.   ◇

Today's inventive playgrounds—designed to encourage socialization and creativity—also include new, safer versions of seesaws (above) and other old favorites. On hot summer days, kids flock to the water area (right).

The New
Rules of
the Game

by Dylan Landis

Jouncing on seesaws, ducking swings, swabbing at bloody knees—for many people over 30, urban childhood centered on a harsh, exhilarating playground. In those days, there were thousands across the country, each with metal swings that whipped around on long chains, and a slide whose high, narrow ladder brooked no indecision at the top: down you went. Of course, it was the child's job to avoid getting thrown by the seesaw, not the seesaw's job to provide a gentle landing.

Low platforms and wide slides help ensure an injury-free day in the park for New York City youngsters (right). Ideally, play areas also should include seating for adults and ramps and equipment for children with disabilities. Below, playground designer Sam Kornhauser admires his creation: a miniature Harlem, complete with tenement, hospital, and fire-engine play structures.

"In the '40s and '50s, we had 12-foot-high swings, 12-foot-high slides, and no safety guidelines at all," says Frances Wallach, a New York City-based consultant on playground safety and design. "I fell off a swing once and broke my elbow on the asphalt. And when they brought me home with a dangling arm, my mother hit me. I was supposed to play *properly*."

Today her mother would probably sue.

Changing Trends

Although it is still a vigorous place, the American playground is being reshaped by some very domestic thinking. First is the belief that people are due the same mantle of safety outdoors that is taken for granted at home. Swings are shortening, and slides growing squat, as safety standards—though voluntary in every state but California—are redefining the playground with newfound caution.

And landscape architects, acknowledging that playgrounds are used by communities, not just by able-bodied children, would rarely break ground these days before asking parents and residents for ideas; new designs, by law, must also extend a ramp or

some other invitation to children with disabilities. Playgrounds are swiftly moving indoors, too, to places where children need diversion (and parents, relief)—including fast-food restaurants, shopping malls, and soon, if one businesswoman has her way, nursing homes. "It would let the seniors interact with their grandchildren, and turn a scary institution into a fun place to visit," says Carol Pollack-Nelson, a psychologist and the co-founder of Kidstation in Silver Spring, Maryland, a new company that is trying to design and sell indoor play centers to residences for the elderly.

Designers have also acquired a growing respect for dramatic play, the kind that typically goes on at home when children play house un-

Kornhauser, a Manhattan designer who is creating playgrounds for seven Harlem public schools. "They herd, traveling from one end to another, playing games of tag that turn into hitting. But if you supply *ideas*, they tend to filter those ideas and play more imaginatively."

Pandering to the Imagination

That is why a new volcano has erupted in Lihue on the Hawaiian island of Kauai. Sixteen feet high, with concrete "lava tubes" funneling the children in and a slide spiraling down inside, the "volcano" was recently built of plastic and timber—entirely by parents and other volunteers. It is the work of Robert S. Leathers, an Ithaca, New York, architect who has led the growing movement in community-built playgrounds. Leathers walked through real lava tubes and asked schoolchildren for ideas before working out the design, much of it wheelchair-accessible. Its wooden towers, passageways, and roofscapes, he says, ar designed to suggest an old Hawaiian village.

More than 900 of Leathers's custom designs have been built nationwide, each one by hundreds of parents, teachers, and neighbors in a highly coordinated

Children of all ages enjoy sliding down a long, curving structure in New York City's Central Park. A popular attraction, the carved stone slide was designed to blend with the natural elements of the park.

der the kitchen table. Today's inventive playground props can be as big as the 80-foot ship that Christopher Clews, a Portsmouth, New Hampshire, architect, has made from recycled truck tires, or as small as the metal steering wheels found on many climbing structures.

"If you give children an asphalt plain, they will act like the wildebeest," says Sam

five-day barn raising. A grassroots notion 20 years ago, community-built playgrounds are nearly mainstream today. No skills are needed, so close is the architect's supervision; lumber, money, and food are donated, and children contribute ideas.

"We're looking at play in a very different way now," says Leathers, who got his start building tree houses as a boy in Maine. "We provide places for the whole family, and that means a lot more than picnic tables. In Kauai, it means an environment that's rich with history, exciting for an adult."

A very different culture is being celebrated at P.S. 200 in Harlem, where Sam Kornhauser has built a new playground atop a huge map, painted on rubber safety matting, that includes all the local geography from New Jersey to Queens. A climbing structure serves as the Triborough Bridge, and the northern end of "Central Park" is a small garden planted by children.

"Even the small act of planting a bulb in October and seeing it come up in April,"

says Kornhauser, "makes that place special to the kids."

Redefining Creativity

City-budget crunches, safety standards, hospitality to the entire family—all are challenging designers to further redefine creativity. Leathers, for example, engaged an engineer, Belinda Roettger, to help develop his "sympathetic swing"—actually two linked, side-by-side swings—in which the parent, vigorously pumping on one, sends the child soaring in the other.

Meanwhile, indoors, many new playgrounds are charging a usually modest admission in exchange for a rain-free, crime-free, well-padded room to romp in. Some are owned by national chains, such as Discovery Zone, which recently snapped up its biggest competitor, the Leaps and Bounds chain started by Mc-Donald's. (As for McDonald's, it still has playgrounds attached to some 4,000 of its restaurants.) Others are entrepreneurial, like Manhattan's PlaySpace, which has a puppet theater, blocks, a sandbox, and a café in two toy-strewn locations. "There's a sense of being indoors and out-doors at the same time," says architect Jonathan Kirschenfeld of Architrope, who, with his partner, Andrew Bartle, designed the glass-enclosed PlaySpace. "It suggests a city built for kids."

In addition to new playgrounds, existing public ones are being reconstructed or refurbished by the hundreds in Los Angeles, Chicago, New York, and

Architects combine natural materials and recycled products to create accessible, safe, and imaginative play areas for children of all ages. In Central Park's Rustic Playground (left), the existing plants and terrain are preserved and blended with play structures to create a "user-friendly" community retreat.

which resemble huge mattress coils. Low, stepped platforms on the newest models of this equipment invite children with disabilities to pull themselves out of a wheelchair and up toward the slides, and the whole extravaganza usually sits on a soft carpet of sand, wood chips, or rubber.

"This structure feeds on the imagination," says Robert C. Johnert, deputy chief of design for capital projects for the New York City Department of Parks and Recreation, which oversees 905 playgrounds. "To

Youngsters sift and build in the sand area, which doubles as a cushion for daring climbers. Architects invite input from community groups when developing a playground design (below).

Design conforms to existing terrain

Low-height designs promote safe play

Soft surfaces for safe play

Tire bouncers encourage cooperative play

Structures linked for interactive play

"Fantasy" structures encourage role-playing

Comfortable adult supervision

Wheelchair accessibility

other cities. Typically they are anchored by a piece of equipment that looks like a toy for a giant toddler. Made of metal, plastic, and sometimes wood, it sprouts tunnels, platforms, ladders, poles, tire swings, steering wheels, upright tic-tac-toe panels with turning X's and O's, and "curly climbers,"

you, it's a boat," he explains. "To someone else, it's a rocket ship."

Revamping Playgrounds

Just as neighborhoods are becoming involved in the design of new playgrounds, they are also being consulted in these ef-

At left, kids tackle a rope maze built by children and parents. Above, an expensive wooden play structure (background) holds little interest for kids who have just discovered an insect-infested tree stump.

forts to revamp old ones. In New York's housing developments, for example, landscape architects now give slide shows of other playgrounds to tenant groups, then try to grant requests when they renovate—placing preschoolers' equipment close by a building, for example, so parents can keep watch from the windows.

And in Chicago, where neighborhood meetings were held for more than 500 renovations, landscape architects engaged in a give-and-take with building residents. They learned, for instance, which colors might invite takeover by gangs, and they taught some basic fund-raising techniques—like inviting a community to blanket a tennis court with pennies—to augment the playgrounds' budgets.

"We were trying to foster a sense of ownership, and it worked," says Robert Megquier, the Park District's director of landscape architecture and management. "You see virtually no vandalism."

But no matter how new and bright the equipment, many designers still feel that natural elements are essential to a good playground. More important than play structures, they say, are water, shrubbery, and especially sand—long scooped out of many urban playgrounds because of the maintenance it demands. A child on slides and swings may spend three minutes, tops, on each activity, explains Robin Moore, Ph.D., a professor of landscape architecture at North Carolina State University in Raleigh. "But when they're playing with sand, water, sticks, vegetation, the attention spans go to 30 minutes, an hour, three hours," says Moore, who spent 10 years researching child's play at a California playground. "And those children are creating something together." ◇

In-Line Skating

by Susan Nielsen

Most adults today remember the metal-wheeled roller skates of old, the kind that would tie with leather straps over sneakers and make loud, scratchy noises on the sidewalk as you rolled along.

Skating on wheels has come a long way since then, and, in its most recent incarnation, it has gone from four wheels of two and two, side by side, to a straight line. In-line skating, so named because the wheels of the skate are in a line, has done nothing short of revolutionizing the sport.

The Innovative Olsons

Patented in 1819, in-line skates were originally popular with ice-hockey players, speed skaters, and cross-country and alpine skiers for off-season training. The modern-day discovery of in-line skating was prompted by brothers Scott and Brennan Olson, diehard semipro hockey players from Minneapolis, Minnesota.

The Olson brothers needed a cross-training tool for practicing hockey during the off-season. After finding a pair of wooden in-line skates at a local hardware store, they applied the wheelbase to the bottom of their hockey boots, a modification that enabled them to practice hockey on dry land.

Unfortunately, the new skates lacked the speed of ice skates. By studying traditional two-by-two roller skates, the Olsons discovered that each wheel had two ball bearings, which act to reduce the friction between the wheel and the axle when the wheel spins. Since the old wooden in-line skates had only one ball bearing, the friction created between

the wheel and the axle slowed down the skates considerably. The innovative Olsons remedied the situation by creating the first in-line wheelbase (three or four narrow wheels lined up in a row) with two ball bearings per wheel. This new arrangement gave the skates the smooth ride and maneuverability of ice skates, plus the durability of conventional roller skates. Thus, the first modern in-line skate was born.

In 1982 the Olson brothers sold their first pair of in-line skates, which eventually came to be called Rollerblades, the registered trade name that has emerged as the common name for the entire sport. Ten years later, in 1992, Rollerblade, Inc., would sell a reported 4.2 million pairs of in-line skates in the United States.

Fun and Fitness

Today 14 million in-line skaters, age 3 to 83, stroke and glide their way to fun and fitness, indoors, outdoors—almost anywhere.

"I take my skates with me when I travel," says Don Phillips, a veteran speed skater and the founder of the Long Island Road and Track Skating Association in New York. "The portability factor is terrific. I'm able to get wherever I need to go in any major city."

"There's a freedom that comes with skating along, in the fresh air, outdoors, with no cumbersome equipment or a care in the world," observes Diane Colleran, who has been "in-lining" for about two years. "And knowing that I'm getting exercise is such a wonderful side benefit." Runners have found another benefit to in-line skating. The low-impact sport takes the stress of jogging off their joints.

"Like many sports, in-line skating can provide muscular development," explains Joseph Kalb, A.T.C., a certified athletic trainer for Queens Exercise & Sports Therapy (QUEST) in Forest Hills, New York. "However," he cautions, "in-lining shouldn't be relied on exclusively for exercise. It should be part of a well-rounded conditioning program."

According to Kalb, in-lining makes the most use of the quadriceps, or thigh muscles; the hamstrings are used to a lesser degree. This can cause an imbalance between the two muscle groups. The best defense? Work the hamstrings with additional exercises.

In-line skating is one of the fastest-growing sports in the United States. Age makes little difference for people in pursuit of a good in-line-skating workout.

What's New

"There are a number of new features for in-line skates," says Maureen O'Neill, public-relations manager for Rollerblade, Inc., a Minnesota-based company that has been instrumental in the growth of in-line skating since the Olson brothers designed the first model. "The skate design advances on almost a daily basis because rollerblading is a sport that has become popular so quickly."

Active Brake Technology (ABT), says O'Neill, is the most important advancement to date. "Braking and stopping were always awkward with in-line skating because of the rudimentary stop brake," she explains. "Before ABT, in-line skaters had to raise one leg and apply pressure on the other to maintain control or to stop. ABT activates the cuff [or bottom rim] of the skate so that it pivots when pressure is applied. This backward pressure releases the brake to the

A row of four wheels is the basic ingredient of an in-line skate.

ground so the skater has an increased ability to control the speed."

Older models of in-line skates had wood wheelbases, which did not provide traction and made stopping and turning difficult. Modern in-line-skate wheels are made of flexible plastic, which provides better shock absorption and a smoother "ride." The wheelbase of an in-line skate balances the skater so the need to constantly shift body weight for control is no longer necessary.

"In-liners want speed and control," explains Danny Fram, part owner of Wheelen Willys Inc., of Wantagh, New York, a retailer who recognized the popularity of the sport almost three years ago. "There is no real stop activity until the skater is finished for the day. In-line skates with ABT provide the speed and movement control in-liners need. Novice skaters feel more balanced, and advanced or expert skaters can control speed and coordination when attempting more-difficult terrain, such as hills and inclines."

Ventilation is another new feature. Traditional boots were made with a heavy plastic material, which caused foot discomfort, sweating, and occasional swelling after prolonged use. The newer boots are made with a more breathable plastic so the foot does not perspire, and the in-liner can more comfortably skate for longer periods of time. And boots are increasingly being produced with buckles instead of laces, which makes it easier for a skater to put on and take off the boot.

"A good in-line boot should fit like a ski boot, with limited heel movement, but not as restrictively as an ice skate," says Tom DeVincenzo, owner of Mercury's Skate & Sport Shop in Babylon, New York.

In-line skaters should also take special note of the wheelbase durometer, which measures the hardness of the wheel. A good skate should have a wheel-durometer rating between 78 and 85, with 78 being the softest. "The softer the wheel, the faster the skate," says DeVincenzo. He suggests a standard wheel size ranging from 64 millimeters to 77 millimeters, and recommends a liner (a breathable boot insert) to increase the ventilation and, therefore, overall comfort.

In-line skates are ideal for both indoor and outdoor skating. However, a harder wheel is best suited for indoors. "The wheel is able to push off from a smooth surface more easily, giving the skater more speed," explains Danny Fram. "A softer wheel, on the other hand, would absorb too much of the hard surface to give the skater that speed."

A softer wheel (durometer rating 78–82), says DeVincenzo, should be used for outdoor skating, because it absorbs more shock, especially on rough or uneven terrain.

In-line skates range in price from $80 for beginning models to as high as $340 for expert and advanced models, depending on the quality of the wheelbase, the

boot material, and special features such as ABT. Professional racers may pay up to $500 for skates. But the percentage of professional skaters is small, so the demand for specialized skates is low.

The proficient in-line skater can readily execute flamboyant moves. The unique construction of in-line skates gives the hotdogger above the speed and control needed to navigate a harrowing obstacle course.

Smart Skating

"A key benefit to in-lining," says Kalb, "is that it increases joint coordination. And as an aerobic exercise, its cardiovascular benefits are terrific." New skaters may not feel so coordinated, however. "As in every new sport, coordination and familiarity with the equipment takes practice, so you will fall," he cautions. Kalb recommends a shoulder roll or a forward fall to the side, as opposed to tipping backward, so the shock is decreased by being dispersed over the entire surface of the body.

The proper equipment can also protect a skater from a fall. "Every sport should be taken seriously, especially a new sport," advises Phillips. He recommends that in-liners always follow the seven points of safety: two knee pads, two wrist pads, two elbow pads, and one approved helmet.

While a forward or shoulder fall is better, Maureen O'Neill believes that in-liners most often fall backward, so it is important to have a helmet especially designed for in-line skating. A certified in-line skating helmet is longer in the back so it provides more protection to the back of the head.

For safety's sake, in-liners should also follow these rules of the road:
- *Skate Smart:* Wear all protective gear.
- *Skate Alert:* Control speed and watch for road hazards, such as sand and heavy traffic.
- *Skate Legal:* Obey all traffic regulations. An in-liner must follow the same rules as any wheeled vehicle.
- *Skate Courteous:* Skate on the right, pass on the left. Always alert someone you will be passing on the left before you do so, and yield to all pedestrians.

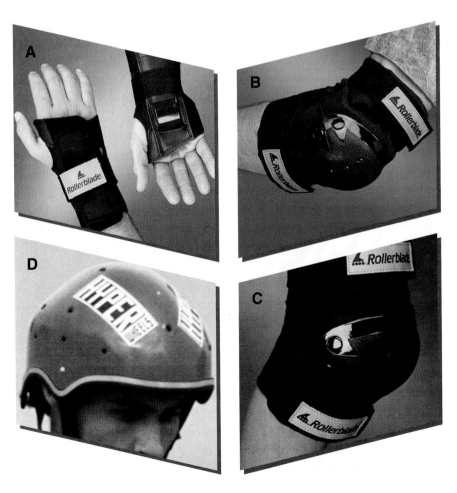

Play It Safe

The safety-minded in-line skater should be sure to always wear protective equipment. For in-line skating, as with many sports, a variety of safety gear is designed with specific risks in mind.

Leather gloves and wrist guards (A) protect the hands and arms from abrasions; some are even equipped with rearview mirrors. Elbow (B) and kneepads (C), made of high-impact molded plastic, are designed for comfort as well as shock absorption. A helmet (D) is absolutely essential. New aerodynamic helmet designs lower wind resistance while providing the head protection needed for such a balance-intensive sport.

Roll with It

The International In-Line Skating Association (ILSA), formed in 1991 to oversee the growth and management of the young sport, represents 20 equipment manufacturers internationally. Among them are Rollerblade, Bauer, and Roces, three of today's most popular manufacturers. "Because it's a sport that has grown so rapidly over the past several years," says ILSA Executive Director Henry Zuver, "we work to promote the safe use of in-line skating and to coordinate first-rate athletic competitions." Additionally, ILSA certifies instructors and lobbies to protect skaters' rights.

"We have worked to defeat proposed skating bans in several cities across the United States," he adds. "It is important to us as an organization to serve the complete recreational, competitive, and safety needs of in-line skaters worldwide."

Millions of Americans share in the fun and fitness that in-line skating provides.

ILSA offers membership programs for recreational and competitive skaters, instructors, retailers, event producers, and corporate sponsors.

For would-be skaters, Team Rollerblade, a group of in-liners sponsored by Rollerblade, Inc., teaches a four-day course each year in August in Santa Monica, California. Up to 500 attendees, at all levels of ability, spend the time learning everything there is to know about in-line skating. Says O'Neill: "It teaches novice skaters the concepts and basics of in-line skating, and encourages more-experienced skaters to advance their skills.

"The program is sold out every year," she adds, "which reflects the amazing popularity of the sport, especially since 1989."

Fitness and recreational aspects of in-line skating are the major growth areas of the sport. "People try it and become eager to advance to the next level," says O'Neill. "There is also an increase in street-skating, stunt-skating, and ramp-skating competitions. More and more in-line skaters are enjoying these more-aggressive types of skating." O'Neill says children ages 6 to 12 represent the largest group of converts. In-

Streets and parks are crowded with in-line skaters. Some in-line enthusiasts are families enjoying an afternoon outing; a few (above) are serious athletes cross-training for a winter sport.

deed, the number of in-line skaters across the country has more than tripled—from 3.89 million in 1992 to 12.5 million in 1993, with no signs of leveling off.

"Ten years ago, you saw maybe 5 to 10 in-line skaters," says Fram. "Three to four years ago, you saw 20 to 30. Today entire families are buying skates, and the parks are crowded with hundreds of in-line skaters."

The sport has much to offer its participants, and, according to Fram, he always knew it. The growth of in-line skating prompted him to open Wheelen Willys three years ago. He adds, with great confidence, "It's a sport that's here to stay." ◇

Housecalls

by Jennifer Kennedy, M.S.

Q *My wrestling coach suggested that I see a doctor about cauliflower ear. I don't think my ear looks like a cauliflower. Is cauliflower ear a nickname for another condition?*

A Repeated contusions or extreme friction on the ear can bring on "hematoma auris," more commonly known as cauliflower ear. The condition is usually found in athletes who participate in sports where forceful head contact is common, such as wrestling or rugby. Ear tissue tears away from the ear's cartilage, leaving a space in which fluid accumulates and where blood may pool and coagulate faster than the tissue can reabsorb it. If this situation is not treated medically, scar tissue may form. Scarring occurs under the skin in white, rounded heads called fibroids, which bear some similarity in appearance to cauliflower. Removing the fibroids requires surgery.

Athletes can avoid cauliflower ear by wearing protective headgear.

Wrestlers, racquetball players, and other sports enthusiasts should always warm up to prepare the body for active play.

Q *My daughter is an excellent tennis player, and has won numerous local tournaments. How would she–or any competitive amateur athlete–go about obtaining a professional sponsorship?*

A Your daughter has taken the first, most important step, which is to win amateur competitions. She should research her sport and find out which tournaments are most heavily scouted by representa-tives of sponsoring companies. The United States Tennis Association (USTA) 18-and-under championships are the most common route for up-and-coming tennis stars.

In many sports, becoming a professional and gaining sponsorships go hand in hand. In team sports, excelling at the college level and earning a right to try out for a professional team is the usual course. In individual sports, winning competitions and gaining visibility is the best way to bring in sponsorship offers.

Often companies making related equipment, clothing, or foods will offer free products and additional stipends to an athlete to use and advertise the products, to compete on a team sponsored by the company, or to just wear the company's name when performing. Companies with products unrelated to the sport may also offer these endorsement contracts.

Q *I know that warming up is an important step in any sport. How would you suggest I warm up before playing an hour-long game of racquetball?*

A One thing to keep in mind is that stretching and warming up are distinct activities, with some overlap in what they accomplish. Warming up involves faster movements that increase your cardiovascular rate and raise your body temperature. Stretching consists of slow, nonaerobic extensions that limber up muscles, tendons, and ligaments. Both get you ready to perform optimally when you start playing, and help minimize the risk of injuries.

For racquetball, like most sports, going through the motions of the sport slowly and easily for some time before competing at full speed is one way to warm up. This approach loosens the muscle groups you need before you try to go all out.

Racquetball is an explosive sport, so you'll want to be sure that your arms, shoulders, legs, neck, and other areas are limber. Stretching involves gentle motions. Done properly, it decreases muscle tension and increases range of motion; done improperly, stretching can cause injuries. A moderate warm-up followed by some careful stretching is often the best combination.

Q *My wife and I have joined a bowling league that plays two nights a week. Does bowling constitute sufficient aerobic activity for the week?*

A It's great that you're active in this way, but you need to supplement your bowling with a more aerobic activity several times per week to get the right cardiovascular conditioning and to burn the proper amount of calories. For example, a person who weighs 160 pounds can burn up to 190 calories by bowling for an hour. Running or swimming, on the other hand, burns many times more calories in the same period of time. Also, unlike running and swimming, bowling increases your heart rate only briefly.

As a general rule of thumb, find an exercise regimen that will enable you to achieve your target heart rate for 20 minutes, three to five times per week.

Q *My 40-year-old husband is in wonderful physical condition. Still, it bothers him that he weighs about 10 pounds more than he did when he was 25. Is such a weight gain considered a normal and healthy part of the aging process or does he have reason to be concerned?*

A This type of weight gain is so common that some people argue that it must be healthy. Nonetheless, this is a controversial research question, one that is perhaps not as important to your husband as are other factors in his lifestyle, such as poor eating habits and physical inactivity.

Between the ages of 22 and 55, the average person gains 1 pound of body weight per year, and loses 10 pounds of lean body mass. Partly as a result, metabolic rate decreases about one-half a percentage point each year as we age.

Anyone can delay this progression by remaining physically active. Americans too often use aging as an excuse for changes that are more accurately attributed to sedentary lifestyle and poor eating habits. If your husband is truly getting sufficient exercise and is eating a healthy diet, he probably does not need to worry about weight gains in the range that you mention.

Q *At my health club, it's not unusual to see guys dressed in layers of clothes (including sweat suits, sometimes plastic ones) working out vigorously in a warm gym. Some of them then sit in the steam room or sauna fully dressed. Is there anything to be gained by exercising this way? Is it dangerous?*

A There is very little to be gained by this, and, yes, it can be dangerous. This approach, especially the use of plastic sweat suits, was more common some years ago, before its shortcomings were as widely known. Exercising in a hot place while overdressed denies the body its natural cooling mechanism—the evaporation of sweat from the skin. Shutting this process off can overheat the body.

People most often subject themselves to the "sweat-out" workout for weight-loss purposes, because it does induce a significant amount of perspiration.

Plastic suits were sold as fitness gimmicks, and are still used by wrestlers or others who need dramatic, short-term weight loss. But the suits do not cause more calories to be burned. Instead, they hamper a workout because the person is overheated. Exercising vigorously this way can cause dehydration and possibly heat exhaustion. And finally, the body will simply replace the lost fluid (and weight) once the person cools down and drinks again.

Do you have a fitness question?
Send it to Editor, Health and Medicine Annual,
P.O. Box 90, Hawleyville, CT 06440-9990.

PSYCHOLOGY

CONTENTS

Over half of all Americans do some volunteer work each year. Many people direct their volunteer work toward a cause about which they feel deeply—such as planting trees in a reforestation project.

For Goodness' Sake!

by Elizabeth McGowan

Probably the last thing Thomas Parker would describe himself as is a do-gooder. Indeed, the 40-year-old former clothing manufacturer scoffs at any suggestion that he owes society anything in return for his own relatively good fortune.

When asked, then, why he recently spent five months as a volunteer instructor at an elementary school in Manhattan's Chinatown teaching fifth graders about the import/export business, he answers bluntly. "I volunteered for selfish reasons," he explains. "Volunteering was a pain-free way to explore something I was curious about. It gave me an avenue to pursue teaching without having to quit a job and without knowing if I had a talent for it." Despite the cynical facade, Parker admits that reaching the children in his once-a-week class made him feel better than almost anything he has ever done. "If the class clicked, I walked out

like I could run down the block." He now teaches junior-high students full-time in the city's public-school system.

The day she started volunteering at Safe House, a domestic-violence shelter in Washtenaw County, Michigan, Mona Kumar, a 19-year-old University of Michigan student who describes her upbringing as privileged and sheltered, was worried that the battered women she counsels would not take her seriously. "I'm still a baby," she explains. "I was afraid they would say, 'You've never been married; what do you know?'" What she has found instead is unconditional acceptance. "They are just so glad that someone is there to give them support. What they need most is a hand on their back or a hug. That's a need I can fulfill for them that has nothing to do with age."

"When my mom was my age, she already had two children," says Jeanne O'Brien, a petite brunette who is the managing editor of a monthly New York City trade magazine. "I really had no responsibility for anything but myself and my cat, and I sort of felt like I wanted to have responsibility for something else."

The problem was that, like many young professionals these days, O'Brien's job is rarely nine to five, so she was hesitant to commit to a cause with an inflexible schedule. She was also wary about getting involved in an activity that would require a lot of emotional attachment. So when O'Brien heard about an opportunity to deliver meals to homebound AIDS patients during only two lunch hours a month, she decided it was something she could handle. "It's not like literacy tutoring, where I have to be there from six to nine every Monday night or I'm going to disappoint somebody. With 'God's Love We Deliver,' we have a buddy system, and if something comes up and I can't make it, I can always swap with another employee. I find it really fulfilling without being a huge time commitment."

We versus Me?

If the rallying cry of the '80s was "Me, Me, Me," the '90s are shaping up to be the decade of "We, We, We." There is a movement of volunteerism sweeping across the towns, cities, and suburbs of America, a renewed belief in the power of the united effort. It is a movement that is a curious hybrid of idealism and realism. Some claim it is a pragmatic response to the sheer magnitude of today's social problems—from homelessness and crime to illiteracy and pollution—plaguing the country, and the seeming incapacity of government to solve them. Others insist that it is simply a matter of a best-kept secret getting out: Americans, they say, have finally discovered that helping others feels good.

Whatever the reasons, volunteerism has, by most accounts, become a national trend, with individuals, institutions, corporations, and college campuses lining up to do their part to make the world a better place.

Volunteers of the '90s represent the diversity that is America, and include people of both sexes, all ages, marital statuses, sexual orientations, and ethnicities; from all professions, philosophies, and nooks and crannies of the nation.

Who Volunteers?

Hard statistics for the total number of Americans who volunteer are difficult to come by, largely because different surveys have different definitions of volunteerism. A 1992 Gallup poll conducted for the Independent Sector, a national coalition of 800 foundations, corporations, and nonprofit organizations, does help shed some light on just how many Americans are donating their time and talent, both formally (through a charitable organization of some sort) and informally (going food shopping for an ailing neighbor, for example).

The poll found that 51 percent of American adults surveyed had done some volunteer work in the previous year. This number has slipped a few percentage points since then, but even revised figures represent a substantial increase over the 1988 level of 45 percent. The 1992 poll also found that more baby boomers volunteered than did people in any other age group—no surprise given their vast numbers.

The urge to do volunteer work may emanate from a curious hybrid of idealism and realism.

And the age category that showed the largest increase in volunteerism was 18- to 24-year-olds.

Upholding a long-standing American tradition, more women volunteered than men. But, surprisingly, women who worked outside the home were more likely to volunteer than women who listed their occupation as homemaker: an impressive 75 percent of the professional, entrepreneurial, and managerial women surveyed donated their time, compared to 47 percent of those who work at home. The poll also found that the number of black volunteers and single volunteers is on the rise, up by 5 percent and 4 percent, respectively.

According to the American Association of Retired Persons (AARP), senior volunteerism is also on the rise. Indeed, organizations are beginning to recruit from groups they used to overlook, like the elderly and people with disabilities. "More and more people are starting to see senior citizens as resources instead of recipients of services," says Judith Helein, director of the office of volunteer coordination at AARP. "And, significantly, senior citizens are starting to see *themselves* that way."

A Long Tradition

The demographics have changed, but the spirit of volunteerism in America is nothing new. As long ago as 1835, Alexis de Tocqueville wrote in *Democracy in America*, of "the extreme skill with which the inhabitants of the United States succeed in proposing a common object for the exertions of a great many men and inducting them voluntarily to pursue," a talent that much impressed the French statesman.

Although grass-roots volunteer efforts are as old as America—our Founding Fa-

Since 1961, Peace Corps volunteers of all ages have traveled to Sierra Leone (below) and countless other sites abroad to provide expertise and to assist in community-development efforts.

thers, after all, volunteered to overthrow the British—government and public support of volunteerism and of the concept of national service historically runs in cycles, according to Charles Moskos in his 1988 book *A Call to Civic Service*.

Often that support coincides with times of economic hardship. In the dark days of the Great Depression of the 1930s, for example, President Franklin D. Roosevelt championed the Civilian Conservation Corps (CCC), an army of young men 3 million strong, who spread across the country building roads and dams. Interest in national service declined in the stable 1950s, and waxed again at the beginning of the turbulent 1960s, when President Kennedy established the Peace Corps, which has made something of a comeback in recent years.

In the 1970s and 1980s, the concept of national service waned amid arguments about whether such service truly constitutes volunteerism, since it usually involves some form of minimal payment. National service nonetheless regained a spotlight during the Bush administration, with the introduction of the Thousand Points of Light initiative. This program adhered to the purist definition of volunteerism, and did not involve payment of any kind. The most recent national-service initiative comes courtesy of President Clinton, who, in September 1994, swore 15,000 Americans into Americorps, a domestic Peace Corps.

While national service benefits only a small number of Americans, its promotion traditionally tends to have a ripple effect on public consciousness. "We've had several presidents in a row who have talked about volunteerism," explains John Thomas, vice president of communications for Independent Sector. "That keeps it out in front of us."

Mark Kessler, deputy director of New York Cares, a volunteer nonprofit agency that organizes volunteer projects in conjunction with other nonprofit organizations, notes that, "People are beginning to realize that the government can't do it all. Whether they think on a block basis, a borough basis, or a city basis, if they want to make their community a better place, they have to take ownership of it."

Maverick Challenges

The service opportunities available today are as diverse as the volunteers who sign up for them. The venerable nonprofit giants like the Salvation Army and United Way are being joined by record numbers of smaller grass-roots organizations, some of which are devoted to issues—such as AIDS—that did not even exist as recently as a decade or two ago. Today's volunteers are tackling everything from illiteracy, homelessness, youth gangs, drunken driving, and domestic violence to environmental disasters, animal rights, and the right to bear arms, among other causes.

Some people start their own volunteer organizations. Sometimes, they even experiment with maverick challenges to the status-quo concept of volunteering. Time Dollars, the brainchild of attorney Edgar S. Cahn, a professor at the District of Columbia Law School, is a system in which participants perform all sorts of services for another person—baby-sitting, home repairs, taking an elderly person to the doctor, reading to someone who cannot see—the possibilities are endless. In return the volunteer receives a time-dollar, which is deposited in a Time Dollars "bank" for exchange at a later date when the original volunteer requires a service performed by another person, who in turn earns his or her time-dollar. For example, a senior citizen who earns a time-dollar by baby-sitting for a toddler can exchange that time-dollar for a ride to the grocery store.

Although critics complain that the program offers no guarantees—who is to say that the program will still be in existence when you want to cash in on your earned time-dollars?—the time-dollar concept is being tried in about 40 states. Its largest ap-

Many volunteers derive great satisfaction from teaching immigrants how to speak English, or from helping illiterate people learn to read or write.

plication is in Miami, Florida, where the Friend-to-Friend program boasts 3,000 participants, including time donors and recipients, according to executive director Anna Miyares.

Corporate Connections

Big, small, experimental, or traditional, all forms of volunteer organizations will likely stand shoulder to shoulder in America's future, according to Cathy Soffin, manager of information services for the Points of Light Foundation, a private organization that promotes volunteerism. The foundation, a spin-off of the Bush initiative, today describes itself as nonpartisan. As Soffin puts it, "The grass-roots organizations probably get the job done more quickly and more easily on the local level, but then you'll always need the biggies to be advocates on the national level, to raise the money, and to direct public attention."

These days, Points of Light is directing a public-attention beam on corporate America, offering training and information services to companies interested in starting community-service programs for their employees. Part of a fast-growing segment of the community-service sector, companies like Campbell Soup, CPC International, Xerox, and Miller-Freeman, to name just a few, have established volunteer programs staffed by full-time paid coordinators.

According to Rose Tobin, who heads Community Connection, Miller-Freeman's volunteer arm, the company funds organizations for which its employees do volunteer work. Employees are also encouraged to take two hours of company time each week to do community service of their own choosing. Community Connection coordinates schedules and acts as a clearinghouse

Retired people perform much of the volunteer work that is conducted during the day, when many younger volunteers are at work. Programs that involve serving lunch at a nursing facility or bringing meals to ill people in their homes help brighten the day of the volunteers and the beneficiaries of their kindness.

for off-hour and weekend volunteer opportunities. Tobin also has the O.K. from the company's top executives to act as an intermediary if a department manager frowns on an employee's volunteer activities, although so far, she says, "that problem has never come up."

Xerox made a strong commitment to employee community service long before it became trendy. Since 1971 the company has given full-pay leaves of absence of up to a year to employees desiring to do community-service work. According to Judd Everhart, manager of corporate public relations, 7 to 10 Xerox employees per year are chosen by a committee of their peers for sabbaticals, only one, he says, "of literally hundreds of projects Xerox people are involved with around the country."

Other companies sponsor one-day efforts like park cleanups, packing boxes in a food bank, or painting a local school. The Los Angeles, California, office of Merrill Lynch, for example, rang in the 1993 holiday season by inviting local senior citizens to make calls on company phones to friends and family anywhere in the world. Merrill Lynch staffers, many of whom are multilingual, volunteered their time to help place the calls. "It was good for morale, but it was also a wrenching process," explains senior vice president Rod Hagenbuch. "You're listening to people talk to friends they haven't spoken with in 40 years. They find out that

people have died, that people have been born." Despite the emotional highs and lows, the Christmas Calling Day was a success, and Merrill Lynch employees voted to do it again this year.

Predictably, corporate volunteerism invites its share of raised eyebrows. Why, skeptics ask, is Big Business suddenly interested in something more than the bottom line? Mark Kessler of New York Cares offers an answer. "Part of it is employee morale, part of it is employee driven. . . . Corporations are also realizing that employees, even if they don't live in the city, spend most of their working lives in the city. Community service helps people feel good about where they work."

In an era of layoffs and downsizing, Xerox's Everhart adds, maintaining community-service programs helps to communicate to employees that their company "is still a decent company, even though it's had to make some tough decisions." Mark Kessler adds that any community-service program can backfire "if a company is just in it for good public relations. If employees sense that a company is being hypocritical, they won't sustain the effort."

Academic Activity

Like the business world, the academic world has recognized that community service fits its mission, which is, in part, to teach students personal values and civic responsibility. On a high-school level, some school districts in communities around the country are now requiring students to perform a varying number of hours of community service to qualify for graduation. Maryland last year became the first state to mandate student volunteerism, a policy that many argue is at best oxymoronic and at worst unconstitutional.

Colleges have taken a less controversial tack, maintaining their students' freedom to choose. Universities nationwide have established volunteer centers that link students with needy organizations in the community. Projects range from a one-day street cleanup, to a spring break spent tracking wildlife for an environmental organization, to tutoring a child for a semester or longer.

Many schools are also experimenting with the concept of service learning. Tim Stanton, director of the Haas Center for Public Service at Stanford University in Palo Alto, California, gives an illustration of how the idea works. "We have a course on the history of poverty and homelessness. The professor has his students intern at homeless-family shelters and use that experience to think about issues of poverty. There's a lot of reading, a lot of writing, and, of course, there's an effort to link the experience with academic thought."

Helper's High?

But whether they sign up on campus, in the corporate boardroom, or on a street corner, with a group or on their own, the bottom line is that volunteer work is done by individuals. Still, the question remains: Why do they do it? "Because I've been very fortunate in my life, and I want to give something back," says Madeline Michalski, a retired nurse, echoing the sentiment of most volunteers interviewed for this article. And, adds Michalski, who volunteers for, among other causes, Meals on Wheels, "it makes me feel good."

What Michalski actually feels, says Allan Luks, author of *The Healing Power of Doing Good*, and executive director of Big Brother/Big Sister, is "helper's high," a phenomenon he compares to the endorphin-induced euphoria reported by runners. Although medical experts believe that he is overstating the case, Luks speaks with the zeal of a missionary about the power of helper's high to act as a buffer to stress, and it "definitely has a link to health."

Do volunteers get fewer colds than other people? The jury is still out. But volunteer recruiters do confirm that the pleasure participants derive from helping is at the heart of most community-service efforts. Recruiters agree, though, that the volunteers of today might be high on helping, but they

A boy confined to a wheelchair benefits greatly from the attention of a Big Brother volunteer. The Big Brother, in turn, derives great pleasure from sharing his interests with someone who appreciates them.

are less starry-eyed and idealistic than the volunteers of yesteryear. They realize that they cannot save the world. Their goal in most cases: to improve their own little corner of the planet.

Increasingly, service is seen as a two-way street, with volunteers expecting both to give something to society and to gain something from the experience. To attract volunteers and to ensure that they keep coming back, organizations are becoming more sophisticated about meeting the individual's needs. Many do extensive interviewing to match the right person with the right project. "We'll look at their background, their accomplishments, likes and dislikes, and what they do now," says Mike Gray, volunteer coordinator for the Salvation Army's St. Louis, Missouri, Division.

"We try to determine their transferable skills," adds Ellen Amstutz, assistant director of the Retired Senior Volunteer Program for the Community Service Society in New York. "We try to be sensitive to what they really want to do. A retired librarian, for example, doesn't necessarily want to do volunteer work in a library. Many people want to explore new terrain."

A Win/Win Situation

Although they still do their share of filing, fund-raising, and envelope stuffing, volunteers today often work directly with client populations, thanks to budget cuts that have denuded many social programs of staff. Whether it is teaching an adult how to read, playing with terminally ill children in a hospital, or counseling the lover of an AIDS patient, most direct-contact positions require some degree of training—you cannot put an untrained volunteer on the phone and expect him or her to talk a distraught teenager out of committing suicide. Volunteerism can be an opportunity to try out a potential career path or to learn new skills. It is also a way to use existing skills in a whole new context.

Other fringe benefits are part of the package. "Volunteering is a tangible way to expand your network, a way to help you get into college, a positive thing to have on your résumé when you look for a job," explains Cynthia Scherer, director of the youth and education outreach program for the Points of Light Foundation. "It's a win/win situation, and there's nothing wrong with looking at it that way."

In a society of singles bars and serial killers, volunteerism can also be a nonpressure way to make new friends or even meet a mate who shares the same values. Indeed, "people contact is the big one," says Ellen Amstutz.

Physical labor is also a hit with volunteers, according to Mark Kessler of New York Cares. "People love community gardening, and they will paint anything that doesn't move." Why? "A lot of us have jobs that are very conceptual. When you paint a park bench, it's instant gratification. You don't have to wait three weeks for polls or marketing surveys."

Which leads to another characteristic of today's volunteers. They are achievement-oriented, and they want results. "What we have learned is that we can't send 10 volunteers to clean up a huge lot and have them only clean up a small corner," explains Kessler. "It's better for us to send in 100 volunteers and have them leave after a day's work and see that lot clean."

Even more important, "you can't waste their time," adds Diana Brownlee, volunteer coordinator for the Greater Chicago Food Depository. "These are busy people. If we're not organized and ready for them when they come, they'll go somewhere else the next time."

Like many organizations these days, the Greater Chicago Food Depository schedules its volunteer sessions on weekends and evenings to accommodate its volunteers' busy work schedules. In fact, offering flexible volunteer opportunities is the raison d'être for New York Cares, which has "Cares" cousins in 20 cities across the United States. Volunteers for New York Cares attend an hour-long after-work orientation that entitles them to receive a calendar each month, listing from 100 to 300 volunteer opportunities from which they can pick and choose. Unable to show up every week? No problem. But Kessler says that after getting their feet wet, many of his volunteers take the plunge, joining organizations with greater obligations. "We call them 'the graduates,'" laughs Kessler.

Jeanne O'Brien, the editor who delivers lunch to homebound AIDS patients twice a month, suspects that she may be among the volunteer commencement class of 1994. "I'm starting to feel like I might be ready for a little more emotional commitment," she says a little tentatively, "like I might be ready to take the next step."   ◇

JURY PSYCHOLOGY

by Elizabeth McGowan

When word leaked out about the Palm Beach, Florida, jury chosen for the William Kennedy Smith rape trial in 1991, the phones started ringing at the offices of Cathy Bennett & Associates, one of the nation's top trial-consulting firms, retained by the defense. "We must have gotten 100 calls from people saying, 'What, are you crazy?'," recalls Robert Hirschhorn, an attorney who helped advise the defense team on juror selection.

It wasn't hard to figure out why the pro-Smith callers were upset—although the Kennedy name is practically synonymous with "liberal," half the jurors who made the cut had stated that Rush Limbaugh, Ronald Reagan, or George Bush were among the people they most admired. "How is the nephew of Ted Kennedy going to get a fair shake from a jury packed with ultraconservatives?" argued the callers.

If Smith supporters were nearly apoplectic about the jury seated, the prosecution was practically doing a pretrial victory dance, according to Hirschhorn. "They were salivating. They thought we were doing it all wrong," explains Hirschhorn. "But we wanted those jurors because they were law-and-order types. We thought they'd be able to hear our side."

There is no way of knowing how great a part Cathy Bennett & Associates' juror advice played in Smith's acquittal. Jury selection is, after all, an inexact science. But one thing is certain: the jury deliberated for a mere 77 minutes before clearing the medical student of all charges.

Trial Consultants

Business these days is booming for trial consultants, a new breed of legal subspecialists who have made headlines—and waves—in connection with the high-profile cases of, among others, the Menendez brothers, O. J. Simpson, and the Branch Davidians. Critics vilify trial consultants as voodoo scientists corrupting the legal system by trying to stack the legal deck in favor of their clients, using methodology better applied to product research than to justice. Advocates laud them as indispensable to ensuring a fair trial in the increasingly publicized and polarized arena of the courtroom, leveling a playing field that is tilted toward the prosecution.

Despite their recent notoriety, trial consultants didn't even exist until the 1970s, when social scientists volunteered their talents to help defendants like antiwar activist Philip Berrigan. Today, as a group, they are decidedly eclectic—a factor that probably contributes to the controversy they inspire. "Our people come from the fields of communications, social psychology, sociology, and linguistics; we have some political scientists, some theater people," says Ronald Matlon, Ph.D., executive director of the American Society of Trial Consultants, whose doctorate is in speech communication. Membership in the society has mushroomed from 19 in 1983 to 350 at last count. Members are asked to adhere to a code of standards, but there's no certification system. Basically anyone can call him- or herself a trial consultant, which has left the field open to accusations of charlatanism—and a fringe of practitioners claiming to be able to read juries based on such tenuous factors as facial characteristics and color preferences.

The tools of mainstream trial consultants, however, are the tools of mass marketing. They use surveys, juror questionnaires, focus groups, and simulated trials to help their clients—whether plaintiff, prosecution, or defense—win their cases. Love them or hate them, trial consultants can take credit for heightening the debate over the ability of juries to do justice, and for leading the charge in jury research—from how individuals process information during the trial, to the dynamics of the deliberation room, to the psychological implications intrinsic to deciding another's guilt or innocence. Most trial lawyers agree that they rely on a mixed bag of common sense, intuition, body language, gut reactions, and demographics to appeal to jurors in the courtroom and to eliminate potentially unsympathetic jurors from their cases.

Attorneys often have little to go on but stereotypes when choosing jurors.

Unabashed Stereotyping?

"Demographic" can often sound a lot like "stereotype," and indeed, unabashed stereotyping in jury selection is a time-honored legal tradition. In the 1930s none other than the renowned Clarence Darrow warned defense attorneys to strike Presbyterians, Baptists, and Lutherans from their juries because they tended to believe in punishment. Darrow maintained that Catholics and Jews were, from the defendant's point of view, a far safer bet.

"If counsel wants to avoid a verdict of intuition or sympathy, generally he would want a male juror," advised distinguished trial attorney Melvin Belli in 1982 in a book on trials. In 1991 the lawyers' manual *Jury Selection: Strategy and Science* stressed a variety of ethnic considerations: "Those of Italian, Spanish, and French descent," it instructed, "are thought to empathize more readily with the human and emotional side of a lawsuit. . . ."

Certain professions have also, over the years, been painted with a broad brush as dangerous to the defense or to the prosecution or both—accountants and engineers (too analytical, might hang the jury, neither side wants them), police officers or anyone related to one (likely to side with the prosecution), doctors (won't rule against another doctor), social workers (sympathetic to the defense), to name just a few.

And nine years after the U.S. Supreme Court declared it unconstitutional to strike jurors on the basis of race (a common practice well into the 1980s, particularly in parts of the South), debate rages over the racial composition of the O. J. Simpson jury. Eight of its original 12 members are black. Critics of the jury-selection process claim that since blacks account for only 11 percent of the Los Angeles population, the Simpson jury is not representative of the California community in which the trial is being held, and has, in essence, been stacked in favor of the ex-football hero.

Although there is some statistical basis for the point of view that blacks are more sympathetic to Simpson than are whites— polls conducted after his arrest found that blacks were only half as likely as whites to believe he was guilty; other polls have found that blacks are more distrustful of the police than are whites, and therefore are more likely to consider that Simpson may have been set up—lawyers and trial consultants surveyed agree that relying on stereotypes alone in choosing a jury, while far from uncommon, is at best unreliable, and can actually backfire.

The tendency to rely heavily on stereotypes, many agree, is strongest in jurisdictions, such as the federal courts, that forbid or greatly restrict attorney participation in voir dire (the preliminary examination to determine competency of a juror). Barred from investigating a potential juror's beliefs, attitudes, or life experiences, an attorney is left with little but stereotypes to go on.

Questions and Answers

Leo Boyle, a partner with the Boston, Massachusetts, law firm Meehan, Boyle & Cohen, and the former president of the Massachusetts Bar Association, practices in the federal courts and specializes in personal-injury cases. He admits that he makes juror decisions based on demographics. He bristles at the term "stereotype," which he says is simplistic and implies racism. Rather, he says, "I look for people about whom the outward signs of their personalities, their jobs, their status in the community, their age, occupation, and neighborhood would make them possibly similar to the person I represent."

In jurisdictions where attorney voir dire is permitted, experts say that asking potential jurors open-ended questions about their beliefs, attitudes, and life experiences encourages elaboration and yields the most-accurate results in screening jurors for biases that the jurors themselves might not be aware they have.

"I almost never ask a question that can be answered yes or no, because I think that whatever information I can get from that answer will probably not be very useful," explains civil attorney Roxanne Barton Conlin, a former president of the American Trial Lawyers Association. "I absolutely want to know what they do in their leisure time, what is their source of news. . . . I like to know if they watch TV, what they like on TV, and why. . . . We think that we can tell something about people if we find out what their activities are, what moves them."

"The big issue is: Does this person have an attitude or life experience that's going to be a barrier to their being able to hear the

Testimony gains credibility if the witness maintains eye contact with the jurors while on the stand. The attorney who cross-examines may try to block the jury's view of the witness.

case from your point of view?" adds Karen Jo Koonan, a trial consultant with the National Jury Project based in Oakland, California. "Sometimes what you really do is get rid of the extreme people on both sides, and you're working with what's left. You don't select a jury; you 'deselect' a jury."

Many lawyers like to use written questionnaires, if jurisdiction allows, to supplement verbal voir dire—prospective jurors in the O. J. Simpson case, for example, were asked to respond to 79 pages of questions. Although experts surveyed say they believe most jurors try to be honest in their responses, many agree that answering the sometimes-personal questions in public can be embarrassing.

As part of their services, trial consultants often assist lawyers in identifying the major issues in a case, and in formulating questions designed to address those issues to weed out biased jurors. Major issues in the O. J. Simpson case, for example, include spousal abuse and interracial relationships; the 79-page juror questionnaire likely included questions to elicit juror attitudes about those issues.

"Basically we try to teach our clients to ask questions that get to the heart of things in a very benign and subtle way. The trick is to leave on the panel people who on the surface your opponent is going to think are bad for you, but that you know from your interview will give you a chance. The goal is to sandbag the other side," explains Joseph Rice, Ph.D., a clinical psychologist and the president of Jury Research Institute, a trial-consulting firm in California.

In the spirit of sandbagging the other side, some experts say they sometimes try to identify "black-and-white" thinkers, jurors likely to decide on a version of events even before the opening arguments in a trial are finished, and then mold all the evidence they hear to fit that story. When it comes to deliberation time, these jurors cannot be budged from their position, and end up hanging the jury or convincing the rest of the panel that their story is true. "I don't want to eliminate them if they're on our side," says Robert Hirschhorn.

Fill in the Blanks

James Rasicot, Ph.D., a Minneapolis, Minnesota, psychologist and trial consultant, says he uses a "visual polygraph" to determine whether a potential juror is lying, an occurrence that he says is on the rise as jurors involved in high-profile cases increasingly profit from their jury experience by

Even passive jurors remember 93 percent of the facts presented during a case.

selling their stories to the tabloids or to talk shows.

"More jurors are coming in with a personal agenda," he says, explaining how his visual polygraph works. "When someone is being untruthful, you'll see more-concentric movements, gestures will be closer to the body, there won't be much eye contact, and their body will turn at angles to you rather than be frontal."

Although some experts believe that weeding out liars and other undesirable jurors from a panel is the single most important factor in ensuring a fair trial, others—like Robert Ladner, Ph.D., a psychologist, sociologist, and president of Behavioral Science Research Corporation in Coral Gables, Florida—believe that concentrating the major effort on jury selection is "paying attention to the molehills and letting the mountains take care of themselves."

Presenting the Case

In reality, Ladner says, attorneys don't really have much control over who sits and who doesn't, since most "legitimate" people use excuse after excuse to get out of jury duty, and many don't even bother to respond to jury-call notices. The jury pool is further limited by the fact that, in some states, certain occupations have automatic exemptions. In New York, for example, 20 professions—including police, clergy, podiatrists, and embalmers—are exempted.

Experts in Ladner's camp believe that energy is better spent improving the presentation of evidence so jurors can more easily understand it. Research has shown that jurors tend to listen to evidence and turn it into stories, stories based on their own life experiences that help them make sense of what they are hearing.

A defendant who doesn't take the stand in his or her own defense similarly risks having the jurors weave fantasy with fact. That's not often a good thing, according to Robert Hirschhorn. "It's contrary to human nature to say a person doesn't have to testify, and you can't hold it against him, because people will. They'll figure, 'If he hasn't done anything wrong, why doesn't he testify?' There will always be questions."

If jurors supplement the evidence with their own imaginations, they also tend to retain most of what they actually have heard. Nancy Pennington, Ph.D., of the University of Colorado in Boulder, found that, collectively (meaning the information retention of the panel as a whole), most juries remember 93 percent of the facts presented during a trial. Other research shows that jurors are influenced by *all* the testimony they hear, even testimony ordered stricken from the record as irrelevant or inappropriate—the reason lawyers are always trying to sneak in statements or questions they know the judge will instruct the jury to ignore.

Jurors will remember that little white lie as well, warns Roxanne Barton Conlin. "I have a list of rules for witnesses, and number one is: Tell the truth. Don't exaggerate, don't shade, don't try to make it better than it is," she explains. "The principle that all of us follow in our daily lives is that if you lie to me about one thing, you're probably lying to me about other things."

Blaming the Victim

Jurors also consider the contributory negligence of a victim, according to Valerie Hans, Ph.D., a social psychologist at the University of Delaware in Newark and the author of *Judging the Jury*. "They take into account who the victim is, what the actions of the victim were, how deserving they were of what happened to them," she explains. For instance, in the first Rodney King trial, in which the four Los Angeles policemen accused of beating King were acquitted, comments made by jurors after the trial suggested that they thought the victim could have avoided the beating by cooperating with the police.

Blaming the victim is particularly typical in rape trials, according to sociologist Gary

Jurors identify with and have sympathy for a defendant they find attractive.

LaFree, Ph.D., chair of the sociology department at the University of New Mexico in Albuquerque. In a study of 350 juror verdicts in rape trials, he found that no evidence—not bloodstains, not torn clothing, not bruises—was as important as the victim's character and behavior in determining the trial outcome. The strongest factors correlated to an acquittal, according to Dr. LaFree, were "the victim's being out at a bar, drinking or drug use, and having sex outside marriage."

The Abuse Excuse

Another variation on the "contributory" theme is what criminal defense lawyer Alan M. Dershowitz, a professor at Harvard Law School in Cambridge, Massachusetts, has coined "abuse excuse." Examples include the recent Menendez and Bobbitt trials.

Admitting to killing their parents, the Menendez brothers painted their father as a pedophile who beat and raped them as they were growing up. Their mother was portrayed as an accessory by virtue of her inaction. A lifetime of parental abuse and fear for their lives, the young men maintained, left them with no choice but to kill their parents in self-defense. Lorena Bobbitt, who admitted cutting off her husband's penis, defended herself on the grounds that, throughout their marriage, she was the target of her husband's emotional, physical, and sexual assaults.

In both cases the victims were as much on trial as the defendants—because of their abusive actions, the defense emphasized, the victims, in effect, caused what happened to them. Bobbitt was acquitted; the Menendez brothers' trial resulted in hung juries—evidence, Dershowitz maintains, that "more jurors are buying" the abuse excuse, a trend he considers dangerous.

Recent research suggests that the fact that both brothers are nice-looking young men probably didn't hurt their chances either. In a 1990 study by psychologist Roger J. MacCoun, Ph.D., mock jurors were more likely to give the benefit of the doubt to and acquit an attractive defendant than an unattractive one.

Thinking through the Story

While there's not much that trial consultants can do to make their clients more attractive, there is much they can do to make the evidence in a trial more presentable. And that's what they get paid to do.

The National Jury Project's Karen Jo Koonan describes the process: "We help the attorney think through the story in a way that laypeople can understand. What's the beginning, the middle, and the end of what happened? Are there holes in the narrative? Who are the good guys, who are the bad guys, and how can the evidence be presented so that the jury will see it in a context?"

The key is to get as much of the evidence lined up within the story line as possible, so jurors don't create their own constructs. To prepare for the opposition, Robert Ladner of Behavioral Science Research Corporation says he hires attorneys "to come after us with both hands and feet, and construct the counterargument as viciously as possible."

Jurors confused by testimony may develop their own sequence of events.

Next step is research, which can involve just about anything: a community survey; a small focus group that listens to presentations from lawyers representing both sides and then discusses the case; or even a full-blown trial simulation.

A mock trial is designed to be as real as possible, with a room set up like a courtroom, and participants playing roles as if it were really a trial—attorneys for both sides make opening statements; evidence is presented, using actual videotaped depositions whenever possible; closing arguments end the proceedings; and the jury deliberates. The results of the mock trial can convince a client to go forward with a real trial, plea-bargain, or settle out of court. (According to Joseph Rice, 75 percent of Jury Research Institute's clients settle before trial.)

During a mock trial, consultants measure the reactions of jurors to witnesses, lawyers, and visual displays. "We focus first and foremost on juror comprehension. Do the jurors understand what the witness is trying to tell them?" explains Joseph Rice.

Rice coaches witnesses to talk directly to the jury. "The audience in a trial is never in front of you, they're off to the side, and you have to turn 90 degrees to look at the people you really should be talking to. It's very uncomfortable, and a good attorney knows that. An opposing attorney will position himself in a courtroom in such a way that the back of the witness is to the jury. Witnesses need to be trained to turn around and talk to the jury." Rice also encourages witnesses to use the courtroom as a classroom, to act as teachers. "We let them get up, move around, use the exhibits, mix it up so it doesn't get dull." Joseph Hirschhorn agrees. "We absolutely ascribe to two things, the KISS principle—Keep It Simple, Stupid—and make it interesting. Jury duty is bad enough for these people."

In addition to prepping the witnesses, adding drama, and getting the story straight, consultants also put the case's lawyers under the microscope. "You're looking for juror reactions to how they phrase questions, the effectiveness of the opening and closing statements," explains Rice, "how aggressive they can be without eliciting sympathy or going against the jury's idea of fair play—and jurors *will* give you an idea of where that line is, how well you can walk it, and at what point you should step over it."

Mock jurors also give feedback on the "fit" of a particular lawyer to a particular case. Dick Sweetnam offers an example of a case he represented when he was IBM's corporate counsel for general litigation. "We used a young lawyer as chief counsel, and the mock jury told us they thought he had to be an actor, that IBM would never use someone that young to try an age-discrimination suit." As a result, IBM changed

The murder trial of O.J. Simpson (near right) helped focus national attention on the process of juror selection. Lyle Menendez's tearful testimony (far right) of the beatings he and his brother allegedly received from their parents represents a classic case of the "abuse excuse." The trial ended in hung juries.

its strategy. Sweetnam says he ended up going to trial "with all my white hair, so there was a little balance sitting at the table."

Deliberations

Mock juries also shed some light on the dynamics of deliberations—real jury deliberations are off-limits to everyone but the jurors themselves and court personnel. Research has found that a typical jury includes some people who dominate the discussion, and some people who don't speak up at all. Foremen or forewomen tend to be those of the highest social status.

According to Robert Gordon, Ph.D., a psychologist who is also a lawyer and the director of the Wilmington Institute of Trial and Settlement, a Dallas, Texas, think tank, "alliances often form among certain jurors to campaign for a particular vote." Here, also, dominant personalities rule.

During deliberations, research shows that 50 percent of the time is spent by jurors talking about themselves. "They will say, 'This is just like when I signed my lease,' or, 'This is just like my aunt who bought a house.' They're going to look at the crime and the evidence in terms of their own experiences," explains Joseph Rice.

No Crystal Ball

Observing how a mock jury reacts to evidence, and predicting how a real jury will decide on the evidence, are, however, two different things, and trial consultants will not claim to have a crystal ball.

Proponents of their services argue that the end result of all the primping, polishing,

electronic monitoring, and research is simply improved communication in the courtroom, which can only be good for jurors.

Opponents, most notably Stephen J. Adler, author of *The Jury: Trial and Error in the American Courtroom*, argue that the end result of all the fancy footwork is a jury system that is being blatantly manipulated, corrupting the concept that real people from all walks of life will rise to the occasion to do justice.

In rebuttal, trial consultants say that that point of view is based on the premise that the system starts out fair. As Joseph Hirschhorn puts it, "In most of the cases we get involved in, the dice are already loaded against our client—there's a presumption of guilt, not innocence." And, perhaps more to the point, adds Karen Jo Koonan, "It's an advocacy system; each side is trying to win. That's what capitalism is all about."

Although lawyers are increasingly seeking their services, the jury on the effectiveness of trial consultants still seems to be out. As Roxanne Barton Conlin puts it, "Do they work? I don't know; there's no way to find out." Why does she use them? "For the same reason I do lots of stuff—I don't want to leave any stone unturned."

Trial consultants are merely the latest wrinkle in a debate that has gone on since trial by jury became an American right. Are juries beacons of democracy, or just panels of 12 people of average ignorance? The debate goes on. But as Alan Dershowitz puts it in *The Abuse Excuse*, "The jury continues to be the worst system for doing justice except for all the others." ◇

Just Part of the Gang

by Erin Hynes

Would you join a club that required you to be beaten up as part of your initiation? Or that multiplied your chances of being imprisoned or killed before you reach adulthood?

For most people, these are ridiculous questions. But thousands of young people eagerly say yes, and join gangs in their neighborhoods and schools. Exact figures are hard to come by—gang members do not typically answer surveys—so most reports come from police departments. One extensive study, made in 1989 by the U.S. Office of Juvenile Justice and Delinquency Prevention, found nearly 1,500 criminal gangs in 35 cities. In Los Angeles, California, the survey reported 26,000 gang members; in Chicago, Illinois, 12,000.

A Violent Life

If your idea of a contemporary gang looks like a scene from *West Side Story*, you're in for a jolt. "In recent years, gangs have gone from being social to being more criminal," says Lieutenant Duane McNeill of the Austin (Texas) Police Department's Gang Suppression Unit. "It used to be that kids from the same ethnic group hooked up to hang out on the street corner or to drink. Now they join to traffic in drugs or firearms, to fence stolen goods, or to sell stolen cars."

The increase in criminal activity over the past decade has made gangs more dangerous for members and nonmembers alike. In the early 1970s, few homicides in the United States were attributed to gangs. But between 1985 and 1989 in Los Angeles alone, there were more than 1,500 gang-related murders. The ease with which teens can buy guns has compounded the problem: in 1989 guns were involved in 61 percent more homicides committed by 15- to 19-year-olds than in 1979.

In many gangs, being a member involves violence from the very beginning—at the time of initiation. "In some gangs the kids take a beating to show they're tough," says Anthony Borbon, a program consultant for the Community Youth Gang Services Project in Los Angeles. "In some, they submit to sexual acts. Or they could be required to go on a drive-by shooting, as a rider, driver, or shooter."

Most of the time, gang violence is directed at members of other gangs who may have infringed on the gang's illegal business or in retaliation for an attack on a member. Nonmembers may become victims of gang violence during drug deals or robberies, or if they somehow offend a gang member—perhaps by giving the member a "bad look" or by unknowingly wearing colors associated with a rival gang.

Sometimes violence is directed at youths within the gang itself. In Chicago, 11-year-old Robert Sandifer was executed by his gang after he killed a 14-year-old girl and shot two other teens. Police believe he was murdered because other gang members were afraid to hide him and feared he'd talk if arrested.

Sandifer's age indicates another change in gangs during the past two decades: they're attracting younger members. "Gangs heavily recruit kids when they're between 12 and 14 years old," says Borbon of the Community Youth Gang Services Project. "Some kids join as early as 10 years

of age." The young kids are used as lookouts or to deliver guns and drugs, because judges often are more lenient with them than with older teens or adults.

And gang members are staying involved longer than they used to, some into their 20s and early 30s. In the past, members would tend to outgrow the gang as they found jobs and started families. Today's gang members may stay on to become gang leaders, helping run the gang's illegal business. That longevity is especially common among members who have been imprisoned, both because they are valued for their toughness and knowledge of criminal practices and because fewer legitimate opportunities are open to them. "We're seeing multigenerational gangs," Borbon re-

> *Most young people who join gangs do so for the sense of belonging that membership provides.*

Today's gangs are considerably more violent than the ones portrayed in West Side Story (above). Back in the 1950s, gang members rarely used guns, and drug abuse was negligible.

ports. "Even older members who might not be as active still claim the philosophy of the gang."

According to Jack Carey, an assistant public defender in Chicago, another new trend is that girls are playing a more aggressive role in gangs than before. "Their role depends on the role of women in the ethnic group," Carey says. "But like other businesses, gangs are becoming a more equal-opportunity employer, especially if it looks like the girl can do the job as well as or better than a man. There are some things girls can do better, like run drugs into a prison or carry weapons, because they're less likely to be searched."

Normal Needs, Dangerously Fulfilled

Despite the risks of gang involvement, those who join do so eagerly. "Very rarely do kids join because they fear for their lives," Borbon says. "For every one who is coerced, there are five or six who want in."

Professionals in psychology and law enforcement agree that young people join gangs for much the same reason they join church youth groups, fraternities, and school clubs. As adolescents begin the transition to adulthood, they cling closely to their peers for a sense of belonging and to start the natural separation from their families. A report by the American Psychological Association (APA) Commission on Violence and Youth explains that kids join gangs to get the things all teens need: "a sense of connection, belonging, and self-definition." Says Assistant Public Defender Carey of Chicago: "It's part of the coming-of-age phenomenon. It's part of the rejection of social norms."

Like members of most youth organizations, gang members have ways of marking themselves, of distinguishing themselves from others. They have their own jargon

Los Angeles has a particularly severe gang problem, with street fights (left) and drive-by shootings having become relatively frequent occurrences. The police (above) have their hands full simply trying to maintain a modicum of control over the streets.

and style of dress. "Members know who is in the gang," says Carey, "by their tattoos, by the colors they wear, by the shoelaces or sweater they wear, by whether they turn their hat to the left or right, by hand signs and handshakes."

And, as in other organizations, members are expected to be loyal—many members consider the bonds with members to be as strong as family ties. And they are expected to conform—the group matters more than the individual. The gang code usually requires that members be honest with each other, share, and—of course—not squeal.

Deviation from the code can bring punishment. Carey tells of one 16-year-old Chicago girl who recently was beaten to death with baseball bats for shorting a fellow gang member on a drug deal.

Her slaying highlights the big difference between delinquent gangs and other groups that teens join—the violence. Why is the need to belong expressed so differently for some youths?

The APA's report on youth and violence suggests several reasons. Noting that 90 percent of gang members are ethnic minorities—primarily black or Hispanic—

As American as Jesse James

With the burst of media attention that gangs have been receiving in the past few years, it may seem like criminal bands—and their violence—are something new. But gangs have been part of American criminal history since Colonial times, when groups of thugs would ride the coach from Philadelphia to wreak havoc in New York City.

Some gang exploits have won a place in our folklore. Nearly everyone knows of Jesse and Frank James, whose outlaw band robbed banks and trains in Missouri in the mid- to late 1800s. During their 15 years of lawlessness, the James gang killed 16 people. Equally famous—and notorious—was the Wild Bunch, whose members included Butch Cassidy and Harry Longbaugh, the Sundance Kid.

While these famous outlaws terrorized the prairies, urban gangs of newly arrived immigrants did battle in the big cities. Irish criminal mobs dominated Lower Manhattan in the mid-1800s. These bands of muggers, thieves, and murderers had names that sound silly by today's standards, but their presence was no less fearsome than that of contemporary gangs. There were the Dead Rabbits, a slang term for a tough guy. And the Shirt Tails, who wore their shirts outside their pants. The Plug Uglies wore tall hats filled with

wool that they pulled down over their ears to protect their heads during fights. The Daybreak Boys, who did their work just before dawn, were responsible for 20 murders between 1850 and 1852. The Molly Maguires, a large gang of murderous Irish miners, virtually ran three Pennsylvania counties for 30 years, beating or killing those who dared oppose them.

Gangs continued to thrive after the Civil War, when New York's Whyos boasted 500 members. Only men who had already killed someone could join. The Whyos passed out a price list for their services: for $15, they'd "chaw an ear off." Murders started at $100.

After World War I, the Irish criminals faded while new immigrants from Italy took over gang crime. Italian mobsters Al Capone and John Torrio both grew up in Chicago slums, where they quickly figured out that fulfilling the middle and upper classes' craving for vice provided a better quality of life than laboring in the stockyards and factories.

In the past, as now, gangs were mostly made up of poor youths in minority groups who didn't have access to traditional paths to success. And back then, as now, gangs attracted youths by offering their members respect, status, and an identity they couldn't get individually.

The special signs and handshakes that allow gang members to recognize one another have the added benefit of creating a sense of camaraderie and exclusivity among the members.

or witnesses—come to see violence as a normal part of life. It cites a study of first and second graders in Washington, D.C., in which nearly half had seen muggings, and a third had seen shootings. Children exposed to violence often come to believe that violence is the way to solve their problems; as a result, once they start school, their aggressive behavior can interfere with learning and making friends. Studies have indicated that other factors may also contribute to aggressiveness, including low birth weight, exposure to lead, head trauma, fetal alcohol syndrome, and attention deficit hyperactivity disorder.

Another factor, says the report, is the acceptance of violent images in film and on television. "There is absolutely no doubt," says the report, "that higher levels of viewing violence on television are correlated with increased acceptance of aggressive attitudes and increased aggressive behavior."

Family and Neighborhood

The report also attributes gang involvement to the breakdown of the family, saying that the "lack of parental supervision is one of the strongest predictors of the development of conduct problems and delinquency." Many gang members come from households headed by a single parent, usually the mother. These single parents are

from low-income areas, the report says, "Part of the explanation for the prevalence of gang membership in these communities may lie in the stressful environment of poverty, unemployment, and economic and social inequality in which these ethnic minority youth live. These stressful conditions may limit youth's access to positive means of meeting developmental needs."

The report points out that children who grow up around violence—either as victims

Some gangs have sought to improve their image by promoting positive values to their peers. In 1993, two Los Angeles gangs put aside their rivalries and recorded a music video titled "Bangin' on Wax."

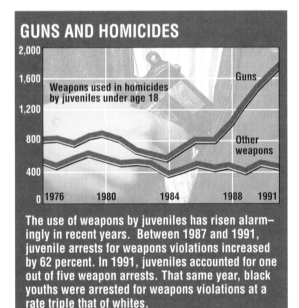

GUNS AND HOMICIDES

Weapons used in homicides by juveniles under age 18

Guns

Other weapons

The use of weapons by juveniles has risen alarm-ingly in recent years. Between 1987 and 1991, juvenile arrests for weapons violations increased by 62 percent. In 1991, juveniles accounted for one out of five weapon arrests. That same year, black youths were arrested for weapons violations at a rate triple that of whites.

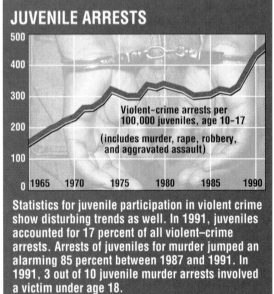

JUVENILE ARRESTS

Violent-crime arrests per 100,000 juveniles, age 10–17

(includes murder, rape, robbery, and aggravated assault)

Statistics for juvenile participation in violent crime show disturbing trends as well. In 1991, juveniles accounted for 17 percent of all violent-crime arrests. Arrests of juveniles for murder jumped an alarming 85 percent between 1987 and 1991. In 1991, 3 out of 10 juvenile murder arrests involved a victim under age 18.

typically beset by problems of their own—they may be alcoholic or drug-dependent, or lack parenting skills. Or they may have to work long hours to make ends meet, and, being unable to afford day care, may leave children to care for themselves or in the care of older siblings.

In low-income neighborhoods, institu-tions that usually provide control—neighbors, the police, churches, and schools—have less influence than in the past. These forces are especially weak in unstable neighborhoods with overcrowded, substandard housing, where new ethnic groups are moving in while long-term resi-dents move out. In these areas, adolescents are most at risk of joining gangs.

Furthermore, as children reach their teens, they may become aware that they have fewer things than other people have, and little opportunity to make up the dif-ference. Under these conditions, teens may be more likely to turn to violence.

For many teens, belonging to a gang that deals in drugs, guns, or car parts gives them the chance to make money and have social status; the violence just comes with the job. "When you can make $700 to $1,000 a day tax-free without a high school diploma, and your alternative is working at a fast-food restaurant for minimum wage, it

has a certain amount of appeal," explains Lieutenant McNeill of the Austin Police De-partment. "They don't look at the end re-sult: that they could end up dead or disabled. They can see a friend get shot and feel bad about it, but the bottom line is that it wasn't them. They be-lieve, like all teens do, that they are invincible."

Even if a gang isn't into organized crime, it may still be into violence. Some-times called "conflict gangs," these groups prove themselves by fighting. Success means having guts and being able to take pain, rather than having material things. Conflict gangs are more common in unstable neigh-borhoods that are too disorganized for or-ganized crime. They also attract youth who lack the intelligence and professionalism needed for organized crime.

While the ways of delinquent gangs seem abnormal to many people, many sociolo-gists contend that delinquent gang mem-bers are merely conforming to the values of their subculture, which differ from or dis-tort the norms of the middle and upper classes. Toughness is valued; for that rea-

Children who grow up around violence come to view violence as a normal way of life.

son, gang members with a prison record are admired. The ability to con people is also important—manipulation, not formal education, is considered "smartness."

Moreover, the gang subculture emphasizes fate, rather than planned effort. Material gain is something someone grabs, or stumbles upon, rather than achieves with steady work. Nor is it considered dishonest for otherwise law-abiding people to buy stolen goods at low prices. Hard work, whether in a school or job, is for those who are considered failures.

It is important to keep in mind that not all kids who grow up amid poverty, crime, and violence join delinquent gangs—the percentage is small. But violent crimes are three times as likely to be committed by gang members as by delinquents not affiliated with a gang.

Perhaps today's gang violence seems so new and shocking because it follows an unusual lull in crime. Throughout U.S. history, most criminals have been in the 14- to 24-year-old age group, so crime fluctuates as the population in that age group fluctuates. During the 1940s and 1950s, the youth population was unusually low. Crime started rising again starting in the 1960s, when the baby boomers born after World War II began coming of age.

Counteractive Measures
Although the population in general is now aging, the percentage of youths is highest in low-income areas, where young people are already at risk for delinquency. Psychologists, sociologists, and law-enforcement officials are experimenting with ways to control gangs, encourage gang members to quit, or prevent kids from joining in the first place.

Members of Common Ground (above), an anti-gang organization, help young people find healthy alternatives to gangs.

To control juvenile crime—including gang crime—some states are considering laws that are tougher on youthful offenders. The Texas legislature, for example, is evaluating bills that would lower the age at which a youth can be tried as an adult from 15 to 14, increase minimum sentences for violent crimes, allow youths as young as 16 to be executed, and give counties the right to institute curfews.

To stop gang violence before it reaches the courts, psychologists and community groups across the United States have set up programs to deter or prevent kids from joining gangs in the first place. The programs vary in their approaches, but usually have several things in common. First, they try to reach at-risk kids as early as possible, before problems develop. Second, they address the various problems that accompany adolescent aggressiveness, including difficulty learning and getting along with others. Finally, they try to involve the child's family, school, peers, and community.

Programs also are in place to help gang members quit their gangs. These, too, vary in their approach, but in general they try to teach young people constructive ways to satisfy their emotional needs. They focus on helping youths develop job skills and find nonviolent ways to handle disagreements. They often provide counseling for participants who are teenage parents, who have family problems, or who are drug-dependent. Anthony Borbon of the Community Youth Gang Services Project in Los Angeles says that programs to help young people quit gangs work if the participant is willing, but that there are not enough programs available. "Those who want out have to find their own way out," he admits. "And it's easier to get in than out." ◇

When HIV Hits Home

by Raymond L. Rigoglioso

Loretta H. didn't learn that her nephew Robert Rimer had AIDS until a year after he was diagnosed. She sensed that Robert, with whom she'd always had a close relationship, was avoiding her. "I was worried about him, but it never really occurred to me that AIDS was the problem," she recalls. Robert's illness was first identified in 1986. "Back then it was an instant death sentence," he says. "I was told I had nine months to live, and I was sick. I was distraught. It was too difficult to discuss right away." Robert finally told Loretta of his diagnosis when he felt he'd regained his strength.

More and more families are facing the kind of bad news that caused a painful si-

The families and friends of people with AIDS often need help coming to grips with the disease.

lence between Loretta and Robert. The Centers for Disease Control and Prevention (CDC) estimates that 1 million to 1.5 million people in the United States are infected with the human immunodeficiency virus (HIV), and increasing numbers of them are developing AIDS.

AIDS is most frequently diagnosed in relatively young people whose illness may profoundly alter the lives of their parents and loved ones. Although most research on the disease's social and emotional impact has centered on patients, the families of people with AIDS also need help coming to grips with the many aspects of this devastating illness.

A Shameful Dilemma

Families face many of the same predicaments as their HIV-positive relatives. Whom should I tell? Will my friends understand? Should I tell my boss? They may feel ashamed and afraid of revealing the diagnosis to friends and colleagues out of fear of rejection or even loss of a job.

Unlike other chronic, life-threatening illnesses, AIDS has a powerful stigma, primarily because the disease first struck homosexual men and intravenous drug users—two historically ostracized groups. A fear of contracting AIDS from casual contact compounds the stigma, although such transmission is virtually impossible. Approximately 99.5 percent of infection occurs through sexual intercourse, shared needles, or transmission from mother to fetus. The virus also could theoretically be spread through contact with saliva, urine, or feces, although no cases of such transmission have been officially documented.

Silence Is Not Golden

Gay men, who make up about 60 percent of people with AIDS in the United States, may face the added burden of revealing their homosexuality to parents when breaking the news of their diagnosis.

"Finding out a son is gay is sometimes more shocking to parents than finding out he has AIDS," says Mardi Fritz, Ph.D., a New York-based psychotherapist who leads grief and healing workshops across the country. Similarly, some parents have no idea their child is an intravenous drug user until they learn he or she has AIDS, Fritz adds.

Some people with AIDS hide the diagnosis from parents or family members because they are afraid of being rejected, or because the relationships are distant. Others try to protect the family from the news, which is a way of sparing themselves from the pain of dealing with AIDS, says psychiatrist Marshall Forstein, M.D., director of HIV Mental Health Services at Cambridge Hospital in Boston, Massachusetts, and instructor in psychiatry at Harvard Medical School in Cambridge, Massachusetts.

AIDS patients and their families should learn as much as possible about HIV and its course of action.

Parents cannot make an HIV-positive child discuss his or her feelings about the disease, but they can seek help for themselves from mental-health professionals, support groups, or other parents who are in the same situation. "Otherwise the isolation and the sense of bearing [AIDS] in silence is devastating," says Dr. Forstein. Indeed, many parents find that talking about their grief to compassionate friends or professionals helps ease the pain over time. Friends, in fact, often turn out to be more supportive and understanding than parents imagined.

Going Through Stages

Families of people with AIDS often feel a tremendous amount of anger—which is both normal and healthy. "I was mad. I hated everybody in the world who didn't have it," says Hilda G., describing her initial reaction to learning that her

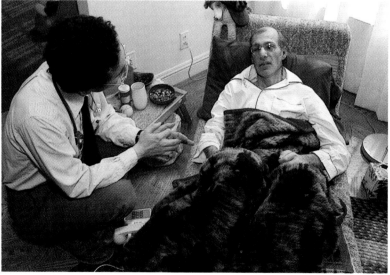

Victims of AIDS sometimes opt to stay home rather than be admitted to a hospital or, in the disease's final stages, enter a hospice. Even at home, professional medical attention is essential.

The shock parents feel upon learning of their child's HIV infection may be compounded by the simultaneous revelation that the child's lifestyle is substantially different than their own. Parental support at this fragile juncture is more essential than ever.

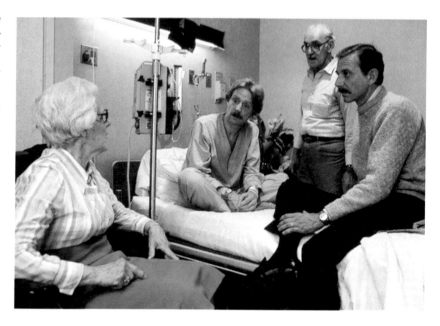

daughter Audrey had AIDS. "I didn't feel that she should get it. It wasn't fair."

Anger becomes decidedly unhealthy when it is directed toward the person with AIDS, his or her lover, homosexuals or drug users as a group, or health-care workers unable to cure a loved one.

Denial is also a common reaction to an AIDS diagnosis. "It's only human to deny illness until we can't deny it anymore," says Dr. Forstein. Denial becomes destructive when it prevents a parent from supporting the family member or acknowledging his or her illness. Guilt, another common reaction, causes parents to blame themselves

for their child's predicament—which, in reality, is something over which they likely had no control.

Depression and grieving are also common reactions to seeing a loved one struggle with AIDS. Parents may find themselves mourning the loss of a son or daughter who is still alive. "Seeing your child getting weaker and weaker, and not being able to

Never Too Old

If you think you are too old to worry about AIDS, think again. Men and women over the age of 50 account for 10 percent of all AIDS cases diagnosed each year. In the early 1980s, almost all of these cases were attributed to transfusions of contaminated blood or to homosexual contact. But HIV infection through heterosexual activity has been rising in older people since 1986. Today heterosexual transmission accounts for 1 out of 10 cases in the over-50 group.

A survey published in the *Archives of Internal Medicine* found that older Americans at risk of contracting AIDS were six times less likely to use condoms than a

comparison group of at-risk individuals in their 20s. "At risk" was defined as having multiple sexual partners, a sexual partner with a known HIV risk, or a blood transfusion between 1978 and 1984. The older group was five times less likely than the younger group to be tested for HIV. The survey was conducted by Ron Stall and Joe Catania, behavioral epidemiologists at the University of California in San Francisco.

The authors say they are not surprised by the results, mainly because AIDS-prevention messages have been geared almost exclusively to young people rather than to the general population.

stop it, is hard to take," says Fritz. "Sometimes families find death easier to face than illness."

Fritz discourages spouses from hiding their grief from each other, or from hiding their grief from other family members. "Society has taught us that we are not supposed to grieve," says Fritz. "The men aren't supposed to cry, and the women aren't supposed to cry too loud."

Family members sometimes cloister themselves behind closed doors, and then emerge as if nothing is wrong. This isolation can make the burden heavier than it needs to be, warns Fritz, who advises family members to grieve with each other, or with groups of other parents or siblings that have lost someone to AIDS. "Don't be with people who make you feel as if you must put on a smile," Fritz cautions.

For some AIDS patients, friends assume the support roles traditionally carried out by family. Parents are advised to comply with their child's wishes concerning his or her care.

So Close but So Far

The way a family manages an HIV diagnosis depends upon the dynamic that was present before the AIDS disclosure. It's no secret that good relationships tend to survive trauma better than strained ones. Un-

fortunately, many people with AIDS are already estranged from family members who reject their drug use or sexual orientation.

As difficult as it may be for some, says Fritz, parents of homosexual men should try to accept that their child is gay, that he may have a lover, and that "this person may mean as much to your son as your spouse does to you."

Fritz also advises parents to ask their son if he has designated a health-care power of attorney in the event that he is unable to make decisions about the use of drugs, life-support systems, or other medical technologies. A detailed advance directive, or living will, can help the person spell out what forms of medical intervention are—and are not—acceptable to him.

Many parents are shocked to learn at the hospital bed that their son has designated his lover to make these delicate decisions. "Parents must honor and treat that person as a spouse," says Fritz, who urges parents to put their son's wishes ahead of their own. If parents learn in advance that their son has designated a friend or lover, they will be better able to support that person when difficult calls must be made.

The Highs and the Lows

AIDS is a chronic disease marked by intermittent hospitalizations and periods of good health. Although, in the absence of treatment, the average time from infection with HIV to serious complications is 10 years, each individual's course is different. Early diagnosis and the availability of drugs that can help prevent opportunistic infections have enabled people to coexist with the HIV virus much longer than was possible in the past.

Learning about HIV through the many resources available to patients and their families can help take some of the fear and mystery out of the illness. "When I finally got my brain to work again, I decided I needed information," said Loretta H., after learning of her nephew's diagnosis. "I called the AIDS Action Committee and read everything I could get my hands on."

One of the most important things families will learn about AIDS is the unpre-

AIDS-education programs and continued medical research have combined to remove—at least to some extent—the stigma associated with AIDS. Nonetheless, far too many people are forced to cope with this devastating disease alone, estranged from family and friends.

dictability of the disease, which can be extremely stressful. "There is a lot of hopefulness along with hopelessness," says Laura Derman, a social worker who oversees home-support services at the AIDS Action Committee in Boston. This makes it especially difficult to plan care.

Where to Find Help

• The National AIDS Hotline provides referrals to local AIDS organizations as well as general information and education. Call 1-800-342-AIDS, 24 hours; 1-800-344-7432, Spanish; 1-800-243-7889, TDD, TTY.

• Parents, Families, and Friends of Lesbians and Gays (PFLAG) provides nationwide support services for families and caregivers of all people with AIDS, gay or straight. Callers will be referred to volunteers in their area. Call 202-638-4200, Mon.-Fri., 9:00 A.M. to 5:00 P.M.

• *The Caregiver's Companion*, a booklet with practical information for caregivers of people with AIDS, is available from Sigrid Burton, P.O. Box 276, Canal Station, New York, NY 10013; 212-226-0169. The cost is $10 plus $2.90 postage and handling.

Derman gives the example of a woman who moved her HIV-infected mother from California to Boston because the daughter believed the illness was in its final stages. The mother, after being hospitalized with pneumonia, eventually recovered and returned to California. "The daughter turned her life upside down and inside out planning for home care and rearranging her work schedule," says Derman.

Learning to Cope
Every family is different, and there is no "right" way to cope with AIDS. Dr. Forstein notes that families who appear to manage best are those who acknowledge the illness and discuss it directly; seek help for themselves; work through their guilt; reach a spiritual acceptance of AIDS without seeing it as a moral issue; don't blame the patient; support each other in difficult times; and respond to the AIDS-stricken person with love and acceptance, rather than fear or judgment.

Indeed, relatives who maintain an open dialogue with each other often find their lives enriched. Loretta, Robert's aunt, points to a conversation that had a profound effect on her life. "Robert came back from counseling and said that 'living with AIDS is what they're teaching, not dying with AIDS.' That's what turned his life around. That made a big impact on me."   ◇

HEALING THROUGH HYPNOSIS

by Sue Berkman

In a small, windowless room in a huge brick-faced building in Brooklyn, New York, a tall, dark-haired man with a clipped mustache is talking to a woman about cigarettes. He notes that women have attained equality with men in the number of cases of lung cancer and heart attacks, largely due to cigarette smoking. He mentions the increased risk of emphysema and upper-respiratory distress. He points out that, apart from the health problems, smoking is simply a nasty habit. It might appear to be an ordinary conversation—were it not for the fact that the woman's hand is raised toward the ceiling and hangs suspended in the air, as if attached to a string. The man pushes down on the woman's upraised hand, but her arm is as rigid as a steel shaft. Her eyes are closed. She makes no sound. She is in a deep hypnotic trance.

For years, stage hypnotists have performed such feats. But the tall man is no entertainer—he is a psychiatrist who has used hypnosis to help patients overcome such problems as physical pain, phobias, and unhealthy personal habits, or as an adjunct to traditional medicine in areas ranging from anesthesia to wart removal. He is also one of some 25,000 hypnotists in the United States who hold a degree in medicine, dentistry, or psychology, and are affiliated with reputable medical institutions. Those ranks are swelling: nearly 50 percent of graduate programs in clinical psychology, 40 percent of medical schools, and 35 percent of dental schools now offer courses or lectures on hypnosis.

Clinical Applications

Many of today's hypnotherapists were once skeptics about hypnosis until clinical evidence emerged showing that something very beneficial was going on. Compared to drugs and conventional treatments, hypnosis has several advantages. Performed properly, it is safe, has no side effects, can be used as often as needed, and allows the patient greater control. Here are some of the specific applications:

Pain. Cancer patients who use hypnotherapy to deaden sensations of pain often reduce their reliance on narcotics, which can suppress breathing and impair thinking processes. Hypnosis also eases the pain and anxiety connected with invasive cancer procedures, such as bone-marrow biopsies. It also helps to control the nausea and vomiting associated with chemotherapy—to the degree that many patients are willing to remain in treatment longer, and thus improve the odds of slowing or stopping the spread of their disease.

When performed properly, hypnosis is safe, has no side effects, and can be used as often as needed.

Anesthesia. Perhaps the best testimony to the power of hypnotic suggestion and hypnotic trance to block pain is its use as the sole means of anesthesia during surgical procedures, such as facial reconstruction, complicated tooth extractions, and cesarean sections. An increasing number of vaginal deliveries are performed today with hypnosis providing the only pain relief.

Immune response. The ability of individuals to increase or decrease the immune-system response by hypnotic suggestion is currently a "hot" area of study. Some investigators believe that it may be possible to teach subjects to target specific components of their immune systems for voluntary control. While results of

Austrian physician Franz Anton Mesmer laid the foundation from which the practice of modern hypnosis ultimately emerged. The word "mesmerize" is derived from his name.

experiments have been disappointing as often as encouraging, researchers remain optimistic because of the important implications for patients with AIDS and cancer.

Circulatory problems. Hypnosis has proven helpful in treating Raynaud's syndrome, a circulatory disorder characterized by cold fingers and toes. In a trance state, patients can visualize their blood vessels widening, thus increasing blood circulation to those areas.

Bleeding. Even moderately hypnotizable people seem to be capable of dramatic control of bleeding. Some subjects image their blood vessels as pipes with faucets that can be turned on and off, while others may picture clothespins pinching off the blood vessels. While this can be useful for small cuts,

it is especially beneficial for larger wounds, since the average time it takes to stop bleeding by using hypnosis may be reduced by half, and the quantity of blood lost is similarly decreased.

Burns. If used within two hours of a serious burn, hypnosis can actually limit the body's inflammatory reaction, and therefore the extent of the burn damage. In addition, hypnosis eases the pain that in itself can hinder healing.

Unwanted behaviors. The relaxed, suggestible state of hypnosis has proved useful in helping people overcome overeating, smoking, nail-biting, bed-wetting, teeth grinding, performance anxiety, and emotionally related sexual dysfunctions.

From Mesmer to Mainstream
In spite of the impressive list of accomplishments, hypnosis can't seem to shed its earlier reputation of mischief and mysticism. The first recorded use of hypnosis

To cure illness, Mesmer had patients grasp iron rods projecting from a magnetized tub while he made comments. The patients would then fall into convulsions, from which they emerged cured.

dates back to 1779 in Paris. There Austrian physician Franz (Friedrich) Anton Mesmer opened a clinic where he treated the sick with "animal magnetism"—a technique wherein Mesmer passed magnets over his patients' bodies with the goal of achieving a more harmonious distribution of the patient's magnetic fluid. Getting the patient into a trance state—mesmerized—was a key component of the treatment; in fact, animal magnetism was probably a classic example of what is today called the placebo effect.

In 1843 English physician Dr. James Braid coined the word "hypnosis" from *Hypnos*, the Greek God of Sleep, and used the technique to assist in painless surgery. His efforts won him few plaudits from his fellow physicians, who remained convinced that rendering patients totally unconscious with chloroform was a better idea, no matter how dangerous the drug might be.

Howard Hall, Ph.D., Psy.D., an assistant professor in the department of pediatrics at Case Western Reserve University and a psychologist at Rainbow Babies and Children's Hospital in Cleveland, Ohio, notes that Mesmer—along with physicians Ambroise Auguste Liébéault, Hippolyte Marie Bernheim, and Pierre Janet—used hypnosis as a psychological approach to curing physical and functional diseases. But, Dr. Hall notes, "modern medicine in the late 19th century, with its emphasis on precision medical instruments and therapeutic drugs, totally captured the attention of physicians, leaving them indifferent to psychological treatments."

Hypnosis further lost favor, says Dr. Hall, because interest turned toward the scientific investigation of the phenomenon of hypnosis itself, rather than on its healing uses. "The new goals of investigation were to define the nature of hypnosis, to identify hypnotizable individuals, and to elucidate what might or might not intensify a hypnotized state. The original focus of hypnosis

> *Most scientists think that hypnosis is a form of concentration so intense that even outside stimuli go unnoticed.*

on treating psychological and organic disease disappeared."

Finally, he adds, the use of hypnosis declined because there was no adequate theory to explain how such psychological factors could influence organic conditions. Physicians who demanded black-and-white answers simply refused to accept the gray areas of hypnotic healing.

How Does It Work?

Scientists have yet to come up with a definition of hypnosis that enjoys consensus. "Hypnosis is one area of medicine where clinical observations have left scientific research in the wake," says Elliot Wineburg, M.D., assistant clinical professor of psychiatry at Mount Sinai Medical Center in New York City. "We can show that it works, but we can't say how."

The most widely held hypothesis is that hypnosis is a form of intense concentration

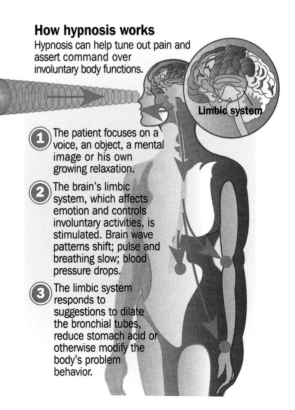

How hypnosis works

Hypnosis can help tune out pain and assert command over involuntary body functions.

Limbic system

1. The patient focuses on a voice, an object, a mental image or his own growing relaxation.

2. The brain's limbic system, which affects emotion and controls involuntary activities, is stimulated. Brain wave patterns shift; pulse and breathing slow; blood pressure drops.

3. The limbic system responds to suggestions to dilate the bronchial tubes, reduce stomach acid or otherwise modify the body's problem behavior.

that allows a person to ignore the bombardment of stimuli from the outside world, eliminating all that is extraneous or that detracts from a goal (stopping smoking, lowering blood pressure, or having an easy labor, for instance).

Others propose that hypnosis directly programs the subconscious mind through hypnotic suggestion, bypassing the conscious mind, which tends to garble information and misrepresent it to the subconscious.

Still others contend that hypnosis triggers certain chemical changes in the brain,

While a subject is hypnotized, his or her response to touch or other stimuli is considerably reduced, and often is blocked altogether. Hypnotized people are, nonetheless, very aware of their surroundings.

releasing neurotransmitters that set into motion a cascade of biological changes that culminate in the desired physical result. The ability of hypnosis to stimulate the release of natural painkilling substances called endorphins, for example, would account for its anesthetic or painkilling properties.

Whatever the preferred definition, all researchers agree on one point: hypnosis is *not* the same state as sleep. "If anything, it is the exact opposite," says Dr. Hall. "You

are often *more* alert and aware than in the normal state." Indeed, a person in a hypnotic trance shows none of the physiological signs of sleep. Breathing, pulse rate—even brain-wave patterns—indicate that the person is very much awake.

Can everybody be hypnotized? Until recently, researchers maintained that about one-quarter of the population make very good subjects, half are moderate to fair, and another quarter are difficult to hypnotize and sometimes cannot be put into a trance by usual methods. Yet many experts contend that probably all human beings are capable of entering a trance—a belief informally supported by the phenomenon of "highway hypnosis," that common dreamlike state resulting from prolonged staring at unbroken stretches of road. Consequently, hypnotherapists working with patients will continue to experiment with many different methods to induce a hypnotic state if traditional ones don't work. This approach has taken some of the elitism away from the hypnosis. "People who are easily hypnotized may like to believe that they are part of a very select group, but most individuals can derive some positive relaxation effects from hypnosis," says Dr. Hall.

To predict just how easily a person will slip into a trance, hypnotherapists use the Hypnotic Induction Profile (HIP), devised in the early 1970s by Herbert H. Spiegel, M.D., one of the country's foremost authorities on hypnosis.

However, the key to successful hypnosis—which means not just the ability to enter a trance, but ultimately conquering the problem at hand—is motivation. "If a person comes to me and remarks, 'I'm here because my wife/husband/mother said that I should try this,' it probably won't work," says Dr. Wineburg.

Unlike authoritarian styles of the past, today's hypnotherapists use subtle suggestion. Most avoid using negative or aversion strategies, such as telling patients that cigarettes will make them violently ill. "Eventually an addicted smoker will find a way around the physical reactions," notes Dr. Wineburg. Most important, each strategy is tailored to the individual patient. For example, suggesting to a patient that her pain will be located at the tip of her little finger would be counterproductive for a pianist or a painter.

Is Hypnosis Safe?

In the movie *The Cabinet of Doctor Caligari*, the doctor hypnotizes a man. The man becomes his zombielike slave, locked up in a box during the day, released during the dark hours programmed to commit murder. Can a subject be rendered powerless, perhaps even to the point of being commanded to commit a crime? That may be a fascinating movie plot, but, thankfully, the facts are quite different. The hypnotized person has at least two ego fractions operating at once: a hypnotized part, on the center of the stage, doing what the hypnotist suggests; and an observing part, in the wings, monitoring what is going on—and quite capable of interrupting the hypnotic state if anything untoward is suggested.

Nor will a subject abstain from any act that is important to health and welfare. "I assure you," says Dr. Wineburg, "that if fire trucks roared onto the street below with firemen shouting, 'Fire!' you would terminate your trance automatically and be out of the window before me."

But what if—and this seems to be a common fear for patients—the therapist drops dead or in some other way leaves the subject in a state of suspended animation? Again the fear is unfounded. Says Dr. Wineburg: "If a person in a trance state is left alone, in time he or she will terminate the trance spontaneously or, at worst, pass into a normal period of sleep."

Most credible professionals in the field are quick to downplay any excessive claims about hypnosis, and point out that anyone looking for an answered prayer

Finding a Hypnotherapist

The American Medical Association endorsed hypnosis in 1958 as a medical technique. A few years later, the American Psychiatric Association and the American Psychological Association also endorsed it. Since hypnosis alone is not treatment, it is important for a patient to choose a doctor who is skilled in his or her original specialty—psychiatry, psychology, medicine, or dentistry—and who has expert training in clinical hypnosis.

Here are some guidelines for choosing a hypnotherapist:

Check credentials—the title "Hypnotist" or, worse, "Master Hypnotist" should be a red flag telling you to be wary.

Avoid large group-hypnosis sessions—it is virtually impossible for a hypnotist to assess hypnotizability and general health of an individual in a crowd.

Avoid guarantees—as long as human behavior is involved, it is impossible for anyone to predict absolute outcomes.

For a list of qualified therapists in your area, send a stamped, self-addressed envelope to:

American Society of Clinical Hypnosis, 2400 East Devon Avenue, Suite 218, Des Plaines, IL 60018; or

Society for Clinical and Experimental Hypnosis, 129-A Kings Park Drive, Liverpool, NY 13088.

should go elsewhere. While one may be able to recall a lost memory in a single session of hypnosis, it may take many weeks of hypnotherapy to deal with a serious weight problem. Unfortunately, there are armies of unscrupulous practitioners who make promises that probably won't be delivered, to patients who end up wasting not only money but time in finding effective therapy. "Hypnosis is not dangerous," says Dr. Wineburg. "A poor hypnotist is." ◇

Housecalls

by Robert Butterworth, Ph.D.

Q *I feel I could benefit greatly from counseling. Should I consult my family physician before seeing a psychologist or psychiatrist?*

A The link between medical care and mental illness was set up early, perhaps because some of the key figures in psychotherapy, such as Sigmund Freud, were physicians. Although the two areas need not go together, physical problems and mental problems can, and very often do, cause one another.

If you have any suspicion that your need for counseling might be interconnected with a physical problem, your personal physician may be the best place to start. Physicians are more knowledgeable these days about emotional problems, and more likely than they were in the past to suggest counseling when needed.

Some physicians may be able to provide you with an appropriate referral to a therapist of the right type. Other physicians may not. If you don't feel the need to see a doctor, look to other sources of referrals to counselors—your friends, school, or an employee-assistance program where you work.

Q *My brother claims that we were raised in a dysfunctional family. I think I had a very happy childhood. What exactly is meant by the term dysfunctional family?*

A The classic definition of a dysfunctional family is a family in which everyone is trying to communicate or wants to communicate, but no one is listening to each other. Words and outward behaviors in dysfunctional families often disguise people's inner feelings.

In a typical dysfunctional family, a great deal of pretending takes place. Family members have too much fear of one another and not enough trust. Because so much of this happens "behind the scenes"—that is, internally—a person growing up in a dysfunctional family may feel that, in many ways, his or her life was normal. Violence, use of drugs, and other self-destructive behaviors often take place within or as a result of dysfunctional households, but such dramatic manifestations of dysfunctionality are probably more the exception than the rule.

Therapists focus on helping members of dysfunctional families communicate with one another. They work to get people to talk and express their emotions, and to teach them how to do so in ways unlikely to make others feel upset.

Q *Is it true that one's concept of time changes with age? If so, why? It seems as though time passed much more slowly when I was a child.*

A We all know that time doesn't change, but one's sense of it does. Most people report that the older they get, the quicker the passage of time appears to be.

To experience time, one has to perceive change. Adults have a broader understanding of the world around them, observe more types of changes, and thus are more aware of change in the course of an hour, a day, or a year. Younger people don't have as long a history or as complex a set of goals dictating their thoughts. They tend to live more fully within the moment. An adult's thoughts reference the past and future much more often and in more-elaborate ways.

Q *Are unruly patients in mental hospitals still restrained in straitjackets? Are there more-humane methods of restraining an irrational person in an institutional setting?*

A For the most part, mental-health institutions have substituted chemical restraints for physical ones. That is, they use medicines such as tranquilizers to calm agitated or violent individuals.

Mental institutions have undergone significant reforms within the past several decades. Patients have more rights, and staff members are more highly trained. Straitjackets are illegal in many states. At the most, the majority of institutions will temporarily use restraining cuffs around the wrist and ankles to control individuals who may physically endanger themselves or others. Regulations dictate how long an institution can use these restraints, and require that other methods be applied to resolve the situation as soon as possible.

Q *I experience overwhelming anxiety every time I have to drive across a long bridge. I'm aware that my fear has no foundation in reality, but that knowledge doesn't seem to stave off my bridge-induced anxiety. Can you suggest a way that I might conquer this fear?*

A Your anxiety is an example of a phobia—a persistent, intense, and illogical fear. But knowing that your fear has no foundation will not resolve it.

If your fear is impairing your ability to function, you should find a therapist to help you overcome it. Alternatively, you may want to try books, tapes, or self-help groups that assist with the same goal. None of these sources will spend much time dwelling on why you have this fear.

Relaxation techniques seem to work best. These may involve deep breathing or hypnotic methods. Such an approach aims at "systematic desensitization"—in other words. progressively learning to pair the feared object or experience with a feeling of calm rather than fear. In your case, for example, you might start by relaxing with a mental image of a bridge, then while looking at pictures of bridges, then while driving near a bridge, then while going over a small bridge, and fi-nally while crossing a big one. If you try, you should be able to break the connection between anxiety and bridges.

Q *Does an alcoholic experience physical withdrawal symptoms when he or she stops drinking? Are they worse than the symptoms experienced by someone withdrawing from heroin?*

A Alcoholics experience profound physical and psychological withdrawal symptoms when they stop drinking. We tend to associate such symptoms much more with illicit, abused substances, such as heroin, in part because these drugs are illegal.

What people experience during withdrawal depends on the individual. During this period the body is detoxifying and in other ways adjusting to the absence of the drug. This often brings on intense cravings, physical and mental pain, hallucinations, and other symptoms. The longer and more heavily a person has abused a drug, the worse the withdrawal symptoms.

Alcohol tends to be a drug that people try to quit "cold turkey"—stopping its use altogether, all at once. This approach brings on the most intense type of withdrawal. Heroin addicts may wean themselves from heroin by using methadone or other drugs as an interim step to going clean, thus spreading the discomfort of withdrawal over a longer period of time.

Do you have a psychology question?
Send it to Editor, Health and Medicine Annual,
P.O. Box 90, Hawleyville, CT 06440-9990.

PRACTICAL NEWS TO USE

CONTENTS

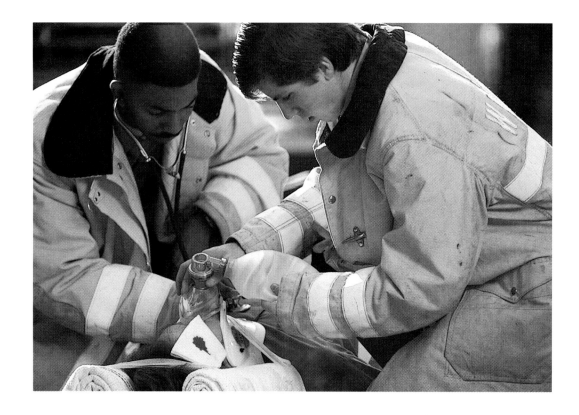

EMTs: Medical Care on the Move

by Preethi Krishnamurthy

A weary driver, nodding off at the wheel, is caught unawares as his car slides off the road and slams into a tree. The impact of the crash throws his head into the steering wheel and knocks him unconscious. Luckily for him, a bystander dials 911 on her cellular phone to report the accident. Within minutes an ambulance arrives on the scene, and two emergency medical technicians, or EMTs, jump into action. One EMT checks the victim's vital signs—pulse, respiratory rate, blood pressure, and body temperature—while the other bandages the driver's head to slow the loss of blood. Once the patient is assessed and stabilized, the EMTs place the bandaged man in the ambulance and

Emergency medical technicians, or EMTs, deliver the vital initial treatment to people injured in car accidents and other calamities that occur outside of hospitals.

roar off to the nearest hospital, sirens blaring and lights flashing.

Whether the emergency is a car accident, a heart attack, or a childbirth in progress,

EMTs represent the vital first line of defense in the chain of medical care. With sophisticated medical equipment in tow, EMTs assess situations, provide preliminary emergency treatment, and transport patients to the hospital, where doctors and nurses take over. As Suresh Dhumale, M.D., an emergency-room physician at Danbury Hospital in Danbury, Connecticut, notes, "Emergency medical technicians have afforded patients the opportunity to receive quality health care during their most critical time."

Chauffeurs No More

Given the crucial nature of such services, it may seem surprising that EMTs are a relatively new addition to the emergency medical field. Not so long ago, ambulance drivers were essentially chauffeurs who received little or no training in medical-rescue techniques. Only in the past two decades have EMTs established a firm foothold in the field of emergency medicine, largely through their work with fire and police departments, private ambulance companies, and hospitals. Today they are widely regarded as virtually indispensable, and most ambulances are staffed by teams of professional EMTs.

The growing need for qualified emergency medical technicians has in turn begotten a host of formal training programs. EMTs can now earn one of three levels of credentials: EMT-Basic, EMT-Intermediate, and EMT-Paramedic (see chart). Participants in these certificate programs must complete intensive clinical and classroom training and pass comprehensive exams.

The title EMT-Basic might suggest a very limited range of expertise, but people with such certification can perform a variety of life-support services. After completing some 100 hours of training, EMTs can perform cardiopulmonary resuscitation (CPR), administer oxygen, and immobilize fractures with splints and backboards. Personnel who undertake an additional 50 hours of training can earn the EMT-Intermediate certification. With this supplemental education, EMTs are capable of more-advanced trauma care. In particular, workers are trained to administer intravenous fluids, a treatment that can help stabilize patients who are weak or dehydrated or who have lost blood.

EMTs represent an absolutely vital first line of defense in the chain of medical care.

The highest level of training is the EMT-Paramedic. Paramedics must complete far-more-rigorous training—up to 2,000 hours—than other EMTs do. In return for such demanding and time-consuming study, paramedics are qualified to perform an array of lifesaving procedures. For example, paramedics can administer electrocardiograms (EKGs) and intravenous drugs to monitor and treat heart-attack victims. In addition, they can penetrate a patient's obstructed airway (and thus establish normal breathing) by performing a procedure called *intubation*, in which a long, narrow tube is inserted through the patient's nose into the trachea.

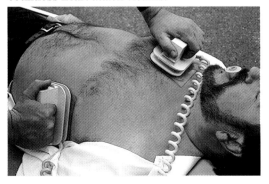

Technology plays an essential role for EMTs. The electric shock provided by a defibrillator, for instance, has helped EMTs save the lives of countless heart-attack victims.

Technology on the Move

The pivotal role that EMTs play in the field of emergency medical care rests largely with their capacity to transport patients rapidly and their ability to increase their patients' chances for survival. Comprehensive training, real-world experience, and a third essential component—technology—help EMTs fulfill this challenge.

The basic requirements for anyone seeking to become an emergency medical technician include good eyesight, or good corrected eyesight; color vision; the ability to lift and carry at least 100 pounds; and, perhaps most importantly, the capacity to work well and remain calm in high-pressure situations. Beyond that, potential EMTs require anywhere from 80 to 2,000 hours of training, depending on the level they wish to reach. The chart below includes the approximate training time required for each level, as well as the devices and techniques each level is permitted to use. Specific time requirements, as well as medical equipment and capabilities, may vary from state to state.

	Hours of Training	Permitted Equipment	Medical Capabilities
EMT-Basic	80 to 120 hours, plus 10 hours of an emergency-room internship	Backboards Suction devices Splints Oxygen delivery systems Stretchers	Clear airways Restore breathing Stop bleeding Treat for shock Administer oxygen Immobilize fractures Bandage wounds Assist in childbirth Treat heart-attack victims Give basic care to poison and burn victims
EMT-Intermediate	An additional 45 to 55 hours	All of the above Antishock garments Defibrillators	All of the above Administer intravenous fluids Assess and treat trauma patients more fully
EMT-Paramedic	750 to 2,000 hours	All of the above Electrocardiographic monitors (EKGs)	All of the above Administer intravenous drugs Perform endotracheal intubations Perform advanced life support and other complex procedures under the guidance of a physician

One of the more important pieces of equipment for an EMT is a device known as a defibrillator. With the aid of these devices, EMTs have saved the lives of thousands of heart-attack victims. The machine consists of two paddles, which, when attached to the victim's chest, administer an electrical shock that can induce the heart to beat in its normal rhythm. Old manual defibrillators were generally reserved for use by highly trained medical personnel, largely because they were difficult to use and required a considerable analysis of the patient's condition. Increasingly, these old devices have been replaced by semiautomatic defibrillators, which minimize the complexity of interpreting heart rhythms. These newer machines analyze the victim's cardiac patterns and provide the necessary shock only when required.

Another lifesaving technology available today is the telecommunications equipment used by EMTs to converse with physicians at a distance. Via radio equipment and cellular phones, hospital-based physicians can advise EMTs on what type of intervention to use, and can even guide EMTs through unusual or difficult procedures. New telemetry technology also allows EMTs to transmit complex medical data, such as a patient's EKG, to a hospital emergency room so doctors can offer more-useful advice to the EMTs and prepare properly for the incoming patient.

Improving Results

New technology has also shortened the arrival time of EMTs to the scene of an emergency. An important metric in the industry is average response time—the time between a phone call for emergency help and the EMTs' arrival at the crisis scene. When

just one minute can translate into the difference between life and death, response speed is crucial.

To win this vital race against time, new transportation methods are being implemented in many areas in order to speed the arrival of EMTs. Virtually every imaginable form of transportation—boats, jet planes, even customized golf carts—has been used by EMTs. Perhaps the most widespread al-

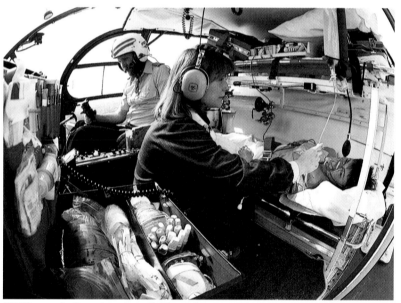

EMTs use helicopters to quickly arrive at remote emergency sites and then rapidly evacuate the injured or ill parties to a hospital. In urban areas, helicopters overfly traffic congestion to expedite EMT arrival at accident scenes.

ternative to the ambulance is the helicopter, which has gained particular prominence in isolated rural areas and in the nation's largest cities. Helicopters were first utilized by medical personnel during the Korean War—where parachuting medical technicians first hatched the term "para-medics." Helicopters were used even more extensively during the Vietnam War. In 1972 medical helicopters were used in the civilian arena for the first time, when an American hospital flew in a patient.

Since then, medical helicopters—staffed with teams of EMTs—have been utilized increasingly in rural areas where hospitals are few and far between. In some dense urban areas, where traffic conditions could seriously impede an ambulance's progress, elite teams of seasoned paramedics respond to serious cases of trauma or to highway accidents and other catastrophes.

Behind-the-scenes improvements in dispatching systems have also trimmed the response time of most emergency medical operations. Computers and advanced telecommunications technology can help track the location of an entire emergency staff—including the positions of para-

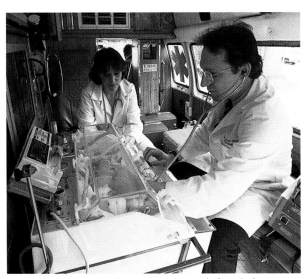

EMTs monitor a premature infant being transported by ambulance from one hospital to another. All EMTs are qualified to assist in childbirth.

medics, pediatric specialists, and burn-unit ambulances—and match these resources to incoming emergency calls. These dispatching systems improve the response time of an emergency medical system; they also help contain costs and deliver better care because expensive equipment and specially trained personnel are used only when truly needed.

The payoff for these systems and the implementation of new transportation methods is large time savings. In 1980 the response time averaged over 18 minutes for an ambulance in New York City—the site of the nation's busiest ambulance service. By 1994 the average response time in the city had dropped to 8.5 minutes. Such dramatic

time savings radically improve the survival rates for most emergency patients, including the victims of heart attacks and strokes.

Physical and Emotional Challenges

Whether utilizing modern technology in a critical medical situation or simply attending to a routine injury, EMTs experience a variety of on-the-job perils. The incidence of injury and emotional stress is far higher for EMTs than for most other professions.

Out on the front lines of emergency medicine, physical risks abound. EMTs often must drive swiftly through crowded city streets and treat patients in such dangerous environments as the debris of a building collapse or the aftermath of a gun battle. In addition to these rather dramatic dangers, EMTs also must protect themselves against a far more prosaic hazard: back injury. Forced to carry heavy equipment and even heavier patients up long flights of stairs, EMTs must use special precautions to avoid a debilitating back injury. Even with protective back braces, a healthy dose of caution, and training on how to carry heavy loads, serious injuries are quite common.

EMTs, like many other health-care professionals, operate in a vacillating emotional environment. They must balance the rewards of saving lives and helping people, with the strains of seeing people die and others suffer in pain. Some municipalities offer counseling sessions on critical-incident stress that enable EMTs to face the issue of death head-on, and hopefully to avoid long-term, destructive emotional consequences.

One topical social issue—the fear and threat of AIDS—has created a very real peril and another source of stress for EMTs. These professionals are at risk through unknowing—and often unavoidable—contact with bleeding patients who may be infected with human immunodeficiency virus (HIV), the virus that causes AIDS. Exposure to HIV-infected blood is one of the primary routes of transmission for the disease. In re-

EMTs balance the rewards of saving lives with the strains of seeing people suffer pain.

CPR: First Step to Saving Lives

While EMTs usually arrive within 10 minutes of the time they are called, this may be too late to save heart-attack victims and others whose breathing and pulse have stopped. (After roughly five minutes without the flow of oxygenated blood, brain cells begin to die.) To fill the gap of time between the call for help and the arrival of EMTs, more and more people are being trained in cardiopulmonary resuscitation (CPR), a potentially lifesaving procedure that can be performed by trained laypeople to help people whose respiratory and circulatory functions have suddenly ceased. CPR, originally developed in the 1950s at Johns Hopkins University in Baltimore, Maryland, was first used successfully in 1958 to save the life of a two-year-old child. Since then, millions of Americans have been trained in CPR. Some experts assert that as many as half of all cardiac-arrest victims could be saved if CPR were initiated immediately.

CPR consists of two alternating components: breathing into the victim's mouth in order to induce respiration, and compressing the victim's chest in order to induce circulation. The procedural steps are often remembered by the mnemonic ABC, for Airway, Breathing, and Circulation. Recent research has produced some minor changes in the recommended course of action. Single rescuers are now instructed to call the Emergency Medical Service before beginning CPR on an adult, whereas, prior to 1992, trainees were taught to provide one minute of CPR before calling for help. The ratio of chest compressions to breaths has also been recently altered to 15 compressions for every 2 breaths, although some experts are suggesting that a 10:2 ratio would be easier for people to remember. Ultimately, the issue of memory is an important one, because the easier the entire process of CPR is to remember, the more likely it is that people will use the procedure correctly to help save lives.

Despite the lifesaving potential of CPR, some difficulties persist. Even when administered correctly, CPR may cause broken ribs or other serious internal damage in the patient. Experts nevertheless are quick to emphasize that such injuries will heal, whereas a nonbreathing person without a pulse is sure to die within minutes in the absence of CPR. In the age of AIDS, trained civilians are often wary of

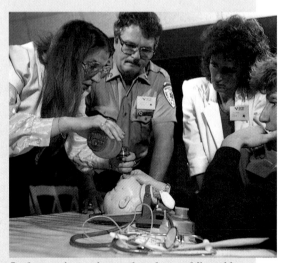

In the precious minutes that elapse while waiting for the arrival of EMTs, a person trained to perform CPR can save the life of a person whose breathing has stopped.

administering CPR to a stranger for fear that the victim could be infected with human immunodeficiency virus (HIV)—the virus that causes AIDS. Because HIV is transferred through bodily fluids, it is technically possible for someone with an open wound in his or her mouth to become infected with the deadly virus during mouth-to-mouth resuscitation. Although there have been no known cases of HIV transmission during CPR, experts suggest that rescuers with open mouth wounds use a facial shield.

For more on CPR and CPR certification, contact your local American Red Cross or American Heart Association chapter.

Inside a Modern Ambulance

One of the driving forces that has changed the face of emergency medicine is the modern ambulance. In the past, ambulances were essentially station wagons or vans that were used to shuttle patients to and from the hospital. Times have certainly changed. Today the ambulance reflects a generation of development in automotive engineering, medical technology, and telecommunications.

Ambulances are now available in a stunning array of sizes and sophistication. Some vehicles are as small as a motorized

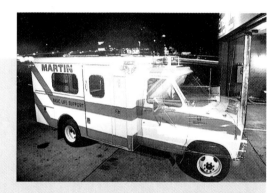

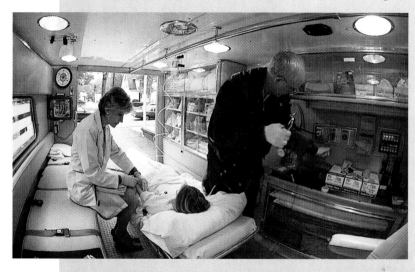

golf cart, while others are the size of an 18-wheel tractor-trailer. A thriving industry of ambulance manufacturers converts truck and van chassis into ambulances.

These vehicles are built to cater to the special demands of emergency medical technicians, with extra-stable suspensions, advanced radio equipment, high-voltage electrical systems, and oxygen storage and delivery systems.

Municipalities and private ambulance companies then equip these ambulances with a host of standard medical equipment, including stretchers, childbirth supplies, ventilators, and heart monitors. Some specialized ambulances carry artificial respirators, defibrillators, incubators, electric intravenous (IV) equipment, cellular phones, fax machines, and refrigerators. Other well-stocked ambulances are actually equipped with televisions and videocassette recorders (VCRs) so EMTs can refine and advance their training (or, perhaps, enjoy a movie) when they are not responding to an emergency call.

sponse, EMTs now don such protective gear as latex gloves and plastic goggles whenever possible.

Rewards of the Job

Though the career risks and strains of an EMT are greater than in most other professions, the rewards are also extraordinary. Few other jobs offer so many opportunities to save lives. EMTs are frequently thrust into situations in which someone's life or health is at stake—whether from a car wreck, a heart attack, or a sudden childbirth. Andres Rodriquez, an EMT with New York City's Emergency Medical Service, recalls a memorable situation in which he and a partner revived a heart-attack victim. Afterward Rodriguez received a letter from the gentleman, personally thanking the EMT for saving his life. Asked to appraise his career choice, Rodriquez replies: "I love this job. I wouldn't give it up."   ◇

HOUSEPLANTS:
Potions in a Pot?

by Marie Hofer

Plants soften a room and make it warm, friendly, and inviting. They symbolize friendship, love, and respect, and play into significant human events—weddings, holidays, death, illness, birthdays. People feel relaxed when they look at or tend their plants. Corporations install interior landscaping to increase worker productivity, decrease absenteeism, and improve morale. The presence of plants in dental and medical waiting rooms somehow has a reassuring effect on patients.

We have always believed that plants make us feel good. And now there is plenty of evidence that plants are every bit as good for us as we think they are.

People-Plant Relationships
The benefits derived from our botanical friends cover a range of psychological and physiological responses. While few studies have focused solely on houseplants, what has been learned so far points to  one salient fact: plants do indeed have an effect on people and their spaces.

In one study, a group of American astronauts and Soviet cosmonauts was asked to suggest ways in which the cramped and stressful interior of space vehicles could be improved. Surprisingly, the inclusion of plants and pictures of nature aboard space vehicles constituted one of the most frequent suggestions.

Back on Earth, plants seem to improve virtually any environment. When flowering plants were installed in the dining hall of a psychiatric hospital, for instance, both the behavior of schizophrenic patients and the attitudes of the staff improved. These positive changes could have been due to the new greenery, although such variables as personnel changes and medications likely played into the improved behavior.

Interestingly enough, plants elicit a relaxation response in people, even when the plants and people

Claims that houseplants provide direct health benefits remain a topic of much debate. Still, the distraction of working with plants, like most hobbies, provides a certain measure of relaxation.

are not sharing the same room. In one study, slides of heavily vegetated nature scenes and slides of urban scenes without vegetation were shown to a group of people. Participants not only reported feeling more relaxed and attentive when they viewed the nature slides, but electroencephalograms (EEGs) revealed the presence of alpha waves—brain activity associated with a relaxed state of mind.

Looking at plants can also speed recovery from stress. In 1979 researcher Roger Ulrich, Ph.D., showed that students who were feeling anxious after a final exam relaxed more quickly when they viewed slides of urban scenes with vegetation than when they saw pictures of urban scenes without vegetation.

And you may not even have to be aware of having seen the pictures of vegetation and nature in order to derive a positive effect. In a study at the National Aeronautics and Space Administration (NASA) that examined the work productivity and stress of astronauts in a space station, pictures of four different

scenes, including a savanna-type nature scene, were placed on the cabin bulkhead. Skin-conductance tests showed that the savanna scene was the most effective in relieving stress, even when the subjects were not aware of having looked at it.

To Your Good Health

The ability of plants to relax us is claimed to produce a variety of positive health effects. Two separate prison studies show that inmates with views of nature as opposed to prison buildings, yards, or other inmates report less often for sick call and have fewer stress-related health complaints. A 1984 study focused on gallbladder-surgery patients whose hospital-room windows offered views of either trees or a brick wall. The study found that patients who could see trees needed less pain medication, appeared to be calmer, and left the hospital sooner than those patients without the leafy view. Critics of these studies point out that other factors—staff changes, for instance—could cause similar effects.

Little Green Air Cleaners

In the 1980s, B. C. Wolverton, Ph.D., then a NASA scientist at the John C. Stennis Space Center in Picayune, Mississippi, started presenting his findings that houseplants are efficient fighters of indoor air pollution. Since then the research has continued, and the surrounding debate has sometimes grown intense.

Wolverton discovered that certain plants excel at removing the noxious fumes that emanate from the synthetic dyes, glues, and other materials found in particleboard, paint, varnishes, furnishings, carpeting, draperies, and plastics. Formaldehyde, benzene, and trichloroethylene are some of the undesirable chemicals that are known to be detoxified by certain plants.

Partly because of their different transpiration rates, plant species vary widely in their ability to neutralize particular chemicals, and some plants may do poorly with one chemical but very well with another. The lady palm *(Rhapis excelsa)*, for example, outpaces the king of hearts *(Homalomena)* in removing formaldehyde and ammonia, but falls behind the same plant in clearing the air of xylene.

Early on, the spider plant *(Chlorophytum comosum)* gained the distinction of being an excellent air purifier—a distinction based primarily on its being the first plant that Wolverton tested. Since then the spider plant has taken a backseat to other home greenery, such as palms and ferns. The Boston fern *(Nephrolepis exaltata)*, for example, removes more than three times as much formaldehyde from the air as the spider plant does.

The quantities of chemicals removed also vary considerably. An areca palm *(Chrysalidocarpus lutescens)* can clean more than 5 grams of acetone in 24 hours. A poinsettia

According to plant advocate B.C. Wolverton (right), houseplants are efficient fighters of indoor air pollution. Greenery in the workplace (below) is claimed to increase productivity and improve employee morale.

(Euphorbia pulcherrima), on the other hand, removes less than 3 milligrams of xylene in the same period.

Hungry Microbes

Part of the air-purifying work is done by the plant and the soil; primarily, though, the task is accomplished by microbes that live on the plant's roots. Houseplants evolved from vegetation that thrives in the subcanopy of the rain forest; such plants depend on microbes to digest organic matter on the forest floor and convert it into nutrients for the plant. Each species of plant fosters a distinctive type of microbial colony on its roots.

These special microbes are closely associated with their host plants. "We know we can wash these plants off, even sterilize them, and put them in a sterile medium," Wolverton says, "and eventually they produce the same microbes that they had when they were in the Amazon Basin or wherever they were." Apparently, according to Wolverton, each plant produces a nutrient solution that controls what type of microbes can grow on its roots.

How soil microbes are able to detoxify many synthetic chemicals has been determined by numerous microbiologists and soil scientists during the past 30 years. Wolverton points out that two natural chemicals derived from decaying vegetation—tannic acids and humic acids—that root microbes have been exposed to for eons have very complex organic structures. "I think the microbes see structures in these molecules that are similar to those found in air pollutants. Therefore, when plant root microbes come in contact with air-polluting chemicals, they recognize them as a substance they can attack."

Ongoing Debate

The application of Wolverton's work to real-world interiors has produced skepticism in some circles. His detractors point out that Wolverton's research has been conducted in small, sealed test chambers, and only on a few chemicals. While no one disputes the fact that plants do remove certain chemicals from the air in such a limited environment, many experts are reluctant to conclude that plants are the solution to indoor air pollution in the average home or office. For one thing, plants have not been shown to eliminate radon, tobacco smoke, or any other of the 100 to 200 different airborne contaminants that the Environmental Protection Agency (EPA) estimates are in the average American home.

The EPA refuses to endorse plants as air cleaners, pointing out that adequate ventilation is a far superior method of cleaning indoor air, and that hundreds of plants would be required to rid an affected home of its pollutants. "If the effect of plant-removal mechanisms is overwhelmed by common ventilation and air-exchange rates," an EPA Indoor Air director stated in a letter three years ago, "we question the practical utility of plants in actually improving indoor air quality." The EPA continues to stand behind the contents of that letter.

Wolverton likewise stands behind his work, and he continues to be in the forefront in this area of research. Most of Wolverton's early critics have faded away, he says. "We've accumulated enough data to answer them," he claims. A German report has since confirmed some of his work, and other researchers are building on it.

"If it works, it looks as though any interior plant will have an effect," says Virginia Lohr, Ph.D., associate professor of horticulture and landscape architecture at Washington State University in Pullman. "You can make the effect greater by changing to species that are more efficient than others, and by using the systems that Wolverton has designed. There's no reason to think that any interior plant in a room couldn't be

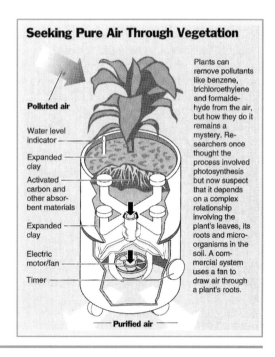

Seeking Pure Air Through Vegetation

Polluted air

Water level indicator

Expanded clay

Activated carbon and other absorbent materials

Expanded clay

Electric motor/fan

Timer

Purified air

Plants can remove pollutants like benzene, trichloroethylene and formaldehyde from the air, but how they do it remains a mystery. Researchers once thought the process involved photosynthesis but now suspect that it depends on a complex relationship involving the plant's leaves, its roots and microorganisms in the soil. A commercial system uses a fan to draw air through a plant's roots.

Removal Rates of Chemicals from Sealed Chamber[1]

PLANT	Xylene	CHEMICAL Formaldehyde	Ammonia
Azalea	168	617	984
Chrysanthemum	201	1,454	3,641
Creeping lilyturf	230	758	4,308
Flamingo lily	276	336	4,119
King of hearts	325	668	5,208
Lady palm	217	876	7,356
Parlor palm	223	660	2,453
Tulip	229	717	2,815
Weeping fig	271	940	1,480
White anthurium	268	939	1,269

[1]Measured in micrograms per hour.

doing the same thing, except perhaps a little less efficiently."

Wolverton applied the air-cleaning technology on a grander, public scale when he designed a sealed atrium in the Northeast Mississippi Community College math and science building in Booneville. In operation for over a year, the atrium houses plants that are fed by wastewater piped in from two staff bathrooms. Air that has been cleaned by the plants is then redirected through the building's central area. An addition to Wolverton's home has been functioning similarly for more than five years.

Still, the average home is a different story. "I'd have to have more information to believe [the effect of plants] is really significant," says Don Williams, Ph.D., a professor of ornamental horticulture at the University of Tennessee in Knoxville, "because most people would not have enough plants to make a lot of difference."

Furthermore, he says, "Plants don't go out and attract these molecules as if they were magnets. They take from the air that's adjacent to them." And then there's the dilution factor. "If you want to dehumidify all the air in your house, for example, [a dehumidifier] doesn't take all the moisture from one area; there's a constant diluting throughout the house.

"Plants give off oxygen, humidify, and trap dust. We feel comfortable living with them, they're not threatening to us, and maybe everything they do is good, but I'm not sure we're not giving them more credit than they deserve."

Ultimately, though, Williams says, "Plants can spend all day long cleaning the air in your home, and then you open the door, and you're back to square one."

Getting Rid of Dry Air

Relative humidity drops in the winter with the onset of cold weather, and drops even lower in the heated indoors. Not only is dry air generally uncomfortable, but it fosters colds and respiratory infections, and sometimes asthma and allergy attacks. For comfort and health, humidity levels between 30 and 60 percent are recommended.

According to research, notes Lohr, plants placed around the edges of a room can

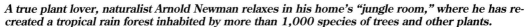

A true plant lover, naturalist Arnold Newman relaxes in his home's "jungle room," where he has recreated a tropical rain forest inhabited by more than 1,000 species of trees and other plants.

raise the humidity from 25 to 30 percent. "The room [in the study] was 35 cubic meters, and the plants filled 1.25 cubic meters," Lohr says, "so you knew there were plants, but it didn't look excessive."

Plants release moisture to the surrounding air by transpiration through their stomates (minute openings in the plant's outermost layer) and by evaporation from the potting soil and water catchers. The rate of water loss depends on the species, temperature, light, relative humidity, and the moisture content of the soil.

You can tell how rapidly a plant is transpiring by how much water you have to add to it. "Transpiration rates are the function of growing conditions of the plant," Lohr says. "If you don't need to water very often, you're not humidifying the air very much."

For building engineers and homeowners who worry that adding too many plants can create a never-ending increase in humidity, Lohr reassures them that plants are self-regulating. "The more humid the air is," Lohr says, "the less they'll transpire. If the air is already humid, they won't add that much more to it."

Mold and spore formation appear to be regulated, too, says Wolverton. "Houseplants evolved under the canopy of the tropical rain forest, where it's warm, dark, and damp," he says. "So nature had to have given them some means of fighting mold and bacteria that might overwhelm them. When we purposely brought the humidity up above 70 percent with plants, we found 55 to 60 percent fewer airborne microbes than in an isolated bedroom without plants where the humidity was 50 to 55 percent."

The Feel-Good Issue

As noted earlier, NASA originally studied plants for their potential to provide psychological benefits to astronauts during long-duration flights.

"I think the major part of what we attribute to psychological benefits is going to be physiological factors," says Wolverton. "We know that plants give off hundreds of chemicals in minute quanti-

Considering the relatively little care they require, houseplants add a great deal of warmth and beauty to virtually any room in the house.

ties. I think we're going to find that this good feeling I get when I sit in my tropical rain forest [sunroom] and do my reports is actually due to these trace levels of chemicals."

These chemicals, more correctly called phytochemicals, have been studied by researchers and observed, but not identified, by Wolverton.

While some phytochemicals are known, no one yet knows why plants give them off or what effects, if any, they have on humans. Or even if all of the effects are good. "One plant may be giving off something harmful," Wolverton hypothesizes. "And there may be 10 others that neutralize it.

"This whole research of plant and human interactions means that we're getting back to where we evolved," Wolverton says. "It's a whole new biological revolution that's emerging." ◇

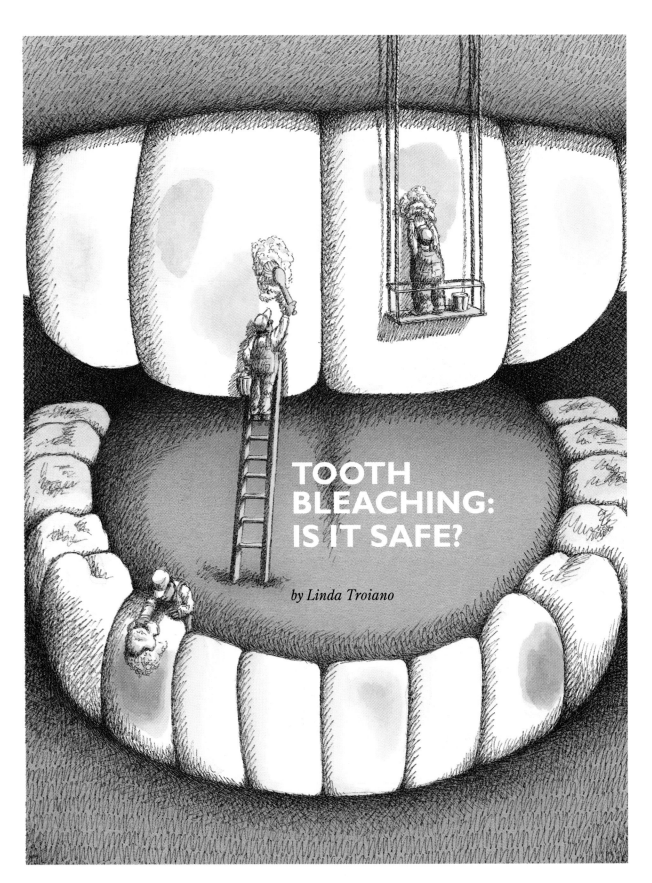

TOOTH BLEACHING: IS IT SAFE?

by Linda Troiano

Vigorous, youth-conscious Americans aren't about to let yellowish teeth and dingy smiles ruin their image. They are having their teeth lightened and brightened by dentists, or they're snapping up the do-it-yourself kits that have proliferated in drugstores across the country over the past several years.

Although many whitening products can be quite effective, some experts are concerned that people are using these preparations without professional supervision. Others worry that the chemicals have not been adequately scrutinized for harmful effects that may occur with long-term use. In fact, the Food and Drug Administration (FDA) is currently evaluating whether tooth bleaches should be classified as cosmetics or as drugs.

Dazzle from the Dentist

Dentists have several methods of restoring a smile's fading dazzle. If the pulp or nerve of a tooth dies due to injury or decay, root-canal therapy is usually in order. In this procedure the pulp is removed, and the resulting canal—now devoid of nerve tissue—is then filled and the tooth is capped. But if damage to the pulp has caused the tooth to change color (generally due to dried blood in the canal), a "walking bleach" technique can be used after the root canal is completed.

In this procedure a highly concentrated solution of 30 to 35 percent hydrogen peroxide is placed into the tooth and then sealed temporarily. Once every week or two, the patient returns to the dentist to have fresh peroxide put in. This continues until the tooth reaches a normal shade (after perhaps one to four trips), at which time the tooth can be permanently filled or capped.

To tackle stains from the outside of the tooth, patients can opt for "power" bleaching by the dentist or a "passive" bleaching system that can be done at home. In the dentist's office, the gums are protected with a dam, a plastic or rubber device with holes through which the teeth project. A peroxide solution is applied to the teeth, and activated with heat or a bright light. The patient must then sit for about 20 to 30 minutes to allow the peroxide to soak in and oxidize the color pigments of the teeth. "It is not painful, but it's not the most comfortable thing in the world either," admits Van B. Haywood, associate professor in the Department of Oral Rehabilitation at the School of Dentistry, Medical College of Georgia in Augusta.

A complete dental examination is essential before beginning any tooth-whitening treatments.

Usually the top six or eight teeth are done first, after which the bottom row is bleached. It may take one to six sessions per arch, although the treatment time can vary greatly because the permeability of enamel differs from person to person, says Sidney Markowitz, D.D.S., the president of the American Academy of Cosmetic Dentistry in Madison, Wisconsin. The cost of brightening teeth is equally unpredictable. On the

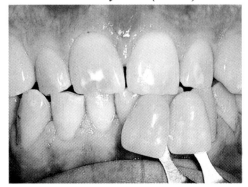

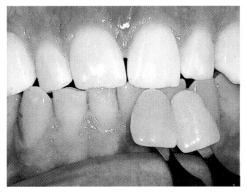

A variety of bleaching techniques is available to whiten dingy-looking teeth (below). Although results can vary, the outcome is truly remarkable in many cases (bottom).

How Teeth Become Discolored

Teeth are rarely as white as freshly fallen snow—they're more apt to have a yellow, brown, or gray cast. For a variety of reasons, though, teeth can darken or turn a surprising array of colors.

Staining of the surface enamel is a major reason teeth become discolored. In between cleanings, plaque forms on teeth. This sticky coating, consisting of saliva, bacteria, and food debris, is a prime cause of tooth decay, and it allows other substances to adhere to and sully a tooth's pearly glow. The top offenders are coffee, tea, and tobacco. Additional stainers include pigmented food and drink like blueberries and red wine, according to New York University College of Dentistry's Dr. John R. Calamia.

Such superficial stains are quite amenable to lightening, as are teeth that change color with the passing of time. Smiles tend to darken with age because the tooth's enamel facade gets a bit worn and translucent. When this happens, dentin, the hard yellowish tissue surrounding the pulp of a tooth, shows through the enamel and gives teeth a yellow or brown patina, explains the American Academy of Cosmetic Dentistry's Dr. Sidney Markowitz.

Other factors that turn teeth unwanted hues of the rainbow are more difficult to whitewash because they affect teeth in their formative stages. For example, when tetracycline is given to a pregnant woman or to children and preteens, "the drug is taken up by the developing buds of baby teeth and/or permanent teeth, and, as a result, they can erupt into the mouth in shades of blue, dark brown, gray, or green. Teeth may even come in with a colored band across them," says Van B. Haywood of the Medical College of Georgia's School of Dentistry.

Until a few years ago, tetracycline wasn't thought to have a darkening effect once adult teeth emerged. But reports now show that when teens or young adults take minocycline (a tetracycline derivative) to help clear acne, they may find that their teeth look grayish by the time they're 25 years old. "The antibiotic darkens the dentin inside teeth," Haywood explains.

Other causes of discolored teeth include traumatic injuries that damage the nerve of a tooth, decay, maldevelopment of dentin or enamel, or excessive fluoridation. Silver-amalgam fillings aren't the problem stainers they were 20 years ago. "That's because a varnish or bonding agent is put into the tooth before the silver filling to prevent it from making the tooth look gray. Today even the amalgam is lighter than it used to be," says Calamia.

average, the typical charge ranges from $250 to $1,000 for a row of teeth—depending on where the patient lives and who the dentist is. Given that tooth-whitening treatments virtually always represent a cosmetic procedure, most dental-insurance policies do not cover them.

Many dentists and patients greatly prefer passive bleaching. For this process the dentist makes a tray that resembles a streamlined version of an athletic mouth guard that is carefully customized to keep bleach away from gums and mouth. At home the patient fills the tray with a 10 percent carbamide peroxide gel and slips it on for one or two hours a day, or even overnight. After a week the patient checks in with the dentist to evaluate progress. This whitening option takes longer than the power system, but the cost may be as low as $500 for both upper and lower arches.

Whichever option is used, teeth tend to become sensitive to hot and cold food and beverages. "But once the treatment ends, so does that side effect," assures Haywood. In the past a liquid bleaching agent was used that irritated the mouth and throat. This problem is less likely to happen now that gels have been developed. Teeth may retain their sparkle for three years or more without a touch-up, depending on how often they are exposed to staining substances.

Three months is the longest amount of time a dentist will allow for either in-office or at-home lightening. If a desirable color isn't achieved by then, patients should consider bonding or veneers, which cover rather than remove stains, says John R. Calamia, D.M.D., director of computer-aided design in esthetic dentistry at New York University College of Dentistry in New York City. This is often the solution for stubborn tetracycline discolorations. In a study conducted last year, Haywood and his colleagues were sur-

Stains that develop while the teeth are in their formative stages are the most difficult to whiten.

prised to find that tetracycline stains lightened up when a bleaching tray was used every night for six months. Further research is in progress to see if this constitutes a good routine practice.

Tooth Bleaching at Home . . . Alone
About three years ago, over-the-counter (OTC) tooth-bleaching kits burst onto the market, and consumers were quick to scoop them up. One of these systems involves a three-step approach consisting of

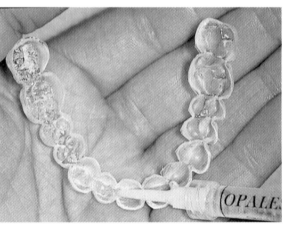

Standard to most tooth-whitening kits is a tray into which the bleaching agent is placed. The tray is then worn over the teeth for a set period of time.

a tooth-roughening acid solution, a bleaching agent, and a polishing cream. The other type of kit is a spin-off of the tray-bleaching devices dentists give their patients, complete with mouth guard and peroxide solution.

Almost as swiftly as these products appeared, questions surfaced regarding their safety. Some concerns center around the complete lack of professional monitoring before and during treatment of patients using OTC kits. Says Haywood: "Without an examination and X rays, there's no way people can tell if color changes are due to superficial stains or other conditions, such as an abscess or decay."

Other possible problems may arise from the one-size-fits-all trays that the patient must wear as part of the tooth-whitening treatment. A poor fit, for example, may keep

A Measure of Precaution

If your teeth have taken on a tinge that you would like to bleach out, take the cautious approach. If you're thinking about using an over-the-counter product, see your dentist first, advises John R. Calamia, D.M.D., of New York University College of Dentistry in New York City.

Here are some factors that must be considered:

• Not all tooth discolorations can be washed away with peroxide. Another procedure, such as bonding, might be more appropriate.

• The teeth should be professionally cleaned before any attempt at whitening.

• Hydrogen peroxide can boost the cancer-causing effects of other substances. Your dentist can discuss any possible risk factors you may have.

• Follow directions precisely. Do not increase the dosage or amount of time that you use the product.

• Advise your dentist if any irritation or sensitivity crops up during the bleaching process.

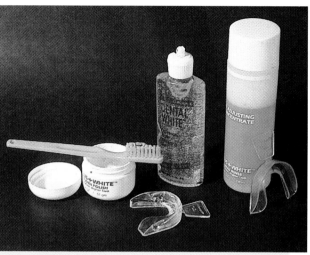

All home tooth-whitening kits work basically the same way: by holding hydrogen peroxide solution against the teeth.

For more information on tooth brightening, contact:

• American Dental Association
211 East Chicago Avenue
Chicago, Illinois 60611-2678.
800-621-8099
or

• American Academy of Cosmetic Dentistry
2711 Marshall Court
Madison, Wisconsin 53705
800-543-9220.

the mouth too far open and lead to jaw soreness. Also, notes Calamia, if the peroxide solution comes into contact with gums because of ill-fitting appliances, the combination can cause gum recession or otherwise irritate soft tissue in the mouth and throat.

Are Whiteners Drugs or Cosmetics?

Dentists have safely used peroxide solutions for decades. But the American Dental Association (ADA) began to worry when home bleaching and long hours of exposure to these chemicals became increasingly popular. According to the ADA's Council on Dental Therapeutics, some studies suggest that concentrated hydrogen peroxides may damage tooth pulp, produce irreversible cell changes, and enhance the effect of certain carcinogens, such as to-bacco. Also, some acidic products may damage enamel, dentin, and dental-restorative materials with regular use or misuse.

Because of these potential hazards, in 1991 the dental association asked the FDA to investigate the safety of tooth whiteners. In turn, the FDA decided to regulate the products as drugs (defined as substances that alter the structure or function of the body). Such a classification meant tooth bleaches could no longer be marketed until the manufacturers proved that the products were safe. Companies bristled at the ruling, and one sued the FDA. The FDA tabled the decision, and the products remain available. The ADA has now developed the published guidelines for manufacturers to submit products for ADA approval for safety and efficacy. ◇

DON'T TOUCH!

by Jenny Tesar

They're the villains of the plant world, ruining spring afternoons on the golf course, summer camp-outs at seaside sand dunes, autumn strolls through colorful woodlands, winter forays to gather firewood—indeed, almost any imaginable type of activity that takes people into the great outdoors. A careless encounter with one of these poisonous plants soon results in an allergic reaction called rhus dermatitis. Its symptoms: a red, blistery rash and a maddening itch.

Each year, millions of people suffer from rhus dermatitis, the consequences of coming in contact with poison ivy, poison oak, and poison sumac. Fortunately, medications are now available to relieve the itching and other symptoms. Even better, by taking a few simple cautionary measures, people can prevent or at least minimize contact with the plants, and hence the discomfort they cause.

Leaves of Three

Poison ivy is not an ivy, nor is poison oak an oak. Like poison sumac, they are members of genus *Toxicodendron* (formerly *Rhus*), in the cashew family, Anacardiaceae. The three species, all native to North America, contain the same oily resin, *urushiol*, a substance so potent that a droplet the size of a pinhead is sufficient to cause 500 cases of rhus dermatitis. Furthermore, urushiol retains its strength for years. Homeowners

cahontas. Smith was the first European to describe rhus dermatitis; he wrote that a plant that looked like English "Yvie . . . causeth redness, itchynge, and finally blysters," and thus "hath gotten itself an ill name."

Poison ivy is the most ubiquitous species of *Toxicodendron*, and the best advice a person can heed—advice that provides both a

Poison ivy, poison oak, and poison sumac are well-known poisonous-to-touch plants. Poison ivy (above), by far the most common of the three, turns a brilliant red in the fall. Two species of poison oak thrive in the United States: one in the East (right) and one in the West. Poison sumac (below) thrives in swampy areas in the eastern U.S.

means of identification and a valuable warning—is "leaflets three, let it be!" A poison-ivy leaf consists of three equal-sized leaflets, each 1 to 5 inches long. The leaves usually are bright, shiny green, but they can be dull or dark, and in autumn, they turn yellow, orange, and red. They may be rounded or pointed, and their margins may be smooth, lobed, or notched.

Another warning signal is the white, berrylike fruits. They develop in early summer, but often remain on the plants through winter. Birds feast on the fruits, then excrete the seeds in their droppings, thus acting as major dispersal agents for poison ivy.

Poison ivy grows in a wide variety of habitats, including gardens, pastures, roadsides, and woodlands. Typically it grows as a vine, traveling horizontally through grass or climbing up walls, fences, and trees. Sometimes it even takes the form of a shrub.

frequently develop rashes after handling gardening tools that touched *Toxicodendron* the previous summer; botanists have even developed rashes after handling century-old herbarium specimens of *Toxicodendron*.

Poison Ivy. This plant's common name can be traced back to Captain John Smith, the English explorer who helped found Jamestown, Virginia, and who claimed that his life was saved by the Indian princess Po-

Poison Oak. There are two species of poison oak. The western species grows as an upright shrub or a vine; it is abundant in forests, fields, and thickets west of the Sierra Nevada. The eastern species, which grows as a shrub, inhabits sandy areas and pine forests throughout the southeastern United States.

Like poison ivy the plants have leaves comprised of three leaflets. In shape the leaflets resemble oak leaves, hence the plants' common names—and a reason for rashes: many New Englanders newly resident to California and homesick for autumn foliage have gathered bouquets of brilliant-red-and-orange "oak" leaves to brighten their homes.

Poison Sumac. The saying "leaflets three" is no help when watching for poison sumac, since this plant's large compound leaves have anywhere from 7 to 13 leaflets. Native to eastern North America, it grows as a shrub or tree, generally at the edge of swamps and bogs—where solid footholds are few, and people have a tendency to grab onto any nearby branch to prevent slipping into the mud.

Poison sumac resembles, but is easy to distinguish from, the far more common non-poisonous staghorn and smooth sumacs. First, the latter usually have between 13 and 25 leaflets per leaf. Second, poison sumac has whitish flowers that give rise to hanging clusters of white fruits, while staghorn and smooth sumacs' greenish or yellowish flowers change to dense upright heads of reddish-brown fruits.

Catching an Itch

Urushiol can get onto a person's skin in any of three ways. The most common way is

One need not directly touch poison ivy or its kin to develop a rash. People frequently develop symptoms simply by playing with a pet whose fur has brushed against a poisonous plant.

through direct contact with a *Toxicodendron* plant. Urushiol is present throughout a *Toxicodendron*; therefore, touching any part of one of these plants, including roots and leafless vines, can result in a rash. And if fingers that touch the plant then touch earlobes, cheeks, and other parts of the body, they will leave behind deposits of urushiol, and the person will have not one but several rashes.

The second way to pick up urushiol is from a pet or object that has brushed against a *Toxicodendron*. A dog or cat that runs through poison ivy, clippers used to cut poison-sumac branches, shoes that have stepped on poison-oak vines—all become contaminated with urushiol. You can also pick up urushiol from another person by, for example, touching the hand that touched the poison ivy.

The third and potentially most hazardous way to contract urushiol is via smoke from burning *Toxicodendron*. You cannot pick up urushiol by standing near a *Toxicodendron*— the oil does not normally travel through air. But during a fire, droplets of urushiol are carried aloft on smoke particles. When the particles settle on a person's skin, rashes develop at the sites of contact. If the smoke is inhaled, rashes can develop in the lungs and respiratory passages. The consequences can be fatal: several years ago a couple in California inadvertently added poison-oak twigs to their campfire; they breathed the smoke, their lungs swelled, and they died.

People vary in their sensitivity to urushiol. An estimated 20 percent of the population appear to be immune to it. Of the remaining 80 percent, some experience only mild reactions, while others have severe reactions to even the slightest contact with urushiol. Additionally, people can become more or less sensitive over time. For example, a person who is immune when young may become allergic as he or she grows older.

Also, some parts of the body are more sensitive than others. The face, inner arms, and webbing between fingers and toes have thin skin, and thus are very susceptible to infection. The palms of the hands and soles of the feet have thicker skin, and are much less susceptible.

People usually do not react to urushiol until they've been exposed to it on several occasions. By then the body has formed antibodies in response to the urushiol. Once acquired, these antibodies are ready to attack future invasions; the formation of an itchy, blistery rash is the result of such an attack.

A rash generally develops within hours after urushiol's contact with the skin, though it may take a week or more to appear in people who are only mildly sensitive. Additionally, the speed at which urushiol is absorbed depends on skin thickness. Thus, it takes longer for a rash to develop on the palms than on the webbing between fingers.

Blisters can grow quite large and begin to weep, or ooze serum. This does not make a person contagious, nor can it spread the rash to other parts of the body; the serum contains no urushiol, and thus is harmless.

> *People can avoid contact with poison ivy by recalling the old adage, "leaflets three, let it be."*

Taking Out the Itch

If you're a victim of rhus dermatitis, here are some steps you can take to relieve pain and itching. Several times a day, rinse the infected area with cool or lukewarm compresses, using a mild vinegar solution (about 1 tablespoon of vinegar per gallon of water). Dry the skin, then apply a nonprescription (over-the-counter) hydrocortisone cream or anesthetic anti-itching cream. Nonprescription oral antihistamines will also relieve itching.

For severe cases, it's advisable to see a physician, who can prescribe topical or oral corticosteroids, such as prednisone. These medications can be extremely effective, especially if their use begins in the early stages of the rash.

Don't scratch! Although scratching won't spread the rash, it can lead to the development of secondary bacterial infections, which could be worse than the rash. If signs of infection develop, gently wash with soap or a soap substitute containing hexachlorophene, then apply an ointment containing neomycin and bacitracin. Repeat three times daily. If no improvement in the rash is apparent within two or three days, see a physician.

Get a Goat

It may not be practical in cities and suburbs, but rural folk faced with large expanses of poison ivy or poison oak might consider keeping a goat or two. Goats find these plants mighty tasty, and they can eat and eat without harming themselves. But keep an eye on the critters—once they plow through the *Toxicodendron*, they'll start devouring plants you'd prefer to cultivate.

Nettlesome Nettles

It may take a few hours or even several days before people begin to see symptoms of an inadvertent brush with poison ivy, oak, or sumac. But nudging stinging nettles results in instant pain. Native to Eurasia, stinging nettles are now common throughout much of North America, appearing along roadsides, in vacant lots, and at the edge of damp woods. They are 3 to 7 feet tall, with erect stems and egg-shaped to heart-shaped leaves.

The stems and leaves are covered with long, needle-sharp bristles. Each bristle has a bulbous base filled with a potent mix of irritants. As bristles puncture and break off in a person's skin, the toxins are released, causing an intense burning sensation, itching, and reddening of the skin. In severe cases, victims may feel faint or even go into shock. Generally, however, symptoms disappear within a few hours.

Victims should use tweezers to remove large bristles; small ones can be removed by pressing sticky tape onto the skin, then peeling the tape off. Itching can be re-

lieved by rinsing affected areas in cool water or treating the areas with hydrocortisone cream; oral antihistamines also will relieve itching.

Still other plants that can cause an allergic reaction if they brush against your skin are ragweed, primrose, scorpionweed, poison wood, wild parsnip, and various lawn and field grasses.

Prevention Is the Best Medicine

The best way to deal with *Toxicodendron* is to avoid it. Know what the plants look like, then keep out of their way. If you anticipate walking through or gardening in places where the plants grow, wear shoes, socks, long-sleeved shirts, gloves, and other protective clothing. Afterward, wipe off the shoes with alcohol, and wash the clothing in hot, soapy water. Similarly clean garden tools, walking sticks, picnic hampers, and anything else that may have come into contact with the plants.

To rid lawns and gardens of *Toxicodendron*, you can use an herbicide recommended by a local agricultural agent or garden center. Ideally, choose something that won't harm nearby plants and animals.

Poison oak and ivy also can be pulled out of the ground, preferably in late fall or early spring, when the vines are leafless—and

when it's cool enough for you to bundle up in lots of clothes! You may have to repeat this operation several times, since the plants have runner roots that may break as you pull on them. Remnants left in the ground will soon develop stems and leaves.

Never burn *Toxicodendron*! Do not take clippings or plants you pull up and add them to a compost pile, either. Bury the stuff, or put it in plastic bags, seal the bags, and take them to a nearby landfill.

If you suspect that you've been exposed to urushiol, wash your skin with plenty of cold water. Don't delay—the longer you wait, the more time the resin has to penetrate into your skin, and the more chances you have to inadvertently spread it around your body. Remember the words of a 17th-century writer: "Prevention is so much better than healing, because it saves the labor of being sick." ◇

IN-HOME TESTS

by Dixie Farley

In-home medical tests that can be purchased without a prescription have become a staple in many American homes. Perhaps the most common in-home device—the fever thermometer, used to determine body temperature—has been a common fixture in the medicine cabinet for decades. More recently a spate of new in-home tests have appeared on drugstore shelves. Some, like home blood-pressure monitors and a take-at-home blood-cholesterol test, help the patient stay focused on a potential medical problem, and may ultimately play a role in thwarting the development of heart and blood-vessel disorders. The benefits of in-home medical tests even extend to prenatal care. A positive result on a home pregnancy test, for instance, almost invariably encourages a woman to seek prompt medical attention.

One in-home test that has all but revolutionized the self-monitoring ability of diabetics is the home meter for testing blood-glucose (sugar) levels. In a matter of seconds, this device electronically analyzes a drop of blood from the finger; based on the reading, the diabetic can adjust his or her medicine, exercise, or diet.

"It's a cornerstone of modern diabetic therapy," says Steven Gutman, M.D., the acting director of the Food and Drug Administration's (FDA's) division of clinical laboratory devices, Center for Devices and Radiological Devices, the division of the FDA responsible for reviewing many in-home test devices.

One common feature of all in-home medical tests is their ability to provide a person with easy access to information about his or her own condition. In many cases, using these devices saves the patient from having to make frequent visits to the doctor or to a laboratory. Moreover, in-home testing helps provide people with an increased sense of control over their health, in partnership with their physician.

Monitoring and Markers

An over-the-counter (OTC) test performs at least one of three functions:

• Doctor-recommended monitoring (e.g., blood pressure, for hypertension; blood glucose, for diabetes control; ovulation, for fertility).

• Detecting markers for possible health conditions when there are no physical signs or symptoms (blood-cholesterol level, for high cholesterol; hidden [occult] blood in stool, for colon or rectal cancer).

• Detecting markers for specific conditions when there are physical signs or symptoms (a specific female hormone in urine after a missed period, for pregnancy).

For any in-home test to receive the approval of the FDA, the manufacturer must convince the agency not only that the test has value (results will benefit consumers), but also that consumers have the knowledge necessary to decide whether testing themselves is appropriate. According to Jur

Home Blood-Pressure Monitor

Strobos, M.D., J.D., director of the FDA's Policy Research Staff, "If the manufacturer does not show that consumers can make this judgment, we assume the test is for screening without preselecting patients. Then we ask, 'Is it appropriate for this use?'"

As might be expected, not all tests on the OTC market are equally useful. Philip Phillips, deputy director of the FDA's Office of Device Evaluation, notes that "Some OTC tests that have been marketed for many years may not be as useful or acceptable as many consumers believe." Eye charts, for example, have been sold for decades and are still found in some drugstores, but you shouldn't rely on them if you think you need eyeglasses or have not had a recent examination. People having eye problems should be examined by an eye-care professional, Phillips advises.

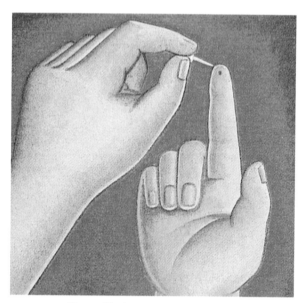
Home Cholesterol Gauge

Incorrect Results

The more recently approved in-home tests are as reliable as professional tests. Still, all tests can generate false positives (indicating someone has a condition that in fact the person does not have) or false negatives (a result that does not identify a condition that is in fact present)—particularly if the user doesn't follow directions.

For example, a positive result on a test for hidden blood in stool could reflect such factors as bleeding gums or last night's T-bone steak. Conversely, an untrained person may perform the test incorrectly, causing hidden blood in stool to go undetected. And in any case, laypeople should bear in mind that the presence of blood in stool does not necessarily mean a diagnosis of colon or rectal cancer.

A false negative can occur with a pregnancy test. When a urine sample has a certain level of human chorionic gonadotropin (HCG) hormone, the test device indicates a probable pregnancy. But pregnant women don't always produce the hormone at the same rate, so a woman could be pregnant but not yet producing enough hormone to prompt the signal from that particular test. Also, levels needed to trigger the signal vary among the different brands of home pregnancy tests. Thus, a test might indicate

no pregnancy in a woman who is in fact pregnant. If the woman continues certain practices, such as smoking, drinking alcoholic beverages, or taking certain medicines, she might risk her baby's health.

After a negative pregnancy test, therefore, a woman should wait the number of days suggested in the instructions, and then test again—making sure she is following the instructions properly. If the second test is negative and she is still not menstruating, she should see her doctor.

In other words, it can be risky for consumers to consider test results as a definite diagnosis. Professional follow-up is needed.

A doctor's diagnosis involves evaluation of the patient's medical history, a physical examination, often other tests, and sometimes consultation with other medical experts. Furthermore, unlike home testing, professional laboratories must meet quality standards, which provide additional reliability and uniformity to test results.

While no test—OTC or professional—is 100 percent accurate, Gutman says that, in a medical setting, "professional, trained people would be expected to interpret test results in a broader context."

The issue of interpreting false results was central to the FDA's decision not to grant OTC status to drugs-of-abuse tests, approved for prescription use only. Gutman says scientists are unsure how these tests

In-Home Dos and Don'ts

To use an in-home test safely and effectively, take these precautions:

• Check the expiration date. If the date is past, do not buy the product. Chemicals in an outdated test may no longer work properly, so the results may not be valid. Do not use a previously purchased test with an expired date.

• Do not leave a temperature-sensitive product in the car trunk or by a sunny car window in hot weather on the trip home from the store. Do not leave it in the car if you go elsewhere.

• Follow the package directions on where to store the product at home.

• Learn what the test is intended to do and what its limitations are. Remember: *No test is 100 percent accurate.*

• Read the insert to learn how to use the product. Review the instructions and pictures until you understand each step.

• Do not guess if something is unclear. Consult a pharmacist or physician, or check the instructions for an "800" number.

• Note special precautions, such as avoiding physical activity or certain foods and drugs before testing.

• Follow instructions exactly, including any specimen-collection process. Sequence is important. Never skip a step. If a step to check the test or calibrate an instrument is included, do it.

• When collecting a urine specimen with a container not supplied in a kit, wash the container thoroughly, and rinse out all soap traces—preferably with distilled water, which generally is purer than other bottled or tap water.

• When a step is timed, be precise. Use a watch that counts seconds.

• Note what to do if the results are positive, negative, or unclear.

• If you have questions about the test results or their implications, consult your doctor or other health professional.

• Keep sharp instruments or tests containing chemicals out of the reach of children. Promptly discard used materials.

Home Pregnancy Test

would affect someone who does not understand false positives and false negatives. Instead of helping people, such a test might hurt them.

"Drugs of abuse," he says, "have a real punch in terms of emotional impact. The harm from a slight error with, say, a cholesterol test is that the user might eat a piece of chocolate cake that he or she might otherwise not have. But a false-positive result in a test for drugs of abuse might lead to a person being fired or divorced, or a youngster being falsely accused."

Preventing Problems

A number of tests unavailable over the counter at pharmacies can be bought from medical-supply firms without a prescription.

"Consumers should be wary about buying these tests on their own," Gutman says. "Many such products, though nonprescription, are intended for use by trained professionals, or for home use only with medical guidance."

However, interpreting results of the newer OTC tests on pharmacy shelves should not be a problem for consumers. Before the FDA will approve OTC sales, test sponsors must prove that consumers can accurately interpret results. OTC tests also must be labeled with appropriate warnings. For instance, if a test is not for use by people with diabetes, a warning must state so.   ◇

TRACE YOUR FAMILY TREE

by Ruth Papazian

W hen it comes to health, the apple doesn't fall far from the family tree: research suggests that an astonishing number of diseases—from rare to common—have some sort of hereditary link.

That is why constructing a family health tree can offer lifesaving glimpses into your future. If you are at risk of inheriting a serious disease, you can get regular checkups to spot early symptoms and increase the chances for a cure. You may also want genetic counseling, to learn the risk of passing a disease on to your children.

Inherited Tendencies
Aside from health problems caused by accident or infectious disease, you can assume that most every disease in your family's background has some sort of genetic basis. These can be divided into two classes: *susceptibility diseases*, in which genes don't cause the problem, but do influence your risk of becoming ill; and *purely genetic diseases*, which people almost invariably develop if they inherit the requisite genes.

Susceptibility diseases typically occur later in life, and include major ailments such as heart disease, diabetes (especially the non-insulin-dependent type), and several types of cancer, including breast, lung, colorectal (colon and rectal), prostate, ovarian, and skin. The inherited tendency to develop a disease probably results from complex interactions among several genes. Also on the list of disorders with a genetic component: rheumatoid arthritis, allergies, asthma, glaucoma, Alzheimer's disease, osteoporosis, and behavioral and emotional problems including schizophrenia, alcoholism, and depression.

Genetics means much more than inheriting your father's hair color and your grandmother's smile. Genes can also exert a lifelong influence on your health. Older relatives are an invaluable resource when seeking information about the lifestyles and medical history of family members.

Although genes set the stage for these disorders, the actual illness is usually caused in part by some environmental factor—cigarette smoke in the case of lung cancer, for example, or high-fat diets in heart disease and non-insulin-dependent diabetes, as well as prostate, colorectal, and perhaps ovarian cancer. Luckily, people who know that a susceptibility disease lurks in their family tree may be able to control those nongenetic risk factors, or at least be on the alert for early symptoms.

For example, if your mother or sister developed breast cancer before menopause, your lifetime risk would be as great as one in three, versus one in nine for other women. (Early onset of any disease increases the probability that heredity played a role.) A family history of breast cancer means you should get annual mammograms beginning at age 35, plus frequent professional exams.

As for purely genetic diseases, there are more than 4,000—most of them rare—that result from defects in single genes. If you have such a disorder in your family tree, your chance of inheriting it depends on the nature of the gene responsible.

For instance, if one of your parents died of a heart attack before age 60, there is a

Testing for Risk

The genes responsible for more than 300 diseases, most of them rare, can now be identified through blood tests. In some cases, these tests detect the gene itself; in others, they identify DNA "markers" that suggest the gene is present. The following is a list of some of the more common diseases that have diagnostic blood tests:
- Cystic fibrosis
- Familial hypercholesterolemia
- Duchenne muscular dystrophy
- Fragile-X syndrome (the most common inherited form of mental retardation)
- Huntington's disease
- Neurofibromatosis (a nerve disease characterized by dozens of skin tumors all over the body)
- Retinoblastoma (an eye tumor that usually occurs in childhood)
- Sickle-cell anemia
- Tay-Sachs disease
- Thalassemia (a blood disorder that occurs most often in people of Mediterranean descent)
- Wilms' tumor (a malignant kidney tumor that usually occurs in childhood)

Source: *Heredity and Your Family's Health* by Aubrey Milunsky, M.D. (Johns Hopkins University Press, 1992)

one-in-five chance that he or she had familial hypercholesterolemia (an inherited extremely high cholesterol level); if so, there is a 50-50 chance you have it, too. The gene responsible for familial hypercholesterolemia is *dominant*: inherit a defective version from one parent, and you'll get the disease, even if your other parent gave you a normal copy.

A health tree with facts about illnesses that run in the family offers a peek into the future.

Familial hypercholesterolemia, which affects one in every 500 people, can clog arteries and lead to a heart attack at an early age. If you have a family history of heart disease, be sure to get your cholesterol level measured. Once detected, an abnormally high cholesterol level can often be controlled with a low-fat diet and cholesterol-lowering drugs.

Familial adenomatous polyposis, another inherited disorder, afflicts one in 8,000 people and almost always results in intestinal cancer. Other dominant diseases include Huntington's disease (the degenerative nervous-system disorder that killed singer Woody Guthrie), adult polycystic renal disease (a kidney disorder), and Marfan's syndrome (characterized by abnormally long limbs and heart problems). Diseases controlled by a dominant gene rarely skip a generation, so you've probably been spared if neither of your parents had the disease, even if a grandparent did.

Ethnic Influence
Fortunately, most purely hereditary diseases are *recessive*: that is, they afflict only those unlucky enough to inherit two copies of a defective gene—one from each parent. The most common of these recessive diseases seem to target certain ethnic groups.

For example, about one in 25 white Americans carries the gene for cystic fibrosis (CF), one of the most common lethal hereditary diseases (for those of northern European descent, the risk is somewhat higher). The gene defect in CF results in a thick, sticky mucus in the lungs; the mucus encourages severe respiratory infections.

A CF carrier—with one abnormal and one normal gene—will be healthy. But if someone with the gene marries another carrier, their offspring will have a one-in-four chance of inheriting two defective copies of the gene and being born with CF. Following the discovery in 1989 of the gene that causes CF, a blood test became available that can tell whether a person is a carrier and whether a couple's fetus will develop the disease.

Purely hereditary diseases (or disorders) that usually affect only men are called X-linked recessive diseases. The best known are hemophilia, color blindness, and Duchenne muscular dystrophy. An X-linked disorder is transmitted from mother to son by a gene on one of her two X chromosomes. Each son has a 50-50 chance of getting the disease from inheriting just a single

The family album can provide valuable insights into the family's medical history. Recent ancestors depicted in old photos sometimes bear discernible signs of inherited medical conditions.

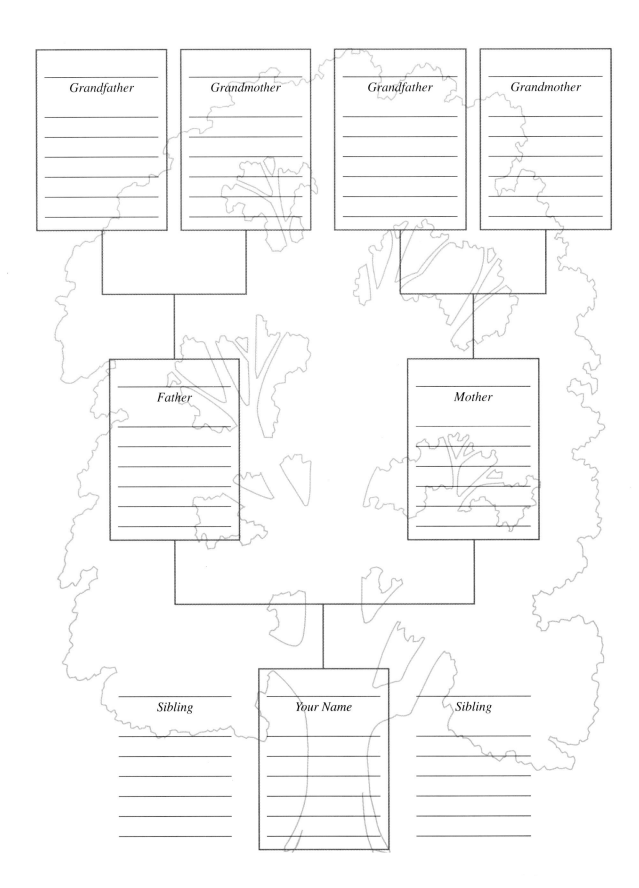

Grandfather

Grandmother

Grandfather

Grandmother

Father

Mother

Sibling

Your Name

Sibling

Family Roots

The risk of certain genetic diseases in specific races or ethnic groups.

Racial or ethnic background	Diseases	Carriers	Afflicted
Italian or Greek	Thalassemia	1 in 10	1 in 400
African	Sickle-cell anemia	1 in 12	1 in 650
Caucasian	Cystic fibrosis	1 in 25	1 in 2,500
Eastern or Central European Jewish (Ashkenazic), Cajun American, or French Canadian	Tay-Sachs disease*	1 in 30	1 in 3,600
Mediterranean Jewish (Sephardic) or Armenian	Familial Mediterranean fever**	1 in 45	1 in 8,000

*Neurological disorder invariably fatal within the first five years of life.
**Repeated bouts of fever and abdominal pain.

Adapted from *Choices, Not Changes: An Essential Guide to Heredity and Health*, © 1977 by Aubrey Milunsky, M.D. By permission of Little, Brown and Company.

copy of the recessive gene. Mom may be a healthy carrier, since her other X chromosome carries a normal copy of the gene, which masks the defective one. But her son, with his X chromosome paired with a Y from his father, isn't as lucky. A woman should suspect she may be a carrier of an X-linked disorder if the disease has shown up in a male relative. Virtually every month, researchers identify a gene linked to yet another hereditary disease; these findings are leading to increasing numbers of blood tests to identify people who carry these genes or who are destined to develop the diseases. To take advantage of these advances, you must first learn whether you or other family members are at risk of developing a hereditary disease.

Building the Tree

Gathering information about illnesses that run in your family is not as daunting as it may seem—especially if you ask relatives for help. Here is a guide for constructing your medical family tree:

1. Make a list of your first-degree relatives (parents, siblings, and children) and second-degree relatives (grandparents, aunts, and uncles). Adding more-peripheral branches to your tree usually isn't worthwhile: the more distant the relative, the less relevant his or her medical fate is to you (you and your second cousin, for example, inherit only about three percent of the same genes). A possible exception: when you need more evidence to confirm a pattern involving a serious health problem such as cancer or heart disease.

2. Construct your family tree, using the sample on the facing page as a guide. Your name and the names of your siblings go on the bottom row. On the row above, put the names of your parents, along with the names of their brothers and sisters. The names of all four grandparents go on the top line. It is customary to put male relatives in squares, and female ones in circles, and to indicate marriages by connecting relatives with horizontal lines.

3. Record the following information for each relative:

• *Date of birth, date of death, and cause of death.* If necessary, you can usually obtain this information from the death certificate. To get a copy, contact the department of vital records in the state where the relative lived. (Be sure to check the family Bible first—birth and death certificates are often tucked inside the covers.)

• *All known illnesses and major surgeries, including the age when they occurred.* This information could be more relevant than the cause of death—if an uncle had a heart attack at age 40, but died 20 years later

The hazardous occupation of an ancestor may have repercussions generations later. Exposure to radiation (above), for instance, can introduce a genetic abnormality into the family tree.

Heredity Risk

The estimated risk for some common disorders that are influenced by inherited genes, but not directly caused by them. Risks are for people with one parent who had the disease. The risk would be greater if a second parent or a sibling also had the disease.

Disease	General population	One parent with condition
	Lifetime risk (percent)	
Alcoholism	5	10 to 20
Alzheimer's disease	2 to 5	19
Asthma	4	26
Cancer, breast	11	22*
Cancer, colon	4	10
Cancer, ovarian	1	5
Cancer, uterine	3	9
Diabetes (non-insulin-dependent)	2	5 to 10
Duodenal ulcer	10	30
Glaucoma	2	4 to 16
Manic-depression	1	25
Migraine	5 to 10	45
Schizophrenia	1	8 to 18

*The risk may be three times as great as in the general population if the mother was premenopausal when her cancer was diagnosed.

©1992 by Consumers Union. Reprinted by permission from *Consumer Reports on Health*.

from an automobile accident, for example. Medical records are the most reliable sources for this information.

Ask relatives who are still living either to give you copies of their medical records or to sign a consent form allowing their doctors to give you this information. To obtain a deceased relative's records, contact the doctor or hospital that treated him or her; those names should be on the death certificate. You may have to provide a letter of consent from your relative's next of kin, as well as a copy of the death certificate.

• *Lifestyle factors that may have contributed to illness.* For instance, heart disease would be less of a genetic threat if you found that the uncle who suffered the heart attack at age 40 was a chain-smoker. Most every family has a self-appointed "historian" who is the repository of family lore. You may be able to learn about relatives' lifestyles by talking to that person.

• *Occupation (optional).* This information may be important if there were job-related factors (such as exposure to toxic chemicals) that may have contributed to illness, miscarriage, or birth defects.

• *Unusual physical characteristics.* Prominent features or chronic skin rashes could hint at certain medical conditions or birth defects (but you'll want to corroborate your hunches with medical records or other documents). Again the family historian may be a good source. Family photo albums can also be revealing: a grandmother's "dowager's hump," for example, probably indicates that she had osteoporosis.

As you research your family medical tree, be prepared for difficulties. Information may be unavailable (some family members may not cooperate, for example), or it may not exist (as when a child died and no diagnosis was ever made), or it may not be ac-

Genealogy: It's All in the Family

Tracing your medical family tree can open the door to the fascinating science of genealogy—the study of ancestry, or family lineage. Much like the research needed to find out your medical heritage, genealogical investigations usually begin by interviewing older relatives. And beyond the family's medical history, you will likely hear fascinating stories about your ancestors and their adventures. Here are some suggestions on what to ask older members of your family:

• *Family Facts:* Where were you and your parents born? What was your grandmother's maiden name? How many brothers and sisters did your grandparents have? Were you named after any relative? Where are your parents and grandparents buried? Did your relatives serve in the military? What kind of work did your parents and grandparents do?

• *Family Life:* What kind of house did you grow up in? How did your family celebrate holidays or other special occasions? How did your family spend the evenings? What were some of the games you played as a child? Do you remember any special foods that your family made?

Do you remember any special trips or vacations that your family took? Were there any special activities that the family enjoyed together?

• *Family Traits:* Are there any physical traits that members of the family share? Whom do you look like the most? Did anyone in the family have artistic or musical talents? Were there any outstanding athletes or scientists in the family? Do people in the family share some of the same habits or mannerisms?

• *Family Legends:* Was anyone in the family famous or infamous? Was anyone in the family present at a famous or historical event? Are there any family heirlooms? What is the history behind them? Does the family have any noble or royal ancestors? Did anyone in the family ever meet a famous historical figure?

• *Family Origins:* Who were the first people in the family to come to this country? Why did they leave the old country? What town did your family originally come from? Are there any relatives still living in the old homeland? How did you or your relatives earn a living when they first arrived here?

Alex Haley's Roots

Popular interest in family history jumped in the late 1970s when the American writer Alex Haley (1921–92) published the book *Roots*, the story of his search for his family's origins.

Haley's search spanned nine years and three continents. He began with stories told to him by his grandmother in Tennessee. She had spoken of their ancestor, "the African," who left his village one day to cut wood, was captured by slave traders, and was shipped to the United States. Haley searched libraries and courthouses for family records. He traveled to London, England, where he studied records of slave ships. And finally, he traveled to a small village in Africa, where the

village historian told him the story of Kunta Kinte—a boy who had been captured while cutting wood and, Haley believed, was his ancestor. Haley's book became a bestseller and was made into a television series that was watched by a record-setting 80 million viewers. It sparked a wave of interest in genealogy as others, like Haley, set out to find their roots.

Today genealogy is enjoying another surge of popularity. There is a growing interest in people's varied ethnic heritage. People are becoming increasingly curious about—and proud of—their background. And that has sent people scurrying to attics, libraries, cemeteries, and computers in search of their family histories.

curate (family legend, for example, may attribute an aunt's pregnancy loss to a miscarriage, when in fact she had an abortion).

A little tact goes a long way. Family members may not want to talk about sad events or what they consider to be the family's dirty laundry. A good approach: "My doctor is interested in Cousin Bobby's condition because it could affect the children I may have. Can you tell me about his problem so that we can calculate the risks?" Offer to share your completed tree with relatives, along with the opinions of medical or genetic experts you consult.

Interpreting the Tree

Now that you've constructed your family tree, here are some tips on interpreting it:

• Your tree's two most important "branches" are your mother and father: each gave you half your genetic inheritance, so their diseases will be most relevant to you and your siblings.

• The earlier a disease develops, the more likely that heredity played a role in it (except for ailments with obvious nongenetic causes such as infections).

• A disease that strikes two or more relatives at the same age is likely to be strongly influenced by heredity.

• A clustering of cases of the same disease on one side of the tree is more likely to suggest that genes play a strong role in causing it than a similar number of cases scattered on both sides. On the other hand, your risk of inheriting a purely hereditary disease like cystic fibrosis would actually be greater when it is present on both your mother's and father's side.

If you have questions about your family tree, you should show it to your doctor. If the doctor suspects a genetic problem, you will probably be referred to a genetic counselor, who can assess your risk of developing the diseases you are worried about, and of passing them on to a child. A counselor can also tell prospective parents if a fetus can be tested for conditions of concern.

Genetic counselors typically have a Master of Science degree in genetics and are certified by the American Board of Medical Genetics. Your family doctor, obstetrician,

For More Help

Free pamphlets

• *Genetic Counseling*, GC Pamphlet, March of Dimes, 1275 Mamaroneck Ave., White Plains, NY 10605

• *Genetic Counseling: Valuable Information for You and Your Family*, the National Society of Genetic Counselors, 233 Canterbury Dr., Wallingford, PA 19086-6617.

• *Where to Write for Vital Records*, Superintendent of Documents, U.S. Government Printing Office, Washington, DC 20402.

Books

• *Heredity and Your Family's Health* by Aubrey Milunsky, M.D. (Johns Hopkins University Press, 1992).

• *How Healthy is Your Family Tree?* A Complete Guide to Creating a Medical and Behavioral Family Tree by Carol Krause (Collier Books, 1994).

Organizations

• The Hereditary Cancer Institute, Creighton University School of Medicine, 2500 California Plaza, Omaha, NE 68178.

• Gilda Radner Familial Ovarian Cancer Registry, Roswell Park Cancer Institute, Elm and Carlton Streets, Buffalo, NY 14263.

• University of Utah Cardiovascular Genetics Research Clinic, 410 Chipeta Way, Room 161, Research Park, Salt Lake City, UT 84108.

• The Hereditary Disease Foundation, 1427 Seventh St., Suite 2, Santa Monica, CA 90401.

or pediatrician can probably refer you to one, or you can contact a major hospital or medical school in your area.

Your medical family tree should be a growing document. As you and your siblings marry and have children, keep adding to it: it can contribute to your health today and to the health of future generations. ◇

Retirement
on the Horizon

by Alice Naude

Most Americans envision retirement as a golden age of relaxation and enjoyment, a well-deserved reward at the end of a long career. And often it can be all of this. Indeed, 90 percent of people who retire voluntarily say they are satisfied with their lives during the retirement years.

But just as the corporate culture and working life are changing in the United States, so, too, is retirement. As companies downsize, many are encouraging their employees to consider early-retirement packages. At the same time, advancements in medicine are increasing the average life expectancy. Retirement is becoming more elastic, an era of life that stretches further than many expected—or, more importantly, planned for.

Traditional pictures of retirement often leave out one important image: stress. "Re-

It's never too early to begin planning for your retirement. A financial adviser (above) can outline an investment strategy and help you prepare now for the future.

tirement is fraught with uncertainty, and it is contingent on the uncontrollable variable—'how much longer will I live,'" says Abraham Monk, Ph.D., professor of gerontology at Columbia University in New York City, and editor of the *Columbia Retirement Handbook*.

Most stress is related to living on a fixed income, one that may not allow for the same lifestyle enjoyed during working years, let alone live up to one's expectations. The other major source of stress is time management. People often have trouble coping with too much time. All retirement experts agree that the best preventive measure for dealing with these stresses is to plan ahead. Not only does planning enable you to enjoy your retirement as it happens, they say, but the very process of

planning will help you see this stage of life realistically and anticipate its pleasures.

Know Thyself
"Most work on retirement planning is in the area of finance," says Helen P. Neuhs, professor of nursing at Pace University in New York City. "But there's a big hole when it comes to lifestyle planning. If your sense of self has always been tied to your work, it's very hard to face a zero schedule."

Neuhs explains that many people plan to do things in retirement that they haven't had a chance to do during their working lives. Then, problems arise when the activities do not provide fulfillment the way the newly retired had anticipated. "People plan to travel," according to Neuhs, "and sometimes discover they don't really enjoy it."

On the other hand, some people never make a clear mental break between work and retirement. "There is the illusion among many professionals that they can get consulting work in retirement," according to Monk. "But most of the time, this doesn't work out."

For a stage of life nearly everyone reaches, retirement involves a lot of highly individual choices. It's important in planning for retirement to think about what you want, and to determine how realistic your expectations are. Neuhs recommends practicing for retirement. "I suggest people start living on the weekends the way they plan to live when they retire," she says. She also recommends talking to older friends who have recently

> *Retirement is a stressful time. Plan now so as to ensure enjoyment and financial security later on.*

begun their retirement. "The important thing to remember," she adds, "is that most people do adjust well to retirement."

Save for the Future

Planning what you will do with your time is an important part of the self-examination that occurs in the years immediately preceding retirement. Financial planning is the other key consideration, and one that should begin significantly earlier. It is never too soon to begin saving for retirement, and, with recent changes in company pension plans, people are becoming active in the finances of retirement at ever-earlier stages in their careers.

"At one time, retirement savings could be thought of as a three-legged stool," says James Norris, author of *The Vanguard Retirement Investing Guide*, a publication of The Vanguard Group, a mutual-fund company based in Valley Forge, Pennsylvania. "Social Security, an employer pension plan, and personal savings each represent a separate element of retirement savings." But this model is changing. In the years to come, Social Security may not be able to maintain its level of benefits. At the same time, employers find traditional company pension programs hard to support.

Between 1988 and 1991, 21 percent of employer pension plans were replaced with

How Confident Are You About Retirement?

Circle the number that best indicates how confident you are about accomplishing each activity in retirement. Rate confidence from low to high on a scale from 1 to 5. To boost confidence in low-rated areas, discuss reasons for your low scores with a retirement counselor or trusted friend.

Financial Security	Confidence
1. Maintaining a comfortable residence.	1 2 3 4 5
2. Having adequate money for health care.	1 2 3 4 5
3. Having adequate money for food.	1 2 3 4 5
4. Having adequate money for travel and leisure.	1 2 3 4 5
5. Saving and investing retirement income.	1 2 3 4 5
6. Applying for Social Security.	1 2 3 4 5
7. Applying for pension benefits.	1 2 3 4 5
8. Choosing the most appropriate pension plan.	1 2 3 4 5
9. Choosing the best time to retire.	1 2 3 4 5

Health	
10. Eating adequately and healthfully.	1 2 3 4 5
11. Obtaining enough rest.	1 2 3 4 5
12. Remaining physically active and independent.	1 2 3 4 5
13. Filling out health-insurance forms.	1 2 3 4 5
14. Obtaining adequate health insurance.	1 2 3 4 5

Attitude and Lifestyle	
15. Coping with changes.	1 2 3 4 5
16. Structuring leisure time.	1 2 3 4 5
17. Adjusting successfully.	1 2 3 4 5

Adapted with permission of Helen P. Neuhs, Ph.D., R.N., Professor of Nursing, Pace University, New York.

Retirement Literature

Booklets

Your Guaranteed Pension and *Your Pension: Things You Should Know About Your Pension Plan*
Pension Benefit Guarantee Corporation
2020 K Street NW
Washington, DC 20006

What You Should Know About Pension Law
Pension and Welfare Benefits Administration
U.S. Department of Labor,
Room South 2524
200 Constitution Avenue NW
Washington, DC 20006

The Medicare Handbook
U.S. Department of Health
1-800-772-1213

General Books on Retirement Planning

The Columbia Retirement Handbook, Abraham Monk, ed. (1994), $60.00, Columbia University Press.

Comfort Zones: A Practical Guide for Retirement Planning, by Elwood N. Chapman (1985), $12.95, Crisp Publications.

Making It Through Middle Age: Notes While In Transit, by William Atwood (1982) $12.95, Atheneum Publishers.

Growing Old, Staying Young: What Medicine and Science are Doing to Make Aging a Natural Part of a Healthier and Longer Life, by Christopher Hallowell (1985), $17.95, William Morrow.

The Complete Retirement Planning Book, by Peter A. Dickinson (1984), $10.95, E. P. Dutton.

Books and Pamphlets from the American Association of Retired Persons (AARP)

Think of Your Future: Retirement Planning Workbook, $24.95 ($18.25 to AARP members).

How to Plan Your Successful Retirement, $9.95 ($6.95 to AARP members).

Your Vital Paper Logbook, $6.95 ($4.95 to AARP members).

AARP Books c/o Acorn Press
P.O. Box 193935
San Francisco, CA 94119
1-800-628-4610

the increasingly popular "defined-contribution plans" such as 401(k) and 403(b) plans. These plans are something of a fusion of two of the stool's legs, with both the employer and the employee contributing money toward a retirement fund. Companies with these plans essentially expect their employees to co-manage their own pension plans.

One benefit of these plans is that money put aside cannot be taxed as long as it remains in the account. The major drawback is that most people do not put aside enough. "In a nation that saves less than 5 percent of its disposable income, it seems unlikely that many workers are saving the 10 to 15 percent of their salaries needed to ensure a comfortable retirement," says Norris.

Because employer pension plans are generally moving in the direction of the "defined-contribution plan," it is important to develop the ability to put aside more money into savings. "The Vanguard Group recommends four basic practices that may help you to save steadily," says Norris. The first suggestion is to "pay yourself first," placing retirement contributions at the top of monthly bills to be paid. One way to make this easier is to "invest automatically." This means having your retirement contributions automatically taken out of your paycheck. Whenever you get a salary increase, "split the raise" by adding half of your pay increase to your retirement contribution. Finally, Vanguard suggests "investing bonuses or tax refunds" instead of spending them automatically.

Stay Informed

Navigating the rules and verbiage of the new employer pension plans can be daunting. Fortunately, once you've leaped in, understanding the system will increase your sense of control over your own life and help minimize the stress caused by worrying about how to pay for retirement. Unfortunately, the burden that individual Americans will need to take on in planning for retirement doesn't end there. Retirement health-care coverage is also changing, calling for added vigilance about what kind of insurance you have.

"In 1993, accounting regulations began to require large companies to carry estimated health-care costs for future retirees as a liability on their books," says Robert Elias, principal with William M. Mercer, a benefits-consulting company in Philadelphia, Pennsylvania. As a result, many companies are putting caps on the benefits they provide—for example, raising eligibility requirements for a retirement health-care plan from 55 years old with 10 years of service in the company to 65 years old with 15 years of service. Other employers may not cover a spouse's health-care costs or may eliminate all coverage before 65, at which point Medicare kicks in, explains Elias.

Think of retirement as a new and challenging job. Enter it well-prepared and enjoy the benefits.

The changing state of health-care reform also adds to the uncertainties. While these changes are unsettling, keeping informed about their implications is the best way to protect yourself. Employers are required to provide you with literature explaining your benefits. Reading and understanding the information that is provided by your employer will minimize the chances of being surprised by certain clauses or "fine print" at the time of retirement.

Use Your Resources

No one can tell you how to plan your retirement. On the other hand, it's something almost everyone goes through. There are numerous resources that can help guide you through the many decisions that need to be made. Some employers provide retirement counseling, though these programs have severely diminished since the 1960s, when they were available as regular employee-assistance programs. Nurse-practitioners increasingly provide mental-health support, and there is a wealth of literature available through bookstores. Also, the American Association of Retired Persons (AARP) provides information and several publications and services for retirees.

Managing the stress of retirement planning is different for each individual. But it is not something you have to go through

alone. Indeed, it is important to remember that many people will be affected by your retirement—spouses, children, and friends. Keep lines of communication open, and discuss decisions with them. Stress is often best minimized by just talking about its source. ◇

Housecalls

by George Valko, M.D.

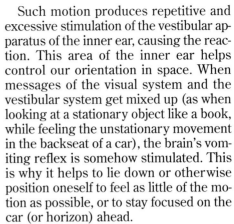

Q *My hair is dry and limp. Using a conditioner seems to help, but now I'm worried that it might be doing more harm than good. What is the latest thinking on hair conditioners?*

A Shampoos and conditioners are generally among the safer consumer products. But washing hair too much can dry it out. This can cause a roughening of the hair surface, split ends, and loss of luster. Other sources of damage are weather conditions, swimming-pool chemicals, bleaching, drying, and even overzealous combing or brushing.

Hair conditioners simulate the return of moisture and other components of the natural "oil" in hair, thereby modifying its surface properties. Even when used too much or improperly, there is little likelihood of harm from conditioners, although they may return the hair to an unwashed look.

Q *My six-year-old son suffers from car sickness, usually within the first couple of miles. Oddly enough, this never happens when he accompanies me on local errands. Do you think that this car sickness is a psychological thing?*

A Motion sickness is real, but it also has a psychological component. In all likelihood, your son's excitement about long trips and his association of long trips with car sickness make the two events more likely to go together. In many cases, motion sickness takes some time to overtake the victim, especially when the condition arises from the subtle motion of a car, boat, or plane.

Such motion produces repetitive and excessive stimulation of the vestibular apparatus of the inner ear, causing the reaction. This area of the inner ear helps control our orientation in space. When messages of the visual system and the vestibular system get mixed up (as when looking at a stationary object like a book, while feeling the unstationary movement in the backseat of a car), the brain's vomiting reflex is somehow stimulated. This is why it helps to lie down or otherwise position oneself to feel as little of the motion as possible, or to stay focused on the car (or horizon) ahead.

Strategies that can help prevent motion sickness include eating a light meal before leaving, and keeping the vehicle well ventilated during the trip. Also, over-the-counter pills and prescription ear patches for motion sickness are effective.

Q *What is the origin of the Hippocratic oath? Are doctors still required to take it? Can a doctor who violates the oath be prosecuted for doing so?*

A Hippocrates (c. 460 to c. 377 B.C.) is considered the Father of Medicine. He required that all his disciples take his oath. Medical students still take it at the time of graduation. Although not a law, the oath is regarded as the basis of medical ethics.

While archaic in some of its tenets, it contains certain key principles for physicians, including the obligation to help and never harm patients, to keep cases confidential, and to refer care to specialists when appropriate.

Q *Why are optometrists and podiatrists referred to as "doctor" even though they have not attended medical school? Do they have a degree equivalent to a doctorate in some other field?*

A You can correctly refer to anyone with a doctoral-level degree as "doctor." The doctorate is the highest degree that a university can bestow in a given profession.

Properly qualified, the professionals you refer to have the degrees Doctor of

Optometry (O.D.) and Doctor of Podiatric Medicine (D.P.M.). Other "doctors" include those with the degrees Doctor of Philosophy (Ph.D.), Veterinary Medicine (D.V.M.), Dental Medicine (D.D.M.), Osteopathic Medicine (D.O.), and Medicine (M.D.).

Q *My toenails have become greatly thickened and somewhat discolored. My podiatrist says this condition is caused by a fungus. Could you elaborate?*

A Onychomycosis is the infection of toenails by a fungus. The fungus invades the hard toenail and causes it to become thickened, misshapen, and dull. Although the nail bed may become elevated and painful, the condition is not considered dangerous. This infection is especially hard to eradicate, because there is no blood supply to the hard nail, and therefore medication cannot penetrate it easily. (For more information on foot problems, see the article "Feet First," beginning on page 16.)

Q *Is there an optimal age at which to begin toilet training a child? Also, is it true that girls are easier to toilet train than boys?*

A Children let their parents know when they are ready to try using the toilet. Thus, the optimal age is when the child is able to express the desire to learn the skill. One of the earliest signs comes when the child can no longer tolerate the feeling of a dirty diaper.

Toilet training also depends on the readiness of the nervous system to place automatic functions under voluntary control. The child not only must be able to sense the need for elimination, but also must have the muscle control to delay it and then start it at will.

Children take this step anywhere from age 1 to late age 3. Conventional wisdom holds that girls toilet train a little earlier than boys. But there are classic gender differences, as well as cultural differences, in all phases of growth and development, and generalizations often do not hold true for a specific child.

Q *My niece somehow acquired head lice in school. Instead of shaving her head, like my mother did to me when I was a child, her mother simply used a special shampoo to kill the lice. Is this an effective treatment?*

A Head lice are tiny insects with the scientific name *Pediculus humanus capitis*. Crab lice live on other hairy parts of the body. Lice bite the skin because they depend on human blood for food. They also lay eggs, called nits, which attach to hair shafts. Lice are passed from human to human when people share combs, hats, clothes, and other objects.

Before the advent of effective shampoos, cutting the hair helped rid the head of places where lice and nits could attach. Lice shampoos are highly effective, but should be used judiciously, because they rely on chemicals to kill the lice. There have been reports that too much exposure to these medicated shampoos can be toxic, especially for people with sensitivities to the chemicals; however, newer lice-shampoo products are less toxic.

Q *Is a black eye just a black-and-blue mark near the eye? Why does it turn so many different shades as it heals? Is a slab of raw meat placed on the eye really helpful for a black eye?*

A black eye is indeed a black-and-blue mark (ecchymosis), which forms when tiny blood vessels are broken in the skin and soft tissues. The mark initially appears black and blue, because of the decreased amount of oxygen in the blood that has leaked from the broken vessels. Further color change reflects the degradation of the blood cells as they break down into their component parts, such as hemoglobin and bilirubin. The phenomenon is similar to the change in

the color of autumn leaves, when chlorophyll breaks down, allowing the nongreen pigments to express themselves.

Applying a slab of cold meat does help because the coolness of the meat works to control swelling. An ice pack would serve the same purpose; the meat has no additional beneficial effects.

Q *A woman I work with claims that the best time to have a face-lift is before you really need it. Is there any truth to that? Are face-lifts safe? Are there alternatives to a total face-lift?*

A Plastic surgeons usually perform a "total" face-lift (facial rhytidectomy) on middle-aged or older people. A face-lift is a cosmetic procedure for lax or sagging skin. The procedure can also lessen wrinkles, which are configurational changes in the skin around the eyes, nose, and mouth. Wrinkles are caused over time by smiles, frowns, and other facial expressions.

In youth, because of underlying elastic fibers, these wrinkles disappear when the expression relaxes, like a rubber band contracting back to its normal shape after a stretch. However, the facial fibers tend to thin out and lose their elastic properties as the skin ages, especially with years of exposure to the Sun. As the skin gradually fails to spring back, it reconfigures around expression lines, and wrinkles slowly become permanent. One can therefore argue that a face-lift done at an early age may keep the skin stretched and delay the onset of the configurational changes that some people consider unflattering.

Because of modern surgical and anesthesiology techniques, face-lifts are considered generally safe. One need not undergo a total face-lift. Some patients opt to have wrinkles and sagging skin removed from just around the eyes, cheeks, and neck; other patients elect to have simple liposuctions (surgical removal of fat deposits), tucks, dermabrasions, or chemical peels.

Q *My daughter is interested in a career in hospital administration. What courses should she take in college? Would she have to become a doctor first? Is hospital administration a field with good job opportunities?*

A Even after a decade or two of growth, hospital administration continues to expand as a field. College courses for students headed in this direction will usually include business courses leading to an undergraduate degree that emphasizes hospital administration. Many hospitals also consider a master's degree in business administration (M.B.A.) a must. Physicians may also choose hospital administration as a career, but an M.D. or D.O. degree is certainly not a requirement for this field.

Just as physicians must pass through a residency in their training, many hospitals also now have administrative residency programs. At the end of such a one- or two-year program, the "administrative resident" may gain a full-fledged administrative position at the training hospital or elsewhere.

Do you have a practical question?
Send it to Editor, Health and Medicine Annual, P.O. Box 90, Hawleyville, CT 06440-9990.

Health and Medicine: Reports '95

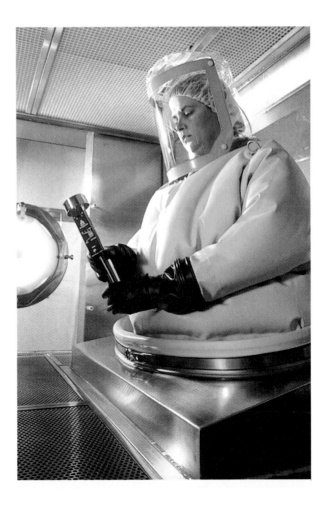

Aging

▶ The Oldest Old

America's elderly population is getting older. According to U.S. Census figures, an estimated 3.5 million U.S. citizens are 85 years of age or older. Between 1960 and 1990, the population of this group increased by 232 percent, while the general population increased by only 39 percent. Among the "oldest old," women outnumber men 2.6 to 1. At the age of 85, life expectancy is 6.4 years for women and 5.2 years for men. Given current mortality rates, 55 percent of girls and 35 percent of boys should live long enough to celebrate their 85th birthday. And women who are 85 years of age can expect that two-thirds of their remaining years will be free of serious disability; for men, that figure is closer to 80 percent. Even up to the age of 95, most of the very elderly live in the community, not in nursing homes.

Despite these rather cheery statistics, most culled from a special report on the "oldest old" published in the *New England Journal of Medicine* (June 23, 1994), increased longevity has its definite downside—including an increased risk of developing Alzheimer's disease. The disease becomes increasingly common with advancing years, and has become a major public-health problem as more people live longer. About one-third of Americans at age 80 have Alzheimer's, compared with only 5 percent at age 65. One notable victim is 84-year-old former President Ronald Reagan. In an effort to heighten public awareness, Reagan publicly disclosed in November 1994 that he is in the early stages of Alzheimer's. The incurable illness, which is characterized by progressive mental and physical deterioration, affects some 4 million Americans.

▶ Depression May Increase Heart Risk

While exercise may decrease depression, one study indicates that increased depression in elderly individuals may play a role in later myocardial infarction (heart attack) or stroke. The results of this study, presented at the American Heart Association's (AHA's) Cardiovascular Disease Epidemiology and Prevention meeting held in Tampa, Florida, in early April 1994, were part of the Systolic Hypertension in the Elderly Program (SHEP). The five-year study's major finding: elderly patients who had a heart attack or stroke had experienced a significant increase in depression during the six months prior to the event.

"It could be that a person feels something before an impending event. This is a fascinating finding, and if it proves true, we may be able to identify individuals at risk by evaluating them for depression," says Sylvia Smoller, Ph.D., of the Einstein College of Medicine in New York City.

At the outset and during the study, nearly 5,000 men and women aged 60 or older with systolic hypertension were measured for depression. People who became depressed during the study were 60 percent more likely to have a subsequent stroke or heart attack, or to develop cancer; they were also 80 percent more likely to die than people who were not depressed.

The study reinforces other data suggesting that people over 60 are more likely to suffer from depression than any other age group, including teenagers. The elderly are also the least likely to recognize or acknowledge that they are depressed. Such "elderly denial" about depression is typical. "It's a cultural thing. The elderly tend to consider depression a symptom of weakness or laziness, instead of as a treatable medical condition," says Martiece Carson, M.D., a neuropsychiatrist at the University of Oklahoma Health Sciences Center in Oklahoma City. Dr. Carson and other experts assert that physicians generally do not look beyond physical complaints to ask probing questions that would reveal depression as the cause of a patient's symptoms.

According to the National Institute of Mental Health (NIMH), 3 percent of Americans over 65 are clinically depressed, while 7 to 12 percent of the elderly suffer from milder forms of depression that impair the quality of life. The situation is far worse in nursing homes, with 20 to 40 percent of patients very depressed.

▶ Averting Falls

Another prevalent hazard among the "oldest old" is the increased likelihood of falling. But although falls are a major cause of death and disability among the elderly, a study reported in the September 30, 1994, *New England Journal of Medicine* found that elderly people can significantly reduce their risk of falling by monitoring blood pressure, taking prescription drugs carefully, and using techniques to increase mobility. The research, led by Mary Tinetti, Ph.D., of Yale University, contradicted earlier studies that suggested that nothing could be done.

"For an older person, this type of fall-prevention strategy can mean the difference between being able to live independently at home and needing nursing-home care or other assistance," says Evan Hadley, Ph.D., of the National Institute of Aging, which helped finance the study.

Nurses and physical therapists, under the guidelines of the study, visited the homes of 153 people 70 years and older, with the intent of "problem finding"—identifying and resolving potential problems. Safer techniques for walking, climbing stairs, and getting out of the bath were taught, as were exercises to improve balance. Physicians were asked to review drug prescriptions and dosages to make sure they were necessary. As a control group, an additional 148 elderly people were visited at home, but the health-care workers took no action to prevent falls.

After one year, 35 percent of the people in the intervention group had suffered falls, versus 47 percent of the nonintervention group.

Those at risk, researchers found, tend to take sedatives, consume more than three prescription drugs a day, and experience problems using the toilet or bathtub. Other typical problems include impaired gait and muscle weakness.

The researchers also discovered that untimely falls contribute to a great deal of pain and suffering among the elderly population, and also lead to serious losses of self-esteem and independence that can even erode the "will to live."

▶ **Weight Training for the Very Old**
A common complaint of the extremely old is frailty, though it is difficult to know the extent to which frailty is the result of disease, of the aging process itself, or of a sedentary lifestyle, and whether frailty is compounded by neglect and depression. A study published in the same June 23, 1994, issue of the *New England Journal of Medicine* indicates that "it's never too late to get in shape," and that weight training can sometimes reverse the effects of frailty.

The study finds that frail people in their late 80s or their 90s move more quickly, climb stairs more easily, and sometimes even give up their walkers after a few weeks of weight lifting to strengthen their legs. The research project, undertaken by the Human Nutrition Research Center based at Tufts University, Boston, Massachusetts, also suggests that one reason the elderly grow chairbound is that their muscles are weak from lack of exercise.

The Tufts study involved 100 men and women living at the Hebrew Rehabilitation Center for the Aged in Boston. The subjects appeared to be typical of nursing-home residents: their average age was 87, and about one-third were in their 90s. Many suffered from a variety of illnesses, including arthritis, lung disease, and high blood pressure. They were randomly assigned either to participate in ordinary nursing-home activities or to work out vigorously for 45 minutes three times a week. Those assigned to work out used exercise machines to strengthen their thighs and knees.

The exercising residents increased their walking speed by 12 percent, and their ability to climb

Older people who exercise regularly decrease their likelihood of falling, increase the ease with which they move about, and generally enjoy a better outlook on life.

stairs by 28 percent. Four who required walkers for mobility were able to walk with only the aid of a cane. The people who worked out were also less depressed and more likely to walk around on their own and to take part in activities.

▶ **Elderly Wimps?**
Contrary to popular belief, the elderly feel pain less acutely and can control pain more effectively than their younger counterparts.

In a study of 68 cancer patients reported in *Psychology Today* (January-February 1994), Michael A. Zevon, Ph.D., and colleagues found that those age 55 and older not only sensed cancer-related pain to a lesser degree, but also endured it with more competence. The subjects accurately predicted the pain's duration or recognized that strong medicine could quell its intensity.

The biggest wimps? Younger men. They reported experiencing the severest pain and feeling most distressed about its onset, the researchers reported to members of the American Psychological Association.

"It could be that cancer contracted in the younger set is more aggressive or that the pain's receptors become less sensitive in old age," muses Dr. Zevon of the Roswell Park Cancer Institute in Buffalo, New York. But not surprisingly, the impact of cancer's pain on the quality of life appears identical in both young and old.

Gode Davis

AIDS

▶ World Overview

Another year of slow progress and some regress in the struggle against acquired immunodeficiency syndrome (AIDS) occurred in 1994. AIDS, which is caused by the human immunodeficiency virus, type 1 (HIV-1), continues to make rapid progress in the developing world, especially in Africa and Southeast Asia; meanwhile, its growth appears to be slowing in most of the industrialized nations. Worldwide an estimated 15 million persons are infected with HIV-1, and the World Health Organization (WHO) estimates that this number will increase to approximately 40 million by the year 2000. The greatest burden of AIDS is falling on developing nations, who have fewer resources to develop prevention programs and to provide adequate care for those who manifest symptoms of the disease.

The situation is worst in Central Africa, where AIDS is becoming a disaster for the future as well as the present. In the developing nations, AIDS is spread primarily by heterosexual activity among people 15 to 45 years old—the same people who are the principal producers of food and other income for these nations. Already the disease is beginning to cause labor shortages that will threaten food production and other forms of economic productivity. In Uganda, for example, it is estimated that half of the sexually active population is HIV-positive, a particularly disturbing statistic in light of the fact that approximately 90 percent of the employment in that country is agricultural. For the foreseeable future, Uganda and other Central African nations will have to produce their own food, because their international credit is limited and will likely become even more so as their economies deteriorate.

Despite the mostly discouraging news from Central Africa, an intriguing anomaly has occurred: a group of prostitutes in Kenya have remained free of any evidence of HIV infection for more than six years, despite being in a line of work in which almost everyone becomes infected. It is estimated that each of the women being studied has been exposed to hundreds or even thousands of HIV-positive men. The uninfected prostitutes do not use condoms more frequently than those who have acquired HIV infection, and they contract other sexually transmitted diseases at the usual rate. Investigators theorize that these people have a natural immunity to the infection—an immunity that, if it were understood, might lead to better methods of prevention. Some Canadian investigators have already shown that the prostitutes who have this apparent immunity to HIV have a different pattern of human leuko-

The Demographics of Death

Since the mid-1970s, HIV has infected more than 17 million people, most of them in Africa. With the epidemic now exploding in Asia, experts say the number of infections worldwide will exceed 40 million by the year 2000.

2000: 40 mil.

1994: 17 mil.

1993: 14 mil.

North America
1 million+

Western Europe
500,000+

Eastern Europe and Central Asia
50,000+

East Asia and Pacific
50,000

South America
2 million

North Africa and Middle East
100,000

South and Southeast Asia
2-3 million

Australia
25,000+

Sub-Saharan Africa
10 million+

250,000 HIV-infected adults

Projected

Source: World Health Organization

cyte group A antigens on the surface of their white blood cells. This finding is being studied intensively.

In industrialized nations the rates of new infection are leveling off, or even declining a bit. Nevertheless, the backlog of approximately 1 million people infected with HIV in the United States alone means that even if no new HIV infections occurred here, the burden of caring for people with AIDS will increase for many years to come, with an immense cost in medical care, suffering, and lost productivity.

Africa has been hit hard by the AIDS epidemic. Particularly alarming is the number of children born with the disease.

▶ AIDS Conference

The 10th International AIDS Conference was held in Yokohama, Japan, in August 1994. This conference has become the best opportunity each year to catch a glimpse of the future of AIDS prevention and control. The news from 1994 was so discouraging that the next such conference was delayed for a year, until 1996, when it will be held in Vancouver, Canada. Scientific advances were limited in their number and scope, and the year provided a continuing warning against optimism to those who believe that either a prevention or a cure for AIDS will soon be found.

There are many fundamental questions about HIV infection and AIDS that remain unanswered. Among these questions are: How does HIV cause the destruction of a person's immune system? Why are some people able to remain resistant to the attack of HIV more than a decade after being infected? Will these people remain free of disease (AIDS) for the remainder of their lives? And what is the best way to use the drugs now available to delay the progress of AIDS?

The drug question has been incompletely addressed because each combination of drugs and doses—and the timing of when to begin the drugs and whether to alternate them—requires a separate clinical trial to resolve these issues in a satisfactory manner. This is an extremely slow and costly process. The most hotly debated session at the conference concerned the wisdom of starting a patient on drugs such as azidothymidine (AZT) before a major drop in the CD4 cell count has occurred. Initial studies suggested that an early start was beneficial, but in 1994 studies from Europe concluded that no benefit was derived from starting treatment before the CD4-cell-count drop occurs.

Current evidence suggests that the virus tricks the immune system into attacking and destroying its own cells through an overproduction of cell-killing substances called cytokines. If this theory is correct, the best therapy may be to use one or a combination of the many medications now available for depressing the immune system. This is a disconcerting approach, especially in a patient whose immune system is already weakened. Further problems arise in determining the optimal time to begin such therapy, and in setting the ideal dose of drug or drugs. Early efforts with immunosuppressive drugs have nonetheless been somewhat encouraging.

Working against this theory is the finding that those people who have been infected with HIV for 12 to 15 years without symptoms apparently mount a vigorous immune response, a response so effective that suppressing it would be ill-advised. The question becomes whether the difference between an effective and an ineffective immune response is due to differences in the intensity of the response or to the type of response; if the latter, it may be difficult to duplicate by therapeutic methods.

AIDS Education. Two approaches to the reduction of the spread of HIV that were reported to be at least partially effective were needle/syringe-exchange programs and explicit, school-based sex-education programs. Both of these approaches have met with resistance in the United States.

Some of the best evidence that needle/syringe-exchange programs for intravenous-drug users slow the spread of HIV comes from studies conducted in New Haven, Connecticut. Most other cities have resisted such programs, although a few cities are now permitting programs to exchange used needles and syringes for clean ones. Such an approach does not increase the number of needles and syringes in circulation.

Explicit sex-education efforts in schools and in the media remain controversial in the United States. Some countries, such as Thailand, claim that they are beginning to control the spread of HIV through large, nationwide mass medical efforts that encourage condom use, and through sex-education and family-life programs from primary school through the college years. Other countries establishing large HIV-education programs include Zimbabwe and South Africa. If these programs are shown to be effective, the existing efforts to prevent HIV infection in the United States will need to be reexamined.

French Research. The basic research finding with the most potential benefit for future efforts at control of the disease was reported by investigators from the Pasteur Institute in France. They claim to have discovered how the HIV virus enters healthy immune cells. First, a protein on the surface of the virus, called GP-120, attaches to CD4 receptors on the surface of lymphocytes. Then the virus extends a string of amino acids—called the V-3 loop—to link with another lymphocyte enzyme receptor, called CD26. Then the V-3 loop acts as a key, enabling the virus to merge with the lymphocyte. After this has occurred, the cell is forced to begin reproducing the HIV virus.

Scientists are both intrigued and cautious about this finding. If true, it opens the door to possible vaccines or treatments aimed at the CD26 receptor, the V-3 loops, or both.

▶ **Vaccine Trials**
High-risk volunteers from two countries with potential AIDS disasters—Brazil and Thailand—will be used to test a new type of vaccine against HIV. These countries were chosen because their residents are at high risk of being exposed to a strain of HIV for which the vaccine has been developed; the two countries agreed to allow the tests. Specifically, uninfected volunteer male homosexuals in Brazil and uninfected volunteer heterosexual intravenous-drug users in Thailand will be studied to determine whether those who receive the vaccine have a reduced risk of contracting HIV infection compared to similar persons who do not receive the vaccine. The vaccines to be tested are known as GP-120 vaccines, because they are based on a protein found in the viral envelope. This type of vaccine has been shown to be safe for humans, based on already-completed trials. The tests will be directed by the WHO's Global Program on AIDS.

In the meantime a U.S. government-appointed committee of 30 experts has reversed a previous decision to start full-scale clinical trials of two vaccines developed in California—one developed by the Genetech company, the other by a joint-funded venture called Biocine. The committee was concerned that there had not been enough studies to understand the mechanism of action of the two vaccines. Furthermore, the committee believes that much more analysis of existing data was needed before recommending the very costly field trials that the vaccines would require. Some experts viewed this action as a setback for privately funded efforts to find a vaccine.

To some experts, the best hope for controlling AIDS seems to be in the development of an effective vaccine for preventing the disease. Other experts believe that the ongoing publicity about a possible vaccine may be setting back efforts to prevent AIDS, primarily because the publicity focuses attention on technological solutions rather than on the behavioral changes needed to prevent the spread of the disease.

▶ **AZT and Fetuses**
There was some encouraging news in 1994 from the report that if HIV-positive women take AZT during pregnancy, the proportion of the infants who acquire HIV from their mothers is reduced from about 25 percent to about 8 percent. The medication is given in

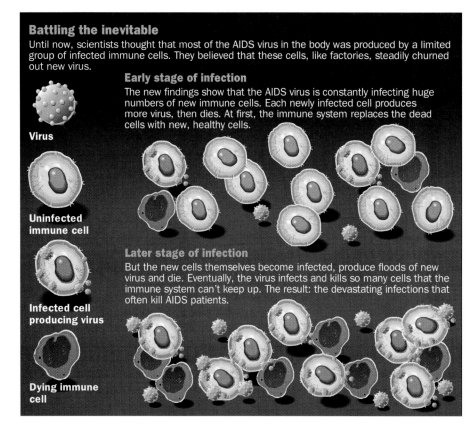

Battling the inevitable

Until now, scientists thought that most of the AIDS virus in the body was produced by a limited group of infected immune cells. They believed that these cells, like factories, steadily churned out new virus.

Virus

Uninfected immune cell

Infected cell producing virus

Dying immune cell

Early stage of infection
The new findings show that the AIDS virus is constantly infecting huge numbers of new immune cells. Each newly infected cell produces more virus, then dies. At first, the immune system replaces the dead cells with new, healthy cells.

Later stage of infection
But the new cells themselves become infected, produce floods of new virus and die. Eventually, the virus infects and kills so many cells that the immune system can't keep up. The result: the devastating infections that often kill AIDS patients.

pill form from the second trimester of pregnancy until labor begins, and then intravenously until the infant is delivered. It is not clear whether the AZT reduces the transmission of infection from the mother to the infant, or whether the AZT reduces the likelihood that the virus will replicate in the newborn.

There are some mild side effects to the babies, including low counts of red and white cells and elevated bilirubin levels in the blood, all of which resolve after the AZT is discontinued. It is not known, however, whether long-term complications will occur in the children from treatment with AZT during the fetal period.

Currently about 7,000 HIV-positive women give birth each year in the United States, and about 1,750 of the infants become infected with the virus. If the number of HIV-positive pregnant women were to remain constant, and if all such women were to be treated, this would leave about 580 infected newborns annually, a reduction of about 1,170 per year.

► Contaminated Blood in Europe

One of the most effective known ways to prevent the spread of HIV is to screen blood that is being prepared for transfusion and to destroy any units that test positive for HIV or one of the hepatitis viruses. In Germany, it was discovered in late 1993 that a blood company, UB Plasma, had ordered far fewer HIV test kits (2,500) than the number of units of blood it sold (7,000). Apparently the company was in financial difficulty, and, in order to save money, it tested blood in pooled batches. When even this was too costly, they used inferior testing methods.

Further investigation discovered that units of blood from UB Plasma had been shipped to 88 hospitals in Germany, Austria, Greece, and Saudi Arabia, and to companies that may have sold units of blood from UB Plasma to Britain, France, Italy, the Netherlands, Portugal, Sweden, and Switzerland. This case revealed how lax the regulations were in Germany: the company had operated without a license for four years, thanks to a loophole in regulations.

There is some concern that some variations of the HIV, including HIV-2 and subtype O (which has as many as 30 strains, mainly from Cameroon, Africa, and nearby areas) may escape detection by current methods used to test blood in U.S. blood banks. Although there are no reported cases of AIDS in the United States due to these HIV variants, efforts are in progress to improve the testing of blood in this regard. As a part of this effort, the Centers for Disease Control and Prevention (CDC) is searching for new variants of the human immunodeficiency virus in other countries, in order to develop tests for these strains, if current tests do not detect them.

Germany is not the only European country to have a scandal about HIV-infected blood. Two years ago, two French officials were put in prison for knowingly distributing HIV-infected blood. In 1994 a former French prime minister, Laurent Fabius, and two of his former cabinet ministers were also placed under judicial investigation. All three have denied responsibility for the distribution of infected blood, but the magnitude of the problems, which caused 1,250 hemophiliacs to become infected, has generated continual pressure to indict all of those possibly responsible.

► HIV Infection and Tuberculosis

From 1985 through 1993, the steady decline in cases of tuberculosis in the United States reversed and began rising, partly due to HIV infection. The type of immunity that is most important in fighting tuberculosis, cell-mediated immunity, is the type of immunity most rapidly destroyed by HIV. People with HIV infection and declining CD4 cell counts lose resistance to tuberculosis before they lose resistance to most of the other "opportunistic infections" that define AIDS. Therefore, clinical tuberculosis may be the first sign of impending AIDS. These HIV-associated cases of active tuberculosis may be due to a recent exposure to tuberculosis organisms from someone else, but they also may result from the failure of the body's immunity to keep long-standing inactive cases of tuberculosis in check. The presence of AIDS makes the risk of reactivation of dormant tuberculosis about 30 times as great as when the person has normal immunity.

Another reason for concern about tuberculosis in the United States is that many of the new tuberculosis infections are resistant to several or all of the antituberculosis treatments. The coexistence of HIV infection and tuberculosis in people, such as drug addicts, whose lifestyles make them difficult to find in order to treat, tends to propagate the drug-resistant forms of tuberculosis.

If the association of tuberculosis and HIV infection is worrisome in the United States, it is far more so for people in Asia, where tuberculosis is a much greater problem than in North America. Epidemiologists at the WHO are discussing the "co-epidemic" of AIDS and tuberculosis in much of the developing world, especially in Asia, where over half the population may have inactive tuberculosis. This means that the potential for HIV infection to stimulate reactivation of dormant tuberculosis is immense. In parts of Asia, according to the WHO, as many as 70 percent of AIDS patients have coexisting active tuberculosis.

James F. Jekel, M.D., M.P.H.

Anesthesiology

▶ Preoperative Fluid Ingestion

Most patients who have undergone surgery recall the strict instructions not to eat or drink anything in the six to eight hours preceding the operation ("nothing after midnight"). The rationale for this restriction rests with the assumption that several hours are needed for the stomach to empty after a meal. An empty stomach at the time of surgery is important for patient safety, since gastric contents could spill into the lungs during anesthesia and, in the most extreme cases, produce a fatal pneumonia. Despite the widespread practice of forbidding food prior to operations, there is compelling evidence that ingesting clear liquids no later than two hours before surgery does not result in an increased gastric-fluid volume at the time of surgery. For this reason, some anesthesiologists are modifying their instructions and allowing certain patients to ingest clear liquids (water, apple juice, black coffee) up until two hours before surgery time.

Anesthesiologists have modified the preoperative fast based on the fact that clear liquids either pass through the stomach into the small intestine or are absorbed across the lining of the stomach into the blood within 30 to 60 minutes from the time of ingestion. Unfortunately, this same rapid emptying of the stomach does not occur following the ingestion of solid foods and of liquids such as milk. Depending on the composition of the solid food, the emptying of the stomach may take several hours (food with a high fat content requires the longest time to pass through the stomach). For this reason, solid food or milk is still forbidden on the morning of surgery.

Preoperative ingestion of clear fluids may have a marked effect on patient comfort, especially with regard to thirst—a problem particularly apparent in children awaiting surgery. The decision to permit ingestion of clear fluids up until two hours before surgery must be individualized and based upon the judgment of the anesthesiologist. Obese patients, pregnant patients, patients in pain, or those receiving pain-relieving drugs may not be able to empty their stomach rapidly enough, making the ingestion of clear fluids potentially unsafe. And in all cases, solid food is still taboo on the day of surgery.

▶ Nitric Oxide

The discovery that human cells generate nitric oxide, a gas previously considered to be merely an atmospheric pollutant, is providing important information about many biological processes. For example, nitric oxide produced by cells lining blood vessels causes the walls of these vessels to relax—an important mechanism in the regulation of blood pressure. Patients who suffer from elevated blood pressure may thus produce inadequate amounts of nitric oxide. Nitric oxide may also play an important role in the normal clotting of blood and in the formation of memory in the brain. For anesthesiologists the most exciting potential value of nitric oxide is its ability to improve oxygenation in newborns with increased blood pressure in the lungs, or in adults who develop respiratory failure following severe trauma (as occurs in an automobile accident) or an infection. In patients who would otherwise die because of their injuries or from lung disease, inhalation of low concentrations of nitric oxide can produce a selective-relaxation effect on the blood vessels of the lungs.

It is too early to determine the true value of nitric oxide to anesthesiologists. Unfortunately, the beneficial effects of nitric oxide on the lungs seem to disappear when inhalation of the gas is discontinued. Nevertheless, it is hoped that treatment with nitric oxide can be used to "buy time" until the lungs can heal.

▶ Mechanism of Anesthesia

For many years the most likely explanation for the mechanism of anesthesia emphasized the fact that molecules of anesthetic dissolve in the lipid components of cell membranes. Although a drug's lipid solubility may correlate with its anesthetic effects, many drugs exist that do not produce anesthesia despite their solubility in lipids.

Recent evidence suggests that anesthetics may act at specific receptor sites that are structurally selective, producing an effect that cannot be accounted for by interactions with membrane lipids alone. For example, several chemically distinct classes of anesthetics (inhaled anesthetics, barbiturates, benzodiazepines) may interact with receptors specific for gamma-aminobutyric acid (an inhibitor of brain function). Likewise, exciting new technology has made it possible to produce genetic changes in nematodes (a type of worm), changes associated with increased or decreased sensitivity to inhaled anesthetics. This finding suggests the existence of specific and perhaps multiple selective molecular receptor sites to explain the mechanism of anesthesia. It is hoped that understanding the mechanism of anesthesia will facilitate the design of drugs that act at selective sites, and thus produce desirable anesthetic effects with few, if any, undesirable side effects.

Robert K. Stoelting, M.D.

Arthritis and Rheumatism

▶ Systemic Lupus Erythematosus

Systemic lupus erythematosus (SLE) is a chronic inflammatory disease that can affect many parts of the body—the skin, the joints, the kidneys, the brain and peripheral nervous system, bone marrow, circulating blood cells, and the heart and blood vessels. A hallmark of SLE is the presence in a patient's blood of abnormal antibodies, collectively known as autoantibodies because they react with the body itself. They include antinuclear antibodies, which are directed against components of cell nuclei, and others that are associated with specific features of SLE. For example, antibodies directed at the membranes of red blood cells may destroy these cells prematurely, leading to hemolytic anemia.

In 1994 several reports examined the link between SLE and a group of antibodies known collectively as antiphospholipid (aPL) antibodies. The question of a link is important because the presence of aPL antibodies has been associated with higher death rates among SLE patients.

The aPL antibodies react to cardiolipin, a component of the cell membrane. First identified in certain patients with SLE, and later in patients without the disease, the aPL antibodies are associated with a group of clinical features known as the antiphospholipid syndrome. Medical problems associated with the syndrome include mid-pregnancy miscarriage and abnormal blood clotting leading to deep-vein thrombosis, pulmonary emboli, strokes, and various forms of central-nervous-system disease. (Excessive clotting is caused by an aPL antibody that, paradoxically, has the opposite effect in the test tube: it inhibits test-tube clotting, and for that reason is known as the lupus anticoagulant.)

In the January 1994 *American Journal of Medicine*, Joao Vianna, M.D., and his associates in London, England, and Barcelona, Spain, reported on a study designed to better define the features associated with aPL. Besides miscarriage and thrombosis, the report describes low blood-platelet counts, pulmonary hypertension, neurological abnormalities, and a skin rash known as livido reticularis (characterized by a netlike pattern of flushed and pale areas). An accompanying editorial by Michael Lockshin, M.D., underscores the probable link between these clinical features and aPL antibodies by noting their similarities in patients with and without SLE.

The importance of the connection was highlighted by Cristina Drenkard, M.D., and her associates at Institute National de la Nutrición, in Mexico City, Mexico, in the June 1994 issue of the *Journal of Rheumatology*. They reported that the presence of aPL in patients with SLE predicts higher death rates. Features of the antiphospholipid syndrome that are specifically associated with the increase in mortality are blocked arteries and low blood-platelet counts. These features can appear even in patients who are treated with anticoagulants. Thus, if treatment is to be improved, better understanding of the mechanisms by which aPL antibodies produce the syndrome is essential.

▶ New Tool for Research

Advances in molecular biology have provided highly sensitive techniques to enhance our understanding of the rheumatic diseases. One such technique, the polymerase chain reaction (PCR), can be used to detect specific messenger RNA (mRNA) from a single cell. Messenger RNA, made from genes in the cell nucleus, instructs the cell machinery to make specific proteins or peptides (protein segments). As a rule, a specific mRNA would be difficult to detect in a single cell. However, the enzyme polymerase, added to cell material, causes the RNA to duplicate repeatedly, eventually producing a measurable quantity.

The extraordinary sensitivity of the PCR technique allows researchers to determine whether an individual cell is making a specific peptide. In 1994 several papers reported on research that applied the polymerase chain reaction to the study of rheumatic diseases. Summaries of a few of these reports follow.

Giant-cell arteritis and polymyalgia rheumatica. In the October 1, 1994, issue of *Annals of Internal Medicine*, Cornelia Weyand, M.D., Ph.D., and her associates at the Mayo Clinic in Rochester, Minnesota, reported on the use of PCR in a search for links between two inflammatory conditions— giant-cell arteritis and polymyalgia rheumatica. Researchers have long debated whether these conditions are separate diseases or two points on the clinical spectrum of a single disease.

Giant-cell arteritis affects the walls of large- and medium-size arteries, particularly those of the head. It causes blockage and, because the ophthalmic artery is often involved, represents a cause of blindness in the elderly. Giant-cell arteritis may also result in stroke or myocardial infarction. Polymyalgia rheumatica produces severe, persistent pain and stiffness of the shoulder, pelvic girdle, and torso. Some patients with polymyalgia rheumatica develop features of giant-cell arteritis; about half of giant-cell-arteritis patients have symptoms of polymyalgia. Both conditions respond to corticosteroids, with giant-cell arteritis requiring significantly larger doses.

PCR was used to search for the production of cytokines, molecules that are involved in inflammatory and immune responses, in the walls of temporal arteries of patients with both diseases. Although biopsies from the temporal arteries of polymyalgia-rheumatica patients show no visual evidence of inflammation, cytokine profiles are strikingly similar to those of patients with typical arteritis. The findings strongly suggest that the two conditions are different aspects of the same disease, although its cause remains unknown.

Lyme disease. In 1994 two different groups reported on PCR use to detect the organism that causes Lyme disease. Arthritis is a hallmark of this disease, which is caused by the spirochete *Borrelia burgdorferi*, and is spread to humans by tick bites. When not treated with antibiotics, about three-fifths of patients have intermittent episodes of arthritis for several years. A smaller number have persistent arthritis for more than a year, and a few have persistent or recurrent arthritis despite antibiotic treatment.

As reported in the January 27, 1994, *New England Journal of Medicine* and the March 15, 1994, *Annals of Internal Medicine*, two groups used PCR to detect nuclear material from the Lyme-disease spirochete in joint fluid from patients with active Lyme arthritis. The subjects included patients with persistent arthritis despite extensive antibiotic treatment. The majority of patients who had been treated with antibiotics tested negative for the spirochete. Thus, PCR may help determine which patients may benefit from additional antibiotics. While a positive PCR does not prove that live organisms are present, a negative result indicates that there may be other explanations for the symptoms.

Sjögren's syndrome. Researchers also used PCR to search for viral material in tissue from patients with Sjögren's syndrome, a connective-tissue disorder associated with rheumatoid arthritis and dryness of the mouth and eyes. As reported in the April 1994 issue of *Arthritis and Rheumatism*, the test reveals some segments of the HTLV-1 retrovirus, but other segments were missing. This suggests that a complete, viable virus was not being formed. An accompanying editorial noted that these findings are consistent with other literature linking retroviruses to the development of some rheumatic diseases. While the study does not prove a viral cause for Sjögren's syndrome, it provides an important new clue to understanding the syndrome.

Herbert S. Diamond, M.D.

Blood and Lymphatic System

Among the exciting developments in the study of blood diseases during 1994 were two discoveries that advance our understanding of blood coagulation. The first is the discovery of a growth factor for blood platelets; the second is the molecular description of the basis for the inherited tendency to develop blood clots.

Both of these advances highlight the central position that hematology plays in molecular medicine. They also demonstrate two aspects of the future of medical care: the importance of the biotechnology industry, and the increasing use of screening tests to diagnose inherited predispositions to disease.

▶ Growth Factor for Platelets

Blood coagulation is the complex process following an injury to a blood vessel that leads to the formation of a blood clot. Within seconds of an injury, small blood cells called platelets adhere to the injured area, forming a sticky clump that stops the leaking of blood. In the minutes following the formation of this platelet "plug," there occurs a sequential activation of a number of soluble blood proteins, called coagulation factors. The function of the activated coagulation factors is to incorporate the protein fibrin into the platelet plug. The resulting blood clot is very tough, remaining in place for days or weeks—however long it takes the vessel to heal. Once the vessel has healed, the fibrin breaks down (a process called fibrinolysis), and the blood clot dissolves. Common disorders related to blood coagulation include bleeding problems, such as hemophilia, and clotting problems, such as deep venous thrombosis (a serious blood clot that occurs most frequently in the legs).

An insufficient number of blood platelets (a condition called thrombocytopenia) is a common and troubling clinical problem that can result in serious bleeding. Thrombocytopenia can occur after chemotherapy; during bone-marrow transplant; or as part of an immune-system disorder, including such infections as AIDS. Thrombocytopenia can be treated with a transfusion of platelets; unfortunately, this expensive procedure has adverse side effects, and does not work in every case.

For many years, hematologists and other researchers have been searching for a growth factor that could be used to stimulate a patient's own bone marrow to produce more platelets. Such a discovery would eliminate the need for a platelet transfusion.

In June 1994, three competing groups comprised of scientists from several medical schools and biotechnology companies simultaneously announced the discovery of just such a growth factor for platelets, which they named thrombopoietin. Thrombopoietin was isolated from the plasma of pigs that were made deficient in platelets (and thus would have high levels of this platelet-stimulating growth factor). The isolated protein was used to clone the gene for thrombopoietin. When injected into normal mice, recombinant thrombopoietin causes a dramatic increase in the level of circulating platelets. Interestingly, the chemical structure of thrombopoietin is similar to the structure of erythropoietin, the growth factor for red blood cells. If further research (including experiments in thrombocytopenic patients) confirms the effectiveness of thrombopoietin, an important new drug in the treatment of blood diseases will exist.

▶ APC and Factor V

The second development in 1994 involves thrombosis. Thrombosis, the unregulated, diseased production of blood clots, is a common clinical problem, and plays an important role in heart disease, stroke, and pulmonary embolism (blood clot in the lung). For many years, physicians have recognized that a predisposition to thrombosis may run in families. A number of molecular mechanisms for inherited thrombosis have been discovered, but prior to 1994, these accounted for only a minority (about 25 percent) of the known families. It was recently discovered that up to 40 percent of the cases of familial thrombosis are due to a resistance to a substance called activated protein C (APC).

APC, a blood protein, is a potent inhibitor of coagulation. Such inhibitors are important because they prevent blood clots from extending down the blood vessel to other sites in the body, sites where the clot may cause harm. APC exerts its anticoagulant effect by destroying a substance called factor V, a vital component in the process of coagulation. The inherited tendency to thrombosis because of a resistance to the effects of APC is caused by a mutation in the factor V molecule, rendering it resistant to destruction by APC. The result is unregulated production of blood clots, and subsequent thrombosis. This mutation is surprisingly common (2 percent of the population). A screening test has been developed that allows physicians to determine if their patients have resistance to activated protein C.

Kevin W. Harris, M.D., Ph.D.

Bones, Muscles, and Joints

▶ Back Surgery

Pedicle-Screw Fixation. The media spotlight glared briefly but harshly on orthopedic surgery in 1994. A major network news program reported on several unfortunate cases in which a promising new device used to stabilize damaged spines actually broke while inside patients. The controversial device was the pedicle screw, a metal implant that some surgeons use to support, or stabilize, a damaged spine that is being repaired with bone grafts.

Bone-grafts are often used to fuse sections of a severely damaged or diseased spine. Often the surgeon implants some type of fixation device in the spine to provide temporary support while the graft heals properly. Pedicle screws were, and still are, one of the most successful of these stabilization devices. A pedicle-screw fixation system utilizes at least two bone screws that are threaded through the pedicles, which form part of the bony arch that surrounds the spinal cord.

The surgical technique used to insert pedicle screws is technically demanding and requires a great deal of surgical training and experience. In addition, this device is designed only for specific types of severe back injury due to fracture or a chronic degenerative spine disease such as spondylolisthesis. Some of the devastating pedi-

A pedicle screw implant (below) supports and stabilizes a damaged spine that is being repaired with a bone graft.

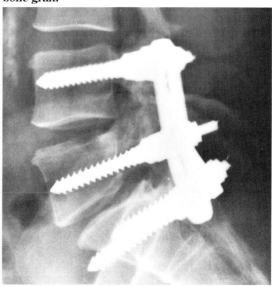

cle-screw failures reported in the media were due to surgeons using the devices inappropriately.

When the controversial news story broke on pedicle screws, the U.S. Food and Drug Administration (FDA) was in the process of investigating the devices. A scientific committee that included some of the nation's leading spine surgeons conducted a study to estimate the success rates and risks associated with them. The study focused on patients who underwent spinal-fusion surgery—with or without pedicle-screw fixation—for either degenerative spine disease or spinal fracture. The researchers found that the use of pedicle screws did increase the rate of successful fusion of damaged vertebrae.

The study also documented one of the greatest benefits of the screws: they enable surgeons to fuse a shorter section of the spine than normally necessary to repair a severely damaged vertebra. As a result, patients receiving the pedicle screws during bone-graft surgery are usually left with greater flexibility and range of motion in their backs than they would otherwise have.

As a result of this study, the FDA's Orthopedic Rehabilitation Devices Advisory Panel voted unanimously to recommend that the FDA approve the marketing of pedicle-screw fixation systems for the express purpose of treating degenerative spondylolisthesis and spinal fractures at qualified research centers. While this recommendation reaffirmed the benefit of pedicle screws, it also sent a clear message to the nation's spinal surgeons: pedicle screws may be inappropriate for other types of back problems, and should be inserted only by experienced hands.

The FDA panel also recommended that the manufacturers of pedicle screws further study the safety and reliability of the materials they use in making the devices. Responding to the concern, manufacturers have already strengthened the devices and added warning labels that specify appropriate use.

Laser-assisted Diskectomy. Disk prolapse is a common and painful disorder of the spine. Spinal disks are the platelike cushions that lie between each of the spine's bony vertebrae. A "prolapse" occurs when the soft, jellylike core of the disk ruptures or bulges out from the spine. If the prolapse leads to pressure on a spinal nerve, it can cause extreme pain and, in rare cases, paralysis or incontinence. While disk prolapse often resolves with bed rest over time, extreme cases are sometimes treated surgically. In an operation known as a diskectomy or disk decompression, portions of the protruding disk are cut away. Traditionally this type of major surgery has required large incisions and considerable recovery time in the hospital.

The good news is that surgeons are now successfully using lasers to speed and ease diskectomy. Instead of performing open-spine surgery, the laser-assisted surgeon can make a simple 1/4-inch incision in the patient's back. The surgeon then inserts an optic fiber that carries energy from the laser to the problematic disk bulge or rupture. As the laser beam cuts through the disk tissue, the beam simultaneously seals surrounding blood vessels.

G. David Casper, M.D., chief of the laser division at the Spine and Joint Center, Southwest Medical Center, Oklahoma City, Oklahoma, reports that, out of 100 patients treated by laser for bulging disks, 87 had either an excellent or good result. Virtually all of the patients were discharged within an hour of the operation, and total operating-room times ranged from 15 to 30 minutes. Even better news: the procedure led to virtually instant pain relief, and most patients were able to resume normal activities in three weeks.

▶ Joint Replacement

Total-hip replacement has been available for more than 30 years, and over 120,000 "total hips" are implanted each year in this country alone. The first artificial hips were used in elderly patients with crippling arthritis. This minimized the stress and wear on the devices, since the elderly were less active than younger patients and were not likely to put as many years on their "new" hips.

Today, with improvements in design and material strength, artificial hips can be implanted in much younger and more-active patients. The early implants were cemented into place with chemical cement that sometimes loosened and led to problems. Newer "cementless" techniques rely on the ability of the patient's own bone to attach to a porous surface etched onto the implant. The result is a firmer fit.

Modular Implants. Another improvement in the fit of artificial hip joints came with the recent introduction of modular implants. Modular implants are literally assembled during surgery from parts that are matched to the dimensions of the patient's own bones and joint cavity. A surgeon may have a choice of more than 6,000 different part combinations to custom-fit the artificial joint. This not only results in a more precise fit, it also enables the surgeon to replace unusually shaped areas of destroyed bone.

Robodoc. Another technique for improving the fit of artificial hips uses "Robodoc," a 250-pound, computer-controlled, high-speed drill. Robodoc can mill out a precise cavity in a patient's thighbone. Into this precise hole, the surgeon inserts the metal-pin portion of the artificial hip. First tested on dogs with hip problems, Robodoc is now being used successfully with human patients. X rays of hip replacements performed using Robodoc show that the resulting fit is much more precise than that achieved by even the best of human surgeons. More than 100 Robodoc-assisted hip replacements have been completed so far, with no complications associated with the use of the robot.

▶ Arthroscopy

Traditionally the repair of serious joint injuries required open surgery, often with a large incision that enabled the surgeon to fully expose the joint. Today many injured joints can be repaired with arthroscopy. In this form of minor surgery, the physician inserts a viewing tube, a light source, and surgical instruments through small incisions near the joint. Because arthroscopy itself causes minimal damage to the joint, the patient is often able to literally walk away from surgery.

Office Arthroscopy. By minimizing recovery time and hospital stays, arthroscopy has produced a tremendous savings in health-care dollars. This trend is being pushed further by moving arthroscopic procedures out of hospital operating rooms and into physicians' offices, where it is performed under local anesthesia. At a recent meeting of the Arthroscopy Association of North America, Neal C. Small, M.D., of Plano, Texas, reported on his first 100 office-based arthroscopies. He noted that the procedure is proving to be safe, convenient, and economical for patients as well as surgeons.

Hip Arthroscopy. At this same meeting, James M. Glick, M.D., and Thomas Sampson, M.D., both of San Francisco, California, reported on 104 patients who have undergone a relatively new procedure—arthroscopy of the hip. (More commonly, arthroscopic procedures are performed on more accessible joints such as the elbow or knee.) Drs. Glick and Sampson found arthroscopy useful for diagnosing and treating loose bodies, torn cartilage, foreign bodies, and synovial pathology of the hip joint.

Arthroscopy of the hip is more difficult than the knee procedures. It involves positioning the patient on his or her side on a regular operating table, with the leg in a traction device. The instruments used in this procedure are considerably longer than those used in arthroscopy of the knee, and they must be inserted around the greater trochanter, the bony bulge of the hip. Still, no significant complications were encountered in any of the 104 reported cases, and success rates were comparable to those seen in traditional hip surgeries.

Jay D. Mabrey, M.D.

Book Reviews

▶ Medicine and the Human Body

• Brookes, Tim. *Catching My Breath: An Asthmatic Explores His Illness.* New York: Times Books/Random House, 1994; 291 pp.—The author remains tethered to his disease, but asthma becomes his teacher as he works to become healthy.

• Cohen, Leah Hager. *Train Go Sorry: Inside a Deaf World.* Boston: Houghton Mifflin, 1994; 296 pp., illus.—A journey through a school for the deaf, introducing an exceptional society that is still deciding how it should live.

• Cytowic, Richard E. *The Man Who Tasted Shapes.* Los Angeles: Jeremy P. Tarcher, 1993; repr. 1994; 288 pp.—A fascinating scientific detective study of *synesthesia,* the condition in which people experience parallel sensations.

• Fisher, Jeffrey A. *The Plague Makers: How We Are Creating Catastrophic New Epidemics— and What We Must Do to Avert Them.* New York: Simon & Schuster, 1994; 256 pp.—A pathologist warns that we are in danger of ruining the antibiotic miracle that made common infections curable.

• Henig, Robin Marantz. *A Dancing Matrix: Voyages Along the Viral Frontier.* New York: Knopf, 1993; repr. 1994; 269 pp., illus.—A look at emerging infections by a medical journalist.

• Hubbard, Ruth, and Elijah Wald. *Exploding the Gene Myth.* Boston: Beacon Press, 1993; repr. 1994; 206 pp., illus.—A disturbing look at how genetic information is produced and manipulated by scientists, physicians, employers, insurance companies, educators, and police.

• Kimbrell, Andrew. *The Human Body Shop: The Engineering and Marketing of Life.* San Francisco: HarperSanFrancisco, 1993; 348 pp.—A provocative look at the dehumanizing pressures to market the human body and its parts.

• Nuland, Sherwin B. *How We Die.* New York: Knopf, 1994; 276 pp.—A doctor's eloquent reflections on death; includes clinical details.

• Pollack, Robert. *Signs of Life: The Language and Meanings of DNA.* Boston: Houghton Mifflin, 1994; 212 pp.—A biologist explains the centrality of DNA in the continuance of life and its medical, social, and political importance in human affairs.

- Rutkow, Ira. *Surgery: An Illustrated History*. St. Louis: Mosby-Year Book/Norman, 1994; 550 pp., illus.—An attractive volume chronicling the art of wounding to heal from prehistory to the present.
- Ryan, Frank. *The Forgotten Plague: How the Battle Against Tuberculosis Was Won—and Lost*. Newport Beach, Calif.: Back Bay/Little, Brown, 1993; repr. 1994; 460 pp., illus.—Details the long search for an unfortunately temporary cure for tuberculosis.

▶ Nutrition

- Carper, Jean. *Food—Your Miracle Medicine*. New York: HarperCollins, 1994; 576 pp.—The author of *The Food Pharmacy* dramatically expands our understanding of food's healing and preventive powers.
- *CSPI/Nutrition Action Newsletter*. Washington, D.C.: Center for Science in the Public Interest, periodical—More helpful nutrition facts from the people who told you all about movie popcorn and Chinese, Mexican, and Italian food.
- *The Low-Fat Way to Cook*. Menlo Park, Calif.: Oxmoor House, 1993; 156 pp., illus.—More than 450 recipes for healthy cooking, plus low-fat techniques.
- Stacey, Michelle. *Consumed: Why Americans Love, Hate, and Fear Food*. New York: Simon & Schuster, 1994; 237 pp.—An examination of our preoccupations with food, with particular emphasis on American food fads of the past 20 years.

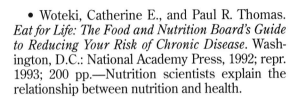

- Staten, Vince. *Can You Trust a Tomato in January? Everything You Wanted to Know (and a Few Things You Didn't) About Food in the Grocery Store*. New York: Simon & Schuster, 1993; 239 pp.—Lighthearted look at the origins, development, and distribution of the foods we love.
- *What Are We Feeding Our Kids?* Washington, D.C.: Center for Science in the Public Interest, 1994; 340 pp.—Why kids get half of their calories from junk food, and what can be done about it.

- Woteki, Catherine E., and Paul R. Thomas. *Eat for Life: The Food and Nutrition Board's Guide to Reducing Your Risk of Chronic Disease*. Washington, D.C.: National Academy Press, 1992; repr. 1993; 200 pp.—Nutrition scientists explain the relationship between nutrition and health.

▶ Fitness and Health

- Friedan, Betty. *The Fountain of Age*. New York: Touchstone/Simon & Schuster, 1993; repr. 1994; 688 pp.—Debunks the myth that the years after 65 are a time of inevitable decline.
- Sobel, Dava, and Arthur C. Klein. *Arthritis: What Exercises Work*. New York: St. Martin's Press, 1993; repr. 1994; 160 pp., illus.—A practical guide for those suffering from osteo- or rheumatoid arthritis.
- Sprague, Ken. *Sports Strength*. New York: Putnam, 1993; 224 pp., illus.—Strength-training routines to improve power, speed, and flexibility for virtually any sport.
- Vedral, Joyce L. *The Twelve-Minute Total Body Workout*. New York: Warner Books, 1993; 192 pp.—For those with little time to exercise.

▶ Psychology

- Calvin, William H., and George A. Ojemann. *Conversations with Neil's Brain: The Neural Nature of Thought and Language*. Reading, Mass.: Addison-Wesley, 1994; 343 pp., illus.—A patient suffering from epilepsy after an auto accident has his doctors explain the workings of his brain and how surgery affects it.
- Dawes, Robyn M. *House of Cards: Psychology and Psychotherapy Built on Myth*. New York: Free Press, 1994; 338 pp.—A controversial book claiming that psychotherapy is based on ideas that sound good and serve therapists well, but have never been scientifically proven.
- Gazzaniga, Michael S. *Nature's Mind: The Biological Roots of Thinking, Emotions, Sexuality, Language, and Intelligence*. New York: Basic Books, 1993; repr. 1994; 220 pp., illus.—A vast body of evidence suggests that innate factors play a major role in determining many aspects of human behavior.
- Hillman, James, and Michael Ventura. *We've Had a Hundred Years of Psychotherapy and the World Is Getting Worse*. San Francisco: HarperSanFrancisco, 1992; repr. 1994; 242 pp.—Fascinating conversations between a Jungian psychologist and an L.A. writer.
- Hunt, Morton. *The Story of Psychology*. Garden City, N.Y.: Doubleday, 1993; repr. 1994; 862 pp.—A lively and comprehensive look at 2,500 years of psychological theory.

• Kramer, Peter D. *Listening to Prozac: A Psychiatrist Explores Mood-Altering Drugs and the New Meaning of the Self*. New York: Viking Penguin, 1993; repr. 1994; 364 pp.—A generally favorable view of the antidepressant Prozac, with case histories.

• Moyers, Bill. *Healing and the Mind*. Garden City, N.Y.: Doubleday, 1993; repr. 1994; 369 pp., illus.—How our emotions can make us sick—and make us well; based on the popular PBS series.

• Pinker, Steven. *The Language Instinct: How the Mind Creates Language*. New York: Morrow, 1994; 494 pp., illus.—The author contends that preverbal language is built into the human brain, and he demonstrates how language works and how children learn it.

• Rose, Steven. *The Making of Memory: From Molecules to Mind*. New York: Anchor/Doubleday, 1994; 355 pp., illus.—A neurobiologist describes, using experiments, the mysterious ability we have to record our experiences and carry them around in our heads.

• Terr, Lenore. *Unchained Memories: True Stories of Traumatic Memories Lost and Found*. New York: Basic Books, 1994; 288 pp.—A leading expert on trauma and memory explains traumatic memory loss and how false memories can be planted.

• Torrey, E. Fuller, et al. *Schizophrenia and Manic-Depressive Disorder*. New York: Basic Books, 1994; 274 pp., illus.—Describes efforts to understand the biological underpinnings of serious mental diseases by studying 66 pairs of twins in which only one is ill.

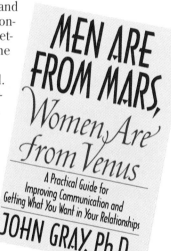

• Williams, Donna. *Somebody Somewhere: Breaking Free from the World of Autism*. New York: Times Books/Random House, 1994; 238 pp.—The author describes her own unique autistic perceptions and how she learned to confront the world.

• Williams, Redford, and Angela Williams. *Anger Kills: How to Control the Hostility That Can Harm Your Health*. New York: Random House, 1993; 228 pp.—The latest research on how to curb harmful hostility that can lead to heart disease and other illnesses.

• Wright, Robert. *The Moral Animal: The New Science of Evolutionary Psychology*. New York: Pantheon Books, 1994; 467 pp., illus.—Explains the evolution of human moral sentiments, and states that morality is an adaptation designed to maximize genetic self-interest.

▶ **Practical News to Use**

• Berger, Gilda. *Alcoholism and the Family*. New York: Franklin Watts, 1993; 128 pp., illus.—An explanation for young people of how alcoholism affects the entire family.

• Gray, John. *Men Are from Mars, Women Are from Venus*. New York: HarperCollins, 1993; repr. 1994; 256 pp.—A psychotherapist explains what men and women need from relationships and how they can better communicate with one another.

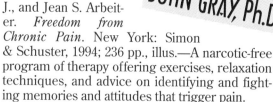

• Kiple, Kenneth F., ed. *The Cambridge World History of Human Disease*. New York: Cambridge University Press, 1993; 1,176 pp.—Definitive study on the history and current state of 158 diseases ranging from AIDS to yellow fever.

• Marcus, Norman J., and Jean S. Arbeiter. *Freedom from Chronic Pain*. New York: Simon & Schuster, 1994; 236 pp., illus.—A narcotic-free program of therapy offering exercises, relaxation techniques, and advice on identifying and fighting memories and attitudes that trigger pain.

• Perl, James. *Sleep Right in Five Nights: A Quick-and-Easy Guide for Conquering Insomnia*. New York: Morrow, 1993; repr. 1994; 288 pp.—Guide to the eight major causes of insomnia, with techniques for inducing sleep and evaluations of sleep medications.

• Pohanish, Richard P., and Stanley A. Greene, eds. *Hazardous Substances Resource Guide*. Detroit: Gale, 1993; 510 pp.—An easy-to-understand guide to hazardous chemicals found in the home, the workplace, and the community; includes sources for further information.

• Prevention Magazine Health Books Eds. *Symptoms: Their Causes and Cures*. Emmaus, Pa.: Rodale Press, 1993; 672 pp.—Lists 265 health concerns and their symptoms, and explains how to treat them and when to see a doctor.

• Rosenthal, Norman E. *Winter Blues: Seasonal Affective Disorder: What It Is and How to Overcome It*. New York: Guilford Press, 1993; 325 pp.—A physician examines SAD symptoms and treatments.

Jo Ann White

Brain and Nervous System

▶ Chronic Nonmalignant Pain

The painful disorder of nonmalignant origin known as reflex sympathetic dystrophy (RSD) is characterized as a pain in any part of the body, usually an extremity, that often follows an injury and does not readily go away. There are two major reasons for exploring this disease at this time. The first reason reflects our increased understanding of the nature and action of chemical signals used in the nervous system, known as neurotransmitters. Our understanding has progressed to the point at which we now know that some of these signals, specifically excitatory neurotransmitters, can potentially be damaging to cells of the nervous system on which they normally act. The second reason illustrates the need to understand the basis of this painful disorder so that adequate treatments, which include the use of antidepressants, anticonvulsants, and potent narcotic analgesic medications, may be applied.

Unlike the pain felt in other pain disorders, the pain of RSD is typically described as burning or aching in nature. Another unusual feature of this disorder is that other normal sensations, such as a light tap, become interpreted as painful (allodynia). Additional features of RSD include tissue swelling and color change (a mottled appearance of the skin and purple discoloration due to blood pooling in veins), both of which worsen when the affected body part is held in an unsupported posture. Still other symptoms include temperature change (usually coolness, despite a sense of burning in the affected area); increased sweating; trophic changes (shiny skin, loss or thinning of hair, brittle nails); abnormalities of movement that include difficulty in the initiation of movements, altered postures, and a variety of tremors; and depression. All of these features seem to worsen with increased physical activity, yet ironically activity is precisely the goal of treatment for this disease.

Now that RSD has become the accepted name for what had previously been considered as several different disorders—Sudeck's atrophy, shoulder-hand syndrome, major and minor causalgia, among others—attention has focused on the way this disorder develops. Local tissue injury and limited movement—such as those found in sprains, strains, and with broken bones—are believed to play a major role in the onset of this disorder because they trigger hyperactivity of the sympathetic nervous system. The hyperactive sympathetic nervous system leads to increased sensitivity to pain and the other features of RSD.

Clinical worsening of RSD may involve its spread to other extremities and symptoms such as fever and skin reactions suggestive of ongoing inflammation. The major goal of therapy is to increase the movement of the affected body part without producing further injury.

Current treatments of RSD are based upon decreasing the sympathetic activity in the affected extremity through the use of physical activity. This is most effective in the early stages of RSD, while there is sympathetically maintained pain (SMP). Sometimes it is necessary to perform a series of sympathetic-nerve blocks, in which a local anesthetic is injected into the area surrounding collections of sympathetic-nerve cells known as sympathetic ganglia, to reduce their hyperactivity and to allow increased movement.

As RSD progresses, SMP becomes sympathetically independent pain (SIP). Sympathetic-nerve blocks are not effective in the treatment of SIP. In SIP, it is believed that there is destruction of the spinal-cord nerve cells that modulate pain sensations through the excessive release of excitatory neurotransmitters. Such changes have been demonstrated in laboratory models of RSD. Therefore, as the disease progresses from SMP to SIP, there is a loss of nerve cells through the release of toxic levels of an excitatory neurotransmitter that is associated with overactivity of the sympathetic nervous system. This step in the progress of RSD provides a focal point for the development of further treatment strategies.

To determine the specific course of treatment, consideration must be given to the severity of the underlying clinical disorder, duration of illness, past response to treatment regimen, side effects, and the likely need for retreatment. RSD therapy includes the use of antidepressants, anticonvulsants, and adequate levels of pain-relieving medications, including potent narcotic analgesics. Antidepressants are helpful, not only in the relief of the reactive depression that accompanies chronic-pain disorders, but also in the reduction of the effects of a neurotransmitter that mediates painful sensation. Anticonvulsants, particularly the new drugs gabapentin (Neurontin), as well as phenytoin (Dilantin) and carbamazepine (Tegretol), also help to reduce sensitivity to these abnormal pain sensations.

Severe pain that does not respond to other measures requires the use of more-potent pain-relieving medications. While, in the past, there has been a social stigma associated with the use of narcotic analgesics, it has recently become more widely recognized that substantial pain even of nonmalignant origin may require these medications for sufficient pain relief to allow increased physical activity. Close observation of the patient, careful monitoring of dosing, insistence on obtaining these medications from a single source, and the knowledge that limited use of these analgesics limits their addictive potential are factors that help to provide control of the patient's pain while limiting the potential for abuse. In some instances, electrical-signal generators implanted over the spine (dorsal-column stimulators), or a pump with a catheter to deliver drugs directly to the nervous system (morphine pump), may be used.

▶ Malignant-Brain-Tumor Therapy

Glioblastoma multiforme (GBM) is the name given to the most malignant type of primary brain tumor. This tumor originates from the astrocyte, a star-shaped cell within the brain. Less-malignant stages of this tumor are referred to as astrocytomas. These tumors commonly cause a spectrum of neurological symptoms that may include headaches, seizures, weakness, incoordination, memory loss, or confusion. GBM is always fatal; there is no cure yet for people affected by this tumor, and efforts to reduce the bulk of the tumor are often severely limited. One of the reasons for this reflects the highly invasive manner by which GBM infiltrates between normal cells of the brain. As a result of this infiltration, attempts at surgical removal of the tumor will also remove normal brain tissue. Similar problems also occur with the use of other treatments, such as radiation and chemotherapy. A newer approach currently under development involves gene therapy.

In gene therapy of GBM, the goal is to add or replace a molecule important in restoring the normal architecture and cell-growth pattern of the brain. Through studies of tumor development, the role of an important molecule, known as p53, has beeen ascertained. This tumor-suppressor molecule is so named for its molecular weight and protein nature. A major function of the intact p53 protein is to control cell replication. Studies have shown that p53 is mutated and inactivated in a variety of human tumors, although it remains normal in nontumor tissues. Normal p53 interacts with other cellular proteins that are thought to mediate tumor suppression. Perhaps mutation of p53 prevents this suppression mechanism, or alternatively, either acts to promote tumor growth or allows the tumor to escape clearance by the immune system.

In gene therapy, one potential goal will be to flood the brain-tumor tissue with increased quan-

tities of the intact p53 molecule. This can be achieved for a specific tumor by genetically engineering cells from the tumor that are taken at the time a surgical sample for diagnosis (biopsy) is obtained. The engineered cells are then reimplanted into the tumor. Gene-therapy approaches are under development for a number of other diseases as well, and success in the fight against GBM will go a long way to influence this treatment approach.

▶ Melatonin: A Natural Sleeping Pill?

There is a normal day-night cycle, or circadian rhythm, in which we commonly sleep at night and are awake during the day. Laboratory studies have shown that in humans, the secretion of melatonin by the pineal gland, deep within the brain, rises during dark phases of the day, and drops during waking hours of daylight.

It has recently been learned that when melatonin is given in an oral form in a dosage of 0.3 milligram (mg), which reproduces the normal nighttime levels of melatonin in the blood, enhanced sleep induction can be obtained. Melatonin cuts the average time to fall asleep (sleep latency)—from 28 minutes in the early afternoon for control subjects receiving a placebo (an inactive replica of the medication), to six minutes in volunteers who took 0.3 mg of melatonin shortly before noon. In addition to reduced sleep latency, melatonin induces a drop in body temperature, another characteristic of the body's changes with nightfall.

In research conducted by Richard Wurtman, M.D., and colleagues at the Massachusetts Institute of Technology (MIT) in Cambridge, it was noted that doses that raise blood levels of melatonin beyond what is needed to make you sleepy normally are more difficult to degrade, so that the subject would experience a sleep "hangover." The reduction in time to fall asleep and the dosage effects are findings that have major practical importance for shift workers, frequent travelers, and patients with sleep disorders.

In contrast to commonly used sleep medications, which usually are forms of the medication class known as benzodiazepines, melatonin does not appear to interfere with an important stage of sleep in which we dream, known as the rapid-eye-movement (REM) stage. Melatonin may also be useful in older individuals, in whom levels needed to induce sleep may no longer be reached. However, additional questions remain regarding whether higher doses can sustain sleep for longer periods of time. Nevertheless, these findings open the door for a newer form of treatment for sleep disorders.

Robert L. Knobler, M.D., Ph.D.

Cancer

▶ BRCA-1

It is well known that certain cancers run in families. One of the most frightening and poorly understood examples of this phenomenon has occurred in families in which a disproportionate number of young women, ages 20 to 40, are afflicted with breast and/or ovarian cancer. After many years of searching, two groups of scientists recently identified a gene that appears to be an essential component in the development of this particular type of breast cancer. The gene has been named BRCA-1 (for *breast cancer gene 1*), and is located on the long arm of chromosome 17 (17q). It is estimated that 2 in every 200 to 400 women in the United States inherit an abnormal copy of this gene. The normal function of BRCA-1 is to regulate the activity of other genes in the cell, turning them on or off when needed. This controls the growth of cells that line the milk ducts of the breast. When BRCA-1 is damaged (mutated), the mutant gene produces an abnormally short protein that cannot carry out this function. As a result the tight regulation of growth is lost, and abnormal processes are allowed to proceed unchecked in the cell. This leads to uncontrolled proliferation of these ductal cells, which can eventually result in the development of breast cancer.

Since there are two copies of every gene in the body (one inherited from the father, and one inherited from the mother), inheritance of one damaged copy of the gene does not automatically lead to the development of cancer, since the other copy (or allele) may be entirely normal and can continue to produce a normal protein. It is only when some other event damages the remaining normal allele (a process called somatic mutation) that the cascade of events can begin that ultimately results in cancer. While it is estimated that up to 85 percent of women who inherit a mutated BRCA-1 gene will develop breast cancer by the age of 70, it is clear that mutation of BRCA-1 alone is not sufficient to cause cancer. In fact, there are a number of women in these "breast- and ovarian-cancer families" who are over 80 years old, have a mutated BRCA-1 gene, and have never developed breast or ovarian cancer. This observation supports the current view that the development of any cancer requires multiple genetic mutations. Normal cells

possess multiple mechanisms that protect the cell from abnormal growth. Several genetic mutations are required to knock out tumor-suppressor genes such as BRCA-1 (or activate tumor-causing dominant oncogenes) before the cell becomes cancerous.

While exciting, these results must be viewed in proper context. Breast cancer is predominantly a disease of older women who have no family history of breast or ovarian cancer. It is estimated that inherited breast cancer caused by a mutant BRCA-1 gene accounts for only 7 to 8 percent of all cases of breast cancer. This genetic mutation is rarely found in the remaining 90 percent or more of women who develop breast cancer and do not have a family history of the disease. For women who come from a breast/ovarian-cancer family, our ability to detect this mutation will benefit them in terms of estimation of personal risk and in providing information that may help in decisions regarding preventive measures that can be taken to avoid one of these cancers.

Unfortunately, this test appears to have little value as a screening tool for women who do not come from such families. Another challenge comes from the observation that the genetic abnormalities do not appear to be of one specific type and do not appear to be limited to one specific area of the gene. This means that tests developed to detect a mutant BRCA-1 gene must be able to detect the presence of any one of a number of different types of abnormalities occurring throughout the 100,000 base pairs that make up the gene, a tall order for any genetic test. The

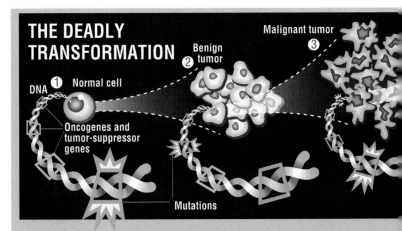

THE DEADLY TRANSFORMATION

DNA ❶ Normal cell
Oncogenes and tumor-suppressor genes
❷ Benign tumor
Malignant tumor ❸
Mutations

❶ DNA contains oncogenes and tumor-suppressor genes. In a normal cell, these genes work together to control cell growth.

❷ Defects in these genes, either inherited or caused by radiation, chemicals, or viruses, eventually let the cell grow into a tumor.

❸ More mutations may cause the cells to become malignant.

common thread is that most of these mutations lead to a shortened and nonfunctioning protein. In the future, it may be more efficient to develop a test for this abnormally short protein rather than to test for an abnormal segment of the DNA.

The identification of BRCA-1 has been the culmination of an intense search for the genetic basis for breast cancer. It is clear, however, that this is but the first step in unraveling the genetic secrets of this common and deadly disease.

▶ Breast-Cancer-Research Scandal

Much of what is considered standard practice in medicine today was not the standard 10 or 20 years ago. Changes in cancer therapy occur as a result of clinical trials demonstrating that a new therapy is superior in some way to the existing therapy. The participation of cancer patients in this process is essential, since what may be true for cancer cells or animals with tumors treated in the laboratory may not be true for people with cancer.

In 1994 approximately 22,000 cancer patients enrolled in clinical trials sponsored by the National Cancer Institute's (NCI's) Cooperative Group network. One of the most accomplished of NCI's cooperative groups has been the National Surgical Adjuvant Breast and Bowel Project (NSABP). Over the past 25 years, NSABP conducted a number of clinical trials that turned out to be landmark studies. Among its many accomplishments, NSABP demonstrated that less-disfiguring lumpectomy (in which only the tumor and a small rim of normal breast tissue are removed) followed by radiation was as effective as a mastectomy (in which the entire breast is removed), and that chemotherapy or hormonal therapy following surgery reduces the risk of relapse and death in women whose breast cancers have not spread beyond the breast at the time of surgery. But for clinical trials to be useful, there must be assurance that the information obtained is accurate and complete.

In 1994 data from the NSABP's mastectomy-versus-lumpectomy study, first published in 1985, were called into question after a physician in Montreal, Canada, was found to have submitted falsified data to the study. Although Roger Poisson, M.D., had entered only 6 of the 2,163 women in this study, further investigations revealed that he had altered data on a total of 99 women enrolled in 14 NSABP studies. This discovery, and the failure of NSABP to detect and report these findings in a timely manner, resulted in a series of catastrophic events—including the removal of Bernard Fisher, M.D., as chairman of the NSABP, temporary suspension of patient enrollment in all NSABP trials, reorganization of the NSABP leadership, congressional hearings on scientific misconduct, and myriad lawsuits and countersuits. While the outcome of the 1985 lumpectomy-versus-mastectomy study was not changed even when the falsified data was removed from the database, the fact that scientific fraud of this magnitude could occur and not be detected or reported for several years was the focus of an intensive investigation by the NCI, the Office of Research Integrity of the National Institutes of Health (NIH), and the U.S. House of Representatives Oversight and Investigations Subcommittee, at that time chaired by Congressman John Dingell. As a result of these investigations, the NCI has intensified its efforts to monitor and detect irregularities in clinical research, and has mandated that all clinical-trial groups have an explicit policy for investigating and reporting research fraud in a timely and thorough manner. Critics charge that the increased scrutiny will only add to the administrative burden associated with clinical trials, discourage physician and patient participation in the process, and significantly delay advances in cancer

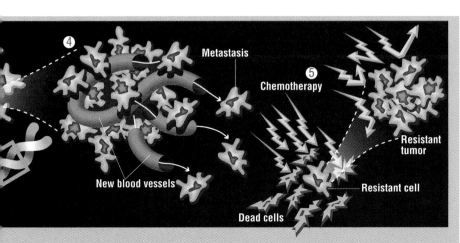

4 The malignant cells stop producing a chemical that prevents blood vessels from forming. New capillaries then grow into the tumor, providing it with nutrients. This also creates a route for malignant cells to break away from the main tumor mass and travel to other parts of the body, where they start new cancers.

5 Chemotherapy can kill the malignant cells, but if there is even one cancer cell that is resistant to the treatment, it will survive and grow into a new tumor. This new cancer will be impervious to the treatment.

treatment. Others feel that the new guidelines establish clear and rigorous standards for the conduct of cancer research, and are essential if the faith of the public in this process is to be restored. All sides agree that this episode has underscored the delicate and critical role that clinical research has in our society today.

▶ Antioxidants

One way in which environmental toxins damage cells is through the generation of oxygen free radicals. Free radicals can damage a variety of cellular components, disrupt normal cellular function, and cause cell death or transformation of the cell into a cancer cell. Fortunately, many elements of our normal daily diet provide us with an ample supply of vitamins that act as antioxidants, which neutralize oxygen free radicals within the cell before they can cause any damage. Laboratory models of cancer, utilizing either cultured cancer cells or tumor cells that have been implanted into a mouse, support the view that antioxidants can reduce the chance that a normal cell exposed to a toxin will undergo malignant transformation (convert into a cancer cell). In addition, epidemiological studies that examine the association of various lifestyle characteristics with the development of cancer suggest that individuals who consume diets rich in fruits and vegetables (which naturally contain high levels of antioxidants) tend to have lower cancer-incidence rates.

As a result of these observations, several large studies were designed to test whether adding vitamin A and/or vitamin E to the daily diet of individuals at high risk could reduce their incidence of cancer. The results of the trials were surprising. In one trial, more than 29,000 Finnish men between the ages of 50 and 69 who smoked at least five cigarettes a day were randomly assigned to receive beta-carotene (a vitamin A analogue), alpha-tocopherol (a vitamin E analogue), both, or neither, to see if the risk of lung cancer could be reduced through the use of these antioxidants. This study was conducted as a double-blind, placebo-controlled, randomized study. This means that neither the men who participated in the trial nor their doctors knew what treatment they were getting, since identical-looking fake pills (placebos) were used, and that neither the individual subject nor his doctor had a choice regarding what treatment was administered (participants were assigned to a treatment group by computer in a process known as randomization). This step was taken to reduce the risk that any individual's bias could influence the outcome of the study. Over an eight-year period, 876 men developed lung cancer. Unexpectedly, the men who received one of the antioxidants (beta-carotene) had a *higher* incidence of lung cancer and a *higher* rate of death from lung cancer than those who did not receive this supplement—exactly the opposite of what was expected. Men who received the other agent, alpha-tocopherol, also did not appear to benefit, since they had the same risk of lung cancer and death as those who received placebos.

In another trial, 864 individuals who had at least one abnormal growth (adenoma) removed from their colon and were at increased risk for recurrence of the adenoma were given beta-carotene (the vitamin A analogue), a combination of vitamin C and vitamin E, all three vitamins, or a placebo for four years. Repeat examinations of the colon were performed one and four years after beginning therapy. The primary goal of the study was to determine if vitamin supplementation could reduce the recurrence rate of the adenomas. Over this four-year period, the proportion of patients who developed recurrent adenomas was equal in those groups who were given vitamin supplementation and in those who were not.

These results emphasize the need for caution when one hears laboratory or epidemiological data used as the sole basis for a claim of therapeutic benefit from one vitamin supplement or another. Other components of fruits and vegetables, such as the high fiber or folate content, are being examined alone and in combination to determine how they may contribute to protection against malignant transformation. Additional studies are under way that will shed further light on this controversial area. Until then, there remains little hard evidence that daily ingestion of high doses of antioxidant supplements is effective in the prevention of cancer.

▶ Angiogenesis

For a cancer to grow or metastasize (spread to other parts of the body), it must have access to blood vessels. Initially tumors are supplied by branches of existing, normal vessels. As the tumors enlarge, they outgrow this blood supply and must create their own blood supply. This process of new blood-vessel growth is termed *angiogenesis*, and has become an area of intense research, not only in the cancer field, but in diabetes and arthritis research as well. Several recent studies have found a correlation between density of blood vessels within the tumor, and risk of relapse and death from breast cancer. Three molecules that stimulate blood-vessel growth (growth factors) have been identified: basic fibroblast growth factor (bFGF), vascular endothelial growth factor (VEGF), and interleukin-8 (IL-8). Abnormally high levels of bFGF

THE BIG KILLERS
Estimates in the U.S., 1994

CANCER	DEATHS	NEW CASES	FIVE-YEAR SURVIVAL RATE	RISK FACTORS
Lung	153,000	172,000	13%	Cigarette smoking; exposure to asbestos, chemicals, radiation, radon.
Colon/Rectum	56,000	149,000	58%	Family history; high-fat, low-fiber diet.
Female Breast	46,000	182,000	79%	Age; family history; no pregnancies; late menopause; early menarche.
Prostate	38,000	200,000	77%	Age; family history; possibly fat intake.
Pancreas	25,900	27,000	3%	Age; smoking; fat intake.
Lymphoma Hodgkin's			78%	Reduced immune function; exposure to herbicides, solvents, vinyl chloride.
22,750	52,900			
Non-Hodgkin's			52%	
Leukemia	19,100	28,600	38%	Genetic abnormalities; exposure to ionizing radiation, chemicals; viruses.
Ovary	13,600	24,000	39%	Age; family history; genetic disorders; no pregnancies.
Kidney	11,300	27,600	55%	Smoking.
Bladder	10,600	51,200	79%	Smoking.
Uterus Cervical			67%	Intercourse at an early age; multiple sex partners; smoking.
10,500	46,000			
Endometrial			83%	Early menarche; late menopause; obesity.
Oral	7,925	29,600	53%	Smoking; excessive use of alcohol.
Skin Melanoma	6,900	32,000	84%	Sunburn; fair complexion; exposure to coal tar, pitch, creosote, arsenic, radium.

Source: American Cancer Society

have been found in the blood and urine of individuals with cancer, while significantly lower levels have been found in normal individuals and those with a history of cancer but whose cancer is in remission. Individuals with cancer who have high levels of bFGF detected in their urine do not survive as long as those who have lower levels of bFGF. Although this kind of result raises the possibility of bFGF serving as a cancer-screening or prognostic test, the differences were not large, there were overlaps between values obtained in normal volunteers and cancer patients, and not every person with cancer had elevated bFGF levels. Additional studies may help to expand upon this promising preliminary observation.

The identification of molecules involved in angiogenesis also provides researchers with another target for cancer therapy. Several natural products—such as DS4152, obtained from bacteria, and TNP-470, extracted from a fungus—appear to be quite potent angiogenesis inhibitors in the laboratory, and have recently entered clinical evaluation in cancer patients. It is quite certain that additional blood-vessel growth factors and angiogenesis inhibitors will be identified as research continues.

Mace L. Rothenberg, M.D., F.A.C.P.

Child Development and Psychology

▶ **Ear Infections and Later Performance**

Children with recurrent middle-ear infections, or otitis media with effusion (OME), have been found by many researchers to perform less well on intelligence and achievement tests than children who experienced fewer infections. It has also been reported that children with OME demonstrate more behavior and attention problems. However, due to the methods used, there appear to be many inconsistencies in results that have been reported. After a close examination of several studies in this area, Joanne Roberts, Ph.D., and researchers at the University of North Carolina at Chapel Hill designed a project to assess OME through age 5. They examined intelligence, academic achievement, classroom behavior, and grade retention.

The study group consisted of 55 children who were normal at birth, attended a research daycare program, and were followed through the first three years of elementary school. The group, 32 males and 23 females, were economically disadvantaged black children. In the study, OME was diagnosed when middle-ear fluid was visible or when movement in the ear's tympanic membrane was reduced or absent.

The authors discovered that the frequency and duration of OME are unrelated to a child's mean intelligence quotient (IQ) and achievement. Teachers nonetheless rated the eight-year-old children who had early histories of recurrent OME as less task-oriented and more distractible. The authors of the study urge caution when interpreting the results. Although the methodology was sound, the sample group was small and homogeneous, and therefore difficult to generalize to the population as a whole. Unfortunately, OME is difficult to study due to the many approaches to treating it and the variety of ways in which patients respond to treatment. The study sample consisted of children who were routinely examined and treated if necessary. Furthermore, children's symptoms and their abilities to cope with OME vary, as does treatment.

▶ **Effects of Fetal Alcohol Syndrome**

Fetal alcohol syndrome (FAS) is a disorder that results from the exposure of an unborn child to alcohol. In 1994 Heather Olsen, Ph.D., from the University of Washington in Seattle, published an article in *Infants and Young Children* in which she describes the effects of alcohol on subsequent child development. The author outlines the characteristics of "fetal-alcohol-affected" children, explains how to recognize these characteristics, and provides recommendations for intervention for this preventable disorder.

FAS is difficult to diagnose at birth; it is often confused with other problems, and must be identified by careful history and physical examination. Characteristics include a pattern of dysmorphic features and abnormalities, prenatal or postnatal growth difficulties, and central-nervous-system dysfunction. There appears to be a wide spectrum of observable effects and subsequent behavior and learning problems. For example, FAS children may be very interactive socially, but they also can exhibit problems making friends. Temper tantrums, antisocial behavior, and learning difficulties may be apparent in these children due to either mental retardation or learning disabilities. To make matters worse, FAS children often live in dysfunctional households and may be at risk for substance abuse themselves.

The intervention recommendations listed are: (1) recognizing and "reframing" the syndrome; (2) creating individualized and flexible programs; (3) building a protective environment by assisting the family, monitoring the child, and teaching functioning skills; and (4) forming a partnership of services.

There is a national effort to reduce the incidence of FAS by the year 2000. Public awareness has certainly been enhanced, but it is difficult to determine the effect that this increased awareness will have or if it will change the drinking habits of pregnant women.

▶ **Childhood Injuries**

Injuries are the primary cause of death in young children in the United States. Results from previous research suggest a relationship between injuries and gender, age, and socioeconomic status. A recent study by David Jaquess, Ph.D., and Jack Finney, Ph.D., of Virginia Polytechnic Institute and State University in Blacksburg, published in the *Journal of Pediatric Psychology*, suggests that children who have a history of injury and who demonstrate behavior problems have a higher incidence of injuries. The study included 50 children—27 boys and 23 girls, between the ages of 3 and 11—who attended a weeklong summer day camp. The children all came from economically underprivileged backgrounds. Ninety-six percent of the participants were white, and the remaining 4 percent were black. The study required two parent-completed injury questionnaires—one filled out during camp and one later—as well as a behavior checklist. The injury questionnaires were designed to measure unintentional injury and whether it was treated by a physician or at home. The behavior problems were recorded using a scale called the Eyberg Child Behavior Inventory (ECBI), which examines 36 behaviors in the areas of opposition, conduct disturbance, and hyperactivity. The best predictor of subsequent injuries was a history of medically treated injuries. The authors note that their results are consistent with previous findings—children with previous injuries appear to be at increased risk for future ones. Oppositional behavior, but not aggression or hyperactivity, occurred more frequently in children who had reported injuries one year later.

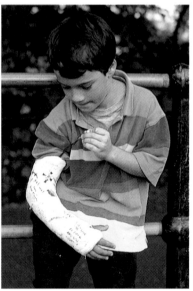

Unlike their less-injury-prone counterparts, youngsters who sustain broken arms (above) or other traumas tend to have an increased risk for future mishaps.

As with any study, there were limitations. For instance, the sample did not represent the school-age population, because the subjects were not randomly selected, and only parent reporting was utilized. Nonetheless, identifying behaviors and situations that place children in high-risk categories may be helpful in reducing accidents among children.

▶ A Child's Understanding of Illness

Researchers, teachers, and parents have wondered where children obtain information about illness, and what they understand. Studies of this subject conclude that children tend to view illness in a developmental sequence, and become more factual about the cause as they grow older. A child's exposure to medicine, medical professions, and his or her own health care certainly enhances the child's understanding of illness.

In an article published in 1994, Susan Johnson, M.D., and her colleagues from the University of California, in San Francisco, were interested in a minority sample's understanding about the causes of AIDS. In order to make comparisons, they also investigated the group's understanding and knowledge of the causes of colds and obesity. The sample consisted of 239 first-, third-, and fifth-graders from an inner-city school district.

As might be expected, the older children (third- and fifth-graders) were more likely than the first-graders to attribute specific "causal agents" to how people catch a cold, become obese, or contract AIDS. These findings are con-sistent with our understanding of how children conceptualize illness. It appears that the complexity of their understanding is directly related to their age. Misconceptions and lack of factual knowledge were observed for colds, obesity, and especially for AIDS. For example, the weather or inadequate clothing, and not an infected individual, was often viewed as the cause of colds. In a similar vein, few children identified lack of exercise as a cause of obesity, citing instead the amount of food consumed as the principal cause.

This study found a greater understanding for colds and obesity than for AIDS. The authors feel this was due to the children's limited experience with the disease.

▶ Pediatrics and Behavior Problems

Parents rely on their child's pediatrician for medical care, parenting advice, and developmental assessment. In the past, primary-care pediatricians had little training in developmental pediatrics, a situation that has changed substantially in recent years. How significantly this education has altered the pediatrician's attitude in assessing possible developmental problems was recently the subject of an article published in *Developmental and Behavioral Pediatrics* by Arthur Dobos, Jr., M.D., and his colleagues from the University of Connecticut School of Medicine in Farmington. The Dobos study repeated a study conducted in 1976–77 that explored perceptions of the number of children seen with developmental problems, the pediatrician's attitudes, and the amount of communication with other disciplines on the part of the pediatrician. The interviews lasted 30 minutes, and were conducted in the offices of the 41 pediatricians (49 took part in the previous study).

From the past study to the present one, the number of children estimated to have learning disabilities, hyperactivity, attention-deficit disorder, speech impairments, hearing impairments, and cerebral palsy remained about the same. However, the number of children with serious emotional disturbances increased more than threefold. In both studies the pediatricians agreed that early identification of potential problems is best. But compared to their counterparts in the late 1970s, pediatricians in the more recent study referred patients to specialists and experts in other disciplines more readily if the child was not achieving certain developmental milestones. For instance, the pediatrician might send a patient to a psychologist, physical/occupational therapist, or to a learning-disability specialist.

▶ Update on Eating Disorders

Eating disorders continue to manifest themselves in adolescence. Simone French, Ph.D., and colleagues from the University of Minnesota, in Minneapolis, examined patterns of behavior in teens with eating disorders and the prevalence of those patterns among a population-based sample. In the study, students were weighed, measured, and asked to complete questionnaires yearly. Eating-disorder symptoms, food patterns, and physical-activity patterns were identified by using an itemized checklist or questionnaire designed to elicit information concerning specific habits. Body-mass index, which is calculated using the teens' height and weight, was measured.

In addition to the social and physical benefits gained from participating in sports, physically active teens develop fewer eating disorders than their less athletic peers.

Females reported frequent low-calorie dieting, binge eating, and weight fluctuations. Males reported binge eating. Few females or males reported extreme dieting behaviors, and both genders reported the greatest preference for and consumption of "junk foods" such as cookies, ice cream, and pizza. Males preferred protein-type foods next, and females preferred "health-type" foods such as celery, fruit, and juice.

Participation in conditioning sports such as jogging, running, walking, and weight lifting were reported more frequently by males.

Females reported equally among leisure sports, conditioning sports, and "typical" sports (baseball, football, hockey). Leisure and conditioning sports were related to preferences for health-type foods. In fact, the participation in sports is more closely related to eating-disorder symptoms than are food choices and symptoms. The authors note that a limitation of their study was the use of self-report measures: people tend to report what is socially desirable or expected as opposed to the truth. Regardless, there seems to be a relationship between physical activity and healthy eating. French and her colleagues suggest that involvement with sports may help preclude the development of an eating disorder.

▶ Hyperactivity and Young Children

The diagnosis of Attention-Deficit Hyperactivity Disorder (ADHD) is usually made in the school-age period. According to the *Diagnostic and Statistical Manual of Mental Disorders IV (DSM-IV)*, some ADHD symptoms can be seen before age 7, but typically children are not diagnosed until years later. The age at which a child can be reliably diagnosed with ADHD was the subject of an article by W. Douglas Tynan, Ph.D., and Jeannette Nearing, B.A., of George Washington University in Washington, D.C. in *Infants and Young Children.* Many professionals believe that children manifest symptoms before the age of 4. Using the available criteria is not appropriate, because it is difficult to differentiate what is "developmentally appropriate" versus what is problematic. Furthermore, problems between the parent and child may contribute greatly to ADHD-like behaviors. The areas to assess include: comprehensive history, cognitive variables, child temperament, parent-child interaction, and external stressors.

As a rule, early diagnosis means early treatment. Improving parenting skills, increasing structure, and decreasing environmental stress can lessen problem behaviors associated with an ADHD child. There are standard measures that predict or assess specific ADHD behaviors, infant and toddler temperament, parent-child interaction, and family-risk variables. These variables, when accompanied with direct observation across settings, must be integrated in order to accurately assess a young child with ADHD-like behaviors before a firm diagnosis is made.

Cynthia P. Rickert, Ph.D.

Digestive System

▶ Aspirin Reduces Colon Cancer Risk

Colorectal cancer is one of the leading causes of cancer mortality in the United States, accounting for nearly 57,000 deaths in 1993. Prevention of this malignancy remains an important goal, since effective therapy for advanced cases does not yet exist. The risk of developing colorectal cancer can be reduced by adhering to a high-fiber, low-fat diet; screening stool for traces of blood; and undergoing periodic sigmoidoscopies or colonoscopies and having any polyps removed.

Edward Giovannucci, M.D., and his colleagues at Harvard Medical School in Cambridge, Massachusetts, recently published a study suggesting that aspirin may prevent colorectal cancer. Their study involved 47,900 male health professionals who were surveyed by questionnaire every two years between 1986 and 1992. The participants were queried about their family history, diet, medication use, and physical activity. The authors found that regular users of aspirin (two or more times per week) had a 32 percent lower risk for developing colon cancer and a 50 percent lower risk of dying from the disease; the longer the aspirin use, the lower the risk. These findings are similar to those of previous studies, which also detected decreases of 30 to 50 percent in colon-cancer incidence with regular aspirin use.

It is unclear whether an 80-milligram (mg) baby aspirin each day is adequate for this protective effect, or if standard doses (325 mg) are necessary. Determination of the minimally effective dose is important given aspirin's potential to cause peptic ulcers and other complications.

Although animal studies have shown that aspirin can prevent the formation of chemically induced cancers, the mechanism of this inhibition is unclear. Aspirin is considered a non-steroidal anti-inflammatory drug (NSAID), a category that includes ibuprofen and other over-the-counter preparations. Another NSAID, sulindac, can shrink polyps in patients with familial polyposis, a rare condition characterized by the presence of hundreds of colon polyps. In the current study, too few men used nonaspirin NSAIDs to draw conclusions about these drugs' potential benefits.

▶ New Drug for Heartburn

Gastroesophageal reflux disease (GERD), the excessive retrograde flow of gastric contents into the esophagus, can lead to heartburn, chest pain, and a sour taste in the mouth. Ten percent of the U.S. population experiences heartburn on a daily basis, and nearly 50 percent of persons suffer from heartburn at least once a month. The Food and Drug Administration (FDA) recently approved cisapride (Propulsid), a new drug for the treatment of nighttime heartburn.

Gastroesophagel reflux disease is caused by an abnormality in either esophageal or gastric motility. The lower esophageal sphincter (LES) is a muscular one-way valve located at the junction of the esophagus and the stomach. Most cases of GERD are related to inappropriate relaxation of this sphincter. Other cases of GERD result from weakness of the LES, poor esophageal contractions, or delayed emptying of the stomach. Despite the fact that few patients with GERD have overproduction of gastric acid, the mainstays of therapy have been drugs that decrease acid production, such as cimetidine (Tagamet), ranitidine (Zantac), and omeprazole (Prilosec).

Cisapride works by increasing the amplitude of esophageal contractions, strengthening the lower esophageal sphincter, and normalizing the timing by which the stomach empties. Cisapride is taken in 10-milligram doses four times a day (before meals and at bedtime), and can be used alone or in conjunction with acid-suppressing drugs.

▶ Toxin Helps Swallowing Disorder

Achalasia is an uncommon swallowing disorder characterized by failure of the lower esophageal sphincter (LES) to relax completely while eating. This causes retention of food and liquids in the esophagus, leading to frequent regurgitation and, ultimately, weight loss. Treatment for this condition has traditionally focused on disrupting the muscle fibers of the LES with a balloon or by surgery.

Researchers at Johns Hopkins University in Baltimore, Maryland, have reported successful therapy of this condition with the injection of botulinum toxin directly into the LES. Botulinum toxin is a neuromuscular blocking agent that causes local paralysis of muscles. Botulinum toxin is derived from *Clostridium botulinum*, the organism that causes botulism. The diluted toxin is extremely safe and is approved by the FDA for the therapy of eyelid-muscle spasms.

In the Johns Hopkins study of 10 patients with achalasia, 90 percent had initial symptomatic improvement after toxin injection, and 60 percent had a good response lasting for more than six months. Since the beneficial effects of botulinum toxin wear off after one year, it will not become the definitive therapy for achalasia. It will, however, provide an alternative for patients who are too ill to undergo traditional treatments.

Arnon Lambroza, M.D.

Ear, Nose, and Throat

▶ Tympanostomy-Tube Controversy

The placement of a tympanostomy, or ventilating, tube in the eardrum is one of the most common operations performed on children. The tympanostomy tube is designed to ventilate the middle ear of children with immature eustachian tubes, preventing the development of a vacuum behind the eardrum; such a vacuum will cause fluid to collect in the middle ear. This fluid may prevent a child from hearing well, and may cause repeated ear infections. The operation is a simple one, performed as an outpatient procedure under local or general anesthesia. Tympanostomy tubes stay in place until they are naturally pushed out by the child's growing eardrum—about 6 to 24 months.

In 1994 a controversial article published in the *Journal of the American Medical Association (JAMA)* indicated that these tubes were inappropriately placed in over one-quarter of the children insured by companies using Value Health Services (VHS) for their utilization review. This article raised a great deal of concern about whether children are being appropriately treated for ear infections and for hearing loss.

The *JAMA* article also raised controversy within the medical community. In an article published in *Archives of Otolaryngology—Head & Neck Review*, a panel of doctors that helped set the standards by which the appropriateness of the tympanostomy operations were judged by the authors of the *JAMA* study took issue with the *JAMA* findings. The doctors also published what they felt were appropriate guidelines for using tympanostomy tubes. They pointed out that the *JAMA* article considered only panel recommendations from 1989, and that many of the doctors on the panel were not permitted to review the results to provide feedback. They further claimed that the company sponsoring the study did not review doctors' records properly.

In the guidelines published in *Archives of Otolaryngology—Head & Neck Review*, the authors stressed that parents should discuss the placement of tympanostomy tubes with both their pediatrician and their ear, nose, and throat doctor. Doctors should offer specific reasons why children will benefit from such a procedure. General situations in which the placement of tympanostomy tubes may be considered include:

- Fluid behind the eardrums that has been present for at least three months, has not disappeared with medical treatment, and is associated with hearing loss or other difficulties.
- Repeated ear infections despite medical treatment.
- A complication of ear infections such as meningitis.
- Problems associated with a poorly working eustachian tube, such as ear ringing, hearing loss, or imbalance, which have not responded to medical treatment.
- More-involved ear surgeries where placement of a tube will increase the chances of the surgery's success.

▶ Restoring Sensation to the Mouth

Patients who have had part of their tongue or back of the throat removed to treat a cancer find themselves devoid of sensation in the affected area of the mouth.

New methods of microvascular oral-cavity reconstruction have been pioneered by Mark Urken, M.D., of Mt. Sinai Medical Center in New York City. In such reconstruction, missing parts of the oral cavity are replaced with sensate skin and muscle taken from other parts of the body.

During the past five years, head-and-neck surgeons have been able to harvest skin from the forearm, and connect the skin's supplying arteries and veins to the arteries and veins in the mouth in order to reconstruct defects present after cancer surgery. Dr. Urken's work concentrates on the possibilities of connecting the nerves in this transplanted tissue to the nerves of the oral cavity. If successful, the patient will regain some level of sensation, enabling him or her to swallow and chew more effectively.

The surgery begins by removing the cancer from the oral cavity, but preserving the arteries, veins, and nerves in order to supply connections for the transplanted tissue from the arm. The tissue to be transplanted, called a radial forearm free flap, consists of skin, underlying soft tissue, and the associated arteries, veins, and nerves. Once the transplanted tissue is harvested, the cephalic vein and radial artery in the forearm free flap are joined to the arteries and veins in the oral cavity that were preserved during the cancer-removal procedure. Thus, the transplanted tissue remains alive and healthy within the mouth. The next step, in which the nerve in the transplanted tissue is reconnected to the nerve in the oral cavity, is performed under a microscope using sutures thinner than a hair. So far, approximately 80 percent of patients recover good sensation following this surgery. The goal, as always, is to help the cancer patient recover full function of the mouth and pharynx.

Edmund A. Pribitkin, M.D.

Emergency Medicine

▶ Taking the Plunge

Millions of Americans, from school-age children to the elderly, have been trained in the lifesaving procedure called cardiopulmonary resuscitation (CPR). Unfortunately, the majority of out-of-hospital heart-attack victims do not survive, despite having received CPR.

Standard CPR, or closed-chest massage, was first described in the late 1950s. Since that time, investigators have attempted to develop improved methods to enhance cardiopulmonary circulation and survival. These techniques include military antishock trousers, high-impulse CPR, the mechanical Thumper, and a pneumatic vest. However, because of impracticality or cost, none of these methods gained wide acceptance.

In the *New England Journal of Medicine* (December 23, 1993), researchers from North Shore University Hospital-Cornell University Medical College in Manhasset, New York, described the benefits of a new device, the CardioPump, which is expected to revolutionize the treatment of heart attack.

Unlike traditional CPR, the CardioPump actively compresses *and* decompresses the heart, and it also causes air to be drawn into the lungs. This active-compression-decompression (ACD) method of CPR does a more efficient job of compressing the stopped heart and restoring the circulation. In this study, twice as many patients were revived after receiving ACD CPR as compared with standard CPR. Also, patients revived with the CardioPump were three times less likely to sustain brain damage after cardiac arrest.

Although widely tested with excellent results, the CardioPump has not received approval by the Food and Drug Administration (FDA), which is waiting for the results of a larger multicenter trial that would assess whether the technique improves long-term outcome. When approved, the CardioPump could become part of the standard equipment of every rescue team in the country.

▶ Disasters: How Prepared Are We?

During the past 25 years, many governments and international relief organizations have made substantial investments in disaster-preparedness and -response activities. Unfortunately, past disaster-relief actions often have been ineffective.

To address the long-standing deficiencies in disaster management, the World Health Organi-

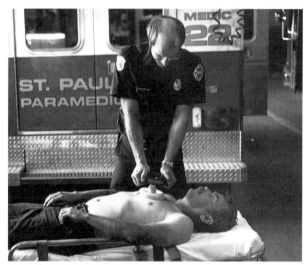

The CardioPump compresses and decompresses the heart each time the rescuer pushes down and pulls up on the device. The firefighter above demonstrates how simple the CardioPump is to use.

zation (WHO) has begun to systematically analyze the process of rapid disaster assessment. WHO has completed work on a number of procedures for evaluating calamities ranging from sudden-impact natural disasters, such as floods and earthquakes, to concentrated outbreaks of infectious disease. The information gained from these studies will greatly assist relief managers. WHO's standardized disaster-assessment methods will allow the rapid identification of the acute public-health needs of populations affected by a disaster. Also, resources can be directed to areas and populations most in need during both the response and recovery phases of the disaster.

▶ Emergency Personnel and Violence

According to a recent study from Tennessee, Ohio, and Washington State, illicit-drug use, a history of violence in the home, and the presence of a gun in the house increase the risk of fatal violence at home. Also, a strong association exists between prior domestic violence and subsequent homicide at the hands of a family member or intimate acquaintance.

Emergency medicine is at the forefront of the community's response to increasing violence. Not only do emergency personnel respond to the victims of life-threatening violence, they also have an opportunity to recognize the signs of domestic violence before it escalates to homicide.

Unfortunately, emergency physicians and nurses may not always recognize these signs, and thus may not provide appropriate referral. To address this issue, health-care-accrediting organizations now require education in methods of recognizing physical assault and domestic abuse of the elderly, spouses, partners, and children.

James A. Blackman, M.D., M.P.H.

Endocrinology

▶ Genes and Diseases

Each cell's unique way of functioning is in part determined by the genes within that cell. A gene is a piece of DNA that encodes information for the cell. What controls the "turning on" of certain genes at certain times is important in determining how that cell functions or whether it continues to function at all. Much research is now focused on the activation or inactivation of genes, and how this process influences the development of disease. Research has also focused on finding which genes are responsible for the hereditary component of disease. For example, physicians have known that familial inheritance is a risk factor for certain diseases, although only through recent advances in molecular techniques have scientists been able to implicate a particular gene with a specific disease. In 1994 several different investigators reported relationships between the mutation of genes and the development of a hereditary form of cancer (medullary carcinoma of the thyroid). Other investigators discovered an interesting relationship between a certain genetic pattern and the attainment of peak bone mass. Peak bone mass is one determinant of risk for osteoporotic fracture.

▶ Medullary Carcinoma of the Thyroid

Medullary carcinoma of the thyroid is a tumor that arises from the gland's C cells, cells so named because they produce the hormone calcitonin. Three forms of medullary carcinoma of the thyroid exist: one that occurs in association with multiple endocrine neoplasia (MEN) Type 2A or Type 2B (an inherited cancer); one that occurs in a familial form; and one that occurs sporadically. Because medullary carcinoma of the thyroid can be inherited by all first-degree relatives, physicians have focused on testing these family members for the disease. This has typically been done by testing for the presence of biochemical markers; the problem is that such tests may give false-positive or false-negative results. False-positive results would influence the physician to advise a patient to undergo surgery to remove the thyroid gland, even though such surgery might not be necessary. False-negative results may influence a physician to delay surgery and retest the patient by the biochemical means one year later.

The problem in helping the physician determine the correct course of action was addressed by some promising discoveries made in 1994. A finding reported in the January 27, 1994, issue of

Nature may help physicians make the decision for surgery without having to rely solely on biochemical testing. The researchers examined the DNA of patients with medullary carcinoma of the thyroid. They found that, in all nine of the tumors from patients with the MEN 2B tumors, there was a mutation in one amino acid—a mutation that was also present in 6 out of 18 tumors from patients with the sporadic form. Thus, it may be that genetic screening of patients suspected of having the tumor will aid in early detection.

In a different study published in the *New England Journal of Medicine* in 1994, the same mutation was found in eight patients who had evidence of disease by pathological examination of the thyroid, but whose biochemical screening tests were normal or borderline abnormal. No mutations were found in six patients who had surgery because of positive biochemical testing. Also, these six patients had no evidence of tumor when the surgical tissue was examined pathologically. The findings from these various studies suggest that genetic testing for the mutation may become increasingly important in the management of patients at risk for the development of medullary carcinoma of the thyroid.

▶ Genes and Osteoporosis

Osteoporosis, a disease characterized by low bone mass, may lead to an increased risk for fractures of the spine, hip, or forearm. Such fractures occur in 1.5 million Americans each year.

Failure to achieve a peak bone mass is one determinant that places a patient at risk for osteoporosis. Since genetic factors influence peak bone mass, investigators have been trying to identify the specific genes involved. If a patient were aware that his or her genetic pattern created a predisposition to having lower peak bone mass, and if such patients could be identified, intervention directed at improving bone mass could be initiated prior to the fracture.

In 1994 some important observations were reported in this area in a study published in *Nature* (January 20, 1994). The investigators studied 250 sets of twins from the Australian cities of Sydney and Melbourne. Seventy were identical twins (identical genes), and 35 were fraternal twins (different genes). The investigators hypothesized that a certain gene pattern for the Vitamin D receptor would help predict the bone density of these twins. Vitamin D is a steroid hormone that is important in bone metabolism, and thus is important in the maintenance of bone mass. The findings were intriguing. The investigators found that twins with the dominant gene pattern, called "BB," for the Vitamin D receptor had lower bone-mineral densities than twins that had the gene pattern "bb." Twins with a pattern "Bb" had a bone mass between the two groups. This study is important because it attempts to identify those at risk for the disease. However, the study has limitations in that it investigates only a particular group, namely Australians of English-Irish descent. Other groups may not have this same pattern, as some more-recent studies suggest. It is also important to note that the difference in the genetic findings of the Vitamin D receptor occurs at a site on the gene whose function is not yet known. Nonetheless, the concept of looking for genetic factors that influence peak bone mass will be helpful in predicting who may develop osteoporosis.

▶ Diabetes

Non-insulin-dependent diabetes is on the increase in the United States, and it already affects millions of Americans. Measures to prevent the development of the disease would improve the lives of those at risk, and decrease the likelihood of their developing heart disease, kidney failure, stroke, and other serious conditions. Two preventive measures that are recommended to all patients are regular physical exercise and maintenance of normal body weight; both measures influence the efficiency by which insulin exerts its effect.

Insulin resistance refers to a condition in which insulin levels exceed what is necessary to transport glucose into cells. Despite high insulin levels, glucose is not transported into the cells. What causes insulin resistance is not known fully at this point, but it most likely has a multifactorial origin. What is known is that insulin resistance precedes the development of non-insulin-dependent diabetes and coexists with it.

Scientists have been investigating pharmacological means to improve the action of insulin and overcome insulin resistance. A 1994 report in the *New England Journal of Medicine* examined the effects of a new agent, troglitazone, in obese patients with insulin resistance and impaired glucose tolerance. These patients were not "true diabetics," but rather they had abnormal glucose transport after the ingestion of a meal. The investigators found that troglitazone improved the glucose status of these patients in the fasting state and after a meal, and improved the effectiveness of insulin in the liver and in skeletal muscle. The study also found that these patients had improvements in the levels of triglycerides and of high-density cholesterol. Overall, the findings suggest that troglitazone may be a promising new medication to prevent the development of non-insulin-dependent diabetes mellitus.

Alison A. Moy, M.D.

Environment and Health

▶ How Deadly Is Dioxin?

On September 13, 1994, the Environmental Protection Agency (EPA) released a long-awaited draft report of its reassessment of the chemical dioxin. The report which more than 100 EPA and outside scientists worked on for three years, confirms the conclusion that dioxin likely causes cancer in people and is a proven animal carcinogen. The report also points to possible noncancer health effects in humans from exposure to dioxin, including developmental and reproductive effects, immune suppression, and disruption of regulatory hormones.

The group of chemical compounds known as dioxins are by-products of combustion, certain kinds of chemical manufacture, chlorine bleaching of pulp and paper, and other industrial processes. Though dioxin is produced in very small amounts, it is quite toxic and has been regarded as a serious pollutant since the early 1970s.

People ingest dioxin when they eat. "We believe that the pathway for exposure to humans is primarily via airborne dioxins that settle on plants, and that are passed on through the food chain and associated particularly with fat," says Lynn Goldman, M.D., assistant administrator for prevention, pesticides, and toxics. "The federal government emphasizes that the benefits from a balanced diet far outweigh any theoretical risks from dioxin exposure." This ingestion results in widespread low-level exposure of the general population to dioxinlike compounds. The EPA is currently conducting a study with the U.S. Department of Agriculture (USDA) and the Food and Drug Administration (FDA) to assess the levels of dioxin found in beef, dairy, pork, and poultry products, the principal sources of exposure to the chemical for most Americans.

On September 13, 1994, the EPA also issued a call for new dioxin data from scientists, industries, state and local governments, hospital facilities, and public-interest groups. Goldman says that "there still are significant data gaps that are critical to our understanding of dioxin. The new data call-in is aimed at filling those data gaps in order to better manage dioxin and protect the public's health." With this additional information and public comments, the EPA's Science Advisory Board will conduct a formal scientific review and will issue the final version of the reassessment in late 1995.

Until the final reassessment is complete, the EPA will not change its direction and programs in regard to dioxin. The agency will, however, continue ongoing efforts to reduce sources of dioxin. To that end, on September 1, 1994, EPA Administrator Carol Browner announced proposed air standards for new and existing municipal-waste incinerators, which are estimated to be the second-largest source of dioxin, after medical-waste incinerators. The standards would reduce dioxin emissions by 99 percent, and severely limit emissions of mercury, lead, cadmium, and other chemicals. When the proposal is enacted in September 1995, existing companies will have one to three years to comply; new companies must immediately adhere to the revised air standards.

▶ Cleaner Lawn Mowers on the Way

On May 4, 1994, the EPA proposed the first-ever national emission standards to safeguard public health by cutting exhaust pollution from gasoline-powered lawn-and-garden equipment, including chain saws, lawn mowers, snowblowers, garden tractors, and leaf blowers.

There are currently 89 million pieces of lawn-and-garden equipment in use in the United States. A 1991 EPA study of nonroad emissions showed that their exhaust is a significant source of ozone and carbon monoxide emissions in many areas of the country.

Exhaust from gasoline-powered lawn equipment is a significant source of carbon monoxide and ozone emissions. Engines that produce reduced levels of pollutants are mandated for the year 2003.

Manufacturers will be expected to meet the proposed standards when they become effective in 1996. These standards will reduce emissions of hydrocarbons, which produce ground-level ozone, or smog. As a respiratory irritant, ozone can cause chest pain and lung inflammation, and can worsen asthma and other existing respiratory conditions. Carbon monoxide, which interferes with the delivery of oxygen to the body's tissues, would also be reduced by the standards.

The reductions would come in two phases. The EPA projects a 32 percent reduction in hydrocarbons and a 14 percent reduction in carbon monoxide as a result of Phase 1 controls by the year 2003, when a majority of the new engines will be in circulation. Phase 1 changes, which use current technology to improve the air-and-fuel mixture for more-complete fuel combustion, are expected to cost consumers less than $5 per piece of equipment. Phase 2 standards are under development and will be announced in 1996.

▶ Particulate Peril

Recent studies show that particulate matter, the airborne hodgepodge of tiny bits of soot, dust, smoke, and acid aerosols, presents a health risk to millions of people. An American Lung Association (ALA) report issued in April 1994 states that more than 18 million children and over 11 million elderly people in the United States may risk adverse health effects, including breathing problems, because they are exposed to particulate-matter air pollution.

Alfred Munzer, M.D., past president of the ALA, says, "Particulate air pollution can lead to lung disease, and our report shows just how many people could be exposed to it." The report investigated people who live in areas with particulate-matter levels below the EPA's current National Ambient Air Quality Standard, but above California's more-stringent air-quality standard.

Particulate matter comes from diesel bus and truck emissions, factory and utility smokestacks, car exhaust, wood burning, mining, construction activity, and other sources. Particulates can impair lung function and are particularly harmful to those with asthma, chronic bronchitis, chronic pulmonary disease, and emphysema.

A study of six cities published in the *New England Journal of Medicine* in late 1993 went a step further, and found an association between fine-particulate air pollution and excess mortality. The study, led by Douglas Dockery, Ph.D., of Harvard University's School of Public Health in Cambridge, Massachusetts, had 8,111 participants. The goal was to estimate the effects of air pollution on mortality while controlling for smoking status, sex, age, and other risk factors. Dockery

Constant exposure to particulate air pollution has been associated with increased risk of impaired lung function, exacerbation of existing respiratory illnesses, and higher death rates.

and his team observed pollution patterns from 1975 to 1988 and compared them with death rates in the six communities. They found significant associations between mortality and the presence of fine, inhalable sulfate particles.

This study, among others, prompted the ALA to file a lawsuit against the EPA in October 1993 for failing to review the adequacy of the federal health-based standard for particulate air pollution. A year later, the ALA won the suit with a ruling that the EPA must accelerate its schedule for reviewing the adequacy of particulate-matter standards. Under the Clean Air Act, the agency was to complete reviews of the standard in 1980, 1985, and 1990. It did not, and had proposed completing the review by the end of 1998. The recent court order will force the EPA to finish the review by January 31, 1997, and, if necessary, to revise the particulate-matter standard.

▶ Persian Gulf Syndrome Update

The unexplained illnesses among Persian Gulf veterans continue to baffle physicians and other specialists. An outside panel of experts led by professors from Harvard University and from Johns Hopkins University in Baltimore, Maryland, met for an April 1994 National Institutes of Health (NIH) workshop to discuss the issue. The outcome: "No single disease or syndrome is apparent, but rather multiple illnesses with overlapping symptoms and causes," they wrote.

Despite this frustrating and repetitive conclusion, more research has been initiated over the past year, and further programs have been set up to assist veterans.

In January 1994, an interagency board—the Persian Gulf Veterans Coordinating Board—was established to resolve the health concerns of Gulf War veterans. The board is headed by the secretaries of the Departments of Defense (DOD), Veterans Affairs (VA), and Health and Human Services (HHS). They oversee and coordinate working groups that will focus on research, clinical issues, and disability compensation.

The DOD and the VA developed the "Comprehensive Clinical Evaluation Protocol" for patients whose diagnosis is unclear after routine medical assessment. In June 1994, the program began to provide an in-depth medical evaluation to all those experiencing illnesses subsequent to their service in the Gulf War. A hot line also was established to gather data, which is sent to 13 DOD medical centers so they can contact individuals to set up exams.

In July 1994, the VA also established three environmental hazards research centers that will focus on the possible health effects of environmental exposures on Persian Gulf veterans. The centers are located at VA hospitals in Boston, Massachusetts; East Orange, New Jersey; and Portland, Oregon.

The ability to deal with all health effects will, of course, be much easier once a definitive solution is found regarding the origin or origins of the soldiers' illnesses. Suspected causes range from exposure to fumes from burning oil wells and depleted uranium in armaments, to possible contamination from Iraqi chemical/biological agents, and, most recently, to drugs experimentally given to protect soldiers against anticipated chemical and biological warfare. In June a group of 26 Gulf War veterans filed a $1 billion lawsuit against 11 companies for injuries the veterans say were caused by biological weapons made from products the companies allegedly sold to Iraq.

While lawsuits are being filed and research goes on, legislation is moving toward passage to provide compensation for Gulf War veterans suffering from the various maladies described by many as Persian Gulf syndrome. In August 1994, such a bill passed the House of Representatives and was sent for further action to the Senate.

▶ Estrogen Mimics

Decreased sperm counts in men? Great Lakes terns and gulls that are becoming biochemical hermaphrodites? A one in nine chance that a woman will get breast cancer? Alligators in Florida with abnormally small penises? Although the evidence is far from ironclad, some scientists have begun to see a common causative thread in these seemingly disparate developments: estrogen, the natural hormone that flows through womens' bodies and that men also produce, though in much smaller amounts. It turns out that a number of human-made chemicals introduced into the environment in the 1940s, such as PCBs (polychlorinated biphenyls), various pesticides including DDT, chlorine compounds that bleach paper, and polycarbonate plastic found in many baby bottles and water jugs, can mimic or block the action of estrogen.

Scientists gathered at a conference in January 1994 sponsored by the National Institute of Environmental Sciences to discuss this topic. This was the third conference that the Institute has convened on this subject, and it attracted a much larger and more diverse group of researchers than the previous meetings. While there is considerable disagreement as to how much estrogen "mimics" are affecting the health of humans and wildlife, no papers claiming that estrogen mimics are not a problem were presented.

There is also agreement that greater research needs to be done in a variety of areas. At the request of the EPA and the U.S. Fish and Wildlife Service, the National Academy of Sciences (NAS) has begun work on a report due out in 1996 or 1997 on hormone-related toxins in the air. The need for increased research is particularly apparent in the effort to identify causes of breast cancer. This is exemplified by two recent studies with conflicting results that investigated the connection between environmental pollutants and women with breast cancer.

The state of New York's Department of Health released a study in April 1994 titled "Residence Near Industries and High Traffic Areas and the Risk of Breast Cancer on Long Island." Data on some 1,400 Long Island women found that those who lived about half a mile from a chemical plant were 60 percent more likely to develop postmenopausal breast cancer than those living farther away. The association was higher for postmenopausal women who lived near chemical plants in 1965–75 compared to 1975–85, when state air-pollution standards became more rigid.

Also in April, a large, long-term study found no link between residues of two chemicals, the pesticide DDT and PCBs, and breast cancer. The study, headed by Nancy Krieger, Ph.D., at the Kaiser Foundation Research Institute in Oakland, California, analyzed blood samples taken from more than 57,000 healthy white, black, and Asian women in the late 1960s, before DDT was banned. In 1990, 150 of these women who had developed breast cancer were compared with a matched group of healthy women. Blood levels of DDE (a by-product of DDT) and PCBs were no higher in breast-cancer patients than in the healthy women.

Due in part to the differing conclusions from these two studies, officials are eagerly awaiting the results from a five-year, $5 million National Cancer Institute (NCI) study of breast cancer on Long Island.

Although the possible scope of problems created by estrogen impostors seems huge, there is also growing evidence that naturally occurring estrogens in plants, called phytoestrogens, may act to suppress the growth of estrogen-dependent cancers such as breast and prostate cancer. French beans, soybeans, and pomegranates all contain phytoestrogens that may combat cancer.

▶ Secondhand Smoke and Children

Children under the age of 5 whose mothers smoke only 10 cigarettes a day show evidence of nicotine and cancer-causing compounds in their blood, according to a study by researchers at Columbia University in New York City led by Frederica Perera, M.D.

"This is the first report that young children with relatively light exposure to environmental tobacco smoke have elevated levels" of markers for nicotine and carcinogens from cigarettes, the researchers wrote in their study, which appeared in the September 21, 1994, issue of the *Journal of the National Cancer Institute*.

The study's finding is of particular concern because the authors say, "There is accumulating evidence that children may be at heightened risk of cancer later in life as a result of exposure to carcinogens during their early development." The researchers estimate that as many as 9 million American children under the age of 5 may be exposed to environmental tobacco smoke.

The study tested the blood of 87 black and Hispanic mothers from New York City, and the blood of their children ages 2 to 5, for by-products of chemicals from smoke that are biological markers of nicotine and carcinogens from cigarettes. Results show that children with smoking mothers had mean levels of carcinogens that were more than twice that of children with nonsmoking mothers and no other regular smokers in the household.

The researchers conclude that the study's results "underscore the potential carcinogenic and public-health hazard of environmental tobacco smoke."

Linda J. Brown

Eyes and Vision

▶ Complications of Cataract Extraction

Jonathan Javitts, M.D., and coworkers at the Worthen Center for Eye Care Research of Georgetown University in Washington, D.C., have published a study that reports on the risk of long-term complications following cataract surgery.

The most-feared complications are retinal detachment and infection; either can lead to total loss of vision. A retinal detachment, the most frequent complication after cataract surgery, occurs if the retina becomes separated from the underlying layer of blood vessels that nourishes it. In this condition the retina is no longer in its normal position, and becomes nonfunctional. It is often repairable, but vision is not always restored to normal levels. Researchers found that patients had a less than 1 percent risk of developing a retinal detachment in the three years after surgery.

The second-most-common complication is postoperative infection of the interior of the eye, or endophthalmitis. Although a rare condition, it often leads to severe loss of vision. Dr. Javitts and coworkers found that endophthalmitis occurred following only 0.08 percent of cases.

Dr. Javitts also considered the relationship of these complications to the transition from in-patient surgery to outpatient surgery that occurred during the 1980s. There was once widespread fear that outpatient cataract surgery might be riskier, but today nearly all of it is performed on an outpatient basis. Dr. Javitts found that the risk for retinal detachment was no different.

▶ Optic Neuritis and Multiple Sclerosis

Optic neuritis, an inflammation of one or both optic nerves, usually affects young patients, women more often than men. In some cases, optic neuritis represents an initial attack of inflammation that will ultimately be diagnosed months or years later as multiple sclerosis (MS).

Investigators involved in a research program called the Optic Neuritis Treatment Trial have previously reported that the early use of steroids accelerates the restoration of vision in the affected eye, and, if administered intravenously, the steroids reduce the frequency of recurrence. In 1994 these investigators reported a startling additional development. During a two-year follow-up study, they found that the patients who had received intravenous steroid therapy had a much lower risk of developing MS than the group of patients who did not receive treatment. It appears that the steroids slow down the development of

MS. Only one other medication, interferon beta, is known to alter the natural course of MS. The patients who most benefited from the steroids were those who had areas of inflammation as seen on a magnetic-resonance-imaging (MRI) study of the brain. The authors conclude that all patients with optic neuritis should undergo an MRI. If vision is markedly reduced, and there is evidence of inflammation in the brain, the patients should receive intravenous steroids, not only to treat the visual loss, but also to delay or perhaps even prevent the development of MS.

▶ Estrogen and Cataracts

The use of postmenopausal supplemental estrogen has frequently been prescribed for the relief of a wide variety of symptoms associated with menopause. Barbara Klein, M.D., and her coworkers in Wisconsin recently evaluated the effect of postmenopausal estrogen on the development of cataracts. Cataracts are more common in women than in men of the same age. Women who develop cataracts are typically postmenopausal and have low levels of estrogen. If it could be shown that postmenopausal supplemental estrogen had a protective effect on the lens of the eye, then this would be a pharmacological method of delaying the development of cataracts.

These researchers found that an older age at menopause directly correlates with a reduced risk of cataracts. They also found that the use of birth-control pills appears to produce lower rates of cataracts, as does the use of estrogen replacements after an early hysterectomy.

▶ Overnight Wear of Contact Lenses

About 24 million Americans currently wear contact lenses. Contact lenses are used on either a daily-wear basis or an extended-wear basis. Corneal infections are the most-feared complication associated with contact-lens use.

Recent advances have led to the development and wide acceptance of disposable contact lenses. When disposable contact lenses were introduced, it was hoped that the frequency of infection would be reduced. Disposable lenses would not need to be sterilized, and thus, handling of the lenses would be minimized.

Oliver Schein, M.D., and his colleagues at Johns Hopkins University in Baltimore, Maryland, evaluated the risk to the wearer of using extended-wear disposable lenses compared to overnight use of reusable extended-wear contact lenses. The authors found that 1 out of 132 individuals wearing disposable soft contact lenses would develop a corneal infection annually, compared to 1 out of 161 individuals wearing reusable extended-wear soft contact lenses. The risk of

New Routes to Clearer Vision

Newer procedures for cataract surgery use smaller and smaller incisions and often replace the clouded lens with one that can be rolled up for insertion, then unfurled. Some techniques can shorten both the operation and recovery period and use only topical anesthesia. However, they require thorough training.

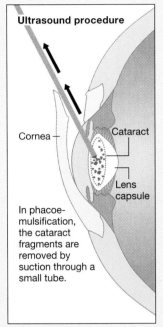

Ultrasound procedure

Cornea

Cataract

Lens capsule

In phacoemulsification, the cataract fragments are removed by suction through a small tube.

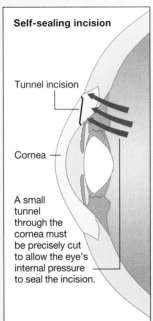

Self-sealing incision

Tunnel incision

Cornea

A small tunnel through the cornea must be precisely cut to allow the eye's internal pressure to seal the incision.

Source: American Academy of Ophthalmology

infection declined by two-thirds when either type of contact lens was worn on a strictly daily basis. These data indicate that contact-lens wearers should adhere strictly to the disposal schedule provided by their practitioner. The safest course for lens wearers is to remove and clean the lenses each day and replace the lenses frequently.

▶ Macular-Degeneration Treatments
Macular degeneration, an age-related disease of the portion of the retina providing straight-ahead vision, is the leading cause of permanent vision loss in older Americans. The benefit of laser treatment has been shown for certain uncommon types of macular degeneration, but has remained controversial for the condition when it exists in the very center of the retina. Laser treatment of this area leads to an immediate reduction in visual acuity. Thus, the patient must choose between immediate loss of vision from treatment, or delayed and usually worse vision loss from no therapy.

The most-recent results of a study of laser therapy sponsored by the National Eye Institute show that laser treatment does not significantly reduce the severe visual loss experienced by most patients. Visual restoration or preservation is a benefit for only a small percentage of those

patients. Patients need to be alerted to this relatively grim prognosis. At present, research into other treatments of macular degeneration continues. In 1994 there were three reports discussing the value of surgical removal of the macular-degenerative tissue. Preliminary work using drugs, particularly interferon alpha, to delay or stop the development of macular degeneration is encouraging.

▶ Radial Keratotomy
Radial keratotomy (RK) is a surgical procedure to eliminate nearsightedness. If the procedure is completely successful, the patient will no longer have to wear glasses.

Over the past decade, the number of patients undergoing RK has skyrocketed, as have the number of ophthalmologists performing the procedure. Despite this apparent widespread acceptance, the long-term implications of the procedure have been controversial. Proponents have suggested that no significant problems occur, while opponents point to several well-publicized complications such as infection and scarring.

Until now, there has been little data on which to draw an informed opinion. George Waring, M.D., and his coworkers at Emory University, in Atlanta, Georgia, published 10-year follow-up data on a group of patients who originally underwent RK as part of a National Eye Institute research study. Dr. Waring found that 70 percent of the patients were not wearing glasses for distance. As would be expected, the patients over age 40 were likely to be wearing glasses for near vision because of aging changes in the eye. This trade-off is expected for most patients who undergo this procedure. The biggest concern with RK is the stability of the surgical effect. Over the decade-long follow-up period, there was a continuing trend away from nearsightedness and toward farsightedness. Such a trend may mean that many patients after age 40 may have to resume wearing glasses even for distance. This trend has led many RK surgeons to undercorrect the patients, leaving some room for this trend to proceed without harming the patient.

No vision-threatening complications have been noted over the decade. Other minor complications have been rare. Only 2 percent of patients had a minor loss of vision that cannot be corrected with glasses. Twenty-two percent of the patients had minimal cataract formation. However, this finding may be related to aging, and thus unrelated to the surgery. But in all cases, patients considering the procedure should carefully discuss the long-term implications of the procedure, and not just the expected benefit of not having to wear glasses.
Michael X. Repka, M.D.

Forensic Medicine

The media frenzy accompanying the O.J. Simpson murder case has inadvertently highlighted another issue that may well take the stand—the controversial forensic technique known as genetic typing, or, more commonly, DNA fingerprinting. Using genetic typing to link a suspect to a crime scene has been a hotly debated legal issue since it was first introduced in a Florida trial court in 1987.

Although the basic science from which genetic typing derives is considered sound by the scientific community, the reliability of the laboratories performing the tests is often questioned, as are the calculations used to create the odds that DNA from two different sources could result in a match. Despite these questions, most experts agree that DNA typing will become a standard forensic tool.

Criminal cases involving the transfer of blood or semen, and the subsequent comparison of DNA types in the evidential specimen with those of the suspect, have been widely reported by the popular press. DNA typing has also been used in helping to identify cadavers by using parentage-testing techniques (where simpler techniques were futile), and in helping to support sexual-assault charges when pregnancy resulted. In addition, DNA typing is widely used today to help establish parentage (usually paternity) in cases where legally acceptable proof is required before a defendant is ordered to pay child support.

Two main types of DNA typing are used in forensic cases: *Restriction Fragment Length Polymorphism* (RFLP) testing, and *Polymerase Chain Reaction* (PCR)-based methods.

▶ RFLP Testing

RFLP, known to molecular biologists for over a decade, requires a minimum quantity of good-quality DNA from small amounts of body tissue or fluid, such as blood, semen, or hair follicles.

The human genome contains several regions with repetitive-sequence DNA—DNA in which a sequence of bases is repeated in a head-to-tail fashion dozens to hundreds of times. Individuals vary considerably in the *number* of times the sequences are repeated; it is the *number of repeats* that forms the basis for telling people apart. This type of DNA variation is called variable number of tandem repeats (VNTR) polymorphism. (In genetics the word "polymorphism" is used to designate detectable genetic variation among members of the same species.)

The regions (technically called *loci*; singular, *locus*) of DNA analyzed by RFLP are highly polymorphic, meaning that the variation among different people is very high. Further, an RFLP test generally employs several DNA probes. Each probe is specific for a different DNA region. The final results thus consist of several *autoradiograms* (images that resemble supermarket bar codes), which are visually compared with those from evidence.

▶ PCR-based Typing

Polymerase Chain Reaction (PCR) specifically copies (or amplifies) a small segment of DNA hundreds of thousands to millions of times, creating an adequate quantity of the genetic material to permit analysis. PCR has revolutionized molecular biology. In just over a decade, PCR has been instrumental in advances in genome mapping and sequencing, disease detection and diagnosis, and in forensic science and medicine.

The PCR method itself is a copying process, not a method of analyzing the DNA. The PCR

In DNA fingerprinting, DNA is extracted from evidence (A) and fragmented by enzymes (B). An electric current pulls the fragments through a gel, separating them into bands (C). After transferal to a nylon sheet (D), the fragments are bathed in a solution of radioactive probes (E), which bind to specific DNA sequences. X-ray film is exposed to the sheet (F), creating a DNA fingerprint (G).

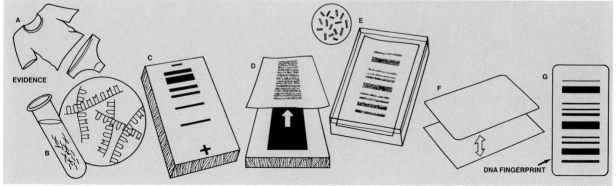

applications that are used in forensic sciences differ from the methods used in genetic mapping or in disease detection primarily in the regions of DNA that are amplified and the actual procedures used to detect the individual differences.

Probably the most widely used PCR-based testing system in forensic analysis is the HLA-DQalpha typing system, developed by Cetus Corporation (now Roche Molecular Systems, RMS). This system analyzes a coding DNA region; 21 different DNA types can be determined using the commercially available RMS amplification and typing kit. An additional typing kit (Amplitype PM), designed to type five separate loci simultaneously using techniques very similar to those employed by HLA-DQalpha, is currently being validated in a number of forensic-science laboratories.

Forensic scientists often encounter specimens that are not only limited in quantity, but also may have been subjected to environmental conditions that can cause DNA degradation. Fortunately, PCR-based methods require a much smaller quantity of specimen material (50 to 100 times less) than what is required for successful RFLP tests. PCR-based methods can also work with specimens containing degraded DNA; the same poor-quality DNA will not always yield RFLP-typing results.

▶ Issues in Forensic DNA Typing

As with any relatively new scientific testing method, DNA typing has ignited some legal controversy surrounding the introduction of its results in court. Adding to the problem is the fact that courts in different states have different criteria for the admissibility of scientific evidence.

Points of controversy have included: 1) whether DNA testing can meet the *Frye* standard, that is, if the technique is generally accepted in the scientific community; 2) whether the testing laboratory has employed validated methods and appropriate quality-assurance procedures in its testing; 3) whether some form of oversight (by government agency) is necessary to assure the public and the courts that both testing protocols and analysts meet preestablished minimum standards; and 4) whether the methods used to calculate profile frequencies in match cases are scientifically defensible.

The federal courts have essentially abandoned the *Frye* standard for the admissibility of scientific evidence, based on the U.S. Supreme Court's decision in *Daubert v. Marion Merrill Dow*. In states that continue to follow the Frye standard, hearings are still held on whether DNA typing meets the standard. The issue can be settled in a particular state only when that state's highest court agrees to hear a case in which the issue is present, and then renders a decision. In any individual case, courts may allow hearings to inquire about such issues as the testing methods used, the competency and experience of analysts, and the quality-assurance procedures.

The adoption of consensus guidelines for lab procedures, recordkeeping, and quality-assurance measures by various professional organizations has helped blunt some of the earlier criticisms. Even so, state and federal regulation of DNA-testing laboratories is likely.

An unresolved point of controversy revolves around the question of calculating the frequency of occurrence of a DNA profile in a DNA-match case. These calculations are based on population studies—the actual typing of hundreds to thousands of people, and computing the frequencies with which the different fragments are observed. The data are also analyzed to ensure that population genetic principles are followed. Generally population studies are carried out separately on different racial/ethnic groups within the general population, such as white, black, or Hispanic. Using these population data to represent the gen-

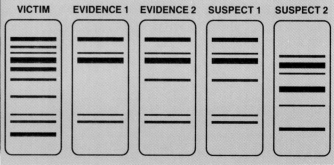

Comparing the unique DNA patterns of individuals has helped officials convict or absolve criminal suspects. At left, a specialist examines several fingerprints. In the case below, the simplified DNA fingerprints implicate suspect 1.

VICTIM	EVIDENCE 1	EVIDENCE 2	SUSPECT 1	SUSPECT 2

eral population, or even a particular racial/ethnic subdivision of it, assumes that the population study has been conducted on a random sample of that group (a difficult proposition to prove).

Some population geneticists believe that DNA-typing data are as yet insufficient to demonstrate that "subpopulations" do not exist within major racial/ethnic groups. The geneticists argue that there may be significant differences in the frequency of a particular DNA type among different subgroups within major racial groups. For example, major differences may exist between Italians and Irish, or between Amish and Norwegians, within the general white population; similar questions can be posed for other population groups.

The population data that have been collected have been analyzed by a number of population geneticists who do not see "subpopulations" as an issue in calculating DNA-profile frequencies. They do not think there is any evidence to suggest that the calculated results would be significantly changed compared with using currently available data.

In DNA-match cases, most experts believe that it is important (even essential) to provide the judge or jury with some basis upon which to interpret the significance (or odds) of the match. This invariably leads to arguments about the method used for calculating the frequency of a matching profile. In 1992 the National Academy of Sciences (NAS) Committee on DNA Typing in Forensic Science recommended an extremely conservative method for computing these frequencies, which takes into consideration any possibility that a frequency in some given case was actually higher in a subpopulation than in the general population.

Many scientists have disagreed with this approach, contending that it is too arbitrary and designed to circumvent a problem that may not, in fact, exist. Even using this conservative approach, however, the frequency of a four-probe DNA-typing match is expected to lie between about 16 people in 10,000 at the lower end, and 16 people in 100 million at the upper extreme.

A few state appellate and supreme courts have sent cases back to trial courts for further hearings (and sometimes new trials) based on the methods used to calculate the frequencies in DNA-match cases.

Even though there is still controversy over some aspects of this testing, forensic DNA typing is here to stay—as much for its ability to demonstrate that specimens do *not* match as for its ability to show that they do. In many ways, genetic typing represents the ultimate method for testing biological evidence.

R. E. Gaensslen, Ph.D.

Genetics and Genetic Engineering

After an intense four-year race, researchers in 1994 identified a long-sought gene that causes the majority of inherited cases of breast cancer. During an unusually productive year, researchers identified two genes linked to inherited colon cancer, a major new tumor-suppression gene, and the genes that cause two of the three major forms of dwarfism. Researchers also demonstrated that juvenile-onset diabetes is caused by a constellation of as many as 18 genes.

▶ Breast Cancer
The elusive breast-cancer gene, called BRCA-1, is carried by about 600,000 American women. These women have an 85 percent risk of developing breast cancer by the age of 65, as well as an unusually high risk of developing ovarian cancer. The gene is responsible for about half of all cases of inherited breast cancer, which in turn accounts for about 5 percent of the 182,000 cases of the disease that occur in the United States each year. About 46,000 women die from the disease each year, making it second only to lung cancer as a cause of death among women. Identification of the gene among these women could allow close monitoring of their health, allowing identification of a tumor at an early, still-curable stage. The five-year survival rate for localized breast cancer is 93 percent; the rate dips to 72 percent if the disease has spread in the breast region at the time of diagnosis, and to 18 percent if the disease has spread to other parts of the body. Equally important, identification of women in families with a history of breast cancer who do not have the gene can relieve anxiety and allow them to forgo unnecessary testing.

The discovery of BRCA-1 was announced in September 1994 by a team headed by Mark H. Skolnick, Ph.D., a geneticist at the University of Utah, and Myriad Genetics Inc., both in Salt Lake City. They located the gene on chromosome 17, one of the 23 pairs of chromosomes that make up the human genetic blueprint. Although they are not yet sure of the gene's function, preliminary results suggest that it is a tumor-suppressor gene—that is, that its normal function is to keep cells from proliferating. Skolnick speculates that a commercial test for the gene could be available in as little as one year. To the disappointment of the researchers, however, they could not find the defective gene in any sporadic (non-familial)

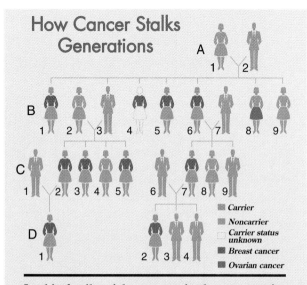

How Cancer Stalks Generations

Carrier
Noncarrier
Carrier status unknown
Breast cancer
Ovarian cancer

In this family, eight cancers in three generations have been linked to defects in BRCA-1. The faulty gene's first known carrier was a man, who passed it along to one son and three daughters. Women who didn't inherit the gene were still susceptible to non-hereditary breast cancer. The noncarriers labeled B1 and C5 both developed cancerous tumors, though at later ages than the carriers.

breast tumors, suggesting that such tumors are caused by a different mechanism.

Also in September, a second team, headed by molecular biologist Douglas F. Easton, Ph.D., of the Institute of Cancer Research in London, England, reported that it had identified the approximate location of a second gene, called BRCA-2, that is thought to be responsible for most of the cases of familial breast cancer not caused by BRCA-1. Some independent evidence suggests that this gene might be related to many sporadic cases of breast cancer, although such a determination awaits isolation of the gene.

▶ Dwarfism
In July 1994, a team headed by John J. Wasmuth, Ph.D., a molecular biologist at the University of California, Irvine, reported the discovery of the gene that causes achondroplasia, the most common form of dwarfism. The disorder, which affects about 1 in 20,000 people, causes alterations in bone growth and development, resulting in an enlarged head, normal-sized trunk, and short limbs. The gene, which is found on chromosome 4 and is called fibroblast growth factor receptor-3 (FGFR-3), was initially identified three years earlier during the search for the gene that causes Huntington's disease; its link to dwarfism was uncovered only recently. FGFR-3 serves as

the blueprint for a growth-factor receptor on bone cells. When it is defective, bones in the limbs are not able to elongate normally.

Although the Irvine researchers developed a test for the gene, they emphasized that it should be used only for prenatal screening of pregnancies at risk for having two copies of the abnormal gene. Even though dwarfs with one abnormal copy of the achondroplasia gene are generally quite healthy, couples in which both parents manifest this form of dwarfism have a 25 percent chance of giving birth to a child with two defective copies of the gene, a condition that is invariably fatal shortly after birth.

In September a team headed by molecular biologists Eric Lander, Ph.D., of the Massachusetts Institute of Technology (MIT) in Cambridge and Albert de la Chapelle, Ph.D., of the University of Helsinki in Finland reported that they had discovered the gene for diastrophic dysplasia, the most common form of dwarfism in Finland, and the third-most-common form in the United States. In Finland, where the disease affects 1 in every 30,000 births, an estimated 2 percent of the population carries the defective gene. This form of dwarfism is associated with twisted, misshapen bones and painful, early-onset arthritis.

Researchers normally search for such genes by studying members of affected families. In this case, they were able to treat the entire Finnish population of 5 million as one big family because virtually all are descended from a small group of "founders" who settled in the area 2,000 years ago. Geneticists believe one of those founders carried the original gene, which they discovered on chromosome 5. Unlike the achondroplasia gene, this one is harmless when the subject carries only one copy. The gene causes disease only when two copies are present. Studies show that the gene is the blueprint for a protein called a sulfate transporter, which researchers had not suspected was involved in the biology of diastrophic dysplasia. Sulfate is an inorganic ion essential to a healthy metabolism. Laboratory studies on cells from patients confirmed that the cells could not, in fact, transport sulfates properly. The discovery thus opens up new possibilities for therapy.

▶ Skeletal Defects
The finding that a fibroblast growth factor receptor is involved in achondroplasia was the first and most important of a striking series of discoveries linking this family of receptors to a variety of skeletal defects. In September 1994, geneticists at the Institute of Child Health in London, England, reported that FGFR-2 is the cause of Crouzon syndrome, a condition characterized by premature fusion of the skull plates. In Novem-

ber 1994, researchers at Johns Hopkins University in Baltimore, Maryland, reported that a different defect in this same gene causes Jackson-Weiss syndrome, a condition marked by abnormalities in the skull and feet. Also in November, geneticists at the University of Pennsylvania in Philadelphia found that a defect in FGFR-1 causes Pfeiffer syndrome, a condition characterized by the premature fusion of bones in the skull during early development. Victims have a tower-shaped head, widely spaced eyes, and finger and toe deformities.

What surprises researchers is that the same receptors are involved in many other facets of growth as well—fibroblasts are present in many tissues in the body—yet the defects in them are manifested primarily in bones. This suggests that there are other genes that control the activity of the receptor genes in various tissues, and that these genes may play a role in the syndromes as well. Identification of these control genes should lead to a much better understanding of the complex process by which development proceeds.

Identification of the genes for these skeletal defects makes possible prenatal identification of children afflicted with them. In most cases the defective genes cause neither deficits in intelligence nor poor health. They simply affect physical appearance. Many, if not most, of these people are able to function successfully in life.

▶ Colon Cancer

Two teams of researchers have independently found two colon-cancer genes that account for 90 percent of inherited cases of colon cancer. Between them the two genes are the cause of one in every six of the 156,000 new cases of colon cancer each year. The genes may also be the cause of about 30 percent of the remaining cases of sporadic colon cancer. Sometime in 1995, the researchers hope to have available diagnostic tests for the presence of the genes. Such tests would allow close monitoring of people carrying the genes, enabling the tumor's detection while it is still operable. The development of such a test is difficult, however, because at least a dozen different mutations in the genes have been observed, and each must be accounted for in any test.

The two teams are headed by researchers from Johns Hopkins University and the University of Vermont, Burlington. The discoveries were announced in December 1993 and March 1994. The two groups have also tentatively identified a third gene that may be responsible for most of the remaining inherited cases of colon cancer.

The functions of the two genes, which occur on different chromosomes, are fairly well known because researchers at Vermont and the Dana-Farber Cancer Institute in Boston, Massachusetts, have been studying the function of identical genes in yeast and bacteria for nearly 20 years. The proteins act much like the spell-check function on a computer, monitoring the replication of DNA to correct mistakes. The first protein scans newly synthesized DNA to check for errors that have occurred during synthesis. If an error is found, the second protein binds to the first and repairs the error. If the first gene is defective, mistakes in DNA formation are not recognized. If the second gene is defective, mistakes are not repaired. Either way, mistakes accumulate until a cancer cell is formed.

Other Cancers. In April 1994, a team headed by researchers at the University of Utah reported the discovery of a gene that appears to be involved in the formation of many types of cancer, including tumors of the lung, breast, bone, skin, bladder, kidney, ovary, and blood. The gene, found on chromosome 9 and named multiple tumor suppressor 1 (MTS-1), is the blueprint for a protein called p16 that regulates a key step in the cell-division process. When functional, p16 inhibits the replication of cells. When it is defective or absent, cells can proliferate much more easily. The researchers found that the gene was defective in nearly half the tumors that they studied. Identification of the gene could lead to the development of new drugs that would mimic its activity and thereby keep cell division in check.

▶ Obesity Gene

In November 1994, researchers at Rockefeller University in New York City identified the gene that, when mutated, causes obesity. The gene is the blueprint for a protein that tells the brain to stop eating once a sufficient amount of body fat is stored. When the gene is defective, the individual keeps eating, even though his or her stomach is full, and thus gains weight. By some estimates, as many as 3 in every 10 Americans are at least 20

Scientists have isolated and cloned a gene in mice that, when mutated, inhibits a protein signal that tells the brain when to stop eating.

percent above their ideal body weight. The researchers hope that it will eventually be possible to administer the healthy form of the protein to control appetite. Identification of the gene in young children could also enable parents to help the children learn how to control their eating behavior at an early age.

▶ Dyslexia

Researchers have discovered the approximate location of a gene that causes the reading disorder dyslexia, a finding that definitively establishes that the disorder is genetic in origin, and that promises early detection of the disorder so that corrective measures can be taken. In dyslexia a person's ability to perceive and process words, numbers, and other symbols is impaired. Often, for example, letters and numbers may appear reversed, making it difficult for a person to absorb the information on a page. An estimated 5 to 10 percent of the population is affected by dyslexia. New interventions can make significant improvements in the reading ability of perhaps half the children treated if the intervention is accomplished at ages 5 or 6. Most children with the disorder are not diagnosed until about the age of 8, by which time no more than 25 percent can be helped. If the disorder is diagnosed much earlier, experts hope an even higher percentage may benefit from the interventions.

Children with dyslexia—a reading disorder with a recently discovered genetic component—have an improved chance of progress if the disability is diagnosed and treated at an early age.

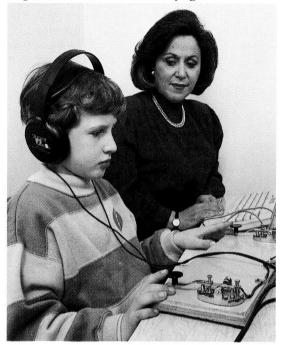

In August, New Jersey researchers reported that a particular region of the brain—the back end of the left side of the brain, in the temporal-lobe area—contains a deficiency in cells that specialize in comprehending rapid sounds. This lack of comprehension, experts say, may be a major factor in the later difficulty in learning to read. In October a team led by researchers at the University of Colorado in Boulder reported that this cell deficiency might be caused by a defective gene located in a region of chromosome 6. The region, they say, could contain from 6 to 200 genes; researchers are racing to discover which one is responsible for the disorder.

▶ Diabetes

British researchers reported in September 1994 that they have identified as many as 18 genes that participate in causing Type 1 (insulin-dependent) diabetes, the most serious form of the disease. Type 1 diabetes results when insulin-secreting cells of the pancreas are destroyed by the body's immune system. Insulin helps cells use and store sugars from the diet; without insulin an individual can quickly fall into a coma and die. Short-term symptoms can be controlled by regular injections of insulin, but complications develop because of the wide swings of sugar concentration in the blood. Complications of diabetes include blindness, kidney disease, heart problems, strokes, and peripheral-nerve damage.

Most genetic diseases are caused by a single defective gene. But diabetes, like heart disease, cancer, and many other disorders, is polygenic, meaning that several genes must be altered for the disease to occur. In many cases, including diabetes and cancer, the victim must be exposed to an environmental trigger, such as a virus or a chemical, for the disease to occur. In the new study, researchers at Oxford University in Oxford, England, studied genetic markers in members of 300 British and American families with a history of Type 1 diabetes. The scientists identified 18 separate locations of genes that play a role in the disorder. One of them, called IDDM-1, is particularly crucial, accounting for 40 to 50 percent of the genetic contribution. Three others play a significant role, much like the supporting actors in a play. The rest are, in effect, bit players. The immediate task is to identify each of the genes and determine precisely what role each specific gene plays in the development of the disease. But even before then, researchers are confident it will be possible to identify individuals whose genetic makeup renders them vulnerable to diabetes, and to intervene to prevent the development of the disease.

Thomas H. Maugh II

Government Policies and Programs

▶ The Clinton Health Plan

For most of 1993 and 1994, the Clinton administration's health-care-reform plan dominated health-care policy. The Health Security Act, the product of extensive executive-branch deliberations, was sent to Congress late in 1993. The health-policy debate was centered in the legislative branch of the federal government, where the Clinton plan and its competitors were dissected, debated, and ultimately abandoned.

In the fall of 1993 and early winter of 1994, groups that would be hurt by the plan voiced their opposition. One group that strenuously opposed the Clinton plan was the private-health-insurance industry, which had been portrayed as responsible for many of the problems in health care. The health-insurance industry's perspective was that the premium costs and coverage problems stemmed from the structural problems in the health-care delivery system over which the health insurers have little control. A major health-insurance trade association, the Health Insurance Association of America (HIAA), developed a series of television commercials that starred the fictional Harry and Louise. These commercials tapped into public anxieties about the increased intrusion of government that the Clinton administration's plan seemed to propose. The health-policy proponents in the Clinton administration were no match for Harry and Louise.

Using slick advertisements, both sides of the health-care debate took to the airwaves to express their views on the proposed—but ultimately abandoned—Clinton plan.

In February 1994, the Congressional Budget Office (CBO), the nonpartisan agency that studies budget and economic issues for the Congress, observed that the federal budget would increase by about one-fourth if the administration's plan were fully implemented. The cornerstone of the Clinton plan was universal coverage, and the primary way universal coverage would be financed was through employer payments. In fact, most employers would have paid 80 percent of the cost of their employees' health insurance.

These payments were to be made to new organizations, called regional health alliances, which, in turn, would reimburse health-care providers. The Clinton administration had not included these transactions in the federal budget. The CBO concluded that the health alliances were federal-government entities, and that both the required premium payments and the federally mandated minimum-benefit package were an exercise of the sovereign power of the federal government. As a result the CBO recommended that the federal budget include both the revenue and spending of the health alliances in the budget.

Press attention focused on the CBO's opinion that the administration's proposal should be included in the budget, and much attention was given to the political problems that this created. Largely ignored was the CBO's praise for the administration's plan. In the official cost report, CBO concluded: "The Health Security Act is unique among proposals to restructure the health-care system both because of its scope and its attention to detail. Some critics of the proposal maintain that it is too complex. A major reason for its complexity, however, is that the proposal outlines in legislation the steps that would actually have to be taken to accomplish its goals. No other proposal has come close to attempting this."

A second blow to the administration's plan came when the business community began to unite in its opposition. The Clinton administration expected opposition from small businesses because employer-provided health insurance is least common among such firms. While the administration sought in its plan to mute small-business opposition through an elaborate series of subsidies, there was no way to bring that sector to actively support the administration's approach without dropping the universal-coverage requirement or moving away from a system in which health insurance was primarily tied to a person's employment.

The Clinton officials had anticipated small-business opposition to their plan, but had counted on support from large business. Most large firms already provide more-generous health insurance for their workers than the Clinton plan would have required. In addition, the Clinton administration threw a significant sweetener to large firms by proposing that the health alliances assume responsibility for health-insurance coverage of workers who took early retirement before being eligible for Medicare. One of the most respected business organizations, the Business Roundtable, dealt a blow to this strategy when it voted 60 to 20 to support a plan based on managed competition that was proposed by Representative Jim Cooper (D-Tenn.). From the administration's perspective, the fatal flaw in the Cooper plan was that it did not mandate universal coverage.

The powerful chairman of the key House Energy and Commerce Committee, John Dingell (D-Mich.), observed that the Business Roundtable vote was the "defining event" in the demise of the Clinton plan in 1994. Following that vote, sentiment in Dingell's committee shifted away from the administration's approach. In June, Dingell announced that his committee could not obtain a majority in favor of any compromise that would effect major reform to the health-care system. This was a major blow to the administration's plan.

The Ways and Means and the Education and Labor committees both approved fairly liberal health-reform bills. The House majority leader, Missouri Democrat Richard Gephardt, molded these bills into a leadership-reform package, but did not bring it to the floor. The strategy was to avoid a House vote on a bill that might be too liberal to get a majority and, instead, to wait for Senate action. Then the differences could be resolved in a conference between the House and Senate.

The wait for Senate action proved long. The key Senate committee was the Finance Committee, chaired by Daniel Patrick Moynihan (D-N.Y.). Moynihan effectively turned health-care reform over to a bipartisan group of moderates on the Finance Committee led by Senators John Chafee (R-R.I.) and John Breaux (D-La.). This group came up with a minimalist reform bill that would gain bipartisan support.

The prospects of getting a bill through Congress dimmed as the November midterm election drew closer. The Republican leadership in the House and the Senate threatened to block consideration of the legislation for the General Agreement on Tariffs and Trade (GATT) if any health-care-reform measure was brought to the floor before the election. Faced with a choice between a minimalist health-care-reform bill, which would prevent consideration of the GATT legislation, or deferring health-care reform until the next Congress, the Senate majority leader, George Mitchell (D-Maine), pulled the plug on health-care reform late in September.

Senator Mitchell concluded that: "The combination of the insurance industry on the outside and a majority of Republicans on the inside provided too much to overcome." Senator Phil Gramm (R-Texas) offered a substantially different assessment: "I think that America rejoices that the president's health-care plan is dead. This is American democracy at its best." With the election of the first Republican Congress in 40 years in November 1994, it was clear that the health-care debate would be dramatically different in 1995.

▶ **Developments in the States**

States were not content to leave it to the federal government to deal with the health-care issues. In 1994 a number of innovations were attempted or under way.

California's Single-Payer-Plan Referendum. In 1994 California voters had the opportunity to vote on whether to institute a major restructuring of the health-care system. Proposition 186 would have created a government-financed health-care system akin to the Canadian model. This proposition would effectively replace private insurance, Medicare, and the California version of Medicaid (Medi-Cal) with a comprehensive health-benefit package. This new system would have been paid for with a business-payroll tax, an increase in the state income tax, a $1-per-pack cigarette tax, and savings achieved by bringing Medicare and Medicaid into the system. California's voters overwhelmingly rejected the proposition.

Oregon's Referendum on Assisted Suicide. Voters in Oregon approved a measure to allow doctors to prescribe suicide pills to terminally ill patients who: (1) have less than six months to live; (2) receive a second opinion from another doctor; (3) make three requests to be allowed to commit suicide; and (4) do not appear to suffer from psychological disorders. With this referendum, Oregon became the first government entity in the world to legalize doctor-assisted suicides. The Netherlands tolerates euthanasia, but technically it is illegal.

State Health-Care-Delivery Proposals. In September, Governor Lawton Chiles of Florida received federal approval for a statewide experiment that would require all beneficiaries of the Medicaid program to participate in managed care. Under this approach, beneficiaries would be required to enroll in commercial health plans that extract deep discounts from doctors and other medical providers. Chiles anticipated that the savings from this approach would enable the state to extend Medicaid protection to 1.1 million additional residents. Implementation of the Florida plan would require the approval of the Florida state legislature. The Florida approach was similar to concepts being tested in a number of states, including Tennessee, Oregon, Rhode Island, Hawaii, and Kentucky. In addition, 40 states have more-limited tests of managed competition. Overall, the U.S. Department of Health and Human Services estimates that enrollment in Medicaid managed-care programs was slightly over 8 million in June 1994, an increase of 63 percent over the previous year.

In Oregon, plans were afoot to extend health-insurance coverage to all residents beginning in 1997. This extension would be financed through employer taxes. Business opposition to this approach was increasing, however, and the Oregon legislature has yet to approve this extension of coverage.

Washington State enacted legislation that would require most employers who have 500 or more workers to provide health insurance by 1999. For this to go into effect, the U.S. Congress would have to waive a federal law, the Employee Retirement Income Security Act (ERISA), that prevents states from regulating health insurance provided by companies that self-insure rather than contract with a commercial insurance company, an HMO, or Blue Cross and Blue Shield. Whether this law should be amended would likely be a major health issue in 1995. The primary opposition is anticipated to come from employers with plans that cover workers in more than one state.

▶ **Other Developments in Federal Policy**
Although reform dominated the congressional agenda in 1994, some legislation was enacted that will make minor changes in health policy.

Dietary-Supplement Legislation. Just before adjournment for the election, the Congress approved legislation limiting the federal Food and Drug Administration's (FDA's) authority to regulate dietary supplements, such as vitamins, minerals, and herbal remedies. For several years, consumers and producers of these goods had bombarded Congress with calls for restrictions on the FDA's authority to regulate these products. These groups were afraid that the FDA would use authority that Congress gave it in the 1990 Nutrition Labeling and Education Act to remove these products from the market. In regulations that took effect on July 15, 1994, the FDA required that health claims on the labels for dietary supplements must be backed up by "significant scientific agreement." While the FDA contended that it had

Proposed legislation would expand health care for female veterans to include periodic Pap smears, breast exams, and mammograms (above).

no intention of taking dietary supplements off the market, many consumers and producers distrusted the agency's ultimate intentions. Congress kept the July FDA regulations in effect, while a seven-member presidential commission reviews them and makes recommendations on how to adjust them. This commission has up to four years to complete its task.

In addition the legislation established an Office of Dietary Supplements within the National Institutes of Health (NIH). The office's mission is to promote scientific study of the benefits of dietary supplements "in maintaining health and preventing chronic disease and other health-related conditions."

Health Assistance for Female Veterans. Congress considered major legislation to expand health care for female veterans, including pre- and postnatal treatment, Pap smears, breast exams, treatment for osteoporosis, and treatment for sexually transmitted diseases and sexual traumas. This legislation got caught up in a debate about whether it would allow the Department of Veterans Affairs to perform abortions. As a result a truncated measure that simply authorized treatment for sexual trauma and mandated that more women be included in Veterans Administration (VA) medical-research studies was finally approved.

Aid for Veterans Suffering from Persian Gulf Syndrome. Congress approved legislation that would allow the Department of Veterans Affairs (VA) to pay disability benefits to veterans disabled by Persian Gulf syndrome, a series of complaints with no known cause that affects some veterans who served in the 1990–91 Persian Gulf War against Iraq. Reported symptoms of the mysterious condition include nausea, hair loss, and heart and respiratory problems. The House had argued that existing law did not authorize benefits for veterans suffering from undiagnosed conditions, while the Senate argued that the secretary of Veterans Affairs already had the authority to pay such benefits. With the adjournment of Congress approaching, the Senate receded largely to the House position, and the bill went to the president.

▶ **Abortion**
Despite the concerns about abortion and the VA women's-health legislation, the abortion issue

was substantially less contentious in Congress in 1994 than in previous years. However, the murder of a doctor and his escort outside an abortion clinic in Florida, and the 1995 killings at a Boston, Massachusetts–area clinic, made it clear that this issue remains a source of profound public contention. Following the Florida murders, Congress moved rapidly to make it a federal crime to use force or the threat of force to intimidate women entering abortion clinics.

For the first time in 18 years, the appropriations bill for the Departments of Labor, Health and Human Services, and Education was approved with no debate on abortion. The traditional language that prohibits the use of Medicaid funds for abortions except to save a woman's life or if the pregnancy was caused by rape or incest was included without debate. The abortion-rights forces avoided the annual debate on this bill to concentrate on protecting the right to abortion in health-care-reform legislation.

Committees in the House and the Senate also approved legislation to codify the right of a woman to an abortion. Currently the legal basis of abortion rights is Supreme Court decisions interpreting certain clauses of the United States Constitution. The new legislation, dubbed the Freedom of Choice Act, did not come to the floor in either the House or the Senate, because of opposition to certain key provisions, including a prohibition on any 24-hour waiting period before a woman could have an abortion.

▶ AIDS Czar Resigns

In July 1994, Christen M. Gebbie, President Clinton's national AIDS-policy coordinator, popularly known as the AIDS czar, resigned abruptly under pressure. Gebbie came to the job with experience caring for AIDS patients, but with no Washington experience.

During the 1992 campaign, Clinton had promised to create an AIDS czar, but had not defined what this czar would do. Even though the Clinton administration sought significant increases in funding for AIDS, an increase of 29 percent in two years for AIDS research, and an increase of 42 percent for prevention and care, advocates felt that not enough progress was being made in an administration that supported a vigorous campaign to end AIDS. Advocacy groups had engaged in confrontational lobbying techniques with the Reagan and Bush administrations, which they had considered adversaries. Faced with a supportive administration, the advocacy groups expected more-rapid action than may have been feasible in an organization as large as the federal government.

James A. Rotherham, Ph.D.

Health-Care Costs

▶ The Reform Debate

From the start of 1994, the push to reform the nation's health-care system dominated all other health-cost issues. The debate primarily focused on how much various reform proposals would cost and how to pay for them. Predictably, the lowest estimates came from proponents of different approaches to reform. Analyses by the Congressional Budget Office (CBO) and such outside experts as Lewin-VHI projected much higher costs. For the Clinton Health Security Act, for instance, the administration calculated a $58.5 billion deficit reduction by the year 2000, while Lewin-VHI projected a reduction of only $24.6 billion, and CBO calculated a $74 billion increase in the deficit. As debate centered on the different projections and whether employers, individuals, or the government should pay the costs of coverage, the push to control the costs of care, which had instigated the reform movement, was all but forgotten.

By the time President Clinton announced in his State of the Union Address in late January 1994 that he would veto any health legislation that did not include universal coverage, the reform battle was already well under way. The plan belatedly delivered to Congress the previous November had provided plenty of fodder for both backers and opponents. The debate excluded the public, though, and focused mainly on the projected costs of reform and how additional coverage could be financed.

The administration and supporters favored a funding mechanism that required employers to pay at least 80 percent of premiums for workers

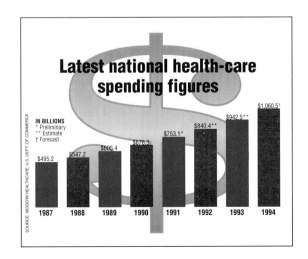

and their families, with government subsidies to aid small firms and those with mainly low-wage earners; subsidies would also aid coverage for the unemployed. The National Federation of Independent Business (NFIB), a trade group for small businesses, vigorously opposed what was labeled the "employer mandate," warning of widespread job losses and failed businesses. The group mobilized an extensive grassroots campaign; small-business owners made their vigorous opposition clear to their local congressional representatives on their home turf.

Despite the efforts of the First Lady, the Clinton health-care plan was ultimately scrapped.

The administration, however, had counted on support from big business to back its proposal. Most large firms currently provide subsidized coverage for employees and, in the interest of holding down their own costs, are actively seeking ways to prevent "cost shifting" by providers to cover care for those with limited or no insurance coverage. In effect, the practice of cost shifting means that those who can pay their bills subsidize the uninsured. Initially, many executives looked to reform to cut their own costs, but that hope was overtaken by fears that health reform would become an open-ended entitlement, leading to higher taxes and uncontrollable increases in the federal deficit.

When the Business Roundtable, which represents the nation's 100 largest employers, met in February, members defied administration efforts to gain support for the Clinton plan, and instead voted to support a rival plan. That plan, proposed by U.S. Representative Jim Cooper (D-Tenn.), did not include an employer mandate, but also did not guarantee coverage for all Americans. Following the Roundtable's lead, the National Association of Manufacturers (NAM) and the U.S. Chamber of Commerce also came out in opposition to the Clinton plan.

Inside Congress, five committees with jurisdiction over government health plans held hearings. Many considered the actions of the House Energy and Commerce Committee, headed by John Dingell (D-Mich.), to be the best test for reform. The committee is viewed as one of the most representative in Congress, both philosophically and geographically. Dingell tried to put together a proposal the committee would approve—recognizing

he would get no Republican votes, because the Republican leadership had pressured members not to support any Democratic plan— by compromising on provisions that caused problems for members.

For instance, Dingell agreed to eliminate price controls for drugs produced by biotechnology firms, and to remove the insurance-coverage mandate for employers with fewer than 10 workers, the group that the NFIB claimed was most vulnerable to the provisions of reform. Even so, by June, Dingell acknowledged his committee would not be able to report a bill for full House deliberation. "The defining event," he later recalled, was the administration's inability to gain the support of big business.

In retrospect, Dingell's failure signaled the beginning of the end for reform during 1994, even though at the time the administration still sounded optimistic about reform prospects. For the first time, major lobbyists on both sides put the chances that anything would pass—including modest insurance-reform measures many suspected would become a last-minute compromise—below 50-50.

Meanwhile, the other four committees did manage to agree to some version of reform. The House Ways and Means Committee crafted a plan that created Medicare Part C to cover the uninsured, while the Education and Labor Committee approved a version very similar to the administration's, as well as a single-payer plan. In the Senate, Edward Kennedy (D-Mass.), chairman of the Labor and Human Resources Committee, also pushed a version that was similar to Clinton's, although the Kennedy plan expanded coverage for mental health and other conditions.

Last to weigh in was the powerful Senate Finance Committee under the leadership of Daniel Patrick Moynihan (D-N.Y.), who had often been at odds with the administration over the hefty cost of the Clinton proposal. What emerged from the Finance Committee was a more mainstream, bipartisan package than any of the other proposals.

Ultimately the final thrust came, not from the committees, but from the efforts of the leadership in both the Senate and the House. House Majority Leader Richard Gephardt (D-Mo.) offered a version that most observers believed was too ambitious to ever gain approval, though many felt Gephardt had taken this approach to leave room for compromise because he believed the Senate version would be more conservative. The result, by that scenario, should have been a mid-ground reform bill.

In the Senate, Majority Leader George Mitchell (D-Maine) worked with a bipartisan "mainstream coalition" to develop a consensus product. Efforts to get a bill approved before summer recess failed, despite Mitchell's pledge to keep members working round the clock. Though the coalition members kept working through the recess, it became increasingly clear that the Republicans would not favor any bill—even the modest insurance reforms that at one time had been so popular. By the end of September, Mitchell proclaimed health reform "dead" for the session, and Congress turned its attention to other issues.

Most of the plans seriously considered by Congress—including the plan introduced in 1993 by the Clinton administration—would have added to the cost burden, CBO analyses suggested. And health economists, pointing to the government's dismal record at predicting the costs of new health programs, worried that history would repeat itself. In that case the costs of providing health coverage to the estimated 39 million uninsured Americans, with hefty government subsidies for small businesses and low-income families, were also seriously underestimated, the critics warned.

As an example of how far wrong government analysts have been, economists recalled that Medicare had been originally projected to cost $9 billion in 1990; it actually cost $67 billion. The prescription-drug benefit in the quickly repealed catastrophic legislation had been projected at $5.7 billion over five years; the following year the government recalculated that cost at $11.8 billion.

▶ Reform Founders

Ultimately, health reform foundered on two unresolved issues: whether employers should be required to pay the costs of health insurance, and what kind of coverage should be required. The split was not along partisan lines, since nearly 100 House Democrats pushed a single-payer, government-financed system, similar to the Canadian system, while other Democrats joined Republicans in opposing the requirement that employers pay the so-called "employer mandate." Members of Congress also failed to agree how quickly reform should be phased in and what measures to take if the market failed to respond as anticipated.

With reform efforts ended for the year, all players quickly placed the blame for the failure elsewhere. Democrats blamed Republicans for their determined effort not to give President Clinton any kind of victory on his number one domestic issue. Republicans attacked Democrats for backing changes they saw as too costly, too dependent on government intervention, and as yet one more potentially budget-breaking entitlement program. Democrats themselves were split, with some favoring a Clinton approach, some opting for a different financing mechanism, and some backing a single-payer system.

The Clinton administration took its share of criticism, starting with the secret process that had been set up to design the plan, and for early attacks on the insurance and pharmaceutical industries—both, as it turned out, were needed as allies in the reform effort. The sheer complexity of the 1,300-plus-page plan was also criticized, as were its designers—notably First Lady Hillary Rodham Clinton and presidential adviser Ira Magaziner—for misreading Congress by offering specific legislative language instead of a blueprint that set goals and parameters for reform.

Senator John Breaux (D-La.), who worked with a core of Senate moderates seeking a plan acceptable to all sides, said he knew reform was gone for the year "when 100 percent became 95 percent," referring to the president's unexpected statement in July that he would accept less than universal coverage.

Nearly everyone blamed—or credited, depending on perspective—the intense lobbying activities of the dozens, if not hundreds, of special-interest groups with a stake in the health-care system. Health care accounts for one-seventh of the nation's economy and, as an industry, ranks among the top employers. As each group worked to protect its own role, the scope of the plan seemed to swell and the complexity increase.

▶ Health Costs Down Anyway

Several other factors undoubtedly contributed to the demise of reform in 1994. One was a stronger economy, which eased fears among those with employer-based insurance who had worried about losing their jobs and thus their coverage. Surveys also showed that while a strong majority of those interviewed backed health reform, most were satisfied with the current system and the care they received, and did not understand what the proposed reform meant for them.

Sweeping changes well under way within the health-care system also relieved the pressure for reform. Though still above the inflation rate, health costs increased at a modest 6 to 7 percent during the year, well below the double-digit growth common in the past. Employers experimented with new ways to hold down their costs of providing care for workers. Throughout the country, doctors, hospitals, and insurers formed

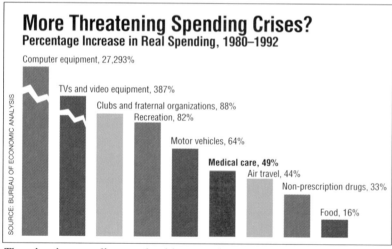

More Threatening Spending Crises?
Percentage Increase in Real Spending, 1980–1992

SOURCE: BUREAU OF ECONOMIC ANALYSIS

Computer equipment, 27,293%

TVs and video equipment, 387%

Clubs and fraternal organizations, 88%

Recreation, 82%

Motor vehicles, 64%

Medical care, 49%

Air travel, 44%

Non-prescription drugs, 33%

Food, 16%

The rise in spending on health care since 1980 has been more than matched by spending on products in other areas of the U.S. economy.

new networks and partnerships, prototypes of many reform proposals.

Another factor was the growing trend of employers to use their purchasing power to drive down costs. Large employers and coalitions of smaller firms, which demanded quality care at reduced costs, pushed consolidation and realignment within the health-care system. New alliances of doctors and hospitals offered discounts to large purchasers, with the promise of increased quality, in return for volume of patients.

A survey by the employee-benefits consulting firm Foster Higgins indicates that cost savings linked to managed care were modest. Overall, preferred-provider organizations (PPOs) cost about 6 percent less than traditional indemnity plans; health-maintenance organizations (HMOs) and point-of-service plans cost about 7 percent less. The higher benefit levels of many managed-care plans offset potential savings, Foster Higgins suggests. In terms of cost to employers, the survey shows that costs increased, on average, 8 percent in 1993—the most-current figures—the lowest in six years. Sixteen percent of employers reported a decrease in benefit cost, while, for 22 percent, costs had remained constant.

Though methods and target groups differed, other surveys reinforced a slowdown in costs. One group, consulting firm Milliman & Robertson Inc., reports that health costs rose a mere 2.5 percent between March 1993 and March 1994. ABR Information Services Inc., which tracks benefits for 12,000 employers, reported in mid-1994 that costs had risen less than 3.5 percent since January 1993. A survey of businesses conducted by the benefits-consulting firm Towers Perrin placed the growth costs at 6 to 7 percent. Many consultants concluded that fear of cost controls in reform proposals played a role in the slowdown.

Even government figures reflected the slowdown. The government reported that total national expenditures for health care accounted for 14 to 14.2 percent of the gross domestic product, slightly lower than the predicted 14.4 percent. A slowdown in the growth of Medicaid, which provided care for more than 32 million poor people in 1993, contributed to the lower figures. In the early 1990s, Medicaid increases exceeded 20 percent, but in 1993 the increase had dropped to 11 percent.

Government figures also show that the number of uninsured grew from 35.4 million to 37.4 million over the past year. Despite new limitations on government spending, expenditures for Medicare and Medicaid—the government health-insurance programs for the elderly, poor, and disabled—account for 16.5 percent of the federal budget. The CBO calculates that within 10 years, at current trends, the programs could consume 26.4 percent of the federal budget.

Analysts are also conducting studies to determine what procedures work and what don't, and to produce care guidelines. Many consumer advocates caution that quality will erode as employers and managed-care plans focus strongly on bottom-line costs. They worry that the lowest-cost care is not always best for patients, and that shortcuts that limit tests, medications, or hospital stays could prove more costly in the long run. Although no definitive studies were completed, anecdotal evidence of deferred, omitted, or uncovered care began to accumulate, fueling those concerns.

Technology and new drugs are often considered overly expensive. The pharmaceutical industry counters critics by reminding them of the high costs of research, development, testing, and finally gaining Food and Drug Administration (FDA) approval of a new drug. The price, officials say, reflects those costs as well as the costs of continuing research for new drugs.

Expensive technology and procedures, such as magnetic-resonance imaging (MRI) and bone-marrow transplants, are also blamed for boosting costs. A study by the Health Care Technology Institute concludes that technology contributes between 11 and 15 percent to each year's health-care-cost increase. General inflation accounts for about half the increase, the analysis shows, and population growth for about 10 percent. In the future a rapidly aging population requiring ever-more-sophisticated care will confound efforts to control these increases.

Mary Hager

Health Personnel and Facilities

▶ The Vanishing Independent Hospital

Cost-driven changes in health-care markets throughout the country are making the familiar independent community hospital a rarity. A recent survey of nearly 24 percent of all U.S. hospitals by a national accounting firm indicates that 71 percent of the hospitals are in the process of developing arrangements to integrate—or already have integrated—with another hospital, physician group practice, managed-care organization, or a specialized health facility such as a home-health agency, nursing home, or ambulatory-surgery center. Eighty-one percent of the hospitals report that within the next five years, they will cease operating as stand-alone institutions. Most of these hospitals will likely merge with another institution or join a network of health-care providers before the end of the century.

As a result of the integration efforts, massive nationwide health-care coalitions are emerging. Columbia/HCA Healthcare is the largest for-profit chain of hospitals in the nation, with medical-care networks in 10 large Sun Belt cities. In the summer of 1994, Columbia/HCA joined Medical Care America, the largest chain of ambulatory-surgery centers in the country.

Regional health-care-delivery systems also are blossoming in many areas. In the Minneapolis-St. Paul, Minnesota, area, 70 percent of the residents belong to three health-maintenance organizations (HMOs), each of which has its own medical facilities. Medica, whose 550,000 enrollees make it one of the largest HMOs in the Twin Cities area, is affiliated with HealthSpan Health Systems Corporation, which has 17 hospitals in Minnesota and northwestern Wisconsin.

The objective of these mergers is to create health-care systems that are large enough to offer convenient, comprehensive health care to large numbers of patients. Ideally, these centralized systems will satisfy the demands of health-care payers for high-quality services at reasonable prices, control and continuously improve the delivery of health services, and provide a single source for the full range of health care.

▶ Primary-Care Focus

In another cost-driven development, newly emerging networks, or integrated delivery systems, are shifting the treatment of many types of acute illnesses to outpatient sites. Hospital members of integrated delivery systems consequently are reconfiguring their facilities to provide more primary care.

Primary care will be the point at which patients enter the health-care system; it will also be the point at which health-care providers determine the mix of services required by each patient. Primary-care providers therefore will direct patients who have unhealthy lifestyles to disease-prevention and wellness-promotion programs. Providers will also coordinate treatment and support activities across all sites of health-care delivery for patients who have long-term, chronic illnesses.

Some hospitals are beginning the transition to primary-care emphasis by converting inpatient units to physician office suites. Bradford Hospital in Starke, Florida, replaced 35 inpatient beds with a primary-care-physician clinic. Afterward the hospital was able to steer patients who are not seriously ill away from visiting the emergency department and into developing a relationship with a family doctor.

A number of hospitals are building extensions that are especially designed for primary-care patients. The new centers have their own entrances and waiting rooms, as well as separate diagnostic, laboratory, and X-ray facilities.

▶ Reengineering Hospital Care

As health-system integration and primary care grow in importance, hospitals find that they need to take a hard look at the ways in which they operate. Hospitals have changed little in structure or organization since the 19th century. They

Rising costs and shrinking budgets have prompted many health-care facilities to change their focus. Florida's Bradford Hospital, for example, has converted much of its space into a primary-care clinic.

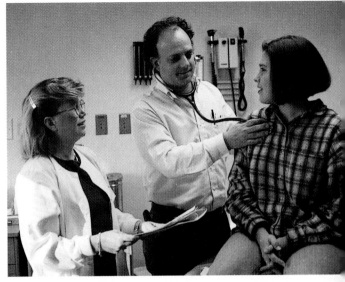

are still organized around departments and functions; they have complex hierarchical structures that slow decision making and hamper cooperation among departments.

A small but expanding movement in the health-care industry is calling for hospitals to completely reorganize themselves so they can cut through the bureaucratic maze and meet more directly the needs of payers and patients. Such a reorganization would require many hospitals to go back to the drawing board and design an institution that responds to specific patient-care needs. Hospitals would identify the health-care activities that must be accomplished in order for patients to achieve satisfactory, positive outcomes as efficiently as possible, and then revamp operations to coordinate performance of the activities.

Such "reengineering" requires from nine months to four years to complete. The process involves an assessment of an institution and its goals, complete retooling of operational functions, revision of individual job descriptions, reassignment of responsibilities for specific duties, and redevelopment of policies and procedures.

▶ **Acceptance of Alternative Medicine**
Every year, individuals make 37 million more visits to providers of unconventional therapy than they do to their primary-care physicians. Even so, health-care facilities in this country have long failed to recognize the benefits of such alternative therapies as Chinese medicine, Tai Chi, chiropractic, herbal medicine, and acupuncture. That may all change since the formation in 1993 of the Office of Unconventional Medicine at the National Institutes of Health (NIH), Bethesda, Maryland. An ever-increasing number of health-care facilities are now seriously exploring forms of alternative medicine, and some have gone so far as to offer unconventional treatment alongside standard methods.

Grant Hospital in Chicago, Illinois, has established a partnership with the Holistic Center, the largest organization of practitioners of holistic medicine in the U.S. The Holistic Center employs 50 staff members who are dedicated to treating the whole person through techniques that address emotional, physical, and spiritual factors.

As a result of the arrangement, Grant Hospital will treat rheumatoid arthritis with acupressure, lifestyle counseling, stress-reducing bodywork, and Chinese medicine, as well as with traditional anti-inflammatory drugs and physical therapy. For irritable colon, the hospital will make use of yoga, Tai Chi, biofeedback, and psychotherapy centered around the body, in addition to the more standard antispasmodic drugs, dietary education, and stress-reduction techniques. The hospital will also send medical interns and residents to the Holistic Center to obtain training in alternative-medicine practices.

▶ **Nursing Shake-up**
An offshoot of the trend toward hospital downsizing and reorganization is large-scale job restructuring involving nurses. Hospitals have been laying off nurses in large numbers. In fact, one hospital reduced its nursing ranks by replacing 200 full- and part-time registered nurses with licensed practical nurses, medical assistants, and patient-care technicians.

Hospitals also have been altering the duties nurses normally perform. In the past, registered nurses were responsible for 75 percent or more of the patient care provided. Now hospitals are employing fewer registered nurses, and those nurses perform only such skilled patient-care duties as catheter insertion and drug administration. Many of the low-skill tasks nurses used to perform, such as bathing and feeding patients, are being done by aides supervised by nurses.

By making more use of aides, hospitals can save large amounts in labor expenses. In California, hospitals reportedly save $25,000 per year each time a nurse's position is filled by an aide. Stanford University Hospital in Palo Alto, California, has saved $25 million since 1989 by reducing the number of registered nurses it hires as patient-care employees from 90 to 60 percent.

▶ **Parish-Nurse Programs**
While fewer nurses appear to be needed in hospitals, increasing numbers are finding work in their local communities as health-care representatives of their church parishes. Parish nurses address the physical, emotional, and spiritual needs of congregation members primarily by helping patients obtain the proper services from health-care providers and support-service agencies.

According to the National Parish Nurse Resource Center in Chicago, there are at least 1,500 formal parish-nurse programs and many other informal efforts. Most of the programs are designed to meet specific requirements of their sponsoring parishes. The activities of the nurses range from conducting health screenings to performing counseling and making referrals.

One parish-nurse program in Pittsburgh, Pennsylvania, has seven part-time nurses who serve 10 inner-city churches. In the past three years, nurses in the program have made 13,000 visits to homes, nursing homes, and senior-citizen centers, and they have referred more than 2,500 people to health and social-service agencies.

Karen M. Sandrick

Heart and Circulatory System

▶ Coronary-Artery Disease

Despite the continued decline in the annual number of deaths from coronary-artery disease (CAD) and from stroke in the United States, the incidence of the total number (both fatal and nonfatal) of heart attacks or myocardial infarctions (MI's) remains steady, and the incidence of chronic heart failure is rising. Since the 1960s mortality from CAD has fallen by nearly 50 percent, thanks to improved treatments and to Americans improving their risk factors for CAD. Nonetheless, over 1 million Americans still die each year from CAD, making it still the most common cause of death by far. Most CAD deaths are due to acute MI or to sudden cardiac death, which is usually the result of an arrhythmia (abnormally fast or slow heartbeat). Over 1.5 million MI's still occur annually in the United States, a number that remains steady despite improved survival rates. Thus, although many more people survive their heart attacks, these people remain at risk for further MI's, arrhythmias, and chronic weakening of the heart muscle (heart failure).

Atherosclerosis is a complex process that ultimately results in plaques or ingrowths of tissue on blood-vessel walls; the narrowed vessels curtail blood flow through the affected arteries. Any tissues "downstream" then suffer from a reduced supply of oxygen and nutrients, and their function is impaired. When the arteries supplying the heart muscle itself are involved, the heart muscle is starved for blood. This condition is termed coronary-artery disease (CAD).

Two reports confirm long-held suspicions that heavy physical exertion can indeed trigger MI, especially in those who are usually sedentary. However, the studies also confirmed that those who were habitually active were at lower risk, even when they greatly exerted themselves. Another study showed that MI risk is greatest on Mondays, presumably a day of high stress. Thus, stress and heavy physical exertion can trigger MI in those with CAD, presumably by causing plaques to rupture, leading to the formation of blood clots at the site of the rupture. These clots then abruptly cut off blood flow through the already narrowed vessel; heart muscle dies quickly if flow is not restored. The result is an MI.

Several 1994 studies bolster evidence that moderate alcohol intake (one to two drinks per day) reduced MI risk by two mechanisms: a rise in protective HDL cholesterol, and a rise in the natural clot-dissolving substance t-PA (which is used to treat MI). A 1994 study concludes that cholesterol levels were not predictive of CAD risk in people over 70 years old, adding fuel to the controversy about how aggressively cholesterol levels should be lowered with medications.

Other recent studies, however, support the aggressive lowering of cholesterol, especially in those with known CAD or those likely to have it. Several studies show that lowering cholesterol with new drugs such as lovastatin (Mevacor), pravastatin (Pravachol), or simvastatin (Zocor) results in reduced atherosclerosis in heart and brain arteries, and fewer MI's.

▶ Myocardial Infarction: Treatment

Of the 5 million Americans with chest pain evaluated in emergency rooms annually, less than 30 percent of those admitted to a coronary-care unit wind up actually having an MI. The problem is that the usual blood tests are not conclusive for up to 24 hours after the pain begins, so large numbers of patients have to be admitted to be on the safe side. Three new blood tests allow for identification of those with MI within a couple of hours, and promise to greatly reduce the number of unnecessary admissions.

Other 1994 research focused on drug therapy during and after MI. The GUSTO trial concludes that the clot dissolver t-PA saves more lives than either streptokinase (the other major "thrombolytic" drug) or a combination of streptokinase and t-PA. The trial found that t-PA opens clotted coronary arteries more effectively in the early phase of MI, leading to the rescue of more heart muscle and a better survival rate. Another study found that t-PA dissolved artery clots more effectively than the other thrombolytic drug, "APSAC" (a streptokinase variant), or than the combination of the two drugs.

Other recent studies report that the blood thinner hirudin (derived from leech saliva) is a more effective blood thinner than the old standby heparin in two important situations: when used with a thrombolytic during MI, and when used during balloon angioplasty. High doses of heparin were found in several studies to produce frequent brain hemorrhages, causing some alarm.

Three large studies show that drugs in the ACE-inhibitor class, such as captopril (Capoten) or lisinopril (Zestril, Prinivil), save lives when given early to MI patients. Two of the same studies found that nitroglycerin-type drugs do not enhance survival in MI, an unexpected finding. Similarly, the role of magnesium as an MI treatment remains controversial after recent trials. Finally, a pilot study reports that a starchlike synthetic molecule called Poloxamer 188 (Rheothrx) improves outcomes when used during MI. The drug acts in a unique way to increase the fluidity of blood and inhibit the aggregation of blood cells.

▶ Angioplasty

Last year, over 300,000 Americans had their CAD plaques treated by angioplasty. In this procedure a catheter (hollow plastic tube) is placed through the skin into an artery in the groin or arm. The catheter is then pushed through the main artery or aorta up to the openings of the coronary arteries at the aorta's origin in the heart itself. Through the catheter a smaller catheter with a balloon on its end is pushed into a coronary artery and beyond the segment narrowed by plaque. The balloon is then inflated as it straddles the plaque, thereby compressing it and widening the path through which the blood flows in the artery. This technique avoids the cost, risk, and discomfort of bypass surgery, which requires open-chest surgery and general anesthesia. There are drawbacks to angioplasty, however: many blockages are not technically suitable for the balloon; 2 to 3 percent of cases result in damage to the artery, which often results in emergency bypass surgery and an MI caused by the procedure; and over 30 percent of blockages opened by angioplasty recur within six months.

Several 1994 reports compared angioplasty and bypass surgery as treatment for those with CAD in multiple arteries (angioplasty has long been recognized as preferable in cases where only one artery is involved). They all found that death and MI rates were similar, that angioplasty costs less (though, with time, the gap narrowed), and that angioplasty patients had more chest pain over time, needed more medications, and required many more repeat angioplasties and bypass surgery than those who underwent bypass initially. Thus, the choice of treatment often falls on the patient to choose between "getting it over with" with bypass surgery, at the cost of the discomfort of major surgery; or using angioplasty to buy time or avoid open heart surgery, at the cost of many more catheter procedures, more chest pain, and more medications.

Recently many ingenious devices have been developed to try and improve on the simple angioplasty balloon. Various drills, cutters, and shavers have been introduced, as have laser catheters that burn through plaque. In addition, several cylindrical, stainless-steel scaffolds called "stents" have been placed in plaque-ridden segments of coronary arteries to prop up the vessel's channel after a balloon has opened up a blockage. Delivered to the artery wall atop the angioplasty balloon, the stent is expanded as the balloon is inflated; the balloon is then withdrawn, leaving the expanded stent firmly imbedded in the artery wall, where it is meant to keep the artery "open."

The first stent available in the United States was approved by the Food and Drug Administration (FDA) in 1993; the second was approved in 1994. The new device, known as the Palmaz-Schatz stent, gained approval on the basis of two 1994 studies demonstrating the stent's ability to reduce the rate of recurrent vessel narrowing, compared with balloon angioplasty alone. This represented a major breakthrough, as no treatment of any kind had ever reduced this troublesome shortcoming of the balloon procedure. In addition, study patients who received the stent had more successful angioplasty procedures with

Boring Holes to Help a Starving Heart

An experimental technique called laser revascularization is being used to create new blood supplies in the heart when other methods have not succeeded. A surgeon uses a carbon dioxide laser to bore 15 to 30 tiny channels through the heart's muscle wall and into the left ventricle, allowing blood to seep in and diffuse throughout the tissue.

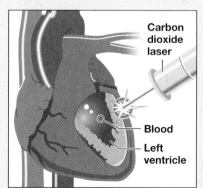
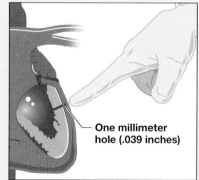
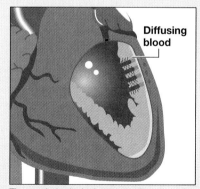

The laser is fired between heart beats, while the heart is gorged with blood. This type of laser is absorbed by liquid, so the blood in the ventricle blocks it from damaging other tissue.

The surgeon presses a finger on the surface for a moment to promote clotting. The channels cut by the laser do not clot because the heart is meant to be suffused with blood.

The new holes in the heart muscle wall act like blood vessels. As the heart beats, it pumps blood into the previously starved ventricle through these channels.

Sources: P.L.C. Systems, Inc.; "Mayo Clinic Heart Book" (William Morrow & Company)

better widening of the arterial narrowing, and fewer complications during and after the procedure. The first stent approved, the Flex-Stent, is intended for use only as an emergency scaffold when a balloon damages an artery to the point that it closes down completely or is about to do so. The Palmaz-Schatz stent is instead intended to improve the outcome of balloon angioplasty from the start, *before* there is any damage to the artery.

▶ Arrhythmias

Arrhythmias include all abnormal heartbeat rhythms, including those that are too fast and those that are too slow. Antiarrhythmic drugs are uniformly toxic, causing a wide variety of side effects and often promoting the arrhythmias they are intended to curtail. While most have been very disappointing or downright dangerous, the drug amiodarone (Cordarone) has recently been shown to increase survival in a variety of settings, though it, too, can cause serious problems. In recent years, studies have shown that amiodarone saves lives when given after MI. In 1994 a study reported that heart-failure patients given the drug lived longer and were admitted to the hospital less, regardless of whether or not they displayed arrhythmias.

Many rapid heart rhythms can be treated electrically. Pacemakerlike devices are implanted under the skin with electrodes tunneled through veins into the heart. Another method involves destroying the areas of heart muscle that create the abnormal rhythms by applying radiowave energy through electrodes inserted into the heart via the groin. These electrical methods are controlling more and more types of arrhythmias, and increasingly sophisticated devices are being developed.

One type of arrhythmia, atrial fibrillation, is the most common chronic arrhythmia. Its incidence rises sharply with advancing age, and it is associated with a variety of other cardiac diseases, high blood pressure, and diabetes. Besides the possibility of cardiac symptoms, atrial fibrillation is a major cause of stroke, due to the possibility of blood clots forming while the atrial chambers of the heart are "fibrillating," or quivering. Several 1994 studies have refined our knowledge of which patients with atrial fibrillation are most likely to have a stroke, and confirmed the benefits of the blood thinner warfarin (Coumadin, others) in preventing this type of stroke. However, studies on aspirin are quite inconclusive; overall a mildly protective effect less than that of warfarin is suggested. Several new reports suggest that amiodarone is likely to be the safest and most effective antiarrhythmic drug for termination or prevention of atrial fibrillation.

Richard L. Mueller, M.D.

Immunology

▶ Directing the Immune System

Like a battlefield commander facing an enemy attack, the immune system must react quickly when the body is invaded by a bacteria, virus, or other such microbial agent. After assessing the exact nature of the threat, the immune system has to marshal the proper defensive response to neutralize the invader.

Recently scientists have gained new insights into a molecular messenger known as interleukin-12 (IL-12), which plays an essential role in immune response. Intensive study of IL-12 is creating a more detailed picture of how the immune system recruits cells and assigns them to fight off invaders. Beyond the basic knowledge that IL-12 is yielding to scientists, it also holds promise as a clinical tool. It may one day underlie strategies for fighting cancer, for shoring up immune systems depleted by the AIDS virus, and for treating certain parasitic and allergic disorders.

Discovered in the late 1980s, IL-12 was the 12th interleukin to be identified. Scientists have now discovered 15 of these messenger molecules, collectively known as cytokines. Like other cytokines, IL-12 exerts biochemical action on the cells of the immune system. Its action centers on white blood cells known as helper T lymphocytes, or T helper cells. These cells execute the crucial task of recognizing the presence of foreign proteins—antigens—that signal the presence of an invading organism. T helper cells then initiate the immune system's main response.

In humans, there are two main types of immune response, each involving different kinds of T helper cells. The humoral response, in which the immune system creates antibodies to mark and destroy infected cells, involves a T helper type 2 cell, or TH-2. This is called the TH-2 response. The other main response, known as cell-mediated immunity, centers on the T helper type 1 cell. Hence, this is known as the TH-1 response, in which other classes of T cells, bearing such no-nonsense names as natural killer cells, are dispatched to destroy the offending virus or bacteria. Exactly why the body has two major immune responses, and how it selects between them, are questions that researchers are still sorting out. But scientists now believe that of the two responses, a strong TH-1 response seems more advantageous in fighting infectious agents and maintaining the body's health. And it is becoming clearer that IL-12 plays a major part in orchestrating the TH-1 response.

In one study that clarified IL-12's role in the immune response, Kenneth Murphy, Ph.D., and his colleagues at the Washington University School of Medicine in St. Louis, Missouri, used a special strain of mice to examine how the immune system responds to invading organisms (mice, like humans, possess both TH-1 and TH-2 cells; in fact, this dual immune capacity was first observed in mice and later confirmed in humans). Murphy and his team observed that roving cells known as macrophages, which serve as the immune system's first line of defense, send out a biochemical message that stimulates the TH-1 response. The actual messenger is IL-12. In particular, IL-12 stimulates production of another key immune signaler, known as interferon-gamma, which in turn stimulates the action of killer cells that seek out and attack intruders.

As immunologists continue to study the basic mechanisms of IL-12, other scientists are attempting to develop new medical therapies that exploit the molecule's key role in the search-and-destroy action of T cells. For cancer patients in particular, IL-l2 may provide effective forms of gene therapy, in which the body's own immune system is brought to bear in destroying cancer cells. In experiments at the Pittsburgh Cancer Center in Pennsylvania, for example, Michael T. Lotze, Ph.D., and colleagues introduced IL-12 into cancerous mice. They observed that the mice not only cured themselves of tumors, but rejected new tumors. The next step, now in its preliminary stages, is to bring this treatment to human patients. IL-12, as one researcher recently observed, "is already demonstrating great promise for manipulating the immune response in cancer and other diseases."

Among those other diseases are infections caused by parasitic organisms. Such diseases are a huge health problem, particularly in developing nations. In the case of schistosomiasis, for example, which is caused by a worm that lays eggs in blood vessels throughout the body of an infected person, the immune system seems to invoke an unfavorable TH-2 response. The resulting build-up of cells in blood vessels actually causes more harm than the original infection. Researchers have noted that, when administered to infected mice, IL-12 stimulates a far more effective TH-1 immune response against the parasite.

Another promising area for IL-12 is in the treatment of AIDS. Recent research has suggested that people infected with HIV (the virus that causes AIDS) show decreased production of TH-1 messenger compounds. Some researchers believe that HIV may shift the immune system toward a TH-2 response, allowing the virus to spread more rapidly and destructively. Scientists examining cells extracted from persons with AIDS have noted that administering IL-12 to the cells seems to restore the cells' ability to fight infection—the ability that is destroyed by HIV. As tests begin in human patients, researchers hope that IL-12 can be used to help weakened immune systems fight off the opportunistic infections that now kill persons with AIDS.

IL-12 has not yet proven itself as a therapeutic tool. Previously other interleukins, such as IL-2, showed initial promise, but proved to be too toxic for use in treatments. At the moment, however, hopes are high for IL-12.

▶ **Prion Diseases: A Cross-Species Threat?**
Recently scientists have gained a new understanding of brain proteins called prions, which—in their normal, healthy form—seem to play a role in nerve signaling. In some cases, however, prions undergo a transformation into an abnormal form. Once changed, these renegade prions begin a ruinous march through the brain, converting healthy prions into abnormal ones and destroying brain tissue as they go. The result is dementia and death.

Scientists have been trying to understand more about the process by which normal prions undergo this deadly transformation. Previously it was believed that a virus or bacterium of some kind must be at work in the conversion of "good" prions into "bad" ones and in the subsequent development of disease. However, because prions contain no cellular or genetic material in which viral replication might take place, investigators have been hard-pressed to explain the

Mad cow disease, a prion disorder that destroys the brains of infected cattle, has devasted some herds in England. Below, a carcass is removed for incineration.

process of conversion. Now, thanks to recent findings by a team of researchers at the Massachusetts Institute of Technology (MIT) in Cambridge and at the National Institutes of Health (NIH), the matter is coming into sharper focus.

The team, led by MIT's David A. Kocisko, Ph.D., managed to reproduce the process of prion conversion in a test tube. By incubating normal prions and their abnormal counterparts—both isolated from hamsters—the researchers demonstrated that prions themselves can cause the conversion. The culture used in the experiment had been painstakingly purified of all cellular material, eliminating the possibility that any virus or stray bit of genetic material had come into play in the infection of normal prions. Exactly how the abnormal prions work their transformations, and how they initiate disease, are matters that have yet to be determined. At present, scientists are particularly interested in the way that prions seem to alter their shape in the course of infection, changing from a twisting, helical structure into a flatter shape.

In humans, prion disease takes various forms, and is known by such names as kuru, Creutzfeldt-Jakob disease, and fatal familial insomnia. These disorders can be caused by inherited genes, by accidental genetic mutation, or by direct infection (for example, Creutzfeldt-Jakob disease was inadvertently transmitted to patients when they were given therapeutic treatments involving hormones or brain tissues derived from infected persons). Similar prion disorders are seen in sheep and goats among other mammals. Cows, for example, suffer a prion disease known as bovine spongiform encephalopathy (BSE), also known as mad cow disease. The worrisome question is whether such diseases can be transmitted from animals to humans.

Such concerns have already had an effect in Europe, where an outbreak of BSE in English cows has caused alarm. Cats in England have been infected with BSE through pet food made from contaminated beef. Could eating beef from infected cows cause prion disease in humans?

That question awaits an answer. However, the recent findings regarding prion conversion will considerably aid subsequent work. The cell-free culture developed by Dr. Kocisko and his colleagues will serve as a valuable experimental model in which prion transmission between species can be tested. It will also help to explain the process by which good prions turn bad. A better understanding of prion disease will hopefully shed more light on how the body falls prey to other neurological disorders, such as Alzheimer's disease and Parkinson's disease.

Christopher King

Kidneys

▶ Dietary Therapy for Renal Disease

Many diseases irreversibly damage the kidneys. Eventually *chronic renal failure* may develop, in which there is sufficient damage to impair the elimination of waste products from the body. If the process continues, *end-stage renal failure* may occur, necessitating dialysis or kidney transplantation to sustain life. In the U.S., well over 200,000 people suffer with end-stage renal disease.

For over 30 years, kidney specialists have recommended low-protein diets to their patients with advanced renal failure, since many of the harmful wastes that accumulate with chronic renal failure originate from dietary protein. Over the past 15 years, it has become commonplace to restrict dietary protein earlier in the course of renal disease, based on yet another rationale: the workload on damaged kidneys is intensified by dietary protein, and this added strain can worsen the injury process initiated by the original renal disease. Limited studies performed on animals and humans in the early 1980s suggest that restricting protein in the initial phases of renal disease may help preserve kidney function.

Low-protein diets are notoriously hard to follow and can have undesirable metabolic effects. In order to determine whether they should be the standard of care in all patients with incipient renal failure, a large multicenter trial was undertaken. The Modification of Diet in Renal Disease (MDRD) study followed the rate of renal-function decline in 840 patients representing many different forms of renal disease. The subjects received normal, low, or very low amounts of dietary protein. The study was fraught with difficulties: differences among patients make group data hard to interpret; renal function is very difficult to quantify accurately; and the rate of decline of renal function may fluctuate for unclear reasons.

The results of the MDRD study, published in March 1994, indicate only a slight benefit of dietary-protein restriction in retarding renal failure. Given the difficulty in implementing such a diet, and bearing in mind that drug therapy may be as beneficial and easier on the patients, it is unlikely that low-protein diets will remain the norm in renal-disease treatment.

▶ Diabetic Kidney Disease

Up to one-half of insulin-dependent diabetics develop kidney disease as a complication of the condition. This form of renal disease, called *diabetic nephropathy*, is the leading cause of end-stage renal disease in the U.S. In diabetic nephropathy, patients have typically had diabetes for at least 10 years before protein is discovered in their urine (proteinuria). Thereafter renal failure develops over a period of a few years.

In animal models of diabetic nephropathy, the pressure in the glomeruli, the small capillary filters of the kidney, is extremely high. A widely used class of antihypertensive drugs, the angiotensin converting enzyme (ACE) inhibitors, can lower intraglomerular pressures. Preliminary studies involving animals and people have shown that this form of treatment may ameliorate the course of diabetic nephropathy.

The results of the largest controlled trial to date to determine with certainty whether ACE-inhibitor therapy should become standard practice in early diabetic nephropathy were reported in the *New England Journal of Medicine* (November 11, 1993). In the study, over 400 patients at risk for diabetic nephropathy were randomly assigned to receive either an ACE inhibitor, known as captopril, or a placebo. The prevalence of hypertension was similar in the two groups. In the group receiving the placebo, hypertension, if present, was controlled with other types of drugs. The study's results suggest that captopril substantially retards the progress of diabetic renal disease; indeed, the risk of progression to end-stage renal failure was reduced by as much as 50 percent over the study period (up to four years). ACE inhibitors should probably be standard therapy for all diabetic patients with early nephropathy, barring contraindications to their use.

Diabetic nephropathy is one of the so-called *microvascular complications* of diabetes. These disorders also include diabetic retinopathy, a cause of blindness, and diabetic neuropathy, which may cause pain and weakness. For years, physicians have debated the extent to which strict control of blood sugar can prevent the development of such devastating conditions. In the recently reported findings of the Diabetes Control and Complications Trial (DCCT), conventional insulin therapy via daily injections promotes normalization of blood sugar for longer periods of time. Over 700 patients at risk for, or in the early stages of, diabetic retinopathy were studied in each treatment group and followed for

an average of 6.5 years. The risk of developing proteinuria, the sentinel sign of diabetic nephropathy, was reduced by 54 percent in the intensively treated group. Although these results argue convincingly in favor of strict glycemic control for diabetics, this form of therapy is not easy to apply. (See also page 22.)

▶ **Genes and Renal Disease**

Essential hypertension, the most common form of hypertension, afflicts 20 percent of the U.S. population. Since the kidney is the central organ of blood-pressure regulation, essential hypertension is widely thought of as a renal disease. Because of its strong tendency to run in families, hypertension is also considered a genetic disorder, although the specific pattern of inheritance is poorly understood.

Findings published in the *New England Journal of Medicine* (November 11, 1993) promise to shed light on the genetics of essential hypertension. The gene for the disease appears to be linked to the gene coding for angiotensinogen, a precursor molecule from which angiotensin II, a hormone that participates in the development of

Over 10,000 Americans receive kidney transplants each year. Above, a surgeon removes a donated kidney from its shipping container.

hypertension, is formed. Identifying genetic markers for hypertension and its associated conditions may eventually lead to improved techniques for identifying and treating people at risk.

Another form of inheritable kidney disease is *autosomal dominant polycystic kidney disease* (ADPKD). The gene that transmits this condition occurs in approximately 1 of every 500 people throughout the world, making ADPKD the most prevalent serious genetic disorder known. People with ADPKD are likely to develop end-stage renal failure, and are prone to complications in other organ systems as well.

Two genetic abnormalities are known to cause ADPKD. One form of the disease, called PKD-1, involves chromosome 16, and is responsible for the vast majority of cases. Scientists are currently on the threshold of cloning this gene—perhaps a first step toward the eventual availability of gene therapy to treat this important disease. The other genetic variant of ADPKD, called PKD-2, has recently been localized to chromosome 4.

David M. Clive, M.D.

Liver

▶ Hepatitis B

A group of investigators presented the results of a multicenter study of lamivudine, a new antiviral drug for patients with chronic hepatitis B. This drug is a nucleoside analogue, a class of substances that mimic the essential ingredients of genes and "deceive" the virus into using them rather than the normal building blocks that are available in cells. In 1993 much attention had focused on another nucleoside, called FIAU, which had caused severe toxicity in a group of hepatitis B patients involved in a previous study.

In addition to showing none of the severe toxic effects of FIAU, lamivudine was found to have a profound suppressive effect on the replication of hepatitis B virus in infected patients. With a few exceptions, however, the suppressive effect was transient, and viral replication recurred upon cessation of therapy. These promising results have led to the formation of a larger multicenter group to investigate the effectiveness and safety of lamivudine, taken for a longer time, both in patients who have never been treated for hepatitis B as well as in patients who have failed to respond to interferon, the drug currently used for this disease. With interferon alone, the response rate is only 40 to 50 percent, and there are significant side effects.

For patients with advanced cirrhosis from hepatitis B where antiviral therapy is "too little, too late" and excessively risky, liver transplantation has been problematic. Rapidly progressive liver disease occurs all too often because of the immunosuppressive therapy needed to avoid rejection of the transplanted liver. Recently treatment of transplant patients with large, frequent doses of hepatitis B immunoglobulin that contain high levels of antibodies to the hepatitis B virus have been found to be somewhat effective in preventing clinically significant reinfection. Some centers that had discouraged transplantation in hepatitis B patients now are actively pursuing this approach. In addition, new antiviral drugs are being tried in patients in whom reinfection with hepatitis B virus does occur.

▶ Hepatitis C

Hepatitis C is the most common chronic hepatitis viral infection in the United States because of the high frequency (75 percent or more) with which acute infection becomes persistent. Advances in the understanding of the molecular biology of this virus continue at an explosive rate. The importance of different major genetic types (genotypes)—of which there are now six, according to the most popular classification scheme—in determining the outcome of infection and response to treatment is becoming more clear. Some genotypes are more often associated with progression to cirrhosis, or failure to respond to interferon treatment, than others. Moreover, within individual genotypes, numerous strains exist, even within the liver and blood of a single patient. This is due to the susceptibility of certain portions of the viral genetic code to mutate readily. Such information has led to the "quasispecies" concept, which holds that by constantly mutating, the virus can escape the immunulogic mechanisms by which infected persons normally would be able to clear viral infections.

A significant impact is being made by the availability of serum analyses for hepatitis C viral RNA, the genetic material of the virus. These analyses free the practitioner from exclusive reliance upon tests for antibodies, which are proteins made by cells of the immune system in response to the virus, and may occasionally be either false-positive or false-negative. In addition to enhancing diagnostic sensitivity, quantitative hepatitis C viral RNA analyses provide a baseline against which future levels of virus can be compared to assess the effectiveness of antiviral therapy. Finally, several studies have shown that the level of viral RNA in the blood can actually help to predict which patients are more likely to respond to interferon, by showing that low RNA levels are a favorable predictor of such a response.

The search for improved therapy for chronic hepatitis C continues. Two major studies, one in Europe and one in the United States, evaluated the effectiveness of ribavirin, an oral antiviral compound. Approximately half the patients normalized their liver-enzyme levels in the blood, suggesting amelioration of the damage to liver cells from the viral infection. Unfortunately, the microscopic appearance of the liver (as obtained by biopsy) was little affected, and, surprisingly, the levels of viral RNA in the blood changed little in patients receiving ribavirin.

It stands to reason, then, that although ribavirin may still prove to have a role as sole therapy for hepatitis C, its principal role may prove to be in combination with interferon or other drugs. Some experts do, in fact, believe that combination therapy will be the way chronic hepatitis C is treated in the future, given the difficulty of eradicating this infection with a single agent. Support for this notion was provided by a published study in which a group of nonresponders to interferon was treated with a combination of ribavirin plus interferon, with a 40 percent response rate.

► Wilson's Disease

In yet another illustration of the power of molecular genetics, the gene for Wilson's disease was discovered recently. This is a rare disease inherited in an autosomal recessive pattern (one gene for it must be inherited from each parent). Victims, who are usually adolescents or young adults, develop various combinations of neurological damage and acute or chronic liver disease as a result of copper overload. The abnormal gene appears to be related to a protein involved in copper transport. The gene has been cloned and sequenced, creating the theoretical future potential for gene therapy—the insertion of normal genes into liver cells to correct the metabolic error that leads to the disease.

► Artificial Liver-Support Devices

Fulminant liver failure is a condition in which a previously healthy liver undergoes sudden and catastrophic deterioration in its basic functions, with a resulting imminent threat to life. Underlying causes include occasional cases of viral hepatitis, drug overdose (especially acetaminophen), and Wilson's disease, among others. Aside from the challenges inherent in the intensive treatment of fulminant liver failure, with all its complications, the physician faces two particular dilemmas. First, it is often difficult to predict when a patient has the potential to recover—or, conversely, when a patient may have "passed the point of no return." The distinction is critical because, ideally, only the latter group should be subjected to liver transplantation. Second, the shortage of donor livers results in potentially fatal delays, even when a decision has been made that transplantation is necessary. Therefore, the availability of a device to provide artificial liver support in fulminant hepatic failure, similar to kidney dialysis, would be a dramatic advance. Such a device would help support some patients until their livers regenerate, and others until they could receive transplants.

One device tested recently uses hollow-fiber perfusive cartridges containing human hepatoblastoma cells through which the patient's blood is passed (hepatoblastoma is a tumor arising from liver cells that have become malignant but retain the functional properties of healthy liver cells). In a series of nine patients with acute liver failure, three patients were maintained successfully on the artificial-liver machine until transplantation could be done; six others were supported until their livers improved spontaneously. Another approach relies upon similar cartridges containing porcine liver cells, with which preliminary successes have also been reported.

Ira M. Jacobson, M.D.

Medical Ethics

► Research on Embryos

The Human Embryo Research Panel, a government-sponsored group composed of scientists, lawyers, ethicists, and private citizens, was convened by President Clinton to address the dilemmas that arise out of research conducted on human embryos, and to develop guidelines in accordance with the panel's findings on this matter. The panel issued a report endorsing government funding for such purposes, concluding that this research is essential for the investigation and analysis of genetic disorders leading to birth defects and other sources of impairment in newborns. Such research could also yield new findings leading to better treatment for human infertility, and could greatly enhance the diagnosis of illness prior to the implantation of a fertilized egg into a woman.

Government funding has been unavailable for such research in the past, because of the controversies surrounding experimentation on human embryos; scientists using private funding have already begun such research endeavors. Opponents of embryo research argue that human embryos, as potential human beings, deserve the respect and dignity accorded to all human beings, and should not be used and discarded for research purposes.

The guidelines developed by the panel focus on research involving embryos in the first two weeks of development. Most embryos for such purposes are made available by *in vitro*–fertilization programs, which usually create more embryos than are necessary for implantation into a particular patient. Typically these embryos are discarded. Under the proposed guidelines, they would become available for government-sponsored research.

More controversial is the recommendation in the proposed guidelines that in "compelling" circumstances, scientists should be allowed to intentionally create human embryos for research purposes rather than use the discards from fertilization programs. However, the proposed guidelines prohibit the manipulation of embryos once implanted into a woman, and they also rule out the implantation of embryos that have already been genetically or chemically altered.

President Clinton, in a preemptive move, ruled out the potential approval of government funding for research involving intentionally created embryos, but left open the possibility of government financing for other embryo research. In 1995 the National Institutes of Health (NIH), under which such financing would be governed, is expected to issue final recommendations concerning human-embryo research.

▶ Genetics Issues

Within the past five years, researchers have been able to identify the genetic marker for nearly 4,000 inherited medical problems in human beings. Recently such findings were used in the case of Brittany Nicole Abshire, born in 1994 to parents Renee and David Abshire of Texas. The Abshires previously lost a child to Tay-Sachs disease, a genetic disorder that leads to painful and progressive illness and ultimately death in early childhood. With new genetic-screening capabilities, scientists were able to check Mrs. Abshire's fertilized eggs prior to implantation in order to rule out the possibility of another child born with Tay-Sachs; without such screening the Abshires would have a one-in-four risk of another Tay-Sachs child. With the new screening techniques, the Abshires were able to ensure that the egg was free of Tay-Sachs markers prior to its implantation into Mrs. Abshire.

While such screening can lead to the prevention of devastating illnesses, it does raise ethical questions concerning its use to screen out less debilitating diseases. For example, with newly found genetic markers for such conditions as breast cancer and Alzheimer's disease, the ethical dilemma arises as to whether to screen out embryos carrying such genetic markers, even if the potential human being might not experience such illness until late in life. Moreover, questions surface as to whether human embryos could be screened for an array of conditions or characteristics in order for parents to "choose" the genetic makeup of their yet-to-be-born children. Such screening could also have an unprecedented impact on insurance coverage, as many argue that insurance companies could mandate such testing in order to better select those they wish to cover. Moreover, the specter of the eugenics movement of the 1920s arises, as parents and society more generally may determine which characteristics are worth reproducing and which are not. Currently few physicians are willing to screen embryos for sex-selection purposes alone, but the implications of such screening have nonetheless led to calls by scientists, ethicists, and other concerned professionals for the development of guidelines to control the use of such screening.

Finally, Ralph Brinster, M.D., a researcher at the University of Pennsylvania in Philadelphia, reported findings concerning efforts to map and alter the genetic makeup of sperm. Dr. Brinster

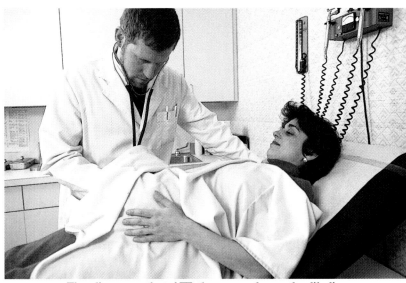

The discovery that AZT therapy reduces the likelihood of transmission of HIV from mother to fetus has prompted a controversy over whether all pregnant women should undergo mandatory AIDS testing.

reported on experiments conducted on mice in which the genetic makeup of sperm was manipulated before its use for impregnation. While proponents argue that such a process could block the inheritance of devastating illness and prevent suffering in an entire lineage, opponents suggest that such genetic manipulation could be subject to abuse, depending on the characteristics selected (and eliminated) by parents and scientists. Such experiments also raise the question of adding certain genes to enhance potential offspring. Once again the ethical concerns center on the potential misuse of such techniques for nontherapeutic purposes, as well as the question of whether parents should have the right to predetermine the genetic makeup of their yet-to-be-born children.

▶ *In Utero* HIV Transmission

Each year, approximately 1,000 to 2,000 infants are born having had HIV, the virus that causes AIDS, transmitted to them by their mothers. A federal study of *in utero* transmission of HIV determined that such transmission may be drastically cut by the administration of the drug AZT (azidothymidine) during pregnancy. A study published in the *New England Journal of Medicine* involving 477 HIV-positive women in the United States and France demonstrated that the rate of HIV transmission from mother to fetus was slowed from 25.5 percent to 8.3 percent when the mothers were given AZT during pregnancy.

The results of this study question what efforts should be undertaken to identify pregnant HIV-positive women. In particular the ethical dilemma arises as to whether there should be mandatory testing of pregnant women in order to identify those whose fetuses would benefit from AZT intervention. At present, women are usually counseled during pregnancy about the potential benefit to their fetus from HIV testing of the mother. However, such testing raises concerns for HIV-positive mothers over the potential discrimination and ostracism they may experience because of their HIV-positive status.

Critics argue that such voluntary counseling programs are insufficient, and that, given the potential of saving an infant from the devastating implications of HIV infection, the situation demands aggressive action. Opponents of forced testing fear that it will drive many women away from prenatal care. Also, they believe that it unfairly singles out pregnant women for mandatory testing, when few other groups in society currently face such involuntary physical intervention. The calls for mandatory testing may ultimately pit the rights of the pregnant woman against the rights of the fetus.

Additionally, controversy erupted in New York State as to whether the current practice of routine HIV testing in the newborn population ought to be "unblinded." This means that HIV-positive infants would be identified, rather than just counted for epidemiological purposes. Currently, such testing does not lead to the identification of specific newborns, but instead is conducted merely to determine the presence of HIV across communities. Supporters argue that such unblinding is imperative, given the nature of the HIV virus and the fact that, with unblinding, HIV-positive infants will receive earlier medical treatment. Opponents once again argue that such identification leads to the mandatory identification of HIV-positive mothers, even if they would wish to forgo such testing for themselves. In this case the interests of the newborn may be in conflict with the interests of the mother. The urgency of this debate has diminished, however, as emphasis has shifted to *in utero* identification and treatment.

▶ Anencephalic and Brain-Dead Patients

The question as to whether any specific treatment obligations exist when patients are diagnosed as either brain-dead or anencephalic surfaced when, in two specific cases, parents demanded that their children receive medical treatment despite the presence of these conditions. Both cases raise profound questions about the obligations of physicians to deliver treatment that they consider futile.

In Florida the parents of Teresa Hamilton, a severely diabetic 13-year-old girl, insisted that health-care providers continue medical treatment, and not withdraw life-sustaining mechanisms, despite the diagnosis that Teresa was brain-dead. Physicians concluded that Teresa deteriorated after lapsing into a coma, and ultimately became brain-dead, a diagnosis made after the irreversible cessation of all brain functions. A patient's cardiovascular and respiratory system may still be maintained artificially after such a diagnosis is determined, but for legal purposes, once such a declaration is made, the patient is considered dead, and physician obligation to continue treatment interventions is negated.

However, the parents of Teresa Hamilton refused to accept such a diagnosis. They insisted that medical intervention continue, believing that their daughter was still alive and could recover from her condition. The Sarasota, Florida, hospital where Teresa was a patient attempted to gain legal permission to proceed with treatment withdrawal. The hospital argued that continuing to treat a brain-dead patient was demoralizing to clinicians, infringed on physician integrity, and represented an inappropriate use of an intensive-care bed. Additionally, it became known that the Hamiltons' insurance had run out, and that the hospital had assumed all costs associated with continuing Teresa's medical interventions.

Ultimately an accommodation was reached. Teresa's parents brought her home, maintaining their daughter on life support paid for by the hospital. The parents were hopeful that once home, Teresa might recover. Physicians, ethicists, and other critics of this arrangement disagreed, arguing that a new precedent had been set that considers brain-dead patients in some way alive, and thus deserving of medical support, despite the fact that they are legally dead. Additionally, many critics found such continued support inequitable and even repulsive, given the nature of the patient's condition, the enormous expenses involved to support this arrangement, and the fact that access to even minimal basic care is beyond the financial means of many people in the United States.

In a Fairfax, Virginia, case, the mother of an anencephalic infant, known as "Baby K," successfully defeated attempts by a Fairfax hospital to stop providing emergency medical assistance to the child when brought to its emergency room. Born in 1992, Baby K had been diagnosed as anencephalic *in utero*, a condition that leaves the child with severe brain damage, and with essentially only a functioning brain stem. Such infants will therefore never be able to think, feel, communicate, or in any other way interact with their environment. The condition is invariably fatal, and the usual course of treatment for such infants is merely comfort care until the child dies.

However, Baby K's mother insisted since the child's birth that whatever aggressive medical interventions were available should be used to maintain her child's life. Doctors treating Baby K reluctantly agreed, but ultimately became uncomfortable with continued aggressive treatment as the baby struggled to survive. Physicians and the mother eventually agreed that Baby K would be discharged to her mother's care, and that the mother could bring the child back to the hospital if acute intervention became necessary. After several emergency admissions, the hospital sought court intervention to clarify its obligation.

Several state courts in Virginia declared that the hospital was legally obligated to deliver emergency medical care to Baby K whenever she arrived at an emergency room. They based their rulings on the federal law known as the Emergency Medical Treatment and Labor Act, a law designed to prevent hospitals from turning away indigent patients in need of emergency services. The courts ruled that under such a law, despite the intent of Congress when passing the law, the hospital had the duty to address the specific acute crisis of Baby K, rather than consider the underlying diagnosis of anencephaly when determining appropriate emergency medical care. The U.S. Supreme Court refused to hear the case, thus leaving in place the lower-court pronouncements obligating the hospital to continue emergency treatment.

▶ Physician-Assisted Suicide

Voters in Oregon approved a precedent-setting bill that legally permits physicians, in certain defined circumstances, to assist patients who wish to commit suicide. Known as Ballot Measure 16, this new law positions Oregon as the first jurisdiction in the world to legally permit physicians to prescribe lethal doses of medication to terminally ill patients. (Physician-assisted suicide is not prosecuted in the Netherlands if it occurs under well-defined conditions, but it still remains technically illegal there.)

Under the Oregon measure, patients and physicians will have to meet carefully defined criteria in order to remain within the bounds of this new law. First, the patient must be an adult, must have a terminal illness, and must have less than six months to live. Also, the patient must be decisionally competent and must request such physician assistance three times, the third time in written form. The presence of depression or any other mental condition affecting the patient's judgment must be ruled out, and a second physician's opinion is necessary to substantiate that these criteria are met. If such conditions are met, the physician is then legally permitted to prescribe a lethal dosage, though not to actually administer it. It will be by the patient's own hands that the lethal dosage is taken.

The measure was designed to address flaws found in similar proposals that were defeated in the states of Washington and California. Supporters of Ballot Measure 16 hail it as a prudent but compassionate response to desperate patients who will ultimately die regardless of what interventions are tried. Critics, however, point to the likelihood that abuse will occur. They question the ability of the state to keep the measure as tightly circumscribed as its current limitations provide. Prior to the actual enactment of the measure, however, a temporary court order was issued to block its implementation while arguments were presented in court to challenge the constitutionality of the measure.

Earlier in 1994 a federal district judge in the state of Washington declared that state's ban on physician-assisted suicide unconstitutional, a decision currently under appeal by the 9th Circuit Court of Appeals. In her decision, Federal Judge Barbara Rothstein declared that the right to assisted suicide was analogous to the right to an abortion, and thus deserving of constitutional protection. A similar lawsuit, by three physicians on behalf of four terminally ill patients, was filed in the state of New York, and is under judicial review. Currently physician-assisted suicide is considered a felony in most states.

Finally, in Michigan, Jack Kevorkian, M.D., the outspoken proponent of physician-assisted suicide, temporarily suspended his efforts to help patients commit suicide, instead trying to win support for a ballot measure to legalize physician-assisted suicide in Michigan. However, he failed to gain sufficient support to place the measure before Michigan voters, and he ultimately resumed his prior activities, assisting 72-year-old Margaret Garrish to commit suicide in November 1994. Ms. Garrish suffered from severe rheumatoid arthritis, advanced osteoporosis, and had previously had both legs amputated and one eye removed. She complained that she could no longer tolerate the pain of her condition, which she said was unrelieved by pain-management techniques. This assisted death occurred immediately following the technical expiration of Michigan's temporary prohibition on physician-assisted suicide. The Michigan Supreme Court is still reviewing the constitutionality of this temporary ban, under which Dr. Kevorkian was initially indicted for previous activities, although two of those indictments were dismissed due to lower-court declarations invalidating the ban.

Currently Dr. Kevorkian has murder charges pending against him, but those charges will not be pressed forward until the Michigan Supreme Court renders its opinion. However, efforts are now under way in Michigan to create a new physician-suicide-assistance ban—one that will be permanent and that will address the flaws associated with the previous ban and its invalidation.

Connie Zuckerman, J.D.

Medical Technology

▶ Improved Mammography

The National Cancer Institute (NCI) reports that clinical trials do not demonstrate that mammography reduces the death rate from breast cancer in women under 50. One reason may be because conventional mammography cannot detect cancers in dense tissue, and younger women have a greater amount of dense breast tissue than do older women. Several technologies now in development may help solve this problem.

Digital Mammography. This method of mammography utilizes advanced techniques for taking and processing X-ray pictures. A research team headed by Martin J. Yaffe, Ph.D., associate professor of radiology and medical biophysics at the University of Toronto in Ontario, Canada, and a team at Lawrence Livermore National Laboratory in California, headed by mechanical engineer Clinton M. Logan, are working on a machine that will use digital electronics, rather than film, to record X rays. Since digital receptors are more sensitive than film, the resulting images will be much clearer.

Currently X-ray films are converted to digital images using a digitizer, a device similar to a photocopy machine. An X-ray film is put into the digitizer, and a light beam scans it. The machine then measures the amount of light that passes through the different areas of the film, assigning values to each: dark areas are assigned low values, and light areas are assigned high values. Once X-ray films are converted to a digital image, they can be displayed on a computer monitor and manipulated to show greater contrast than the original picture. This makes it easier to find abnormalities in women with dense breast tissue.

Fischer Imaging Corporation in Denver, Colorado, is building a machine that will combine these processes so that X-ray images are instantly digitized during a mammogram, eliminating the film step completely. This will provide radiologists with a higher-quality image for analysis.

In addition, digital mammography using the new machine will expose women to less radiation, since the machine scans the breast in sec-

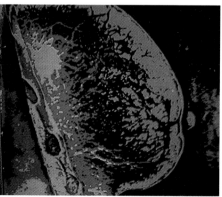

A large breast tumor shows up clearly in a conventional mammogram (pink area above). Digital and laser mammography techniques will make it easier to detect less-obvious abnormalities.

onds. Digital systems also require a lower X-ray threshold, because the X rays do not need to react to photochemicals, as they do in conventional mammography.

Fischer hopes to start clinical trials on prototype machines in the second half of 1994, with commercial availability in 1995, pending approval by the Food and Drug Administration (FDA).

Software for Analyzing Digitized Mammograms. To further analyze digitized mammograms, several research groups are working on computer software that can read and manipulate the images. One software package, developed by Philip Kegelmeyer, a scientist at Sandia National Laboratories/California in Livermore, scans the digitized mammogram, measures the size and shape of tissue structures, and looks for unusual patterns. The computer then determines if an area shows potential signs of disease. Kegelmeyer's system specializes in recognizing patterns that indicate stellate lesions, which result in breast cancer 95 percent of the time.

Clinton Logan and his co-workers are also developing software that will analyze digitized mammograms. Their package will focus on microcalcifications—the tiny, calcium-rich mineral deposits that occur in 50 percent of American women with breast cancer.

A pair of British biophysicists hope to produce software that detects architectural distortions of the breast, which are very subtle signs of breast cancer. Sue Astley, Ph.D., and Peter Miller, Ph.D. from the University of Manchester in England, believe that by comparing a woman's left and right breasts, they can identify variations that indicate the presence of disease. Since most women's breasts exhibit a high degree of normal asymmetry, this task will be difficult. So far the program is designed to divide each breast image into anatomical segments, and then compare the analogous fatty and granular regions.

Government/Industry Alliance. In 1994 the U.S. government and private industry joined the effort to develop better ways to detect breast cancer. An alliance encouraged by the NCI, the National Association of Breast Cancer Organizations, and the National Institutes of Health (NIH) brings together government organizations such as the Central Intelligence Agency (CIA) and the

Pentagon with defense contractors such as Martin Marietta Corporation. The alliance hopes to combine highly specialized optical-processing lenses, telescopic technology, and computer software used for defense and intelligence missions to generate more-detailed images of breast tissue. "If we can use the Hubble telescope to see craters on Mars, we should be able to find a tiny lump in a woman's breast," says Dr. Susan Blumenthal, M.D., deputy assistant secretary for women's health in the Department of Health and Human Services. One technology of particular interest to the group is Martin Marietta's Automatic Target Recognition system. It uses a high-powered optical processor with laser lenses to lock onto a target and translate it into a high-quality image on a screen.

Using Light Instead of X Rays for Mammography. To detect tumors in breast tissue, a University of Pennsylvania research team is experimenting with laser light instead of X rays. In preliminary studies the scientists shone a red laser through a substance similar to living tissue. They then blinked the light off and on to produce waves or ripples of brightness 3 to 4 inches in length—long enough to show bending and diffraction caused by passing through the substance. Physicist Arjun Yodh, Ph.D., and biophysicist Britton Chance, Ph.D., from the University of Pennsylvania in Philadelphia, discovered that these waves adhere to the same rules of diffraction that govern sound and light waves when they pass through different mediums. In the future, scientists might be able to use this method to create a model of breast tissue—by shining the blinking laser through a woman's breast, an image could be created showing the different types of tissues present.

New Guidelines for Conventional Mammography. Until the new technologies are available for use by the general public, conventional mammograms are still the most effective method for breast-cancer screening. To ensure that women receive the safest and most-reliable mammograms, the FDA has enacted strict guidelines requiring all mammography facilities to be accredited and federally certified by October 1, 1994. These regulations are in direct response to the Mammography Quality Standards Act enacted by the U.S. Congress in 1992. They describe standards for quality assurance and control, radiological equipment, personnel qualifications, and medical recordkeeping.

▶ Performing Surgery in Virtual Reality

Surgeons can now practice new medical procedures and complex operations on patients without ever touching a living body—human or animal. Using computer-based simulators and technology known as virtual reality, physicians can see, feel, and operate on different parts of a human body as if they were real.

Until now, virtual reality was best known to followers of the space program—it was originally developed to train astronauts—and to enthusiasts of high-tech video games. In the latter case, game participants wear a helmet or a pair of goggles that contains two miniature televisions. These televisions are aimed at the wearer's eyes—the image participants see appears to be three-dimensional. Since no other images can penetrate the headgear, participants often feel as if they have entered another world. Some games also provide a special glove or a joystick that participants use to "grasp" or move objects.

Prostate Surgery. Universities and new high-tech companies are taking the concepts behind virtual-reality games and applying them to real-world medical situations. High Techsplanations, Baltimore, Maryland, has created a prostate-surgery simulator that uses stereoscopic lenses to turn a flat picture of the prostate and surrounding anatomy into a three-dimensional image. A physician looks at this picture through the lenses while moving a device that functions like a real instrument, such as a scalpel. If the doctor accidentally cuts a blood vessel during the "operation," it bleeds in the onscreen picture. A text box then displays what the surgeon did wrong.

High Techsplanations is also developing a simulator to teach physicians how to perform a digital rectal exam and identify the symptoms of prostate cancer and benign prostatic hyperplasia (BPH). A sensor is attached to a doctor's finger; he or she then inserts the finger in a rectal model linked to a computer screen. As the physician moves his or her finger through this simulator, the position of the sensor is displayed onscreen as it corresponds to the internal structure of the model. In this way a doctor learns how a particular internal structure of the rectum should feel.

Laparoscopic Surgery. Cine-Med, a company in Woodbury, Connecticut, that produces medical-training videos, is now developing a "virtual clinic" in which surgeons can improve their operating skills. One part of this system allows surgeons to practice laparoscopic surgery. Traditionally in this type of minimally invasive operation, a tiny camera and instruments are inserted in a small incision in the abdomen. The surgeon then looks at a television screen to guide the instruments and perform the surgery. In Cine-Med's virtual-reality system, the instruments are contained in a black box fitted with sensors. The sensors track the instruments as they are moved by the surgeon and display the instruments on a monitor. A three-dimensional moving picture of the organs being operated on is also shown. Eventually Cine-Med hopes to incorporate actual CAT-scan and MRI data into its virtual clinic. A surgeon can then plan and practice an operation for a particular patient based on real data.

Laparoscopic simulators are especially effective training tools for surgeons, since this type of surgery is a two-dimensional task that can be difficult to visualize. For example, if a surgeon is working with a long instrument with a pivoting point, the tip of the tool moves to the right when the doctor moves his or her hand to the left.

Eye Surgery. Eye surgeons will also soon be able to practice obscure procedures or prepare for complex operations using virtual reality. Georgia Institute of Technology in Atlanta and the Medical College of Georgia in Augusta are collaborating on a simulated operating microscope that provides realistic close-up views of the operation being performed along with a simulated surgical

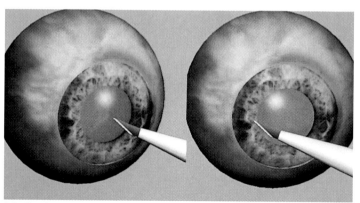

Medical students can practice highly delicate surgery using the computer-based technology called virtual reality. Above, eye surgery is "performed" on a three-dimensional simulation of a pair of eyes using a simulated scalpel.

tool held by a physician that provides the feel of contacting and cutting eye structures. Keith Green, Ph.D., of the Medical College of Georgia, a member of the team developing the eye simulator, says that the device will allow for more-realistic practice by surgeons than would operating on donor eyes: since donor eyes are no longer alive, they do not feel and react as live tissue does.

Robotic Surgery. Robots are being combined with some virtual-reality systems. Scientists at the University of Auckland, New Zealand, and McGill University, Montreal, Canada, along with researchers at the Massachusetts Institute of Technology (MIT), Cambridge, are working on a system in which a surgeon holds an instrument that is connected to a "master" robotic arm. The surgeon looks at a computer screen displaying

the surgical site, and moves the instrument accordingly. The "master" transmits the doctor's motions to a computer, which then sends the information to a "slave" robot, which actually performs the surgical procedure. The system is designed for eye surgery, and will allow a physician to perform an operation on a patient in another room or even another country.

Visible Human Program. To enhance the growing use of surgical simulators, the NIH's National Library of Medicine plans to release an atlas of digital cadavers. This computerized library will have descriptions and images of every part of the human body, male and female, and will show organs and physical structures in ways not possible in real life. For example, a person will be able to "travel" through the body using passageways between organs and other parts of the body. The project is known as the "visible human program," and will be available on the Internet by the end of 1994. Forty gigabytes of computer disk space will be required to run the entire atlas.

Benefits of Virtual-Reality Surgical Simulators. Proponents note that the virtual-reality simulators will decrease the learning curve for medical students, while providing valuable practice for working surgeons before they undertake a costly or risky procedure. This in turn may result in fewer malpractice cases and shorter hospital admissions. In addition, simulators will allow surgeons to be tested equally on various procedures, leading to standardization and licensing in particular disciplines.

▶ New Devices Help Heart Patients

In 1994 the FDA approved the first implantable heart pump for temporary use in patients awaiting heart transplants. The HeartMate Left Ventricular Assist Device (LVAD) is a product of Thermo CardioSystems, Incorporated (TCI), of Woburn, Massachusetts, and is one of two types of LVADs they manufacture. Both consist of an implantable device that pumps blood through the left side of the heart (which moves most of the blood in the body), and an external power source. The pump approved by the FDA uses a pneumatic air device to supply its power. This dishwasher-sized machine sits next to the patient's bed or can be rolled along next to the patient as he or she walks around. The other TCI LVAD, which has received FDA approval for use in humans for testing purposes only, runs off a 12-volt battery pack and control panel that can be worn on the hip, allowing a patient to leave the hospital while waiting for a donor heart.

In both systems the implantable pump is inserted in the patient's abdomen. A tube runs to the heart's left ventricle—the lower-left chamber—so that the pump can help it move blood, at 80 beats per minute, into the aorta, the main artery of the body. Meanwhile, the natural heart continues to perform other functions, including producing peptides and regulating blood flow.

The pump is invaluable for people suffering from congestive heart failure. These people's hearts are too weak to pump blood at the rate required for normal activity. Fluid may build up in their lungs, making patients short of breath and fatigued. The TCI HeartMate restores the proper circulation of blood through the body. This indirectly helps other organs heal and regain the strength they lost when the blood and oxygen supply in the body was diminished.

FDA Commissioner David A. Kessler believes the TCI HeartMate implantable pump "will save the lives of many transplant candidates who now

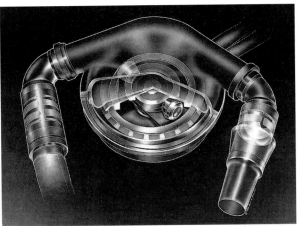

In 1994, the U.S. Food and Drug Administration approved the HeartMate (above). This device is the first implantable heart pump for temporary use in transplant candidates awaiting donor hearts.

die because there are not enough donor hearts." Every year 20,000 Americans need a heart transplant, but only 2,000 donor hearts are available. Although the TCI device is approved only for patients already on a transplant list and in danger of dying within two days, the manufacturer hopes a future version may someday provide a permanent alternative to a heart transplant.

To date, the TCI HeartMate pump has been implanted in over 230 Americans, with the average implant lasting 76 days. Test data submitted before the pump's approval show that 71 percent of patients who used it as a bridge before transplant were still healthy two months after receiv-

ing the transplant. Other data indicate that 90 percent of patients who received the TCI Heart-Mate were still alive one year after receiving a heart transplant, compared to 67 percent of transplant patients who did not use the pump.

The TCI battery-operated heart pump still in testing has been used in 19 patients since 1991—one man lived with it for 503 days before receiving a transplant.

Implantable heart pumps are a cost-effective option for both patients and hospitals, since patients implanted with the pump can be moved out of intensive care to less expensive hospital rooms while awaiting transplants.

Coronary Stents. The FDA recently approved two coronary stents designed to keep open the arteries of people suffering from atherosclerosis (hardening of the arteries). Atherosclerosis is characterized by the buildup of fatty plaque in the arteries of the heart. This can lead to chest pains, heart attacks, and death.

Cook Incorporated, Bloomington, Indiana, received approval in 1993 for use of the Gianturco-Roubin Flex-Stent Coronary Stent for patients whose heart arteries close during balloon angioplasty. Balloon angioplasty is a procedure in which a balloon-tipped catheter is threaded through a leg or arm artery to the blocked coronary artery. The balloon is inflated to open the artery, and is then removed. Sometimes, when the balloon is removed, the artery does not stay open. When this happens, the Cook implantable stainless-steel "scaffold" is inserted using another balloon catheter. When this catheter is removed, the 1-inch mesh stent is left behind.

Doctors perform approximately 300,000 balloon angioplasties annually in people with atherosclerosis. Clinical data submitted as part of the approval process for the Cook Flex-Stent indicate that it reduces the number of heart attacks caused by arteries reclosing during angioplasty. In addition, fewer bypass operations are necessary when the stent is used.

Johnson & Johnson (J&J), New Brunswick, New Jersey, received approval for a similar device in August 1994. Clinical trials indicate that the J&J device has a 90 percent success rate in keeping clogged arteries open.

Cardiologists are excited about the potential for coronary stents. Over 1,600 doctors and nurses have signed up for courses sponsored by J&J that will teach medical professionals how to use the new stent. The J&J device co-inventor, Richard Schatz, M.D., research director for interventional cardiology at Scripps Clinic and Research Foundation, La Jolla, California, says it will take a year to train 4,000 physicians in its use.
Abigail Polek

Medications and Drugs

▶ New Drugs for Psychiatric Patients

During 1994 two new drugs, risperidone (Risperdal) and venlafaxine (Effexor), were added to those drugs available for the treatment of the psychiatric patient.

Risperidone, manufactured by Janssen Pharmaceutica, Titusville, New Jersey, has been approved by the Food and Drug Administration (FDA) for managing psychotic disorders. Its main use is in the treatment of schizophrenia, especially in those patients who are not responding to other, more-traditional antipsychotics such as haloperidol (Haldol) and clozapine (Clozaril).

Schizophrenia is a complex psychiatric problem in which an individual has disorders of thought, delusions, hallucinations, absence of emotional reaction, problems with relationships, and an inability to function in society on a daily basis. It is thought to affect between 0.6 percent and 3 percent of the population in the United States. The disease usually begins in late adolescence or early adulthood and occurs in both males and females.

Risperidone has been shown to be as effective as other traditional drugs, and it has fewer side effects. Also, risperidone treats all the symptoms of schizophrenia, including social withdrawal, lack of facial expression, and lack of motivation—symptoms that often are not controlled by traditional drugs.

The main side effects of risperidone are excessive muscle movement, dizziness, sleepiness, agitation, anxiety, headache, and nausea. However, fewer movement disorders are reported with risperidone as compared to other antipsychotics. Especially important is that, so far, risperidone has not been associated with tardive dyskinesia (TD), a serious syndrome characterized by abnormal involuntary movements of the tongue, jaw, eyes, lips, head, arms, legs, and torso. TD affects 20 to 30 percent of people taking antipsychotic drugs.

The second new psychiatric drug, venlafaxine, is marketed by Wyeth-Ayerst Laboratories, Philadelphia, Pennsylvania, and is used for the treatment of depression—one of the most common of the mental disorders. Depression is characterized by a depressed mood, lack of interest or pleasure in activities, fatigue, feelings of worthlessness, and changes in weight and sleeping habits. The condition affects approximately 10 to 20 percent of women and 5 to 10 percent of men over a lifetime.

There are many drugs used to treat depression. Venlafaxine, although not superior to any other agent, has been shown to work well in the management of depression. It is another choice for those patients who may not have responded to other antidepressants.

The most common adverse effects of venlafaxine are nausea, sleepiness, dry mouth, dizziness, and nervousness. Higher doses of venlafaxine have been associated with increases in diastolic blood pressure and with a small increase in cholesterol levels.

Venlafaxine must be taken three times daily with meals. This may make it less convenient for patients than most other antidepressants, which can be taken once daily.

▶ Easy Dosing for ADHD, Narcolepsy

Adderall, a product from Richwood Pharmaceutical Company, Florence, Kentucky, is a safe and effective alternative treatment for attention-deficit hyperactivity disorder (ADHD). In fact, it is the first new product in 20 years for the treatment of this disorder.

ADHD is characterized by hyperactivity, inattention, and distractibility. It is more common in boys than in girls, and is usually diagnosed when the child first enters school.

Stimulants, especially methylphenidate (Ritalin) and pemoline (Cylert), have been mainstays in the treatment of ADHD. It is believed that they help restore a chemical balance in the area of the brain that controls the child's ability to focus or pay attention. All drugs for the treatment of ADHD work best when used in conjunction with behavior modification and environmental control.

The main advantage of Adderall is its convenient dosing schedule. It can be taken once or twice a day, which may eliminate the need for administering the drug during school hours.

Adderall has also been used to treat narcolepsy, a rare sleep disorder characterized by uncontrollable sleepiness.

The most common side effects of Adderall are insomnia and loss of appetite. They occur most typically when the medication is first started, and usually decrease within about two weeks.

▶ New Treatment for Narcotic Addiction

Levomethadyl acetate hydrochloride (Orlaam), by Biodevelopment Corporation, Arlington, Virginia, recently was approved for the treatment of narcotic addiction. It is similar to methadone (Dolophine), and is dispensed through outpatient treatment programs approved by federal and state authorities.

Levomethadyl acetate, which has been shown to be as effective as methadone, is more advantageous in that it has to be administered only every other day or else three times weekly, while methadone must be administered daily. This frees the patient from having to visit the clinic daily, and eliminates take-home doses of methadone, which are often misused.

The major disadvantages of using levomethadyl acetate are that doses must be calculated carefully, and that it may take up to 10 days to suppress withdrawal symptoms from the previously used illegal drug.

The side effects of levomethadyl acetate are similar to those seen with methadone: constipation, abdominal pain, insomnia, jerking movements, changes in mood, slowed heartbeat, low blood pressure, abnormal dreams, swelling of the hands or feet, blurred vision, hot flashes, and sexual difficulties in males.

Although symptoms can occur after the use of levomethadyl acetate ceases, most patients can tolerate abrupt withdrawal because of the long duration of action of the drug. Patients are considered candidates for the discontinuation of levomethadyl acetate when they have eliminated illegal drug use, achieved occupational and social stability, and have made appropriate lifestyle changes.

▶ Earlier Relief from Pain of Shingles

Shingles, or herpes zoster, is a viral infection that affects over 600,000 Americans yearly. It causes severe pain and skin rash and lesions, most commonly on the chest and back. Shingles occurs years after the initial infection with the chickenpox virus. This virus remains dormant in the nerves for years before it is reactivated. The elderly and those with weakened immune systems are most likely to develop shingles.

Until 1994 acyclovir (Zovirax) had been the only treatment for shingles. However, a new drug, famciclovir (Famvir), by SmithKline Beecham Pharmaceuticals, Philadelphia, Pennsylvania, is now available for the treatment of

Researchers are working to develop a vaccine that would confer lifetime immunity to the chicken-pox virus, thereby eliminating shingles—the later-in-life manifestation of the virus.

herpes zoster. Famciclovir is absorbed and converted to penciclovir, a drug that acts against the herpes virus. It enters the herpes-infected cell and does not allow the cell to replicate, effectively stopping the spread of the virus.

Famciclovir reduces recovery time, quickens the time needed for the lesions to heal, and limits the duration of pain. It is especially effective in shortening the duration of post-herpetic neuralgia, the pain that may continue for months after the lesions are healed. At three times daily, famciclovir is also easier to administer than is acyclovir, which requires doses five times daily.

In the elderly, famciclovir is safe, although the dosage may need to be adjusted in those patients with moderate to severe renal impairment. The most common side effect of famciclovir is headache; fatigue, vomiting, diarrhea, and nausea may also occur.

▶ Treating AIDS and Related Infections

A new antiretroviral drug, stavudine (Zerit), by Bristol-Myers Squibb Company, Princeton, New Jersey, was approved by the FDA for the treatment of advanced HIV infection. Stavudine, although not known to be superior to other antiretroviral drugs, is yet another choice for those patients who either do not respond to the existing drugs or are intolerant of them.

Stavudine, also known as d4T, is similar to other drugs used for the treatment of HIV, such as zidovudine (Retrovir), more familiarly known as AZT; didanosine (Videx); and zalcitabine (Hivid). Stavudine works by getting into the viral cells and preventing them from reproducing. After six weeks of taking stavudine twice daily, the most common side effects of diarrhea, fever, night sweats, and fatigue disappeared in 80 to 100 percent of patients; weight gain may also occur.

The main side effects of stavudine are pain, numbness, cramping, tingling, prickling, or burning sensations of the extremities. These effects usually occur after at least five weeks of treatment, and are usually reversible if the dose is decreased or the drug discontinued.

At this time, there is no information on the use of stavudine with other drugs. Adding stavudine to AZT therapy is not expected to increase AZT's effectiveness or decrease its toxicity.

Trimetrexate (Neutrexin), by U.S. Bioscience Inc., West Conshohocken, Pennsylvania, has been brought on the market for the treatment of moderate-to-severe *Pneumocystis carinii* pneumonia, a common AIDS-related infection of the lungs. Trimetrexate is to be used only in those patients who, for some reason, cannot take co-trimoxazole or who have not responded to treatment with co-trimoxazole. Trimetrexate must be given intravenously for 21 days. Another drug, leucovorin, must be given simultaneously to limit trimetrexate's toxicity. Trimetrexate inhibits an enzyme in the AIDS virus, leading to disruption of cell activity and cell death.

The major side effect of trimetrexate is a decrease in platelets and white blood cells. This is more likely to happen when the patient is given high doses or when the patient has liver or kidney disease. Other side effects include nausea and vomiting, fever, mouth sores, itching, and skin rashes. When the drug is taken with leucovorin, these side effects are usually minimal.

More studies are needed before the roles of trimetrexate and leucovorin in the treatment of *Pneumocystis carinii* pneumonia are fully understood.

▶ Drug for High Cholesterol

Fluvastatin sodium (Lescol), by Sandoz Pharmaceutical Corporation, East Hanover, New Jersey, is the most recent addition to the class of drugs known as HMG-CoA reductase inhibitors. These agents are classified by the National Cholesterol Education Program Adult Treatment Panel as drugs for the treatment of high cholesterol.

Fluvastatin is indicated as a supplement to a cholesterol-lowering diet to treat elevations of total cholesterol and LDL cholesterol. Lowering serum cholesterol may reduce the risk for coronary disease, and may, in fact, prevent or even reverse lesions already in the arteries of the heart. Patients receive cholesterol-lowering drugs when dietary measures and weight loss do not lower serum cholesterol sufficiently.

Fluvastatin is the first entirely synthetic HMG-CoA reductase agent available. This allows the drug to produce adequate lowering of cholesterol without many of the adverse reactions seen with the other agents such as lovastatin (Mevacor) and simvastatin (Zocor).

Few side effects with fluvastatin have been reported. The most commonly seen problems are headache, stomach discomfort, nausea, fatigue, and an increase in liver enzymes.

Prior to the initiation of cholesterol-lowering drugs such as fluvastatin, most patients are start-ed on the American Heart Association's Step One diet for at least six months. If this measure does not lower cholesterol, fluvastatin may be started. It may take up to four weeks for the drug to yield its maximum benefit. If, after this time, more of the drug is needed, the dose may be increased.

▶ New Therapy for Xerostomia

Oral pilocarpine hydrochloride (Salagen), made by MGI Pharma, Minneapolis, Minnesota, recently has been approved for treatment of radiation-induced xerostomia (dry mouth) in patients with head and neck cancer. This drug represents a major breakthrough for those suffering from dry mouth.

In addition to its radiation-induced occurrence, dry mouth also occurs frequently in the elderly, and it is a side effect of as many as 400 drugs. Patients experience not only the sensation of dry mouth, but frequent mouth infections, burning, lip cracking, and difficulty in eating, swallowing, speaking, and even denture wearing. Some have reported an increase in tooth decay.

In patients with functional salivary glands, the oral preparation of pilocarpine should be effective in relieving dry mouth. Unfortunately, many patients who have undergone radiation therapy for head and neck cancer have had many of their salivary glands destroyed by the treatment. These people may only partially respond to pilocarpine. Adverse effects of pilocarpine may include a drop in blood pressure, sweating, urinary frequency, dizziness, visual disturbance at night, nausea, and flushing.

▶ Topical Therapy for Psoriasis

Calcipotriene ointment (Dovonex), by Westwood-Squibb Pharmaceuticals Inc., Princeton, New Jersey, recently became available for the topical treatment of psoriasis. Psoriasis is a chronic inflammatory skin disorder that occurs in approximately 1 to 2 percent of the population. Chronic plaque psoriasis, in which scaling and red plaques occur on the scalp, knees, elbows, and sometimes nailbeds, is the most common form of psoriasis. Psoriasis does not compromise overall health, but it may cause a person great anxiety about his or her appearance.

Topical treatment of psoriasis has three main benefits: it exposes the skin to drugs with therapeutic benefit; it uses preparations to soften the skin; and it uses agents such as salicylic acid to remove the skin plaques. Standard therapy for psoriasis includes the use of tar or steroid preparations. Tar therapy is messy, and steroids become increasingly less effective over time.

Calcipotriene is a synthetic version of vitamin D_3. Clinical trials have shown good results in people with plaque psoriasis involving less than 40 percent of the body. Calcipotriene inhibits proliferation of psoriasis and enhances differentiation of human skin cells.

Calcipotriene is absorbed into the body and is broken down by the liver; therefore, the drug has limited toxicity. Skin irritation, peeling, rash, and burning are the most commonly reported adverse effects. Use on the face is not recommended, due to increased skin sensitivity in this area. Calcipotriene ointment is especially well tolerated for short-term therapy of psoriasis.

▶ Drugs for Heart-Bypass Surgery

Aprotinin (Trasylol Injection), a new drug from Miles Inc., West Haven, Connecticut, is designed to decrease bleeding and the need for transfusions in high-risk coronary-artery-bypass-graft (CABG) surgery. More than 200,000 Americans undergo coronary-bypass surgery each year, and bleeding requiring blood transfusions is a common complication. A patient that receives fewer transfusions has a lower risk of infection and associated adverse reactions.

In clinical trials, aprotinin use led to an almost 50 percent reduction in blood loss, and a similar decrease in the need for transfusions. Aprotinin is ideal for patients on aspirin therapy, patients undergoing repeat surgery, and patients with rare blood types.

Aprotinin has been shown to cause serious allergic reactions in some patients; therefore, the drug should be reserved for high-risk patients.

▶ Cystic Fibrosis

The most common fatal, genetically inherited disease is cystic fibrosis (CF). For years, cystic fibrosis was usually fatal by age 5, but advances in therapy and diagnosis now allow many CF patients to live to adulthood. The disease primarily involves the respiratory tract. Thick mucus accumulates in the lungs and causes obstruction of breathing and chronic lung infections. The majority of CF patients die from pulmonary complications.

The discovery of the CF gene in 1989 has allowed the development of new therapies. Human recombinant DNase (dornase alfa [Pulmozyme]), by Genentech, South San Francisco, California, is the first biotechnology drug available for the treatment of CF. Dornase alpha is an enzyme that decreases the thickness of the mucus secretions in the lung, thereby improving lung function and decreasing the risk of infections.

Clinical trials have shown the agent to be both safe and effective in reducing sputum viscosity, and thus facilitating its elimination. Most patients also benefit from a decreased amount of bacteria in the lung fluids, and therefore have a decreased infection rate in the lung.

Side effects from dornase alpha are expected to be low because the agent is a recombinant human protein and not from an animal source.

▶ Acute Lymphoblastic Leukemia

Pegaspargase (Oncaspar), by Enzon, Piscataway, New Jersey, was recently released for use in patients with acute lymphoblastic leukemia (ALL) who have shown hypersensitivity to L-asparaginase, the traditional treatment for this condition. Patients allergic to L-asparaginase previously had no real options for continued treatment of their disease.

Pegaspargase is generally used in combination with other chemotherapeutic agents. The agent works by decreasing the amount of asparagine in the blood. Asparagine is necessary for the leukemia cancer cells to survive. Without adequate amounts of asparagine, the number of leukemic cells decreases.

Clinical trials using pegaspargase have shown promising results. The most frequently reported adverse effects include nausea, vomiting, fever, fatigue, and increases in liver enzymes.

▶ Long-acting Treatment for Asthma

Approximately 10 million Americans suffer from asthma. The first choice of therapy for these people is a class of drugs known as the inhaled beta-2 agonists, taken in conjunction with anti-inflammatory agents such as steroids. The limiting factor of the available beta-2 agonists is that they work for only up to eight hours.

Salmeterol xinafoate (Serevent), recently introduced by Allen & Hanburys, Research Triangle Park, North Carolina, is a long-acting beta-2 selective-inhalation agent. The drug works by dilating the airways, allowing easier air exchange and breathing. Patients should be advised that the drug does not provide immediate relief, and therefore they should not readminister the drug before the next scheduled dose. Following a dose of salmeterol, relief usually begins in 10 to 20 minutes, with a peak effect in approximately 3 to 4 hours, and persistence of activity for 12 hours.

Reported adverse effects include increased heart rate, tremor, and headache. Experts disagree as to whether overuse of any of the beta-2 agonists causes a worsening of disease, or if worsening disease causes overuse. Caution is nonetheless advised against overuse, and notification of physicians upon any worsening of asthma conditions or symptoms is recommended.

Cheryl A. Stoukides, Pharm.D., and
Michelle M. Emery, R.Ph.

Mental Health

▶ Extent of Mental Disorders

The most comprehensive survey to date of emotional health in the United States found that nearly one-half of all adults had suffered from a mental disorder at some time in their lives, and almost one in three had experienced such a condition in the year preceding the survey. These results, based on interviews conducted between 1990 and 1992 with a national sample of 8,098 people, significantly exceed previous estimates of the prevalence of mental disorders. Survey participants ranged in age from 15 to 54 years old.

Researchers who conducted the survey expressed particular concern about the one in six persons who develop three or more mental disorders during their lives. Emotional turmoil usually worsens over time for these individuals. They account for a majority of the lifetime mental conditions reported by the sample, and for many of the disorders that had occurred in the prior year.

Between 3 and 5 percent of those contacted required immediate psychiatric treatment, says study director Ronald C. Kessler, a sociologist at the University of Michigan in Ann Arbor. He and his coworkers published their investigation in the January 1994 *Archives of General Psychiatry.*

Most people who had experienced a mental disorder still managed to meet responsibilities at home and work during that period, and were able to recover on their own, Kessler reports.

Major depression is the most common disorder picked up by the survey, affecting 17 percent of the sample at some time in their lives, and 10 percent in the previous year. Next comes alcohol dependence, with 14 percent citing a history of this condition, and 7 percent reporting it in the past year. Phobias, ranging from fear of heights to avoidance of any social activity, reach a lifetime prevalence of approximately 12 percent, with a slightly lower rate for the previous year.

Unlike past national surveys of mental disorders, the new investigation relied on the latest official psychiatric definitions of these conditions, and gathered a variety of data on each participant's family and social life.

A large majority of those who had suffered at some point from a mental disorder had not received medical or mental-health treatment for their condition. More than 80 percent of those who reported a disorder in the previous year had failed to receive appropriate professional help.

Wealthier and better-educated individuals tend to report lower rates of mental disorders. However,

The majority of American adults suffering from a mental disorder fail to receive professional help; those who do usually benefit from the experience.

blacks cite a lower prevalence of serious mental conditions, such as major depression and manic depression, than do whites. And people living in rural areas note fewer instances of multiple psychiatric disorders than do city dwellers.

▶ Delayed Sex-Abuse Memories

An increasing number of adults now claim, often after entering psychotherapy, that they have recovered long-buried or -repressed memories of sexual abuse inflicted on them as children. These delayed recollections have sparked numerous lawsuits against both accused perpetrators and psychotherapists alleged to have orchestrated "false memories" of sexual abuse in their clients.

Psychologists who use laboratory experiments to study the way memory normally functions have entered this emotional debate, arguing that what people remember about most incidents in their lives becomes distorted over time and can prove highly inaccurate. But traumatic memories may work differently, reports Bessel A. van der Kolk, M.D., a psychiatrist at Massachusetts General Hospital in Boston. The terror triggered by sexual abuse may—at least in some instances—interfere with brain circuits that handle the conscious recall of events, van der Kolk argues. This interference may then create conditioned fear responses that are stored as visual images or physical sensations in other brain areas. Recovered memories of confirmed instances of childhood sexual abuse typically emerge first in perceptual fragments that help to generate a coherent story over weeks, months, or even longer, according to a study the Boston psychiatrist presented in May at the annual meeting of the American Psychiatric Association in Philadelphia, Pennsylvania.

Sexual abuse that begins early in life and lasts for many years generates the most fragmented perceptual memories of trauma, he contends. This process of splitting up memory is often aided by altered states of consciousness that victims enter during sexual abuse, such as a feeling of psychological separation from one's body.

Intensive interviews were conducted with 43 adults, most of them women, who responded to a newspaper ad seeking survivors of severe trauma in childhood or later. Periods of severe or moderate amnesia for these experiences had occurred in 29 participants. A total of 37 individuals gathered evidence indicating that their memories were accurate. This included a sibling's confirmation that childhood sexual abuse had occurred in the family, admission of guilt by an alleged abuser, or medical and police records of a car accident that resulted in the death of loved ones.

Everyone in the study reports having remembered traumatic incidents first in fragmentary perceptions that they developed into verbal accounts over time. One woman began by having panic attacks, feelings of being smothered, and uncomfortable sensations of genital rubbing that led to memories of sexual abuse by her mother and uncle.

Amnesia most often broke in response to a changed relationship with a perpetrator of sexual abuse (such as that person's death), the initiation of a romantic relationship, or accidentally encountering sights or sensations related to a past trauma. Recovered memories first appeared during psychotherapy in about one-quarter of the adults studied by van der Kolk's group.

Post-traumatic stress disorder, which includes emotional detachment from others, angry outbursts, and a constant sense of being under threat, occurred only in six persons who had failed to put together a meaningful story from their perceptual memories. A thorough recollection of trauma apparently protected the others from experiencing severe stress reactions, van der Kolk asserts. Memory of personal events is still susceptible to distortion over time, and, in some cases, inaccurate memories of having been sexually abused as a child may emerge, he adds.

▶ Nature and Treatment of Depression

Researchers have yet to clarify the differences between endogenous depressions, thought to result mainly from biological influences, and reactive depressions, considered to be the consequences of highly stressful life experiences. Equally distressing events sometimes precede both forms of depression, which has caused some psychiatrists to question the usefulness of dividing depression into these two categories.

A possible explanation for this puzzling situation was presented in two studies published in the July 1994 *Archives of General Psychiatry*. A large majority of all first bouts of major depression came on the heels of stressful personal experiences, according to these investigations. Thereafter, cases of endogenous depression flare back up in response to minor forms of stress, while people with reactive depression require highly stressful events to send their mood plummeting once again.

An initial episode of major endogenous depression may cause brain changes that markedly lessen the amount of stress needed to spark later recurrences, the researchers assert.

In one study, directed by George William Brown, Ph.D., a psychologist at the University of London, England, 127 women hospitalized for their first bout of major depression received diagnoses of either endogenous or reactive depression. Interviewers asked the women about stressful events and difficulties in their lives over the previous six months. A second set of interviews occurred about four years later, when most participants had suffered at least one more episode of depression.

About 60 percent of first-time cases of both endogenous and reactive depression followed a highly stressful event in the preceding six months. Although 70 percent of subsequent instances of reactive depression followed recent stressful experiences, only one-third of recurrences in the endogenous group show a link to severe stress.

Similar findings emerged in a study directed by Ellen Frank, Ph.D., a psychologist at the University of Pittsburgh in Pennsylvania.

Preliminary data from another project indicate that a majority of people who suffer either from chronic depression or "double depression"—recurring bouts of major depression that occur on top of a constant, low-grade sadness—show much improvement when offered adequate treatment with antidepressant drugs.

These positive responses are particularly striking because the depressed participants received no psychotherapy, reports Martin Keller, M.D., a psychiatrist at Brown University in Providence, Rhode Island. Keller directs the ongoing multicenter study, which is the largest clinical trial to date of drug treatments for double depression. He and his colleagues described their preliminary findings in August 1994 at the annual meeting of the American Psychological Association.

From 3 to 5 percent of people living in the United States suffer from chronic depression at some time in their lives. In these cases, periods of major depression or a more moderate, but still serious, depression last for at least two years.

Keller's team reported on the results of 12-week antidepressant-drug trials with 89 individuals

Hyperactive children seem unable to resist moving about excessively—a finding supported by recent brain-scan studies.

suffering from chronic major depression, and 123 with double depression. Volunteers had been depressed for an average of 17 years. Although most had attended college, about one-third were unemployed, and a large majority were unmarried.

Participants received either sertraline, a drug that works much like Prozac (fluoxetine), or imipramine, which belongs to a different class of antidepressant drugs. Clinicians adjusted each individual's drug dosage, if needed, on a weekly basis.

About two-thirds of both depressed groups displayed a substantial lessening of psychiatric symptoms by the end of the 12-week trial. The two antidepressants produced roughly comparable results.

Few of those taking part in the study had received adequate treatment with any antidepressant previously, according to Michael Thase, M.D., a psychiatrist at the University of Pittsburgh who helped administer the trials. Those who had obtained prior psychotherapy or drug treatment did not show a superior response to either of the antidepressants, he adds.

▶ Inside Hyperactive Brains

Researchers estimate that from 3 to 5 percent of school-age children suffer from attention-deficit hyperactivity disorder (ADHD), more commonly known as hyperactivity. This condition also occurs in teenagers and adults, although its prevalence in those groups remains unclear. A variety of symptoms characterize this condition, including an inability to pay attention to others at home and at school, excessive movements that seemingly cannot be controlled, and impulsive behaviors such as constantly interrupting others.

Two brain-scan studies published in the May 1994 *American Journal of Psychiatry* provide new clues to the biological underpinnings of ADHD.

One investigation suggests that hyperactivity may result from disturbances in areas at the front of the brain involved in regulating automatic muscle activity. An inability to refrain from making such movements when necessary, rather than a short or fragmented attention span, may lie at the heart of ADHD, argues Jay N. Giedd, M.D., a psychiatrist at the NIMH, and his colleagues.

His team used magnetic-resonance-imaging (MRI) scans to study the size and shape of the corpus callosum—a bundle of nerve fibers that connects the left and right sides of the brain—in 18 boys with ADHD and in 18 boys with no psychiatric disorders. MRI creates a powerful magnetic field from which sensors pick up data on brain anatomy that get transformed into pictures.

Specific areas at the front of the corpus callosum were much smaller in the hyperactive group. These regions maintain connections to parts of the brain that help to suppress bodily movements, the researchers say, and probably enhance the ability to fight off impulses to engage in fidgeting or other hyperactive behaviors.

In the second study, scientists found that stimulant medications offer substantial help to adults suffering from ADHD, although reasons for the effectiveness of these drugs remains unclear. Energy use in the brains of hyperactive adults, as measured by another type of imaging device, is largely the same before and after successful stimulant treatment, reports a team led by John A. Matochik, M.D., a psychiatrist at the NIMH.

Matochik's team gave one of two stimulants to 21 men and 16 women, all diagnosed with ADHD. Before drug treatment and from 6 to 15 weeks after treatment began, positron-emission-tomography (PET) scans were taken of each volunteer's brain. PET scans measure the amount of glucose used throughout the brain, which provides an indication of how hard different brain regions are working. This information gets transformed into color-coded pictures of brain activity.

About two out of three participants became less restless and showed improved attention after the drug trial. Yet PET scans found similar patterns of glucose use in the brains of those helped by medication and in those whose condition stayed about the same.

Further studies of stimulant treatment for adult ADHD must include the use of inactive "placebo" pills with some participants, recruit larger samples, and look at aspects of social functioning as well as attention and restlessness, the researchers note. In addition, scientists must keep in mind that hyperactive adults often suffer from other mental disorders, such as alcoholism or dependence on illegal drugs, that have a greater impact on their lives.

► Genetics of Manic Depression

Over the past seven years, scientists have failed to confirm initial reports that linked manic depression to defects in two separate areas of the human genetic code. But a new study, published in the June 21, 1994, *Proceedings of the National Academy of Sciences*, finds that a gene predisposing its bearers to manic depression apparently lies on chromosome 18, one of the 23 pairs of chromosomes on which genes are arrayed.

From one-quarter to one-third of all individuals suffering from manic depression probably possess this gene, asserts study director Wade H. Berrettini, M.D., a psychiatrist at Thomas Jefferson University in Philadelphia. Manic depression afflicts more than 2.5 million Americans at some time in their lives. This condition consists of episodes of severe depression that alternate with periods of elation and frenzied, sometimes self-destructive, behavior.

Berrettini's team studied several generations within 22 families, each of which had at least six members diagnosed with manic depression. A total of 395 people took part in the investigation. Of that number, 167 suffered from manic depression or, in a few cases, depression without mania.

In eight families the researchers note that psychiatrically ill members displayed genetic changes at the same location on chromosome 18. Genetic material was isolated from blood samples and then marked with enzymes that snip chromosomes at precise spots, allowing scientists to compare the chemical arrangement of these areas in different people.

The chromosome-18 area identified by Berrettini and his coworkers contains about 100 genes, but researchers suspect that only two of the genes may be involved in manic depression. One gene is in charge of a protein that prepares certain brain cells to receive chemical messages. The other gene helps to regulate some of the body's hormonal responses to stress, which change markedly in many cases of depression and manic depression.

Preliminary family studies conducted at Indiana University School of Medicine in Indianapolis and at the National Institute of Mental Health (NIMH) in Bethesda, Maryland—unpublished when Berrettini's results appeared—link the same chromosome-18 region to a similar proportion of people suffering from manic depression.

► Nature and Treatment of Schizophrenia

A study published in the October 14, 1994, issue of *Science* presents evidence suggesting that schizophrenia may derive from abnormalities in the thalamus, a structure located deep within the brain, and a number of other areas that maintain nerve connections to the thalamus. Previous research indicates that the thalamus helps to filter sensations, focus attention, and process many types of information. Brain disturbances centered on the thalamus could easily create the wide array of symptoms observed in schizophrenia, argues Nancy C. Andreasen, M.D., a psychiatrist at the University of Iowa Hospital and Clinics in Iowa City.

Andreasen and her colleagues took MRI scans of the brains of 47 healthy men and 39 men diagnosed with schizophrenia. A special method was then used to produce an average schizophrenic brain and an average healthy brain. Areas of differences between these brains were then located.

The most disparity appears in the thalamus and nearby tissue that leads to the areas at the front of the brain involved in thinking and memory. The thalamus of the average schizophrenic brain was significantly smaller than the same structure in the average healthy brain. Also, Andreasen's group found, as have other researchers, that schizophrenics have smaller brains with larger fluid-filled spaces than do healthy individuals.

It remains unclear how the differences picked up in the MRI images relate to brain function, such as the transmission of chemical messengers involved in schizophrenia. Another question regards the extent to which deficits in the thalamus and related regions actually cause schizophrenia, or whether they arise from the long-term use of powerful drugs prescribed to treat schizophrenia.

Whatever causes schizophrenia, a drug approved for use in the United States beginning in 1994 shows promise in treating this debilitating condition. The medication, called risperidone, often eases hallucinations, delusions, apathy, and other symptoms while avoiding harmful and sometimes dangerous reactions caused by other so-called antipsychotic drugs, according to a study in the June 1994 *American Journal of Psychiatry.*

Risperidone blocks the action of two substances that serve as chemical messengers in the brain, serotonin and dopamine. But scientists cannot yet explain the precise way in which the new drug diminishes symptoms of schizophrenia.

Stephen R. Marder, M.D., a psychiatrist at the West Los Angeles Veterans Affairs Medical Center in California, and Richard C. Meibach, M.D., a psychopharmacologist at Janssen Research Foundation in Titusville, New Jersey, directed the eight-week trial project.

Bruce Bower

Nobel Prize 1994
in Physiology or Medicine

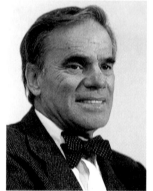

Drs. Martin Rodbell (left) and Alfred G. Gilman received the Nobel Prize in Physiology or Medicine for their discovery of G-proteins.

Two Americans, biochemist Martin Rodbell, Ph.D., and pharmacologist Alfred G. Gilman, M.D., Ph.D., received the 1994 Nobel Prize in Physiology or Medicine for their discovery of "G-proteins." Drs. Rodbell and Gilman, who worked independently of one another, "have opened up a new and rapidly expanding area of knowledge," noted the Nobel committee in its announcement.

▶ Cellular Signaling

The human body contains several trillion cells. For decades, scientists have studied how cells interact with each other and how they respond to signals from their external environment. Each cell is surrounded by a membrane—a barrier that separates the interior of the cell from the world outside. The surface membrane contains groups of proteins known as *receptors*—molecules that specialize in receiving chemical signals from hormones, neurotransmitters, and other sources. During the 1950s American scientist Earl Sutherland clarified the mechanism by which cells process and act on signals from the outside. In a constant series of split-second reactions, hormones and other chemical signals bind to receptors on the cellular membrane, acting as a "first messenger." In many cases, this signal is converted inside the cell to form a "second messenger," a substance that starts a cascade of molecular events, triggering biochemical responses within the cell. For discovering the second-messenger compound known as cyclic AMP—the first such compound to be identified—Sutherland received the Nobel Prize in 1971.

While working at the National Institutes of Health (NIH) in Bethesda, Maryland, during the late 1960s and early 1970s, Dr. Rodbell followed up on Dr. Sutherland's work. Rodbell studied how cells form second messengers such as cyclic AMP. At the time, scientists believed that the transmission of signals from the exterior to the interior of cells involved only two substances—an enzyme and a receptor. Rodbell concluded that there must be a third biochemical step involving another molecule in the cell membrane. He called this molecule a "transducer." The transducer, Rodbell theorized, acts as an intermediary, or "middleman," receiving messages from receptors, modifying the signal, and sending the signal on to an amplifier protein, which in turn initiates the formation of cyclic AMP.

Like many groundbreaking scientific ideas, Rodbell's theory of a signal-transducing molecule met with considerable resistance from the research community. Eventually, however, Rodbell and his collaborators were able to demonstrate that the presence of a transducer is essential to the process of cell signaling. Rodbell determined that there are several different transducing molecules. Rodbell observed that, in modifying and transmitting signals within the cell, these molecules react with an energy-rich compound known as guanosine triphosphate, or GTP.

▶ Finding the Protein

Thanks to the work of Dr. Rodbell, the existence of transducing protein molecules had been established. However, isolating the proteins and determining their exact chemical nature was another story. That was the task that Dr. Gilman, then working at the University of Virginia School of Medicine in Charlottesville, set for himself and his colleagues in a series of experiments during the late 1970s.

Using leukemia cells whose genetic makeup had been altered through mutation, Gilman and his team studied the formation of cyclic AMP in these cells. They found that one type of mutated leukemia cell possessed a normal receptor and a normal amplifier protein that generated cyclic AMP as a second messenger. However, nothing happened when the cell was challenged with an outside signal; the cell failed to respond in the usual way. The reason, Gilman determined, was that these mutated cells lacked the transducing protein. When extracts from other, normal cells were added to these mutated cells, they regained the ability to synthesize cyclic AMP in response to external signals.

In 1980 members of Gilman's team were able to isolate and purify the first transducing protein. Because they had observed that the proteins cannot act without the energy supplied by GTP, the researchers gave the proteins the name by which they are now known: G-proteins.

Since the isolation of the first G-protein, scientists have discovered several different kinds of transducing molecules. These proteins are composed of three separate peptide chains, which are designated *alpha*, *beta*, and *gamma*. Because these peptides can be combined in numerous configurations, it is possible that as many as several hundred different kinds of G-proteins might exist. The study of "signal transduction"—the various biochemical mechanisms by which incoming signals are processed and acted upon inside the cell—is one of the busiest areas in current biomedical research. Thanks to the initial discoveries of Drs. Rodbell and Gilman, there is now a far more detailed understanding of the role of G-proteins as an "on/off switch" for cellular actions. A wide range of biological activities depend on G-protein function.

▶ Function and Malfunction

By some estimates, G-proteins play an essential role in as many as one-third of all signal-transduction processes. For example, they form part of the molecular pathway that enables cells to respond to signals from hormones such as epinephrine and glucagon, which help to metabolize fat and glucose. They are involved in the cellular processing of acetylcholine and other neurotransmitters, which transmit nerve impulses. Scientists, in examining the biochemistry of vision in humans and other higher animals, are studying the role of G-proteins in the light-absorbing molecules known as visual pigments, which are found in the retina. These proteins help the eyes process light, and they transmit visual stimuli to the brain.

In a further indication of the importance of G-proteins, more than half the medications now being used in clinical medicine are targeted at the receptor systems that communicate with G-proteins. These include medicines called beta-blockers, which are used to treat high blood pressure and irregular heartbeat.

When G-proteins fail to function properly, disease often follows. One such instance is cholera, an infectious disease of the gastrointestinal system. The cholera bacteria produce a toxin that acts as an enzyme, altering the function of G-proteins. As a result, instead of fulfilling their usual function of switching on to activate amplifiers and then switching off, the G-proteins remain stuck in the "on" position, like a traffic light stuck on green. With this impairment of cellular function, water and salt in the intestines are not properly absorbed, leading to the severe diarrhea and dehydration by which cholera kills its victims. A similar alteration of G-protein function occurs in cases of infection by the bacterium *E. coli.*

G-proteins have been implicated in other diseases. For example, G-protein malfunction may play a role in symptoms associated with diabetes and alcoholism. In some cases the formation of tumors also appears to be characterized by overactive G-proteins. Scientists are currently investigating the possible role that G-proteins and similar protein structures in the cell might play in the development of various forms of cancer.

As yet, no specific therapies have been developed as a result of the work of Drs. Rodbell and Gilman. However, these two scientists have laid the foundation for ever-increasing knowledge of the means by which the cell membrane functions as a "switchboard" in processing incoming signals. Gradually, scientists are developing a detailed picture of the cellular pathways—in effect, drawing a wire-by-wire diagram. As Dr. Gilman told a reporter shortly after the Nobel prizes were announced, "When we know the whole diagram, we'll know how every cell is controlled." This knowledge could lead, within a few decades, to the development of drugs designed to target specific molecules within the body, immeasurably improving the accuracy and effectiveness of drug therapy.

Martin Rodbell, Ph.D., was born on December 1, 1928, in Baltimore, Maryland. He earned his undergraduate degree in biology in 1949 at Johns Hopkins University in Baltimore, where he also pursued graduate work in chemistry. He earned his doctoral degree in biochemistry from the University of Washington in 1954. In addition to his duties at the NIH in Bethesda from 1970 to 1985, Dr. Rodbell was a visiting professor at the University of Geneva, Switzerland. In 1989 Dr. Rodbell moved to the National Institute of Environmental Health Sciences in Research Triangle Park, North Carolina, where he was head of the signal-transduction laboratory. He retired from his post in June 1994.

Alfred G. Gilman, M.D., Ph.D., was born on July 1, 1941, in New Haven, Connecticut. He earned his bachelor's degree from Yale University in New Haven, and his M.D. and Ph.D. degrees from Case Western Reserve University, Cleveland, Ohio. In 1977, after postdoctoral research at the National Heart, Lung and Blood Institute in Bethesda, Dr. Gilman became a professor of pharmacology at the University of Virginia School of Medicine in Charlottesville. In 1981 he moved to the Texas Southwestern Medical Center in Dallas, where he now heads the Department of Pharmacology.

Christopher King

Nutrition and Diet

▶ New Diabetic Guidelines

In the May 1994 issue of *Diabetes Care*, the American Diabetes Association (ADA) announced updated and progressive nutrition guidelines, which replace the previously recommended standard meal plan. For the 14 million Americans with diabetes, these new guidelines offer greater flexibility in food choices and add more enjoyment to meals.

The main thrust of the new guidelines is an emphasis on the need for an individualized meal plan based on each person's type of diabetes, medication, personal food preferences, and other health problems such as lipid levels or obesity.

In order to meet each diabetic's needs, the ADA recommends that a meal plan be individually prescribed by a registered dietitian. First the dietitian should develop a nutrition assessment that considers the cultural, ethnic, and financial needs of the patient. Second, treatment goals that take into consideration blood-glucose levels and other medical conditions should be set. Finally, the dietitian should regularly monitor treatment goals and modify the patient's meal plan as necessary to achieve the goals.

Liberalizing Sugars. The hallmark of the dietary treatment of diabetes for the past 100 years has been the restriction of refined sugar and sweets. Individuals with diabetes were taught to avoid sugars and to obtain their carbohydrate intake from bread, pasta, potatoes, and other foods rich in complex carbohydrates. However, scientific evidence shows that sugar is not more quickly digested and absorbed than complex carbohydrates, and therefore does not cause havoc with blood-glucose control.

The new guidelines allow the moderate use of sugar as a substitute for other carbohydrates. The total amount of carbohydrates, rather than their source, appears to be the most important factor affecting postmeal blood-glucose levels. Since dietary fructose (sugar derived from such foods as fruits and honey) causes smaller increases in blood glucose than table sugar and most starches, it may be a more desirable sweetener in the diabetic diet. However, large quantities of fructose (about 40 percent of total calories consumed) may raise serum cholesterol and triglyceride levels. Therefore, individuals with elevated lipids should limit their intake of fructose as a sweetener, but need not avoid consumption of fruits and vegetables. In regard to other nutritive sweeteners such as molasses, corn syrup, fruit-juice concentrate, and sugar alcohols (sorbitol, mannitol, and xylitol), the ADA reports no scientific data that suggest that these sweeteners are better or worse than table sugar in affecting blood-glucose levels.

Flexibility in Meal Planning. Based on the ADA's 1986 guidelines, diabetic diets have been developed with approximately 12 to 20 percent of total calories from proteins, up to 60 percent from carbohydrates, and 30 percent or less from fats. The new ADA guidelines allow more flexibility in planning a diabetic diet, with emphasis on individual goals for blood glucose, lipid levels, and weight. The new guidelines recommend that 10 to 20 percent of total daily calories be derived from proteins, and the remaining 80 to 90 percent be divided between carbohydrates and fats. The ADA recommends that polyunsaturated fats comprise up to 10 percent of the calories, and that less than 10 percent come from saturated fats.

Individuals who maintain an acceptable weight and normal cholesterol and triglyceride levels may be prescribed a meal plan with 30 percent or less of the calories from total fat, and with less than 20 percent of these calories from saturated fat. On the other hand, individuals who are overweight, which is often the case in Type 2 (non-insulin-dependent) diabetes, may require a lower-fat diet—20 to 25 percent total fat. Furthermore, the National Cholesterol Education Program Step II diet, which allows less than 7 percent of calories from saturated fat and less than 200 milligrams of cholesterol daily, may be recommended for diabetic individuals who have elevated LDL cholesterol levels.

The aim of nutrition therapy for diabetes management is to implement a meal plan that will achieve as normal a blood-glucose level as possible while meeting other individual health goals.

Realistic Weight Goals. The new ADA guidelines recommend setting realistic weight goals. A moderate reduction of 250 to 500 calories per day coupled with regular exercise and behavioral changes may lead to positive long-term lifestyle changes. The ADA, recognizing that traditional diets have not been effective in attaining long-term weight maintenance, recommends a variety of weight-loss techniques. Mild to moderate weight loss of 10 to 20 pounds has proven effective in improving blood-glucose control even if the goal body weight has not yet been reached. Overall, emphasis is best placed on achieving and maintaining normal blood-glucose and lipid levels in concert with realistic weight goals for each patient.

New Food-Group Selections. New diabetic-education materials reflect the changes in the dietary guidelines by offering a greater selection of carbohydrate choices. Now foods are ranked by their "glycemic index," a measurement of their ability to increase blood-glucose levels. A higher glycemic index means that there will be a larger increase in blood glucose when a standard size serving of the food is eaten. Interestingly, carrots, cereals, grains, most fruits, and even nonfat frozen yogurt have a higher glycemic index than does ice cream. This is because foods containing fat are digested more slowly than most other foods, and thus glucose reaches the bloodstream more slowly.

▶ Broccoli versus Tumors

Broccoli first received rave reviews in 1992, when researchers at Johns Hopkins University in Baltimore, Maryland, announced that the vegetable contained sulforaphane, a chemical that stimulates the formation of anticancer enzymes in laboratory cultures of human cells.

Results of the continued research were published in the April 1994 issue of *Proceedings of the National Academy of Sciences*. Paul Talalay, M.D., and Gary Posner, Ph.D., chief investigators of the study, reported that sulforaphane inhibits the development of breast cancer in rats exposed to dimethyl benzanthracene (DMBA), a potent carcinogen. When tumors did form, they were small in size and number. The sulforaphane used in the investigation was a synthetic version developed by Dr. Posner.

Researchers have speculated that sulforaphane—both natural and synthetic—protects against cancer by enhancing the action of "phase 2 enzymes." The phase 2 enzymes deactivate carcinogens and assist in their elimination from the body. It appears that the process of deactivating the carcinogens makes them less reactive and reduces their ability to damage a cell's DNA. By protecting the cell's DNA, a critical step in cancer development is blocked.

If broccoli is not one of your favorite vegetables, do not despair: sulforaphane is present in the entire family of cruciferous vegetables—cauliflower, brussels sprouts, turnips, cabbage, and

Although rich in vitamins and minerals, vegetables often are considered boring and unappetizing. By trading in her fork for chopsticks, the child above makes eating vegetables an adventure.

kale. Researchers have not yet determined how much sulforaphane is present in each of these vegetables, but they do know that the chemical is not destroyed by conventional cooking or by preparation in a microwave oven.

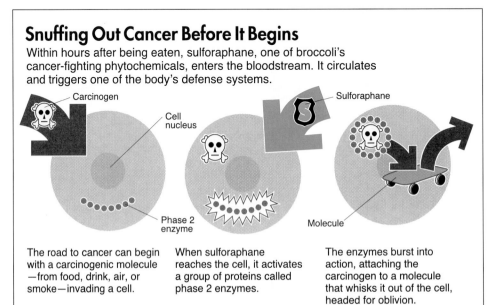

Snuffing Out Cancer Before It Begins

Within hours after being eaten, sulforaphane, one of broccoli's cancer-fighting phytochemicals, enters the bloodstream. It circulates and triggers one of the body's defense systems.

The road to cancer can begin with a carcinogenic molecule —from food, drink, air, or smoke—invading a cell.

When sulforaphane reaches the cell, it activates a group of proteins called phase 2 enzymes.

The enzymes burst into action, attaching the carcinogen to a molecule that whisks it out of the cell, headed for oblivion.

According to the investigators, the next areas of research will determine which vegetables provide the most protection, how the handling and storage of the vegetables may affect their protective qualities, and what type of anticancer protection each variety of vegetable provides. Sulforaphane and its synthetic form will eventually be used in human studies to determine if the chemical will inhibit the development of cancer in people who are at higher risk for the disease. Also, the researchers hope to develop more-powerful synthetic forms of sulforaphane to maximize its anticarcinogenic effect. Since synthetic forms will first need comprehensive safety testing, clinical trials on humans will not start for several years.

Nutritionists now recommend three to five servings of vegetables per day to obtain adequate fiber, beta-carotene, vitamin C, and myriad phytochemicals (disease-fighting substances in plants). The new research on sulforaphane adds support to that recommendation, with an added note to choose your greens wisely.

▶ Trans Fatty Acids

A fatty-acid molecule is composed of a chain of carbon atoms with hydrogen atoms attached. Most unsaturated fatty acids are "*cis* fatty acids," which means that the hydrogen atoms are on the same side of the carbons. Manufacturers hydrogenate (add hydrogen atoms to) polyunsaturated oils in order to produce a solid fat such as margarine or to improve the shelf life of a product. Hydrogenation of fatty acids makes them more saturated. During the hydrogenation of an unsaturated fatty acid, some of the hydrogen atoms are added on opposite sides of the carbons. This process alters the structure of the fatty-acid molecule, producing a "trans fatty acid" (*trans* means "across"). A trans fatty acid is more saturated, and thus a more solid fat. It is capable of raising serum cholesterol, although less than butter and other saturated fats.

Many Americans are wondering if butter is a better choice than margarine. To quell consumer concerns, the Nutrition Committee of the American Heart Association (AHA) released dietary recommendations on trans fatty acids in April 1994. The committee recommends that consumers choose soft margarine over stick margarine. Stick margarine is more hydrogenated and thus contains more trans fatty acids. The AHA recommends that, when shopping, consumers purchase margarine with no more than 2 grams of saturated fat per tablespoon. The committee believes that margarine is still a healthier choice than butter because margarine is made from vegetable oil, and therefore does not con-

The Spread Narrows

Margarine's advantage over butter for cholesterol-lowering diets may be less than once thought. Research now suggests that trans fatty acids as well as some saturated fatty acids (areas colored in orange) can raise blood cholesterol. Areas in yellow show the percentage of saturated and unsaturated fatty acids that have a neutral or beneficial effect on cholesterol levels.

MARGARINE

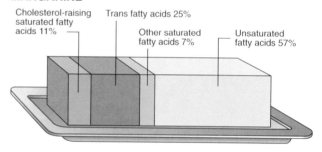

Cholesterol-raising saturated fatty acids 11%
Trans fatty acids 25%
Other saturated fatty acids 7%
Unsaturated fatty acids 57%

BUTTER

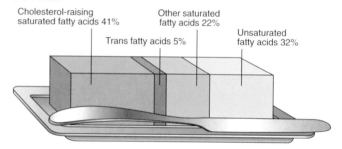

Cholesterol-raising saturated fatty acids 41%
Other saturated fatty acids 22%
Trans fatty acids 5%
Unsaturated fatty acids 32%

tain cholesterol. Since butter contains both saturated fat and cholesterol, it likely has a greater potential to raise cholesterol levels and cause arterial-plaque formation. The bottom line is that no solid fats are healthy, and even margarine intake should be limited.

For healthy Americans over the age of two years, the AHA Nutrition Committee continues to advise limiting total fat to less than 30 percent of total daily calories consumed. To limit the intake of trans fatty acids, the AHA suggests that individuals restrict their daily intake to between 5 and 8 teaspoons of fat, preferably from liquid oils. Consumers can further reduce their intake of trans fatty acids by avoiding processed foods such as crackers, cookies, cakes, chips, and other baked products, which typically contain partially hydrogenated oils. Let the buyer beware: trans-fatty-acid content is not listed on food labels; however, it is part of the total fat listed under unsaturated fat.

▶ Americans Growing Heavier

Since 1960 the National Center for Health Statistics has conducted a series of surveys known as the National Health and Nutrition Examination Survey (NHANES), to examine the incidence of overweight in adults in the United States. Discouraging results from the most recent survey, NHANES III phase 1 (1988–91), were published in the July 20, 1994, issue of the *Journal of the American Medical Association (JAMA)*.

NHANES III is a two-phase, six-year survey (1988–94) designed to oversample Mexican Americans, blacks, children, and the elderly in order to obtain more-accurate estimates for these subgroups. The results of the first phase of the survey are based on 8,260 adults interviewed at their home or in a mobile NHANES examination center. Trained health technicians measured the weight and height of each subject according to standardized procedures.

Criteria for determining overweight were based on body-mass index (BMI), which is calculated as weight in kilograms divided by height in meters squared. In keeping with past surveys, overweight was defined as a BMI measure greater than 27.8 for men and 27.3 for women.

The survey provided estimates on the prevalence of overweight for the total U.S. adult population, and for three race groups—non-Hispanic whites, non-Hispanic blacks, and Mexican-Americans. According to the survey, approximately 33.4 percent (one-third) of adults are considered to be overweight. When compared to the previous survey, NHANES II, the data reveal an alarming 8 percent increase in the incidence of overweight in white men and women. There was a slightly lower increase in the prevalence of overweight in black men and women.

NHANES III phase 1 reveals little difference in the prevalence of overweight in non-Hispanic white men (32.3 percent) and non-Hispanic black men (30.9 percent); the incidence was higher in Mexican-American men (35.5 percent). When women were compared across race groups, non-Hispanic white women had the lowest prevalence of overweight (32.9 percent), while the incidence was much higher in Mexican-American women (46.7 percent) and non-Hispanic black women (48.6 percent).

The survey also examines the effect of aging on trends in overweight by sex and race. The incidence of overweight appears to increase with each decade of life up to age 70 in both non-Hispanic white and Mexican-American men. However, the age-weight correlation is much less pronounced in non-Hispanic black men.

Non-Hispanic white women experience the lowest incidence of overweight for every decade of aging, with the highest prevalence occurring from ages 50 through 59 years. In Mexican-American women, weight gain accelerated between the ages of 40 and 49, while the highest incidence of overweight for non-Hispanic black women was between 60 and 69 years.

Results from NHANES III phase 1 indicate that approximately 58 million adults are currently overweight (about 26 million men and 32 million women). The average weight of adults aged 20 through 74 years increased by almost 8 pounds between NHANES II (1976–80) and NHANES III phase 1 (1988–91).

The results from NHANES III phase 1 are discouraging. Overweight is linked to a variety of health problems. In 1986 alone, illnesses associated with overweight cost Americans more than $39 billion in health care expenses. Federal health officials have set a national health goal of decreasing the incidence of overweight to 20 percent or less by the year 2000. Given the results of NHANES III phase 1, this objective may be a difficult goal to meet.

Among the reasons for the trend in overweight in the United States are insufficient awareness and knowledge of food intake, increase in meals eaten in restaurants, and inadequate physical activity. A 1991 survey on exercise revealed that about 58 percent of American adults exercised irregularly or not at all.

Historically, overweight individuals have been difficult to treat. Studies have shown that 90 to 95 percent of all people who lose weight on traditional diets gain the weight back within five years. Health experts also note that commercial weight-loss programs rarely produce long-term success, and many of them are downright dangerous. Pediatricians can help prevent children from acquiring excessive weight by educating parents and children on the importance of nutrition and regular physical activity. Overweight children and adolescents should be referred to family-based weight-management programs supervised by registered dietitians.

▶ Finnish Antioxidant Study

Results from a controlled six-year study conducted by the National Cancer Institute (NCI) and the National Public Health Institute in Finland were published in the *New England Journal of Medicine* in April 1994. The purpose of the investigation was to determine if supplemental beta-carotene and vitamin E reduce the incidences of lung cancer and other cancers. The findings that the antioxidant vitamins did not provide protection against lung cancer, and that they might even be harmful, stunned the scientific community. Several earlier studies had indicated that increased intakes of beta-carotene and vitamin E were linked to a lower risk for lung cancer.

The subjects in this investigation were 29,000 Finnish men, aged 50 to 69 years old, who smoked an average of one pack of cigarettes daily for an average of 36 years. Each man was randomly assigned to one of four groups. One group was given 20 milligrams of beta-carotene per day; one group was given 50 milligrams of vitamin E per day; another group was given both beta-carotene and vitamin E supplements daily; and a fourth group was given a placebo. The groups were monitored for five to eight years.

The research yielded some startling results: not only did the supplements provide no health benefits, but the men taking beta-carotene were found to have a *greater* incidence of lung cancer and heart disease than the men who did not take them. Also, the group that was given only supplemental vitamin E experienced more deaths from strokes than the group that did not take it. Curiously, the men who received vitamin E had a slightly lower incidence of prostate cancer. The investigators reported that the men taking both beta-carotene and vitamin E supplements also did not have a lower incidence of lung cancer.

Health experts agree that this study does not prove that antioxidant vitamins do not lower risk of cancer. While it was a well-controlled study, it had some flaws. First, the subjects were heavy smokers for many years and had a much higher chance of developing lung cancer. The investigators note that the duration of the study may not have been long enough for the supplements to reverse damage done by a lifetime exposure to cigarette smoke. Also, it is possible that beta-carotene and vitamin E may confer protection against lung cancer in nonsmokers or newer smokers.

Also, a large number of subjects dropped out of the study—almost one-third left the investigation or died. The subjects who dropped out or died were included in the statistical analysis. This raises the possibility that the results may have been skewed.

The investigators, as well as other researchers in the scientific community, feel that it is unlikely that beta-carotene actually increases the risk for lung cancer. However, the increased risk for stroke in the vitamin E subjects merits careful scrutiny. Until more is known, health experts advise that individuals with high blood pressure or bleeding problems should be warned against taking supplemental vitamin E.

Many earlier studies have shown an association between diets rich in fruits and vegetables that contain beta-carotene and a reduced risk of cancer. Further research will help determine whether it is the beta-carotene that confers protection against cancer, or whether it is a combination of beta-carotene, vitamin C, other carotenoids, fiber, and a host of phytochemicals found in fruits and vegetables.

Maria Guglielmino, M.S., R.D.

Obstetrics and Gynecology

▶ Infertility

Great advances have been made in treating infertility, although the high cost of new treatments limits their availability. In addition, research into infertility has been hampered by controversies over fetal research and embryo manipulations. Ethical concerns have also been raised about preying on the vulnerability of desperate couples who may opt for experimental treatment without necessarily being fully informed about the experimental nature of the treatment or about the small chance of actually taking home a healthy baby. Despite such concerns the new advances represent breakthroughs for couples who, without some of the new technologies, would have had little—if any—chance at becoming biological parents. Among some of the new technologies available to couples:

Zona Pellucida Drilling. By drilling tiny holes in the surface of an egg during *in vitro* fertilization (fertilization of an egg outside of the uterus), scientists can fertilize eggs with small numbers of sperm. This allows couples in which the male has a very low sperm count to successfully conceive.

Egg Donation. A number of infertility programs offer donor eggs. Eggs are harvested after giving a healthy young woman fertility drugs to cause her to produce several eggs. The mature eggs are harvested, usually with ultrasound guidance to identify the ovarian follicles in which they have grown. The eggs are then fertilized in the lab, usually with the sperm of the male partner in an infertile couple, and then placed in the recipient woman. This procedure is philosophically a bit more like using a sperm donor than so-called surrogate parenting, in which the donor woman produces the egg and carries the pregnancy. In egg donation, it is the adoptive mother who carries the pregnancy, and hence becomes the "birth" mother. The donor mother may be known to the adoptive family or may remain anonymous. This procedure makes pregnancy an option for women whose ovaries have been destroyed by surgery or cancer-treating drugs or for women who are congenitally incapable of forming healthy eggs. The widest and most controversial use of egg donation, however, is in women past the age of menopause. While most infertility clinics have a cutoff age of 50 for recipients, several instances of women well over 50 delivering healthy infants by this technique have occurred.

Infertility research and advances continue to raise controversy. While the majority of infertility clinics are reputable, some have been accused of manipulating statistics on success, citing high "pregnancy" rates when what consumers actually need to know is the "take-home-baby" rate. The American Fertility Society has developed standardized definitions for purposes of compiling statistical comparisons and standards for infertility clinics.

Payments and economics raise another important issue. High-tech infertility treatments are expensive in two ways. First, the treatments themselves may cost several thousands of dollars per attempted pregnancy. In a 1994 article in the *New England Journal of Medicine*, the cost per "take-home baby" was estimated at $44,000 to $211,000. A second, more indirect cost of assisted reproduction is that of multiple gestations. In one study, 2 percent of singleton births, 35 percent of twins, and 77 percent of triplets and higher multiple births resulted from assisted reproduction. The average cost per pregnancy in the study was $9,800 for a singleton pregnancy, $38,000 for twins, and $109,800 for triplets. (In a separate study, it was noted that nationally, multiple births grew by 26.6 percent between 1970 and 1993.)

▶ Ultrasound

Ultrasound is a medical diagnostic method in which sound waves are emitted from a transducer and "bounced back" from tissue interfaces to form pictures in computer-integrated circuitry. Ultrasound images can be either static shadow pictures or moving, "real-time" images of internal structures. Ultrasound has been particularly useful in looking at fetuses *in utero*. It is an invaluable part of infertility treatment that allows eggs to be harvested out of a woman's ovaries through the vaginal wall, avoiding surgery for *in vitro* fertilization. Ultrasound is increasingly used for gynecologic scanning; it is a useful tool for evaluating enlarged ovaries and assessing the uterine lining. However, few studies have yet demonstrated that ultrasound actually improves pregnancy outcome or detects ovarian and other cancers soon enough to actually impact mortality rates.

▶ Evolving Contraceptives

Contraceptive development has been slow in the United States due to both political controversy about safety and product liability and the cumbersome approval process for new medications or devices on the part of the Food and Drug Administration (FDA). However, the addition of Norplant (five-year implantable capsules) and Depo-Provera (quarterly injections) to the contraceptive armamentarium within recent years may represent a new wave of expanding contraceptive options. According to *The Contraceptive Report*, there are a number of contraceptive methods available abroad—but not in the United States—and new methods are being developed abroad, which may further expand American options within the coming years.

Implants. Norplant II is a two-implant system, similar to the six-implant Norplant, that lasts for three to five years. Single-rod systems are being tested, including biodegradable pellets and implants. Some physicians have encountered difficulty removing the implants; concerns about removal and side effects such as irregular bleeding, coupled with high purchase and insertion

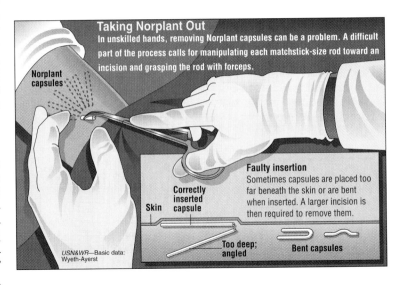

Taking Norplant Out
In unskilled hands, removing Norplant capsules can be a problem. A difficult part of the process calls for manipulating each matchstick-size rod toward an incision and grasping the rod with forceps.

Norplant capsules

Faulty insertion
Sometimes capsules are placed too far beneath the skin or are bent when inserted. A larger incision is then required to remove them.

Correctly inserted capsule

Skin

Too deep; angled

Bent capsules

USN&WR—Basic data: Wyeth-Ayerst

prices, have limited the number of women using Norplant in the United States.

Barrier Contraceptives. Concerns about the transmission of human immunodeficiency virus (HIV), the virus that causes AIDS, have fueled an interest in barrier contraceptives. A major obstacle to the use of the most common barrier contraceptive—condoms—is the unwillingness of many men to use them. Methods under study include a contraceptive sponge with enhanced antimicrobial activity; disposable diaphragms; the so-called "female condom," which covers the cervix and entire perineum; and cervical caps with outflow valves.

Male Methods. Injections of testosterone, sometimes combined with other hormones, block sperm production in many men. Research continues in these methods. In initial research, Chinese and

Indonesian men experience higher rates of azoo-spermia (lack of sperm) with most of the methods currently being tested than do Caucasian men.

In the meantime the FDA has approved poly-urethane condoms for use in the United States, which will be a boon for people allergic to latex, as well as possibly being more aesthetically acceptable to some men. Several other materials and condom designs are being tested.

▶ Calcium Update

A National Institutes of Health (NIH) Consensus Development Conference on "Optimal Calcium Intake" met in 1994 to review recommendations on calcium intake. The panel of experts conclud-ed that most Americans consume well below the current recommended dietary allowance (RDA) for calcium. The panel came up with increased recommendations for most groups, with amounts given in milligrams (mg) per day (see the table).

Recommended Dietary Allowances for Calcium Intake

Group	Current Typical Intake (mg/day)	Current RDA (mg/day)	Optimal (mg/day)
Infants (to 6 mo.)	300	400	400
Infants (6 mo.–1 yr.)	300	600	600
Children (1–10 yrs.)	800–1,000	300	800
Girls (10–20 yrs.)	700	800	1,200–1,500
Boys (10–20 yrs.)	1,200	800	1,200–1,500
Adult women	600	800	1,000
Adult men	800	800	800
Pregnant, lactating women	1,200	1,200	1,200
Postmenopausal women	600	800	1,500

▶ Menopause Management

Hormones: The Controversy Continues. The contro-versy over estrogen therapy for menopause contin-ues. Estrogens clearly are beneficial in maintaining bone density and protecting against heart disease in women after menopause; in many women, estrogen also alleviates hot flashes, improves sleep, and possibly improves overall well-being. Hip fractures and heart attacks, major sources of illness, disability, and death in older women, are reduced dramatically in women on long-term estrogen therapy. There is also data suggesting that women with Alzheimer's disease improve on estrogen therapy, possibly because estrogen may stimulate neuron development in the brain.

However, side effects such as breast tender-ness, fluid retention, and vaginal bleeding make many women avoid estrogen-replacement therapy. In addition, estrogen can cause excessive buildup and even cancer of the uterine lining (endometrial cancer) unless a woman also takes an additional type of hormone called a progestin. But progestins often cause side effects of irritability and weight gain. Furthermore, the progestins commonly used in the United States actually undo some of the cardiovascular protective effect of estrogen. Some women and their doctors choose to forgo the progestins altogether, feeling that a small chance of endometrial cancer is worth avoiding the side effects and disadvantages of an added progestin. Finally, the effects of both estrogen and progesterone on breast tissue are unclear.

Most studies do not show any increase in breast cancer on long-term hormone-replacement thera-py, but a few studies indicate there may be a slight increased risk with long-term use. It also is not entirely clear whether the problem, if it exists, is related to estrogen, proges-terone, or—most likely—to the specific chemical struc-ture of the actual formulation of hormones in women with certain genetic predisposi-tions (see accompanying sec-tion on breast-cancer gene). During 1994 a national study group of cancer specialists called for more research on the specific issue of whether women who have survived breast cancer should be offered estrogen in light of the hormone's benefits and the lack of firm scientific data that estrogens actually cause breast cancer.

The dilemma faced by women deciding whether to undergo estrogen-replacement therapy may not be resolved for many years. In the meantime, women and their doctors must seriously weigh the issues and come up with an individualized treatment plan based on the woman's risk fac-tors for osteoporosis, heart disease, and cancer.

▶ Tamoxifen

Controversy has also surrounded the drug tam-oxifen, commonly used to treat breast-cancer patients and to prevent cancer recurrences. Ta-moxifen, a form of estrogen, seems to confer some of the bone and cardiovascular benefits of estrogen. Unfortunately, it also acts like an estro-gen on the uterine lining, resulting in a slightly increased risk of uterine-lining cancer. A large national trial of tamoxifen as a breast-cancer preventive agent momentarily stopped enrolling patients after several endometrial cancers were detected in women in the trial; enrollment of patients resumed after the consent forms were revised to reflect this risk, and after the protocols were revised to include endometrial surveillance. The risk of endometrial cancer from using tamoxifen is low, but most oncologists and gynecologists are recommending that women on long-term tamoxifen therapy have regular uterine-lining assessments either with office endometrial biopsies or vaginal-probe ultrasound.

▶ Closing in on Cancer Genes
Researchers in Utah and North Carolina have isolated the gene responsible for inherited breast cancer. For years, scientists have been closing in on the gene, which seems to be a common denominator for families in which multiple women spanning several generations have breast cancer. The gene, dubbed BRCA-1, appears to be on the 17th chromosome, and can be inherited from either a paternal or a maternal chromosome. However, only 5 to 10 percent of breast-cancer cases occur in familial clusters, while 90 percent or more are sporadic, occurring in women with no family history.

Physicians and ethicists have concerns about finding genes that establish that an individual is at high risk of breast-cancer development. A woman who finds out she is carrying the gene could certainly be targeted for close surveillance; some doctors would support preventative mastectomy in such women. However, insurers might balk at paying for preventative surgery. Furthermore, women known to be BRCA-1 carriers could be subject to job and insurance discrimination, as well as to psychosocial aftermaths such as depression. Women carrying the familial breast-cancer gene are not alone, however. Geneticists are identifying genes for familial ovarian cancer and colon cancer as well. The overwhelming majority of such cancers are thought to arise from a complex web of environmental and lifestyle factors.

▶ RU-486
RU-486, the "abortion pill" developed in France, has advanced into clinical trials in the United States. Currently RU-486 is available in France and Britain, offering a medical alternative to early surgical abortions, and potentially moving abortion out of surgical clinics and into private physicians' offices. Sidestepping the controversy surrounding RU-486 altogether, several physicians are pursuing a combination of methotrexate (a drug currently used for arthritis treatment and cancer chemotherapy) and misoprostol, which is also highly effective in inducing early abortion.

Linda Hughey Holt, M.D.

Occupational Health

▶ Drug Use in the Workplace
Many U.S. companies have implemented drug-testing and employee-counseling programs as part of an overall antidrug effort, at an annual cost of approximately $1.2 billion. But more research is needed before the effectiveness of these programs can be judged, according to a report by a committee of the National Research Council and the Institute of Medicine. As reported in the Winter 1993–94 edition of *Issues of Science and Technology*, data collected in the National Household Survey on Drug Abuse show that occupational differences do exist in drug and heavy alcohol abuse, but the disparities seem to be more a function of the personal qualities of the individuals rather than of the work environments.

The study shows that workers in the construction and retail-trade industries have far higher rates of both drug and alcohol abuse than do manufacturing workers or those workers classified as professionals. Although all employment groups have similar rates of heavy alcohol use, the prevalence of illicit-drug use is significantly higher among the unemployed, especially men.

Alcohol is the most commonly abused substance at work. In 1991, 7.6 percent of male workers drank on the job, compared to 4.6 percent of female workers. Marijuana is the most prevalent illegal drug—4.5 percent of men and 0.9 percent of women report having used it at work in 1991. Less than 1.0 percent reported using any other illegal drug at the workplace.

▶ On the Job
The National Institute for Occupational Safety and Health (NIOSH) identifies homicide as the third-leading cause of injury death in the workplace in the United States during the 1980s. About 12.1 percent of all injury deaths on the job were homicides—only motor-vehicle (23.1 percent) and machine-related (13.4 percent) accidents account for more deaths.

According to a study in the February 1994 issue of the *Journal of Occupational Medicine*, more than 7,500 work-related homicides occurred during the 10-year period ending in 1989, with men accounting for 80 percent of the victims. The rate for men (1.02 per 100,000 workers) was more than three times the rate for females. Approximately 74 percent of the homicide victims were white workers; 19 percent black; and 6 percent other races. Nonetheless, the work-related homicide rates for black workers (1.42 per 100,000) and for workers of other races (1.57 per 100,000) were more than twice the rate for white workers.

Nearly one-third of all civilian occupational homicides occur in three areas: grocery stores; eating and drinking establishments; and the justice, public-order, and safety system, which includes courts, police and fire protection, correctional institutions, and legal counsel. The homicide rate for the taxicab industry is about 40 percent greater than the rate for all workers, and more than three times greater than the rate for liquor stores, the industry with the next-highest rate. Women are at particularly high risk for occupational homicide in liquor stores, gasoline stations, and grocery stores. Stock handlers and baggers are the only occupations in

Causes of All Workplace Deaths 1980–1989

- Other 28.3%
- Motor vehicles 23.1%
- Machines 13.4%
- Homicides 12.1%
- Falls 9.5%
- Electrocutions 7.1%
- Struck by falling objects 6.5%

Safety research and injury-prevention measures have gone a long way toward reducing work-related injuries. Still, workplace deaths—including homicides—occur far too often.

which the rate for women exceeds that for men.

The authors of the study point out that in some cases, crude rates of homicide mask high rates among certain subpopulations of workers. For example, although crude rates for automobile mechanics (8.86 homicides per 100,000) and construction laborers (0.80 per 100,000) are low, black workers in these occupations are at higher risk of work-related homicides—2.57 per 100,00

for black auto mechanics, and 2.28 per 100,000 for black construction workers.

This study and others point out certain characteristics of employment that increase a worker's risk for occupational homicide: handling money; working alone or in small numbers; and working in the late evening or very early morning.

▶ HIV and Work Performance

A number of studies conducted since the late 1980s indicate that perhaps one-third of HIV-infected individuals who display no medical symptoms nonetheless experience mild loss of attention, memory, and reaction time on laboratory tests. More-recent data suggest that in some cases, these lapses impede day-to-day functioning at work. As reported in the February 26, 1994, issue of *Science News*, a study undertaken at the University of California, San Diego, School of Medicine shows that symptom-free HIV-infected men more often report unemployment or a recent drop in job performance if they also exhibit mild neuropsychological problems.

The study included 378 men ranging in age from 18 to 50. Of those, 252 were HIV-positive, but displayed no significant medical symptoms; 37 were HIV-positive with some immune-cell irregularities and other signs of progression toward AIDS; and 89 were HIV-negative controls. Each participant was evaluated on attention, memory, language skills, spatial perception, and intelligence. At least a mild degree of impairment was evidenced by about 50 percent of the symptomatic HIV group, by 33 percent of the symptom-free group, and by 16 percent of the controls. Unemployment reached 22 percent in the symptomatic group, compared to 10 percent among the neuropsychologically healthy HIV-positive group. Moreover, 28 percent of employed HIV-positive men showing some signs of neuropsychological deficits cited a marked drop in their ability to perform job duties, compared to only 6 percent of their unimpaired counterparts.

▶ Water-based Paints

A study reported in the March 1994 *Occupational and Environmental Medicine* indicates that the introduction of water-based paint has improved the work environment for housepainters. The study group consisted of 255 male housepainters, aged 20 to 65, and two industrial populations, in total 302 men, without exposure to water-based paints. Hygiene measurements were performed during normal workdays when only water-based paints and no solvent-based paints were being used. The study group says that the work environment was better when working with water-based paints. There were more complaints of frequent urination when working with water-based paints, but taste and/or olfactory problems were less common. General as well as work-related eye and skin irritation were more common among the housepainters than among the control group. For other symptoms, no significant differences were found. The study concludes that water-based paints cause less discomfort and airway irritation than the earlier solvent-based products, and adverse general health effects seem to be negligible.

▶ Nurses

Three recent studies have focused on the tolerance of nurses for shift work and their ability to handle the physical workload. A report in the May 1994 *International Archives of Occupational and Environmental Health* studied 15 female nurses, aged 21 to 29 years, who are employed in an intensive-care unit. The study aimed to evaluate their psychophysical adaptation to a rotating shift system where the length of the shift was modified according to the workload (including night shifts of 10 hours), and with the start of the morning shift delayed until 7:00 A.M. Subjective evaluations, performance measures, blood pressure, and heart rate were recorded at the start, middle, and end of the work shifts on the last four days of the shift cycle, which comprised one morning, one afternoon, and two consecutive nights.

The results show that rotating shifts did not alter the normal circadian rhythms of the body. Lengthening of the night shift to 10 hours was considered acceptable in terms of work efficiency, provided that the workload is somewhat reduced and that there are enough rest pauses to compensate for fatigue and sleepiness. Shortening of the day shift to seven hours appears to be conducive to job performance, the study says.

A Danish study reported in the February 1994 *Occupational Medicine-Oxford* concludes that assistant nurses were more likely to suffer genital prolapse and herniated lumbar-disk problems than the overall female population because of the stress of heavy lifting while taking care of patients. The incidence of surgery due to herniated lumbar disk and genital prolapse was investigated using two population groups: 28,619 assistant nurses aged 20 to 69 years, and more than 1.6 million controls in the general Danish population.

In a related study reported in the March 1994 *Journal of Occupational Medicine*, researchers investigated the physical workload and musculoskeletal complaints of nurses in nursing homes. Thirty-six female subjects from three nursing homes in the Netherlands participated in the observational study. The researchers note that 60 percent of the observed time was spent on non-patient-related activities, which alternate rapidly and seldom last for more than four minutes. Twenty percent of the work time was spent in "poor" work postures, especially during patient care and during the performance of household and other preliminary tasks. Perceived exertion is highest during patient care. Nurses complained most of back (41 percent), arm/neck (35 percent), and leg (20 percent) pain. The study concludes that not only patient-related activities, but also household tasks, ergonomic layout of the ward, and work stress deserve continuing attention in the effort to improve work postures and other potentially strenuous aspects of nursing work.

▶ Oil Workers

Nonfatal work-related injury rates are 49 percent higher among oil- and gas-field workers than among workers in all U.S. industries combined, and these injuries are 2.8 times more severe in terms of lost workdays, according to a study in the June 1994 *Journal of Occupational Medicine*. Using data collected by an international trade association for the three-year period from 1988 to 1990, the researchers analyzed incidents on both on- and offshore drilling rigs. Of the 551 reported injuries, 99.4 percent were nonfatal.

Nonfatal injuries are four times more likely to be reported in the U.S. than overseas, while injury rates on offshore rigs were higher than land-based injuries both in the U.S. and abroad. Three occupations—floormen, roustabouts, and derrickmen—have higher risks for both fatal and nonfatal injuries, with rates 4 to 10 times higher than for all other occupations combined.

Upper extremities account for 31 percent of the nonfatal injuries, a larger proportion than any other body part. Head or neck injuries account for the greatest proportion of fatal injuries, about one-third. The researchers conclude that offshore-petroleum-drilling workers face extremely hazardous conditions, conditions further exacerbated by high stress and anxiety levels, the need to manage large pieces of equipment, long working hours or shifts, and a slippery work area.

▶ Construction Workers

According to a study in the February 1994 *Journal of Occupational Medicine*, the construction industry had a fatality rate of 25.6 per 100,000 full-time workers, more than 3.5 times the rate for all industries in the United States for the 10-year period ending in 1989.

During the time frame used in the study, 59 percent of nonfatal injuries occurred to workers under 35 years of age, with the highest rate among those in the 20- to 24-year-old group. Machine operators and laborers had the highest and second-highest rates of injury respectively. Almost 63 percent of the injuries resulted in strains or sprains (34 percent); cuts, lacerations, or punctures (17 percent); or fractures (11 percent). The back was the most frequently injured body part. Along with fingers, legs, and eyes, these four groups made up 50 percent of the total. Sprains or strains to the back, and cuts, lacerations, or punctures to the finger, accounted for approximately 23 percent of the total injuries to workers from 1981 through 1986.

Four sources of injury accounted for 47 percent of the total: metal items (18 percent), working surfaces (16 percent), nonpowered hand tools (7 percent), and wood items (6 percent). The leading types of incidents were overexertion (24 percent), being struck by objects (22 percent), falling from elevations (13 percent), and being struck against an object (9 percent).

Of the fatalities, 47 percent were in workers under 35 years of age, but workers over 65 had the highest rate. Eighty-one percent of the total fatalities were white workers, 9 percent were black, and 7 percent were Hispanic; 3 percent of the fatalities were to people of another or unknown race or ethnicity.

Construction workers had the highest fatality rates in the general workforce, with the exception of farmers, foresters, and fishermen. The divisions within the contruction industry with the greatest frequencies of death were precision production/craft/repair (48 percent), laborers (27 percent), and transport operatives (12 percent).

The three leading causes of death for construction workers were falls (25 percent), electrocutions (15 percent), and motor-vehicle-related incidents (14 percent).

The study concludes that there is a need to focus additional safety research and injury-prevention measures on the construction industry in general, and on specific divisions within the industry that have been identified in this and other reports. The authors note that the national health objective for the year 2000, as set by the Public Health Service, includes these goals, and that NIOSH recently established an initiative to accelerate research that would help reduce work-related injuries and fatalities in the construction industry.

Neil Springer

Pediatrics

▶ Bouncing Off the Walls

A common belief holds that sugary foods cause hyperactivity in children. Two recent studies provide new evidence that this axiom of child rearing is incorrect. Researchers from the University of Iowa in Iowa City assumed total control of a family's diet for several weeks, with neither participants nor researchers aware of whether the week's meals were sugar-filled or sugar-free. Another group from Yale University in New Haven, Connecticut, studied children known to be hyperactive, and used aspartame rather than sugar, as a sweetening agent.

The presumed reaction to sugar has been attributed to a rise in blood-sugar levels shortly after ingestion, followed by low blood-sugar levels several hours later, or to an allergic response. For aspartame the apparent increase in activity level has been attributed to an increase in the level of the amino acid phenylalanine in the blood, which in turn alters the transport of other essential amino acids to the brain.

To the disappointment of those who cling to the notion that too much sugar revs kids up, neither study found any effect of sweeteners on behavior or thinking. Parents should nonetheless regulate the amount of sweets that their children consume. Besides the obvious link between sugar and dental cavities, excessive sugar intake by children can lead to obesity, prevent children from eating a balanced diet, and cultivate poor eating habits.

Although studies dispute the claim that sugary foods cause hyperactivity, it's wise to restrict sugar intake, which can lead to cavities and obesity.

► Risk of Whooping-Cough Vaccine

The whooping-cough (pertussis) vaccine is given to infants along with vaccines for diphtheria and tetanus. For infants, whooping cough is a serious disease that can result in brain damage and even death from inadequate oxygenation.

A British study in 1976 found that children with serious neurological illness, seizures, or encephalitis were more likely to have received diphtheria-tetanus-pertussis (DTP) vaccine during the previous seven days than were children who did not receive the vaccine. Despite criticism about the methodology of this study, and subsequent studies that failed to demonstrate the same association, the public and some in the medical profession continue to be concerned about the pertussis vaccine.

As a result of the 1976 study, vaccination rates in Great Britain declined from 77 percent to 30 percent. An epidemic of pertussis followed, with a dramatic increase in death and permanent brain damage due to whooping cough. In the United States, similar public fears may account in part for the current low immunization rates of young children, although the American Academy of Pediatrics and the Centers for Disease Control and Prevention (CDC) have never deviated from the recommendation for immunization of infants with the pertussis vaccine, arguing that the risk of *not* being immunized is far greater than the small (if any) risk from the vaccine. The U.S. Congress has enacted the Vaccine Compensation Act to provide payment to parents whose infants may have been harmed by the pertussis or other vaccines.

A recent study from Washington and Oregon finds no increased risk for serious acute neurological illness in the seven days after the DTP vaccine was administered to 218,000 children ages one month to two years. The question of risk will become less important as a new acellular pertussis vaccine, which causes fewer side effects (fever, pain at the site of injection, and irritability) becomes available.

► Fresh Air for Cystic Fibrosis

Cystic fibrosis is the most common fatal inherited disease among whites in the United States. Its major symptoms arise from chronic obstruction and infection of the airways and from digestive disorders. The digestive problems can be treated successfully with dietary adjustment, pancreatic-enzyme replacement, and vitamins; unfortunately, most individuals die in early adulthood from cardiorespiratory complications.

Some of these complications can be ameliorated by the drug Pulmozyme, the first new treatment for cystic fibrosis in three decades. Pulmozyme is a genetically engineered copy of the human enzyme recombinant human deoxyribonuclease (also called dornase alfa), which is normally present in saliva, urine, and pancreatic secretions, and is responsible for the digestion of extracellular DNA. Abnormally high concentrations of DNA make the secretions in the lung thick and sticky; the secretions then obstruct the flow of air. It is thought that Pulmozyme, administered directly into the lungs by aerosol, chops up this extracellular DNA, facilitating clearance of airway secretions.

A consortium of researchers from over 50 research hospitals sought to determine whether once- or twice-daily administration of Pulmozyme would benefit patients with cystic fibrosis. A total of 968 adults and children were treated over 24 weeks. The researchers found that the drug reduces (but does not eliminate) respiratory symptoms, and does so without serious side effects. Further studies are required to determine whether the modest but significant improvement brought about by Pulmozyme outweighs the drug's high cost.

► Insights into Childhood Infections

Roseola. Roseola, a common disease in young children, is characterized by high fever for about three days; when the temperature returns to normal, a body rash typically appears. In 1988 reports from Japan indicated that roseola was caused by human herpesvirus-6 (HHV-6), which is related to the viruses that produce chicken pox and cold sores.

It is now known that HHV-6 infection is nearly universal in infancy and early childhood, although it has many different manifestations. These include red eardrums, cold symptoms, stomach and intestinal upset, and, almost always, high fever. When the characteristic rash develops (about 20 percent of cases), the diagnosis of roseola is made. Otherwise the illness is indistinguishable from that caused by other infectious organisms. The presence of HHV-6 is detectable only by sophisticated laboratory tests that normally are conducted only for research purposes. A research team from the University of Rochester School of Medicine recently concluded that HHV-6 infection is a major cause of visits to the emergency department, of seizures due to sudden rise in body temperature, and of infant hospitalizations.

Kawasaki Syndrome. Kawasaki syndrome is the leading cause of acquired heart disease among children in Japan and the United States. Although Kawasaki syndrome has been reported in adults, 80 percent of patients are five years old or younger. Researchers continue to search

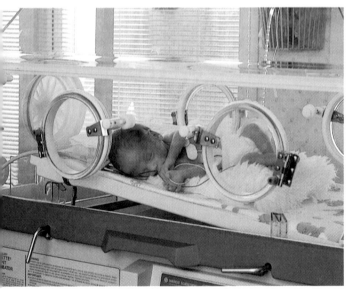

Extremely premature babies require intensive health-care resources and also face increased risk for permanent developmental disabilities.

for the cause of this disease. Although Kawasaki syndrome is considered an infectious disease, no one has identified the causal organism. A recent study in the *Lancet* reports the isolation of a new strain of the bacterium *Staphylococcus aureau* that produces a toxin in a majority of patients with Kawasaki syndrome.

Previous studies have associated Kawasaki syndrome with bacterial toxins acting as super-antigens, substances that stimulate the body's immune system to mistakenly attack its own tissues. The hallmarks of Kawasaki syndrome are similar to other "autoimmune" diseases: fever, rash, achy joints, and irritation of the lining of the eyelids and mouth. The potential symptom of utmost concern is the ballooning out (aneurysm) of the blood vessels in the muscle of the heart. Rupture of these aneurysms results in almost-certain death from heart attack.

Newer treatments are aimed at preventing this self-destruction by administration of intravenous immunoglobulin (IVIG), which may inactivate the toxins so that they do not become superantigens. If treatment is started in the first 10 days of the disease, fever lessens, and the aneurysms do not develop. Superantigens produced by bacterial toxins likely play a role in a large number of other diseases that have long puzzled doctors. A better understanding of superantigens will likely lead to improved and more-specific treatments for Kawasaki syndrome.

▶ Micropreemies: How Do They Fare?
While technological advances have allowed very small prematurely born infants a better chance of survival over the past decade, there has been concern that their quality of life may be limited by injury to the brain. The smaller and more premature infants are, the more susceptible they are to complications resulting in developmental disabilities.

A specialist in newborn care at Case Western Reserve University in Cleveland, Ohio, followed a group of the smallest premature infants—all of whom weighed under 750 grams (1 pound, 7 ounces) at birth—until they were of school age. She and her colleagues found that these children were at serious disadvantage in every skill required for adequate performance in school. Twenty-one percent had subnormal mental abilities, and 45 percent required special-education services in school. Fifteen percent had major neurosensory impairments, such as cerebral palsy, blindness, and deafness.

Although these children represent less than 1 percent of live births and only a small proportion of children needing special-education support, they nevertheless do require enormous expenditure of neonatal health-care resources (in the newborn intensive-care units), and place a significant educational burden on the child, family, and school system. The prevention of extreme prematurity is thus a critical issue.

▶ Hot Red Ears
In most cases of childhood otitis media (inflammation of the middle ear), the doctor sees a reddish eardrum and prescribes an antibiotic. Yet most ear infections are caused by viruses, which are not effectively treated with antibiotics. Unfortunately, it is difficult to tell whether an ear infection is viral or bacterial in origin simply by looking at the eardrum. As a result, many children receive antibiotics unnecessarily.

After the acute infection subsides, fluid often persists in the middle ear for weeks or months. Sometimes this fluid becomes thick, leading to a "glue ear." Since the middle-ear ossicles do not conduct sound well in this thickened fluid, temporary hearing loss can occur. In the past, experts have advised doctors to treat this condition with antibiotics. New guidelines from a federal health agency and the American Academy of Pediatrics caution against use of antibiotics for this condition, since otitis media usually resolves on its own without treatment. Furthermore, the guidelines suggest that medications are used too early in most cases, that antibiotics sometimes cause rashes and diarrhea, and that antibiotic therapy may increase the likelihood of a child developing an immunity to the drugs. Antibiotics have been shown to be only 14 percent more effective than "watchful waiting" in correcting the problem.

Experts recommend hearing tests and antibiotics if the symptoms persist for more than three months. Surgery, which costs about $2,100, is recommended if symptoms persist for more than six months. Currently surgery for otitis media, in which a small tube is put through a small slit in the eardrum to drain fluid, is the most common surgical procedure among children under age 15. A recent study of ear, nose, and throat specialists in the United States found that tubes were inserted into eardrums unnecessarily in one-quarter of the cases.

▶ Tuberculosis on the Rise in Children

Since the late 1980s, a significant increase in *Mycobacterium tuberculosis* infection has occurred in children under the age of 15. Tuberculosis (TB) in children is considered an indicator that TB prevention and control efforts are failing. Indeed, public-health officials have a diminished capacity to identify adults with TB promptly and, once they are identified, to make them noninfectious by providing appropriate antibiotic therapy. New pediatric TB cases represent a significant proportion of the pool from which future cases of TB will emerge.

By race and ethnicity, the largest increases in TB case rates have occurred in Hispanic children, followed by increases among black children. Case rates among white children have remained unchanged, while those among Asian and Pacific Islanders, Alaskan natives, and American Indians have actually declined. The highest increase in case rates occurred in children from two to four years old, reflecting the fact that younger children progress more rapidly to active disease once infected with *M. tuberculosis*.

Two factors—immigration and the AIDS epidemic—account for part of the jump in pediatric TB cases since 1985. In recent years, 25 percent of children with TB in the United States were foreign-born. This is not surprising, given that the World Health Organization (WHO) reports that TB is the leading cause of death from infectious disease in those older than 5—responsible for an alarming 2.7 million deaths yearly. Fortunately, 50 to 60 percent of foreign-born children with TB are diagnosed soon after entering the U.S.

The second factor raising the rates of TB in children is AIDS. Children with AIDS are extraordinarily prone to develop active TB infection. To date, prevention-control strategies have not adequately targeted this population.

Another alarming fact is that strains of *M. tuberculosis* are emerging that are resistant to the antibiotics usually used to treat TB, making it more difficult to contain the disease.

James A. Blackman, M.D., M.P.H.

Plastic Surgery

▶ Tattoo Removal by Laser

For some 5,000 years, people have been decorating their bodies with tattoos. For probably just as long, the desire to remove these pigment-injected areas has haunted people who have grown tired of their permanent skin embellishments. Attempts at removal have invariably had less-than-desirable effects, primarily because all methods that effectively erased the tattoo left behind an unsightly scar. Fortunately, thanks to recent technological advances in lasers, surgeons now have the capacity to remove the dye materials from a tattoo without the postoperative disfigurement that typically occurs with traditional tattoo-removal methods.

To achieve scar-free tattoo removal, surgeons use a pulsed-dye laser called the Q-switched Nd:YAG, in which the beam penetrates through the patient's skin. The energy emitted by the differing wavelengths of the laser beam is absorbed by the various colors present in the tattooed skin. The high force of this concentrated "blast" bursts the dye particles. The disintegrated particles of dye are then rapidly engulfed, or "eaten," by scavenger cells called macrophages, an essential part of the body's immune system. Macrophages circulate throughout the bloodstream in search of substances to consume; the laser-tattoo-removal process stimulates the macrophages into action. As the microparticles of dye are gradually

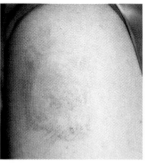

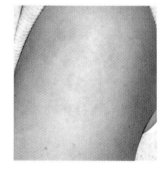

A tattoo (top) can now be removed with no residual scar by means of monthly laser "shots," which penetrate the skin, causing the dye particles in the tattoo to burst. Scavenging white blood cells slowly remove the pigment from the area (center) and, within four to six months, the tattoo is gone (bottom).

removed from the site, the skin in the tattooed area slowly lightens.

Scar-free tattoo removal does involve a certain amount of time—typically four to six treatments performed at monthly intervals in an office setting. Gradually the pigment is totally removed, and no visible scar tissue remains.

▶ Cosmetic Skin Enhancement

Practically since the beginning of time, people of both sexes have relentlessly pursued the Fountain of Youth—a pursuit more often than not dominated by the quest for younger-looking skin. In ancient Egypt, Cleopatra was said to have bathed in sour milk as a means of maintaining her skin tone. In the days of the elegant French royal court, noble ladies applied aged wine to their faces to keep their skin smooth and blemish-free. Even now, cosmetic companies sell billions of dollars worth of facial creams and body lotions.

Over the past year, scientists have discovered that Cleopatra and the French noblewomen might have been on to something. Indeed, mild, nontoxic acids gleaned from fruits (malic acid from apples, citric acid from oranges) have been effectively used on the face to peel the upper layers of skin, imparting to the skin a renewed texture. Chemically similar substances—lactic acid from sour milk, tartaric acid from grapes—yield similar effects.

Collectively, these breakdown products of fruits are known as alpha-hydroxy acids. For cosmetic purposes, these acids are transformed into a neutralized solution and applied directly to the face or other skin area under treatment. The solution causes the upper layers of the skin to shed. Applications are repeated at prescribed intervals over a period of one to six months. Gradually the composite nature of wrinkles and skin pores improves. This slow process, often performed on a daily basis by patients at home, has the added benefit of allowing the patient to participate in his or her own treatment.

For patients with acne or its resultant scars, alpha-hydroxy acids applied in this way reduce the enlarged pores and fine wrinkles. In certain cases the physician may wish to apply a stronger peeling agent (typically a 70 percent solution). This in-office procedure, called a "micropeel," seems to amplify the aesthetic results and speed the entire skin-improvement process. Aside from an occasional tingling sensation for no more than five minutes, patients experience no discomfort or pain from this treatment. Reports of sensitivity to alpha-hydroxy acids have been rare. It is likely that such products will be widely used and accepted in the near future.

C. Andrew Salzberg, M.D.

Podiatry

▶ An Alternative to Injections

A relatively new technique allows podiatrists to avoid the use of needles when administering anti-inflammatory drugs to treat the swelling that often accompanies sports injuries and other foot problems. Through a process called hydrocortisone phonophoresis, the podiatrist spreads hydrocortisone cream on the affected area and then administers ultrasound, which drives the medication beneath the top layer of skin. In other words the ultrasound waves allow the treatment cream to penetrate the skin, and no injection is needed. When the medication is applied by this method about three times a week, patients get the same relief from inflammation and pain as they would with hydrocortisone shots, while experiencing far less apprehension and discomfort. This technique has the added advantages of focusing the treatment on an isolated area of the foot and of shortening rehabilitation time. Phonophoresis may be used as part of the treatment for sprains, plantar fasciitis (stretched or torn ligaments along the bottom of the foot), painful scar tissue, bursitis, heel spurs, arthritis, and various sports injuries.

▶ Diagnostic Techniques

Ultrasound is also an increasingly popular tool for diagnosing diseases and injuries of the foot—particularly in detecting plantar fasciitis and heel problems—as well as for monitoring the healing process of soft-tissue injuries inside the foot. Similarly, magnetic resonance imaging (MRI) is proving effective in detecting conditions such as stress fractures and postsurgical infection, problems that might go unnoticed in preliminary X rays. MRI may also be performed to determine the extent of a tumor within the foot. This scanning procedure, which utilizes non-ionizing magnetic fields and radio waves, is painless and is done in the doctor's office; what's more, its results are available immediately.

▶ New Products

A number of products recently introduced on the podiatric market offer new types of relief. In some cases the new products are simply an improvement of old ones. People who have foot surgery now may recuperate wearing high-top ambulatory boots, or "walking casts," that are far lighter and more comfortable than conventional plaster casts, and allow patients fairly normal mobility soon after their operations. Other new products are being used by some podiatrists in treating black patients, who often experience hyperpigmentation around surgical scars and other healed cuts on the feet.

The third area of development is technological, within the field of biomechanics. Many podiatric offices now contain "scanners," machines that use computer technology to measure patients' feet for casts and orthotics (custom-made prescription shoe inserts that are used to compensate for structural problems of the foot or to cushion painful areas such as corns, bunions, or the heel). The patient places his or her foot onto a surface of the machine, which records information about the foot's structure. The machine then sends that information electronically to a lab, where the cast or orthotic is made immediately, and then shipped to the patient within a day or two. More than a half dozen other firms are developing scanners and researching how computers might further aid in the diagnosis and treatment of foot problems.

▶ Concerns of an Aging Population

Podiatrists have always tended to treat a high number of older patients, since many problems of the feet worsen over time and/or occur in later years. However, the proportion of aging people in the U.S. population is increasing: the famous "baby boom" generation is now well into middle age and approaching old age, and that demographic shift means that podiatrists, along with other medical professionals, must be increasingly attuned to diseases associated with age.

Some podiatrists use liposuction—the surgical removal of fat from a part of the body—to obtain fat for reimplantation into the feet's fat pads, which naturally thin with age. Fat replacement is only one type of treatment now frequently advised for the feet of older patients; also common are prescription creams designed to replace lost moisture in the skin, to soften built-up calluses, and to increase the skin's elasticity (which decreases over time); elective bunion surgery and other corrective procedures to prevent structural deformities from causing pain and aggravating related problems; and special foot exercises prescribed to alleviate arthritis pain, increase joint flexibility, and strengthen bones in the foot.

Podiatrists also are concerned with postmenopausal women whose hormonal changes, such as declining levels of estrogen (a hormone that slows calcium loss from the bones), affect the feet along with the rest of the body. Since calcium-depleted bones are subject to fracture, podiatrists are increasingly recommending diet changes and nutritional supplements.

Suzanne M. Levine, D.P.M.

Public Health

▶ Emerging Infections

Since the Institute of Medicine issued a report on emerging infections in 1992, the world has become increasingly aware of the growing problem of infectious diseases. As recently as two decades ago, the major infectious diseases were thought to have been almost eliminated as serious problems, despite the warnings of a few scientists. Factors that have worked against the control of infectious diseases include: the population explosion; urbanization; increasing rapid worldwide travel; migration and refugees; increasing resistance to antibiotics and insecticides; changes in industry and technology; decreasing diagnostic acuity of new or unfamiliar infectious diseases; changing lifestyle patterns; increasing exposure to new organisms as tropical rain forests are invaded and cut down; and widespread lack of concern about infectious diseases, which in many areas has reduced support for public-health measures. There are several categories of emerging infections:

New Organisms. Some of the emerging infections are caused by newly discovered organisms, such as *Legionella pneumophila*, which causes Legionnaires' disease (first recognized in 1976); *Borrelia burgdorferi*, which causes Lyme disease (recognized as a problem beginning in 1975); and the human immunodeficiency virus-type 1 (HIV-1), which was isolated in 1983, and which causes acquired immune deficiency syndrome (AIDS—first recognized in 1981).

New Variants. A second category of emerging infections is new species or subspecies of organisms that have been known for some time. An example of this is the Muerto Canyon virus, a hantavirus related to viruses first discovered in Korea in the early 1950s. The Muerto Canyon virus, however, causes a rapidly progressive pneumonia that is very different from the disease caused by the Korean hantaviruses. The hantavirus pulmonary syndrome was discovered when an epidemic of a highly fatal pneumonia was discovered, primarily in New Mexico and Arizona, in 1993.

New Pathogens. A third category of these diseases is organisms whose type had been known before, but that have only recently been shown to cause human disease, such as cryptosporidium, which in 1993 caused thousands of cases of dysentery in Milwaukee, Wisconsin, by infecting the public water supply; and the 0157:H7 strain of *E. coli*, which caused the outbreak of sometimes-fatal hemolytic-uremic syndrome after being transmitted through incompletely cooked hamburger meat in 1993.

Resurgent Infections. A fourth category of emerging infections is those that had been serious problems in the past, have not been very serious in recent decades, and now have become somewhat resurgent. Examples in this category include tuberculosis and Type A beta hemolytic streptococcus.

Antibiotic Resistance. A fifth category of emerging infections includes those bacteria and other organisms that have become resistant to increasing numbers of antibiotics. This list includes tuberculosis and a new strain of cholera, as well as many more-common infections and the organisms that cause pneumonias, meningitis, dysentery, blood poisoning, and sexually transmitted diseases. Malaria is increasingly resistant to the malaria-prevention medicines, such as chloroquine, that are taken by visitors to the tropics.

All of these problems would be serious enough without the major complications added by wars and rebellions, such as those occurring in Bosnia and Rwanda in 1994. In Bosnia, the biggest public-health impacts of the war have been direct injuries from the hostilities, as well as malnutrition and intestinal diseases, including hepatitis A.

▶ Cholera and Dysentery in Rwanda
Because of the civil war in Rwanda, 3 million to 4 million refugees have fled to nearby Tanzania and Zaïre, where they have clustered in huge camps with inadequate food, water, and sanitation. Given such bad sanitation, it is hardly surprising that the intestinal diseases known as cholera and shigella dysentery have devastated

the camps. Relief workers were calling for help in creating 60,000 latrines, and bringing in safe water and food.

A cholera patient is treated with replacement fluids containing salts and sugar. This can be done either by administering intravenous fluids during the peak few days of the diarrhea, or by giving the solution orally, which is almost as effective. If the fluids and salts lost by diarrhea can be rapidly replaced, the patient will soon recover. However, both treatment methods were in short supply. The cases of shigellosis were even more difficult to treat, because the causal organisms were resistant to antibiotics, and more than simple fluid replacement was required.

▶ Plague in India
Few diseases cause as much fear as the great scourge of the Middle Ages, the "Black Death"—bubonic and pneumonic plague. Caused by the bacterium *Yersina pestis,* plague is fundamentally a disease of small rodents, usually rats in cities, and it is spread from rat to rat, and eventually to human beings, by rat fleas. Because fleas leaving dead rats are likely to bite human beings on the lower limbs, the infection starts there and moves up to the lymph nodes where the legs join the torso. These nodes become very large and tender (the "buboes" of bubonic plague), and then break down and drain pus. This form of the disease has a moderate mortality rate.

The most dangerous form of plague occurs when the organism gets into the bloodstream and causes a plague pneumonia, known as pneumonic plague, a highly fatal condition. Unfortunately, the victims of pneumonic plague also tend to spread organisms from their noses and mouths by droplet infection, so that those caring for them may get pneumonic plague by direct spread, without going through the bubonic stage first.

Beginning in late August 1994, India suffered a major outbreak of plague. Three major regions of the country were affected: Maharashtra State (which includes Bom-

Thousands of refugees died when disease swept the overcrowded camps to which they had fled to escape the brutal civil war in Rwanda. The lack of medical supplies and the squalid conditions in the refugee camps exacerbated the desperate situation.

bay); Gujarat State (including the industrial port city of Surat); and the city of Delhi. Approximately 700 cases of plague with a positive test for antibodies to *Yersina pestis* were reported to the World Health Organization (WHO) through mid-October 1994, although the actual number of suspected cases was well over 5,000, and the known deaths were more than 50. The human cases began following a reported rat die-off. In some areas, the rodent population was unusually large due to a number of factors: the squalor of the shantytowns around big cities; inadequate food-storage facilities, in part due to damage from earthquakes; piles of garbage due to inadequate refuse disposal; and the migration of rodents following monsoon rains.

When the bubonic form of the plague was followed by the appearance of the pneumonic form of the disease, which is uniformly fatal if untreated, people fled Surat in a panic, in some cases carrying the disease with them to new areas.

Many nations enacted various levels of quarantine or surveillance of travelers from India until the epidemic was brought under control. No spread of plague was detected by any other country, and the epidemic eventually ended.

Although it has been almost 30 years since the last plague outbreak in India, no one believes it will be that long again, unless fundamental changes are made. In addition to reducing overcrowding and environmental problems around cities, India will have to rethink the reverence shown to rats and other rodents.

▶ Beta Hemolytic Streptococcus A

Americans were shocked to read of a "flesh-eating" bacterium that killed at least 11 people and

In August 1994, a major outbreak of bubonic and pneumonic plague began in India. By the time it ended two months later, more than 50 had died.

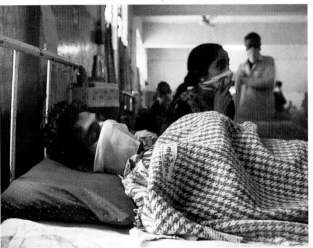

caused serious illness in an equal number of others in Gloucestershire and other counties in England. The official term for the extensive tissue damage produced by an aggressive form of beta hemolytic streptococcus, type A, is "necrotizing fasciitis." This is a type of fast-moving gangrene in which the bacterium's toxins destroy muscle and fat tissue in a rapidly spreading pattern until the condition is treated. Those who die may succumb to overwhelming infection, or they may develop a "toxic-shock syndrome," much like the toxic-shock syndrome due to the staphylococcus bacterium in the early 1980s. In toxic-shock syndrome, a buildup of toxin from the streptococci causes a collapse of blood pressure and a general shutdown of the body's organs, and results in a high mortality rate. In the United States, there were scattered cases of a similar illness, with at least one cluster of cases in Los Angeles and Orange counties, California.

▶ Dangerous Cruises

Some of the most vivid examples of the problems of emerging infections in 1994 manifested themselves on cruise ships. People go on cruises expecting a relaxed, enjoyable time; the last thing they expect is that illness or death will result. Yet this is exactly what happened to many passengers on the cruise ship *Horizon*, which traveled to Bermuda during the spring and summer of 1994. Between the end of April and mid-July 1994, 42 passengers developed a pneumonia within two weeks of sailing on the *Horizon*. Of these, Legionnaires' disease was confirmed in 14 patients and strongly suspected in the other ill passengers.

The sick patients in these outbreaks had 16 times the odds of having used the whirlpool baths compared to those who were not ill; moreover, legionella organisms were recovered from the whirlpool baths on the ship. The ship's owners subsequently followed the recommendations of the Centers for Disease Control and Prevention (CDC), hyperchlorinating the ship's drinking-water supply, removing the existing filters from the whirlpool baths, and discontinuing the use of the whirlpool baths.

Another cruise ship, the *Viking Serenade*, was hit by a devastating outbreak of shigellosis, a bacillary dysentery caused in this instance by the bacterium *Shigella flexneri 2a*. The *Viking Serenade*, which had intended to make a Baja California cruise, canceled that trip and all subsequent ones until the ship was deemed safe. The CDC reported that 586 (37 percent) of the 1,589 passengers and 584 (98 percent) of the 594 crew members who completed a survey were sick with fever, diarrhea, and/or vomiting. One 78-year-old

A severe outbreak of pneumonia among dozens of passengers on the Horizon cruise ship (left) was caused by Legionnaires' disease bacteria that had contaminated the craft's water system.

Salmonellosis can also be a problem in homemade ice cream. In late 1993, an outbreak of diarrheal disease, also due to *Salmonella enteritidis*, occurred among attendees of a hospital picnic. Homemade ice cream, prepared using six raw eggs, was the presumptive source.

man died from the disease. Shigellosis is usually spread by contaminated water, but it can be acquired by consuming contaminated food. The food served aboard the *Viking Serenade* was investigated also.

▶ Salmonellosis in Ice Cream

An outbreak of diarrheal disease known as salmonellosis was spread by Schwan's ice cream, made in Marshall, Minnesota. The ice cream involved was made in August and September 1994, and the first cases occurred in October.

It is not known how many people became ill. About 400,000 gallons of Schwan's ice cream are made weekly, and the products are distributed throughout the continental United States, so the potential for the spread of salmonellosis was tremendous. More than 2,000 cases have been reported to the Minnesota Department of Health. Infections from the ice cream were reported in 16 states, and suspected ice-cream-associated cases were reported from another 16 states. Although the final number of people who fell ill from the contaminated product will never be known, one outbreak of salmonellosis in 1985, caused by milk produced at a single dairy plant, caused approximately 197,000 infections.

The offending bacterium is *Salmonella enteritidis*. The apparent source of the infection was contaminated tanker trucks that had previously carried raw eggs, a frequent source of salmonella infections. Usually ice-cream mix is pasteurized (heated to a temperature that kills bacteria, but does not change the flavor of the food) just before it is packaged; in this case the ice cream was pasteurized and then shipped in the tanker trucks to another facility to be packaged. The commissioner of the U.S. Food and Drug Administration (FDA) called this practice an "unacceptable risk to the public which must be corrected."

▶ New Human Diseases

New Horse Virus. In Queensland, Australia, a virus that had never before been known to affect either human beings or horses killed 14 racehorses and their trainer, in addition to making two other people ill. The virus is a member of the paramyxovirus family, to which human measles also belongs. The virus caused an acute respiratory infection.

Ehrlichia. A previously unrecognized strain of *Ehrlichia*, a tick-borne disease-causing bacterium, was identified by the CDC in 1994. This organism, which causes a disease called human granulocytic ehrlichiosis, killed several people in Minnesota and Wisconsin in 1994. Among other kinds of damage, the disease destroys granulocytes, an important type of human white blood cell. Ehrlichiosis features fever, headache, muscle aches, nausea, and vomiting. It may be confused with influenza or Rocky Mountain spotted fever, but the condition does not produce the spotted fever's characteristic rash. The illness apparently begins 10 to 14 days after a tick bite, the event during which the infectious organism is transmitted to the human host.

New Hantavirus. A young Florida man developed a severe respiratory illness in 1994 that closely resembles the hantavirus pulmonary syndrome first identified in the southwestern United States in 1993. However, tests of his antibodies showed that the virus causing his illness was not the Muerto Canyon virus, which caused the 1993 outbreak, but instead was a new strain of hantavirus. Public-health investigation revealed that the virus probably was spread by the cotton rat *(Sigmodon hispidus)*, whose range extends throughout the southeastern and south-central United States. The hantavirus pulmonary syndrome is severe, with a 50 percent mortality rate in young people.

▶ Laboratory Infections

Scientists who work with hazardous infectious agents in laboratories typically take great care to avoid coming into contact with the organisms themselves, and to avoid spreading these laboratory agents to others. However, familiarity and lack of previous problems with an agent may breed a certain level of carelessness. In 1994 a visiting scientist at Yale University in New Haven, Connecticut, was working with a deadly virus when a plastic test tube containing the virus broke in a high-speed centrifuge, infecting him despite the fact that he was wearing a gown and gloves. He did not report the accident as required, because he thought he had satisfactorily cleaned up all contaminated surfaces.

Fortunately, there was little danger to the public from the initial accident, as it occurred in a level-3 laboratory with negative pressure, where the exhaust air passes through a fine filter. A few days later, while visiting friends in Boston, Massachusetts, the scientist developed a fever and thought he had a recurrence of malaria. However, physicians at Yale detected an unusual disease caused by the deadly arenavirus, and immediately administered intravenous ribavirin, which is effective against the infection. The Yale scientist recovered completely from the illness.

The causative organism was an RNA arenavirus called the Sabia virus, named after the town in Brazil where it was discovered when a woman there died after being infected with it. Similar viral infections are transmitted by rodents, so it is presumed the arenavirus is, too. Scientists are considering requiring that this virus be limited to study only in a class-4 laboratory, in which agents are studied using robot arms and similar protections in a completely contained environment.

▶ Vaccine Levels

The efforts to improve the level of immunization of children against common diseases has not gotten off to a good start. A federal program called the Childhood Immunization Initiative aims to get 90 percent of U.S. children immunized. The program is intended to provide funds for distributing free vaccines to clinics and private doctors to help every child have access to immunization, but the vaccine manufacturers are often slow to deliver the vaccine to private physicians. Some states, such as South Carolina, are adding state funds to enable private physicians to join the program and take some of the burden off public clinics. Other states, such as Pennsylvania, are not waiting for the federal funds, but instead are establishing their own systems.

James F. Jekel, M.D., M.P.H.

Rehabilitation Medicine

▶ Hope for Paraplegics

A study that has implications for the treatment of paralysis examined the role played by locomotion centers in the spinal cord in initiating leg movement. The elicitation of such locomotion centers has been documented in some animals, but not in people. To elicit their function in people, the study used subjects who had been rendered paraplegic following recent (not more than six-week-old) spinal-cord injury. The subjects were placed on a treadmill with the belt moving slowly (1 mile per hour), their body weight suspended by means of a parachute harness, and their feet touching the moving belt.

The electrical activity generated by muscular contractions was recorded by surface electrodes placed on the skin over the calf and shin muscles. Surprisingly, the patterns of electrical activity elicited from these muscles resembled those patterns created by healthy persons while walking. In fact, movements very similar to the overall leg motion of walking could be observed in the paraplegic patients.

The amplitude of the recorded electrical activity was lower than that found in normal walking motion. With training, the amplitudes became higher, and the elicited muscular action more closely resembled the electrical potentials found in persons without paralysis. The amplitude was not related to the degree of weight suspension. After four weeks of training, some of the partially paralyzed patients could walk a short distance without a moving belt.

These results show that the function of the spinal locomotion center can be elicited without receiving impulses from the supraspinal center in the brain. The findings will bear on future functional-rehabilitation methods for persons with spinal-cord injuries.

▶ Falls among the Elderly

One-third of people over 65 years of age fall each year. Fifteen percent of these falls result in serious injuries, half of which are hip fractures. Fatalities resulting from these injuries make falls the sixth-leading cause of death in this age group. Furthermore, the nonfatal consequences of a fall include fear, loss of function, and the possibility of, or necessity for, nursing-home care.

Previous efforts to address this problem by preventing falls and related injuries did not lead to noteworthy results, because the interventions did not specifically address the risk factors for falls. Now a controlled study involving 350 people about age 70 has assessed the effects of reducing or eliminating multiple risk factors. The study focused on muscle fitness, drugs and other medication, and diet rather than cardiac and similar causes. (If a person does not lose consciousness immediately preceding a fall, usually a cardiac cause is not to blame.)

Muscle Fitness. Previously, exercise had not been shown to change the frequency or consequences of falls. However, in this study the risk of falling decreased with a program of progressive resistive exercises. The researchers found that these exercises must be done once a day for 20 minutes to decrease the risk; older persons should rest one second between each muscle contraction to allow refilling of the striated muscles with blood. It takes four to six weeks for the exercises to bring about a noticeable improvement in muscle strength.

Medication. People receiving more than four prescriptive drugs also have an increased risk of falling. Older persons who have fallen should be checked for this type of polypharmacy. If patients receive a sedative, particularly a long-lasting one, it is imperative that they be counseled as to the possible cross-reactions, and observed until the risk of falling is reduced.

Diet. Dietary measures can prevent some of the most serious consequences of a fall. For example, when nursing-home residents received calcium and vitamin D supplements, the incidence of hip fractures from falls decreased.

Overall, the incidence of falls went down 30 percent with the measures outlined in the study. Of course, not all falls can be prevented. Still, medical personnel, family members, and all those around the elderly have to participate in fall prevention to make it a truly effective effort.

▶ Running to Prevent Disability

A study that followed comparable groups of runners and inactive persons over an eight-year period found that a regular regimen of running produces a general increase in strength that plays a major role in the prevention of disability from falls among the elderly.

In this study, the number of fractures did not differ strikingly between runners and inactive people because some runners suffered fractures from falls. But the runners suffered far fewer fractures caused by osteoporosis than did people who were not physically active. Those who were inactive had more fractures of the vertebrae, hips, and wrists due to osteoporosis, while runners had ankle and similar fractures caused by running injuries. Overall, the fractures of the runners caused much less disability, as they often healed quickly. In contrast, osteoporotic fractures heal poorly or not at all. Finally, no increased incidence of arthritis of the hips and knees was observed in people who were runners.

The study also shows that the increase in general strength promoted by running is a greater factor in preventing falls and disability than are coordination exercises.

▶ Risks for Older Drivers

The number of licensed drivers over age 72 is increasing steadily, and with it the concern about the criteria used in issuing driver's licenses to older people. A study of 283 drivers age 72 and older suggests that some of these criteria should be reevaluated. Of those in the group, 13 percent reported a crash or moving violation within one year. These 283 drivers underwent various physical and mental examinations to find out what factors are associated with driving incidents. The factors most frequently associated with such incidents were:

• Poor performance on the depth-perception sections of the state driving examination.

• Poor physical condition. (The fewer blocks a person was able to walk, the more likely the person was to be involved in a moving violation or in an automobile mishap.)

• Foot abnormalities that affect the way the driver applies pressure to the brake, accelerator, or clutch.

All factors were adjusted for driving frequency and driving time. When the results were analyzed, the association of these risk factors with moving violations was as follows: among drivers with none of the factors, 6 percent were involved in incidents. When one factor was present, the incidence was 12 percent; when two factors were present, 26 percent; and when all three factors were present, 47 percent.

These factors have a greater correlation with driving incidents than do standard evaluation methods for judging driving fitness, such as the visual-acuity examination, or even the presence of such chronic diseases as diabetes. For instance, the ability to dissect a pentagon on the depth-perception section of the state exam has a higher association with driving incidents than does a poor performance on the standard driving examination.

When a driver's license is issued, factors most closely associated with driving incidents should be carefully examined and, if possible, corrected. Furthermore, criteria for withholding a license should be reevaluated.

Willibald Nagler, M.D.

Respiratory System

▶ Asthma

The incidences of asthma and of deaths from this disease have increased markedly in recent years. According to a report published by the American College of Chest Physicians, asthma prevalence has increased: the Centers for Disease Control and Prevention (CDC) reports a 40 percent rise in the asthma death rate between 1982 and 1991. This disturbing trend is occurring while understanding of the disease is growing and the range of available therapies is increasing.

Behind the trend are factors that include the overuse and abuse of bronchodilators, increased air pollution, poor management by physicians (especially the underutilization of steroid anti-inflammatory drugs), disregard of asthma symptoms by patients, and patients' failure to follow treatment regimens. Factors that warn of serious, potentially fatal asthma include genetic predisposition to the disease, a pattern of frequent hospitalizations or emergency-room visits in the preceding year, and previous life-threatening attacks. Some recent reports have highlighted the role of psychological factors in fatal asthma.

Growing attention is being focused on indoor air pollution. Indoor pollutants include environmental tobacco smoke (ETS, or "secondhand" smoke); dust mites and molds, which can provoke allergies; nitrogen dioxide, produced by burning fossil fuels; and volatile organic compounds, such as fumes from solvents. A study of moderate to severe asthmatics who were exposed to ETS or combustion products from gas stoves, woodstoves, or fireplaces shows a connection between exposure and symptoms.

Nocturnal asthma is common. Up to 39 percent of asthma patients report waking every night, and 94 percent at least one night a month. Factors in nighttime attacks include cooling of the airways, increased airway muscle tone, changing hormone levels, and stomach acid backing up into the airway (gastroesophageal reflux). Timing medication correctly is crucial to controlling nocturnal asthma.

The central role of inflammation in asthma is widely recognized, and treatment is increasingly directed at controlling it. Anti-inflammatory and antiallergic agents, such as inhaled or oral steroids and preparations such as cromolyn and nedocromil, are the cornerstones of therapy. Better education to help patients recognize and manage acute attacks will reduce both illness and deaths from asthma.

▶ Therapy in Lung Disease

Improvements in inhalers have made these devices easier to use and more efficient in delivering bronchodilators and anti-inflammatory medications. Many patients find standard metered-dose inhalers (MDIs) difficult to use; in fact, only 36 percent of patients use them properly. The success rate increases to 64 percent with breath-activated devices and spacers, which improve airflow from the inhaler.

Patients who have difficulty in using MDIs were helped in April 1994 by the introduction of a new ipratropium bromide solution (Atrovent Inhalation Solution, manufactured by Boehringer Ingelheim Pharmaceuticals, Inc., Ridgefield, Connecticut). Delivered by nebulization, this product blocks contraction of the bronchial wall, and can be used with standard bronchodilators (beta-adrenergic agonists such as albuterol, which relax bronchial spasms) for improved results without additional side effects.

In February 1994, the Food and Drug Administration (FDA) approved the sale of Serevent (Salmeterol xinafoate, manufactured by Allen & Hanburys, Division of Glaxo, Inc.), the first commercially available long-acting inhaled bronchodilator. Serevent, which was studied in more than 35,000 patients, is approved for twice-daily use in maintenance treatment of asthma and for the prevention of exercise-induced asthma, but not for use in acute bronchospasm.

By delivering medications directly to obstructed or collapsed airways, inhalers can improve the quality of life for people with respiratory disorders.

Pharmaceutical companies have also developed an MDI that does not rely on chlorofluorocarbon (CFC) propellants. CFCs are being phased out worldwide because they damage the atmosphere's ozone layer, which screens out harmful ultraviolet radiation. The new inhaler uses hydrofluoroalkanes, which have virtually no impact on the environment.

▶ Treatment for COPD

Chronic obstructive pulmonary disease (COPD) continues to be a serious health problem with a high mortality rate. It includes a range of conditions marked by chronic air-flow obstruction, including chronic bronchitis and emphysema. In the early stages, therapy is preventive, aimed at keeping the disease from becoming fully established. Cessation of smoking, a major cause of COPD, is especially effective. Later therapy is aimed mainly at reducing symptoms, and includes bronchodilator and anti-inflammatory medications. In some cases, lung transplantation has been effective.

In emphysema, patients complain of unrelenting shortness of breath, first during physical activity, and then, as the disease progresses, at rest. The shortness of breath, or dyspnea, develops as air is trapped in the lungs behind obstructed or collapsed airways. This trapped, stale air places the chest wall and main muscles of respiration at a mechanical disadvantage during breathing. Inhaled bronchodilators and anti-inflammatory agents provide relief, but many patients eventually must depend on supplemental oxygen to perform daily activities.

Surgery may provide relief for patients with advanced emphysema. In a presentation to the American Thoracic Society in May 1994 and to the Society of Thoracic Surgeons in February, 1994, Joel Cooper, M.D., of the Washington University School of Medicine in St. Louis, Missouri, reported on volume-reduction surgery, in which lung tissue damaged by emphysema is removed. The function of the remaining lung tissue improved, and the chest wall and muscles of respiration returned to a more natural position, leading to relief of dyspnea. Most patients resumed daily activities without supplemental oxygen.

Volume-reduction surgery was attempted in the 1950s, but the mortality rate was so high that it was abandoned. Cooper's promising outcomes result from careful selection and preparation of patients for surgery and improvements in anesthesia and surgical techniques. Nevertheless, Cooper emphasizes that the procedure only relieves symptoms—the underlying disease is unchanged, and it is not clear how long the improvement will last.

▶ Building-related Illness

People can and do get sick from buildings, especially buildings in which they work. "Building-related illness" is a broad term covering health problems caused by indoor air quality. Such illness is a particular concern in office buildings and similar structures, where workers spend hours behind closed (often sealed) windows.

Building-related illness may result from a particular problem, such as contamination. For example, bacteria or fungi that contaminate air-conditioning or humidification systems can cause illnesses such as Legionnaires' disease (caused by a bacterium) or hypersensitivity pneumonitis (caused by a fungus). These diseases have characteristic symptoms—fever, chills, muscle pains, and (in Legionnaires' disease) cough, headache, and diarrhea. Building-related illness can also consist of less specific problems in "sick" or "tight" buildings with poor ventilation. In these cases, symptoms are difficult to ascribe to a particular disease. They may include fatigue, dry throat, itching eyes, dry skin, chest tightness, wheezing, sneezing, stuffy nose, headache, difficulty in concentration, dizziness, and nausea.

Not all workplace complaints are caused by poor indoor air quality. But when the problems persist and affect a substantial number of workers, building inspections can help find the cause and suggest solutions.

▶ Infections

Tuberculosis, particularly multiple-drug-resistant (MDR) tuberculosis, remains a significant problem, especially in inner-city areas with high rates of homelessness and infection with HIV, the virus that causes AIDS. There is also growing awareness of another group of infectious agents, nontuberculous mycobacteria (NTM). NTM often take hold as an opportunistic infection in patients whose immune systems have been damaged by HIV, and in people with a history of lung disease. In recent years, NTM infections have also been identified in patients without these problems. For example, a June 1994 article in the *American Journal of Respiratory and Critical Care Medicine* described NTM infections in a group of elderly middle-class patients, most of whom were nonsmokers and many of whom were women. Their symptoms included coughing and weight loss.

Most of the patients in this study responded to multidrug therapy, which is the standard regimen. The antibiotic clarithromycin has been found effective as a single drug for the treatment of *Mycobacterium avium intracellulare*, one of the most common agents of NTM infections.

Maria L. Padilla, M.D.

Sexually Transmitted Diseases

▶ Sexual Behavior in the '90s

In the most comprehensive survey on sexual practices in the United States since the 1950s Kinsey report, a research team led by University of Chicago sociologists found Americans to be far less sexually active than previously thought. Among the findings: most people are monogamous. Indeed, nearly 75 percent of married men and 85 percent of married women say they have never been unfaithful. Over a lifetime, the average man has six sexual partners, the average woman two. The specter of AIDS has put a crimp in some people's sex lives: 76 percent of those who have had five or more partners in the past year say they have changed their sexual behavior, by either slowing down, getting tested for AIDS, or using condoms faithfully.

Still, other recent surveys have shown that a sizable proportion of the U.S. adult population engages in sexual behaviors that expose them to the risk of acquiring sexually transmitted diseases (STDs). Furthermore, engaging in one risky behavior is associated with engaging in other risky behaviors, and thereby increases the likelihood of STD acquisition. Among the sexually active adults studied, 13 percent had had sex with more than one partner in the year preceding the study, but only 8 percent of this group had used condoms consistently. Researchers conclude that concern about AIDS, behavior changes in response to AIDS, and perceptions of risk for contracting AIDS remain low for the highest-risk groups.

Unfortunately, a minority of physicians ask patients about their sexual history. While 49 percent ask about STDs, only 31 percent ask about condom use, 27 percent about sexual orientation, and 22 percent about numbers of sexual partners. Many feel their patients would be offended by such questions. The reluctance of physicians to assess risky sexual practices of patients underscores the need for public-health agencies to assist physicians in improving risk assessment and risk-reduction-counseling efforts.

▶ Global Differences in STD Rates

In Northern and Western Europe, there has been a dramatic decline in the incidences of STDs, particularly gonorrhea and syphilis. In Sweden, for example, there has been an 80-fold reduction in reported cases of gonorrhea in the past 20 years.

In fact, infection has become so rare that, without the importation of new cases from outside the country, it would probably die out. This change is likely due to a combination of early-age sex education at school, behavior change, condom promotion, and the wide availability of STD treatment in Europe.

The situation in North America is less encouraging. While certain geographic areas and population groups have low levels of STDs, others continue to experience high rates, particularly inner-city minority populations in the United States. While there has been a steady decline in the incidence of gonorrhea, rates are 50 times higher than in some parts of Europe. Syphilis made a dramatic comeback in the late 1980s, and remains prevalent among high-risk groups. Drug addiction, exchange of sex for drugs, and poor access to health care have been closely associated with the syphilis epidemic.

The incidence of STDs in developing countries is very high, making them the second-most-frequent cause of death in women 15 to 45 years of age (after death associated with childbirth). Only a combination of medical, behavioral, and societal interventions is likely to have a positive impact in reducing STDs among high-risk groups.

▶ Female Condoms

The current epidemic of STDs, including AIDS, has stimulated renewed interest in barrier methods of contraception. The lack of female-controlled barrier methods known to protect against AIDS and other STDs—and to prevent pregnancy—has led to the development of the female condom, a device designed for both purposes.

Condoms for use by men were first described in the 16th century for protection against venereal disease. By the 18th century, condoms were generally available and even advertised. Two hundred years later, there is a female equivalent of the condom.

Invented by a Danish physician in 1984, the female condom has been available for years in European countries, though it was just approved recently by the Food and Drug Administration (FDA) in the United States. The only version now available, the Reality, is made by Wisconsin Pharmacal of Jackson, Wisconsin, and sells for about $3.00. The device is a 7-inch-long polyurethane sheath with a ring on each end. The inner ring is inserted into the vagina, much like a diaphragm, while the other ring remains outside.

In approving the female condom, the FDA insisted that the label indicate that the male condom is the more-effective contraceptive. Nevertheless, the female condom, when used during every act of sexual intercourse, is only slightly less effective than the male condom. Unfortunately, the female condom is about three times as expensive. However, given the well-documented reluctance of many men to wear condoms, it may provide some women with their only means of protection. A recent study found that among sexually active women, only 20 percent have partners who use condoms. It is estimated that faithful use of the female condom may reduce the annual risk of acquiring AIDS by more than 90 percent among women who have intercourse twice weekly with an infected male.

The female condom can be very effective in preventing pregnancy as well as STDs in the women whose partners refuse to use a condom. The annual failure rate with perfect use is about 5 percent, similar to rates for the diaphragm and the cervical cap.

▶ Contraception and STDs in Teens
Although a large percentage of sexually active teenagers are taking precautions against pregnancy, most are using oral contraceptives that offer no protection against STDs. A study by the Alan Buttmacher Institute indicates that sexually active young people (ages 15 to 24) are more than twice as likely to choose oral contraceptives as they are to choose condoms. Of those surveyed, 50 percent use birth-control pills, 22 percent use condoms, 9 percent use other contraceptive methods, and 19 percent do not use any method. Two-thirds of the 12 million new STD infections in the United States each year occur in people younger than 25.

Young people are at higher risk for STDs for several reasons. Compared to adults, teens are less likely to know the facts about sexually transmitted diseases; they have less access to health care; and they are more likely to feel uncomfortable about discussing and using personal protection during sexual activity. With more teens becoming sexually active at an early age, U.S. health officials expect the epidemic of STDs to escalate. Peggy Clark, recent president of the American Social Health Association, says that to combat this trend, we must provide confidential and comprehensive STD screening, treatment, and counseling.

▶ Dangers of *Chlamydia trachomatis*
Chlamydia trachomatis is currently the most common sexually transmitted infection in the United States. At least 15 different variants of this bacterial agent cause disease. In addition to causing genital-tract infection, some types of this condition can be transmitted to infants during passage through the birth canal. The presence of chlamydia in newborns causes inflammation of the eye tissues; blindness in chronic, untreated cases; and pneumonia. Sexually active adolescents and young adults are at very high risk for *C. trachomatis* infection.

If sexually transmitted diseases are undetected and untreated, they have severe long-term consequences. In a study in Washington State, researchers examined the fallopian tubes of ectopic-pregnancy patients. They found that those patients with a history of chlamydia were more likely than those with no such history to have moderately or severely damaged tubes. They concluded that reversing the increasing incidence of ectopic pregnancy will depend in part on prevention of infection with chlamydia through protective methods such as condoms. Wisconsin has initiated a pilot study to evaluate universal screening for chlamydia in women younger than 22, and to notify male partners of infected patients.

▶ Prevention Approaches That Work
The prevention of STDs requires that individuals at elevated risk make and maintain behavior changes to limit their vulnerability. Two approaches are feasible: face-to-face interaction and community-level change efforts. Intense individual intervention is time-consuming, relatively expensive, and likely to be delivered to only a small proportion of individuals at risk. Community-wide interventions are potentially capable of reaching large numbers of people and producing population-wide risk reduction.

Researchers from the Medical College of Wisconsin in Milwaukee evaluated the face-to-face approach among women with multiple sexual partners who use injected drugs—a clearly high-risk group. After three months of intense, individualized risk education, the women demonstrated behavior changes that significantly reduced their vulnerability to STDs.

The same researchers conducted trials of interventions designed to reduce risk at the community level. Nominated leaders among the gay communities in four cities were invited to attend a five-session group intervention that provided them with information they could use to sensitize friends to the risks of unprotected sex. Each leader agreed to speak with 14 or more friends or acquaintances about risk-reduction behavior. A follow-up nine months later found a 33 percent reduction in risky sexual practices.

These studies demonstrate that both face-to-face and community-wide educational approaches can produce substantial reductions in sexual practices that confer risk for STDs.

James A. Blackman, M.D., M.P.H.

Skin

▶ Low-Fat Diet and Skin Cancer

A surprising and important new association has been established between diet and skin cancer. Researchers from Baylor College of Medicine in Houston, Texas, and the Veterans Affairs Medical Center of Houston published results of a two-year study on the effects of dietary fat on the risk for skin cancer. They assigned 76 patients with a past history of skin cancer to either a normal or a low-fat diet. During the two-year period, they observed a reduced number of skin cancers in the patients on the low-fat diet. Unfortunately, the number of patients in the study was too small, and the length of follow-up was too short, to make this trend statistically significant.

The researchers also monitored the appearance of new actinic keratoses. Actinic keratoses are concentrated areas of sun-induced skin damage. They are considered precancers, because on rare occasions (estimated at between 1 and 10 percent), actinic keratoses transform into skin cancer. Thus, a reduction in the number of newly developed actinic keratoses can be assumed to eventually result in a reduced number of subsequent skin cancers. This study documents a significant reduction in the development of new actinic keratoses by patients on the low-fat diet. The reduction in precancers occurred even though total calories, percentages of saturated versus unsaturated fat, and the amount of sun exposure remained the same in both groups.

The Committee on Diet and Health of the National Research Council currently recommends a low-fat diet to reduce the risk of cancer as well as of heart disease. This study offers another argument for pursuing a low-fat diet. The next step is to investigate the mechanism by which dietary fat promotes the development of skin cancer.

▶ Toxic Epidermal Necrolysis

Toxic epidermal necrolysis (TEN) is a severe, life-threatening form of allergic skin reaction that, even with the best treatment available, has a fatality rate of 25 to 30 percent. Patients suffering from TEN develop widespread necrosis of the skin. As with severe burns, the full thickness of epidermis first dies, then peels away to reveal the raw, oozing, unprotected dermis. This leads to a loss of the skin's important barrier function. Fatalities usually result as a consequence of a bacterial infection that enters through the damaged skin, and then invades the bloodstream.

More than 90 percent of TEN cases appear to result from allergic reactions to drugs. More than 100 different medications have been implicated as causative factors. The most common offending classes of drugs are antibiotics, anticonvulsants, and the nonsteroidal anti-inflammatory agents. The mechanism by which drugs induce TEN remains unknown. It is believed that the causative agent is not the drugs themselves, but an as-yet-unidentified breakdown product (called a toxic metabolite) of the original drug. It is hypothesized that toxic drug metabolites cause activation of lymphocytes, which create the actual damage to the epidermis.

In 1994 researchers reported the results of studies on a case of TEN that greatly bolstered the toxic-metabolite theory. In their case, TEN was caused by carbamazepine, an antiseizure drug. The patient's lymphocytes displayed no reaction when they were exposed to the carbamazepine. However, the same lymphocytes were activated by exposure to the chemicals from the experimental metabolism of the drug. Thus, in keeping with the toxic-metabolite theory, metabolites of the drug, and not the drug itself, were capable of activating the immune system.

▶ Gastric Ulcers and Rosacea

Helicobacter pylori, a bacterium sometimes found in the stomach, has been strongly associated with the development of peptic- (gastric-) ulcer disease. At the summer 1994 meeting of the American Academy of Dermatology in San Francisco, California, Robert B. Skinner, M.D., presented evidence that this same bacterium may be a causative factor for acne rosacea.

Acne rosacea is a common skin disease characterized by facial flushing and the development during adulthood of an acnelike facial eruption. Left untreated, this disease can lead to a persistently red and ruddy facial complexion. Sometimes a particularly dramatic case causes enlargement of the nose, a phenomenon known commonly as W. C. Fields-type nose, or, more technically, as rhinophyma. Hot, spicy foods and alcohol have long been known to aggravate rosacea, suggesting that a link may exist between rosacea and the bowel. *H. pylori* bacteria in the stomach have been shown to increase the production of hormones by the gastric mucosa.

These gastric-mucosa hormones have now been shown not only to increase acid production in the stomach, but also to trigger facial flushing. It is interesting to note that tetracycline antibiotics have long been recognized as the backbone of rosacea therapy. Tetracycline is also highly effective in eliminating *H. pylori* from the bowel. Thus, the same therapy now used for gastric ulcers (oral bismuth, metronidazole, and tetracycline) may also prove to be an excellent combination for rosacea.

A fair-skinned child who acquires a severe sunburn may have a heightened risk of developing melanoma later in life.

▶ Topical Treatment for Psoriasis

New hope for psoriasis patients may come from an old thyroid medication. Propylthiouracil, a drug used for many years to treat hyperthyroidism, has now been shown to be effective in the treatment of psoriasis. In 1993 Alan Elias, M.D., F.R.C.P.C., and K. Dangaran, M.D., and colleagues from the University of California, Irvine College of Medicine showed that two antithyroid medications—propylthiouracil (PTU) and methimazole—were effective oral drugs for treating psoriasis. In 1994 the same researchers documented the effectiveness of PTU for the topical treatment of psoriasis. The topical PTU was applied three times daily for four to eight weeks to nine patients with chronic localized psoriasis; all nine showed significant improvement. The improvement was restricted to the areas of psoriasis treated; those areas of psoriasis treated with placebo ointment showed no improvement.

The mechanism of action of PTU on psoriasis is still unknown. It is thought to be related either to its complex effects on the immune system or to its direct suppression of epidermal proliferation. No adverse effects were noted on the thyroid function of the nine patients in this study.

PTU is likely to be a safe therapy. The years of PTU usage in high oral doses for the treatment of hyperthyroidism have established an excellent safety record for this drug. It is unlikely that its topical form will display new and unexpected toxicity. Future studies to understand the mechanism of action of topical PTU promise to yield new insight into the cause of psoriasis.

▶ Childhood Sunburns and Melanoma

It is widely accepted that exposure to the Sun is a key causative factor for all types of skin cancer, including melanoma. It is also believed that the total lifetime cumulative dose of sunlight is an important risk factor leading to nonmelanoma types of skin cancer. In contrast, the risk for melanoma is usually correlated, not with the total cumulative dose of lifelong sun exposure, but rather to a history of childhood sun exposure. It is frequently speculated that a single severe sunburn in childhood will elevate an individual's lifetime risk for melanoma. Results of a study by Emily White, Constance Kirkpatrick, and colleagues from the University of Washington in Seattle, regarding risk factors for melanoma in patients from Washington State, seriously question these previous assumptions.

Their study involved interviewing 256 melanoma patients and 273 randomly selected nonmelanoma control patients. The results confirm the accepted conclusions of previous studies that having (1) fair, "always burns, never tans," type of skin; (2) increased numbers of moles; (3) high education level; and (4) high socioeconomic status are all risk factors for melanoma. However, their data regarding childhood sun exposure and the risks for melanoma produced some surprising conclusions. Childhood exposure seemed to be a significant risk factor for melanoma only in the fair-skinned patients who are unable to form a tan. Among patients who are able to form a deep tan, their results actually suggest a reduced risk for melanoma.

Unexpected results like these demand more investigation to verify their accuracy. This study highlights the complexity of the interactions of the Sun with the human body. It also raises many questions. Are all of the effects of sunlight on human skin negative? Is it possible that mechanisms have evolved in populations with the ability to tan that actually protect against melanoma if the skin and/or immune system is properly stimulated by sunlight early in childhood? Are sunscreens always helpful to all skin types, at all ages, and in all climates? Certainly these are important questions for future studies.

Edward E. Bondi, M.D.

Substance Abuse

▶ Controversy Over Legalization

The legalization of drugs is an issue that evokes strong emotions from many people, including those who treat substance abuse and dependence. In 1994, when M. Joycelyn Elders, M.D., then the surgeon general of the United States, stated that the concept of legalization of drugs should be explored, a storm of protest and controversy erupted. In response to this controversy, the *New England Journal of Medicine* published contrasting views by eminent individuals on the costs and benefits of drug legalization. On the side of legalization were Lester Grinspoon, M.D., and James Bakalar, J.D., of the Harvard Medical School in Cambridge, Massachusetts. On the side against legalization was Herbert Kleber, M.D., of the Center on Addiction and Substance Abuse at Columbia University in New York City. Both sides presented papers that offered cogent arguments for their respective positions.

Grinspoon and Bakalar assert that the "war on drugs" has been a failure and has resulted in increased crime and social tension. The authors feel that a drug-free society is an impossibility. They argue that education, rather than prohibition, is the best way to prevent drug abuse. In contrast, Kleber feels that current efforts to reduce the supply and demand for drugs are effective, although not perfect. He also feels that the increased availability of drugs would lead to increased use and greater dependency, with serious consequences for many individuals and for society at large. He is particularly concerned about the legalization of cocaine, a very dangerous drug, and the legalization of marijuana, which he feels is especially dangerous to teens.

▶ Is Addiction Genetically Determined?

People who have family members with alcoholism appear to be at higher risk for developing alcoholism themselves. Approximately one-third of children of alcoholic parents become alcoholics. (However, it is important to point out that two-thirds of the children of alcoholics do *not* become alcoholic.) Studies on alcoholism in twins and adopted children suggest that having alcoholic parents increases one's risk of becoming alcoholic significantly: approximately fourfold in men and twofold in women. The factors that account for the increased risk remain unknown. There is much interest in the identification of specific factors that may correlate with the development of this illness.

One factor may be the amount of alcohol it takes to get a person intoxicated. More than 10 years ago, Mark Schuckit, M.D., of the University of California at San Diego found that young men with a family history of alcoholism tend to be less sensitive to the intoxicating effects of alcohol than are a matched group of men without such a family history. In 1994 Dr. Schuckit published a 10-year follow-up study of these young men. More of the family-history-positive men developed alcoholism than did the family-history-negative men. However, he found that those men in both groups who are less sensitive to the effects of alcohol are also more likely to have become alcoholics. The author suggests that a high tolerance for alcohol leads to the need to drink more to feel intoxicated. Since a high percentage of family-history-positive individuals are less sensitive to alcohol, they have a greater likelihood of becoming alcoholics, especially if they live among heavy drinkers. In conclusion, Dr. Schuckit points out that the factors that determine alcoholism are complex and probably due to an interaction between genetic tendencies and environmental influences.

▶ Alcoholism Treatment

When alcoholics stop drinking, they often develop signs and symptoms of the alcohol-withdrawal syndrome. This syndrome may manifest itself through such symptoms as agitation, hyperactivity, tremor, fever, elevated blood pressure, and insomnia. In severe cases, there may be seizures, confusion, psychosis (delirium tremens), and even death. Fortunately, the alcohol-withdrawal syndrome is usually treatable by administering a sedative medication, such as a benzodiazepine (Valium, Librium, and others). Benzodiazepines are superior to other medications because of their low toxicity and their anticonvulsant effects.

Clinicians are striving for ways to optimize the use of medications for treating alcohol withdrawal. It has been observed that many patients receive sedative medication for withdrawal even when they do not require it. A study by Richard Saitz, M.D., M.P.H., and his colleagues at Harvard Medical School suggests that sedative medications are optimally used when the dose is titrated according to symptoms by using an established "withdrawal-severity scale." The researchers studied 101 mostly male patients who were admitted to a veterans hospital in order to undergo detoxification. One group received a standard amount of medication; the other received medication only in response to a high withdrawal-severity-scale score. The staff members who treated the patients were unaware of the group to which a given patient belonged.

Although the group that received medication according to their "score" on the withdrawal scale were given less medication over a shorter period of time, the severity of withdrawal between the two groups was comparable. This method, the researchers assert, allows physicians to correlate dosage amount to the patient's symptoms, thus avoiding overmedication or undermedication.

In a retrospective study, researchers from the University of Michigan in Ann Arbor found that, compared to young patients, elderly alcoholics were more likely to experience medical problems and to demonstrate significantly more signs and symptoms of withdrawal. Elderly patients were, for instance, more subject to high blood pressure, weakness, and impaired thinking than were the younger group of patients—problems that necessitated longer hospital stays. Regardless of age, the withdrawal-medication requirements of the two groups were similar.

After detoxification, alcoholics are quite vulnerable to relapse. Recent research suggests that alcoholics who take an opioid-blocker (antagonist) medication in the first several weeks after detoxification may reduce their risk of returning to drinking. The medication that has been primarily studied is naltrexone, an opioid blocker used to treat narcotic dependence. In two double-blind, placebo-controlled clinical studies, naltrexone, along with psychosocial therapy, reduced relapse drinking in newly abstinent alcoholics.

Another study published in 1994 provides further evidence for the effectiveness of opioid antagonists in the treatment of alcoholism. A pilot study by Barbara Mason, Ph.D., and her colleagues at the University of Miami in Florida examined abstinence in 21 recently detoxified alcoholics receiving either a placebo or two doses of nalmefene, an opioid blocker. Medication was administered such that neither patients nor staff knew which medication they were receiving. The researchers found that patients receiving nalmefene were more likely to remain abstinent and, if they did relapse, to drink less. This study confirms the previous findings showing that opioid blockers may reduce relapse in alcoholics. A possible advantage of using nalmefene instead of naltrexone is that the former has a less damaging effect on the liver.

► Cocaine Treatment

Although recent data from the National Household Study on Drug Abuse indicates that cocaine use has declined somewhat from its peak in the late 1980s, the drug nonetheless continues to be widely used. Cocaine is highly addictive, and there have been concerns that cocaine treatment has only limited success. One factor that appears to be important in successful cocaine treatment is the participation of the addict's family or friends in the treatment program. Researchers from the University of Vermont in Burlington, led by Stephen Higgins, Ph.D., found a 19-times-greater success rate in achieving abstinence for addicts whose spouse, parent, sibling, or friend offered support and participated in treatment along with the addict. The researchers followed 52 men and women who were cocaine-dependent, and treated them with behavioral therapy for 12 weeks. Patients chose a "significant other" to participate with them in the therapy. Those with the partner had a much-improved chance of remaining abstinent from cocaine. Although further research needs to be done, the results suggest a potential method for improving treatment success for cocaine addicts.

► Adolescent Substance Abuse

The use of illicit drugs and alcohol by adolescents is a problem of increasing concern. In many areas of the country, illicit drugs and alcohol are easily available to youth and teens. A recent study by Joe Westermeyer, M.D., and his colleagues at the University of Minnesota in Minneapolis attempted to better describe the characteristics of adolescents who use drugs and alcohol. The researchers examined 100 youngsters between the ages of 14 and 20 who entered substance-abuse treatment programs. They found a

As part of its nationwide antidrug effort, Project DARE arranges for police officers to speak to students about the dangers of using drugs.

trend toward entering treatment at a younger age, although the age at which drug use began remained stable. Those adolescents who began their drug use at an early age were more likely to come from single-parent households, to have a family history of substance abuse, and to have a low socioeconomic status. The authors also found a high prevalence of psychiatric disorders in this group of teens, with an alarming 42 percent having attempted suicide.

One major national effort to prevent substance abuse in youth is the Drug Abuse Resistance Education (DARE) program. Project DARE was originally developed in Los Angeles, California, in 1983, through a collaboration between the Los Angeles Police Department and the Los Angeles County school system. The program was made available to other locales and has been adopted by half of the school districts in the country. The project primarily targets students in elementary or junior high school, with the idea of providing drug education to them before they are likely to be exposed to drugs. Instead of teachers, specially trained police officers provide instruction in the classroom.

The DARE project enjoys broad-based support from parents' groups, educators, and law-enforcement officials, even though few studies have examined how well the program succeeds in preventing teen drug use several years after DARE training—the time when teens are more likely to be exposed to drugs. Researchers from the Research Triangle Institute in North Carolina and the University of Illinois in Chicago studied elementary-school students from 24 pairs of schools in Illinois matched for socioeconomic status and location. Students from schools offering Project DARE were compared with students from schools that did not offer the DARE program. The researchers followed the students over a three-year period and compared the use of alcohol and tobacco and the attitudes toward drug use between the groups who did and did not receive DARE training.

The results, according to the researchers, are "unfortunate." The students who received DARE training showed no reduction in alcohol or tobacco use at intervals of one, two, and three years after the course, compared to those who did not receive DARE training. There was also no long-term impact of DARE on social and psychological risk factors for illicit drug use. The authors of the study indicate that their results are in agreement with other studies that show limited success of DARE instruction. They stress the need to strengthen the effectiveness of the program, and perhaps modify the curriculum or grade level of students receiving the program.

▶ New Research on Self-Help Groups

Alcoholics Anonymous (AA), Narcotics Anonymous (NA), and other self-help groups are a mainstay of chemical-dependency treatment for many individuals. Yet there has been little objective research to determine which specific aspects of self-help groups reduce drug and alcohol use, promote abstinence, and improve an individual's well-being. To help overcome this lack of knowledge, William Miller, Ph.D., and Ernest Kurtz, Ph.D., of the psychology department at the University of New Mexico in Albuquerque surveyed addiction professionals regarding their beliefs and understanding of the operation of AA and other "12-step" self-help groups. The authors discovered that addiction professionals often misunderstand the basic tenets of AA and other self-help movements. The authors emphasize that clinicians who have a clearer understanding of these tenets of AA can make better referrals for their patients.

Two recent studies explored the relationship between self-help-program philosophy and program effectiveness. In a case study of 12 individuals who joined 12-step programs, John Peteet, M.D., of Harvard Medical School explored the reasons that these programs work for some people and not for others. He found that those who are willing to identify themselves as alcoholics or addicts, and those who wish to address spiritual needs, do well in traditional 12-step programs such as AA or NA. Dr. Peteet points out that those who have an agnostic or antireligious view of life may find the philosophy behind the 12-step programs unacceptable.

Marc Galanter, M.D., and his colleagues at the New York University School of Medicine in New York City studied the Rational Recovery (RR) movement, a self-help program similar to AA, but without AA's stress on spirituality. RR offers a cognitive orientation, which emphasizes independence. Researchers sent questionnaires to 433 RR members across the United States. Seventy-seven percent of members reported at least one month of abstinence; 58 percent reported six months of abstinence. One notable statistic was that only 53 percent of the RR subjects believed in God or the existence of a "universal spirit"; this finding is in sharp contrast with the general population, of which 94 percent believe in God. Respondents had a high regard for RR, felt a strong group identity, and reported that it was more effective than AA. The authors conclude that Rational Recovery can promote abstinence and may be a viable self-help alternative for individuals who are uncomfortable with AA's spiritual orientation.

Robert M. Swift, M.D., Ph.D.

Teeth and Gums

▶ Diagnosis of Periodontitis

Periodontitis is a gum disease caused by a bacterial infection of the connective tissues and bone that support an individual's teeth. Left unchecked, periodontitis will destroy these tissues, causing the teeth to loosen. Ultimately, enough tissue may be destroyed to require removal of the teeth.

Dentists have traditionally evaluated patients for the presence or extent of periodontitis by X rays or clinical probing. X rays of the teeth generally reveal the amount of bone that has been destroyed by periodontitis. Since the oral cavity is a complex three-dimensional unit, X rays can grossly underestimate the amount of bone damage. Also, radiation-safety standards do not allow short-interval repeated use of dental X rays.

The magnitude of the damage caused by periodontitis may also be determined by the use of a periodontal probe. This small calibrated rod is gently placed between the tooth and gum tissue to measure the extent of tissue destruction. This approach, while giving a more accurate assessment, is still very limited because it determines only the aftermath from previous exposures to the infection. It does not allow the dentist to determine whether periodontitis is currently progressing.

When gum tissues are infected and inflamed, an exudate called gingival crevicular fluid (GCF) is produced. It has long been known that increased levels of inflammation result in more production of GCF. Recently, biomedical techniques have allowed clinical scientists to identify a variety of substances within GCF. Clinical trials now provide data implicating some of these substances as indicators of active periodontitis.

The components of GCF may be divided into five groups: substances produced by bacteria thought to be responsible for initiating periodontitis; substances associated with generalized inflammation; enzymes capable of causing direct tissue damage; enzymes produced during cell damage or death; and enzymes produced by specific immune cells that may be suppressed during periodontitis.

While a case can be made for the use of each of these elements to determine the presence of periodontitis, measurement of enzymes produced by damaged cells appears to hold the most promise. Aspartate aminotransferase (AST) is an enzyme released by a cell when it dies. AST blood levels have been used for years to assess heart or kidney damage. Commercial tests for dental chairside use have recently been developed to measure AST levels in GCF.

AST in GCF is definitely associated with inflammation of the gum tissues. However, while controlled laboratory experiments show a direct correlation of AST levels with progression of periodontitis, clinical trials suggest that the test is not completely capable of distinguishing between advancing periodontitis and gingivitis, a more common inflammation. Gingivitis affects only the surface gum tissues; it does not involve the tissues supporting the teeth.

▶ Advances in Orthodontics

Orthodontics is the dental specialty dedicated to selective movement of teeth to produce better function and aesthetics. Orthodontic tooth movement is achieved by applying relatively light force on teeth over a period of time.

The teeth are secured into the jawbone by a connective-tissue ligament. Orthodontic forces apply pressure that allows the teeth to slowly move through the jawbone. Orthodontists create the forces needed for tooth movement by placing small wires containing specific bends into brackets secured to the teeth. The bends are designed so that the wire is placed under tension. As the wire straightens, it directs forces to the appropriate location on the teeth to be moved.

The wire must, of course, be anchored within the mouth. Traditionally this anchorage has been achieved by securing the wire to several large teeth. While successful, this method poses problems in that the anchored teeth move at least a short distance in the opposite direction. This movement disperses applied forces in an uncontrollable manner, and potentially alters alignment of the anchor teeth, which then require correction later in therapy.

A new approach to orthodontic anchorage involves attaching a solid metal button to the bone on the roof of the mouth. A small incision is made through the soft tissue on the roof of the mouth; the base of the metal button is then secured to the surface of the exposed bone with adhesive. The incised tissues are repositioned, allowing the extended end of the button to protrude a few millimeters into the oral cavity. After several weeks of healing, the orthodontist may use the button as a solid, stationary anchor without fear of reciprocal movement. Preliminary studies demonstrate the ability to provide faster and more predictable tooth movement using this anchor system. Trials are now being conducted to evaluate long-term efficiency and safety of the system. If these trials yield positive results, approval by the Food and Drug Administration (FDA) for marketing is anticipated in the near future.

In other orthodontic news, computer programs have been developed to digitize predetermined skeletal points on the young orthodontic patient. Then, guided by an extensive database that takes into account sex, race, skeletal age, and genetic facial patterns, the program plots a series of jaw-growth projections. These projections assist the orthodontist in anticipating such things as final jaw size and upper- and lower-jaw relationships. This information allows the orthodontist to better plan the need for tooth extractions and the amount of tooth movement needed to achieve desired function and aesthetics.

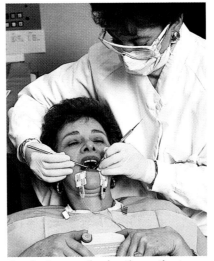

In electroanesthesia, the patient controls the pain incurred during minor dental procedures by transmitting impulses of electricity to nerves in the treatment area.

▶ Smoking and Gum Diseases

An increasing amount of evidence has shown that the oral bacteria of cigarette smokers are not different from those of nonsmokers. However, well-controlled long-term human studies have confirmed that smokers are nonetheless more likely than nonsmokers to have gum disease. They have also shown that gum disease, when present, is more severe in smokers than in nonsmokers, regardless of how frequently they see their dentist or how compliant they may be with their oral-hygiene procedures.

Many biological factors may be involved in producing these findings. An intact, healthy immune system, for example, may be capable of holding infection in check and limiting the progress of gum disease. Cigarette smoking has been shown to inhibit neutrophil function, reduce antibody production, and alter lymphocytes, all important components of the immune response.

Local tissue factors associated with response to irritation and healing are also adversely affected by cigarette smoking. It has been demonstrated that the function of cells making up the gum tissue is significantly depressed when exposed to cigarette smoke. Nicotine, a major constituent of cigarette smoke, has also been shown to kill connective-tissue cells in the gum tissue and to reduce the amount of blood flow to the gums.

Gum disease in nonsmokers is typically characterized by an inflammatory response that includes redness, edema of the gum tissue, and bleeding from the tissue following such minor mechanical manipulation as brushing and flossing. Cigarette smokers with gum disease exhibit decreased color change and a reduced tendency to bleed, most likely due to the suppression of the gum tissue's inflammatory response. This absence of key clinical symptoms causes diagnostic problems, particularly in younger patients with early disease.

▶ Electroanesthesia

For many diseases in the oral cavity, the abundant and sensitive nerve supply of the teeth and gums makes treatment without anesthesia an uncomfortable experience for most people. Local anesthesia is a very effective method to control nerve conduction. However, the traditional process of obtaining profound local anesthesia requires the injection of an anesthetic agent adjacent to the receptive nerves. These nerves lie deep within the connective tissues of the mouth. The penetration of the anesthetic needle and the expansion of the connective tissue by the anesthetic solution is an unpleasant experience for some patients. This fact, coupled with the time necessary to obtain profound anesthesia and the post-therapy time necessary to recover normal nerve conduction, makes the injection of local anesthetics a less-than-ideal approach in some clinical situations. Dentists are constantly searching for a method to obtain easily reversible local anesthesia of the teeth and gums. Recent success in the use of transcutaneous (through the skin) electrical nerve stimulation for control of chronic pain has heightened the interest in use of electroanesthesia for dental therapy.

A dental electroanesthesia machine consists of a small battery-powered generator capable of producing at least three electrical waveforms at a variety of frequencies. The appropriate electrical impulse is transmitted to the treatment region by wires that are attached to a sponge, clamp, or adhesive electrodes. As the electrical impulse is transmitted, it is typically described by the patient as an intense vibration, not unlike the sensation when one's "leg goes to sleep."

Clinical trials have shown that electroanesthesia is effective in adult patients 35 to 80 percent of the time. Minor dental procedures on the gum tissue can generally be accomplished under electroanesthesia more successfully than can procedures on teeth. More success has been shown for procedures on front teeth than on back teeth.

The ability to obtain adequate anesthesia by electroanesthetic techniques for endodontic (root canal) therapy is limited. Generally, surgical procedures or tooth extractions cannot be accomplished with electroanesthesia.

▶ Diagnosis of Dental Caries

Dental caries (decay) has traditionally been diagnosed by the dentist with the use of X rays and a dental explorer, a sharp wire instrument that is inserted with finger pressure to determine if a cavity in the tooth structure is present. Both approaches are based on the assumption that dental caries is a nonreversible, progressive process that requires mechanical treatment—excavation and placement of a restoration (filling). Newer information defines dental caries as a symptom of a bacterial infection that can be reversed or arrested by appropriate therapy.

Acceptance of this premise has led the dental profession to work toward refining diagnostic approaches for determining the presence of active disease prior to the development of cavities in the tooth surface. Transillumination with high-power fiber-optic lights has been shown to detect with great accuracy early evidence of beginning demineralization on the chewing surfaces of the teeth. An endoscopic device coupled with a video camera for image magnification and enhancement has also been shown to be effective in the early diagnosis of small lesions in the tooth enamel. Argon lasers have similarly been shown to be effective in early detection of decay. Modifications of dental X-ray technology, such as digital imaging, xeroradiography, and computer enhancement are being evaluated in an attempt to improve early detection of dental caries. Diagnostic techniques based upon the difference in electrical resistance between healthy and diseased tooth structure are also being investigated.

Earlier detection of decay allows the dentist to choose treatment options other than mechanical excavation and restoration. Alterations in diet, application of anticaries or remineralization agents such as fluoride or chlorhexidine, or placement of sealing agents to retard bacterial penetration may be used in specific situations in which early infections are identified.

Saliva has been shown to act as a remineralization agent in areas of early caries activity. Studies demonstrate that chewing sugarless (sorbitol) gum within five minutes of eating, and continuing for at least 15 minutes, increases the salivary-flow rate, the pH, and the buffering capacity of the saliva. Significant reductions in the pH of the decay-causing bacteria have occurred when sorbitol gum is routinely used after eating.

Kenneth L. Kalkwarf, D.D.S., M.S.

Tropical Medicine

▶ Fighting River Blindness

In many developing nations, the local river is a community's busiest place. People use the waterways not just for fishing and swimming, but also for bathing, washing clothes and dishes, and just socializing. Unfortunately, many Africans and Latin Americans share their riverbanks with the blackfly *Simulium damnosum,* which is the carrier of a parasitic nematode worm, *Onchocerca volvulus.* When an infected fly bites a person, it can transmit the parasite, which then grows into a threadlike worm in its new human host.

The resulting infection causes a devastating illness called onchocerciasis, or "river blindness," after one of its most serious complications. Experts estimate that at least 18 million people are infected by onchocerciasis at any one time, and more than 80 million people live in areas where they are exposed to infected blackflies.

When a blackfly bites, it makes a tiny opening in a person's skin, and drinks the blood that oozes out. As the fly feeds, immature *O. volvulus* nematodes, or larvae, escape from the fly's mouthparts and enter the open wound. Once inside a person's skin, the larvae travel to lower skin layers. Reacting to the presence of foreign material, the person's body walls off the maturing nematodes inside hard nodules. In 8 to 12 months, the parasites mature into threadlike adult worms. Typically, there are three to eight worms of both sexes entangled in each nodule. An adult female is between 12 and 16 inches long, and the male is slightly smaller.

After mating, each adult female can produce hundreds of larvae a day. These first-stage larvae, called microfilariae, leave the nodules and move through the skin. Some penetrate into the eye, where they can cause permanent blindness. Much of the damage to the eye is done by a person's own immune system as it reacts to the microfilariae. Elsewhere in the body, these larvae cause severe skin irritation and thickening, loss of pigment, and lymph disorders.

The skin micofilariae wait for the arrival of a blackfly to continue their life cycle. When a blackfly feeds on an infected human, microfilariae enter the fly's body. There they develop through three larval stages, at which point they are ready to enter a new human host.

Vaccine Development. In 1976 the World Health Organization (WHO) launched the Onchocerciasis Control Program in West Africa. The program's continuing mission is to stop the transmis-

More than 18 million people suffer from "river blindess," an infection caused by a tropical parasite. In some villages, 15 percent of the adults are permanently blinded by the disease.

sion of *O. volvulus* and, in doing so, to eliminate onchocerciasis as a major public-health problem in eastern and western Africa.

The primary target for control is the *Simulium* blackfly, which can be killed in its immature, aquatic stages with insecticide sprays. Several insecticides have been used with varying degrees of success. But over time, populations of blackfly larvae develop resistance to the chemicals. In places where such resistance develops, health officials have switched to more-toxic chemicals, such as the insecticide Chlorphoxim. However, Chlorphoxim is toxic to many beneficial insects and animals as well as to the blackfly. Health officials have also used bacteria (*Bacillus thuringiensis* H-14) that infect and kill the blackfly larvae. Unfortunately, the bacteria do not work well in fast-flowing rivers.

Treatment for Onchocerciasis. The chemical compound diethylcarbamazine (DEC) is effective against microfilariae that are present either in a person's skin or lymph system. However, the drug causes a massive extermination of microfilariae in the skin, which in turn can cause a serious reaction. In most patients, this reaction amounts to no more than intense itching and a rash. However, some people experience high fever, headache, malaise, nausea and vomiting,

joint and muscle pain, cough and breathing difficulties, and a dangerous fall in blood pressure.

Another onchocerciasis treatment, ivermectin, is more familiar to North Americans as a veterinary drug used to prevent and treat heartworm in dogs. It was approved by WHO in 1989 for treatment of humans infected with *O. volvulus*. In contrast to DEC, ivermectin has very mild or no side effects. Importantly, only a single oral dose is needed to complete the treatment—as compared with DEC, which requires three doses spread over time.

However, neither drug kills the adult nematode worm. So treatment must be repeated every year, or the adult females will repopulate their host's skin. Because follow-up care is especially difficult in remote areas, new alternatives are desperately needed to control—and eventually eliminate—onchocerciasis.

Antigen Production and Vaccine Development. Experts believe that the most vulnerable point in the "river blindness" parasite's life cycle may be when it first enters the human body. This is when a person's immune system has the best chance of fighting off infection. With this in mind, the Edna McConnell Clark Foundation's Program in Tropical Medicine is organizing research toward developing an effective vaccine targeted against two developmental stages of the *O. volvulus* parasite: the infective, third-stage larva, which is ready to enter the human host through the bite of a blackfly; and the fourth-stage larva, which is in its first stage of development in the host.

But to develop a vaccine, scientists first need an antigen, irradiated, harmless larval parasites that can be recognized by a person's immune system. Once the immune system has been exposed to such an antigen, the system is primed and ready to recognize and attack the real larval parasite, which bears the same antigen on its surface.

To amass the amount of antigen needed for research, scientists have developed insectaries in West Africa where they rear infected flies and harvest *O. volvulus* larvae at their crucial stages. Humans are the only hosts for the later stages of the *O. volvulus* worm. So animal studies can be done only by using closely related species. Despite such difficulties, scientists have developed and tested 12 antigens, both individually and as a mixture. Early testing suggests that dead larvae may themselves be useful as a vaccine.

In the spring of 1994, 60 of the world's leading experts on onchocerciasis met in Woods Hole, Massachusetts. Encouraged by the progress of recent years, they recommended the continued search for antigens that may be fashioned into an effective vaccine.

Milan Trpis, Ph.D.

Urology

▶ The Prostate

Treatment for enlarged prostate, a condition that affects more than half of all men over 50 years old, has continued to heat up—literally. Gaining wider acceptance is the technique of laser ablation, in which infrared laser light burns away excess prostate tissue. The laser light is directed from a small generating machine through a fine tube running up an endoscope placed in the urethra. The laser-emitting tip then removes some of the swollen prostate tissue surrounding the urinary pathway. The procedure takes about 30 minutes, and is conducted using spinal or local anesthesia. The body absorbs the ablated tissue.

Laser ablation joins a host of treatments—including microwave and ultrasound therapies and laser-induced coagulation—that shrink tissue without surgery. Still, surgery (transurethral resection of the prostate, or TURP) continues to be the most effective method for shrinking an enlarged prostate. A recent study in the *New England Journal of Medicine* reaffirms the value of both TURP and watchful waiting in treating benign enlarged prostates.

In August 1994, the U.S. Food and Drug Administration (FDA) approved a blood test for detecting prostate cancer by measuring the level of a protein known as prostate-specific antigen (PSA). Experts caution that the test may miss some cancers, and it also can detect extremely small cancers that, in some cases, would best be left untreated (in part because some prostate cancer grows at such a slow rate that it could take many years to become dangerous).

In other prostate news, researchers from Johns Hopkins University in Baltimore, Maryland, discovered a genetic flaw associated with prostate cancer. The flaw appears to prevent the body from producing an enzyme that protects against carcinogens that lead to this cancer.

▶ Urinary-Tract Infections

A study published in the March 9, 1994, issue of the *Journal of the American Medical Association* has proved what many have suspected: drinking cranberry juice can reduce the incidences of, and speed up the resolution of, urinary-tract infections (UTIs) in some women. Researchers from Harvard Medical School in Cambridge, Massachusetts, studied two groups of randomly selected women. Members of one group drank cranberry-juice cocktail daily for six months, while members of the other group drank a beverage containing cranberry flavoring but no cranberry juice. Women who drank cranberry juice developed fewer UTIs—42 percent of the number developed by women who drank the placebo. Furthermore, the chance that a woman with a UTI who drank cranberry juice would continue to suffer from the disorder was substantially decreased compared to those women who drank the placebo. The study also ruled out any effect of vitamin C.

▶ Erectile Dysfunction

One of the more successful treatments for erectile dysfunction is accomplished by injecting drugs directly into the penis, causing it to fill with blood and become erect. The commonly prescribed drug is prostaglandin El, or alprostadil. About half the men who begin this therapy discontinue it, however, because they dislike injecting themselves. These men may soon have a new alternative in the form of an intraurethral pellet. Now in the final stages of testing, the 3-millimeter pellet dispenses alprostadil from inside the urethra with the aid of a device that inserts it about 1 inch up the penile shaft. Experts say that, compared to erection based on injection, erection based on the pellet involves more of the penile tissues—and is thus more natural—but with slightly less rigidity.

The FDA has approved a new two-piece implantable prosthesis that inflates in the penis to simulate erection. The device comprises two cylinders that are implanted in the penis, and a small pump that is implanted in the scrotum and connected by a tube to the cylinders. Gently squeezing the pump (through the skin) causes fluid stored in a reservoir at the base of each cylinder to fill the cylinders, expanding them along with the penis. The fluid returns to the reservoir when the user bends the penis downward. The new device will benefit patients who must avoid the abdominal surgery needed for three-piece devices (in which a separate fluid reservoir is implanted in the abdomen).

▶ Interstitial Cystitis

Interstitial cystitis (IC) is a painful, inflammatory disease of the bladder wall that affects mostly women. Research at Tulane University in New Orleans, Louisiana, has pointed to a possible association of bacteria to the disease. Studies conducted by Gerald J. Domingue, Ph.D., found bacterial DNA and evidence of an as-yet-unidentified microorganism in bladders of IC patients. He theorizes that the bacteria may be killed by the body's immune response, which may, in turn, cause the bladder inflammation typical of IC.

Donald W. Cunningham

Index

Main article headings appear in this index as bold-faced capital letters; subjects within articles appear as lower-case entries. Both the general references and the subentries should be consulted for maximum usefulness of this index. A Cumulative Index of feature articles from the 1992, 1993, 1994, and 1995 editions of this volume appears on pages 348 and 349.

A

AA (Alcoholics Anonymous) 328
AARP *see* American Association of Retired Persons
Abortion
  government policies 267–68
  RU-486 testing 306
Accidents *see* Occupational health; Safety
ACD CPR 251
ACE inhibitor (drug)
  diabetic kidney disease 28, 279
  heart attack treatment 274
Acetaminophen (drug)
  drug interactions 38
Acetone
  indoor air pollution 191
Achalasia 249
Achilles tendon
  medical terminology 54
Achondroplasia 262
Ackerknecht, Erwin H.
  medical terminology 49
Acne
  alpha-hydroxy acid treatment 313
  drug interactions 41
Acne rosacea 324–25
Actinic keratoses
  skin cancer 324
Activated protein C
  thrombosis 235
Active-compression-decompression (ACD) method
  cardiopulmonary resuscitation 251
Acute lymphoblastic leukemia
  medications and drugs 292
Adderall (drug)
  hyperactivity 289
Addiction (to drugs) *see* Substance abuse
Additives, Food
  candy 82–83
Adductor muscles 129
Adenoma
  antioxidants 244
Adenomatous polyposis
  medical family tree 211, 249
ADHD (Attention-deficit hyperactivity disorder) *see* Hyperactivity
Administration, Hospital 224
Adolescents *see* Teenagers
ADPKD (Autosomal dominant polycystic kidney disease) 211, 279
Advertising
  health insurance 265
  tobacco industry 59 *illus.*, 61 *illus.*, 63
Aerobic exercise
  bowling 143
  health clubs 123
  in-line skating 138
  swimming 115
Aerosol propellants
  air pollution 321
Africa
  AIDS infection 228
  palm kernel oil extraction 76 *illus.*
  Peace Corps 148 *illus.*
  Rwandan refugees 315

  tropical medicine 331–32
African-Americans *see* Blacks
Aggressive behavior
  causes 164
  domestic violence 251
  gang violence 160–66
AGING 226–27
  alcohol-withdrawal syndrome 327
  depression 226
  exercise 319
  falls 226–27, 318–19
  foot care 19–20, 314
  Fountain of Age (book) 238
  HIV infection 169
  living longer 226
  malnutrition 101
  overweight 302
  pain perception 227
  predicting driving accidents 319
  retirement 217–21
  sleep 241
  swimming 116–17
  tooth discoloration 198
  vitamin requirements 94
  weight training 227
  wrinkles 224
Agriculture, United States Department of
  body-weight guidelines 99 *table*
  candy in the Food Pyramid 82
AIDS 228–31 *see also* HIV
  children's understanding 247
  contaminated blood in Europe 231
  contraceptive use 304
  family reactions to HIV 167–71
  female condoms 323
  government policies 268
  interleukin-12 therapy 277
  in utero transmission 230–31, 282–83
  medications and drugs 290–91
  National AIDS Hotline 171
  nontuberculous mycobacteria 321
  on-the-job risks to EMTs 186
  10th International AIDS Conference 229
  transmission during CPR 187
  tuberculosis among children 312
  tuberculosis infection 231
  vaccine trials 230
  world population trends 228–29
Air conditioning
  Legionnaires' disease 316
Air pollution
  aerosol propellants 321
  environment and health 254–56
  houseplants 191, 193–94
Alcohol *see also* Substance abuse
  chocolate candy 86
  drug interactions 39–40
  fetal alcohol syndrome 246
  genetic risk of alcoholism 214 *table*, 326
  G-protein malfunction in alcoholism 298
  mental health survey 293
  reduces heart attack risk 103, 274
  use in the workplace 306
  withdrawal symptoms 179, 326–27
Alcoholics Anonymous (AA) 328

Alcoholism and the Family (book, Berger) 239
Allergy
  houseplants 192
  rashes from plants 203–5
  sun-drug interactions 41
Allodynia
  pain 240
Aloe vera
  burn treatment 72
Alpha-fetoprotein
  testicular cancer 34
Alpha-hydroxy acids
  cosmetic skin enhancement 313
Alpha-tocopherol
  antioxidants 244
Alpha waves
  relaxation 190
Alprostadil (Prostaglandin E1) (drug)
  erectile dysfunction 333
Alternative medicine
  Healing and the Mind (book) 239
  health personnel and facilities 273
  hypnosis 172–77
  osteopathic physicians 42–48
Alzheimer's disease 12
  genetic risk 214 *table*
  public health 226
AMA *see* American Medical Association
Ambulance 188 *illus.*
AMBULATORY SURGERY 29–30
  procedures increase 11
American Academy of Cosmetic Dentistry 200
American Association of Retired Persons (AARP)
  retirement planning 220
  volunteer work 148
American Cancer Society
  smoking education 63
American Dental Association (ADA) 200
American Dietetic Association (ADA) 101
American Heart Association
  fats in diet 78
  secondhand smoke deaths 60
American Medical Association (AMA)
  hypnosis 177
  osteopathic physicians 48
American Psychiatric Association 177
American Psychological Association 177
American Red Cross
  swimming classes 120
American Society of Clinical Hypnosis 177
American Stop Smoking Intervention Study for Cancer Prevention 63
AmeriCorps 148
Amiodarone (Cordarone) (drug)
  arrhythmia 276
Ammonia
  air-cleaning houseplants 191, 193 *table*
Amnesia
  childhood sexual abuse 294
Amphetamine (drug)
  weight loss 97–98
Ampicillin (drug)
  drug interactions 39
Analgesics
  drug interactions 41
  narcotics 240–41
Anemia
  systemic lupus erythematosus 233
Anencephaly
  medical ethics 283–84
ANESTHESIOLOGY 232
  dentistry 330–31
  hypnosis 173, 175
  liquids before surgery 30, 232
  nerve block 30, 241
  nitric oxide 232

  outpatient surgery 29–30
  receptor sites 232
Aneurysm
  diagnosing 64–65
  Kawasaki Syndrome 311
Anger Kills (book, Williams and Williams) 239
Angiogenesis
  tumor development 244–45
Angioplasty 275–76, 288
Angiotensin converting enzyme (ACE)
  diabetic kidney disease 28, 279
Angiotensin II (hormone)
  essential hypertension 279
Annals of Internal Medicine
  rheumatic disease research 233–34
Anorexia nervosa 98–99
Antacids
  drug interactions 40
Antibiotics
  drug interactions 39, 41
  ear infections 311
  Lyme disease 234
  resistant disease organisms 315
  tooth discoloration 198–99
  toxic epidermal necrolysis 324
  tuberculosis 231
Antibodies
  diabetes 25 *illus.*
  immunology 276
  systemic lupus erythematosus 233
Anticoagulant drugs *see* Blood-thinning drugs
Anticonvulsant drugs
  reflex sympathetic dystrophy 240
  toxic epidermal necrolysis 324
Antidepressant drugs 289
  drug interactions 38–41
  reflex sympathetic dystrophy 240
  treatment study 294–95
Antigens
  AIDS 229
  diabetes 25 *illus.*
  Kawasaki Syndrome 311
  onchocerciasis vaccine 332
Antihistamines
  drug interactions 37, 40–41
Anti-inflammatory drugs
  aspirin 40, 249
  NSAIDs 37, 40, 249
  respiratory system 320–21
  sun-drug interactions 41
Antioxidants
  cancer 244
  chili peppers 71
  nutrition and diet 12, 302–3
  vitamins 89, 91
Antiphospholipid syndrome 233
Antipsychotic drugs
  schizophrenia 296
Antiretroviral drugs
  AIDS 290–91
Antismoking spray 63
Anxiety
  drug interactions 40
  hypnotherapy 174
  phobias 179
APC (blood protein) 235
Appetite 97–99
Aprotinin (Trasylol) (drug)
  bypass surgery 292
Aquatic Exercise Association 120
Arbeiter, Jean S.
  pain 239
Arch (foot) 17 *illus.*, 21
Areca palm (*Chrysalidocarpus lutescens*)
  health benefits 191
Arenavirus
  laboratory infections 318
Argon lasers
  diagnosis of dental caries 331
Arrhythmia
  drug interactions 36, 41
  treatments 276

Cumulative Index

This listing indexes feature articles that have appeared in the 1992, 1993, 1994, and 1995 editions of *Health and Medicine.*

Acknowledgments

CANDY: HOW SWEET IT IS!, page 81
Reprinted from *FDA Consumer*, July/August 1994.

FEET FIRST, page 16
Reprinted with the permission of *The Walking Magazine* © 1994.

IN-HOME TESTS, page 206
Reprinted from *FDA Consumer*, December 1994.

THE NEW RULES OF THE GAME, page 131
Copyright © 1994 by The New York Times Company. Reprinted by permission.

STRETCHING . . . THE TRUTH, page 127
Reprinted with permission of the *University of California at Berkeley Wellness Letter,* © Health Letter Associates, 1994.

TRACE YOUR FAMILY TREE, page 209
American Health © 1994 by Ruth Papazian.

VITAMINS: CHARTING YOUR COURSE, page 92
Reprinted with permission of the *University of California at Berkeley Wellness Letter,* © Health Letter Associates, 1994.

WHEN HIV HITS HOME, page 167
Reprinted from the April 1994 issue of the *HARVARD HEALTH LETTER,* © 1994, President and Fellows of Harvard College.

Manufacturing Acknowledgments

We wish to thank the following for their services: Composition and Color Separations, Gamma One, Inc.; Text Stock, printed on Champion's 60# Courtland Matte; Cover Materials provided by Holliston Mills, Inc., Decorative Specialties International, Inc., and Ecological Fibers, Inc.; Printing and Binding, R.R. Donnelley & Sons Co.

Illustration Credits

The following list acknowledges, according to page, the sources of illustrations used in this volume. The credits are listed illustration by illustration—top to bottom, left to right. Where necessary, the name of the photographer or artist has been listed with the source, the two separated by a slash. If two or more illustrations appear on the same page, their credits are separated by semicolons.

3 © Michael Heron/The Stock Market
8 © Jane Grushow/Grant Heilman; © Blaine Harrington/The Stock Market
9 © Moore/The Image Works; © D. Greco/The Image Works
11 © Mark Joseph/Tony Stone Images
13 © Steven Peters/Tony Stone Images
14- © Kevin Horan/Tony Stone Images
15
16 © Antonia Deutsch/Tony Stone Images; © Gary Nolton/Tony Stone Images
17 © Krames Communications
18 © Francois Sauze/Science Photo Library/Photo Researchers
19 Left column: © George Kavanagh/Tony Stone Images; right column: both illustrations: © Krames Communications
20 Illustrations: © Krames Communications; © Connie Hansen/The Stock Market
21 Photo: © Philip & Karen Smith/Tony Stone Images; illustration: © Krames Communications
22- Artwork: Lewis E. Calver/© 1986 *Discover Magazine*
23
24 All photos: © Terry Wild Studio
25 Art: Copyright © 1994 by The New York Times Company. Reprinted by permission; photo: © Terry Wild Studio
27 © Larry Mulvehill/Photo Researchers; © Will & Deni McIntyre/Photo Researchers
28 © Rick Lance/Phototake
31 © Joe Cornish/Tony Stone Images; insets: top: graph from *Science News*, February 26, 1994; bottom: © Andrew Syred/Science Photo Library/Photo Researchers
33 © Nancy Ney/FPG
36 Photos, clockwise from top left: © William Whitehurst/The Stock Market; © Chris Sorensen/The Stock Market; © Mauritius GMBH/Phototake; © Michael Krasowitz/FPG
37 © David Woods/The Stock Market
38 © Guy Marche/FPG
41 © The Stock Market
42 © Mark Perlstein
43 © Hattie Young/Science Photo Library/Photo Researchers
45 Illustrations courtesy of the American Osteopathic Association
47 © Paul Biddle & Tim Malyon/Science Photo Library/Photo Researchers
49 © The Granger Collection
50 © The Bettmann Archive; © The Granger Collection
51 © Meaad Kulyk/Science Photo Library/Photo Researchers; © The Bettmann Archive; © Francis Leroy, Biocosmos/Science Photo Library/Photo Researchers
52 Left column: © The Bettmann Archive; © Peter Cull/Science Photo Library/Photo Researchers; right column: © The Bettmann Archive; © John Bavossi/Science Photo Library/Photo Researchers
53 All illustrations: The Bettmann Archive
54 Bottom left: © The Granger Collection; other illustrations: © The Bettmann Archive
55 Bottom left: © The Granger Collection; other illustrations: © The Bettmann Archive
57 © Damien Lovegrove/Photo Researchers
58 © The Bettmann Archive; © Rossi Xavier/Liaison
59 © UPI/Bettmann; © The Bettmann Archive
60 © Reuters/Bettmann; © UPI/Bettmann
61 © Rossi Xavier/Liaison; © Chris Kleponis/Sygma
62 © Paul S. Howell/Liaison
63 © Stephen J. Krasemann/Photo Researchers
64 © Matt Meadows/Peter Arnold
66- © Ian O'Leary/Tony Stone Images
67
68 © Jane Grushow/Grant Heilman
69 © Eduardo Fuss
70 Both photos: © Eduardo Fuss
71 © Muriel Orans
72 © Henley & Savage/The Stock Market; © Jane Grushow/Grant Heilman
73 © Eduardo Fuss; © Pedro Coll/The Stock Market

74 Both photos: © Eduardo Fuss
75 © Bob Ward/International Stock Photo
76 © Marc & Evelyne Bernheim/Woodfin Camp
77 © Chris Collins/The Stock Market
78 © Tom Pantages
79 © Vano/Photobank
80 © David Young-Wolff/Photo Edit
81 © Victor Scocozza/FPG
82 © S. Lousada/Photo Researchers; © Mary Stadtfeld/Unicorn
83 © Jon Feingersh/The Stock Market
84 © Marshall Prescott/Unicorn
85 © Don Mason/The Stock Market
86 © H. Mark Weidman
87 © Jim Shippee/Unicorn; © Eric Berndt/Unicorn
88 © Dennis Galante/Envision
89 © Henley & Savage/The Stock Market
90 © Steven Needham/Envision
91 © G. Ryan & S. Beyer/Tony Stone Images
94 © Envision; © Anthony Blake/Tony Stone Images
95 © David Pollack/The Stock Market
96 © Howard Sokol/Tony Stone Images
97 © Mike Malyszko/FPG
98 © Charles Petit/Photo Researchers; © Jeff Christensen/Liaison
99 © Thomas Ives/The Stock Market
100 © Matthew Klein/Photo Researchers
102 © Diane Graham-Henry/Tony Stone Images
103 © Andy Levin/Photo Researchers
104- © Arthur Tilley/Tony Stone Images
105
106- All illustrations: © Courtesy of Special Olympics International
107
108 © UPI/Bettmann
109 © Courtesy of Connecticut Special Olympics
110 Top photo: © Courtesy of Special Olympics International; bottom photos: © Wide World Photos
111 Both photos: © Courtesy of Special Olympics International
112 © Courtesy of Special Olympics International
113 © Courtesy of Special Olympics International
114 © Jim Leynse/Saba
116 © Daemmrich/The Image Works; © Bachmann/Photo Researchers
118 © Will & Deni McIntyre/Photo Researchers
119 © Oser Saar-Media/Sipa; © Ann States/Saba
120 © D. Greco/The Image Works
121 © Bruce Ayres/Tony Stone Images
122 © Shahn Kermani/Liaison; © Andy Levin/Photo Researchers
123 Courtesy, East Bank Club
124 © Lew Long/The Stock Market
125 © Will & Deni McIntyre/Photo Researchers
126 © E. Sander/Liaison
127 © Lance Nelson/The Stock Market
128- Artwork: © Lisa Natoli
129
130 © Lori Adamski Peek/Tony Stone Images
131 © Michael Heron/The Stock Market; © Richard Howard
132 Both photos: © Richard Howard
133 © Richard Howard
134 © Richard Howard
135 © Richard Howard; © Christopher Clews
136 Both photos: © Richard Howard
137 © David Madison/Tony Stone Images
138 © Lawrence Migdale/Photo Researchers; © The Stock Market; © Jerry Wachter/Focus on Sports; © Courtesy of Rollerblade, Inc.
139 © Ollie Ready/Focus on Sports
140 Bottom left: © Ollie Ready/Focus on Sports; other photos: © Courtesy of Rollerblade, Inc.
141 © Focus on Sports
142 © Michael Kevin Daly/The Stock Market
143 © Bob Daemmrich/The Image Works
144- © David Madison/The Stock Market
145
146 © Miller Freeman Inc.

148 Grolier Library File
149 © Daemmrich/The Image Works
150 © Bill Aron/Photo Edit
151 © Moore/The Image Works
153 © Mark Ryden
155 © Billy Barnes
156 © Mark Ryden
157 © Mark Ryden
158 © Mark Ryden
159 © Fred Prouser/Sipa; © Lee Celano/Reuters/Bettmann
160 © RIHA/Liaison
161 © Photofest
162 © Burrows/Liaison; © Andrew Lichtenstein/Impact Visuals
164 © Jim Tynan/Impact Visuals; © Steve Starr/Saba
165 Photos: © Jon Levy/Liaison; © John Chiasson/Liaison; charts from *Newsweek*, August 2, 1993. © 1993, Newsweek, Inc. All rights reserved. Reprinted by permission.
166 © Jim Tynan/Impact Visuals
167 © Stuart Franklin/Magnum
168 © P.F. Bentley/Black Star
169 © Alon Reininger/Woodfin Camp
170 © Alon Reininger/Woodfin Camp
171 © Erich Hartmann/Magnum
172 © Ann Cutting/Photonica
173 © Tim Jonke/The Image Bank
174 © The Granger Collection; © Bettmann Archive
175 © Richard Gage/*U.S. News & World Report*
176 © T.J. Florian/Rainbow
178 © ATC Productions/The Stock Market
179 © William S. Helsel/Tony Stone Images
180- © Peter Beck/The Stock Market
181
182 © Gabe Palmer/The Stock Market; © Kenneth Murray/Photo Researchers
183 © Adam Hart-Davis/Science Photo Library/Photo Researchers
184 © David Weintraub/Photo Researchers
185 © David Weintraub/Photo Researchers
186 © Joseph Nettis/Photo Researchers
187 © The Stock Market
188 © The Stock Market; © Paul Shambroom/Science Source/Photo Researchers
189 © Jerry Howard/Positive Images; © Michael Kingsford/Envision
190 © Frances M. Roberts; © Walter Chandoha
191 Top: © Jerry Howard/Positive Images; center right: © Alex Brandon/NYT Pictures; bottom: © Chuck Wyrostok/Appalight
192 © Curt Wilcott/Liaison
193 Al Granger © 1991 by The New York Times Company. Reprinted by permission.
194 © William H. Allen, Jr.; © E. Sander/Liaison
195 © Ariel Skelley/The Stock Market; © Grace Davies/Envision
196 © Scott Pollack
197 Both photos: © Courtesy of Ultradent Products, Inc.
198 Top photos: © Arthur Beck/Photo Researchers; bottom photo: © Bonnie Rauch/Photo Researchers
199 © Courtesy of Ultradent Products, Inc.
200 © Lisa Loucks Christenson/Absolute Stock
201 © Michael P. Gadomski/Photo Researchers; inset: © Jean Anderson/The Stock Market
202 © Jean Anderson/The Stock Market; © J.H. Robinson/Photo Researchers; © Gilbert Grant/Photo Researchers
203 © Erika Stone/Photo Researchers
204 © Joyce Photographics/Photo Researchers
205 © John Kaprielian/Photo Researchers
206- Artwork: Sandra Dionisi © 1993 by The New York Times Company.
208 Reprinted by permission.
209 © Dan Bosler/Tony Stone Images
210 © Barbara Kirk/The Stock Market
211 © Ariel Skelley/The Stock Market
212 Art by William Donovan
214 © UPI/Bettmann

217 © John Lund/Tony Stone Images; © Ken Fisher/Tony Stone Images
218 © Frank Herholdt/Tony Stone Images
219 © Turner & De Vries/The Image Bank
221 © Don Bonsey/Tony Stone Images
222 © Esbin-Anderson/The Image Works
223 © Margaret Miller/Photo Researchers
224 © J. Gerard Smith/Photo Researchers
225 © Blaine Harrington/The Stock Market
227 © Will & Deni McIntyre/Photo Researchers
228 © *Newsweek*, August 28, 1994, Christopher Blumrich/World Health Organization
229 © Thomas Haley/Sipa
230 © Rod Little/*U.S. News & World Report*
235 © Courtesy of Jay D. Mabrey, M.D.
237 © Courtesy of Houghton Mifflin
238 © Courtesy of Harper Collins; © Courtesy of Workman Press, Inc.
239 © Courtesy of Free Press; © Courtesy of Harper Collins
242- © Joe Lertola/*Time* Magazine
243
245 Table: © *Time* Magazine; source: American Cancer Society
247 © Mark Clarke/Science Photo Library/Photo Researchers
248 © Chromosohm/Sohm/Stock Boston
251 © Steve Woit/NYT Pictures
254 © Superstock
255 © Ben Osborne/Tony Stone Images
258 © 1994 by The New York Times Company. Reprinted by permission.
260 Photo: © Jeffrey MacMillan/*U.S. News & World Report*
262 Art from *Newsweek*, December 6, 1993. © 1993, Newsweek, Inc. All rights reserved. Reprinted by permission.
263 © Jeffrey Friedman/The Rockefeller Center
264 © Hank Morgan/Science Source/Photo Researchers
265 © John Mantel/Sipa
267 © Lynn Kantor/Bronx VA Medical Center
268 © *Medical Tribune*
269 © Ira Wyman/Sygma
271 © *Consumers' Research*
272 © Courtesy of Bradford Hospital, Florida
275 © Frank O'Connell/© 1994 by The New York Times Company. Reprinted by permission.
277 © Sinclair Stammers/Science Photo Library/Photo Researchers
279 © Will & Deni McIntyre/Photo Researchers
282 © Andy Levin/Photo Researchers
285 © Howard Sochurek/The Stock Market
287 © Hank Morgan/Photo Researchers
288 © Courtesy of Thermo CardioSystems, Incorporated
290 © Ovak Arslanian
293 © Bruce Ayres/Tony Stone Images
295 © Superstock
297 © Jeffrey Markowitz/Sygma; © Timothy Sharp/Sygma
300 Photo: © Stephen Frisch/Stock Boston; artwork: © *Newsweek*, April 25, 1994, Blumrich
301 © 1991 by Consumers Union of U.S., Inc. Reprinted by permission from *Consumer Reports*, March 1991.
304 © Rod Little/*U.S. News & World Report*
307 Photo: © J. Bernot/Stock Boston; graph: copyright © 1994 by The New York Times Company. Reprinted by permission.
309 © Bob Daemmrich/The Image Works
311 © Stevie Grand/Science Photo Library/Photo Researchers
312 Photos © Courtesy of C. Andrew Salzberg, M.D.
315 © Thierry Orban/Sygma
316 © Sipa
317 © Joe Tabacca/AP/Wide World
320 © Stephen Feld
324 © Everett Collection
325 © David James/Tony Stone Images
327 © Bob Strong/The Image Works
330 © Michael A. Schwarz
332 © Eugene Richards/Magnum